Lecture Notes in Computer Science   16477

Founding Editors

Gerhard Goos
Juris Hartmanis

Editorial Board Members

Elisa Bertino, *Purdue University, West Lafayette, IN, USA*
Wen Gao, *Peking University, Beijing, China*
Bernhard Steffen, *TU Dortmund University, Dortmund, Germany*
Moti Yung, *Columbia University, New York, NY, USA*

The series Lecture Notes in Computer Science (LNCS), including its subseries Lecture Notes in Artificial Intelligence (LNAI) and Lecture Notes in Bioinformatics (LNBI), has established itself as a medium for the publication of new developments in computer science and information technology research, teaching, and education.

LNCS enjoys close cooperation with the computer science R & D community, the series counts many renowned academics among its volume editors and paper authors, and collaborates with prestigious societies. Its mission is to serve this international community by providing an invaluable service, mainly focused on the publication of conference and workshop proceedings and postproceedings. LNCS commenced publication in 1973.

Simone Ferlin-Reiter · Romain Fontugne ·
Johanna Ullrich
Editors

Passive and Active Measurement

27th International Conference, PAM 2026
Virtual Event, March 23–25, 2026
Proceedings

 Springer

Editors
Simone Ferlin-Reiter
Karlstad University
Karlstad, Sweden

Romain Fontugne
IIJ Research Laboratory
Tokyo, Japan

Johanna Ullrich
Interdisciplinary Transformation University
Linz, Austria

ISSN 0302-9743   ISSN 1611-3349 (electronic)
Lecture Notes in Computer Science
ISBN 978-3-032-18267-8   ISBN 978-3-032-18268-5 (eBook)
https://doi.org/10.1007/978-3-032-18268-5

Preface

We are excited to present the proceedings of the 27th Annual Passive and Active Measurement Conference, PAM 2026. With this program, PAM continues its tradition as a venue for thorough, compelling, but often early-stage and emerging research on networks, Internet measurement, and the emergent systems they host. This year's conference took place on March 23–25, 2026, virtually hosted by the Interdisciplinary Transformation University Austria. Hosting PAM as a virtual conference is a tradition we proudly continued, as it lowers the barrier for participation and reduces the impact of long-distance travel on the environment.

This year, we received 57 double-blind submissions, of which 51 were admissible for review. After four double-blind reviews per paper, the Technical Program Committee (TPC) selected 18 papers for publication. As with last year, submissions could be of either long or short form, and our ultimate program featured 9 long papers and 9 short papers. Finally, 9 of the accepted papers were shepherded by members of the TPC who were reviewers of each paper. The proceedings of PAM once again illustrate how network measurements can provide essential insights for different types of networks and networked systems and cover topics such as applications, performance, network infrastructure and topology, measurement tools, and security and privacy. They thus provide a comprehensive view of the current state of the art and emerging ideas in this important domain.

We built a TPC that included a mix of experience levels, backgrounds, and geographies, bringing well-established and fresh perspectives to the committee. Each submission was assigned to four reviewers. As program chairs, we would like to thank our TPC members for volunteering their time and expertise with such dedication and enthusiasm. We would like to extend a special token of gratitude to our shepherds, and to all authors for having all final versions complete and fully submitted by our camera-ready deadline!

Special thanks to our hosting organization this year, the Interdisciplinary Transformation University in Linz, Austria. Thanks to the PAM steering committee for their guidance in putting together the conference. Finally, thank you to the researchers in the networking and measurement communities and beyond who submitted their work to PAM and engaged in the process.

March 2026

Simone Ferlin
Romain Fontugne
Johanna Ullrich

Organization

General Chair

Johanna Ullrich   Interdisciplinary Transformation University, Austria

Program Committee Chairs

Simone Ferlin-Reiter   Red Hat AB, Karlstad University, Sweden
Romain Fontugne   IIJ Research Laboratory, Japan

Steering Committee

Michael Agarwal   KU Leuven, Belgium
Marinho P. Barcellos   University of Waikato, New Zealand
Fabian E. Bustamante   Northwestern University, USA
Michalis Faloutsos   University of California, Riverside, USA
Anja Feldmann   Max Planck Institute for Informatics, Germany
Oliver Hohlfeld   University of Kassel, Germany
Jelena Mirkovic   University of Southern California, USA
Giovane Moura   SIDN Labs, The Netherlands
Cristel Pelsser   UCLouvain, Belgium
Steve Uhlig   Queen Mary University of London, UK

Program Committee

Alessandro Finamore   Huawei Technologies, France
Alexander Gamero-Garrido   University of California, Davis, USA
Anna Sperotto   University of Twente, Netherlands
Anne Josiane Kouam   Inria, France
Antonia Affinito   University of Twente, Netherlands
Aristide Akem   University of Oxford, UK
Ben Du   University of California, Los Angeles, USA
Burkhard Stiller   Universität Zürich, Switzerland

Carlos Gañán   ICANN/Delft University of Technology,
                                    Netherlands
Casey Deccio   Brigham Young University, UK
Daphne Tuncer   Institut Polytechnique de Paris, France
Eman Ramadan   University of Minnesota, USA
Emilia Weyulu   Max Planck Institute for Informatics, Germany
Esteban Carisimo   Northwestern University, USA
Etienne Khan   University of Twente, Netherlands
Fabricio Rodriguez   Telefónica Research, Spain
Francisco Germano Vogt   Universidade Estadual de Campinas, Brazil
Ha Dao   Max Planck Institute for Informatics, Germany
Hammas Bin Tanveer   University of Iowa, USA
Hannah B. Pasandi   University of California, Berkeley, USA
Haoyu Wang   Huazhong University of Science and Technology,
                                    China
Idilio Drago   University of Turin, Italy
Ioana Livadariu   SimulaMet, Norway
Johan Mazel   ANSSI, France
Johanna Ullrich   SBA, Austria
Johannes Zirngibl   Max Planck Institute for Informatics, Germany
Kevin Vermeulen   CNRS, École Polytechnique, France
Lars Prehn   Google, Ireland
Maciej Korczynski   Grenoble Alpes University, France
Marcel Flores   Netflix, USA
Minzhao Lyu   University of New South Wales, Australia
Mirja Kühlewind   Ericsson Research, Germany
Moritz Müller   SIDN and University of Twente, Netherlands
Olaf Maennel   University of Adelaide, Australia
Oliver Gasser   IPinfo, Germany
Orlando E. Martínez-Durive   IMDEA Networks & NetAI, Spain
Pawel Foremski   IITiS PAN/DomainTools, Poland
Philipp Richter   Akamai Technologies, Germany
Polly Huang   National Taiwan University, Taiwan
Ramin Sadre   UCLouvain, Belgium
Remi Hendriks   University of Twente, Netherlands
Ricky K. P. Mok   CAIDA/University of California, San Diego, USA
Sarah Wassermann   Hornetsecurity, France
Savvas Kastanakis   University of Twente, Netherlands
Shuai Hao   Old Dominion University, USA
Solange Rito Lima   University of Minho, Portugal
Stephen McQuistin   University of St Andrews, UK
Taha Albakour   Max Planck Institute for Informatics, Germany

Tanya Shreedhar	TU Delft, Netherlands
Thomas Krenc	IIJ Research Laboratory, Japan
Tijay Chung	Virginia Tech, USA
Tobias Fiebig	Max Planck Institute for Informatics, Germany
Tobias Urban	Institute for Internet Security; Westphalian University of Applied Sciences, Germany
Vadim Safronov	University of Oxford, UK
Vasanta Chaganti	Swarthmore College, USA
Wei Sun	Wright State University, USA
Yevheniya Nosyk	KOR Labs, France
Yufei Zheng	University of Massachusetts Amherst, USA
Zachary Bischof	Georgia Tech, USA

Contents

DNS

Wireless and Mobile

Security and Privacy

Virtualization

Routing

Prefix Top Lists Reloaded: A Temporal Prefix Ranking Dataset

Savvas Kastanakis[1]([⊠]), Rick Fontein[1], Shyam Krishna Khadka[1], Ebrima Jaw[1], Cristian Hesselman[1,2], and Mattijs Jonker[1]

[1] University of Twente, Enschede, The Netherlands
{s.kastanakis,r.l.h.fontein,s.k.khadka,e.jaw,c.e.w.hesselman,
m.jonker}@utwente.nl
[2] SIDN Labs, Arnhem, The Netherlands
cristian.hesselman@sidn.nl

Abstract. Accurate Internet measurements depend on well-defined targets. A popular mechanism for target selection is domain-based top lists, e.g., the Tranco or Cisco Umbrella lists. Such lists have a few shortcomings such as the lack of aggregation across related domain names and high volatility over time. Prefix Top Lists (*PTL*) were introduced in 2019 to address these issues, by aggregating domain names into IP prefixes and applying a Zipf-based ranking model to improve stability and representativeness, nonetheless, the original *PTL* resource was discontinued, leaving a gap in publicly available prefix-level data.

In this replication study, we revive and enhance the *PTL* resource by incorporating a broader range of domain-based top lists. Our approach involves mapping domain names to IP prefixes using DNS resolution and BGP routing data, ranking prefixes through a Zipf-based weighting system, and conducting three use-case studies to promote the applicability of *PTLs*. We release the complete *PTL* toolchain as open-source software and publish weekly *PTL* snapshots under https://openintel.nl/data/prefix-top-lists, ensuring sustained, versioned and publicly accessible prefix-level rankings for the measurement community.

1 Introduction

Internet measurements typically begin with careful target selection [21]. Researchers often rely on Domain-based Top Lists (DTLs), such as Cloudflare Radar [14], Cisco Umbrella [13] and Google CrUX [18] to identify key Internet properties. However, these lists exhibit rank fluctuations, do not group related infrastructure under a single entity, and lack a consistent weighting mechanism, making it challenging to interpret their significance [26]. Specifically, DTLs fluctuate significantly over time and treat separate domain names under the same Autonomous System (AS) or organization (e.g., google.com and google.co.uk) as distinct entities, despite serving the same function [21]. Additionally, these lists do not reflect the relative importance of ranked entries, making it unclear how much more significant one domain name is compared to another. For example, a low-traffic but persistent domain name might be ranked similarly to a widely

S. Ferlin-Reiter et al. (Eds.): PAM 2026, LNCS 16477, pp. 3–16, 2026.
https://doi.org/10.1007/978-3-032-18268-5_1

used, high-impact one, despite their vastly different influence on the Internet ecosystem.

To address these challenges, the ***Prefix Top Lists (PTL)*** method introduced in [21] aggregated domain names into IP prefixes, and employed a Zipf-based ranking [27] to reflect relative importance, and reduce temporal volatility. *PTLs* complement DTLs by shifting focus to the infrastructure-level, capturing how services are actually deployed across IP space. By exposing this infrastructure, *PTLs* reveal patterns of concentration and operational dependencies that domain-based top lists cannot capture. This makes *PTLs* a complementary resource that enables network measurement studies [9, 21, 25].

PTLs are operationally important because key Internet processes, e.g., routing, hijack propagation, DNS and CDN deployment and security enforcement, occur at the prefix and AS level. This view is essential for understanding patterns of centralization, exposure to routing risks, and operational diversity. Since prefixes are the units of routing and control in BGP, *PTLs* provide a stable and interpretable lens into the Internet's structural hubs, making them well-suited for measurement tasks that require network-aware target selection. While the initial study relied on DTLs from Cisco Umbrella, Majestic and the since retired Alexa, we expand this scope to include additional sources that offer varied perspectives on domain name importance, including: Tranco, Google CrUX and Cloudflare Radar [13, 14, 18, 19, 23].

However, despite its value, the original *PTL* resource [5] was discontinued, creating a void in publicly available prefix-level data. This absence limits the ability of researchers and operators to conduct longitudinal studies and reproduce previous analyses, highlighting the need for a renewed and expanded approach to prefix-based ranking methodologies. In this work, we aim to *revive* and *enhance* this valuable resource, and commit to sustaining it for the research community.

Specifically, we replicate and extend the *PTL* methodology by reconstructing and improving prefix-level aggregation, while adhering to the respective ACM replication guidelines [10]. Our replication approach is as follows:

1. We gather recent DTLs, i.e.,: *Umbrella, Majestic, CrUX, Tranco, and Radar*.
2. We leverage public *DNS* and *BGP data* through the OpenINTEL platform [24] to map domain names to their respective IP prefixes and ASes.
3. We implement both a *Zipf-based ranking model* and a *presence-based frequency model*, allowing flexible aggregation strategies based on domain name rank or multi-list presence.
4. We explore the applicability of *PTLs* across three study domains: a) DNS name server deployment, b) BGP prefix hijacks prevalence, and c) Post-Quantum Cryptography (PQC) adoption.
5. We provide the complete *PTL* toolchain as open-source code under https:// github.com/kastanakis/prefix-top-lists and publish weekly *PTL* snapshots via the long-standing OpenINTEL platform at https://openintel.nl/data/prefix-top-lists, ensuring stable, versioned, and long-term availability of both the methodology and the datasets.

By reviving and enhancing *PTLs*, we aim to create a robust resource that will benefit the Internet measurement ecosystem. We commit to continually updating the *PTL* data and maintaining accessibility.

1.1   Enhancements Over Original PTL Study

While our work is rooted in the original *PTL* methodology introduced at IMC 2019 [21], we introduce several important advancements that significantly improve both the quality and the scope of prefix-level Internet measurements.

First, rather than, as in the original study, relying on in-house DNS resolution, we ingest public DNS data from the OpenINTEL project [24]. This relieves us and anyone seeking to reproduce our results from having to perform DNS queries, and is designed so others can access the same underlying data.

Second, we expand the range of DTLs used to construct *PTLs*. Whereas the original work relied on Alexa, Majestic, and Umbrella, our study incorporates a more diverse set of DTLs, including Tranco, Google CrUX, and Cloudflare Radar, which capture a more diverse and modern view of popular Internet infrastructure.

Since the original *PTL* work, several shortcomings of DTLs have been addressed by efforts such as Tranco [23], which stabilizes domain name rankings via aggregation across multiple sources, and CrUX [18], which offers accurate, user-centric web performance telemetry. While these advances reduce volatility and increase representativeness at the domain level, they do not resolve a distinct challenge: the disconnect between domain names and network infrastructure. As such, *PTLs* and modern DTLs offer complementary perspectives on Internet measurement.

In addition to the methodological improvements, we also broaden the scope of the use-case analyses. While the original *PTL* work focused solely on DNS name server deployment, we further demonstrate the applicability of *PTLs* to two additional contemporary challenges [12,20]: the measurement of prefix hijack incidents and the analysis of Post-Quantum Cryptography (PQC) adoption trends. These use cases illustrate the continued relevance of prefix-based aggregation for both operational and security-focused network measurement.

Furthermore, we are committed to the ongoing public availability of our data and tooling to promote reproducibility and longitudinal research. We plan to release updates on a weekly basis, aligned with the release cycles of source datasets such as Umbrella and Tranco, and archive historical snapshots to support longitudinal analysis. Collectively, these enhancements position our replication as a robust, flexible, and sustainable resource for the measurement community.

2   Prefix Top Lists (*PTLs*)

This section describes our approach for generating *PTLs*, from input DTLs and DNS/BGP data to the final prefix rankings, as illustrated in Fig. 1.

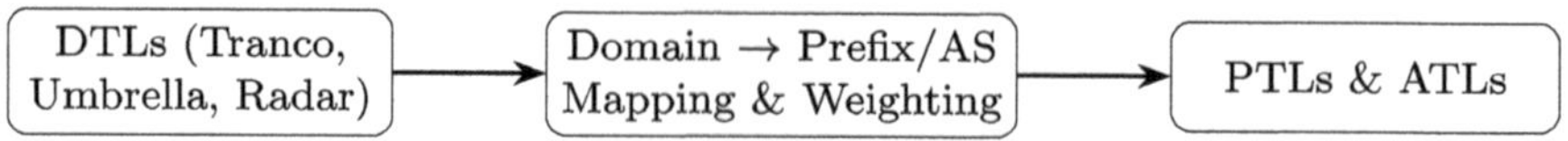

Fig. 1. Overview of the PTL/ATL generation pipeline.

Table 1. Top 10 domain names from Tranco and Umbrella (Apr 17, 2025), with Zipf-based weights averaged over a 7-day rolling window. Rank ranges reflect Tranco's long-term aggregation and Umbrella's real-time DNS activity; limited overlap (in bold) shows how source choice affects observed domains.

Tranco Domain	Weight	Top Rank	Bottom Rank	Umbrella Domain	Weight	Top Rank	Bottom Rank
google.com	0.0693	1	1	**google.com**	0.0510	1	10
microsoft.com	0.0346	2	2	**microsoft.com**	0.0238	1	375
mail.ru	0.0231	3	3	data.microsoft.com	0.0108	3	223025
facebook.com	0.0173	4	4	events.data.microsoft.com	0.0086	4	42786
root-servers.net	0.0138	5	5	**apple.com**	0.0063	6	288
dzen.ru	0.0115	6	6	office.com	0.0061	6	3458
amazonaws.com	0.0099	7	7	clientservices.googleapis.com	0.0053	14	31
apple.com	0.0086	8	8	live.com	0.0049	8	89958
youtube.com	0.0077	9	9	e2ro.com	0.0043	5	61
googleapis.com	0.0069	10	10	windowsupdate.com	0.0042	8	121494

2.1 Domain Top List Generation

Existing domain-based top lists [13, 14, 18, 19, 23] have the following properties. They: a) generally rank domain names based on proprietary metrics; b) differ in methodology and underlying data; and c) are prone to short-term fluctuations [21, 26]. To improve their stability, we follow the conventions of the original work and apply a Zipf-based weighting scheme [27] to each list individually.

Zipf's law has been used to model the popularity of web content and domain access patterns [8, 11, 16, 17], where a few top-ranked domain names receive disproportionately high attention while the majority receive very little. By assigning Zipfian weights, we ensure that higher-ranked domain names have a stronger influence on the final ranking, while still accounting for long-tail entries. To formalize this intuition, we compute a normalized Zipfian weight for each domain name based on its rank position. For a given rank k in a list of size N, the Zipf weight w_k (using $s = 1$, consistent with the original study [21]) is:

$$w_k = \frac{1/k^s}{\sum_{n=1}^{N} 1/n^s}$$

Here, the numerator $1/k^s$ reflects that higher-ranked domains receive more weight than lower-ranked ones, while the denominator $\sum_{n=1}^{N} 1/n^s$ acts as the normalization constant that scales these values across the entire list. This normalization ensures that the weights sum to one and that lower-ranked domain names contribute progressively less to the overall distribution.

To further stabilize the data, we aggregate weights using a seven-day sliding window (consistent with the original PTL methodology [5]). For each domain name, we compute the average Zipf weight over the preceding week. Domain names that do not appear in a given list on a particular day are assigned a weight of zero for that day. This smoothing process reduces the impact of daily fluctuations and ensures that transient spikes or drops in popularity do not dominate the resulting prefix rankings. The final averaged weights form the input to our DNS resolution and prefix aggregation steps.

The DTLs for April 1–7, 2025, based on the Tranco and Umbrella datasets [13,23], are shown in Table 1. Tranco provides stable domain name rankings by aggregating data from multiple sources over a rolling window, effectively smoothing out short-term fluctuations. In contrast, Cisco Umbrella derives its rankings from real-time DNS query data observed at recursive resolvers, which captures a broader spectrum of activity and as a result, Umbrella rankings exhibit significantly higher variance, reflecting the dynamic DNS nature at the edge.

2.2 DNS Resolution and Routing Data

Unlike the original *PTL* study, which performed custom DNS resolution in-house, we use publicly available DNS datasets. This approach saves us and those seeking to generate their own *PTLs* with our tooling from the operational complexity of deploying and managing a custom resolution pipeline. We use data from the OpenINTEL project, which makes various types of DNS data available for academic research [24]. We specifically rely on forward DNS (fDNS) measurement data, which OpenINTEL collects daily by querying sizable lists of domain names for address records (i.e., A and AAAA) and others. Among its public data are top-list based measurements for Tranco, Majestic, CrUX, Umbrella, and Radar. OpenINTEL also embeds BGP-related data such as the covering prefix and origin AS of the resolved IP addresses making it particularly suitable for our replication study.

2.3 Prefix Top List Generation

We construct a Prefix Top List (*PTL*) by augmenting the DTL from Sect. 2.1 with DNS data obtained from OpenINTEL (see Sect. 2.2) over the same seven-day sliding window. Each domain name d is assigned a normalized weight w_d according to its Zipfian rank in the input *DTL*. Domain names frequently resolve to multiple IP addresses—e.g., due to global load balancing, CDN distribution, or DNS-based failover. We denote the set of addresses associated with a domain name d as:

$$I(d) = \{i_1, i_2, \ldots, i_m\}$$

We assume that each IP address in $I(d)$ shares equal responsibility for serving d, and thus evenly divide the domain name's weight across its resolved addresses. Each address $i \in I(d)$ receives a proportional share of $\frac{w_d}{|I(d)|}$. OpenINTEL maps

(a) Prefix Top List (Zipf)

Prefix	AS	Weight	# of Domains
2a00:1450:400e::/48	15169	0.0705	20473
2a02:26f0:1180::/48	20940	0.0264	34724
142.250.0.0/15	15169	0.0193	18853
142.251.36.0/24	15169	0.0186	7502
2603:1000::/25	8075	0.0166	14324
2606:4700::/44	13335	0.0141	47681
162.159.128.0/19	13335	0.0110	14101
172.217.23.0/24	15169	0.0107	8405
151.101.204.0/22	54113	0.0102	18848
172.217.0.0/16	15169	0.0090	10008

(b) Prefix Top List (Presence)

Prefix	AS	Weight	# of Domains
2606:4700:3030::/48	13335	0.0215	167066
23.227.38.0/23	13335	0.0173	72047
2606:4700:20::/44	13335	0.0156	73091
104.26.0.0/20	13335	0.0112	75479
2606:4700::/44	13335	0.0105	62653
141.193.213.0/24	209242	0.0088	23516
2620:127:f00f::/48	13335	0.0081	58288
188.114.96.0/24	13335	0.0080	116787
188.114.97.0/24	13335	0.0080	116782
2a06:98c1:3120::/48	13335	0.0074	112756

(c) AS Top List (Zipf)

ASN	Weight	# of Prefixes
15169	0.1576	390
13335	0.1550	442
16509	0.1161	3389
8075	0.0646	208
20940	0.0636	829
54113	0.0438	200
32934	0.0366	352
14618	0.0265	291
16625	0.0259	580
396982	0.0214	1995

(d) AS Top List (Presence)

ASN	Weight	# of Prefixes
13335	0.2654	540
16509	0.1271	3522
8075	0.0393	222
14618	0.0274	299
396982	0.0207	2050
20940	0.0186	879
24940	0.0182	60
16276	0.0178	170
209242	0.0174	254
15169	0.0171	396

Fig. 2. Top 10 entries from the Prefix Top Lists (PTL) and AS Top Lists (ATL) generated using two methods: Zipf-based ranking and presence-based frequency.

DNS address records to one or more BGP prefixes $P(i)$ based on publicly available BGP routing data. Typically, an address will map to a single, most-specific prefix, but multi-origin entries can occur as well. We use these metadata to compute the weight of each prefix p by summing the contributions of all addresses that map to it:

$$W(p) = \sum_{\substack{d \\ i \in I(d) \\ P(i)=p}} \frac{w_d}{|I(d)|} \tag{1}$$

This yields a weighted ranking of BGP prefixes based on the volume of popular domain names they serve, defined as the Prefix Top List (*PTL*). We then aggregate these prefix-level weights to the AS level. Let $P(AS)$ denote the set of prefixes originated by AS AS. The total weight assigned to AS is:

$$W(AS) = \sum_{p \in P(AS)} W(p) \tag{2}$$

This yields a weighted ranking of ASes based on the volume of popular prefixes they serve, defined as the AS Top List (*ATL*). Unlike traditional domain-centric lists, these rankings (i.e., *PTL* and *ATL*) highlight which prefixes and ASes play central roles in hosting or distributing the most frequently accessed web services.

Our approach generates two types of Top lists: ranked (Zipf-based) and presence-based. For the ranked *PTLs* and *ATLs*, we apply a Zipfian weighting scheme to domain-based top lists from Tranco, Umbrella, and Majestic, assigning greater weight to higher-ranked domain names. In the presence-based variant, we ignore domain ranks and instead assign weights based only on whether a domain name appears in each input list. The resulting value reflects the domain's normalized appearance frequency across sources. We then aggregate these weights to prefixes and ASes following the same method used for the Zipf-weighted lists. These variants are constructed using a broader set of sources, including CrUX and Cloudflare Radar in addition to Tranco, Umbrella, and Majestic, to better reflect raw domain appearance frequency across diverse datasets.

Figure 2 shows the top 10 prefixes and ASes under each ranking variant, illustrating the differences in outcome between Zipf-based and presence-based methods. Zipf-based rankings (subfigure a) are dominated by Google prefixes, making Google (AS15169) the top AS in the corresponding ATL (subfigure c), due to a few highly ranked services like YouTube and Google Search. In contrast, the presence-based PTL (subfigure b) surfaces more Cloudflare-operated prefixes, with Cloudflare (AS13335) topping the presence-based ATL (subfigure d), reflecting its support for many moderately popular or regional domain names. These patterns illustrate how aggregation shapes AS-level rankings and highlight differing strategies: centralized hosting vs. widespread coverage.

To comply with the original methodology and due to space constraints, we focus our analysis on the Zipf-based ranked lists. However, we release the presence-based variants to support research that prioritizes breadth of coverage over popularity [6], e.g., assessing geographic diversity, evaluating the spread of services across hosting providers, or tracking technology adoption in the long tail.

2.4   Considerations for DNS Resolution

OpenINTEL provides broad DNS and BGP coverage across multiple top lists, but like any passive measurement platform, it is not exhaustive. Some domain names may remain unresolved, and not all resolved IP addresses map cleanly to BGP prefixes, particularly in cases involving sparse or short-lived announcements. Although we do not supplement the dataset with active DNS resolution in this study, our methodology is compatible with such extensions. We consider this a pragmatic trade-off between reproducibility and completeness.

As a result, our mapping approach requires additional care in handling incomplete data. Some domain names may be delegated (i.e., have an NS record) and be included in a DTL due to query volume even though no address records exist, or failed to resolve due to transient errors. We disregard such names, consistent with the original study [5]. To preserve ranking integrity, we normalize weights after filtering. Once non-resolvable domain names are removed, the remaining weights are rescaled to sum to 1.0, preventing bias toward any specific prefix or AS.

3   Temporal Analysis of Prefix Top Lists

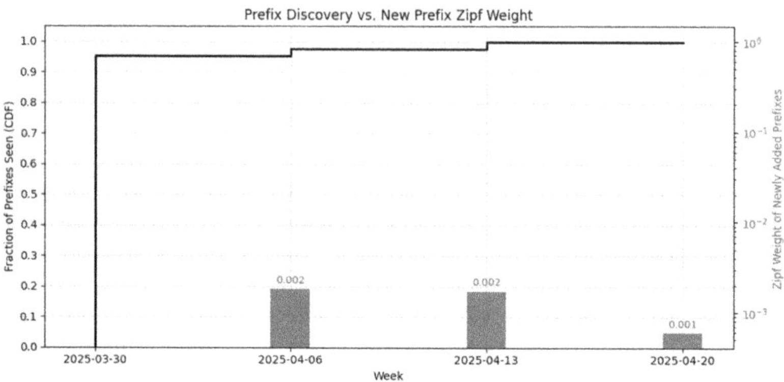

Fig. 3. Growth of Unique Prefix Coverage by *PTL*. The left y-axis shows the CDF of discovered prefixes on a linear scale, representing the proportion of total unique prefixes observed over time. The right y-axis shows the cumulative Zipf weight of newly added prefixes on a logarithmic scale, emphasizing the diminishing contribution of lower-ranked domain names.

In this section, we analyze the growth of *PTLs* over an one-month period, using four weekly snapshots. Our analysis begins in mid-March, 2025, coinciding with the start of our data collection. For each weekly snapshot, we identify newly discovered BGP prefixes (i.e., those not present in earlier lists) and quantify their relative importance by accumulating their Zipf weights.

Figure 3 shows the cumulative prefix discovery across the four weeks. The black step line (left y-axis) indicates the fraction of total prefixes observed over time, while the red bars (right y-axis, log scale) show the Zipf weight of newly added prefixes. Prefix coverage increases rapidly in the first snapshot (March 30), capturing over 90% of all observed prefixes. Subsequent weeks (April 6, 13, and 20) add only a few new prefixes, contributing marginal Zipf weights of 0.002, 0.002, and 0.001, respectively, demonstrating the long-tail of domain name popularity.

Prefix weights also remain stable across time. Although we do not calculate explicit weight deltas (as in the original study), the minimal changes in cumulative Zipf weight indicate low volatility across snapshots. This behavior mirrors the original findings [5] and reflects that prefixes associated with highly ranked domains tend to be discovered early and persist across measurement periods. As a result, most of the PTL's structure converges quickly, which is consistent with the intended stability of prefix- and AS-level rankings. A more extensive, longer-term stability analysis is beyond the scope of this paper but represents a natural direction for future work.

4   Applications of Prefix Top Lists

To demonstrate the practicability of the revived *PTL* resource, we evaluate its utility in three network measurement domains: a) Border Gateway Protocol (BGP) security, b) Post-Quantum Cryptography (PQC) compliance, and c) Domain Name System (DNS) resilience.

It is important to note that *PTLs* are not intended as direct replacements for DTLs. The use cases in this section illustrate analyses that benefit specifically from a prefix- or AS-level perspective, which cannot be reliably inferred from domain-level rankings alone.

4.1   Exposure to Suspicious Routing Events

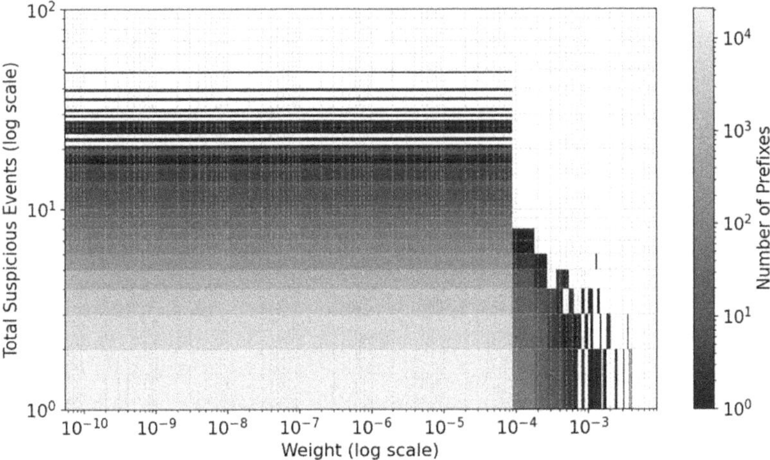

Fig. 4. Heatmap showing the density of prefixes based on their weight and the total number of suspicious events observed in 2024. Both axes are log-scaled, and color reflects the number of prefixes in each bin.

To evaluate the relationship between prefix popularity and routing security incidents [20], we analyzed suspicious routing events using the Global Routing Intelligence Platform (GRIP) from Georgia Tech's INET-Intel platform [1].

We queried GRIP's API for suspicious events through the whole duration of 2024 involving each prefix in our Zipf-weighted *PTL* for April 1–7, 2025 (compiled in Sect. 2.3). For each prefix, we retrieved the total number of Multiple Origin AS (MOAS) events flagged with high suspicion scores (>80) occurring between January 1 and December 31, 2024. Although there is a temporal offset between the *PTL* snapshot and the MOAS event data, Sect. 3 shows that popular prefixes remain stable across neighboring periods, making it reasonable to relate the 2025 snapshot to 2024 routing events. If a prefix had no associated events, it was recorded with a count of zero. The result is a mapping between *PTL-ranked* prefixes and their corresponding number of suspicious events.

Figure 4 presents the results as a log-log heatmap. The x-axis shows the popularity as derived from the *PTL* rankings, and the y-axis shows the total number of suspicious events associated with each prefix. The color of each bin indicates how many prefixes fall into that weightevent range, using a logarithmic color scale: brighter areas (yellow) represent higher concentrations of prefixes, while darker areas (purple) indicate sparsely populated regions. While most high-weight prefixes (right) experience few or no suspicious events, lower-weight prefixes (lower left quadrant) exhibit higher counts. This exploratory view suggests that less prominent infrastructure may be more prone to routing anomalies or targeted hijacks. In contrast, prefixes with both high weight and high event counts are rare but may signal critical infrastructure under persistent targeting.

4.2   Investigation of PQC Deployment

Table 2. PQC compliance across popularity tiers. A prefix is classified as compliant if at least one domain within it successfully completes a PQC handshake.

Prefix popularity tier	PQC-compliant prefixes
Top 100 prefixes	71%
Top 1,000 prefixes	48%
Top 10,000 prefixes	29%
All prefixes	6%

To assess the early adoption of post-quantum cryptography (PQC) [12], we integrate TLS handshake testing into our generated *PTL* for April 1–7. Our methodology aligns with recent community-driven scanning efforts [7,15] and serves as a practical baseline for monitoring PQC adoption at the prefix level.

Building on the Open Quantum Safe (OQS) project [3], we deploy a custom TLS 1.3 scanner based on OpenSSL [4] with the oqsprovider module enabled. This setup allows us to attempt handshakes with hybrid key exchange groups. Specifically, we test the following popular [2,7] groups: `mlkem768`, `X25519 MLKEM768`, `SecP256r1MLKEM768`, `x25519kyber768`. For each domain name in the *PTL* dataset, the scanner attempts to negotiate a connection using each hybrid group. To capture whether a prefix exhibits any evidence of PQC readiness, we apply a binary rule: if at least one domain name within a prefix successfully completes a PQC handshake, we classify the entire prefix as compliant. This consideration reflects the prefix-oriented nature of our study, where the presence of a single PQC-capable domain name demonstrates that the underlying infrastructure can support PQC, even if deployment is not uniform across all hosted domain names.

Table 2 summarizes PQC compliance rates across prefix popularity tiers, from the top 100 to the full set of observed prefixes. We observe a strong decreasing trend: while 71% of prefixes in the top 100 tier host at least one PQC-capable domain name, this rate drops sharply with rank. The compliance rate falls below 30% for prefixes ranked beyond 10,000 and below 6% overall. This suggests that PQC adoption is currently concentrated among prominent prefixes, indicating an uneven and early-stage deployment pattern. These findings offer a prefix-level view of PQC adoption, showing that support is emerging but concentrated in popular, likely well-resourced prefixes.

4.3   Evaluation of DNS Resilience

To replicate the DNS analysis from the original *PTL* study [5], we evaluate name server placement compliance with RFC 2182 [22] across the April 1–7 *PTL*. As the RFC requires name servers to span multiple prefixes, we identify each zone's hosting prefixes and treat zones located within a single prefix as non-compliant.

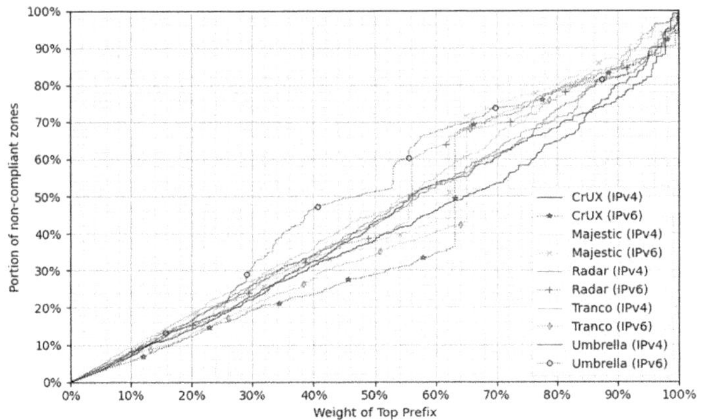

Fig. 5. CDF of non-compliant DNS zones sorted by prefix weight.

Figure 5 shows the cumulative distribution of non-compliant zones across our ranked *PTLs*, broken down by *DTL* and IP version. On the x-axis, prefixes are sorted by their cumulative weight, from most popular (left) to least popular (right). The y-axis represents the fraction of non-compliant zones. The IPv4 distribution is relatively smooth, suggesting that non-compliance is more evenly spread across prefixes. In contrast, IPv6 displays step-like jumps, indicating that misconfigurations are concentrated within a small number of top-ranked prefixes.

Notably, Umbrella (IPv6) shows the earliest and most pronounced jump, starting around the 30% mark, whereas the other top-listed zones demonstrate similar but smaller spikes that occur later, roughly after the 55% weight mark for Radar and after 60% for Majestic, Crux and Tranco. These findings align with the original *PTL* study and confirm that many popular domain names, do not adhere to robust DNS deployment practices, especially in the IPv6 space. An additional breakdown by domain name rank is provided in Appendix B.

5   Conclusion

In this study, we revived and enhanced the *PTL* resource originally introduced at IMC'19. Our findings corroborate key insights from the original work, including the early discovery of high-impact prefixes and the long-tail distribution of domain name popularity. Through three applied use cases, we demonstrate that *PTLs* offer a meaningful lens into the structure and stability of the Internet's edge. We publicly release our tooling and data to support further reproducibility and future research, and commit to continually updating the *PTL* dataset.

Acknowledgements. This research received funding from the Dutch Research Council (NWO) under the projects UPIN and CATRIN.

A   Ethics

This work does not raise any ethical issues. We consulted the original Prefix Top Lists authors, who acknowledged our replication effort without objections. All TLS handshakes were performed using non-intrusive probes with rate limiting in place to avoid overwhelming any individual host. The measurements were conducted over an extended period to distribute load, and no content was fetched beyond the handshake itself.

B   Breakdown by Domain Rank

This appendix complements Sect. 4.3 by showing the distribution of DNS non-compliance across domain ranks. Figure 6 shows the cumulative distribution of non-compliant zones across domain-based top lists. As in the original study [21], the curves are mostly linear, indicating that non-compliance to RFC2182 [22] is fairly evenly distributed across domain ranks. However, meaningful differences emerge between sources and IP versions.

IPv6 consistently shows higher rates of non-compliance than IPv4, with Umbrella (IPv6) exhibiting the steepest slope reflecting its inclusion of many ephemeral or operational domains with poor NS redundancy. In contrast, lists like Tranco and Majestic show slightly lower non-compliance at the top, likely due to their emphasis on stable, long-lived web domains. These patterns confirm that poor topological diversity in NS placement is not confined to the tail of domain rankings but remains a widespread issue, especially in IPv6 environments.

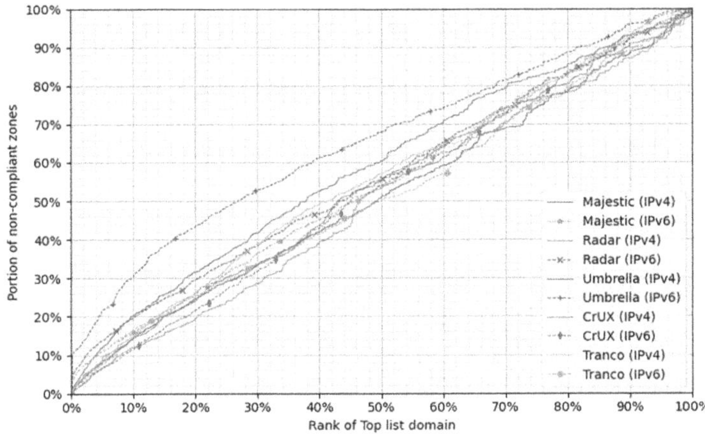

Fig. 6. Share of DNS zones with non-compliant NS placement, sorted by DTL-ranked domains.

Crucially, the variability across lists also reinforces the motivation for prefix-based aggregation. While domain-level rankings reflect differing views of popularity and usage, they do not account for shared infrastructure or hosting patterns. *PTLs* address this by elevating the analysis to the prefix level, smoothing out list-specific biases and surfacing systemic configuration issues tied to underlying infrastructure regardless of which domains are affected.

References

1. GRIP: Global routing intelligence platform (2024). https://grip.inetintel.cc.gatech.edu/. Accessed 31 Jul 2025
2. Cloudflare research: Post-quantum key agreement (2025). https://pq.cloudflareresearch.com/. Accessed 01 Aug 2025
3. Open quantum safe (2025). https://openquantumsafe.org/. Accessed 07 Aug 2025
4. OpenSSL (2025). https://www.openssl.org/. Accessed 07 Aug 2025
5. Prefix top lists (2025). https://prefixtoplists.net.in.tum.de/. Accessed 30 Jul 2025
6. Prefix top lists datasets and code (2025, to be released upon publication)
7. Sites using PQC, March 2025 (2025). https://www.netmeister.org/blog/pqc-use-2025-03.html. Accessed 01 Aug 2025
8. Adamic, L.A.: Zipf, power-laws, and pareto-a ranking tutorial. Xerox Palo Alto Research Center, Palo Alto, CA (2000). http://gingerhpl.hp.com/shl/papers/ranking/ranking.html (2000)
9. Amos, R., Acar, G., Lucherini, E., Kshirsagar, M., Narayanan, A., Mayer, J.: Privacy policies over time: curation and analysis of a million-document dataset. In: Proceedings of the Web Conference 2021, WWW 2021, pp. 2165–2176. Association for Computing Machinery, New York (2021). https://doi.org/10.1145/3442381.3450048
10. Association for Computing Machinery: Artifact Review and Badging (2025). https://www.acm.org/publications/policies/artifact-review-and-badging-current. Accessed 30 Jul 2025

11. Berners-Lee, T.: The fractal nature of the web (1998). https://edshare.soton.ac.uk/392/3/DesignIssues/Fractal.html. Accessed 01 Aug 2025
12. Bernstein, D.J., Lange, T.: Post-quantum cryptography. Nature **549**(7671), 188–194 (2017)
13. Cisco Systems, I.: Cisco umbrella popularity list. Website (2025). https://umbrella.cisco.com/. Accessed 30 Jul 2025
14. Cloudflare, I.: Cloudflare radar: Internet traffic trends. Website (2025). https://radar.cloudflare.com/. Accessed 30 Jul 2025
15. Fabrizio, G., Sperotto, A., Van Rijswijk-Deij, R.: Measuring the impact of post-quantum cryptography on complex applications: a case study on federated identity management. In: 2025 9th Network Traffic Measurement and Analysis Conference (TMA), pp. 1–10 (2025). https://doi.org/10.23919/TMA66427.2025.11097002
16. Kepner, J., et al.: New phenomena in large-scale internet traffic. In: Massive Graph Analytics, pp. 241–285. Chapman and Hall/CRC (2022)
17. Krashakov, S.A., Teslyuk, A.B., Shchur, L.N.: On the universality of rank distributions of website popularity. Comput. Netw. **50**(11), 1769–1780 (2006). https://doi.org/10.1016/j.comnet.2005.07.009, https://www.sciencedirect.com/science/article/pii/S1389128605002513
18. Google LLC: Chrome user experience report (CrUX). Website (2025). https://developers.google.com/web/tools/chrome-user-experience-report. Accessed 30 Jul 2025
19. Majestic: Majestic million: The top 1 million websites. Website (2025). https://majestic.com/reports/majestic-million. Accessed 30 Jul 2025
20. Mitseva, A., Panchenko, A., Engel, T.: The state of affairs in BGP security: a survey of attacks and defenses. Comput. Commun. **124**, 45–60 (2018)
21. Naab, J., Sattler, P., Jelten, J., Gasser, O., Carle, G.: Prefix top lists: gaining insights with prefixes from domain-based top lists on DNS deployment. In: Proceedings of the Internet Measurement Conference, IMC '19, pp. 351–357. Association for Computing Machinery, New York (2019). https://doi.org/10.1145/3355369.3355598
22. Patton, M.A., Bradner, S.O., Elz, R., Bush, R.: Selection and operation of secondary DNS servers. RFC 2182, July 1997. https://doi.org/10.17487/RFC2182, https://www.rfc-editor.org/info/rfc2182
23. Pochat, V.L., Van Goethem, T., Tajalizadehkhoob, S., Korczyński, M., Joosen, W.: Tranco: a research-oriented top sites ranking hardened against manipulation. arXiv preprint arXiv:1806.01156 (2018)
24. van Rijswijk-Deij, R., Jonker, M., Sperotto, A., Pras, A.: A high-performance, scalable infrastructure for large-scale active DNS measurements. IEEE J. Sel. Areas Commun. **34**(6), 1877–1888 (2016). https://doi.org/10.1109/JSAC.2016.2558918
25. Ruth, K., Kumar, D., Wang, B., Valenta, L., Durumeric, Z.: Toppling top lists: evaluating the accuracy of popular website lists. In: Proceedings of the 22nd ACM Internet Measurement Conference, IMC '22, pp. 374–387. Association for Computing Machinery, New York (2022). https://doi.org/10.1145/3517745.3561444
26. Scheitle, Q., et al.: A long way to the top: significance, structure, and stability of internet top lists. In: Proceedings of the Internet Measurement Conference 2018, pp. 478–493 (2018)
27. Wikipedia contributors: Zipf's law—Wikipedia, the free encyclopedia. Website (2025). https://en.wikipedia.org/wiki/Zipf%27s_law. Accessed 30 Jul 2025

Detecting and Characterizing DDoS Scrubbing from Global BGP Routing: Insights from Five Leading Scrubbers

Shyam Krishna Khadka[1(✉)] [iD], Suzan Bayhan[1] [iD], Ralph Holz[1,2] [iD], and Cristian Hesselman[1,3] [iD]

[1] University of Twente, Enschede, The Netherlands
{s.k.khadka,s.bayhan,r.holz,c.e.w.hesselman}@utwente.nl
[2] University of Münster, Münster, Germany
[3] SIDN Labs, Arnhem, The Netherlands

Abstract. Many scrubbers use the Border Gateway Protocol (BGP) to route Distributed Denial of Service (DDoS) traffic to their infrastructure, allowing them to drop the DDoS traffic and forward legitimate traffic to the Autonomous Systems (ASes) the scrubber protects. Despite their importance, the prevalence and operational behaviors of BGP-based DDoS scrubbing services remain poorly understood, such as the extent to which protected ASes always have a scrubber on their path or activate a scrubber on-demand when an attack occurs. We bridge this gap by detecting scrubbing activations and deactivations in public BGP data, where they manifest themselves as a scrubber dynamically appearing as the first upstream of an origin AS or as an origin AS for a particular prefix. We use 30 days of BGP data from the RIS route collectors, focusing on the global top five scrubbing providers, such as Cloudflare and Akamai. We also characterize their behavior, including protection modes, on-demand mitigation strategies, and RPKI/IRR practices. We find that prefixes that always use a scrubber are dominant compared to those that activate a scrubber on-demand. We also observe that 48% of the prefixes that scrubbers temporarily originate during an attack are not covered by valid RPKI ROAs (12.5% Invalid and 35.5% Notfound), which highlights a potential operational gap in current scrubbing practices regarding routing security. These insights are conservative because we only consider public BGP data and AS path changes that are most likely to be scrubbing events (e.g., those observed by two or more route collector peers). We believe our work is useful for security researchers and policymakers, for instance, to better understand DDoS protection levels of ASes in a particular country or region.

Keywords: DDoS · Scrubbing · BGP

1 Introduction

With the rise of Distributed Denial of Service (DDoS) attacks, many commercial DDoS "scrubbing" providers have come into existence. They often use the Border

© The Author(s), under exclusive license to Springer Nature Switzerland AG 2026
S. Ferlin-Reiter et al. (Eds.): PAM 2026, LNCS 16477, pp. 17–43, 2026.
https://doi.org/10.1007/978-3-032-18268-5_2

Gateway Protocol (BGP) to redirect DDoS traffic to their infrastructure and then drop the DDoS traffic and forward legitimate traffic to the Autonomous Systems (ASes) the scrubber protects. We refer to such ASes as "protected ASes" and to their prefixes as "protected prefixes".

Scrubbers offer two modes of protection: always-on and on-demand [1,9,25, 47,53]. The first means that a protected AS always routes all of its inbound traffic through a scrubber, and the protected AS does not have to make any changes in BGP to activate/deactivate the scrubber. In the case of on-demand protection, the protected AS dynamically activates and deactivates the scrubbing service by adding it to the path during a DDoS attack and removing it afterwards. As a result, the scrubber only occasionally appears on the path to the protected AS.

Different ASes might use different types of protection depending on their requirements, such as costs, operational complexity, and criticality of their services. We spoke with several scrubbers, and one of the top ones indicated that always-on is the default model. In contrast, other scrubbers have on-demand as their default setup (e.g., Nawas [41]), where the scrubber dynamically appears and disappears as an upstream in AS paths and the protected AS originates its own prefixes. Others report on the use of on-demand scrubbers that originate a protected prefix rather than the protected ASes being the origin [7,29,54].

Despite the presence of a large number of BGP-based DDoS scrubbers globally, a significant research gap remains because we have no insight into the prevalence of always-on and on-demand protection on the Internet. Khadka et al. [31] study global adoption of BGP-based scrubbing for the top five providers using public BGP data, but explicitly limit themselves to cases where the protected AS remains the origin and do not distinguish on-demand from always-on. Also, we know little about the operational characteristics of on-demand scrubbers, for instance, in terms of frequency and duration of their activation and how they handle routing security objects, such as in the Resource Public Key Infrastructure (RPKI) and the Internet Routing Registry (IRR). For example, a scrubber's RPKI practices are important when it originates the BGP announcements for protected prefixes. This is because protected AS must authorize the scrubber's AS Number (ASN) in its Route Origin Authorizations (ROA) [5] or otherwise ROA-validating ASes [24] might reject the route toward the scrubber, undermining DDoS mitigation.

Obtaining these insights is useful for multiple stakeholders. For example, the Mutually Agreed Norms for Routing Security (MANRS)+ working group could use them for their "DDoS Attack Prevention" metric. This metric reflects the DDoS protection practices of an AS [38], and is needed to implement MANRS+' stricter routing security compliance and auditing controls. Also, researchers can use insights into BGP-based DDoS scrubbers to gain a better understanding of the operation of the scrubber, for instance, to better distinguish BGP anomalies from DDoS scrubbing events. Additionally, insights into on-demand DDoS scrubbing can improve BGP monitoring platforms such as GRIP [22] and Radar [44], which network operators use to detect and prevent routing incidents like leaks or hijacks. For example, if the operators can more reliably distinguish legitimate scrubbing events from actual hijacks, they can reduce the number of false positives in their results.

We answer the following Research Questions (RQs) to obtain these insights:

- **RQ1:** Which type of scrubbing is more dominant on the Internet: always-on or on-demand?
- **RQ2:** What are the characteristics of on-demand scrubbers? For example, to what extent do they originate a protected prefix on behalf of the ASes they protect, and to what extent do they propagate BGP announcements for protected prefixes as an upstream of a protected AS?
- **RQ3:** What are the RPKI and IRR management practices of scrubbers that originate the prefixes of their protected ASes?
- **RQ4:** What hints can we get about DDoS attacks based on the BGP behavior of on-demand scrubbers? For example, how long do DDoS attacks last, and how often do they take place?

To address these research questions, we design a method to detect scrubbing activations and deactivations in public BGP data, for instance, to capture a scrubber dynamically appearing as the first upstream (hereafter referred to simply as *upstream*) of an origin AS or as a scrubber becoming an origin AS for a particular prefix. We use the BGP data from the RIS project, which has 21 active route collectors gathering BGP data from about 1,300 BGP peers. We analyze 30 days of BGP routing data, combining daily Routing Information Bases (RIBs) snapshots with detailed analysis of BGP updates of 5-minute granularity. We focus on the global top five DDoS scrubbing providers: Cloudflare, Akamai Prolexic, Vercara (formerly Neustar), Imperva, and Radware.

Our detection method is intentionally conservative: it identifies only those events in public BGP data that are most likely attributable to scrubbing activations and deactivations. For example, we require that two or more route collector peers observe an AS path change that signals the activation of a scrubber, such as when the scrubber starts to originate the protected prefix rather than the protected AS. This approach aims to prioritize accuracy and minimize false positives, increasing confidence that the observed cases reflect actual DDoS scrubbing (de)activations.

Our contributions and main findings are as follows:

- We develop and implement a methodology that detects scrubbing by using BGP dumps and BGP updates, thereby providing insights into DDoS scrubbing and its operational practices. Our study focuses on the global top five scrubbers on the Internet, but it can be used for any scrubber as long as the ASN it uses for scrubbing is known.
- We observe that the number of prefixes using always-on protection is higher than those using on-demand protection, with 11,408 vs. 5,649 prefixes, corresponding to 0.8% and 0.4% of all routed prefixes as of 30 May 2025. We note that the actual number of on-demand protected prefixes may be higher, since some prefixes might not have been activated during our study period.

- We map out the different protection modes of on-demand scrubbers. We find that there are about 10 times more cases where a scrubber appears as an upstream provider of a protected AS than cases where a scrubber originates the prefix of a protected AS, with 1,070 and 104 prefixes observed, respectively. We also identify 4,475 prefixes that are likely to change their origin to scrubbers during DDoS protection, based on our ROA analysis of scrubber ASNs.
- We find 48% of prefixes that the scrubbers temporarily originate for DDoS protection are either RPKI Invalid (12.5%) or do not have records (35.5%) in the Route Origin Authorization (ROA) objects, which highlights a potential operational gap in current scrubbing practices regarding routing security.

The remainder of this paper is structured as follows. Section 2 provides information about always-on and on-demand scrubbing. We discuss related work in Sect. 3 and introduce our methodology in Sect. 4. We present our results scrubbing (de)activation dynamics and their characteristics in Sect. 5, and discuss our results in Sect. 6. We end with conclusions and future work in Sect. 7.

2   Background on DDoS Scrubbers

A DDoS scrubber connects to its protected AS through mechanisms such as GRE tunnels [48], dedicated links [1], or peering arrangements [8], which the protected AS uses to advertise its routes to the scrubber. DDoS scrubbers provide two modes of protection: always-on and on-demand [1,9,25,47,53]. We divide the latter into two subtypes: on-demand scrubbing for a prefix activated by changing the origin of the prefix to the scrubber or by changing the upstream of the origin AS of the prefix in an AS path [9,26,46]. In both scrubbing modes, only the inbound traffic comes through the scrubber, while the outbound traffic from the protected AS continues to exit normally through its ISP toward the Internet [15]. The activation and deactivation of on-demand scrubbing can be manual, where a protected AS modifies BGP configurations directly [57]; fully automated, as in Cloudflare's Magic Transit [11]; or partially automated, triggered by flow-monitoring alerts and executed via tools such as API calls to scrubbing providers [2,56].

2.1   Always-On Scrubbing

In always-on scrubbing, the protected AS always routes its traffic through a scrubbing service, such that the scrubber's AS always appears on the path toward the protected AS. In this case, a scrubber AS appears as the upstream of the protected AS in AS paths.

Consider a real-world example from our analysis, involving an AS path with ASNs *[513 25091 25091 13335 24864]* for prefix *2.58.145.0/24*, with *AS24864* the originating AS, and *AS13335* a known scrubber (Cloudflare). If *AS13335* always appears as an upstream for the prefix *2.58.145.0/24*, we say the prefix uses always-on mode of scrubbing and is a protected prefix.

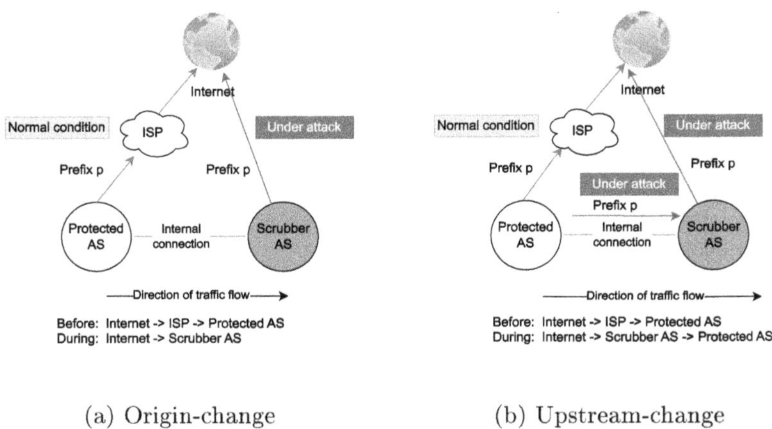

(a) Origin-change   (b) Upstream-change

Fig. 1. Two ways of on-demand scrubbing we distinguish: a) Origin-change, where the scrubber originates the protected prefix, and b) Upstream-change, where a scrubber comes as an upstream of the protected AS.

2.2 On-Demand Scrubbing Through Origin Changes

In on-demand scrubbing through origin changes, a scrubber AS originates the protected AS' prefixes on behalf of the protected AS during a DDoS attack (as shown by the red arrow in Fig. 1a). Because this action involves a temporary change of the origin of the protected prefix, we call this mode "origin-change".

In scrubbing through origin changes, the scrubber ASN appears as the origin of a protected prefix in the BGP AS path during a DDoS attack. As a result, all Internet traffic first goes to the scrubber, which delivers clean traffic to the protected AS using an internal connection. A few research papers discuss this method [7,54], but they lack detailed empirical evidence of inferring such cases.

As an example, consider AS path with ASNs *[3492 52025 32097 12200 33070]* for prefix *148.62.86.0/24*, where *AS33070* is the originating AS. In our data, we observed scrubber *AS19905* (Vercara) starting to originate that prefix, presumably to absorb a DDoS attack. As a result, the AS path changes to *835 3257 19905* for prefix *148.62.86.0/24*. After around 35 min, Vercara stops originating the prefix, and the origin reverts to *AS33070* (or to another ASN different from the scrubber that is authorized to originate), presumably when the DDoS attack is over.

For routing security, the prefix owner must authorize the scrubber's ASN in its ROAs [5] to prevent routing anomalies and allow scrubbing to operate safely [5]. ROAs are cryptographically signed objects in RPKI specifying which AS may originate which prefixes and up to what length. Without such ROAs, ROA-validating ASes may reject the scrubber's announcements, undermining mitigation. A prefix is RPKI-valid if a ROA exists that authorizes the scrubber's ASN and the announced length does not exceed the ROA's maximum; it is

Invalid if the ROA specifies a different ASN or a shorter length. A Notfound state indicates no covering ROA.

Similarly, ASes using IRR-based filtering must ensure their route objects are updated to include the scrubber's ASN. A route object specifies the IP prefix and originating ASN that an AS intends to announce in BGP. Since many network operators have not yet deployed RPKI-based filtering, IRR-based filtering remains the most widely used method, even among networks participating in the MANRS routing security initiative [19,37].

2.3 On-Demand Scrubbing Through Upstream Changes

In on-demand scrubbing through upstream changes, the protected AS originates its BGP prefix and advertises the prefix to a scrubber for mitigation during a DDoS attack, as shown in Fig. 1b

As an example of upstream-change-based scrubbing, consider the AS path with ASNs *[2914 9744 45753]* for the originated prefix *182.16.18.0/24*, which we found in our data. First, the originating *AS45753* changes its upstream to scrubber *AS19905* (Vercara), presumably because of a DDoS attack. As a result, we see a new AS path for the prefix with ASNs *[2652 1299 2914 19905 45753]*. After around 47 min (presumably when the attack is over), the origin *AS45753* reverts its upstream to *AS9744*. In this example, we found that the protected AS used the same upstream before and after the attack, but they might differ if the AS has multiple upstream providers.

A protected AS can implement upstream-changes in three ways [21,26,46], which are essentially traffic engineering techniques [17]: i) the protected AS withdraws its announcement to its ISP and advertises it toward the scrubber, ii) the protected AS prepends its ASN on the AS path toward its ISP, causing the traffic to flow through the scrubber during the attack because of the shorter path toward the scrubber, and iii) the protected AS announces a more specific prefix (e.g. /24) toward the scrubber and a less specific prefix (e.g. /22) toward its regular ISP, thus deaggregating the a larger prefix into smaller ones to control routing and traffic flows. As a result, the routing will choose the route towards the scrubber.

3 Related Work on Scrubbing

We are unaware of prior work that provides insight into the prevalence of different scrubbing services, on-demand scrubbing services, and the operational practices of on-demand scrubbers based on public BGP and RPKI data. In general, the aspects of DDoS scrubbing that use BGP are relatively underexplored.

Khadka et al. [31] investigate the model in which the scrubber appears as an upstream provider of a protected AS. However, their study does not consider on-demand protection or differentiate between on-demand and always-on modes, as it samples data only one day per month. While the DDoS scrubbing providers they examine overlap with ours, the research questions and methodology differ in important ways. In contrast, we sample BGP data every five minutes, allowing us to distinguish on-demand from always-on protection, detect cases where a scrubber appears as the origin of a protected prefix, and assess the RPKI and IRR status of these prefixes.

Tung et al. [55] propose a method for distinguishing DDoS attacks from other BGP anomalies and for analyzing scrubber behavior during such attacks. However, their study is limited to a single attack affecting three prefixes of one AS, and only identifies ASes that had previously experienced attacks. In contrast, our method detects DDoS scrubbing activity, providing insights in different modes of scrubbing regardless of prior attacks.

Jonker et al. [29] state that a DPS (DDoS Protection Service) provider announces an IP subnet of its protected AS, but they primarily focus on diverting traffic to the scrubber using the DNS rather than providing empirical evidence for BGP-based scrubber behavior. Testart et al. [54] state that DDoS scrubbers originate the prefixes of protected ASes during an attack, but their focus is on identifying and characterizing ASes that repeatedly and intentionally hijack IP prefixes.

Chung et al. [7] analyze the RPKI-based ROA deployment history. The paper looks at one snapshot of Routeviews data and finds 15 prefixes that are announced by DDoS protection ASes but belong to other ASes. Authors classify such announcements as "wrong" BGP announcements. As their primary focus is not on exploring RPKI practices of scrubbers, the study does not analyze the BGP updates that we perform to identify scrubbing cases.

Livadariu et al. [32] analyze the use of RPKI in conjunction with Remotely Triggered Black Hole (RTBH) filtering at Internet Exchange Points (IXPs), which is related but different from DDoS-handling using scrubbers. In addition, their study does not examine the RPKI practices of scrubbing providers. Chung et al. [7] study the deployment and coverage of RPKI longitudinally, where they examine a single routing snapshot, looking at 3 DDoS mitigation providers: Verisign, Neustar (now Vercara), and Level 3.

4   Methodology to Detect and Characterize Scrubbing

The goal of our methodology is to detect always-on and on-demand scrubbing (de)activations and to map out the properties of on demand-scrubbers, using public BGP data, such as BGP updates from RIS and RPKI data. We start the design of our methodology by identifying the five leading scrubbers and their ASNs, which we selected for our study. Next, we describe our approach for detecting on-demand scrubbing.

We classify on-demand scrubbing into "same-day" and "cross-day" events. Same-day scrubbing occurs when activation and deactivation signals for a prefix happen within a single day (24 h), while cross-day scrubbing spans two consecutive days (48 h). Both categories include origin-change and upstream-change (de)activations (Sects. 2.2 and 2.3). We make this distinction for methodological simplicity: same-day events are detected directly from BGP updates within a

Table 1. ASNs of scrubbers and the references to verify them.

Scrubbers	Cloudflare	Akamai	Vercara	Imperva	Radware
ASNs	13335	32787	19905	19551	198949
References	[9, 14, 42]	[1, 10, 21, 39]	[30, 53]	[58]	[31]

24-hour window, whereas cross-day events require first comparing RIBs across consecutive days to identify prefixes that disappear the next day. This approach reduces the sample size for subsequent BGP update analysis by focusing only on these disappearing prefixes. We elaborate on the motivation for this approach further below. To facilitate reproducibility, we make our source code and analysis scripts publicly available[1].

4.1 Identifying Scrubbers and their AS Numbers

We focus on five leading scrubbers: Cloudflare, Akamai Prolexic, Vercara, Imperva, and Radware. We use them because they are among the global top five in terms of bandwidth [18] capabilities to mitigate DDoS attacks, and are also recognized as leading scrubbers in the 2021 Forrester wave market analysis [23]. Prior research has similarly considered these scrubbers [28, 29, 31].

Following the approach of Khadka et al. [31], we determine the ASNs that the five scrubbers use for scrubbing by inspecting multiple sources: documentation of the scrubbers; checking AS path changes involving Akamai, Cloudflare, and Vercare as scrubbers against known past DDoS incidents; blogs; and contacting operators from Akamai, Cloudflare, and Radware. We also identify "sibling" ASNs, which are other ASNs of the five scrubbers that they do not use for scrubbing. We employ the CAIDA AS rank API [6], augmenting it with bgp.tools [3] to capture siblings missed by CAIDA, for this purpose.

We summarize the ASNs of scrubbers in Table 1, which includes the sources (e.g., blogs, past incidents) we used to confirm the identified ASNs. For example, we determined that Akamai's ASN is 32787 for DDoS protection, which we also verified from their website [1], and by validating past DDoS scrubbing events [21, 30, 39].

4.2 Detecting Always-on Scrubbing

We consider a prefix as protected by always-on scrubbing if its AS path has a scrubber as an upstream (second last AS in the path) for 30 days in a row, as seen in BGP Routing Information Bases (RIBs) data. This definition infers always-on protection based on our limited observation window and the typical minimum subscription length of 30 days reported in the product sheets of several scrubbers [36, 51, 52], but it does not provide direct evidence of uninterrupted protection.

---

[1] https://github.com/shyamkkhadka/scrubbing_detection.

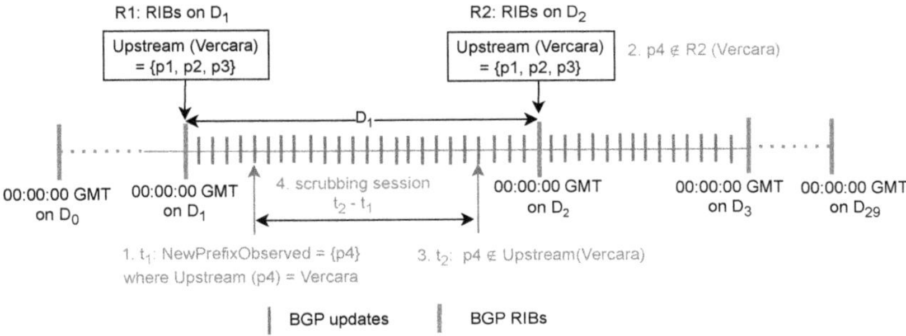

Fig. 2. Steps to detect on-demand scrubbing activated for prefix p4 at t_1 and deactivated at t_2 on day D_1 (same-day scrubbing). The protected AS activates the scrubber for prefix p4 through an upstream change.

We collect RIBs data containing AS paths with the scrubber ASN anywhere on the path using a daily snapshot from all RIS route collectors at 00:00:00 GMT from 1st May to 30th May, 2025. The RIBs data provides a snapshot of the global routing data as seen by all RIS public route collectors at 8-hour intervals, one of which is at 00:00:00 GMT.

Next, we find the records where the scrubber ASN appears as the second last AS in the AS path for all 30 days. This indicates that traffic always passes through the scrubber before reaching the protected AS. We drop any routes where the origin AS matches the scrubber ASN or any of its sibling ASNs, thus ensuring that only prefixes originating from non-scrubber ASNs are included.

4.3   Detecting Same-Day on-Demand Scrubbing

A same-day scrubbing is an on-demand scrubbing which is activated and deactivated within the same day. Figure 2 shows an overview of our methodology to detect same-day on-demand scrubbing for the upstream-change case. Our objective is to determine whether a prefix was scrubbed on a given day rather than how frequently it was scrubbed on a day. We therefore do not track individual cycles of activation, deactivation, or reactivation of a prefix in a day. Instead, we focus on detecting and characterizing scrubbing events at the daily level.

We consider a window of 24 h (from 00:00:01 GMT until 23:59:59 GMT) because DDoS attacks are often short-lived. For example, Cloudflare's Q2 2025 notes that 92% of attacks are mitigated within 10 min [12]. Similarly, Netscout reports that only 1.88% of attacks last more than 12 h [43]. A short-lived DDoS attack can, however, still span the boundary between two days, for instance, if it occurs a few minutes before and after midnight. We term such cases as cross-day scrubbing, which in our analysis is limited to the attacks spanning at most two consecutive days, and explain it in Sect. 4.4.

Daily BGP RIBs: We first collect daily snapshots of BGP RIBs data at 00:00:00 GMT (red lines in Fig. 2) and filter out private prefixes, default routes, reserved, and unallocated prefixes using Team Cymru's bogon lists [4], ensuring that only valid BGP prefixes are included in our analysis.

Next, we extract the AS paths of protected prefixes that have one of the five scrubbers we study as an origin or as an upstream. These prefixes are potentially being scrubbed at the time of the snapshot, which we use as a reference point to spot new scrubber activations in the next 24 h, both activations based on origin changes and on upstream changes. In the example of Fig. 2), our daily snapshot tells us that scrubber Vercara acts as an upstream for prefixes p1, p2, and p3 at 00:00:00 GMT on day D_1. In such cases, we also check that the origin is not a sibling of the scrubber, ensuring that we identify prefixes belonging to other ASes rather than the scrubber itself.

Activation Signals: Next, we identify scrubber activation signals up to 23:59:59 on day D_1 by monitoring BGP updates that the route collectors dump every five minutes (blue lines in Fig. 2). We use BGP updates instead of RIBs dumps because RIS collectors generate RIBs data only every eight hours, whereas BGP updates provide all routing changes at five-minute intervals, capturing any route changes that occur within each interval.

We say that scrubbing was activated for a prefix p during day D_1 if (1) p was not in the RIBs snapshot of D_1 and (2) either one of the five scrubbers began originating announcements for p before 23:59:59 (scrubber activation through an origination change) or if the scrubber appeared as an upstream in p's AS path before 23:59:59 (activation through an upstream change). Step 1 in Fig. 2 illustrates this step for prefix p4.

For example, in our data we observed a prefix *182.16.18.0/24* where scrubber *AS19905* (Vercara) appeared as an upstream in AS path *[29504, 15935, 174, 3257, 19905, 45753]* at 11:17:45 on 2025-05-12 in the BGP update files. Since this prefix was not in the RIBs snapshot of 00:00:00 GMT on 2025-05-12, we say scrubbing was activated for it on that day.

De-activation Signals: We consider a scrubber to deactivate for a particular prefix p on day D_1 when (1) the scrubber stops originating p and the protected AS or an AS different from the scrubber starts announcing p (deactivation through origin change) before 23:59:59 on D_1 or (2) when the scrubber is not an upstream any longer for p before 23:59:59 on D_1 (deactivation through upstream change). We determine whether such a deactivation event has occurred by examining the RIBs snapshot of day D_2 and comparing it to BGP updates of D_1. For example, prefix p4 is no longer in the RIBs snaphot of D_2 (step 2 in Fig. 2), which means that scrubbing was deactivated for it somewhere in day D_1. In such cases, we analyze BGP updates on D_1 to identify the precise time at which the scrubber disappeared from the AS paths (step 3). In our data, we observed that the scrubber (*AS19905*) is no longer an upstream for the prefix *182.16.18.0/24* on the path toward *AS45753* on 2025-05-13, which our method flags as a deactivation.

Scrubbing Session: We define a scrubbing session as the time elapsed between the first observation of an activation signal for a particular prefix by a route

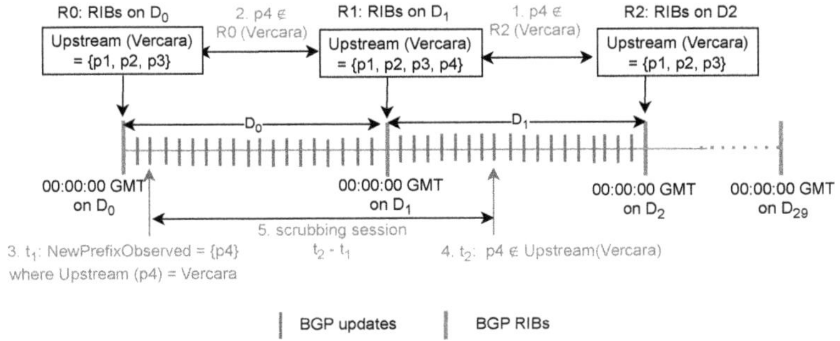

Fig. 3. Steps to detect on-demand scrubbing activated for prefix p4 on day D_0 and deactivated on day D_1 (cross-day scrubbing). The protected AS activates the scrubbing for p4 through an upstream-change.

collector peer and the last observation of that change (step 4 in Fig. 2). For example, we observed a BGP update where scrubber *AS19905* first appeared on the AS path *[48362, 1299, 6453, 19905, 45753]* for prefix *182.16.18.0/24* on 2025-05-12 at 11:17:45 GMT (activation based on upstream change). The last time we saw it was at 11:32:49 GMT on that same day (deactivation), which means the presumable scrubbing session (and DDoS attack) for that prefix is around 15 min.

Accuracy of (de)activation Signals: We require that at least two route collector peers observe the BGP updates corresponding to an activation or deactivation event before we flag it as such, to avoid relying on a single collector that may have stale data. For example, we saw the scrubbing activation signal for *182.16.18.0/24* at 215 collector peers. Our rationale is that seeing the same (de)activation event at multiple collectors increases the probability that a scrubber indeed started or stopped scrubbing because the BGP changes spread across the Internet. We limit the threshold to two collector peers to minimize operational effort.

We ignore scrubbing sessions of less than 1 min because they could be route flapping cases involving a scrubber, where an AS originates its prefix to a scrubber and withdraws rapidly over a short period of time. We choose 1 min because the recommended BGP Minimum Route Advertisement Interval (MRAI) is 30 s [27], and network operators can change that interval. The MRAI timer controls how frequently a BGP speaker can send updates to a peer, enforcing a minimum interval between consecutive advertisements of the same prefix.

4.4 Detecting Cross-Day on-Demand Scrubbing

We detect scrubbing that activates on a certain day and deactivates the following day (cross-day) by combining coarse and fine-grained analyses of BGP data, as shown in Fig. 3. We use a 48-hour window for our analysis, comparing RIBs from two consecutive days. Although the number of days to consider is not fixed, this window is sufficient to capture relevant scrubbing events [12,43].

We use the same concepts as in the case of same-day scrubbing (Sect. 4.3) in terms of methods for BGP data collection, scrubbing session, (de)activation signals, and accuracy of (de)activation signals. The differences are about examining changes in BGP RIBs and the activation signal in cross-day scrubbing.

We consider scrubbing to be activated for a prefix p before day D_1 if (1) p was in the RIBs snapshot of D_1 but not in RIBs snapshots of D_0 and D_2 and (2) either one of the five scrubbers began originating announcements for p before 00:00:00 on D_1 (scrubber activation through an origination change) or if the scrubber appeared as an upstream in p's AS path before 00:00:00 D_1 (activation through an upstream change). The detection method involves the following two steps.

Changes in BGP RIBs: As a coarse-grained analysis, we examine changes in the snapshots on reference day D_1 compared to those of days D_0 (previous day) and D_2 (following day) to identify the prefixes whose origin or upstream has changed. Steps 1 and 2 in Fig. 3 illustrate this step for prefix p4. This prefix might be being scrubbed because it is in the snapshot of D_1, but not in the snapshot of D_0 and D_2. We investigate that further in the next step. As an example, prefix *46.184.88.0/24* appeared in our analysis with upstream *AS19905* in the RIBs snapshot collected on 2025-05-03 at 00:00:00 GMT. We checked the prefix's upstream on 2025-05-02 and 2025-05-04 at 00:000:00 GMT, where it had a different upstream (*AS47794*) on both days, which means it might have been scrubbed using an upstream-change-based activation.

Activation Signals: Next, our fine-grained analysis involves monitoring BGP updates for the prefixes that are potentially being scrubbed before and after the D_1 snapshot, as identified in the previous step. We analyze BGP updates from 00:00:00 GMT on day D_0 to 23:59:59 GMT on day D_1, to find the activation and deactivation times for prefix p4 (t_1 and t_2 in Fig. 3, respectively), which are the times the scrubber (dis)appeared as an origin or as an upstream in BGP updates. Steps 3 and 4 in Fig. 3 illustrate this process.

In our data, we observed that the first time a route collector saw the prefix *46.184.88.0/24* with scrubber *AS19905* as its upstream was 2025-05-02 03:19:13 GMT (step 3), and the last time was 2025-05-03 23:59:35 GMT (step 4). We flag this prefix as a scrubbed prefix across days starting on 2025-05-02.

4.5   Identifying Potential Origin-Change Using ROA Configurations

In addition to detecting dynamic scrubbing (de)activation through BGP origin changes (see Sects. 4.3 and 4.4), we also identify prefixes that are likely to use origin change-activated scrubbing by analyzing their ROA objects. For this analysis, we examine ROA objects published by the five RIRs (RIPENCC, APNIC, ARIN, LACNIC, and AFRINIC) in which the scrubbers are registered as the origin ASN for prefixes. We then check how many of these prefixes have ROAs listing a different ASN as the origin. We use the ROA data on 30th May 2025, the end date of our study period. We exclude any ASNs that are siblings of the scrubber.

Our method is grounded in the operational requirement that only ASNs authorized in a prefix's ROAs can validly originate it under RPKI. Hence, if a prefix has a ROA authorizing the scrubber's ASN as well as ROAs for the protected AS' ASN, then this strongly indicates that the scrubber originates the prefix during DDoS mitigation. Such ROAs allow the scrubber to announce the prefix during an attack while remaining compliant with RPKI and ROA-based routing security standards. Consequently, origin change-activated scrubbing requires protected ASes to create these ROAs, as documented in scrubbers operation guides, RFCs, and mailing lists [13,16,20,35,40].

4.6 Analyzing RPKI and IRR Management Practices of Scrubbers

Finally, our methodology aims to characterize the RPKI and IRR management practices of scrubbers that protected ASes activate through origin changes. This is important because ROA-validating ASes may drop announcements with RPKI statuses Invalid or Notfound (see Sect. 2.2) [24]. In addition, ASes that perform IRR-based filtering may also reject announcements if they cannot retrieve a matching IRR record, which might reduce the effectiveness of scrubbing.

We examine the prefixes that we obtained from our same-day and cross-day scrubbing detection methodologies (see Sect. 4.3 and Sect. 4.4) to characterize such practices.

RPKI Practices. We assess if an origin-change activated scrubber properly implements ROA management practices by validating the ROAs at the dates when scrubbing was activated for a prefix, with the outcome being RPKI-valid (practices properly implemented), RPKI-Invalid (practices not properly implemented), or RPKI-Notfound (practices not implemented). We use the RPKI archive for this purpose, a publicly available repository of cryptographically signed ROA objects collected from all RIRs [49]. We analyze and verify the ROA records from the five RIRs .

IRR Practices. For a scrubber-originated prefix that has RPKI statuses Invalid or Notfound, we also determine whether an ASN was registered as an origin in IRRs by examining the prefix's route objects in the IRRs operated by the five RIRs and by inspecting RADb (Routing Assets Database) using the RADb API [45]. While the five RIRs collectively cover all global IP address allocations and thus provide broad visibility, their IRRs alone are insufficient to capture all existing route object registrations because many operators maintain entries in third-party IRRs for operational or historical reasons. To improve coverage and completeness, we include RADb, one of the largest and oldest public IRRs operated by Merit Network.

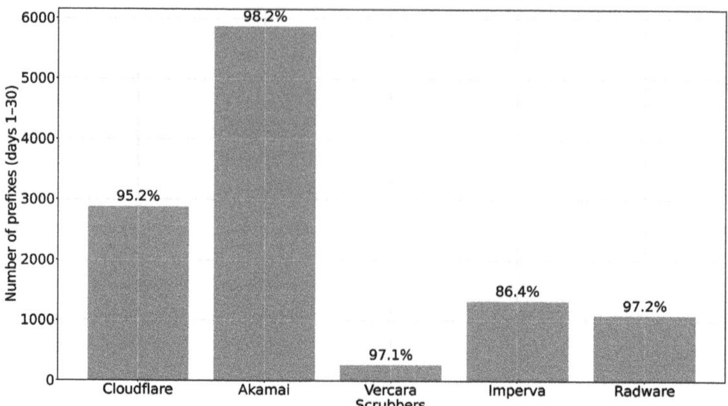

Fig. 4. Always-on protected prefixes. The y-axis shows the number of prefixes that retain the scrubber on their AS paths each day over our 30-day study period. The percentages above the bars indicate the share of always-on protected prefixes relative to prefixes for which the scrubber appeared as an upstream on the first day.

5 Results on Detecting and Characterizing Scrubbing

This section presents our findings on detecting and characterizing scrubbing, which we obtained by applying our methodology to the global top five scrubbers. Our study period is 2025-05-01 (1st May) until 2025-05-30 (30th May).

5.1 Always-On Scrubbing

Figure 4 shows the number of prefixes using always-on protection, as identified through our methodology (Sect. 4.2). We observe that Cloudflare and Akamai account for the largest number of always-on protected prefixes, which are 2,876 and 5,861, respectively. Imperva and Radware have a more moderate number of always-on protected prefixes (1,325 and 1,082). In contrast, Vercara covers only 264 prefixes in always-on mode, indicating a more limited deployment.

The bars in Fig. 4 show how many prefixes consistently retained a scrubber on their AS paths throughout the 30-day observation window. The proportions of always-on protected prefixes relative to the total number of protected prefixes for a particular scrubber on the first day are 95.2%, 98.2%, 97.1%, 86.4%, and 97.2% for the five scrubbers, respectively. For example, for Cloudflare, we find 2,876 prefixes that were always scrubbed in our study period, which corresponds to 95.2% of the prefixes that Cloudflare protected on 1st May.

These results confirm that the majority of prefixes remain protected for at least one month, consistent with our definition of always-on scrubbing described in Sect. 4.2. The only notable deviation is observed for Imperva, of which 86.4% had that scrubber on their AS path for 30 consecutive days.

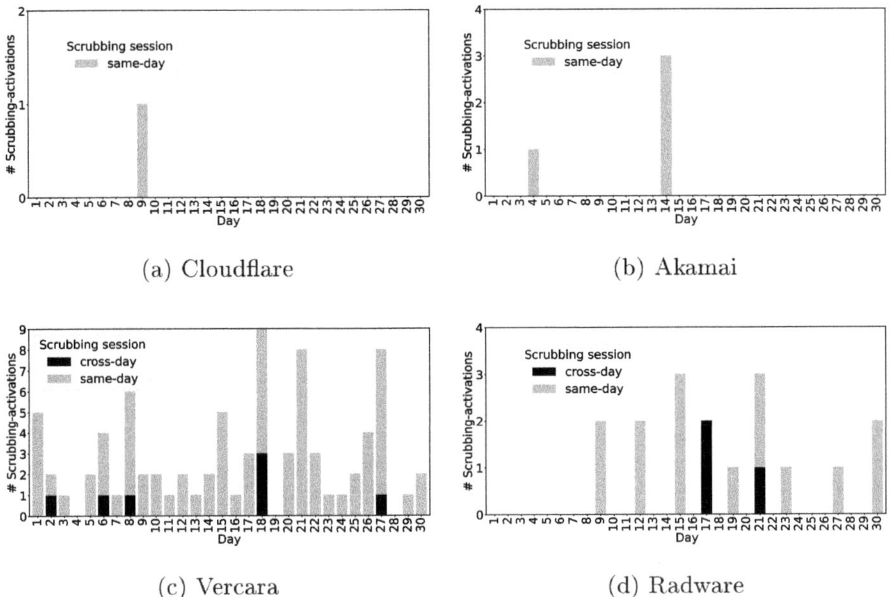

(a) Cloudflare   (b) Akamai

(c) Vercara   (d) Radware

Fig. 5. Origin-change-based scrubbing activations for four scrubbers. We did not find any origin-change activations with Imperva. The y-axes use different scales for readability.

Key takeaway: We identify 11,408 prefixes with always-on protection from the five scrubbers, with an average of 94.8% of prefixes present on the first day remaining continuously protected over the 30-day period.

5.2   On-Demand Scrubbing: (de)activation Through Origin Changes

We address two research questions in this section. First, we investigate how widely origin change-activated scrubbing is being used (RQ2 in Sect. 1), for which we use the methodology we discussed in Sects. 4.3 and 4.4. Next, we determine what the ROA and IRR management practices of origin change-based scrubbers are (RQ3) using the methodology from Sect. 4.6.

Figure 5 shows the number of prefixes that were protected using origin change-activated scrubbing for our four scrubbers, with same-day scrubbing and cross-day scrubbing for the 30 days of our study period. We found no such cases for Imperva, so we did not plot them. Cloudflare and Akamai each have a very small number of prefixes that they protect using origin-change activations: 1 and 4 prefixes, which were activated and deactivated on the same day. We did not observe any cases of cross-day scrubbing for them.

We observe a large number of origin-change activations involving Vercara and Radware, with 82 and 17 total activations, respectively. Of these, same-day and cross-day scrubbing account for 75 and 7 activations for Vercara, and 14 and 3 activations for Radware.

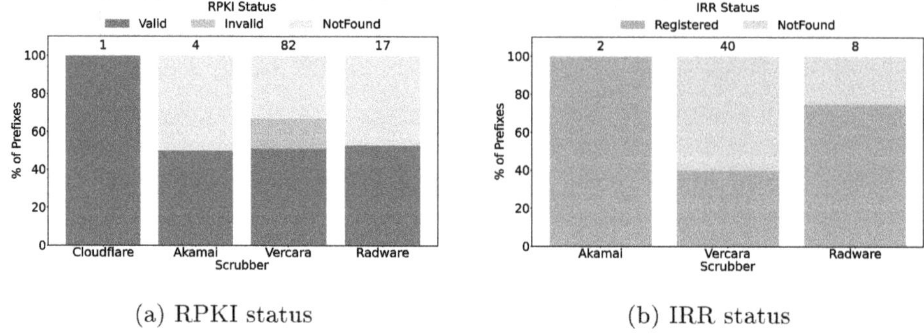

(a) RPKI status   (b) IRR status

Fig. 6. (a) RPKI status of prefixes protected by origin-change-based activations. The numbers at the top of the bars indicate the total number of prefixes originated by each scrubber. (b) IRR registration details of prefixes having RPKI-Invalid or Notfound statuses in five RIRs and RADb. Numbers at the top bars indicate the total number of prefixes originated by each scrubber with RPKI-Invalid or Notfound statuses.

Key takeaway: Out of the five scrubbers, the protected prefixes of Vercara and Radware seem to use the origin-change model mostly. We suspect that the origin-change-based activations are used in a limited way, as we did not observe this behavior for the other three major scrubbers.

RPKI Management Practices of Scrubbers. We examine the ROA status of all prefixes on the Internet to determine whether scrubbers were authorized to originate them, using the methodology we described in Sect. 4.6.

Figure 6a shows the distribution of RPKI statuses for four of our five scrubbers that originate prefixes of protected ASes (Imperva has no prefixes protected by origin-change activations). Cloudflare and Akamai have a very low number of protected prefixes they originate: 1 and 4, respectively (top of the bars).

We observe that 51% of the prefixes originated by Vercara for scrubbing are RPKI Valid, while 16% (13 prefixes) are RPKI Invalid, and 33% (27 prefixes) are NotFound. All of the Invalid cases are due to an origin AS mismatch, meaning that the prefix originated by the scrubber does not have a ROA authorizing the scrubber's ASN as the origin. For Radware, we find a larger proportion of NotFound prefixes compared to valid ones, accounting for 53% and 47%, respectively, with no Invalid cases observed.

Key takeaway: Out of 104 scrubbed prefixes, 52% of scrubbed prefixes were RPKI Valid, 12.5% are invalid, while 35.5% were not found, indicating that the scrubbers do not strictly follow RPKI/ROA practices. This may reduce mitigation effectiveness, as ROA filtering [5] ASes could filter routes from these scrubbers.

IRR Management Practices of Scrubbers. Among the five scrubbers we studied, we observed that Akamai, Vercara, and Radware originated prefixes with RPKI-Notfound or Invalid status. For Vercara, out of 40 prefixes with RPKI status Invalid or Notfound, we found that 16 (40%) were registered in at least one of the six IRRs we examined, while 24 (60%) were absent from all six IRRs. Radware originated 8 prefixes with Invalid or Notfound RPKI status, 6 of which were registered in one of the IRRs. Overall, we observed that 24 out of 50 prefixes (48%) that underwent scrubbing and had Invalid or Notfound RPKI status were registered in at least one of the six IRRs, whereas 52% were not present in any of them.

We speculate on two reasons for such a high percentage of prefixes not found in IRRs. First, they might be registered to other IRRs beyond our study. Second, the scrubbers might have some private agreements (e.g., Letter of Authorization [33,34]) with their protected ASes and their upstreams to originate the protected ASes' prefixes under an attack.

Key takeaway: Only 48% of the total number of prefixes that underwent scrubbing are registered into one of the 6 IRRs we examined. Since the scrubbers are not authorized to originate these prefixes based on either ROA or IRR data, such routes may have been dropped during a DDoS attack by ASes performing ROA or IRR-based filtering, potentially limiting scrubbing effectiveness.

On-Demand Scrubbing from ROA Configurations. We use our methodology of Sect. 4.5 to identify prefixes that are likely to use on-demand scrubbing based on the origin-change model. Figure 7 shows the distribution of ROAs in which prefixes are registered with both scrubbers and other ASNs as origins across five RIRs. Among the scrubbers, we observe that Vercara has the highest number of such prefixes across all five RIRs (amber bar in the figure), which potentially shows it protects many prefixes that use origin-change-based on-demand scrubbing. We counted the number of such prefixes in all five RIRs and aggregated them. In our case of Vercara, we see that the ROAs registered in five RIRs is the maximum (3,237 prefixes), having ROAs for both the scrubber and other ASNs. Radware comes next with 935 such prefixes registered in the five RIRs.

Figure 7 also complements our findings in Sect. 5.2, where we observed a high number of origin change-based activations for Vercara and Radware from BGP data. We observe a very low number of such cases for Akamai and Cloudflare, indicating low usage of origin change-based on-demand scrubbing cases by them. We aggregate such prefixes across five RIRs and find a total of 4,475 prefixes that are likely to use origin-change-based on-demand scrubbing.

Key Takeaway: We identify up to 4,475 prefixes with ROAs authorizing scrubbers, suggesting that these prefixes likely employ origin-changeâĂŞbased on-demand scrubbing. Notably, Vercara and Radware account for the majority of such cases, with 3,237 and 935 prefixes, respectively.

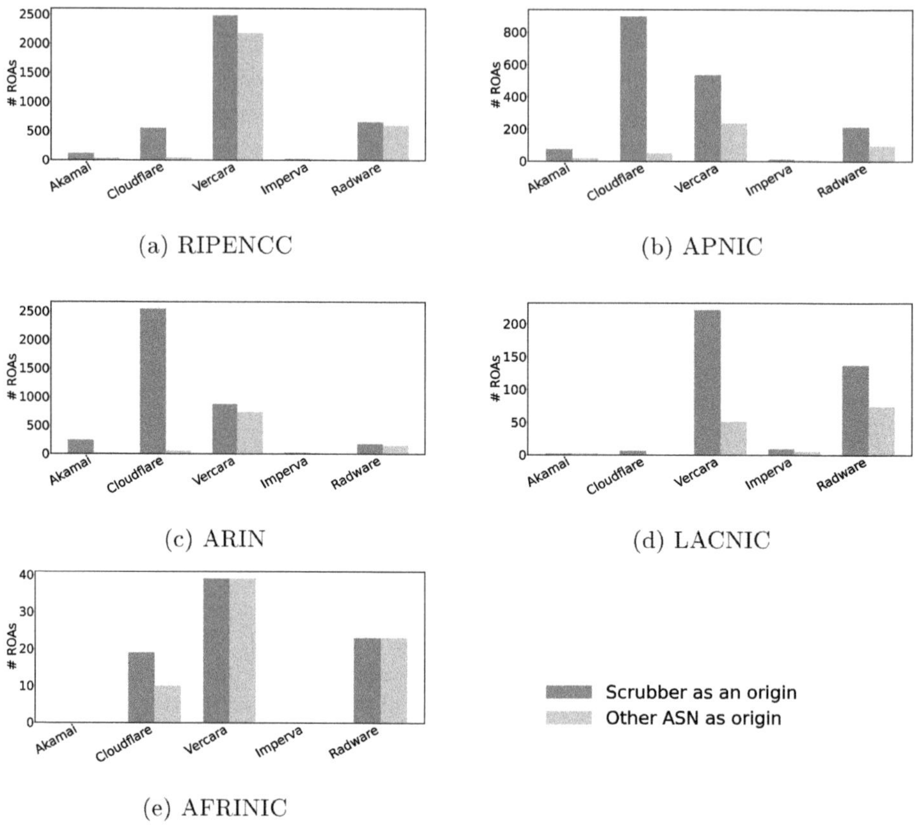

Fig. 7. Distribution of ROAs listing the prefixes with scrubber as the origin in five RIRs, highlighting how many of these prefixes also have ROAs registered under other ASNs, indicating potential for origin-change during on-demand scrubbing.

5.3 On-Demand Scrubbing: (de)activation Through Upstream Changes

We assess the extent to which a scrubber appears as an upstream of a protected AS for scrubbing purposes, which gives the prefixes that were upstream change-activated. Figure 8 shows that Cloudflare regularly engages in this type of scrubbing, with the daily number of scrubbed prefixes ranging from a minimum of 2 to a maximum of 16. We observe that the frequency of activation and deactivation cycles for protected ASes of Cloudflare is higher than the other scrubbers. Akamai and Imperva follow Cloudflare in terms of regular scrubbing, as we did not see any activations for them for some days. Vercara showed a high number of prefixes scrubbed on the 13th May: 282 prefixes. Radware also scrubbed a relatively low number of prefixes: 38 prefixes in 30 days.

Key Takeaway: We observe daily DDoS scrubbing activity in our study period that follows the scrubbing activation model based on upstream-changes, with

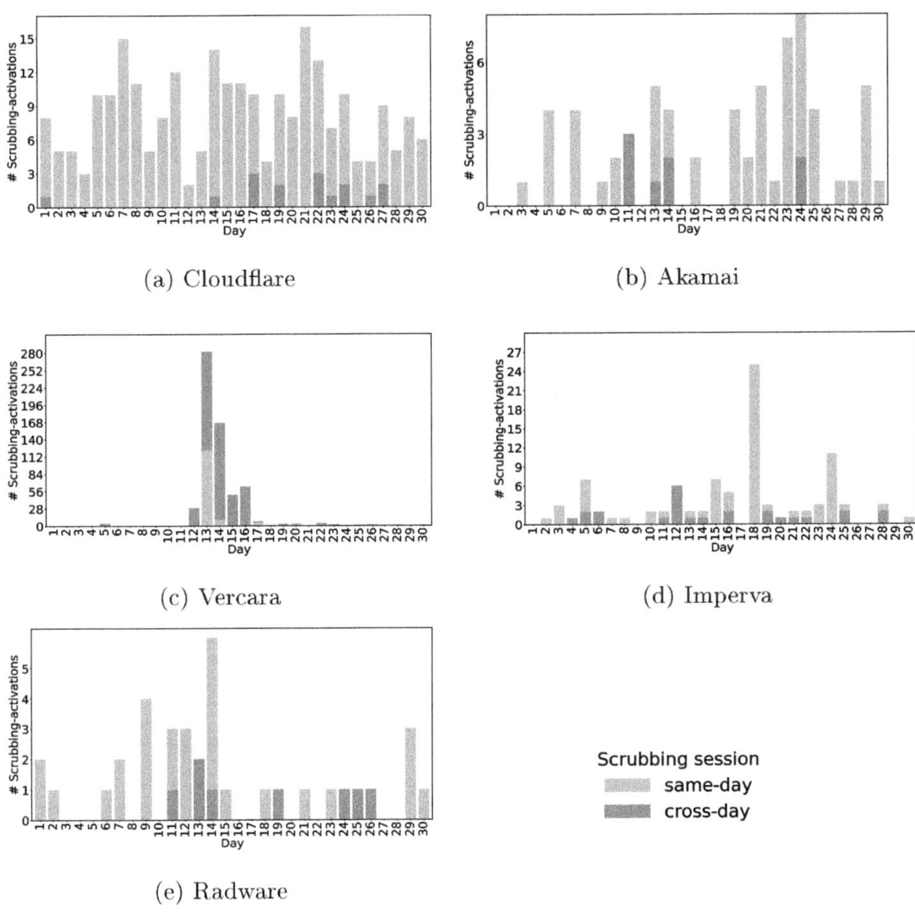

(a) Cloudflare

(b) Akamai

(c) Vercara

(d) Imperva

(e) Radware

Fig. 8. Upstream-change-based scrubbing activations for five scrubbers. The y-axes use different scales for readability.

Cloudflare and Akamai accounting for the largest share of daily scrubbing activity.

5.4 Hints About DDoS Attacks from Behavior of on-Demand Scrubbing

This section provides an initial characterization of DDoS attacks mitigated by on-demand scrubbers by examining the frequency and maximum duration of scrubbing activations. We then analyze the distribution of scrubbing sessions with their durations, total scrubbing activations, and the top five scrubbed prefixes during our study period. To do this, we aggregate scrubbing events across all five scrubbers, including both origin-change and upstream-change activations that occur within the same day or across consecutive days (cross-day) over the

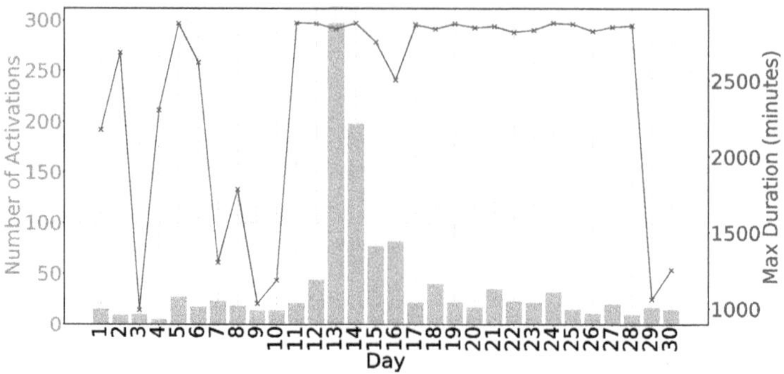

Fig. 9. Aggregated scrubbing events across all five scrubbers, showing daily activation counts and the maximum scrubbing session duration.

30-day study period. While these scrubbing durations offer useful hints about the periods during which prefixes may be under mitigation, they should be interpreted with caution, as scrubbing can remain active for reasons unrelated to actual attack activity (e.g., operator caution, delayed deactivation, human error, contractual arrangements, or pricing and notification policies).

Frequency: We define scrubbing frequency as the number of prefixes that are activated per day in our 30-day study period. Although we found cases where a protected AS activates scrubbing for the same prefix multiple times a day, we do not consider these repeated activations for determining frequency. This is because our focus is on detecting and characterizing scrubbing events at the daily level rather than tracking the (de)activation cycles of individual prefixes within a day, and also simplifies our methodology.

The frequency of scrubbing activations indicates the number of DDoS attacks in a day.

Maximum Duration: The maximum duration of a scrubbing session indicates the maximum duration of the DDoS attacks that the scrubber presumably handled during activation. We consider determining the exact activation and deactivation times, and thus the precise duration of the mitigation, as future work.

Figure 9 highlights the daily frequency of scrubbing activations and the maximum scrubbing session durations. We observe that the maximum duration of scrubbing in our 30-day study period is 2878.68 min (48 h) for three prefixes that were originated by *AS28846* on 2025-05-11. Since we limited our study window to 48 h, we missed scrubbing sessions that take longer, but these are rare as we discussed in Sect. 4.3.

The maximum duration of a scrubbing session within a day in our study period is 1,346 min (22 h and 26 min) for prefix *66.248.170.0/24* on 2025-05-20. The minimum duration of the scrubbing session was 1 min for the prefix *2401:e380:10::/48* originated on 2025-05-21 at 05:49:55. We observed 291 scrubbing activations on 2025-05-13, which is the maximum in our study period.

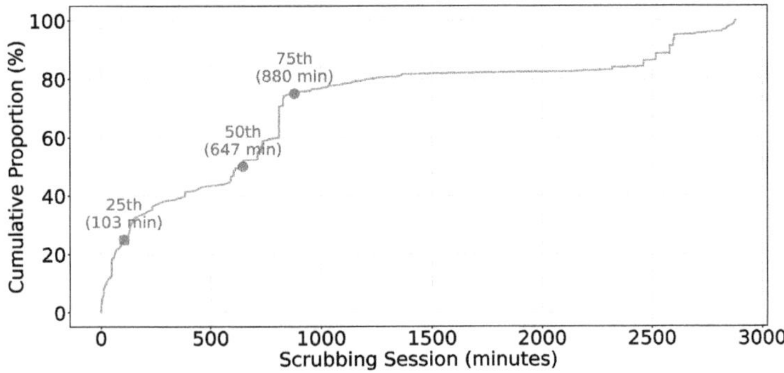

Fig. 10. Cumulative distribution of scrubbing sessions.

Distribution of Scrubbing Sessions with their Durations: Figure 10 shows
the cumulative distribution of the durations of scrubbing sessions. We see that
25% of them lasted less than 1 h and 45 min (around 103 min). This indicates that
short-lived attacks are quite common, and many scrubbing operations resolve
quickly. Half of the scrubbing sessions ended within about 10 h and 45 min
(around 647 h), while the other half persisted longer. Additionally, we see 25% of
scrubbing sessions lasted longer than around 15 h (around 880 min). These findings also validate our assumption of considering 24 h as the maximum duration
of a DDoS attack in Sect. 4.3. While some scrubbers report mitigation within
10 min [12,43], we find that AS operators often keep scrubbing active longer. We
learnt from NaWas [41] that this is done as a precaution, beyond the immediate
duration of the attack.

Total Scrubbing Activations. Table 2 shows the number of scrubbing activations that the five scrubbers faced in a month, along with the number of
origin-change-activated and upstream-changed activations. We see that Vercara
handled the largest number of activations (703), suggesting they handled the
most DDoS attacks. The next highest is Cloudflare (250 activations). Radware
went through the lowest number activations (55) for the prefixes it protects.

Table 2. Origin-change and upstream-change activations for the five scrubbers.

Scrubbers	#Origin-changed	#Upstream-changed	#Total
Cloudflare	1	249	250
Akamai	4	66	70
Vercara	82	621	703
Imperva	0	96	96
Radware	17	38	55

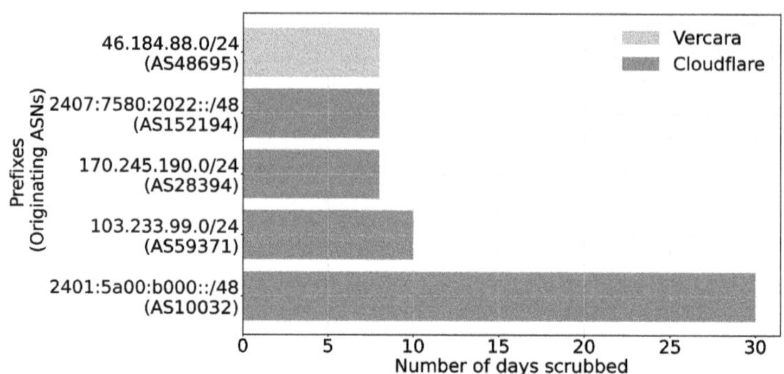

Fig. 11. The top five prefixes in terms of the number of days they underwent scrubbing, their originating ASes, and their scrubbers.

Top Five Scrubbed Prefixes: Figure. 11 shows the top five protected prefixes in terms of the number of days that they underwent on-demand scrubbing in our study period. We observe that Cloudflare handled the majority of the top prefixes with the longest scrubbing time, while Vercara was responsible for a smaller subset. The prefix *2401:5a00:b000::/48* underwent upstream-change-based scrubbing at least once in the 30 days of our study period, with different durations. The originating ASN of that prefix under normal conditions (not scrubbing) is *AS10032* (BDX DC Services (HK) Limited), which is a data center company.

Key Takeaway: We observe that the daily duration of scrubbing sessions ranges from a minimum of 1 min to a maximum of approximately 22 h for same-day scrubbing, while the maximum is around 48 h for cross-day scrubbing, with 25% of sessions lasting less than 1 h and 45 min.

6   Discussion and Limitations

First, we answer the four research questions (RQs) that we raised in Sect. 1. Then, we present the limitations of our study.

RQ1: Dominance of DDoS Scrubbing Protection Types. Our study of a 30-day period and based on the global top five scrubbers shows that there are more protected prefixes that use always-on than on-demand scrubbing. We observe that the number of always-on protected prefixes is 11,408. We find 1,174 prefixes use on-demand protection, which we inferred by analyzing BGP data. In addition, we assess that the number of prefixes that are likely to use on-demand scrubbing is 4,475 based on our analysis of ROA records. Among these, 54 prefixes with RPKI-valid status underwent scrubbing in the origin-change cases we analyzed. In total, we thus identify 5,649 prefixes that either use on-demand scrubbing (from BGP data) or are likely to use so (from ROA records).

RQ2: Characteristics of On-Demand Scrubbing. We observe on-demand scrubbing occurring daily on the Internet. Among the two models of on-demand protection (origin-change and upstream-change), we find that upstream-change is more prevalent, with 104 and 1,070 prefixes, respectively. This differs somewhat from prior studies [7,29,54], which primarily discuss the origin-change model of on-demand scrubbing. We see that only 2 scrubbers (Vercara and Radware) out of five in our study mostly change the origin of prefixes of their protected ASes under a DDoS attack. One reason for the dominance of the upstream-change model could be that it gives the owner AS of a prefix flexibility and control to originate their prefix themselves, rather than delegating the prefix origination task to the scrubber AS. In this way, the protected AS also does not need to create ROAs for scrubbers for its prefixes.

RQ3: RPKI and IRR Management Practices. We observe that 52% of the prefixes that underwent the case of origin-change have RPKI Valid status, while the remaining 48% of the prefixes have RPKI Invalid(12.5%) or Notfound (35.5%)status, which shows that the scrubbers that mostly follow the origin-change model do not strictly follow RPKI and ROA practices. This might affect their DDoS mitigation services and put their protected ASes at risk because other ASes on the Internet that filter Invalid RPKI announcements can drop such BGP announcements. Additionally, we observe 48% of total prefixes that underwent scrubbing are registered in IRRs. The remaining 52% are not found in IRR records. Some ASes that rely on IRR-based filtering may reject or ignore the scrubbed routes, reducing the effectiveness of the mitigation. We suspect that some private agreements exist between the scrubber and the protected AS, allowing the scrubber to originate the protected AS's prefixes. Without such agreements, the routes originated by scrubbers for scrubbing would likely be dropped by other BGP peers of the scrubber that enforce RPKI or IRR-based filtering.

RQ4: Hints About DDoS Attacks from Scrubbing. We observe daily scrubbing sessions with scrubbing durations ranging from as short as 1 min to as long as 22 h in a day, which hints at a wide range of DDoS attack durations that the scrubbers handle. Notably, 25% of the scrubbing sessions have a duration of less than 1 h and 45 min, which illustrates that short-lived DDoS attacks occur frequently. These insights into DDoS attacks could inform regulators and policymakers about the DDoS-protection levels of ASes within a region or a country.

Limitations. There are inherent limitations to using publicly available BGP data. For example, limited coverage and bias in the data collection of RIS route collectors [50], which means we miss some scrubbing-protected prefixes in our analysis. Also, some inaccurate records in IRR data [19] affect our findings about IRR management practices of the scrubbers.

Beyond these inherent dataset limitations, we acknowledge the other limitations related to our methodology. First, we lack ground truth data about DDoS scrubbing to validate our findings about the prefixes that underwent scrubbing.

Getting data from scrubbers or from their protected ASes would help us to assess our methodology and validate our findings. Our second limitation is that we might misclassify a prefix that a scrubber originates or a protected AS advertises its announcement to a scrubber temporarily for its testing purpose, as a protected prefix.

7 Conclusion and Future Work

We have presented a methodology that detects scrubbing by combining BGP dumps and BGP updates, thereby providing insights into always-on and on-demand DDoS scrubbing for the global top five scrubbers. Our methodology tracks the changes in BGP paths to infer on-demand scrubbing. We characterize on-demand scrubbing by investigating its different modes of operation and the RPKI and IRR management practices of scrubbers.

We show that a scrubber does not always originate its protected ASes' prefixes to handle an attack. The scrubbers also perform mitigation by allowing the protected ASes to originate their prefixes themselves, with the scrubber coming as the first upstream provider of the protected AS. In fact, we observe that this model is more prevalent during our study period, as reflected in the BGP data.

As future work, we plan to evaluate the effectiveness of scrubbing by measuring the time between the start of a DDoS attack and scrubbing activation, as well as between attack termination and scrubbing deactivation. We plan to get the DDoS attack datasets from scrubbers or from network operators who are using the scrubbing service to know the precise DDoS attack start and termination time.

Acknowledgment. We want to thank the anonymous reviewers for their valuable feedback on our paper. This research was funded by the Dutch Research Council (NWO) as part of the projects CATRIN (NWA.1215.18.003) and UPIN (CS.004). CATRIN is part of NWO's National Research Agenda (NWA).

Ethical Considerations. Our work raises no ethical concerns. Our analysis relies on publicly available datasets.

References

1. Akamai: Prolexic - Comprehensive DDoS Attack Protection. https://www.akamai.com/resources/product-brief/prolexic. Accessed 13 Nov 2025
2. Akamai Services Descriptions | Akamai. https://www.akamai.com/site/en/documents/corporate/akamai-services-descriptions.pdf. Accessed 13 Nov 2025
3. BGP.tools. https://bgp.tools/
4. Bogon Reference HTTP. https://www.team-cymru.com/bogon-reference-http. Accessed 10 Oct 2025
5. Bush, R.: Origin Validation Operation Based on the Resource Public Key Infrastructure (RPKI). RFC 7115 (Jan 2014). 10.17487/RFC7115. https://www.rfc-editor.org/info/rfc7115

6. CAIDA: AS Rank (March 2024). https://doi.org/10.21986/CAIDA.DATA.AS-RANK

7. Chung, T., et al.: RPKI is coming of age: A longitudinal study of RPKI deployment and invalid route origins. In: Proceedings of the Internet Measurement Conference, pp. 406–419 (2019)

8. Cloudflare Docs: About | cloudflare network interconnect docs (2024). https://developers.cloudflare.com/network-interconnect/about/

9. Cloudflare Magic Transit Docs: Advertise prefixes (2024). https://developers.cloudflare.com/magic-transit/how-to/advertise-prefixes/. Accessed 14 Nov 2025

10. Cloudflare Radar: AS32787 overview (2024). https://radar.cloudflare.com/as32787

11. Flow-based monitoring for Magic Transit. https://blog.cloudflare.com/flow-based-monitoring-for-magic-transit/. Accessed 19 Nov 2025

12. Hyper-volumetric DDoS attacks skyrocket: Cloudflare's 2025 Q2 DDoS threat report. https://blog.cloudflare.com/ddos-threat-report-for-2025-q2/. Accessed 28 Sept 2025

13. Get started · Cloudflare BYOIP docs. https://developers.cloudflare.com/byoip/get-started/. Accessed 10 Oct 2025

14. BGP zombies and excessive path hunting. https://blog.cloudflare.com/going-bgp-zombie-hunting/. Accessed 20 Nov 2025

15. Magic Transit Reference Architecture. https://developers.cloudflare.com/reference-architecture/architectures/magic-transit/. Accessed 20 Nov 2025

16. RPKI and Cloud DDoS Protection - Corero Network Security. https://www.corero.com/rpki-and-cloud-ddos-protection/. Accessed 14 Oct 2025

17. Darwich, O., Pelsser, C., Vermeulen, K.: Detecting traffic engineering from public BGP data. In: International Conference on Passive and Active Network Measurement, pp. 307–334. Springer (2025)

18. DDoS providers. https://x.com/eastdakota/status/1937828176056521011/photo/1. Accessed 10 Sept 2025

19. Du, B., et al.: Irregularities in the internet routing registry. In: Proceedings of the 2023 ACM on Internet Measurement Conference, pp. 104–110 (2023)

20. Gilad, Y., Goldberg, S., Sriram, K., Snijders, J., Maddison, B.: The Use of maxLength in the Resource Public Key Infrastructure (RPKI). RFC 9319 (Oct 2022). https://doi.org/10.17487/RFC9319, https://www.rfc-editor.org/info/rfc9319

21. GitHub Survived the Biggest DDoS Attack Ever Recorded. https://www.wired.com/story/github-ddos-memcached/. Accessed 14 Oct 2025

22. Global Routing Intelligence Platform. https://grip.inetintel.cc.gatech.edu/. Accessed 17 Sept 2025

23. Holmes, D.: The forrester wave^{TM}: DDoS mitigation solutions, q1 2021 (2021). https://allofsecurity.pl/wp-content/uploads/2021/03/The-Forrester-Wave-DDoS-Mitigation-Solutions-Q1-2021.pdf. Accessed 14 Jan 2025

24. Huston, G., Michaelson, G.: Validation of Route Origination Using the Resource Certificate Public Key Infrastructure (PKI) and Route Origin Authorizations (ROAs). RFC 6483 (Feb 2012). https://doi.org/10.17487/RFC6483, https://www.rfc-editor.org/info/rfc6483

25. Imperva: Advanced DDoS Protection & Mitigation Services. https://www.imperva.com/products/ddos-protection-services/. Accessed 11 Mar 2025

26. Imperva Documentation Portal. https://docs.imperva.com/bundle/cloud-application-security/page/introducing/network-ddos-protection.htm. Accessed 14 June 2025

27. Jakma, P.: Revisions to the BGP 'Minimum Route Advertisement Interval'. Internet-Draft draft-ietf-idr-mrai-dep-04, Internet Engineering Task Force (Sep 2011). https://datatracker.ietf.org/doc/draft-ietf-idr-mrai-dep/04/, work in Progress
28. Jonker, M., Sperotto, A., Pras, A.: DDoS mitigation: a measurement-based approach. In: NOMS 2020–2020 IEEE/IFIP Network Operations and Management Symposium, pp. 1–6. IEEE (2020)
29. Jonker, M., Sperotto, A., van Rijswijk-Deij, R., Sadre, R., Pras, A.: Measuring the adoption of DDoS protection services. In: Proceedings of the 2016 Internet Measurement Conference, pp. 279–285 (2016)
30. BGP Flowspec Doesn't Suck. We're Just Using it Wrong. https://www.kentik.com/blog/bgp-flowspec-doesnt-suck-were-just-using-it-wrong/. Accessed 17 July 2025
31. Khadka, S., Bayhan, S., Holz, R., Shokoohi, S., Barcellos, M.: A first look at the adoption of BGP-based ddos scrubbing services: a 5-year longitudinal analysis. In: Proceedings of the 2025 International Conference on Network and Service Management (2025)
32. Livadariu, I., Fontugne, R., Phokeer, A., Candela, M., Stucchi, M.: A tale of two synergies: Uncovering rpki practices for rtbh at ixps. In: International Conference on Passive and Active Network Measurement, pp. 88–103. Springer (2024)
33. Letter of Agency (LOA) · Cloudflare BYOIP docs. https://developers.cloudflare.com/byoip/concepts/loa/. Accessed 10 Oct 2025
34. L3/L4 DDoS Mitigation | F5 Distributed Cloud Technical Knowledge. https://docs.cloud.f5.com/docs-v2/ddos-and-transit-services/how-tos/network-firewall/l3l4-ddos-mitigation. Accessed 10 Oct 2025
35. Lumen RPKI Guide. https://assets.lumen.com/is/content/Lumen/rpki-customer-notification?Creativeid=1c967bb7-1321-4be8-92c0-74097e840849. Accessed 14 Oct 2025
36. MANRS: DataSheet Emergency OnboardingDDoS. https://real-sec.com/wp-content/uploads/2022/02/DataSheet_Emergency_OnboardingDDoS.pdf. Accessed 06 Oct 2025
37. MANRS: MANRS. https://manrs.org/. Accessed 01 Sept 2025
38. MANRS: MANRS+ Controls. https://manrs.org/wp-content/uploads/2023/12/MANRSPlus_Controls.pdf. Accessed 01 Sept 2025
39. Mike Hicks: Akamai Prolexic Routed Outage Analysis. https://www.thousandeyes.com/blog/akamai-prolexic-routed-outage-analysis. Accessed 05 Feb 2025
40. nanog: Re: It can be challenging to advise DDoS mitigation subscribers on their RPKI-ROA needs, https://seclists.org/nanog/2024/Oct/73. Accessed 10 Oct 2025
41. NBIP. https://www.nbip.nl/en/nawas/faq/. Accessed 06 Oct 2025
42. Phil Gervasi: How Kentik Visualizes the BGP Propagation of a DDoS Mitigation (2022). https://www.kentik.com/blog/how-bgp-propagation-affects-ddos-mitigation/. Accessed 14 Nov 2024
43. How Long Does a DDoS Attack Last?. https://www.netscout.com/blog/how-long-does-ddos-attack-last. Accessed 28 Sept 2025
44. Cloudflare Radar. https://radar.cloudflare.com/. Accessed 17 Sept 2025
45. RADb. https://www.radb.net/. Accessed 28 Sept 2025
46. Choosing the Best Diversion For Your Needs (2019). https://support.radware.com/app/answers/answer_view/a_id/1018554/related/1. Accessed 05 Dec 2025
47. Radware Doc: DDoS Protector Cloud Service. https://www.radware.com/getattachment/bfc20642-47c5-4e1a-adb4-40350695541e/ds-checkpoint-ddos-protector-cloud-service.pdf.aspx (2024). Accessed 12 Nov 2025

48. Radware Support: How to setup GRE tunnels (2019). https://support.radware.com/app/answers/answer_view/a_id/1018552/~/how-to-setup-gre-tunnels. Accessed 05 Dec 2024
49. RIPE RPKI. https://ftp.ripe.net/rpki/. Accessed 17 Aug 2025
50. Sermpezis, P., Prehn, L., Kostoglou, S., Flores, M., Vakali, A., Aben, E.: Bias in internet measurement platforms. In: 2023 7th Network Traffic Measurement and Analysis Conference (TMA), pp. 1–10. IEEE (2023)
51. DDoS Hyper: DDoS Protection Solution | Lumen. https://www.lumen.com/en-us/security/ddos-hyper.htm.html. Accessed 10 Oct 2025
52. eSecurity Planet. https://www.esecurityplanet.com/products/distributed-denial-of-service-ddos-protection-vendors/. Accessed 10 Oct 2025
53. Team, Vercara: UltraDDoS protect - FAQs (2024). https://vercara.com/resources/ultraddos-protect. Accessed 19 Nov 2025
54. Testart, C., Richter, P., King, A., Dainotti, A., Clark, D.: Profiling BGP serial hijackers: capturing persistent misbehavior in the global routing table. In: Proceedings of the Internet Measurement Conference, pp. 420–434 (2019)
55. Tung, T.M., Wang, C., Wang, J.: Understanding the behaviors of BGP-based DDoS protection services. In: Man Ho Au et al. (ed.) Network and System Security, pp. 463–473. Springer International Publishing (2018)
56. DDoS Protection Services | Cloud-based DDoS Mitigation | UltraDDoS Protect. https://vercara.digicert.com/ddos-protection. Accessed 19 Nov 2025
57. Release Note: DDoS Protection for Networks - Manually divert your ranges | Imperva Cyber Community. https://community.imperva.com/discussion/release-note-ddos-protection-for-networks-manually-divert-your-ranges. Accessed 19 Nov 2025
58. Wallace Lee: DDoS Protection for Networks: Combatting Local Preference from ISPs | Imperva (2020). https://www.imperva.com/blog/ddos-protection-for-networks-combatting-local-preference-from-isps/. Accessed 16 July2025

Routing Under Siege: How Traffic Engineering Decisions Facilitate Prefix Hijackings

Renan Paredes Barreto[1(✉)] [iD], Leandro Márcio Bertholdo[2] [iD], and Pedro de Botelho Marcos[1] [iD]

[1] Federal University of Rio Grande (FURG), Rio Grande, Brazil
`{renan.paredes,pbmarcos}@furg.br`
[2] Federal University of Rio Grande do Sul (UFRGS), Porto Alegre, Brazil
`leandro.bertholdo@ufrgs.br`

Abstract. The reliability and security of Internet routing are increasingly challenged by applications with strict service requirements, where connectivity and traffic engineering play a central role. While operators apply traffic engineering to optimize performance and resilience, these decisions can inadvertently amplify routing security risks. Existing mechanisms such as BGPSec, RPKI, and ASPA remain insufficient due to limited deployment, leaving open questions about how traffic engineering practices and connectivity affect routing security. To address this, we propose a methodology that combines measurements from both the control and data planes. We use the PEERING Testbed to announce prefixes on the Internet using different traffic engineering techniques, such as AS Path Prepend, more specific announcements, and selective route announcements, and hijack our prefixes to understand the interplay between traffic engineering and prefix hijackings. Our results show that prepending can increase the impact of a hijack from 17% to 67%, and that the way an AS connects to other networks—its connectivity structure—can also determine its exposure to prefix hijacks. We further demonstrate that hijacking via more specific prefixes is particularly effective, achieving up to 100% of both control and data plane targets. Based on these findings, we provide a comprehensive view of the current announced address space, showing that 61.4% of the address space may be facing a higher exposure to prefix hijackings due to ASes' traffic engineering practices.

Keywords: BGP · Traffic Engineering · Security

1 Introduction

Traffic delivery is a fundamental component of current Internet operations. As the Internet evolves in both scale and importance, its underlying infrastructure faces increasing complexity and growing traffic volumes. This growth is driven by the need to meet application requirements, enhance users' quality of experience, and ensure network resilience [42].

S. Ferlin-Reiter et al. (Eds.): PAM 2026, LNCS 16477, pp. 44–70, 2026.
https://doi.org/10.1007/978-3-032-18268-5_3

To handle these complexities, Autonomous Systems (ASes) rely on two approaches: increasing their connectivity by establishing links with multiple transit providers and Internet eXchange Points (IXPs), and applying traffic engineering to optimize the use of this expanded footprint. While these strategies improve performance, resilience, and traffic delivery, they can also increase routing security risks, specifically the risk of a prefix being hijacked.

A hijack event occurs when an AS announces a prefix it does not legitimately own, thereby diverting traffic. Such incidents can disrupt services or serve as vectors for more severe attacks, underscoring the fragility of the global routing system, even after decades of operational experience with BGP. Historical cases, such as the 2008 hijack of YouTube by Pakistan Telecom [27] and the 2010 route leak by China Telecom [17], illustrate how misconfigurations or malicious intent can lead to global outages. More recent incidents targeting cloud and financial services [24, 37] show that the threat persists today, with studies reporting an average of 17 suspicious hijacks per day [19]. While prefix hijacks have been widely studied, the specific role of operational practices such as AS Path prepending, prefix length manipulation, and selective peering remains poorly understood. This gap motivates our investigation into how everyday traffic engineering decisions influence routing security at the inter-domain level.

When announcing their prefixes, ASes commonly apply traffic engineering techniques such as AS Path Prepending (ASPP), selective announcements, and the use of more- or less-specific prefixes.[1] Each technique influences route preferences differently and can inadvertently increase exposure to hijacks. For example, ASPP artificially lengthens AS paths, making it easier for a hijacker to originate a shorter path. Selective announcements restrict the propagation of portions of the AS's address space, reducing routing diversity and leading to longer paths in parts of the Internet. More or less specific announcements are a two-edged sword: using less specific prefixes helps reduce the routing table size but increases vulnerability to more specific-prefix attacks.

Mechanisms such as RPKI and ASPA have been developed to improve the validation of route origins and AS paths. However, their adoption is still far from universal. As of early October 2025, roughly 57% of global IPv4 and 63% IPv6 routes are covered by valid RPKI ROAs [23], while fewer than 150 ASes worldwide (>0.2%) have published ASPA objects [9]. This limited deployment leaves nearly half of the global routing table—and thus the vast majority of AS-level connectivity relationships—outside the scope of origin or path validation. In practice, this means that more than 60% of the address space can still be successfully hijacked, mostly by more specific-prefix attacks, as our measurements confirm later in this paper. These figures highlight the need to look beyond cryptographic validation and examine how operational decisions, particularly connectivity and traffic engineering practices, influence routing security.

In this work, we investigate how traffic engineering practices and AS-level connectivity influence the likelihood and impact of prefix hijacking. To this end,

---

[1] Other mechanisms, such as BGP communities or the MED attribute, can also be used but depend on neighbor support and are less widely applicable.

we utilize the PEERING testbed [34] to emulate prefix hijackings in scenarios where the prefix owner employs different traffic engineering techniques with varying connectivity levels. We then perform measurements on both the data plane and the control plane to analyze the impact of the prefix hijacking. In addition to investigating the role of each traffic engineering technique, we assess the connectivity characteristics of the attacker and the victim that influence the success of the hijacking. Additionally, we investigate traffic engineering strategies for mitigating prefix hijackings and the properties of ASes that accept the forged route. Finally, based on our findings, we analyze Internet routing data to determine the degree of exposure of current BGP announcements. Our goal is to offer practical guidance for operators who must weigh the operational benefits of traffic engineering against its security risks.

We summarize our main contributions as follows: We show that using a single AS path prepend increases the likelihood of a hijack to 17%; when additional prepends are applied, this value can rise to 67%. We also observe that hijacks with more specific prefixes are particularly damaging, in some cases capturing 100% of the control plane targets. Furthermore, our analysis indicates that only 33.25% of the announced Internet address space with vulnerable characteristics are covered by ROAs where the max length attribute matches the length of how the AS is announcing the prefix.

2   Background

The *Border Gateway Protocol* (BGP) is the standard inter-domain routing protocol of the Internet. It enables ASes to exchange reachability information and decide which routes to use for forwarding traffic [32]. Route selection follows a deterministic sequence of criteria [32], including the longest prefix match[2], highest *local preference*, shortest AS path, lowest origin type, and lowest Multi-Exit Discriminator (MED), among others. These criteria define how BGP determines the "best" route to each destination and also provide opportunities for traffic optimization through *traffic engineering* (TE).

BGP allows operators to control both outbound and inbound traffic through traffic engineering (TE). Outbound TE influences how traffic leaves an AS by selecting which external routes to use (e.g., based on the local preference). Inbound TE, on the other hand, affects how other ASes route traffic toward the network, typically by manipulating the announcements an AS advertises. Because BGP lacks a native mechanism for inbound path control, operators rely on indirect techniques through route attributes manipulation, such as AS Path Prepending, selective announcements, BGP communities, and prefix-length manipulation. Each of these methods leverages specific BGP decision rules to balance performance, cost, and resilience, but they may also introduce security side effects.

A *prefix hijack* occurs when an AS illegitimately announces IP prefixes it does not own or forges AS paths to redirect traffic [2]. Depending on the attacker's

---

[2] Used for prefix lookup but not part of the BGP protocol.

intent and configuration, hijacks may take the form of subprefix, exact-match, or interception attacks. These incidents can disrupt connectivity or enable traffic redirection and inspection.

3   Problem Statement

The increasing interconnection density and the widespread use of complex routing policies among ASes have created new challenges for routing security, particularly in the form of prefix hijacking, which we analyze in this study. While BGP defines clear decision rules, operators routinely adjust them through traffic engineering policies to balance performance, enforce business relationships, and optimize costs. However, these operational choices, which influence how routes propagate, can sometimes make it easier for malicious actors to exploit announcements and successfully perform a prefix hijack.

In this context, ongoing community efforts focus on the use of cryptographic validation mechanisms to enhance routing security. The main examples are *RPKI* [4] and *ASPA* [1,40]. RPKI (Resource Public Key Infrastructure) aims to authenticate prefix ownership, while ASPA (Autonomous System Provider Authorization) validates the interconnection relationships between adjacent ASes, thereby improving routing security against prefix hijacking. Although these protocols have existed for some time, their adoption remains limited: only about 57% of IPv4 and 63% of IPv6 routes are covered by valid ROAs (Route Origin Authorization), and fewer than 150 ASes worldwide (>0.2% of all ASNs) have published ASPA objects [1,18].[3] Moreover, misconfigured ROAs—such as those with overly broad *maxLength* attributes—can still permit hijacks using more-specific prefixes. Thus, despite these advances, routing security still depends heavily on operational practices and AS-level connectivity rather than cryptographic validation alone. If properly integrated into day-to-day operations, these mechanisms could significantly reduce the risk of routing attacks such as prefix hijacking.

We hypothesize that certain inbound traffic engineering (TE) techniques can unintentionally increase the likelihood of a prefix being hijacked. Specifically, we consider three widespread practices that influence BGP route selection in distinct ways: (i) **AS Path Prepending**, where repeating an ASN makes a route less attractive to peers; (ii) **Selective Announcements**, where advertising a prefix to fewer neighbors reduces visibility and resilience; and (iii) **Prefix Length Manipulation**, where the use of less-specific prefixes allows attackers to override legitimate aggregates.

These cases exemplify how operational and policy-driven decisions—often made to improve performance or cost efficiency—can inadvertently weaken routing security. This motivates our experimental analysis, where we use the PEERING testbed to systematically evaluate how connectivity and TE practices affect hijack success under real-world conditions.

---

[3] In the case of ASPA, low adoption is expected since it is still a draft.

4   Methodology

Our goal is to understand how traffic engineering and connectivity decisions relate to prefix hijacking. To that end, we use the PEERING testbed [34] to emulate realistic hijacking scenarios and measure their effects on both the control and data planes. The methodology has two phases, summarized in Fig. 1.

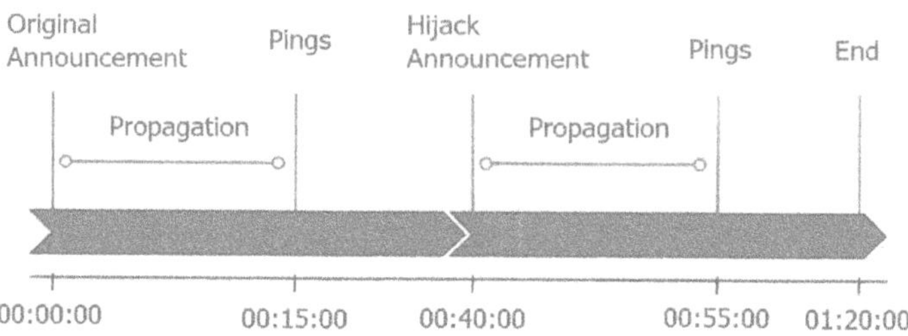

Fig. 1. Timeline of steps executed for every experiment round.

Phase 1—Original Announcement. The experiment begins with the victim AS announcing its prefix, referred to as the *original announcement*. We then start monitoring control plane changes using RIPE RIS Live [28]. Before starting the data plane measurements, we wait 15 min to ensure that route propagation stabilizes. This propagation interval follows the methodology of Rizvi et al. [33]. After this period, we perform data plane measurements for 25 min, targeting responsive hosts located in multiple ASes. Once these measurements are completed, we proceed to the second phase of our methodology.

Phase 2—Hijack Announcement. In the second phase, the hijacker AS attempts to partially or fully hijack the address space of the *original announcement*. We refer to this stage as the *hijack announcement*. During this phase, we repeat the same control plane and data plane measurements performed in Phase 1 to quantify the propagation and impact of the hijack. We evaluate the effectiveness of the attack as the fraction of vantage points that switch from the legitimate to the hijacked route, as observed in both control- and data plane measurements.

4.1   Announcement Configuration

Using our methodology, we evaluate three inbound traffic engineering techniques—AS Path Prepending (ASPP), selective announcements, and more-specific announcements—as proposed in Sect. 3. Below, we detail the announcement configuration for each technique as well as for the hijack announcement.

AS Path Prepending. We perform experiments considering prepend sizes between 0 and 3 for the *original announcement*. For example, a prepend size of 1 means the ASN of the prefix origin is repeated once, resulting in an AS

Path length of 2 (e.g., 65000_65000). We limit the maximum prepend size to 3, as this is the upper bound supported by the PEERING testbed.

Prefix Length. To evaluate the impact of prefix length, we emulate scenarios where the legitimate announcement originates as a /23 and as a /24 prefix. Our evaluation is limited to these two lengths because PEERING allocated a /23 prefix to us, preventing tests with less-specific aggregates (e.g., /22). Although more-specific prefixes (e.g., /25 or more specific) could technically be announced, their global propagation is known to be severely limited [5,29].

Selective Announcements. To measure the effects of reduced route propagation, we design scenarios where the prefix is advertised to only a subset of available neighbors. Specifically, we consider three configurations: (i) announcements to all neighbors, (ii) only to transit providers, and (iii) only to IXPs. We further vary the number of transit providers to assess how reduced connectivity influences exposure to hijacks.

Hijack Announcement. Regardless of the scenario, the hijacker always announces the prefix as a /24, without using ASPP, and advertises it to all available neighbors.

4.2 Vantage Point Selection

The PEERING Testbed has connectivity in multiple locations, referred to as *muxes*. In total, it operates **52** *muxes* spread across **20** *countries* in **6** *continents*. For our experiment, we selected a subset of *muxes* based on three criteria: proper route propagation quality, stability, and geographical diversity. We evaluate route propagation and stability by measuring the visibility of our prefix announcement from each PEERING *mux*, considering the number of RIPE RIS monitors that received an announcement for our prefix. From each region, we then chose the *mux* that achieved the highest visibility. Applying these criteria, we selected five *muxes* from a total of 39 analyzed: *amsterdam01* (Europe), *ufmg01* (South America), *neu01* (North America), *vtrjohannesburg* (Africa), and *vtrseoul* (Asia).

Table 1. Connectivity information for each PEERING testbed mux from [31].

Mux	Transit Providers	IXP Presence	Private Peerings	Total of Directly Connected ASes
amsterdam01	2	1	107	726
ufmg01	1	1	2	103
vtrseoul	1	—	—	1
vtrjohannesburg	1	—	—	1
neu01	1	—	—	1

Considering the second hop—i.e., the peers listed in PEERING's public peers table, as shown in Table 1.—*amsterdam01* stands out as the most connected node, and *ufmg01* follows. In contrast, the Vultr-hosted *muxes* (*vtrseoul* and *vtrjohannesburg*) and *neu01* each report only a single directly connected AS in PEERING's dataset. This disparity reflects the distinct nature of their underlying infrastructures: the Vultr nodes are hosted on commercial cloud environments, known for extensive upstream connectivity to Tier-1 providers and IXPs in their respective regions. As such, even though Johannesburg Vultr PoP has 470 connected ASes and Seoul Vultr PoP has 66 connected ASes, they are one more hop away. Conversely, the research-oriented nodes—*amsterdam01*, *ufmg01*, and *neu01*—are typically connected through academic or non-commercial networks, which offer more limited, yet stable, interconnection footprints.

4.3   Measuring the Impacts

To measure the potential impact of prefix hijacking, we collect data from both the control and data planes. Control plane data provides visibility into routing decisions and path selection by ASes, allowing us to identify the extent of a hijack by comparing announcements and updates against BGP route-selection criteria. Because control plane data alone offers limited visibility, we complement our analysis with data plane measurements.

Control Plane. We measure the control plane impact of a prefix hijack by quantifying the number of RIPE RIS monitors affected by the event. Specifically, we first identify how many monitors receive the *original announcement*. Then, during the *hijack announcement*, we measure how many of these monitors switch their preferred route to the one originated by the hijacker. Our dataset includes approximately 400 BGP monitors distributed worldwide.

Data Plane. To broaden our visibility, we perform active measurements using a hitlist derived from the ANT IP list [10]. To avoid over-representation of large ASes, we include all addresses from ASes with up to five entries in the list and select a limited, geodiverse subset for ASes exceeding this threshold. We use the MaxMind GeoIP database [25] to geolocate the hosts and apply the following selection criteria:

1. Remove hosts with unavailable geolocation data;
2. Select one host per continent, one per country, and one per city.

After applying these filters, we obtain a list of 127,421 responsive targets across 45,462 ASes, ensuring both geographical diversity and reduced bias from large ASes. We probe these targets using the *nping* tool [14] with *ICMP echo requests*, and capture the responses via *tcpdump* [16]. We then analyze the collected packets to determine whether the responses were received through the interface of the *original announcement* or through that of the *hijack announcement*.

4.4   Limitations

Our methodology, while enabling controlled and reproducible experiments, has limitations. The experiments rely on the PEERING testbed, which does not allow the manipulation of intermediate AS path links or impersonation of third-party ASNs, restricting our analysis to *type-0 hijacks* [36]. We also limited our evaluation to IPv4, as we did not have an IPv6 prefix available. Also, we have not evaluated the use of *BGP Communities* because to the lack of support from neighboring ASes, and the *MED* attribute due to the lack of support from the PEERING testbed. Since the hijacker ASN and prefixes belong to PEERING-controlled resources and no ROAs were created or modified, RPKI-based filtering was not applied. At the time of the experiments, the PEERING resources allocated to our setup did not support ROA creation, preventing us from running experiments with RPKI validation. In addition, data plane observations depend on ICMP responses, which can bias results toward networks that allow echo replies.

Finally, the PEERING topology abstracts away economic relationships between ASes and may not fully represent Internet-scale routing diversity. Additionally, the evaluated techniques (AS-path prepending, prefix-length manipulation, and selective announcements) were tested in isolation rather than combined[4]. Despite these constraints, the approach provides a controlled environment to quantify how operational and connectivity choices influence prefix hijack susceptibility.

4.5   Ethics

It is important to emphasize that none of the prefix announcements made during the experiments interfered with real user traffic, as the PEERING platform does not have any clients. Additionally, we include contact information in the data plane measurements to allow ASes to request exclusion from probing. We also limit the ping rate per second to prevent overloading of vantage points or measurement targets.

5   Traffic Engineering Decisions and Connectivity Impacts

Our goal is to investigate how the use of each inbound traffic engineering technique and connectivity aspects relate to the impact of a prefix hijacking event. To that end, we use the PEERING Testbed to emulate scenarios where an AS announces a prefix using different traffic engineering techniques and another AS attempts to hijack the prefix. We conduct our experiments from multiple locations with varying connectivity levels to also analyze how connectivity affects the impacts of prefix hijacking. We performed the prefix length experiments

---

[4] Although it is expected that ASes not to alter ASPP made by the origin (unless specified by the origin to do so), this could not always be the case. As such, ASes could remove ASPP when propagating announcements, causing noise in the experiments.

using an IPv4 prefix between 16/11/2024 and 22/11/2024. ASPP experiments were executed between 24/01/2025 and 05/02/2025, and selective announcement experiments between 17/02/2025 and 18/02/2025. During the experiments, we used ASNs 61574 and 61575, along with the prefix 184.164.226.0/23 and its sub-prefixes.

5.1 AS Path Prepend

To analyze the security impacts of using ASPP, we emulate scenarios with prepend sizes ranging from 0 to 3 applied to the *original announcement*[5]. In

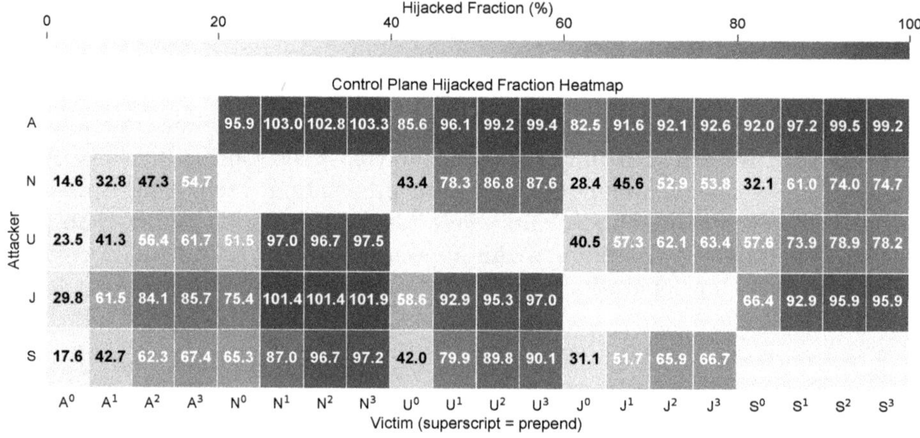

a Control plane results (ASPP).

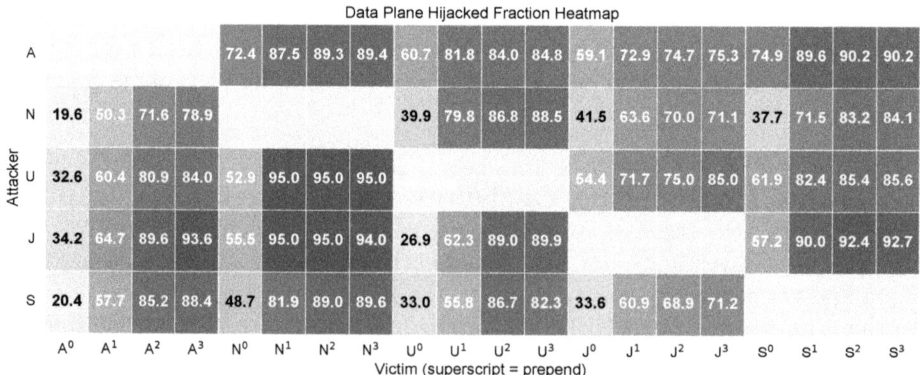

b Data plane results (ASPP).

Fig. 2. Results for control plane monitors and data plane targets using ASPP.

---

[5] We limit the number of prepends to 3 as this is the maximum amount allowed on the PEERING Testbed.

all cases, the *hijack announcement* is performed without any traffic engineering technique. For each prepend configuration, we conducted experiments where each *mux* was alternately configured as the victim and the attacker. We measure the impact of the attack on both the control plane and the data plane. In the control plane, we count the number of RIPE RIS monitors adopting the hijacked route; in the data plane, we count the number of hosts from our hitlist that reply to the hijacker.

Figures 2a and b summarize the results for the control and data planes, respectively. In each heatmap, the Y-axis represents the PEERING *mux* acting as the hijacker: (A) *amsterdam01*, (N) *neu01*, (U) *ufmg01*, (J) *vtrjohannesburg*, and (S) *vtrseoul*. The X-axis represents the victim *mux* and its inbound traffic engineering (ITE) configuration. For instance, A^2 indicates that *amsterdam01* announced its prefix with two prepends.

An exceptional case appears for *neu01*, which exhibits values exceeding 100%. This anomaly arises because the number of routes observed in the *original announcement* was smaller in the RIS Live dataset than in the experiments N^1, N^2, and N^3. We attribute this discrepancy to route-filtering policies affecting announcements originated from *neu01*, which do not apply to other *muxes* such as *amsterdam01* or *vtrjohannesburg* when they advertise the same prefix. This behavior highlights how local operational policies and connectivity conditions can influence visibility in control plane measurements, thereby affecting the observed hijack ratio.

Overall, the results reveal a consistent pattern: larger prepend values systematically increase the hijack success rate, confirming that excessive prepending substantially weakens the attractiveness of a route, irrespective of the propagation layer.

Prepend size directly amplifies the impact of a hijack, as shown in the control plane measurements presented in Fig. 2a. For instance, when *amsterdam01* acts as the victim without prepends (A^0), between 14.6% (*neu01*) and 29.8% (*vtrjohannesburg*) of monitors were hijacked; with three prepends (A^3), these numbers rose to 54.7% and 85.7%, respectively. In the data plane, as shown in Fig. 2b, the proportion of hijacked targets increased from about 20% to more than 90%. These results, consistent with previous studies [3], also reveal some heterogeneity across *muxes*: while control plane hijacks react more promptly to prepend changes, the data plane sometimes diverges, indicating that route propagation and effective traffic redirection do not always evolve synchronously. This lack of synchrony can, in part, be explained by differences in the AS sets of control-plane monitors versus those probed in the data plane.

Prepend Size Produces Little Variation for Less Resilient Origins. Considering *neu01* as the victim, this *mux* exhibits weaker connectivity compared to *amsterdam01*. When *amsterdam01* acts as the attacker, 95.9% of monitors were hijacked without prepends (N^0), and with only one prepend (N^1), the number already rose to 103%, meaning that the number of hijacked monitors exceeded those that had observed the victim's original announcement. This indicates that *amsterdam01* already provides shorter paths to a larger set of RIPE monitors than *neu01*, making hijacks more effective regardless of prepend count. Consequently, ASes with limited connectivity, such as *neu01*, remain highly vulnerable even with minimal prepend usage. In practice, this amplifies the potential impact of a hijack while simultaneously restricting available mitigation options, emphasizing the role of network connectivity in routing security.

A similar trend is observed when *ufmg01* acts as the victim: the results for one, two, and three prepends (U^1, U^2, U^3) are nearly identical, suggesting that additional prepends beyond this point do not significantly alter the outcome. An important observation regarding both *neu01* and *ufmg01* is that these *muxes* operate within academic networks—one in the United States and the other in Brazil. Given that the RIPE RIS infrastructure includes only two collectors in the United States and one in Brazil, out of a total of 27 worldwide, this limited vantage-point distribution may introduce a measurement bias. Such bias could influence the observed behavior, as these academic *muxes* may exhibit lower visibility compared to those hosted within large commercial networks, where route propagation toward RIS collectors is typically more extensive.

Finally, to further investigate how connectivity influences hijack exposure, Fig. 3 summarizes the overall distribution of hijack impact across all *muxes* for both the control and data planes. The figure illustrates how vulnerability is unevenly distributed: each *mux* exhibits a distinct range and median of hijacked visibility, reflecting its connectivity and propagation reach. The wide dispersion observed for *neu01* confirms its limited resilience—even without prepends, hijack ratios remain high due to weaker upstream connectivity and reduced route diversity. Conversely, better-connected *muxes*, such as *amsterdam01*, show lower medians and narrower spreads, indicating greater route stability and reduced hijack exposure.

The green boxplots (control plane) indicate the number of RIS collectors that recorded the hijack, out of a maximum of 407 active monitors. In contrast, the orange boxplots represent data plane results and show a greater variability in outcomes, indicating that even when control plane propagation stabilizes, traffic redirection may remain inconsistent. The numbers above each median (in the data plane) denote the total number of hijacked hosts observed from 127,421 ICMP probes (histlist size). At the same time, those in parentheses correspond to the median number of affected ASes. Together, these results emphasize that resilience against prefix hijacking depends not only on traffic engineering policies but also on a network's position in the global topology and on the geographical distribution of collectors and vantage points.

5.2   Prefix Length

Prefix length plays a crucial role in the outcome of hijack events, since more specific prefixes are generally preferred in BGP route selection. To evaluate its impact, we define two scenarios for each mux pair. In the first, the victim announces a /23 prefix for the *original announcement*. In the second, the victim announces a /24. In both cases, the attacker uses a /24 prefix to execute the hijack attempt.

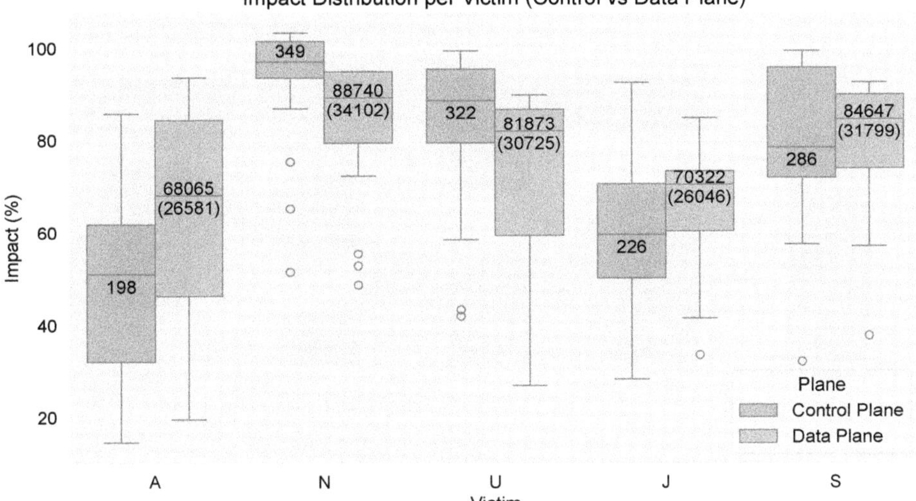

Fig. 3. Aggregate impact of prepend experiments across all victim *muxes*. Green boxplots represent the number of RIPE RIS collectors that observed the hijack, while orange boxplots represent the number of data plane hosts (above) and ASes (below) that suffered the hijack. Median values indicate the central hijack ratio observed for each *mux*.

An important observation is that not all RIS-Live monitors that observed the *original announcement* also accepted the hijack announcement; conversely, some monitors that did not observe the original may observe the hijack. This behavior stems from visibility limitations: announcements from the victim do not necessarily reach the same subset of RIS-Live monitors as announcements from the attacker. Consequently, the set of prefixes seen as hijacked can differ from the set observed in the *original announcement*—either appearing larger (because the attacker's announcement reaches additional monitors) or smaller (because some monitors never see the hijack).

In Fig. 4a, we observe that **hijacks involving more specific prefixes are consistently successful.** When the victim announces a /23 prefix, and the attacker announces a /24, the attacker effectively captures all traffic, leaving the victim with no reachability. This behavior is corroborated by the data plane results, where all experiments involving /23 victims resulted in a 100% hijack success rate[6]. Here, an important distinction emerges between the control and data planes: while the data plane consistently reports complete traffic redirection (100% ICMP responses via the attacker), the control plane observations from

---

[6] The experiment *amsterdam01* vs. *seoul*, in which the victim announced a /24 prefix, failed to propagate. Thus, failed to produce valid control plane and data plane results.

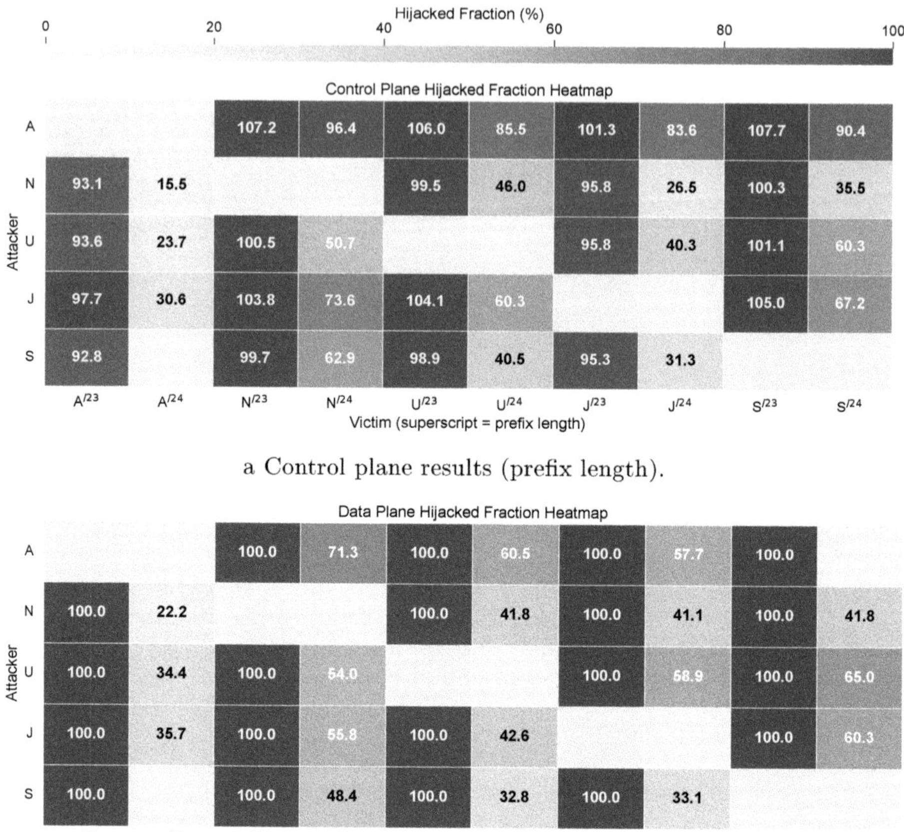

a Control plane results (prefix length).

b Data plane results (prefix length).

Fig. 4. Results for control plane monitors and data plane targets while varying the victim's prefix length. The Y-axis indicates the hijacker *mux*; the X-axis indicates the victim *mux* and configuration (e.g., $A^{/23}$ denotes *amsterdam01* announcing a /23).

RIS Live reveal a discrepancy of approximately 10%, reinforcing the visibility differences among approaches[7].

Although more specific prefixes, such as /24, can reduce the impact of a hijack, they do not necessarily guarantee protection. Their effectiveness depends strongly on the underlying network connectivity, as illustrated by the data plane results for *amsterdam01* and *neu01*, representing the best- and worst-connected *muxes*, respectively. The former experienced minimal impact, with only 22âĂŞ35% of monitored hosts redirected to the attacker ($A^{/24}$), whereas the latter showed a substantially higher impact, with 48âĂŞ71% of hosts con-

---

[7] The experiment *vtrseoul* vs. *amsterdam01*, in which the victim announced a /24 prefix, failed to produce valid data plane results.

verging toward the attacker ($N^{/24}$). However, using /24 prefixes as a defensive strategy presents inherent limitations: once an announcement is fully disaggregated into /24s, no further mitigation is possible, since most ASes filter prefixes longer than /24. Moreover, widespread /24 announcements inflate global routing tables (RIBs), potentially exposing memory constraints in routers and increasing operational overhead. Managing numerous /24s also complicates configuration and reduces the use of prefix length for traffic engineering, forcing operators to rely on alternative mechanisms to steer traffic.

For attackers, /23 and less-specific prefixes remain particularly attractive targets for hijacking, as observed for $A^{/23}$, $N^{/23}$, $U^{/23}$, $J^{/23}$, and $S^{/23}$. While a hijack of a /22 using a /23 could still be mitigated by announcing a /24, an attack employing a /24 prefix largely removes the victim's ability to recover traffic—again depending on the victim's connectivity. Therefore, connectivity plays a decisive role not only in the extent of hijack propagation but also in the feasibility of any mitigation strategy.

Similar to the prepend experiments, Fig. 5 presents a boxplot with an overview of the results for each mux. For all muxes, the maximum values are similar, confirming the effectiveness of a hijack using a more specific prefix.

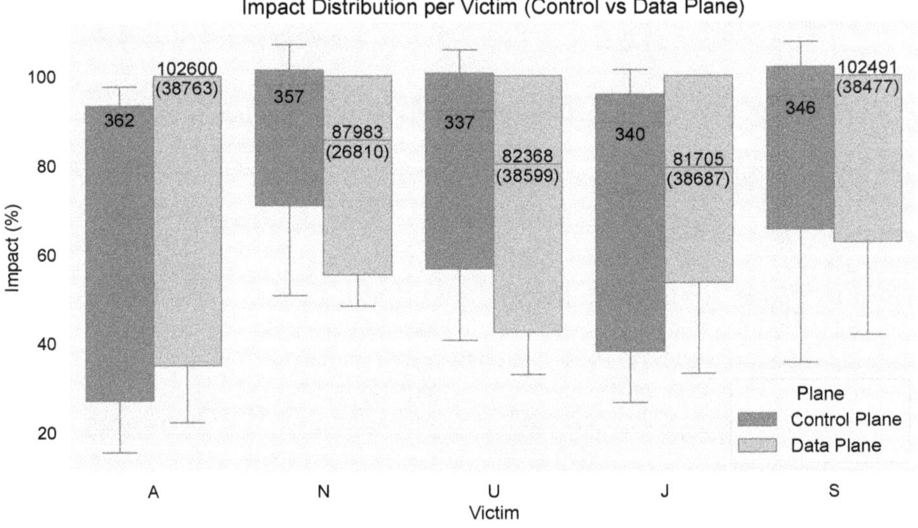

Fig. 5. Impact of prefix length experiments for each victim. Median values for RIS Monitors and Data Plane Hosts are shown. The number of affected ASes in the Data Plane is shown in parentheses.

5.3   Selective Announcements and Connectivity

Selective announcements are a common traffic engineering technique in which an Autonomous System advertises only a subset of its prefixes to specific peers or upstream providers. While helpful in controlling inbound traffic, this approach can also reduce reachability if not carefully planned, since limiting prefix visibility may unintentionally restrict access from portions of the Internet.

In the PEERING testbed, each *mux* offers distinct peering options. Among them, *amsterdam01* provides the largest number of peers and was therefore selected as the victim site for these experiments. Other *muxes* lack sufficient connectivity to support selective announcement configurations and were excluded from this analysis.

In these experiments, both the victim and the attacker announced prefixes of equal length, without applying AS path prepending. Selective announcements were propagated through *amsterdam01*'s peers—AMS-IX (Amsterdam Internet Exchange)[8], Bit BV, and Coloclue—using different peer combinations; for instance, the victim announced to AMS-IX and Bit BV while excluding Coloclue.

Table 2 presents the results obtained from the selective announcement experiments. The table reports the total number of monitors that observed the victim's selective announcement, the number of monitors that accepted the hijacked route, and the proportion between these two groups. The data plane results show the number of hosts that replied to probes in each configuration. For example, when the victim announced the prefix only to AMS-IX, the advertisement was visible to just 18 RIS Live monitors. In comparison, the attacker's announcement reached 345 monitors—corresponding to a hijack success rate of 1,916%.

Table 2. Selective announcement results with amsterdam01 as victim.

Experiment Configuration			Control Plane Monitors		Data Plane Targets	
Origin	Hijacker	Peers/IX	Total	Hijacked	Total	Hijacked
amsterdam01	neu01	AMS-IX	18	345 (1,916%)	1165	98252 (84.34%)
amsterdam01	neu01	Bit BV	371	65 (17.52%)	98872	21726 (21.97%)
amsterdam01	neu01	AMS-IX, Bit BV	371	65 (17.52%)	98939	21853 (22.08%)
amsterdam01	neu01	Coloclue, Bit BV	386	63 (16.32%)	98794	21681 (21.94%)
amsterdam01	neu01	AMS-IX, Coloclue, Bit BV	386	65 (16.83%)	98779	21818 (22.08%)
amsterdam01	neu01	Coloclue	391	39 (9.97%)	98884	20967 (21.20%)
amsterdam01	neu01	AMS-IX, Coloclue	391	39 (9.97%)	98716	20980 (21.25%)

In the case of announcements directed only to peering and not to transit providers (e.g., AMS-IX), it becomes evident that restricting announcements exclusively to IXPs significantly reduces the visibility of the victim's prefix and amplifies the impact of a prefix hijack, since for most monitors the attacker's announcement is the only one visible. Conversely, increasing the number of neighbors does not necessarily mitigate the impact of a hijack, as observed in the configurations involving AMS-IX, Coloclue, and Bit BV.

---

[8] The selective announcement was advertised only through open peering agreements, i.e., the announcement was sent exclusively to the route servers, and not to the private peering sessions that PEERING maintains at AMS-IX.

When announcing only to Coloclue, 391 monitors observed the original announcement, and only 39 (9.97%) were hijacked. In contrast, announcing to a subset including Bit BV but excluding Coloclue resulted in 371 monitors observing the original announcement, with 65 (17.52%) being hijacked. Contrary to expectations, announcing to all three peers—AMS-IX, Bit BV, and Coloclue—did not improve resilience compared to excluding Bit BV: 386 monitors observed the original announcement, while 65 (16.83%) were hijacked.

This behavior could be the result of local preference or routing policies along the AS path, demonstrating that the number of neighbors does not directly correlate with security. In fact, relying on a single neighbor provided better results than using two neighbors and an IXP. Showing the characteristics of the neighbors can influence the impact of a hijack. Therefore, ASes must consider not only the number of neighbors they maintain but also the routing policies of those neighbors when evaluating potential benefits. While maintaining multiple peering agreements may increase operational costs, it can also, in some cases, strengthen security.

Another interesting observation is that the quality of transit appears to have little influence on the hijack's outcome: the data plane results were similar across all combinations of transit providers, around 22%. This occurred even though Coloclue purchases transit from regional networks—Atom86(AS8455), Fusix Networks (AS57866), LeaseWeb (AS38930), and TrueFullstaq (AS15703)), whereas Bit BV relies on two Tier-1 providers—Arelion (AS1299) and NTT (AS2914).

6   Traffic Engineering for Prefix Hijacking Mitigation

In the event of a prefix hijack, the primary objective of the victim is to reduce or eliminate its impact. To this end, several mitigation strategies can be employed, often by modifying how the prefix is announced to the rest of the Internet.

Networks can choose different approaches to mitigate a prefix hijack event, including attempting to handle it in-house or outsourcing to a third party. For the first approach, previous studies already pointed out that operators contact other networks and/or deaggregate prefixes [36]. We will focus on the latter to evaluate the effectiveness of prefix deaggregation and discuss the possibilities of removing prepends and using selective announcements. To evaluate prefix deaggregation, we extend our experiments with an additional step:

Mitigation Announcement: The victim initiates a mitigation attempt, referred to as the *mitigation announcement*. In this stage, the victim announces more specific prefixes than in the *original announcement*, aiming to reduce the impact of the hijack. Measurements and data collection are again performed in both the control plane and the data plane. We present our results in Table 3.

One promising mitigation strategy for a victim mirrors that of an attacker: announcing a more specific prefix than the other party, if possible. Mitigation using a prefix of equal length to the hijack announcement will rely on local preference and AS path length to influence route selection. While announcing a

Table 3. Results for amsterdam01 as the victim while it uses a /23 prefix and mitigates with a /24. The attacker in this scenario is using a /24 prefix.

Experiment Configuration			Control Plane Monitors			Data Plane Targets		
Origin	Hijacker	Victim Prefix Length	Total	Hijacked	Recovered	Total	Hijacked	Recovered
amsterdam01	neu01	/23	391	364 (93.09%)	295 (81.04%)	102631	102600 (99.96%)	73270 (71.39%)
amsterdam01	ufmg01	/23	390	365 (93.58%)	264 (72.32%)	103050	103019 (99.96%)	62746 (60.88%)
amsterdam01	vtrseoul	/23	390	362 (92.82%)	286 (79.00%)	102983	102963 (99.98%)	78777 (76.49%)
amsterdam01	vtrjohannesburg	/23	389	380 (97.68%)	250 (67.78%)	102801	102785 (99.98%)	59558 (57.93%)

prefix with the same length as the attacker can reduce the impact, it does not guarantee full traffic recovery.

Another possible mitigation step is to remove prepends. Tracing back to the prepend results shown in Fig. 2a, in the case of *amsterdam01* vs. *neu01*, the impact of using three prepends compared to zero prepends was 40.09% of the monitors. Removing prepends is therefore only partially effective. In the best-case scenario observed in our experiments, *amsterdam01* vs. *neu01*, 14.57% of the monitors would still be hijacked even after this mitigation attempt.

Selective announcements could be used, or removed, but the effect might not scale with the number of neighbors receiving the announcement. Although the choice of which neighbors receive the prefix announcement directly influences the impact of a prefix hijack.

In the case of *amsterdam01*, announcing to both ASes and the IXP resulted in a worse outcome than announcing to a single AS, as shown in Table 2. This indicates that, in some scenarios, an AS can use selective announcements to reduce the impact of a hijack. However, this approach may also increase operational costs, depending on the agreements established with each peer.

Takeaway: Although ITE provides viable mitigation options, our experiments show that when the attacker and victim use the same prefix length, mitigation does not eliminate the impact. Thus, removing prepends or adjusting selective announcements can help reduce the severity of a hijack, but cannot guarantee complete recovery. The most effective scenario occurs when the victim can announce a prefix more specific than that of the attacker.

7   Propagation and the Impact of Local Preference

ASes that accept a hijack could route traffic towards the hijacker instead of the correct destination, sending data from their clients or neighbors towards a possibly malicious actor. In this Section, we focus on ASes that accepted the hijack announcements. We define any AS that is neither the victim nor the attacker but selects the hijacker's route as an *impacted AS*.

7.1   Attack Propagation

BGP announcement takes time to propagate and converge. This delay defines how long a prefix takes to become visible, how quickly a hijack takes effect, and how quickly operators must apply mitigation techniques. Understanding this process is essential to assessing how fast impacted ASes divert their traffic from the victim to the attacker. To achieve this goal, Fig. 6 presents a cumulative graph depicting the time in seconds for a hijack to reach the maximum number of RIS Live monitors during our experiments.

In our experiments, we allowed announcements to propagate for 15 min before starting the data plane measurements. As shown in Fig. 6, for 74.3% of the experiments, the hijack announcement achieved the maximum number of RIS Live monitors in under 5 min. We observed some monitors sending updates long after an announcement was made or changed. This could be due to the monitor having intervals in which it sends updates.

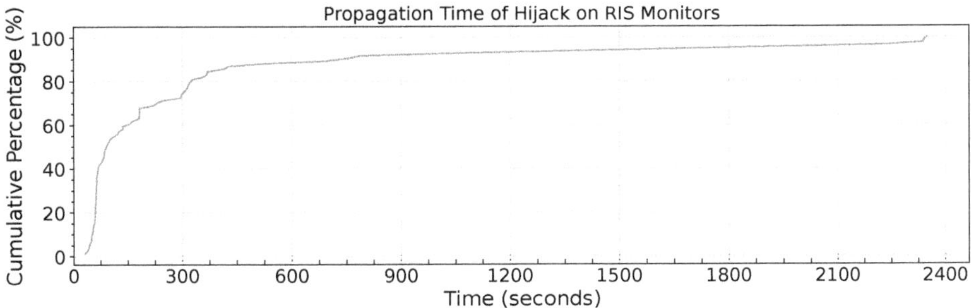

Fig. 6. Cumulative distribution of propagation times for experiments.

Considering that RIS Live includes approximately 400 monitors, it does not capture the behavior of all ASes on the Internet. Nevertheless, it provides valuable insight into how announcements propagate. In this case, any mitigation attempt that seeks to prevent the attacker from spreading the hijack announcement must occur as quickly as possible—ideally within 3 min, which would correspond to 62.99% of our experiment configurations.

Takeaway: Extrapolating this result as the time it takes for an announcement to propagate to all ASes shows that real-time mitigation tactics are required. Mitigation attempts under 3 min since the beginning of the attack can also prevent the attacker from acquiring all possible targets.

7.2   Distance and Local Preference

An impacted AS may accept a hijack announcement due to its distance from the victim, which can be measured either topologically (number of hops in the AS path) or geographically. In BGP route selection, shorter AS paths are generally preferred. Consequently, an AS that is topologically closer to the victim is less likely to accept the hijacker's announcement than one located farther away.

We observed this behavior in the prepend experiments, where increasing the prepend size led to more monitors being hijacked. To analyze this effect further, we examine the path lengths of both the victim and the attacker for the monitors that accepted the hijack, to determine how many cases can be explained by differences in AS path length.

Table 4. Comparison between victim announcement AS path size to the hijacker AS path size in the event of a successful hijack during prepend experiments.

Experiment Configuration			Hijacker Path Size		
Origin	Hijacker	Prepend Size	Shorter	Equal	Longer
amsterdam01	neu01	0	21	18	18
amsterdam01	neu01	3	200	6	5
amsterdam01	ufmg01	0	35	44	13
amsterdam01	ufmg01	3	233	3	4
amsterdam01	vtrseoul	0	12	41	16
amsterdam01	vtrseoul	3	246	1	14
amsterdam01	vtrjohannesburg	0	42	44	31
amsterdam01	vtrjohannesburg	3	326	0	10
neu01	amsterdam01	0	254	49	45
neu01	amsterdam01	3	340	0	32

In Table 4, we observe that several hijacked monitors had a shorter AS path to the attacker than the victim. In the scenario where *neu01* was the victim, most hijacked monitors selected the attacker even without the use of ASPP, indicating that the longer AS path of the victim played a decisive role.

It is important to note, however, that some monitors still selected the hijacker's announcement even when the attacker's AS path was longer. This behavior can be explained either by local preference policies applied by ASes along the path. Looking at *neu01* again, we can see that, without using prepends, 45 monitors were affected by the hijack from *amsterdam01* due to local preference, since both the attacker and victim announced prefixes of equal lengths.

Takeaway: Although topological distance does impact the chance of an AS accepting a hijack announcement instead of keeping the route to the victim, we can also observe that local preference in the AS paths will also be a factor that can minimize or amplify the effects of a hijack.

8   Investigating the Security of Current TE Practices

Building on the results presented in Sect. 5, we now examine the current state of BGP announcements to assess their potential vulnerability to prefix hijacking. We determine whether a part of the address space is vulnerable to a hijack according to criteria related to prepend usage, prefix length, and number of peers/providers. We separate our analysis into two parts: (1) The overall safety of address space by ITE usage and connectivity; (2) The address space covered by RPKI.

8.1   Methodology

We evaluate on ASPP usage, prefix length, and connectivity. For the prepend technique, we base our analysis on the best-case scenario observed in our experiments, with *amsterdam01* as the victim, and extrapolate the susceptibility of the address space to hijacks. We adopt the lowest prepend value seen in the RIB. For example, if an AS announces the same prefix with prepends to one neighbor but without prepends to another, we classify the prefix as having no prepends. We classify announcements as follows:

- 0 or 1 prepends are considered *safe*;
- 2 prepends are considered *at risk*;
- 3 or more prepends are considered *not safe*.

For prefix length, we classify a /24 prefix as *safe* and a /23 prefix as *at risk*, since a /24 attack is possible, but disaggregating a /23 requires less effort than attacking less specific prefixes. Prefixes less specific than /23 are classified as *not safe*.

For connectivity, we again use *amsterdam01* as a reference, since it consistently showed the strongest resilience both as a victim and as an attacker in our experiments. We consider two neighbors (either providers or peers) as the minimum threshold for being classified as *safe*.

We classify the safety of each announcement based on the worst outcome among the three criteria. For example, an AS that propagates a /24 prefix with strong connectivity will still be marked as *at risk* if it uses 2 prepends. Similarly, we classify a prefix as *not safe* if it is announced as a /20 without prepends.

To perform this analysis, we disaggregate all prefixes observed in the RIB into /24 s. This approach allows us to evaluate what portion of the address space falls into the categories of *safe*, *at risk*, or *not safe*. We base our analysis on a snapshot collected on October 14th, 2025, at 12:00:00 UTC, using the RouteViews collector *2nd SAOPAULO* [41].

Considering the coverage of ROA objects, we classify the address space being announced in three categories: i) when the max length of the ROA matches exactly the prefix length announced on the Internet; ii) when the max length of the ROA is /24 but the prefix is not being announced as /24; and iii) when the max length of the ROA is different than /24 and the prefix is not being announced following with the max length. Additionally, we analyze the address space without ROA coverage.

8.2   Results

First, we analyze the results for each case separately: the use of prepends in the address space, the number of peers or providers, and the prefix length. We then combine these dimensions with RPKI coverage to present the intersection of results, providing an overview of the current state of the address space. We provide the results for each characteristic in Table 5.

Table 5. Details of Address Space by each characteristic: Usage of ASPP, Prefix Length, and Peers/Providers.

Characteristic	Safe	At Risk	Not Safe
ASPP	90.65%	3.48%	5.87%
Peers/Providers	82.46%	N/A	17.54%
Prefix Length	5.34%	1.45%	93.21%

ASPP. Considering the prepend usage in the observed address space, we obtained positive results. Considering the snapshot used, the majority of the address space is announced without prepends or with only a single prepend. Only 3.48% of the address space falls into the *at risk* category due to the use of two prepends, while 5.87% is classified as *not safe*.

Peers and Providers. When analyzing the number of peers and providers for each AS originating a prefix, the results indicate that most ASes are on par with, or better than, *amsterdam01*. In total, 82.46% of the address space originates from ASes with at least two peers or providers, which we classify as *safe* in this regard.

A small fraction of the address space (less than 0.1%) originates from ASes not listed in the ASRank API. We classify them as *not safe*. Furthermore, 17.54% of the address space is announced by ASes with only a single peer or provider, which we also classify as *not safe*.

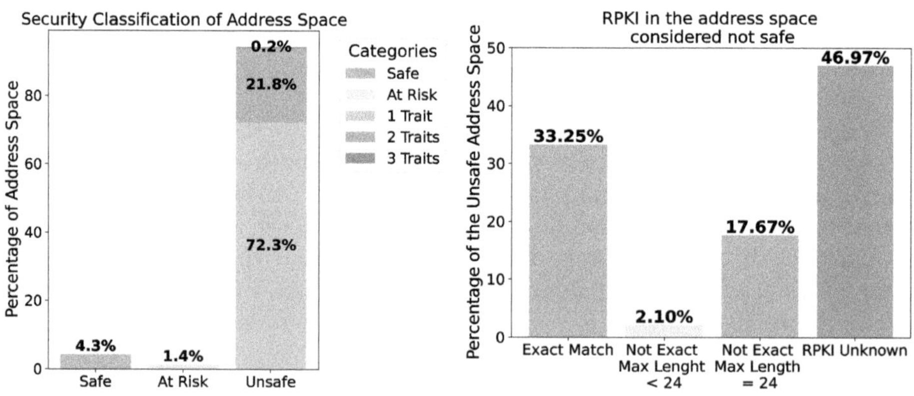

a Classification of the Address Space.   b RPKI Coverage of the Unsafe Address Space.

Fig. 7. Security of the address space by characteristics (ASPP, Prefix Length, and Peers/Providers) and RPKI coverage of the address space considered unsafe.

Prefix Length. The results for prefix length are less favorable. While we must reiterate the operational challenges of disaggregating prefixes, the analysis shows that most of the address space is not announced as /24. Only 5.34% of the address space is covered by /24 announcements and 1.45% by /23. Consequently, the vast majority (93.21%) of the address space is announced in prefixes less specific than /23.

This behavior stands out compared to the other results and highlights a key vulnerability that adversaries could exploit. Hijacks using more specific prefixes remain the most straightforward vector for malicious networks.

The Address Space Safety. When we intersect the characteristics of the address space, we can classify it into portions that are *safe*, *at risk*, or *not safe*, based on the use of prepends, the number of peers and providers, and the prefix length. Figure 7a shows that a large part of the address space remains vulnerable to type-0 hijacks either because of ITE or peers/providers. Only 4.3% of the address space does not fall within the characteristics we define as unsafe.

RPKI Coverage. Considering the address space marked as not safe, we can intersect with RPKI coverage. We can observe in Fig. 7b that 17.67% of the address space with unsafe characteristics has ROAs that allow a /24 prefix but are not contained in announcements that are exact matches to the max length attribute. While 46.97% of the address space deemed unsafe is announced in prefixes with unknown status for ROAs. Thus, 60.95% of the address space seen in the RIB is vulnerable even when accounting for RPKI. Lastly, only 33.25% of the address space considered unsafe is covered by ROAs and is contained in announcements that are the exact match of the max length attribute.

9 Related Work

Usage of ITE. The challenges of routing continue to be present, with new routes due to infrastructure [11] or new connections between ASes. This leads to the use of traffic engineering techniques [15, 21] to achieve the goals of the network, such as performance or costs. As such, not only guidelines have been proposed for ITE [6, 12, 13], but also solutions to automate ITE, aiming to decrease latency and increase resilience [22].

Security and Mitigation. The risks associated with the use of these techniques are not fully understood. Although the security issues of prepending were raised previously [3], we expand on previous knowledge by including data plane analysis to view the impact outside of BGP monitors. We also evaluated the impact of other traffic engineering techniques, such as selective announcements, prefix length, and connectivity.

The previous study focused on control plane data, and a different set of PEERING muxes, but we can highlight differences and similarities in the results. Amsterdam01 is the best-performing mux in both studies, and the impact of a hijack increases with ASPP usage. Unlike the previous research, even muxes with weaker connectivity (VtrSeoul) can affect better-connected muxes (Amsterdam01) when the victim uses fewer than three prepends. The earlier study also observed, in some cases, a steep change in the hijack impact, increasing from 0% to 96% when moving from 2 to 3 prepends, thus allowing to signal three prepends as unsafe ASPP usage. Our current results for both the data plane and control plane show a more gradual increase, making it more challenging to set a precise threshold for unsafe ASPP usage.

Even though the community is deploying security mechanisms, they do not resolve the issue completely [30]. RPKI adoption, despite growing, still does not cover all the routed address space [8,35,38] or could be the source of vulnerabilities when the certification authority itself acts maliciously [20].

To complete the situation, hijacks do occur [7,19,26,37,39], inflicting damage on ASes, applications, and users. Therefore, it is necessary to expand the knowledge regarding the security of implications of traffic engineering techniques and AS connectivity, to provide network operators with the necessary information to achieve their routing objectives efficiently and securely.

10   Final Remarks

Inbound traffic engineering techniques are one of the approaches that ASes rely on to meet application requirements and enhance users' quality of experience. However, these techniques could impact the suitability of a prefix being hijacked. These events occur when an AS announces a prefix it does not own, allowing traffic to be diverted to the hijacker.

Although there are mechanisms to improve the validation of route origins, these can face limitations in adoption or, in the case of RPKI, relaxed attributes to facilitate necessary changes in prefix announcements. In this paper, we used the PEERING Testbed to instantiate ASes and conduct experiments to evaluate how the use of ASPP, prefix Length, and selective announcements affects the impact of a prefix hijack, using data from both the control and data planes. In this section, we revisit the experimental results, state our final considerations, and outline possible directions for future research.

Our experiments show that traffic engineering practices can significantly alter the impact of prefix hijacks. ASPP, in particular, increases the likelihood of hijacks by artificially lengthening AS paths, with more vulnerable ASes being heavily impacted even at small prepend sizes. As such, prepend values above two should generally be avoided.

The use of prefixes more specific than the victim's is consistently effective for hijacking. Although disaggregation to /24 offers better protection, it introduces operational challenges such as larger routing tables and increased management workload.

Our measurements quantify the amplification effect of operational choices: AS Path prepending can raise hijack success from 17% to 67%, and attacks using more specific prefixes (/24) can compromise up to 100% of reachable targets.

Selective announcements and peering choices exhibit non-linear behavior and may either mitigate or aggravate hijack exposure. This demonstrates that security depends not only on the number of neighbors but also on their routing policies.

Well-connected ASes, such as *amsterdam01*, can mitigate the effects of ASPP and selective announcements, while poorly connected ASes, such as *neu01*, remain vulnerable even without prepends. On the attacker's side, strong connectivity amplifies the impact of hijacks, allowing them to dominate route selection quickly. We also observed that restricting announcements to a carefully chosen subset of neighbors can sometimes improve security, indicating that the quality of peering and the policies of connections matter more than their absolute number.

Considering the ASes that accepted the hijack, most hijacked ASes preferred the attacker's route because to shorter AS paths, especially when the victim used prepending. However, we also observed hijacks being accepted even when the attacker's path was longer. In these cases, BGP's longest-prefix matching does not apply (since prefix length was equal), which suggests that *local preference policies* drove route selection. This highlights how AS-level policies, beyond basic BGP rules, can both amplify or mitigate the effects of hijacks.

Traffic engineering remains widely used to optimize costs and performance, but it creates non-negligible risks. Our analysis indicates that 94.3% of the IPv4 address space is deemed unsafe. Considering the IPv4 address space deemed unsafe, only 33.25% of it is covered by prefixes with ROAs with an exact match.

Not only are there vulnerable prefixes, but hijack propagation also occurs in less than three minutes. During our experiments, 62.99% of the hijacks achieved peak impact in the control plane in three minutes or less. Underscoring that mitigation must be applied almost in real time to prevent full route convergence toward the attacker. Operators should weigh the benefits of ITE against these security risks, perhaps applying stricter protection measures only to the most critical prefixes.

Beyond the main findings summarized above, our results reveal differences between control plane and data plane visibility, confirming that evaluating only one plane can lead to incomplete conclusions—some hijacks affect data plane paths even when control plane monitors remain unaffected. Lastly, ITE-based mitigations remain partial solutions—while disaggregation to /24 or the removal of prepends can recover part of the traffic, they also increase routing-table size and management complexity. These observations highlight the importance of integrating operational awareness and real-time monitoring into future routing-security mechanisms.

We plan to expand the experiments to IPv6 to assess whether differences in protocol characteristics and network topology produce distinct results for each traffic engineering technique. To enrich the data plane analysis, we intend to capture both incoming and outgoing packets, enabling us to compute round-trip times (RTT). Another possibility is to evaluate the time needed for each ITE to mitigate a hijack, to establish if there is any meaningful difference. Lastly, we plan to explore the role of RPKI adoption and validation. By manipulating PEERING Route Origin Authorizations (ROAs), we can design announcements that should be protected by RPKI and evaluate the extent to which current deployments reduce the impact of hijacks.

References

1. Azimov, A., Bogomazov, E., Bush, R., Patel, K., Snijders, J., Sriram, K.: BGP AS_PATH Verification Based on Autonomous System Provider Authorization (ASPA) Objects. Internet-Draft draft-ietf-sidrops-aspa-verification-18, Internet Engineering Task Force, July 2024. Work in Progress. https://datatracker.ietf.org/doc/draft-ietf-sidrops-aspa-verification/18/
2. Ballani, H., Francis, P., Zhang, X.: A study of prefix hijacking and interception in the internet. In: Proceedings of the 2007 Conference on Applications, Technologies, Architectures, and Protocols for Computer Communications, SIGCOMM '07, pp. 265–276. Association for Computing Machinery, New York (2007). https://doi.org/10.1145/1282380.1282411
3. de Botelho Marcos, P., Prehn, L., Leal, L., Dainotti, A., Feldmann, A., Barcellos, M.: As-path prepending: there is no rose without a thorn. In: ACM IMC 2020 (2020). https://doi.org/10.1145/3419394.3423642
4. Bush, R., Austein, R.: The Resource Public Key Infrastructure (RPKI) to router protocol. RFC 6810, January 2013. https://doi.org/10.17487/RFC6810
5. Bush, R., Maennel, O., Roughan, M., Uhlig, S.: Internet optometry: assessing the broken glasses in internet reachability. In: Proceedings of the 9th ACM SIGCOMM Conference on Internet Measurement, IMC 2009, pp. 242–253. Association for Computing Machinery, New York (2009). https://doi.org/10.1145/1644893.1644923
6. Chang, R., Lo, M.: Inbound traffic engineering for multihomed ass using as path prepending. IEEE Netw. **19**(2), 18–25 (2005). https://doi.org/10.1109/MNET.2005.1407694
7. Cho, S., Fontugne, R., Cho, K., Dainotti, A., Gill, P.: BGP hijacking classification. In: 2019 Network Traffic Measurement and Analysis Conference (TMA), pp. 25–32 (2019). https://doi.org/10.23919/TMA.2019.8784511
8. Chung, T., et al.: RPKI is coming of age: a longitudinal study of RPKI deployment and invalid route origins. In: Proceedings of the Internet Measurement Conference, IMC '19, pp. 406–419. Association for Computing Machinery, New York (2019). https://doi.org/10.1145/3355369.3355596
9. RPKI client: ASPA (2025). https://console.rpki-client.org/aspa.html
10. Fan, X., Heidemann, J.: Selecting representative IP addresses for Internet topology studies. In: ACM IMC 2010. ACM (2010). https://doi.org/10.1145/1879141.1879195
11. Fanou, R., Huffaker, B., Mok, R., Claffy, K.C.: Unintended consequences: effects of submarine cable deployment on internet routing. In: Sperotto, A., Dainotti, A., Stiller, B. (eds.) PAM 2020. LNCS, vol. 12048, pp. 211–227. Springer, Cham (2020). https://doi.org/10.1007/978-3-030-44081-7_13
12. Feamster, N., Borkenhagen, J., Rexford, J.: Guidelines for interdomain traffic engineering. SIGCOMM Comput. Commun. Rev. **33**(5), 19–30 (2003). https://doi.org/10.1145/963985.963988

13. Gao, L., Rexford, J.: Stable internet routing without global coordination. SIG-METRICS Perform. Eval. Rev. **28**(1), 307–317 (2000). https://doi.org/10.1145/345063.339426
14. Garcia, L.M.: Fyodor. Nmap (2024). https://nmap.org/
15. Gill, P., Schapira, M., Goldberg, S.: A survey of interdomain routing policies. SIGCOMM Comput. Commun. Rev. **44**(1), 28–34 (2014). https://doi.org/10.1145/2567561.2567566
16. The Tcpdump Group: Tcpdump and libpcap (2024). https://www.tcpdump.org/
17. Hiran, R., Carlsson, N., Gill, P.: Characterizing large-scale routing anomalies: a case study of the China telecom incident. In: Roughan, M., Chang, R. (eds.) PAM 2013. LNCS, vol. 7799, pp. 229–238. Springer, Heidelberg (2013). https://doi.org/10.1007/978-3-642-36516-4_23
18. Hlavacek, T., Shulman, H., Vogel, N., Waidner, M.: Keep your friends close, but your routeservers closer: insights into RPKI validation in the internet. In: 32nd USENIX Security Symposium (USENIX Security 23), Anaheim, CA, August 2023, pp. 4841–4858. USENIX Association (2023). https://www.usenix.org/conference/usenixsecurity23/presentation/hlavacek
19. Holterbach, T., Alfroy, T., Phokeer, A.D., Dainotti, A., Pelsser, C.: A system to detect forged-origin hijacks. In: 21th USENIX Symposium on Networked Systems Design and Implementation (NSDI 24). USENIX Association (2024)
20. van Hove, K., van der Ham-de Vos, J., van Rijswijk-Deij, R.: rpkiller: threat analysis of the BGP resource public key infrastructure. Digit. Threats **4**(4) (2023). https://doi.org/10.1145/3617182
21. Kastanakis, S., Giotsas, V., Livadariu, I., Suri, N.: Replication: 20 years of inferring interdomain routing policies. In: Proceedings of the 2023 ACM on Internet Measurement Conference, IMC '23, pp. 16–29. Association for Computing Machinery, New York (2023). https://doi.org/10.1145/3618257.3624799
22. Koch, T., Yu, S., Agarwal, S., Katz-Bassett, E., Beckett, R.: PAINTER: ingress traffic engineering and routing for enterprise cloud networks. In: Proceedings of the ACM SIGCOMM 2023 Conference, ACM SIGCOMM '23, pp. 360–377. Association for Computing Machinery, New York (2023). https://doi.org/10.1145/3603269.3604868
23. MANRS: MANRS observatory (2025). https://observatory.manrs.org/#/roas/
24. Manrs, M.K.: Another BGP hijacking event highlights the importance of MANRS and routing security, April 2018. https://manrs.org/2018/04/another-bgp-hijacking-event-highlights-the-importance-of-manrs-and-routing-security/
25. MaxMind, I.: GeoIP and GeoLite database documentation (2025). https://dev.maxmind.com/geoip/docs/databases/. Accessed 6 Oct 2025
26. Milolidakis, A., Bühler, T., Wang, K., Chiesa, M., Vanbever, L., Vissicchio, S.: On the effectiveness of BGP hijackers that evade public route collectors. IEEE Access **11**, 31092–31124 (2023). https://doi.org/10.1109/ACCESS.2023.3261128
27. RIPE NCC: YouTube hijacking: a ripe NCC RIS case study, March 2008. https://www.ripe.net/about-us/news/youtube-hijacking-a-ripe-ncc-ris-case-study/
28. NCC RIPE: RIS Live (2024). https://ris-live.ripe.net/
29. NLNOG BGP Filter Guide: Filtragem de prefixos pequenos (2025). https://bgpfilterguide.nlnog.net/guides/small_prefixes/
30. Oliver, L., Akiwate, G., Luckie, M., Du, B., Claffy, k.: Stop, DROP, and ROA: effectiveness of defenses through the lens of DROP. In: Proceedings of the 22nd ACM Internet Measurement Conference, IMC '22, pp. 730–737. Association for Computing Machinery, New York (2022). https://doi.org/10.1145/3517745.3561454

31. PEERING: Peering sessions | peering - the BGP testbed. https://peering.ee.columbia.edu/peers/. Accessed 15 Oct 2025

32. Rekhter, Y., Hares, S., Li, T.: A Border Gateway Protocol 4 (BGP-4). RFC 4271, January 2006. https://doi.org/10.17487/RFC4271

33. Rizvi, A., Bertholdo, L., Ceron, J., Heidemann, J.: Anycast agility: network playbooks to fight {DDoS}. In: 31st USENIX Security Symposium (USENIX Security 22), pp. 4201–4218 (2022)

34. Schlinker, B., Arnold, T., Cunha, I., Katz-Bassett, E.: Peering: virtualizing BGP at the edge for research. In: Proceedings of the 15th International Conference on Emerging Networking Experiments and Technologies, CoNEXT '19, pp. 51–67. Association for Computing Machinery, New York (2019). https://doi.org/10.1145/3359989.3365414

35. Sermpezis, P., Kotronis, V., Dainotti, A., Dimitropoulos, X.: A survey among network operators on BGP prefix hijacking. SIGCOMM Comput. Commun. Rev. **48**(1), 64–69 (2018). https://doi.org/10.1145/3211852.3211862

36. Sermpezis, P., et al.: ARTEMIS: neutralizing BGP hijacking within a minute. IEEE/ACM Trans. Netw. **26**(6), 2471–2486 (2018). https://doi.org/10.1109/TNET.2018.2869798

37. Siddiqui, A.: KlaySwap – another BGP hijack targeting crypto wallets (2022). https://manrs.org/2022/02/klayswap-another-bgp-hijack-targeting-crypto-wallets/

38. Testart, C., Richter, P., King, A., Dainotti, A., Clark, D.: To filter or not to filter: measuring the benefits of registering in the RPKI today. In: Passive and Active Measurement Conference (PAM), March 2020 (2020). https://catalog.caida.org/paper/2020_filter_not_filter

39. Testart, C., Richter, P., King, A., Dainotti, A., Clark, D.: Profiling BGP serial hijackers: capturing persistent misbehavior in the global routing table. In: Proceedings of the Internet Measurement Conference, IMC 2019, pp. 420–434. Association for Computing Machinery, New York (2019). https://doi.org/10.1145/3355369.3355581

40. Umeda, N., Kimura, T., Yanai, N.: The juice is worth the squeeze: analysis of autonomous system provider authorization in partial deployment. IEEE Open J. Commun. Soc. **4**, 269–306 (2023). https://doi.org/10.1109/OJCOMS.2022.3233833

41. University of Oregon: University of Oregon route views archive project (2022). http://archive.routeviews.org/. Accessed 12 Jun 2022

42. Zerwas, J., Poese, I., Schmid, S., Blenk, A.: On the benefits of joint optimization of reconfigurable CDN-ISP infrastructure. IEEE Trans. Netw. Serv. Manage. **19**(1), 158–173 (2022). https://doi.org/10.1109/TNSM.2021.3119134

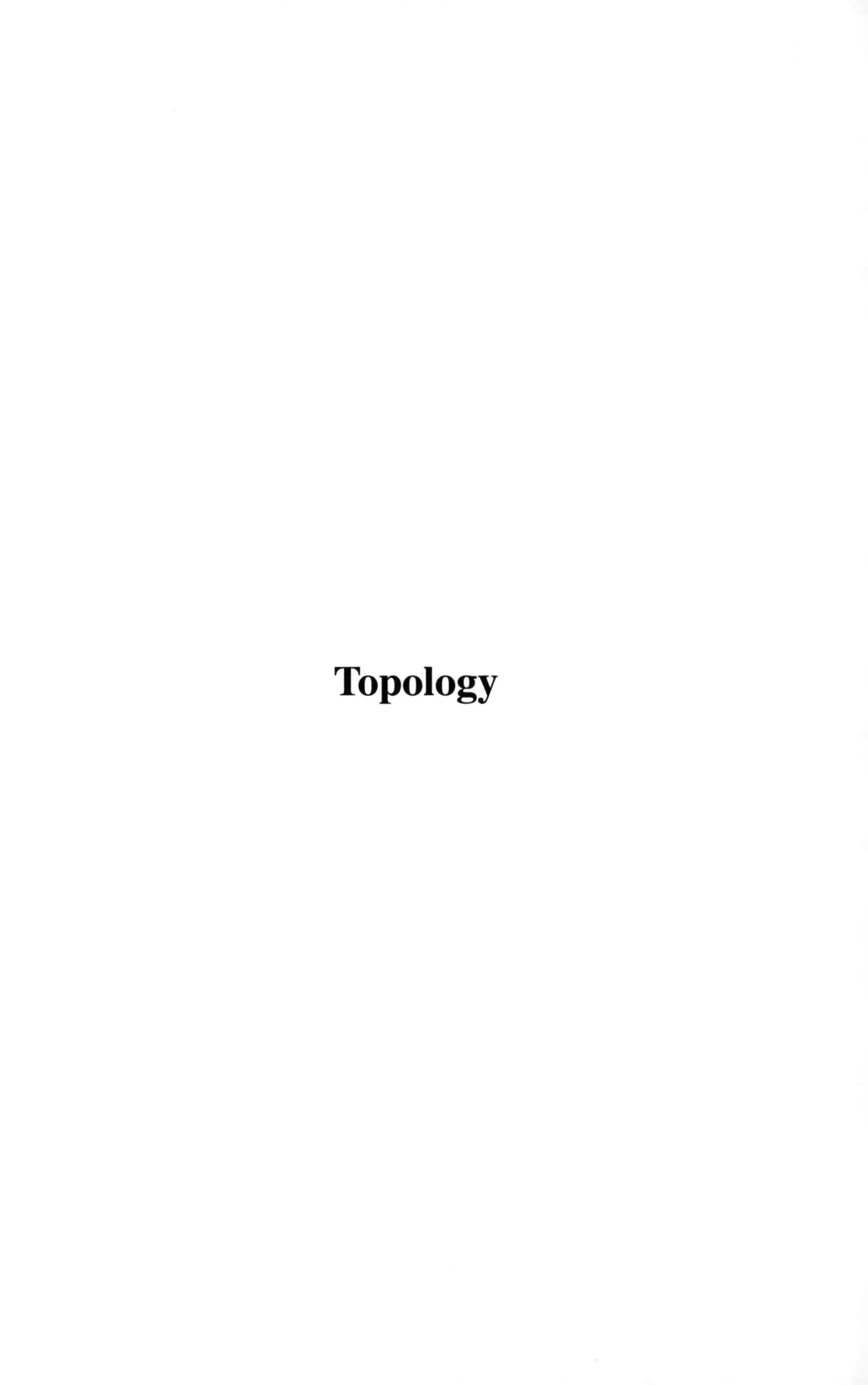

Topology

En Unión y Libertad: Subnational Strategies for Hosting Government Services

Esteban Carisimo[1]([envelope]) [iD], Mariano G. Beiró[2][iD], Lukas De Angelis Riva[3][iD], Mauricio Buzzone[3][iD], and Fabián E. Bustamante[1][iD]

[1] Northwestern University, Evanston, USA
{esteban.carisimo,fabianb}@northwestern.edu
[2] Universidad de San Andrés & CONICET, San Andrés, Argentina
mbeiro@udesa.edu.ar
[3] Universidad de Buenos Aires, Buenos Aires, Argentina
{ldeangelis,mbuzzone}@fi.uba.ar

Abstract. We present the first empirical study of subnational hosting strategies, using Argentina's 24 provinces as a case. Starting from official landing pages, we analyze ≈1.2k domains (collected Oct 2023 – Apr 2024), classifying serving networks by operational control (sovereign, domestic third-party, global) and examining authoritative DNS and HTTPS deployment. We relate these choices to 31 demographic, economic, technological, and political covariates – associations only, not causal claims. We find substantial heterogeneity: some provinces operate sovereign infrastructure; others rely on domestic incumbents or outsource to global providers. Federal capacity is rarely used, with provinces favoring bespoke or repurposed networks (including utility backbones). Legacy telecom footprints remain strong predictors of hosting choice even within a shared national umbrella. We also observe frequent splits between hosting and nameservers and uneven HTTPS hygiene. Taken together, the study offers a reusable measurement template and benchmarks that make sovereigntyperformance trade-offs measurable below the nation level.

En unión y libertad

Argentina's National Motto

1 Introduction

Accessing government services, from paying taxes and renewing licenses to scheduling health appointments, depends on reliable, Internet-facing infrastructure [35,79]. Citizens increasingly expect commercial-grade performance and availability [20], yet public agencies face additional constraints: legal data custody [28], long-term archival [82], and institutional accountability through proactive disclosure [29]. Choosing a hosting strategy that balances performance with

S. Ferlin-Reiter et al. (Eds.): PAM 2026, LNCS 16477, pp. 73–102, 2026.
https://doi.org/10.1007/978-3-032-18268-5_4

control forces governments to navigate trade-offs between engineering realities (e.g., scalability, latency, resilience) and policy obligations (e.g., data protection, durable archiving, open publication) [35, 79].

Many agencies rely on global clouds and CDNs for scalability, built-in DDoS mitigation, and broad footprints, at the cost of visibility and control over server placement, data residency, and network interconnections. Running infrastructure in-house preserves autonomy but requires specialized staff, capital investment, and long-term maintenance. Prior work has examined how national governments approach these trade-offs and documented sharp differences in outsourcing rates and provider choice [62].

This paper shifts the lens to subnational governments (provinces and states). Operating under the same federal legal and infrastructural umbrella, these jurisdictions manage their own digital portals—property registries, benefits, public health alerts—and independently choose where and how to host them. Local infrastructure, political priorities, and budgets can diverge sharply from national norms.

Argentina is a federal country with 23 provinces and one autonomous city (CABA), each with constitutional authority over its digital infrastructure. Spanning 2.8 million km^2—from dense urban corridors to sparsely connected Andean and Patagonian regions—it offers a natural setting to observe decentralized choices under a shared national framework. Despite a national fiber backbone (REFEFO) [12] and a federally operated data center, provinces are free to choose their own hosting arrangements.

Study Design. Building on Kumar et al. [62], we adapt their nation-level approach to the subnational tier. Starting from each jurisdiction's official landing page, we crawl to depth seven and analyze >1,200 domains (Oct 2023Apr 2024), classifying serving ASNs by operational control—*sovereign* (Sovereign), *local third-party* (Local), or *global third-party* (Global). We also examine authoritative DNS and HTTPS deployment and relate these choices to 31 demographic, economic, technological, and political covariates (associations only). "Government services" comprise domains under official provincial portals (e.g., *.gob.ar, *.gov.ar) and first-party subdomains linked from them; we exclude social media, SaaS dashboards, and ad/analytics endpoints. Crawls ran from three Argentine vantage networks, and provider classifications were stable across vantage (§3).

Why Argentina – and Why it Generalizes. Beyond its scale and diversity, Argentina mirrors a broader Latin American and Caribbean (LAC) pattern in which subnational governments deliver a growing share of public services under heterogeneous capacities and budgets. In LAC, the subnational share of consolidated public spending rose from ≈13% to ≈25% between 1985–2015, and in federations such as Argentina and Brazil it exceeds 40%—placing provinces at the critical edge of digital service delivery [87]. Argentina combines (i) *autonomy*—provinces and agencies retain genuine purchasing and operational control; (ii) *contrast*—a federal backbone (ARSAT's REFEFO) [12] coexists with local and global third-party providers; and (iii) *observability*—government transparency initiatives publicly listing all digital resources make infrastructure choices measurable at scale [29]. This makes it a compelling laboratory for infrastructure choices under shared national policy but uneven local capacity, with lessons for other federal and quasi-federal contexts.

By surfacing these patterns, we show how subnational governments, often overlooked in Internet measurement, shape the geography of public-sector infrastructure. Our results provide both a methodological template and policy-relevant benchmarks for assessing digital sovereignty below the national level. To anchor our claims, we add a lightweight latency sanity check across hosting classes and a cache-locality audit that verifies whether 'global' providers serve from in-country PoPs. *Our goal is not only to characterize one country, but to offer a reusable template that researchers and agencies can apply to states, regions, or municipalities elsewhere.*

This paper makes three contributions. First, it offers the first empirical study of hosting strategies by subnational governments, revealing substantial variation in choices made under shared national policies, infrastructure, and legal frameworks. Second, it provides an annotated map of provincial dependencies by analyzing over 1,200 government domains across 24 jurisdictions, classifying serving providers (Sovereign, Local, Global), authoritative DNS operators, and TLS configurations, and relating these to 31 socioeconomic and political variables. Third, it uncovers evidence of legacy and localization effects, including the imprint of pre-Internet telecom monopolies, the repurposing of utility/education/telco ASNs for government services, and the limited use of federally funded capacity (e.g., ARSAT), raising questions about coordination, performance, and control.

Our key findings are as follows. Heterogeneous strategies: 11 jurisdictions rely primarily on Local, 7 on Global, and the remainder on Sovereign for URLs/bytes,[1] with domains showing similar splits—there is no single national template. Underuse of federal capacity: only 8 of 24 provinces use ARSAT at all, never exceeding 2% of bytes. Province-operated footprints: 15 provinces serve content from province-run or affiliated networks, with byte shares ranging from $\approx 1.594\%$, indicating wide variation in operational maturity. Incumbent imprint: hosting patterns align with historical Telecom and Telefónica regions, where incumbents still retain substantial shares. DNS and TLS gaps: DNS is mostly outsourced (Local 41%, Global 35%); 48% of domains use different providers for web hosting and authoritative DNS; and in 14/24 jurisdictions domains employ neither anycast nor multi-AS redundancy. HTTPS is enforced on 64% of domains, yet 19% remain HTTP-only, with failures often due to certificate-chain or hostname errors.

---

[1] 'Bytes' denotes retrieved content size from our crawl, not network traffic volume.

2 Subnational Digital Infrastructures: Policy, Constraints, and the Argentine Case

We outline national digital programs, noting converged front-end standards but decentralized back-end hosting. We highlight the role of subnational governments in transaction-heavy services, summarize four constraints on their infrastructure choices, and position Argentina as a regional example. We close by showing how these approaches extend to other federations.

2.1 National Digital Programs

Many national digital programs emphasize unifying the front-end of government websites—through design systems, accessibility rules, and UX guidelines [1–9,36,53,93]. By contrast, decisions about hosting, traffic delivery, and data residency are often decentralized or weakly enforced. Some countries have experimented with stronger, sovereignty-motivated approaches (e.g., government-operated platforms or localization mandates), but these vary in scope and longevity.[2] In short, while national frameworks set common front-end baselines, the infrastructure layer frequently remains a patchwork of agency, vendor, and subnational choices. We describe these programs to contextualize observable hosting outcomes; we do not evaluate policy efficacy or compliance.

2.2 Why Subnational Governments Matter

Subnational governments in LAC deliver most education, health, security, and local administrative services. Their share of consolidated public spending grew from 13% to 25% between 1985 and 2015 [87]. Argentina sits in the high-decentralization tier: provinces and municipalities account for roughly 40% of public expenditure [85,87]. Provinces therefore run transaction-heavy, always-on digital services—tax portals, licensing, appointments—where performance directly affects citizen engagement. Here, "government services" denotes public-sector domains and first-party subdomains linked from official portals; regulated private providers are excluded.

At the same time, subnationals often face binding constraints: limited and rotating IT staff, fiscal dependence on transfers, and weak cross-jurisdiction ICT governance [87]. These pressures create incentives to outsource to large platforms and CDNs, trading capital costs for operating expenses—but sometimes sacrificing control, auditability, or data residency. We therefore treat hosting as an *organizational choice under constraints*. Our focus complements national-level studies by showing how local capacity, incumbent footprints, federal offerings, and market structure jointly shape outcomes.

---

[2] Illustrative examples include: (i) the UK's GOV.UK PaaS, which centralized hosting for some agencies (decommissioned in Dec. 2023); (ii) Russia's personal-data localization rules requiring storage of residents' data within national borders; (iii) India's *MeghRaj* (GI Cloud) framework with in-country data requirements; and (iv) Europe's *Gaia-X* initiative for federated, interoperable infrastructure to bolster data sovereignty. These are illustrative, not endorsements; scopes and timelines differ.

2.3 Challenges for Subnational Digital Services

Policy evidence and practice point to four recurring constraints that shape hosting choices for provinces and municipalities:

Institutional Capacity. Teams are small and rotate frequently, with documented hiring freezes (2018–2019), difficulties attracting and retaining skilled staff, and reliance on temporary contracts, eroding portfolio governance and continuity [31,77,87].

Fiscal Constraints. Vertical fiscal imbalance and reliance on intergovernmental transfers limit the predictability of capital expenditures. Cloud models shift costs from capital to operational expenditures ("pay-as-you-go") and reduce anticipatory budgeting; an IDB-cited study finds an in-country data center model could be $\approx 54\%$ costlier than leveraging global cloud providers, and that IXPs and cache placement can reduce bandwidth costs and latency [35,84,85]. We therefore treat budget exposure as context, not as measured spend, and later weight outcomes using domain/URL/bytes aggregates as proxies for footprint and content heft.

Fragmented Procurement & Governance. Policy recommendations encourage a transition from agency-by-agency purchasing toward a "government-as-one-client" model. Multiple, disconnected platforms hinder reuse, and e-procurement maturity remains uneven across LAC [14,77,80].

Risk Management & Resilience Gaps. Siting, power redundancy, and regularly tested disaster-recovery and business-continuity procedures are often under-specified, despite guidance to provision reserve capacity, diversify and duplicate critical systems, and run exercises [78,91,95]. Operationally, we map these risks to two measurable dimensions—authoritative DNS anycast/AS-level diversity and failover/DR posture—which we quantify in §5.

These measured constraints then interact with existing telecom footprints and federal programs (e.g., ARSAT's REFEFO backbone [12]), helping explain the heterogeneous hosting choices we document across provinces.

Recent events underscore the stakes: in May 2024, extreme flooding in Rio Grande do Sul (Brazil) led the state IT company (PROCERGS) to shut down its data center, taking multiple state services offline until gradual restoration [10,16,39]. Beyond that case, comparative guidance highlights that exposure to hydrological risk, placement of backup power, reserve capacity, and the frequency of continuity testing are first-order design choices for subnational digital infrastructure [78,91].

2.4 Argentina in Regional Perspective

Argentina intensified its national digital policy in 2016 with the *Plan de Modernización del Estado*, which authorized the National Office of Information Technologies (ONTI) to establish technical standards and offer guidance throughout the public sector [83]. ONTI subsequently published and updated accessibility and technology standards—e.g., the 2019 *Disposición ONTI 6/2019* on Web

Content Accessibility Guidelines (WCAG) 2.0 and the *Decálogo Tecnológico*—that continue to shape how public websites are developed and maintained [72,73]. However, these policies largely leave infrastructure choices (where and how to host, use of clouds and CDNs, resilience practices) to each agency or jurisdiction. As a federation of 23 provinces and one autonomous city—with independent administrative and budget processes—Argentina mirrors broader LAC reforms that emphasize clearer assignment of responsibilities and intergovernmental transfers while calling for stronger subnational management capacity and digitalization [87]. Federal infrastructure such as ARSAT's *Red Federal de Fibra Óptica* (REFEFO) provides important backbone capacity, but does not itself determine provincial hosting strategies [12]. These policies set design baselines while leaving hosting to agencies and jurisdictions; our analysis observes the resulting deployment choices, not compliance.

2.5   Argentina as a Case Study

Why Argentina – and Why It Generalizes. Three features make Argentina a natural case study: (1) federative structure, (2) articulation between federal and subnational governments in digital policies, and (3) availability of federally funded digital infrastructures. **Federative structure**, it is a federation of 23 provinces and one autonomous city with independent administrative and budget processes; provinces and municipalities execute on the order of 40% of consolidated public spending, in line with a broader regional shift in LAC where the subnational share rose from 13% to 25% between 1985 and 2015 [85,87]. This places provinces at the front line of transaction-heavy digital services. **Policy articulation: centralized design, decentralized infrastructure** the policy design separates front-end standardization from back-end infrastructure discretion, creating cross-provincial variation in hosting models, cloud and CDN reliance, and resilience practices that can be observed and measured [77]. **Federally funded digital backbones**, federal infrastructure such as ARSAT's *Red Federal de Fibra Óptica* (REFEFO) provides backbone capacity without prescribing provincial hosting strategies, interacting with heterogeneous provincial telecom footprints and local IXP and cache opportunities [12,35]. From this landscape, we derive testable hypotheses: (H1) Incumbent fixed-line footprints predict provider choice; (H2) Federal capacity (e.g., ARSAT) sees limited uptake relative to local/global options; (H3) Capacity constraints correlate with platform outsourcing; (H4) Cache locality moderates the sovereignty – performance trade-off. Sections 5–6 test these associations.

How the Case Generalizes. Argentina presents a set of features shared by both Latin American countries and nations outside the region. The federal division of powers, centralized design guidance with decentralized control of hosting infrastructure, and the coexistence of a public backbone alongside domestic and global cloud and CDNs create a set of characteristics that can be extended to other countries. These features closely resemble those found in other Latin American and Caribbean federations with extensive territories (e.g., Brazil, Mexico) and in unitary states (e.g., Colombia, Chile). However, this is not exclusive to Latin America, as similar features are shared by OECD countries (e.g., U.S. states, Canadian provinces, and Spain's autonomous communities). We then examine how capacity constraints, capital and operational expenditure trade-offs, fragmented procurement, and resilience and continuity planning—shape Argentina's subnational digital hosting, and derive actionable design implications for any jurisdiction where subnational entities choose hosting under national policy frameworks [35, 77, 87].

3   Methodology and Dataset

This section describes our methodological framework (Sect. 3.1), the process for compiling and scraping government domains (Sect. 3.2), and the non-network variables used to explain hosting decisions (Sect. 3.3).

3.1   Methodology

Our methodology builds on the work of Kumar et al. [62], who analyzed national government hosting across 61 countries. We adapt and extend their approach to focus on subnational entities.

Scraping Approach. We start from each jurisdiction's official landing page and crawl up to depth 7, following the depth criteria applied in Kumar et al. [62] and Singanamalla et al. [89]. Because public sites often embed third-party content (e.g., YouTube, X), we restrict the dataset to *first-party* resources via a multi-step filter: (i) allowlist government domains at the eTLD+1, (ii) retain only internal URLs, and (iii) drop known third-party embeds/trackers. Table 1 details these rules. We canonicalize URLs (lowercasing, query-param normalization), deduplicate exact resources, honor `robots.txt`, and justify depth-7 as a coverage/tractability trade-off with a saturation check.

Table 1. Steps used to identify government-owned domains.

Approach	Description
Government TLDs	Matches `.gob.ar` or `.gov.ar` domains
Domain Matching	Checks if hostname matches known gov domains
TLS SAN Matching	Identifies gov domains via certificate SANs

Government Domain Identification. We first label as government resources those with domains under known government top-level domains (TLDs), as proposed by Singanamalla et al. [89]. In Argentina, these TLDs include both `.gob.ar` and `.gov.ar`[3].

For domains outside the `.gob.ar`/`.gov.ar` TLDs (e.g., state-owned firms like `ypf.com`), we apply manual and certificate-based heuristics to confirm government ownership before resolving to IPs and mapping to ASNs.

Vantage Points. We fetch pages from in-country vantage points to reflect domestic path selection, cache affinity, and CDN mapping. We deploy three vantage points in the Buenos Aires metropolitan area: one on a large university (albeit running on three VMs) and two residential nodes in major access ISPs – Telecom Argentina (AS7303) and Telecentro (AS27747) – which serve approximately 27% and 10% of the user base, respectively [63]. This placement captures the CDN choices applied to Argentina-based users, including in multi-CDN settings. Our scraping did not include vantage points in every province, as we assume that hosting strategies will not change on a per-province basis.

Attribution and Metrics. We record the server IP address for every fetched resource and attach per-resource metrics. IP addresses are mapped to origin Autonomous Systems (ASes) using CAIDA's prefix-to-AS dataset [22]. For each URL, we log bytes served—the on-disk size retrieved by the crawler for first-party HTML and same-origin static assets during rendering—not traffic volume; we report URLs, domains (eTLD+1), and bytes per provider to capture structure, scope, and content heft. To contextualize provider reliance, we report three aggregates per site, each highlighting a different aspect of government hosting: (i) distinct serving URLs—capturing application surface and fragmentation; (ii) distinct domains (eTLD+1)—capturing administrative scope and delegation; and (iii) total bytes served—capturing content and storage footprint. All aggregates are broken down by AS/provider. Together, these measures reveal the structural dependence of government sites on specific networks and platforms.

Provider Taxonomy (Control, not Location). Our approach groups the serving ASN for each domain into three categories based on operational control: (1) Government/SOE (Sovereign), (2) Third-Party Local (Local), and (3) Third-Party Global (Global). Sovereign covers ASNs dedicated to government use or run by state-owned enterprises (e.g., ARSAT). Local includes commercial ASNs registered and primarily operating in Argentina. Global refers to multinational networks with an international footprint. These labels reflect ownership and control—not physical server location. For instance, ARSAT remains "Sovereign" even with broad peering, while global CDNs with local PoPs remain "Global." Classification is supported by registry and documentary sources.

Our provider taxonomy combines documentary verification with registry checks. First, government and state-owned networks were manually classified by searching official sources (laws/decrees, corporate registries, and agency pages) that establish public ownership or control. Second, we label as Local firms incorporated in Argentina, i.e., companies registered under Argentine jurisdiction.

---

[3] While `.gob` is the natural extension for "government" (gobierno) in Spanish (Argentina's official language), many Spanish-speaking countries also use `.gov` as a legacy convention influenced by the United States.

Third, we label as Global global platforms that operate across multiple continents (e.g., multi-region cloud/CDN providers). Within our measurement corpus, we did not identify foreign providers serving Argentina's government content other than these Global.

3.2 Dataset

We compiled an official seed list of landing pages for Argentina's federal government and its 24 subnational jurisdictions. For the federal branch, our starting point was the executive-branch CSV that lists ministries and secretariats (e.g., Ministry of Economy), federal agencies (e.g., ENACOM), and state-owned enterprises (e.g., Nucleoeléctrica Argentina S.A.)[4]. We complemented this automatically harvested list with a manual review of the legislative and judicial branches (Senate, Chamber of Deputies, Supreme Court, Public Prosecutor), using official organograms to locate each branch's top-level portal.

At the provincial level, we followed the same approach: most provinces publish organograms or directories that link to ministries, secretariats, and agencies. Where a consolidated list was unavailable, we extracted candidate URLs from official organizational charts and then manually verified coverage by spot-checking each province's directory pages. State ownership of companies is generally traceable from these official disclosures—for example, the federal CSV identifies YPF as dependent on the Ministry of Economy and the Secretary of Energy. Provinces likewise publish their lists of publicly owned companies: for example, the Province of Buenos Aires documents its ownership of power-generation firms such as Centrales de la Costa Atlántica S.A.[5]

Terminology. A *landing page* is a top-level portal listed in an official organogram. A *domain* is counted at the eTLD+1 (e.g., `salta.gob.ar`). *URLs* are distinct first-party pages discovered during the crawl. *Bytes* denote the on-disk size retrieved for first-party HTML and same-origin static assets during rendering (not traffic volume).

We crawled **202** federal and **1,446** subnational landing pages between Oct. 2023 and Apr. 2024, yielding **57,730** first-party URLs across **1,244** eTLD+1 domains (8.8 GB). Figure 1 shows landing-page coverage by province.

Table 2 summarizes where content lives by suffix class. We apply the same control-based taxonomy to *authoritative DNS operators* (sovereign/local/global) and evaluate HTTPS deployment and certificate chain/hostname quality across all domains.

At the time of writing, the Milei administration is restructuring the executive branch (e.g., ministry mergers; AFIP → ARCA). To gauge URL stability, we compare two snapshots of *federal top-level portals and agencies* (Aug. 23,

---

[4] Latest disclosure of Argentina's executive branch composition: https://mapadelestado.jefatura.gob.ar/back/api/datos.php?db=m&id=9&fi=csv. Accessed Feb. 15, 2025.

[5] Latest disclosure of the Province of Buenos Aires state-owned enterprises: https://www.gba.gob.ar/infraestructura/empresas. Accessed Dec. 2, 2025.

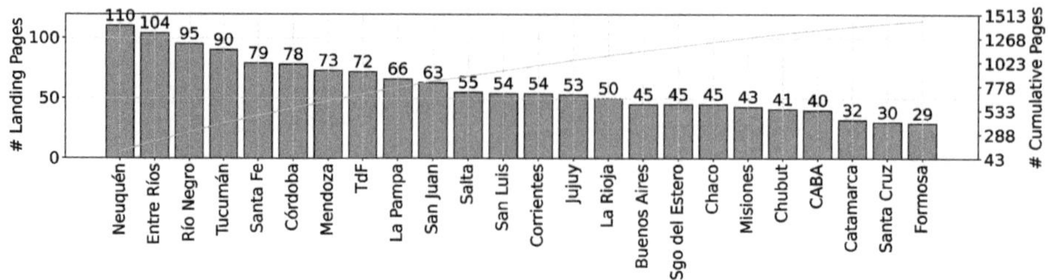

Fig. 1. Landing pages collected per province (bars) and cumulative share (line).

Table 2. Share of URLs, domains, and bytes by suffix class. Categories mix second-level domains under `.ar` (e.g., `gob.ar`) and global TLDs (e.g., `.com`). Percentages may not sum to 100 due to rounding.

Metric	gob.ar	gov.ar	com.ar	.com	edu.ar	org.ar	.ar	.org	.net	.tv	.app
URLs	46.5	32.1	11.1	3.1	2.6	2.3	1.1	0.6	0.2	0.0	0.0
Domains	47.1	34.1	11.9	0.0	2.3	2.0	1.0	0.8	0.3	0.1	0.1
Bytes	48.2	27.2	12.7	2.9	2.5	0.6	1.6	3.9	0.4	0.0	0.0

2023, pre-election; Sep. 3, 2025, mid-term): the Jaccard distance is 0.35 (similarity 0.65), with **158/243** URLs unchanged and **85/243** changed (new entities, mergers, decommissions, or rewrites). Thus, while the federal web evolved, a *majority* of portals remained stable across the period.

We release the seed list, suffix-class rules, and per-province aggregates upon request to support replication.

3.3   Contextual Variables

To explain variation in hosting choices, we compile 31 contextual variables across four categories:

We organize these non-network variables into four categories: demographic, economic, technological, and governmental. The dataset includes 31 variables for the federal government and 24 provincial jurisdictions, with a complete version available in Appendix B. All data were collected from authoritative sources, including Argentina's communications regulator (ENACOM), the National Institute of Statistics and Censuses (INDEC), and several United Nations agencies.

The following paragraph provides a brief overview of the variables within each pillar.

Demographic Variables. This pillar includes 11 indicators: inequality (Gini coefficient) [76], Human Development Index (HDI) [86], average years of schooling [52], share of the population with tertiary education [44], total population [45], urbanization rate [46], migration rate [33], life expectancy [51], illiteracy rate [32], poverty rate [49], and financial inclusion [13]. Most of these variables come from INDEC's national census and routine surveys, supplemented by data from United Nations sources and provincial agencies. We use these variables to test whether each jurisdiction's social profile influences the government's choice of global, local, or in-house hosting strategies.

Economic Variables. This pillar tracks 8 indicators: GDP per capita [19], unemployment rate [50], public expenditure as a share of GDP [81], public debt as a share of GDP [60], fiscal balance (tax result) as a share of GDP [43], inflation rate [48], and public-sector employment [56]. This compilation was obtained from several authoritative sources, including INDEC, academic research centers, the Congressional Budget Office, and national ministries. We use these variables to test whether a province's economic performance affects its government's content-delivery strategies.

Technological Variables. This pillar covers 9 indicators: overall Internet-penetration rate [34]; fixed-line Internet access rate [47]; mobile Internet access rate [47]; household Internet-penetration rate [47]; enterprise Internet-penetration rate [47]; average connection speed [34]; number of peering facilities [23]; number of registered ASes[6]; and the share of government domains among the country's 100k most-visited websites [37]. We use these metrics to test whether the strength of a jurisdiction's Internet infrastructure influences its preference for global, local, or government-run hosting strategies.

Governmental Variables. This pillar tracks three indicators: (i) the democracy score, derived from the Varieties of Democracy (V-Dem) methodological guidelines [92]; (ii) congress diversity, measured as the entropy of party representation in each provincial legislature; and (iii) political diversity, defined as the number of active political parties [24]. We use these variables to test whether a jurisdiction's political profile influences its preference for global, local, or in-house hosting strategies.

4   Serving Infrastructures

In this section, we examine the hosting choices of Argentina's subnational governments. We focus on their preference for self-hosting versus third-party providers (Sect. 4.1); their use of federal- or province-owned infrastructure (Sect. 4.2); the prevalence of legacy fixed-line incumbents in content delivery (Sect. 4.3); and their reliance on local hosting providers (Sect. 4.4).

4.1   Government-Run Vs. Third-Party Hosting

We quantify, for each jurisdiction, the fraction of *URLs*, *domains*, and *bytes* served by Sovereign (sovereign), Local (third-party domestic), and Global (third-party foreign) providers (Fig. 2). Using *bytes* as the primary metric and a *plurality* decision rule, 11 provinces predominantly rely on Local, 7 on Global, and

---

[6] Computed with a script that combines LACNIC delegation files, RDAP records, and geolocation APIs from OpenStreetMaps, Geoapify, and OpenCageData.

the remainder on Sovereign; *domains* show a similar split.[7] There is no single national template; for illustration, CABA serves 38.1% of domains, 33.5% of URLs, and 48.9% of bytes via Sovereign.

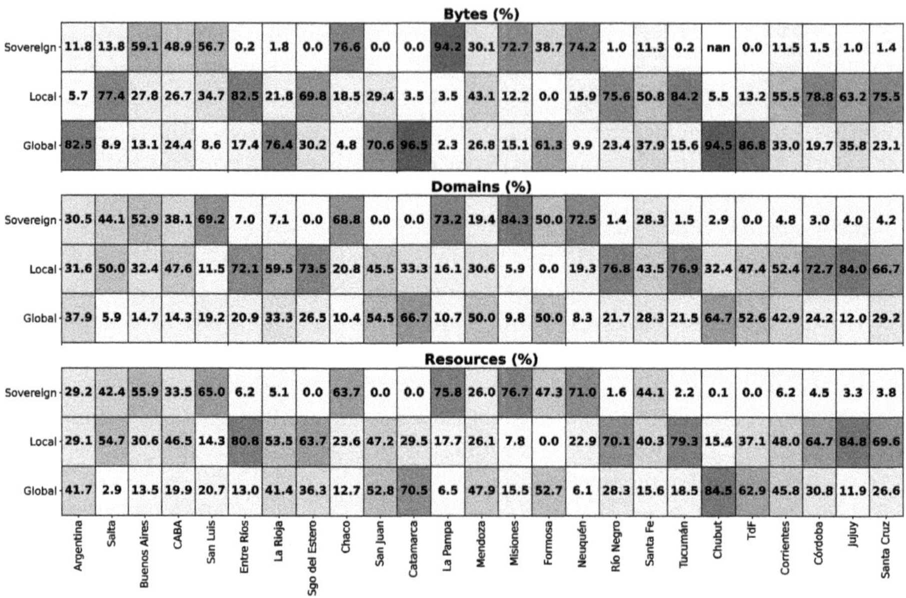

Bytes (%)

	Argentina	Salta	Buenos Aires	CABA	San Luis	Entre Ríos	La Rioja	Sgo del Estero	Chaco	San Juan	Catamarca	La Pampa	Mendoza	Misiones	Formosa	Neuquén	Río Negro	Santa Fe	Tucumán	Chubut	TdF	Corrientes	Córdoba	Jujuy	Santa Cruz
Sovereign	11.8	13.8	59.1	48.9	56.7	0.2	1.8	0.0	76.6	0.0	0.0	94.2	30.1	72.7	38.7	74.2	1.0	11.3	0.2	nan	0.0	11.5	1.5	1.0	1.4
Local	5.7	77.4	27.8	26.7	34.7	82.5	21.8	69.8	18.5	29.4	3.5	3.5	43.1	12.2	0.0	15.9	75.6	50.8	84.2	5.5	13.2	55.5	78.8	63.2	75.5
Global	82.5	8.9	13.1	24.4	8.6	17.4	76.4	30.2	4.8	70.6	96.5	2.3	26.8	15.1	61.3	9.9	23.4	37.9	15.6	94.5	86.8	33.0	19.7	35.8	23.1

Domains (%)

	Argentina	Salta	Buenos Aires	CABA	San Luis	Entre Ríos	La Rioja	Sgo del Estero	Chaco	San Juan	Catamarca	La Pampa	Mendoza	Misiones	Formosa	Neuquén	Río Negro	Santa Fe	Tucumán	Chubut	TdF	Corrientes	Córdoba	Jujuy	Santa Cruz
Sovereign	30.5	44.1	52.9	38.1	69.2	7.0	7.1	0.0	68.8	0.0	0.0	73.2	19.4	84.3	50.0	72.5	1.4	28.3	1.5	2.9	0.0	4.8	3.0	4.0	4.2
Local	31.6	50.0	32.4	47.6	11.5	72.1	59.5	73.5	20.8	45.5	33.3	16.1	30.6	5.9	0.0	19.3	76.8	43.5	76.9	32.4	47.4	52.4	72.7	84.0	66.7
Global	37.9	5.9	14.7	14.3	19.2	20.9	33.3	26.5	10.4	54.5	66.7	10.7	50.0	9.8	50.0	8.3	21.7	28.3	21.5	64.7	52.6	42.9	24.2	12.0	29.2

Resources (%)

	Argentina	Salta	Buenos Aires	CABA	San Luis	Entre Ríos	La Rioja	Sgo del Estero	Chaco	San Juan	Catamarca	La Pampa	Mendoza	Misiones	Formosa	Neuquén	Río Negro	Santa Fe	Tucumán	Chubut	TdF	Corrientes	Córdoba	Jujuy	Santa Cruz
Sovereign	29.2	42.4	55.9	33.5	65.0	6.2	5.1	0.0	63.7	0.0	0.0	75.8	26.0	76.7	47.3	71.0	1.6	44.1	2.2	0.1	0.0	6.2	4.5	3.3	3.8
Local	29.1	54.7	30.6	46.5	14.3	80.8	53.5	63.7	23.6	47.2	29.5	17.7	26.1	7.8	0.0	22.9	70.1	40.3	79.3	15.4	37.1	48.0	64.7	84.8	69.6
Global	41.7	2.9	13.5	19.9	20.7	13.0	41.4	36.3	12.7	52.8	70.5	6.5	47.9	15.5	52.7	6.1	28.3	15.6	18.5	84.5	62.9	45.8	30.8	11.9	26.6

Fig. 2. Hosting choices by jurisdiction: share of URLs, domains, and bytes served via Sovereign, Local, and Global.

Distributions vary widely across jurisdictions. For *URLs*, Local spans 0–84% (mean 42.3%), Global 2.2–84.5% (31.2%), and Sovereign 0–76.7% (26.5%). For *domains*, Local spans 0–84% (44.1%), Global 5.9–66.7% (29.2%), and Sovereign 0–84.3% (26.7%). For *bytes*, Local spans 0–84.2% (39.0%), Global 2.3–96.5% (36.8%), and Sovereign 0–94.2% (24.5%).

Sanity Checks (Summary). (i) *Latency*: from three Buenos Aires area vantage points, median TTFB/ping differs across classes as expected (Global ≈ Local when served from in-country PoPs; Sovereign varies with provincial backhaul). (ii) *Cache locality*: for each domain in Global, we resolve/trace to confirm in-country CDN PoPs when present.

4.2 Federal and Province-Operated Infrastructures

ARSAT's REFEFO backbone and the Benavídez data center are widely reachable, yet provincial uptake is limited. At the federal tier, ARSAT is the #2

---

[7] Replacing plurality with a $> 50\%$ threshold leaves conclusions qualitatively unchanged.

network by domains, URLs, and bytes; at the provincial tier, only 8/24 jurisdictions use ARSAT at all—typically for a single domain—and it never exceeds 2% of bytes (max: Jujuy). This pattern suggests organizational or procurement factors dominate raw reachability.

Argentina's federal government owns ARSAT, founded to operate geostationary satellites [55] and later expanded to build the Federal Optical Fiber Network (REFEFO), a country-wide backbone [12], and to run a national data center. The Benavídez facility (inaugurated in 2012 [11]) connects directly to REFEFO, providing paths to all provinces. Given this federally funded capacity, we examine whether governments leverage ARSAT's network and data center to host federal- and province-level websites.

Table 3. Top networks serving the federal government by URLs, domains, and bytes.

ASN–ASName	URLs		Domains		Bytes	
	#	Rank	#	Rank	MB	Rank
13335–Cloudflare	1,561	1	12	1	1,618.0	1
52361–ARSAT	**410**	**2**	**10**	**2**	**83.5**	**2**
8075–Microsoft	231	8	9	3	20.8	7
16814–NSS	369	3	7	4	16.2	12
27823–Dattatec	321	4	7	4	16.7	11
266700–HCDN	300	5	4	8	50.2	3
6121–Ministry of Justice	136	12	2	10	34.2	4
7049–Silica Networks	168	9	2	10	21.3	5

At the federal level (Table 3), ARSAT ranks second by all three metrics (10 domains; 410 URLs; ∼83.5 MB). At the provincial level, the picture changes markedly.

As shown in Fig. 3a, only a third of provinces (8/24) use ARSAT to host content, and it is never used to serve more than 2% of bytes (Jujuy). Each of these provinces relies on ARSAT for a single domain; by number of URLs, the largest is Mendoza (115 URLs). Despite uneven coverage, a reduced measurement campaign using 60 in-country RIPE Atlas vantage points found the 90th-percentile probe-to-Benavídez RTT $\leq$ 40 ms; suggesting that latency is unlikely to be the primary driver of hosting decisions.

Turning to province-operated infrastructures, Fig. 3bshows that 15 provinces serve content from their own or affiliated networks. Across 23 such networks, byte shares range widely—from La Pampa at 94.2%, Neuquén at 74.2%, and San Luis at 56.7% to La Rioja at 1.5%.

Zooming in (Table 4), six provincial governments operate eleven dedicated networks for content delivery (e.g., AS27967 in Buenos Aires; AS52318 in CABA), while others repurpose pre-existing province-owned infrastructures: four leverage utility networks (e.g., AS262150 in Córdoba), five rely on telecom networks (e.g., AS263774 in Misiones), and two use educational networks (e.g., AS52440 in San Luis). Reuse can deliver control at low capex but may inherit

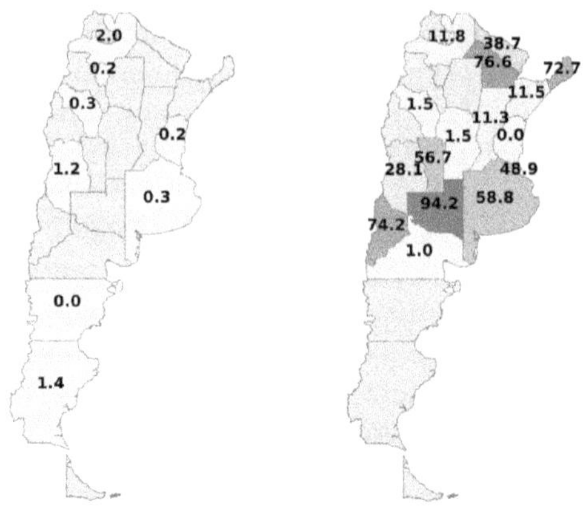

(a) federal-owned in-
frastructure   (b)   province-owned
infrastructure

Fig. 3. Share of provincial bytes delivered via (a) federal-owned (ARSAT) and (b) province-owned networks.

design constraints; we evaluate resilience proxies (authoritative-DNS anycast/AS diversity and failover posture) in Sect. 5.

4.3   Incumbents' Fingerprints

In the early 1990s, Argentina privatized the state telco ENTEL [67,69] and split the country into two service regions—north ("upper") and south ("lower")—with the City of Buenos Aires divided between them [68]. The northern region was awarded to Telecom Argentina (then a Telecom Italia/France Télécom JV) [70]; the southern region to Telefónica de Argentina [71]. Although Internet service (commercial from 1994 [75]) was not regulated as a public service, fixed-line incumbents quickly leveraged their plant and customer bases to dominate last-mile access (Fig. 4).

Present-day government hosting patterns track the historical Telecom/Telefónica demarcation. Assigning each province to its legacy incumbent's service area, the incumbent's share of *domains* hosted within its home zone mirrors the legacy split. Using *bytes* yields the same qualitative result, with province-level variation (e.g., Santa Cruz 29.2→7.3%, Córdoba 65.2→75.3%). We treat this as an *association*, not a causal claim.

Two mechanisms are consistent with this pattern: inherited access/backhaul footprints and institutional familiarity (procurement/sales channels). Server *location* may differ (e.g., CDN PoPs) and does not determine class; we account for cache locality and latency when interpreting performance.[8]

---

[8] We observed anecdotal evidence of locally hosted government servers (e.g., Río Gallegos for Santa Cruz). Geolocation for these hosts was inconsistent across databases, and we lacked in-province active measurements; we therefore do not rely on these anecdotes in our analysis.

Table 4. Fraction of bytes served by each province-owned network.

ASN–ASName	Province	%	Role
27967–Buenos Aires Gov	Buenos Aires	58.8	Gov
269906–Chaco Digital	Chaco	0.0	Telco
52373–ECOM Chaco	Chaco	76.6	Telco
3449–University of Buenos Aires	CABA	0.5	Education
269766–Council of Magistracy	CABA	1.6	Gov
267816–Public Prosecutor's Office	CABA	3.5	Gov
52318–ASIGCBA	CABA	43.3	Gov
270044–Corrientes Telecom	Corrientes	11.5	Telco
262150–EPEC	Córdoba	1.5	Utility
272834–ENER	Entre Ríos	0.0	Utility
263791–REFSA	Formosa	38.7	Utility
52308–Waters of the Colorado	La Pampa	94.2	Utility
28048–Internet for All	La Rioja	1.5	Telco
264808–Ministry of Finance	Mendoza	12.3	Gov
27894–Judiciary Branch	Mendoza	15.8	Gov
263774–Marandú	Misiones	72.7	Telco
262222–OPTIC	Neuquén	74.2	Gov
267820–NEUTICS	Neuquén	0.0	Gov
265687–ALTEC	Río Negro	1.0	Telco
264848–Gov. Financial Service	Salta	10.9	Gov
265651–Ministry of Finance	Salta	0.9	Gov
52440–University of La Punta	San Luis	56.7	Education
52293–Santa Fe Gov	Santa Fe	11.3	Gov

4.4   The Role of Local Providers

Beyond the two fixed-line incumbents, a handful of domestic networks account for most provincial outsourcing—e.g., Claro (AS11664; also AS19037/AMX), NSS/iPlan (AS16814), and Dattatec/DonWeb (AS27823). We use *bytes* as the primary metric, sort the heatmap by each ASN's *aggregate* byte share across provinces, and annotate the top five. Single-province providers are common (11 provinces), but only four exceed 5% of bytes; we list these explicitly in Table 5 and discuss operational risk in Sect. 5.

Figure 5 highlights local providers with multi-province reach. Besides Telecom Argentina (AS7303) and Telefónica Argentina (AS10834), major domestic networks include Claro (AS11664/AS19037) and NSS/iPlan (AS16814). Regional patterns emerge: Gigared (cable along the Paraná River) serves Chaco, Corrientes, Santa Fe, and Entre Ríos, while Dattatec/DonWeb (AS27823) appears in 22 provinces and reaches up to 69.7% of URLs and 36.0% of bytes in Salta. Results are similar when ranking by domains instead of bytes.

We also examine providers dedicated to a *single* province. This preference appears in 11 provinces; among 18 such networks, only four exceed 5% of bytes: AS52312 (TV MUSIC HOUSE, Jujuy), AS264738 (Sebastián Souto, Santa Cruz), AS27879 (IyT, Mendoza), and AS61449 (RESEARCH, Misiones). Several others are very small and, in some cases, are personal or boutique

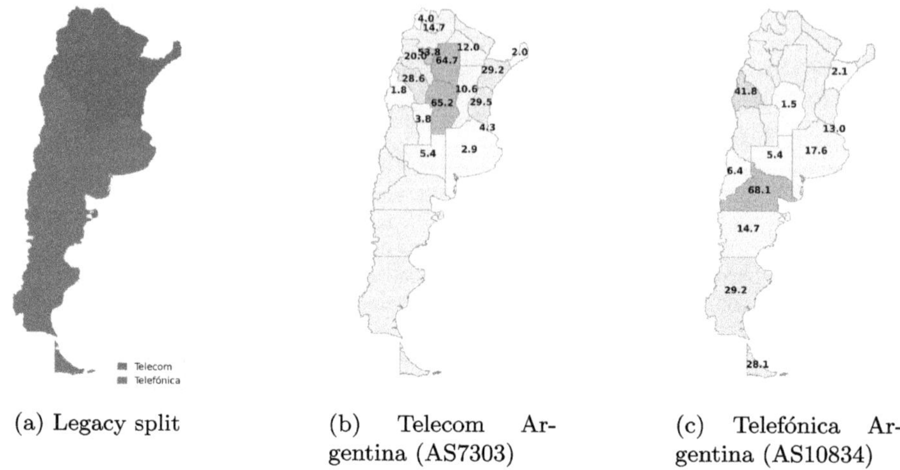

(a) Legacy split   (b) Telecom Argentina (AS7303)   (c) Telefónica Argentina (AS10834)

Fig. 4. Share of provincial *domains* hosted by each incumbent. Panel (a) shows the 1990 legacy split; (b)–(c) show present-day provincial shares.

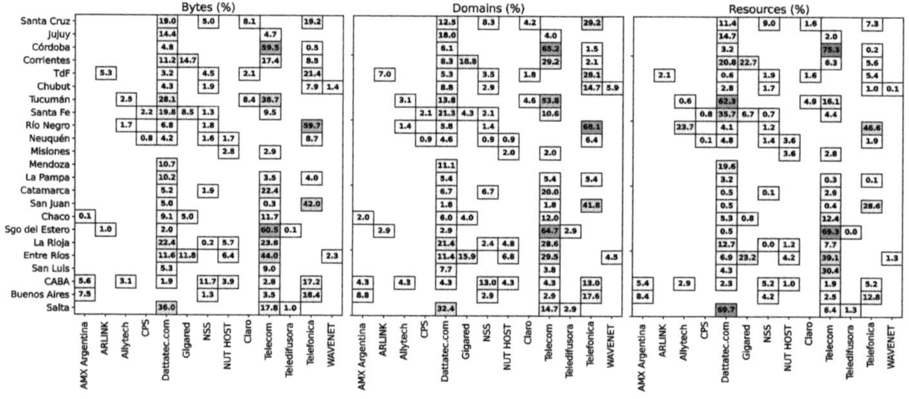

Fig. 5. Share of URLs, domains, and bytes served by each *local* network that serves more than one province. Rows (ASNs) are sorted by total byte share across provinces.

ASNs (e.g., 265781—Pala Pablo Federico; 264689—Luciano Gabriel Chersanaz). Appendix C provides per-AS details (Table 10).

Takeaways. Hosting strategies vary: most use local third-party providers, some rely on global CDNs, and others have government-run footprints. Federally owned capacity (ARSAT, REFEFO) appears underutilized, with only 8 of 24 jurisdictions using ARSAT and never exceeding 2% of bytes, suggesting procurement or operational issues. Fifteen provinces serve content through province-operated networks, often using utility or telco ASNs, resulting in a large variation in bytes (1.5% to 94%) and affecting resilience and maintainability. Legacy incumbents—Telecom and Telefonica—influence provincial domain

Table 5. Single-province providers exceeding 5% of bytes.

ASN–ASName	Province	Bytes (%)
52312–TV MUSIC HOUSE	Jujuy	>5
264738–Sebastián Souto	Santa Cruz	>5
27879–IyT	Mendoza	>5
61449–RESEARCH	Misiones	>5

hosting, aligned with historical service regions. Future analysis should consider economic factors in hosting decisions, such as hosting costs and budgets, and foreign currency exposure in countries with volatile exchange rates.

5 Domain Name Infrastructures and Certificates

We examine two further components of the delivery stack: authoritative DNS (Sect. 5.1) and HTTPS (Sect. 5.2).

5.1 Name Servers Choices

Domain management introduces additional choices—third-party DNS, anycast, multihoming, and load balancing. We focus on three questions: (1) how often governments outsource nameservers, (2) whether they deploy redundancy, and (3) how DNS choices align with web-hosting choices.

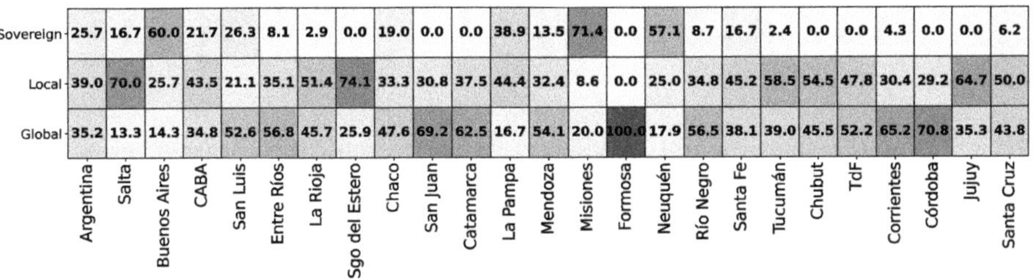

	Argentina	Salta	Buenos Aires	CABA	San Luis	Entre Ríos	La Rioja	Sgo del Estero	Chaco	San Juan	Catamarca	La Pampa	Mendoza	Misiones	Formosa	Neuquén	Río Negro	Santa Fe	Tucumán	Chubut	TdF	Corrientes	Córdoba	Jujuy	Santa Cruz
Sovereign	25.7	16.7	60.0	21.7	26.3	8.1	2.9	0.0	19.0	0.0	0.0	38.9	13.5	71.4	0.0	57.1	8.7	16.7	2.4	0.0	0.0	4.3	0.0	0.0	6.2
Local	39.0	70.0	25.7	43.5	21.1	35.1	51.4	74.1	33.3	30.8	37.5	44.4	32.4	8.6	0.0	25.0	34.8	45.2	58.5	54.5	47.8	30.4	29.2	64.7	50.0
Global	35.2	13.3	14.3	34.8	52.6	56.8	45.7	25.9	47.6	69.2	62.5	16.7	54.1	20.0	100.0	17.9	56.5	38.1	39.0	45.5	52.2	65.2	70.8	35.3	43.8

Fig. 6. Nameserver outsourcing strategies across Argentina's jurisdictions, classified by sovereign, local, and global providers.

Outsourcing Nameservers Management. We map which provinces manage or delegate their authoritative name servers. Figure 6 shows the share of domains using sovereign, local, or global providers. On average, 23.5% use sovereign platforms, 41.1% local providers, and 35.4% global operators. Self-hosting is uncommon: only Buenos Aires, Misiones, and Neuquén use sovereign NSs for most domains, and eight provinces never do so.

Mix and Match. We then examine whether provinces separate web-hosting and DNS providers. Many do, since some vendors offer only one service. Figure 7

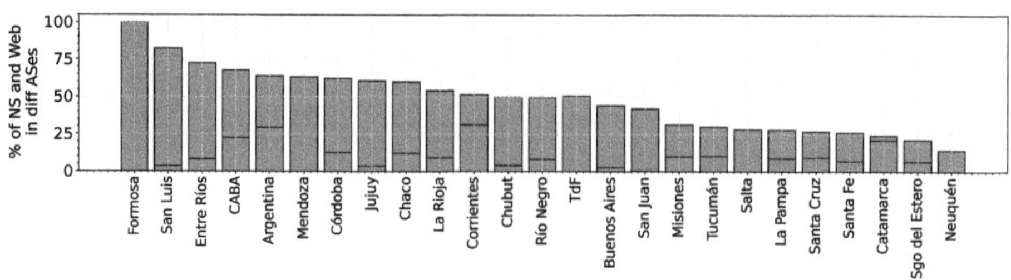

Fig. 7. Percentage of different hosting infrastructures for web and nameservers across Argentinian jurisdictions.

reports the share of domains whose web and name servers sit in different ASes; the average (median) split is 48% (50%).

Motivations vary. Formosa and Entre Ríos, which host most content on sovereign or local networks, outsource DNS to global providers. CABA adopts a hybrid model, operating its own NSs while advertising a third-party NS as apparent failover. These cases illustrate how provinces balance local control with external resilience.

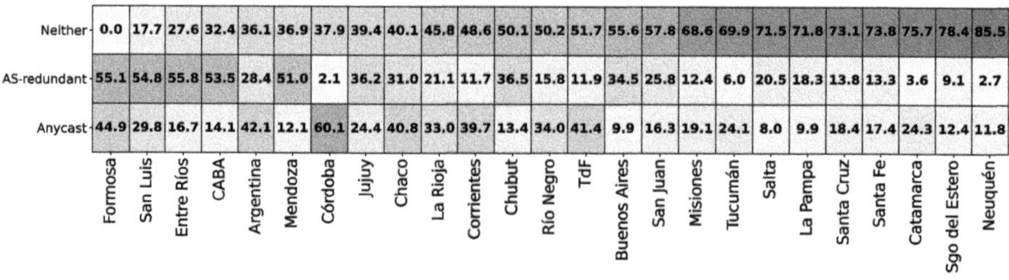

	Formosa	San Luis	Entre Ríos	CABA	Argentina	Mendoza	Córdoba	Jujuy	Chaco	La Rioja	Corrientes	Chubut	Río Negro	TdF	Buenos Aires	San Juan	Misiones	Tucumán	Salta	La Pampa	Santa Cruz	Santa Fe	Catamarca	Sgo del Estero	Neuquén
Neither	0.0	17.7	27.6	32.4	36.1	36.9	37.9	39.4	40.1	45.8	48.6	50.1	50.2	51.7	55.6	57.8	68.6	69.9	71.5	71.8	73.1	73.8	75.7	78.4	85.5
AS-redundant	55.1	54.8	55.8	53.5	28.4	51.0	2.1	36.2	31.0	21.1	11.7	36.5	15.8	11.9	34.5	25.8	12.4	6.0	20.5	18.3	13.8	13.3	3.6	9.1	2.7
Anycast	44.9	29.8	16.7	14.1	42.1	12.1	60.1	24.4	40.8	33.0	39.7	13.4	34.0	41.4	9.9	16.3	19.1	24.1	8.0	9.9	18.4	17.4	24.3	12.4	11.8

Fig. 8. Percentage distribution of nameserver redundancy mechanisms across Argentinian jurisdictions, classified into Anycast, AS-level redundancy, and no redundancy.

Redundancy Strategies. We also measure redundancy in authoritative DNS via two mechanisms: anycasted NS prefixes and placement of NS records across multiple ASes. Figure 8 shows the share of domains using anycast, AS-level redundancy, or neither; domains may employ both, so totals can exceed 100%.

Redundancy practices vary widely. Córdoba records the highest anycast adoption, yet every province uses anycast for at least some domains. AS-level diversification is also common, with pronounced peaks in Mendoza, Entre Ríos, and the Autonomous City of Buenos Aires (CABA). Despite these examples, 14 of the 24 jurisdictions place more than half of their domains in the "neither" category, indicating that a substantial portion of provincial namespaces still lack basic DNS resilience.

5.2 HTTPS Adoption

We next assess HTTPS adoption across the 24 provinces and the federal government. We classify domains into four categories: HTTP-only; HTTPS-only; both with redirect (80→443); and both without redirect.

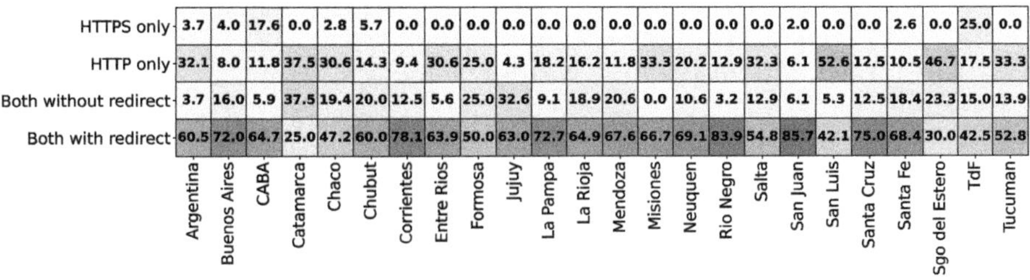

	Argentina	Buenos Aires	CABA	Catamarca	Chaco	Chubut	Corrientes	Entre Rios	Formosa	Jujuy	La Pampa	La Rioja	Mendoza	Misiones	Neuquen	Rio Negro	Salta	San Juan	San Luis	Santa Cruz	Santa Fe	Sgo del Estero	TdF	Tucuman
HTTPS only	3.7	4.0	17.6	0.0	2.8	5.7	0.0	0.0	0.0	0.0	0.0	0.0	0.0	0.0	0.0	0.0	0.0	2.0	0.0	0.0	2.6	0.0	25.0	0.0
HTTP only	32.1	8.0	11.8	37.5	30.6	14.3	9.4	30.6	25.0	4.3	18.2	16.2	11.8	33.3	20.2	12.9	32.3	6.1	52.6	12.5	10.5	46.7	17.5	33.3
Both without redirect	3.7	16.0	5.9	37.5	19.4	20.0	12.5	5.6	25.0	32.6	9.1	18.9	20.6	0.0	10.6	3.2	12.9	6.1	5.3	12.5	18.4	23.3	15.0	13.9
Both with redirect	60.5	72.0	64.7	25.0	47.2	60.0	78.1	63.9	50.0	63.0	72.7	64.9	67.6	66.7	69.1	83.9	54.8	85.7	42.1	75.0	68.4	30.0	42.5	52.8

Fig. 9. Percentage distribution of HTTPS adoption across Argentinian jurisdictions, classified into HTTPS only, HTTP only, both with and without redirect.

Figure 9 presents a heatmap categorizing HTTPS adoption across the federal government and the 24 Argentine provinces. Our findings reveal that the "Both with redirect" configuration is the most prevalent, with an average adoption rate of 63.7% across the 25 jurisdictions, ranging from 25% to 89.4%. In contrast, the proportion of domains using only HTTP is lower at 18.5% on average. However, there is a significant disparity: 7 provinces have more than one-quarter of their domains operating as HTTP only, and 3 provinces exceed one-third.

Table 6. Counts and percentages of HTTPS connection errors.

Error Type	Count	%
Invalid or missing CA chain	51	37.0
Hostname mismatch	28	20.3
Max retries	21	15.2
Self-signed certificate	12	8.7
Read timed out	12	8.7
Expired certificate	10	7.2
SSL wrong version number	2	1.4
Connection reset by peer	1	0.7
Self-signed in chain	1	0.7

To understand HTTPS gaps (Table 6), we group failures into availability errors (e.g., "Max retries," "Read timed out"—HTTPS unavailable) and certificate errors, which dominate. Certificate issues include broken chains, hostname mismatches, self-signed or expired certificates, incorrect SSL versions, and invalid roots.

These patterns suggest difficulty renewing certificates and maintaining services, reflecting a tendency to treat deployments as one-off launches rather than systems requiring ongoing operational upkeep.

6 Explainability Analysis

Sections 3–5 describe our measurement pipeline (seed and crawl construction, provider classification by operational control, and DNS/TLS hygiene checks).

Here, we examine which *non-technical covariates*—demographic, economic, technological, and governance variables (see § 3.3)—are statistically associated with the observed hosting shares. We fit linear regression models to quantify these associations across provinces. While these models reveal consistent patterns in the data, they do not prove causality due to unobserved confounders and the limitations of provincial-level aggregation.

6.1   Model Specification and Model Selection

We fit one model per provider class (Sovereign, Local, Global) and metric (bytes, domains, URLs). Let $y_{p,c}^{(m)} \in [0,1]$ denote the fraction served by class c, for province p and metric m. The specification of the model is:

$$y_{p,c}^{(m)} = \alpha_c^{(m)} + X_p^\top \beta_c^{(m)} + \varepsilon_{p,c}^{(m)}, \tag{1}$$

where X_p is the vector of covariates for province p (standardized to mean 0 and variance 1), $\beta_c^{(m)}$ is the vector of coefficients for class c and metric m, $\alpha_c^{(m)}$ is an intercept term, and $\varepsilon_{p,c}^{(m)}$ is an error term.

In our linear regression framework, each coefficient $\beta_c^{(m)}$ indicates the change in hosting share associated with a one-unit change in the corresponding predictor, holding all other variables constant. We make no causal claims: coefficients should be interpreted as conditional correlations given the included covariates. Potential confounding, omitted variables, and reverse causality may remain.

6.2   Model Fit

Given that the number of samples is low ($n=24$ provinces), we constrain the complexity of the model via forward stepwise selection [94]: features are added one at a time, choosing the one that most improves predictive performance in a leave-one-out cross-validation (LOOCV) framework, minimizing LOOCV mean squared error (MSE). In LOOCV, n-1 samples are used to train the model, and the held-out sample is used to evaluate performance; this process is repeated for each sample, and then the results are averaged. The procedure stops when no further improvement is possible. Then, the model is refit on the selected features to obtain final coefficient estimates.

The predictive capacity of the model is assessed using Pearson's correlation between observed and predicted hosting shares in a LOOCV (leave-one-out cross-validation) framework. We report these values in Table 7: we observe that sovereign-share models exhibit the highest out-of-fold correlations, while global/local shares are harder to predict.

6.3   Key Associations

The statistical significance of each coefficient is assessed via its t-statistic, which is computed as the ratio of the estimated coefficient to its standard error. A

Table 7. LOOCV Pearson correlation (r) between observed shares and predictions, by provider type and metric.

Provider	Metric		
	Bytes	Domains	URLs
Global	0.35	0.25	0.20
Local	0.37	0.20	0.22
Sovereign	0.76	0.83	0.70

higher absolute value of the t-statistic indicates a stronger relationship between the predictor and the hosting share, pointing out that the observed association is less likely to have occurred by chance. In Table 8, we report the features retained after forward stepwise selection for each model, along with their t-statistics, sorted by their importance, and including only those features with $|t| > 2$ (i.e., significant at approximately the 5% level under a two-tailed test).

Table 8. Features retained after forward stepwise selection. Entries show t-statistics from the *refit* on the selected set, including only those features with $|t| > 2$.

Provider Type	Bytes	Domains	URLs
Global	—	Internet speed (-2.1)	Internet speed (-2.0)
Local	Mobile Internet (-2.3)	Mobile Internet (-2.1)	Mobile Internet (-2.3)
Sovereign	Household Internet (-6.0) Illiteracy (5.6) Public employment (3.9) Inequality (-3.6) Internet speed (2.9)	Household Internet (-4.4) Tertiary education (-3.9) Illiteracy (3.2) Tax result (-3.1) GDP per capita (2.8) HDI (2.8) Congress diversity (2.8) Internet speed (3.0)	Household Internet (-4.1) Illiteracy (4.4) Tax result (-3.0) GDP per capita (2.5) Inequality (-2.1)

We also use SHAP (SHapley Additive exPlanations) [65] to explain the individual predictions of each model. SHAP computes feature importance by measuring how much each feature contributes to moving a prediction away from the baseline (mean) prediction, conditional on other included features. SHAP is based on cooperative game theory, specifically the concept of Shapley values, which fairly distribute the "payout" (prediction) among the "players" (features) based on their contributions. Analyzing the SHAP explanations offers a robustness check against the t-statistics derived from our model's fitted regression coefficients.

Figure 10 shows SHAP summaries for three selected models. In this plot, each point represents a single observation from the dataset. The horizontal position of a point indicates the SHAP value (contribution to the prediction), with positive values on the x-axis increasing predictions and negative values decreasing them. The color of each point represents the feature's value for that observation. Features are ranked vertically in the plot by their mean absolute SHAP value, with the most important features at the top.

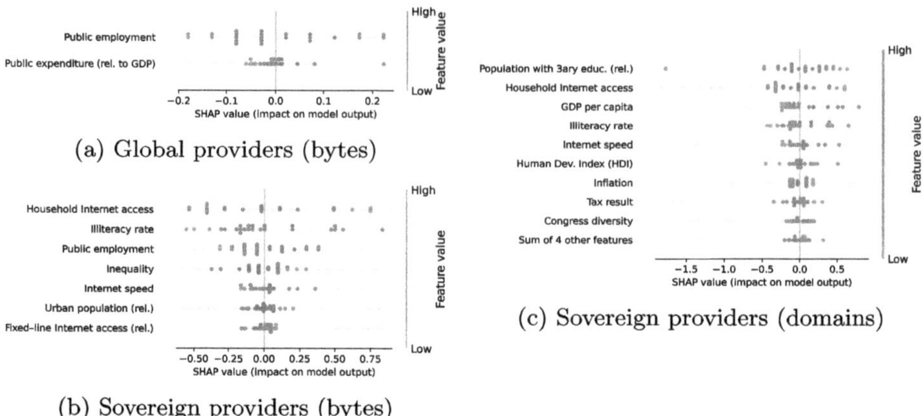

Fig. 10. SHAP summaries for three selected models. Features are ordered by mean absolute SHAP (average impact on predictions across provinces). Each point is a province; color encodes the direction of the feature's contribution.

We observe in panel (b) that lower household Internet access is *associated* with higher local shares; panel (a) points out that higher public-employment levels are *associated* with greater global shares. For sovereign shares, higher illiteracy and lower tertiary attainment are *associated* with larger sovereign shares. These SHAP-based patterns align with the t-statistics in Table 8: household Internet emerges as the dominant predictor for sovereign hosting, while illiteracy and education variables also appear with consistent signs and magnitudes. However, we note that these patterns are correlational and may proxy for underlying factors (e.g., fiscal capacity, institutional maturity) not explicitly modeled here.

7 Discussion

As with any study, our work has limitations. Below, we summarize the key limitations in concrete terms and offer steps to address them in follow-on work.

Scope of Observation. Our dataset is restricted to pages reachable from the portal seeds and to content crawled up to seven levels deep. We therefore do not capture non-web infrastructure such as VDI or remote desktop systems, internal admin portals, private APIs, backend databases, cloud control planes, enterprise CDNs, log systems, or data-residency clauses. Any conclusions should be read as statements about the public web footprint only, not the complete content delivery approach of each government.

Portal-seed and Discovery Bias. Our list compiles public information from official portals and published organograms; we then scrape services linked from those pages. Services that are unlinked, contractor-hosted microsites, campaign pages, or payment gateways might not have been covered. To reduce this bias, future work should combine portal crawling with passive DNS data, registrar zone lists, certificate transparency logs, and coordinated disclosures from agencies.

Measurement Design and Proxy Limits. Our analysis of DNS records, TLS observations, anycast detection, and AS mappings offers valuable indirect insights into how and where content is served. However, these are not direct metrics of user experience, uptime, or redundancy as per contracts. The accuracy of inferences can depend on the locations of the vantage points and the timing of the experiments. To mitigate these limitations, increasing probe diversity, extending sampling over time, and correlating with client-side measurements would reduce these vulnerabilities.

Aggregation and Sample Size. Province-level aggregates can hide important agency-level heterogeneity: different ministries or services within the same province often make distinct hosting choices. Statistical analyses based on only 24 provinces also have limited degrees of freedom and low statistical power; thus estimated effect sizes should be treated as exploratory

Missing Contextual Covariates and Generalizability. We do not examine procurement records, costs, vendor selection rationales, or political drivers that motivate hosting choices. Without those covariates, causal interpretations are constrained. Institutional contexts also vary across countries, making our findings may not generalize without careful consideration of market structure and regulatory differences.

8   Related Work

Governments increasingly shape Internet infrastructure and online services—from granting access [26] and imposing politically motivated shutdowns [17] to delivering e-government portals [41, 42, 90] and enforcing privacy rules [30, 38]. The measurement community has tracked these shifts accordingly.

Closest to our setting, Kumar et al. [62] map hosting choices for *61* countries, highlighting diverse mixes of on-premises and third-party providers. Jansen et al. [54] analyze government infrastructures in six states with tense neighbor relations. Hsiao et al. [42] study external dependencies of public-facing sites in the G7, and Jonker et al. [57] show that many Russian sites were domestically hosted pre-invasion and later lost Western providers—a pattern consistent with our observations. Reliance on single third-party DNS operators is documented by Sommese [90] and Houser [41]; other work examines HTTPS adoption [89], privacy risks [88], and cookie practices [38]. More broadly, consolidation across hosting, DNS, CDNs, and certificate authorities has gained notable attention from various perspectives far beyond government services [40, 58, 59, 61, 64].

To our knowledge, this is the first study to quantify *subnational* diversity in hosting choices within a single country under a shared legal and infrastructural framework, while also incorporating DNS and HTTPS hygiene and linking outcomes to non-technical covariates. Finally, our Argentina-focused analysis contributes to recent efforts to deepen understanding of Latin American network infrastructure [15,18,21,25,27,66,74].

9   Conclusions

Subnational governments shape public-sector infrastructure in ways that defy a single national template. In Argentina, we observe wide diversity – some provinces invest in sovereign footprints, others lean on domestic incumbents or global platforms – with patterns that reflect historical legacies and institutional autonomy as much as technical capacity. We report *associations*, not causal effects, and contextualize sovereigntyperformance trade-offs with latency and cache-locality sanity checks.

Beyond this case, we distill a reusable measurement template (domain discovery → provider classification by operational control → DNS/HTTPS hygiene and resilience proxies) and subnational benchmarks others can replicate. Limits include portal-seed bias and that "bytes" measure retrieved content size, not traffic. A natural next step is a second country (or two) and deeper performance/cost slices to test which invariants travel.

Acknowledgements. This work was supported in part by NSF grants CNS-2246475 and CNS-2107392. The views expressed are solely the authors'. We thank the reviewers and our shepherd for their helpful feedback.

A   Ethical Considerations

Our study reveals provincial infrastructure choices while minimizing harm: we limited collection to public, client-facing pages, performed a single, user-like crawl with no logins or vulnerability probing, and kept our load on government servers negligible. Our results are reported only in aggregate—domain-to-provider mappings are omitted to prevent reconstruction of targets—and the compiled seed dataset will be shared only for replication under a non-redistribution agreement. By constraining granularity, omitting sensitive attribution, and controlling data access, we comply with ethical best practices for Internet measurement while enabling independent validation.

B   Explanatory Variables

Table 9 summarizes the variables that have been considered to explain the hosting decisions of the provinces, grouped by type and including their sources and descriptions.

Table 9. Summary of variables, sources, and descriptions

Type	Variable	Source
Demographic	Inequality	Observatorio Federal Urbano, Ministerio del Interior, Obras Públicas y Vivienda [76]
	HDI	United Nations Development Programme [86]
	Avg. years of schooling	INDEC [52]
	Population with tertiary education	INDEC [44]
	Population	INDEC [45]
	Urban population	INDEC [46]
	Migration rate	Dirección Nacional de Población, Ministerio del Interior [33]
	Life expectancy	INDEC [51]
	Illiteracy rate	Dirección General de Estadística y Censos, GCBA [32]
	Poverty	EPH (INDEC) [49]
	Financial inclusion	BCRA [13]
Economic	GDP per capita	Bolsa de Comercio de Rosario [19]
	Unemployment rate	EPH (INDEC) [50]
	Public expenditure	Oficina de Presupuesto del Congreso [81]
	Credit	KPMG Consulting [60]
	Tax result	IIEP – UBA [43]
	Inflation	INDEC [48]
	Public employment	Jefatura de Gabinete de Ministros [56]
Technological	Internet penetration	ENACOM [34]
	Fixed–line Internet access	INDEC [47]
	Mobile Internet access	INDEC [47]
	Household Internet access	INDEC [47]
	Enterprise Internet access	INDEC [47]
	Internet speed	ENACOM
	Peering facilities	CAIDA [23]
	Registered ASes	LACNIC + RDAP + OSM + Geoapify + OpenCageData
	Government websites	Google CrUX [37]
Governmental	Democracy score	Transparencia Electoral [92]
	Congress diversity	—
	Political diversity	Cámara Nacional Electoral [24]

C   Hosting Providers Operating in a Single Province

Table 10 presents the 18 hosting providers operating hosting content of a single province.

Table 10. List of local providers serving exactly one province. Notably, TV MUSIC HOUSE JUJUY (AS52312) and Sebastian Souto (AS264738) account for the largest share of served bytes for the governments of Jujuy and Santa Cruz, respectively.

ASN-AS Name	Province	URLs	Dom.	Bytes
52312-TV MUSIC HOUSE JUJUY	Jujuy	64.0	60.0	45.9
264738-Sebastian Souto	Santa Cruz	15.0	8.3	45.7
27879-IyT	Mendoza	11.9	8.3	20.3
61449-RESEARCH	Misiones	2.1	2.0	5.8
262187-Patagonia Green	Entre Ríos	2.6	2.3	4.6
28009-Davitel	Neuquén	5.4	4.6	3.9
272150-TELECOMUNICACIONES	Entre Ríos	2.6	2.3	3.1
27747-Telecentro	CABA	3.8	4.3	2.8
61493-BAEHOST	Mendoza	2.8	5.6	2.7
265781-PALA PABLO FEDERICO	Santa Fe	1.0	2.1	2.1
27983-Red Intercable Digital	TdF	0.7	1.8	1.5
52236-G2K ARGENTINA	Jujuy	1.8	2.0	0.6
264689-Luciano Gabriel Chersanaz	Santa Cruz	3.3	4.2	0.5
22927-Telefonica de Argentina	Mendoza	0.7	5.6	0.4
52351-Integral Insumos	Santa Fe	1.0	2.1	0.4
7049-Silica Networks	Tucumán	1.7	1.5	0.3
265749-RBA	La Rioja	1.4	2.4	0.2
61443-KPMG Argentina	Neuquén	0.6	0.9	0.2

References

1. Digital service standard. www.digital.gov.au
2. Estándares digitales y guías. digital.gob.cl
3. An introduction to federal website standards. digital-gov-static-prod.app.cloud.gov
4. Nz government web standards. www.digital.govt.nz
5. Section 508 of the rehabilitation act. www.section508.gov
6. Web standards. webstandards.ca.gov
7. Government technology standards and guidance. www.gov.uk (2016)
8. Guía de estándares de calidad e interoperabilidad de los datos abiertos del gobierno de colombia. herramientas.datos.gov.co (2020)
9. Digital accessibility best practices guide. www.gov.br (2023)
10. Agência Brasil: Centro de dados da procergs é invadido pela água e desligado; há risco de interrupção de serviços. agenciabrasil.ebc.com.br (05 2024)
11. ARSAT: Arsat en el tiempo. www.arsat.com.ar (2025)
12. ARSAT: Red federal de fibra óptica. www.arsat.com.ar (2025)
13. Banco Central de la República Argentina: Informe de inclusión financiera - Feb 2020. www.bcra.gob.ar (2020)
14. Benavides, J.L., M'Causland Sánchez, M.C., Flórez Salazar, C., Roca, M.E.: Public procurement in latin america and the caribbean and idb-financed projects: A normative and comparative study. Tech. rep, IDB (2016)

15. Berenguer, S.S., Carisimo, E., Alvarez-Hamelin, J.I., Pintor, F.V.: Hidden internet topologies info: Truth or myth? In: LANCOMM (2016)
16. Bertholdo, L.M., Paredes, R., de Lima Marin, G., Loureiro, C.A., Kashwakura, M.K., de Botelho Marcos, P.: Analyzing the effect of an extreme weather event on telecommunications and information technology: Insights from 30 days of flooding. In: Proc. of PAM (2025)
17. Bischof, Z.S., et al.: Destination unreachable: Characterizing internet outages and shutdowns. In: Proc. of ACM SIGCOMM (2023)
18. Bischof, Z.S., Rula, J.P., Bustamante, F.E.: In and out of cuba: Characterizing cuba's connectivity. In: Proc. of IMC (2015)
19. Bolsa de Comercio de Rosario: Cómo fue el desempeño del pib per cápita. www.bcr.com.ar (2025)
20. Boston Consulting Group: Trust imperative 4.0: Genai–the trust multiplier for government. Tech. rep. (2024)
21. Brito, S.H.B., Santos, M.A., Fontes, R.d.R., Perez, D.A.L., Rothenberg, C.E.: Dissecting the largest national ecosystem of public internet exchange points in Brazil. In: Proc. of PAM (2016)
22. CAIDA: Routeviews prefix to as mappings dataset (pfx2as) for ipv4 and ipv6. www.caida.org (2008)
23. CAIDA: Peeringdb dump - 1 Jan 2025. publicdata.caida.org (2025)
24. Cámara Nacional Electoral: Listado de partidos políticos reconocidos. www.argentina.gob.ar (2025)
25. Carisimo, E., Fiore, J.M.D., Dujovne, D., Pelsser, C., Alvarez-Hamelin, J.I.: A first look at the latin american ixps. ACM SIGCOMM Computer Communication Review (mar 2020)
26. Carisimo, E., Gamero-Garrido, A., Snoeren, A.C., Dainotti, A.: Identifying ases of state-owned internet operators. In: Proc. of IMC (2021)
27. Carisimo, E., Kumar, R., Wang, C.J., Klein, S., Bustamante, F.E.: Ten years of the venezuelan crisis - an internet perspective. In: Proc. of ACM SIGCOMM (08 2024)
28. Congreso de la Nación Argentina: Ley 25.326 (protección de datos personales). argentina.gob.ar (2000)
29. Congreso de la Nación Argentina: Ley 27.275 (acceso a la información pública). argentina.gob.ar (2016), boletín Oficial
30. Dabrowski, A., Merzdovnik, G., Ullrich, J., Sendera, G., Weippl, E.: Measuring cookies and web privacy in a post-gdpr world. In: Proc. of PAM (2019)
31. Dener, C., Ghunney, L.E., Johns, K., Nii-Aponsah, H.: Govtech maturity index: The state of public sector digital transformation. Tech. rep, World Bank (2021)
32. Dirección General de Estadística y Censos, GCBA: Indicadores de analfabetismo 2014. www.estadisticaciudad.gob.ar (2014)
33. Dirección Nacional de Población: Análisis de la movilidad residencial interna en argentina. www.argentina.gob.ar (2023)
34. ENACOM: Acceso a internet fija - 2022 t2. indicadores.enacom.gob.ar (2022)
35. García Zaballos, A., Iglesias Rodríguez, E.: Cloud Computing: Opportunities and Challenges for Sustainable Economic Development in Latin America and the Caribbean. IDB (2018). https://publications.iadb.org/publications/english/document/Cloud-Computing-Opportunities-and-Challenges-for-Sustainable-Economic-Development-in-Latin-America-and-the-Caribbean.pdf
36. de Gobierno Digital, D.: Guía para el diseño de interfaces web institucionales. digital.gob.cl (2019)

37. Google Chrome User Experience Report: Crux - top sites lists. github.com (2025)
38. Gotze, M., Matic, S., Iordanou, C., Smaragdakis, G., Laoutaris, N.: Measuring web cookies in governmental websites. In: Proc of. ACM Web Sciences (2022)
39. Governo do Estado do Rio Grande do Sul: Procergs reativa data center e prevê retorno de serviços a partir de 27 de maio. estado.rs.gov.br (05 2024)
40. Habib, R., Ruth, K., Akiwate, G., Durumeric, Z.: Formalizing dependence of web infrastructure. In: Proc. of ACM SIGCOMM (2025)
41. Houser, R., Hao, S., Cotton, C., Wang, H.: A comprehensive, longitudinal study of government dns deployment at global scale. In: Proc of IEEE DSN (2022)
42. Hsiao, H.C., et al.: An investigation of cyber autonomy on government websites. In: Proc. of the WWW (2019)
43. IIEP, Universidad de Buenos Aires: Reporte especial - resultado fiscal de las provincias. iiep.economicas.uba.ar (2024)
44. INDEC: Censo 2022 - educación: población con nivel terciario completo. www.indec.gob.ar (2022)
45. INDEC: Censo 2022 - población total por provincia. censo.gob.ar (2022)
46. INDEC: Población urbana por provincia (cuadro n° 020210). www.indec.gob.ar (2022)
47. INDEC: Acceso a internet - informe 2024. www.indec.gob.ar (2024)
48. INDEC: índice de precios al consumidor - dic 2024. www.indec.gob.ar (2024)
49. INDEC: Informe de pobreza (eph). www.indec.gob.ar (2024)
50. INDEC: Mercado de trabajo - eph 3.er t 2024. www.indec.gob.ar (2024)
51. INDEC: Esperanza de vida al nacer. www.indec.gob.ar (2025)
52. INDEC: Promedio de años de escolaridad. www.indec.gob.ar (2025)
53. ITIF, TicTac: Evaluación de los sitios web del gobierno colombiano. www.ccit.org.co (Sep 2020)
54. Jansen, B., Kadenko, N., Broeders, D., van Eeten, M., Borgolte, K., Fiebig, T.: Pushing boundaries: An empirical view on the digital sovereignty of six governments in the midst of geopolitical tensions. Government Information Quarterly (2023)
55. JGM: Arsat – empresa argentina de soluciones satelitales sociedad anónima (arsat). www.argentina.gob.ar (2025)
56. JGM: Información provincial sobre empleo público. mepp.jefatura.gob.ar (2025)
57. Jonker, M., Akiwate, G., Affinito, A., Claffy, k., Botta, A., Voelker, G.M., van Rijswijk-Deij, R., Savage, S.: Where.ru? assessing the impact of conflict on russian domain infrastructure. In: Proc. of IMC (2022)
58. Kashaf, A., Dou, J., Belova, M., Apostolaki, M., Agarwal, Y., Sekar, V.: A first look at third-party service dependencies of web services in Africa. In: Proc. of PAM (2023)
59. Kashaf, A., Sekar, V., Agarwal, Y.: Analyzing third party service dependencies in modern web services: Have we learned from the mirai-dyn incident? In: Proc. of IMC (2020)
60. KPMG Argentina: Créditos y depósitos provinciales. assets.kpmg.com (2012)
61. Kumar, R., Asif, S., Lee, E., Bustamante, F.E.: Each at its own pace: Third-party dependency and centralization around the world. In: Proc. of ACM SIGMETRICS (2023)
62. Kumar, R., Carisimo, E., De Angelis Rivas, L., Buzzone, M., Bustamante, F.E., Qazi, I.A., Beiró, M.G.: Of choices and control: a comparative analysis of government hosting. In: Proc. of IMC, November 2024
63. Labs, A.: Visible asns: Customer populations (est.) – argentina. stats.labs.apnic.net (2025)

64. Liu, E., Akiwate, G., Jonker, M., Mirian, A., Savage, S., Voelker, G.M.: Who's got your mail? characterizing mail service provider usage. In: Proc. of IMC (2021)
65. Lundberg, S.M., Lee, S.I.: A unified approach to interpreting model predictions. Advances in neural information processing systems 30 (2017)
66. Mazzola, F., Marcos, P., Barcellos, M.: Light, camera, actions: characterizing the usage of ixps' action bgp communities. In: Proc. of CoNEXT (2022)
67. MECON: Decreto 62/90. mepriv.mecon.gob.ar
68. MECON: Decreto 60/90. mepriv.mecon.gob.ar (2025)
69. MECON: Ley 23.696. mepriv.mecon.gob.ar (2025)
70. MECON: Origen y ámbito de acción - telecom. mepriv.mecon.gob.ar (2025)
71. MECON: Origen y ámbito de acción - telefónica. mepriv.mecon.gob.ar (2025)
72. Ministerio de Modernización: Decálogo Tecnológico ONTI: Versión 1.1.0. Tech. rep., Presidencia de la Nación (Argentina), Buenos Aires, Argentina (Nov 2019), publicado el 8 de noviembre de 2019
73. de Modernización, M.: Disposición onti 6/2019 (accesibilidad web 2.0). www.argentina.gob.ar (Sep 2019), boletín Oficial, 30 de septiembre de 2019
74. Müller, L., Luckie, M., Huffaker, B., Claffy, K., Barcellos, M.: Challenges in inferring spoofed traffic at ixps. In: Proc. of CoNEXT (2019)
75. NIC.ar: 30 años de nic.ar. nic.ar (2025)
76. Observatorio Federal Urbano: Coeficiente gini - provincias. ofu.obraspublicas.gob.ar (2025)
77. OECD: Digital Government Review of Argentina: Accelerating the Digitalisation of the Public Sector. Paris (2019). https://doi.org/10.1787/354732cc-en
78. OECD: Good Governance for Critical Infrastructure Resilience (2019). https://doi.org/10.1787/02f0e5a0-en
79. OECD: Good practice principles for public service design and delivery in the digital age. Tech. rep. (2022)
80. OECD: Digital transformation of public procurement: Good practice report. Tech. rep., Public Governance Directorate (2025)
81. Oficina de Presupuesto del Congreso: Gasto público provincial sobre pib. opc.gob.ar (2024)
82. P.E.N.: Decreto 1131/2016 (gde). argentina.gob.ar (2016)
83. P.E.N.: Decreto 13/2016 (modificación del decreto 357/2002). www.argentina.gob.ar (Jan 2016), sancionado el 5 de enero de 2016; publicado en el Boletín Oficial el 6 de enero de 2016
84. Porto, A.: Transferencias intergubernamentales y disparidades fiscales a nivel subnacional en argentina. Tech. rep, Inter-American Development Bank (2016)
85. Porto, A., Puig, J.P.: On the fiscal behavior of subnational governments. a long-term vision for Argentina. Tech. rep., Buenos Aires, Argentina (2022). https://aaep.org.ar/works/works2022/4588.pdf
86. Programa de las Naciones Unidas para el Desarrollo: El mapa del desarrollo humano en argentina. www.undp.org (2023)
87. Radics, A., Eguino, H.: Próximos pasos para la descentralización y gobiernos subnacionales en américa latina y el caribe. Tech. rep., IDB (Oct 2018), https://publications.iadb.org/publications/spanish/document/Proximos-pasos-para-la-descentralizacion-y-gobiernos-subnacionales-en-America-Latina-y-el-Caribe.pdf
88. Samarasinghe, N., Adhikari, A., Mannan, M., Youssef, A.: Et tu, brute? privacy analysis of government websites and mobile apps. In: Proc. of the WWW (2022)
89. Singanamalla, S., Jang, E.H.B., Anderson, R., Kohno, T., Heimerl, K.: Accept the risk and continue: Measuring the long tail of government https adoption. In: Proc. of IMC (2020)

90. Sommese, R., Jonker, M., van der Ham, J., Moura, G.C.M.: Assessing e-government dns resilience. In: Proc. of CNSM) (2022)
91. Swanson, M., Bowen, P., Phillips, A., Gallup, D., Lynes, D.: Contingency planning guide for federal information systems. Tech. rep, NIST (2010)
92. Transparencia Electoral: Mapa de integridad electoral. transparenciaelectoral.org (2025)
93. U.S. General Services Administration: Federal website standards. standards.digital.gov
94. Wasserman, L.: All of statistics: a concise course in statistical inference. Springer Science & Business Media (2013)
95. World Bank: Building resilience against disasters in latin america and the caribbean. www.worldbank.org (2023)

Unpacking Internet Ossification: A Large-Scale Study of Path-Impairing Middleboxes Across IPv4 and IPv6

Fahad Hilal[1]([✉]), Taha Albakour[1], Oliver Gasser[2], and Kevin Vermeulen[3]

[1] Max Planck Institute for Informatics, Saarbrücken, Germany
`fhilal@mpi-inf.mpg.de`
[2] IPinfo, Washington, USA
[3] LIX, CNRS, Ecole Polytechnique, Palaiseau, France

Abstract. The end-to-end principle that limits on-path devices to simple tasks such as forwarding and routing has been one of the backbones of the Internet's architecture. This is, however, being challenged as Internet paths now contain devices that inspect, filter, modify, or even discard packets. Some of these carry out benign and positive undertakings such as balancing resources and thwarting attacks, while others interfere with packets in unexpected ways leading to broken paths, thus inhibiting the deployment of new protocols or even extensions.

While Internet ossification has already been studied in prior work, we propose to address new research questions enabled by recent Internet-scale middlebox mapping techniques. Combining Internet-scale measurements, measurements towards popular domains, repeated measurements, and longitudinal measurements, both in IPv6 and IPv4, we provide a multi-dimensional study on path-impairing middleboxes in the Internet. Our findings reveal that six times fewer IPv6 prefixes are affected than IPv4 prefixes by path-impairing middleboxes, and that there is an opportunity to switch between IPv4 and IPv6 to evade path-impairing middleboxes. Looking into the nature of path-impairments, we find that up to 87% relate to the usage of Multipath TCP. We also present the first results about the dynamics of these middleboxes, at both short (over hours), and long (over years) time windows. We show that path-impairing middleboxes have a consistent behavior over hours and that their number has tripled since 2022 for IPv6. We complement our measurements with operator perspectives and set up a service designed to help operators uncover and address unintentional path-impairments in their networks. Finally, we highlight default configurations as one potential contributor to path-impairments.

1 Introduction

The end-to-end principle, which calls for the communication between endpoints to be untouched in transit, is now a relic of the early Internet. In the current Internet, several on-path devices exist that no longer limit themselves to forwarding and routing. This paradigm shift has been brought on by the invasion

S. Ferlin-Reiter et al. (Eds.): PAM 2026, LNCS 16477, pp. 103–134, 2026.
https://doi.org/10.1007/978-3-032-18268-5_5

of *middleboxes*. These devices deviate from the "simplicity in the network core and complexity at the endpoints" principle. They exist as standalone physical entities or as functions embedded in network devices, to perform tasks other than those expected of routers [14], like thwarting attacks (firewalls), improving connection latencies (TCP accelerators), or balancing resources (load balancers). They are widespread across network types–deployed as commonly as standard devices in enterprise networks [62], and have been long present in cellular ones [67].

While most middleboxes are aimed at fulfilling benign and positive objectives, some have negative side-effects. Firstly, these add more complexity to paths, often creating hidden points of failure thereby confounding debugging of network breakdowns. Moreover, these may interfere with new protocols or extensions in unpredictable ways inhibiting their evolution. Non-conformant packets may be filtered, modified or even dropped. TCP has been in constant tussle with such devices as they continue to subject its extensions to unexpected tampering [23,27,32,34,38,65]. Additionally, alternative transport protocols, such as the Datagram Congestion Control Protocol (DCCP) [43] or the Stream Control Transmission Protocol (SCTP) [63] continue to be alienated by middleboxes, and despite standardization, fail to see large-scale deployments. As such, protocol designers have to work around the innovation-inhibiting middlebox-ridden Internet to ensure that proposed protocols and extensions are middlebox-resistant or come packed with adequate fall-backs. QUIC [16,21,40,60,68], TLS 1.3 [37,44,58,64] and MPTCP [5,28,29,50] are good examples.

In this paper, we address research questions concerning such packet-rewriting middleboxes that make modifications to IP and TCP headers, referring to them as path-impairing middleboxes, that prior work partially answered or did not answer at all (Sect. 2). While prior work has provided valuable insights into path-impairing middelboxes, it has largely remained limited to the path dimension and to one-off snapshots of impairments. Our study advances the state of the art by taking a broader and more systematic perspective beyond individual paths to the level of affected networks and prefixes, thereby providing a more thorough view of the scope of impairments. We also add longitudinal analyses of path-impairing middleboxes over multiple years, and an examination of their short-term dynamics over the scale of hours. We complement our measurements with direct engagement with operators to contrast observed behaviors with operational practices. We find some path-impairments might also be unintentional, and explore potential causes. We make the following contributions:

- **Quantification of affected paths, prefixes, ASes:** We conduct an in-depth study quantifying the effects of path-impairing middleboxes on the Internet finding a substantially lower fraction of impaired IPv6 paths, leading to six times fewer impacted IPv6 BGP prefixes and 13 times fewer affected ASes compared to IPv4.

Table 1. Comparison of research questions answered by prior work.

Research question	Work	Internet-scale		Popular domains	
		IPv6	IPv4	IPv6	IPv4
How are paths and ASes affected by path-impairing middleboxes?	[27]	×	×	×	✓
	[34]	×	×	×	×
	Sect. 4, Sect. 5	✓	✓	✓	✓
Which path-impairing middlebox behaviors do we observe?	[27]	×	×	×	✓
	[34]	×	×	×	×
	Sect. 6	✓	✓	✓	✓
Where on path are the path-impairing middlebox behaviors applied?	[27]	×	×	×	✓
	[34]	✓	✓	×	×
	Sect. 7	✓	✓	✓	✓
Is there a vantage point dependence for observing traffic impairments?	[27]	×	×	×	×
	[34]	✓	✓	×	×
	Sect. 4.5, Appendix A	✓	✓	✓	✓
Which short and long-term dynamics path-impairing middleboxes have?	[27]	×	×	×	×
	[34]	×	×	×	×
	Sect. 8	✓	✓	✓	✓
How can we engage with network operators to aid de-ossification?	[27]	×	×	×	×
	[34]	×	×	×	×
	Sect. 9	✓	✓	✓	✓

- **Measuring the prevalence of path-impairing middleboxes:** We analyze nearly 250 million IPv6 and 156 million IPv4 paths, revealing 277.6k and 377.4k impaired paths, respectively, with up to 87% of these showing the stripping of the Multipath TCP extension.
- **Measuring opportunities to switch between IPv6 and IPv4 to evade path-impairing middleboxes:** We find that for 6.1% domains impaired over IPv4 switching to IPv6 might allow for impairment-free paths allowing the connection to benefit from TCP extensions like MPTCP.
- **Transience:** We examine the short-term stability of path-impairing middlebox behavior over an unprecedented timescale of hours, discovering that the majority of path-impairing devices remain consistently active in the short-term, thereby continually disrupting Internet traffic.
- **Middlebox evolution:** We track the path-impairing middleboxes over a two-year period and show that while previously identified middleboxes remain stable, the IPv6 numbers have tripled.
- **A service to help operators:** Our survey with network operators shows that operators might be unaware of path-impairing middleboxes in their network. To help operators and to aid deossification, we set up a service where network operators can look up IP addresses from their networks filtering TCP options:

path-impairments.mpi-inf.mpg.de

2   Research Questions

We identify three core questions about middleboxes that prior work partially answered: (1) How many paths are affected by path-impairing middleboxes? (2) Which path-impairments are observed?, and (3) Which ASes host path-impairing middleboxes?

For each of these questions, we must look at different dimensions to provide a complete answer: (a) consider both IPv4 and IPv6; (b) collect measurements at Internet-scale; and (c) perform measurements to diverse targets, to understand not only which web services of the Internet are impacted by path-impairing middleboxes, but also which ASes.

Whereas prior work [27, 34] overlooked this multi-dimensional aspect, we provide a more complete picture taking the opportunity to answer new research questions. For instance, collecting measurements at Internet-scale to find how many paths are affected allows us to answer the following: When a middlebox is observed on a path to an AS, do we also observe it for other paths to it? Another example is that if we combine IPv4 and IPv6 measurements to popular domains to answer which path-impairments are observed to them, we can answer the practical question: Could the domain operator (or even the client) switch between IPv6 and IPv4 to use certain TCP features (*e.g.*, Multipath TCP) that would otherwise be disabled by a path-impairing middlebox?

Additionally, we also answer new research questions related to the temporal behavior of middleboxes, namely their temporal dynamics at both short-term, over hours, and long-term, over years. Finally, we engage directly with network operators to confront our observations with operator perspectives. The research questions and their related sections are summarized in Table 1.

3   Measurement Setup and Analysis Heuristics

In this section, we provide an overview of our approach for detecting middleboxes and their path-impariments. We describe our measurement setup for identifying path-impairing middleboxes, and interference classification. We also provide a summary of the path-impairing behaviors that we consider in this study.

3.1   Detecting Path-Impairing Middleboxes

To detect path-impairing middleboxes, we run multiple path measurements towards a diverse set of targets. These measurements share a similar setup with regard to the tool we use, heuristics, and our vantage point selection.

Yarrpbox: To identify path-impairing middleboxes, we use Yarrpbox—a tool for high-speed Internet-scale middlebox detection [33]. To identify on-path interferences and the responsible devices, Yarrpbox adopts a traceroute style of probing sending TTL limited probes in a randomized fashion. These encode state information such as the destination IP and TTL, and other fields not used to store state are set to fixed values across all probes. It relies upon RFC 1812 [7] (RFC

4443 [19] for IPv6) and RFC 792 [57] which state that on-path routers upon receiving expired TTL packets should quote the IP header and its complete payload or the first 64 bits from the IP payload in ICMP (ICMPv6) Time-exceeded responses, respectively. Extracting the encoded state from the ICMP responses followed by comparing quoted fields to those initially set, it highlights applied on-path alterations. By inspecting the encoded TTL, it estimates the path-impairing middlebox's location. Moreover, Yarrpbox also adopts Paris traceroute [6] style of probing. In this work, we extend Yarrpbox and build support for Explicit Congestion Notification (ECN). This allows us to also test for ECN negotiation in TCP SYNs.

Highest Confidence Middleboxes: To identify the hop and the corresponding address where an impairment is applied, we adopt prior work's Highest Confidence Middlebox metric [34]. Using this metric, the very first hop within the trace that reports an on-path interference is initially flagged as a 'potential middlebox hop' and the replying IP address at the hop as the 'potential middlebox'. If the last responding hop before the potential middlebox hop immediately precedes it (no missing hops) and quotes at least the same size of the packet as the potential middlebox hop, it is classified as a Highest Confidence Middlebox IP address (HCMB IP). However, we relax this metric up to the AS level: if the last responding hop before the potential middlebox hop is not immediately before it but despite missing or inconsequential replies is still in the same AS, then although the middlebox's exact hop-based location is unknown (and its address not determined), the middlebox location is still correct at the AS level. We refer to such middlebox IP addresses as HCMB IPs throughout the text unless we explicitly specify the use of the more stringent metric.

Vantage Points: All our measurements are carried out from nine vantage points (VPs) across six continents. Eight out of these are in the AWS network located across six continents, situated in India, Brazil, Germany, the US west coast, South Africa, Australia, Sweden and the US east coast, whereas one VP is at our university in Europe. All the scans from AWS are performed at 1 kpps owing to the lower availability of resources and to prevent blocking by AWS. We carry out scans from our university VP at higher rates, 5 kpps for IPv6 and 20 kpps for IPv4. Our VPs are well suited for observing path-impairing middleboxes. Eight of our nine VPs are hosted in AWS, a network with about 560 peers and 18 upstream providers at the time of writing [9]. Compared to eyeballs–which typically have just 1–3 upstreams, AWS enables visibility into a broader range of ASes and paths. At the same time, its moderate peering footprint avoids overly direct routes that would mask in-transit interference. As such, AWS offers path diversity while still preserving sufficient AS-level depth to surface path-impairing middlebox behavior that would be otherwise missed.

3.2   Interference Classifications

We revise two classifications from prior work [27] to classify middlebox interference. The high level one looks at if it is benign, path-impairing, or if we cannot conclude. The low level one focuses on path-impairing behavior and describes the different consequences on the traffic.

Benign, Path-Impairing, and Inconclusive Impairments: We limit our analysis of on-path middlebox interferences (modifications to fields or option removals) to more critical path-impairing ones. Unless explicitly stated, we ignore benign interferences similar to prior work [27,34]. Therefore, we do not consider other fields with no guarantees of remaining unaltered on Internet paths such as the Traffic Class in IPv6 [22], the DSCP from IPv4 [53], or when the transport protocol is not harmed (i.e., TCP MSS data alterations). We consider the following set of IP and TCP header fields and TCP options collectively referring to them as the critical set and on-path interferences to them as impairments: IP Payload Length, IP Total Length, TCP Sack Permitted, TCP Receiver Window, TCP MP Capable Sender Key, TCP Timestamp, TCP MSS, TCP Sack Permitted, TCP MP Capable, TCP NOP (addition for overwriting TCP options), and TCP Sequence Number.

We also ignore interferences termed as inconclusive by Edeline and Donnet [27] like the TCP Checksum, which predominantly result from alterations to the fields over which the value is computed. However, we also find isolated cases where the TCP Checksum is solely altered. Upon detailed investigation, this seems to stem from on-path routers setting a random checksum for the quoted packet when the destination is unreachable. Although unexpected, these are not instances of path-impairing behavior. Additionally, although Edeline and Donnet treat all IP Total Length modifications as inconclusive, we find instances where the field and its IPv6 counterpart, i.e., the IP Payload Length, are altered without any additions to or removals from the packets. These seem to result from potential router misconfigurations leading to flipping of the expected byte order [34]. We treat such cases of only length field alterations as impairments as these could lead to undefined behavior or packet drops. For instance, in 99% cases of sole Total Length alterations no traffic is seen after the reporting hop.

Path-Impairing Middleboxes Behaviors: We break the path-impairing behaviors into four sets based on the path condition they create [27]: Negotiation Disruption (ND), Disrupted Traffic (DT), Disabled feature (DF), and Potential for Traffic Block (PB).

ND behavior encompasses instances of on-path changes of one-way state announcements. It consists of on-path devices that also implement certain feature-disabling policies, which in the face of load balancing or asymmetric paths, and in absence of robust fallbacks, could result in inconsistent protocol states. SACK-Permitted removals, and alterations to the MP Capable sender's key fall in this category. While interferences that can cause disruptions to transport control mechanisms and/or result in performance degradation are mapped to DT.

DT includes tampering with the TCP Sequence Number and the TCP Receiver Window. Altering end-host assigned Sequence Numbers on forward

Table 2. Overview of large-scale measurements toward BGP prefixes.

Family	Targets	Hop IPs	Hop ASes	Tested Paths
IPv6	20.2M	1.5M	14.3k	251.6M
IPv4	11.7M	1.2M	29.2k	156.9M

Table 3. ASes (percentage of announcing ASes) experiencing impaired traffic, affected prefixes in them (percentage of all announced), and the prefixes for which the path-impairing middlebox's location is determined. Overall, substantially fewer ASes are affected over IPv6.

Family	Affected ASes (%)	Affected Prefixes (%)	HCMB
IPv6	339 (1%)	1,808 (0.9%)	1,002
IPv4	4,565 (6.1%)	11,423 (1.1%)	5,151

paths and failing to do so on the reverse paths could result in packet drops, thus unnecessarily triggering congestion control mechanisms. Similarly, altering the Receiver Window Size in the worst case could disturb flow-control mechanisms leading to the endpoint being overwhelmed thereby triggering delayed ACKs or even dropped packets at the endpoint. These events could also potentially result in unnecessary retransmissions pushing the network towards congestion and culminating into network inefficiency and increased latencies.

Stripping TCP options/disabling TCP features like explicit congestion notification (ECN) is DF.

PB includes sole modifications to the length fields of the IP header which could lead to packet drops. As we found that over IPv6, 71% (99% for IPv4) of such alterations lead to traffic drops, we conservatively call them PB. We do not explicitly look at blocks due to the presence of MP Capable, as all our scans carry the option. Nevertheless, prior work [27] found such instances to be very rare (0.1% of all tamperings applied to the MP Capable) with MP Capable stripping the most common choice. Finally, the "Multi" category includes middlebox behaviors that include instances of impairments from more than one of the aforementioned categories.

4   How Are Paths and ASes Affected by Path-Impairing Middleboxes?

In this section, we broaden the analysis of path-impairing middleboxes beyond individual paths to examine their impact on prefixes and ASes. While path-level statistics reveal the immediate presence of impairments, they do not capture whether middleboxes affect all prefixes of an AS, whether certain types of ASes are more prone to impairments, or how results may depend on vantage point diversity. We perform Internet-scale measurements and study (i) the relative

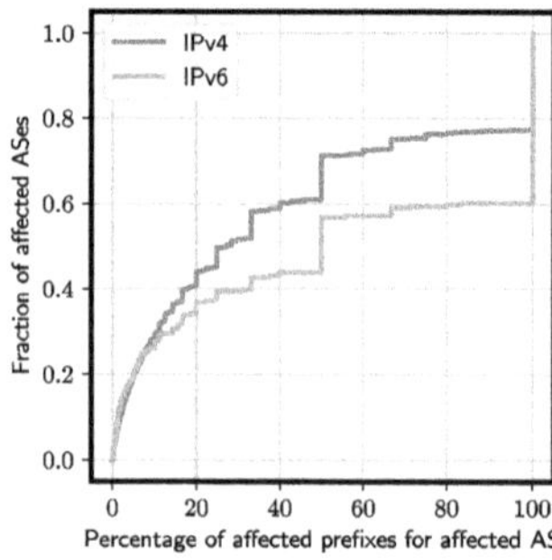

Fig. 1. Affected ASes vs prefixes.

Table 4. Affected ASes by network type. Percentages out of the total ASes of each type. ASes of type content are substantially less affected over IPv6.

AS Type	IPv6	IPv4
Access	163 (0.7%)	1,257 (7.1%)
Transit/Access	77 (0.2%)	1,721 (5.2%)
Content	19 (0.5%)	256 (7.4%)
Enterprise	44 (0.1%)	1,098 (8%)
Tier-1	3 (25%)	8 (66.7%)
n/a	33	225

prevalence of impairments in IPv4 and IPv6 across paths, prefixes, and ASes (ii) the extent of prefix-level affectedness within impaired ASes, (iii) which categories of ASes are impacted, and (iv) how vantage point location influences the observed set of impaired prefixes and ASes.

4.1 Dataset

To perform our Internet-scale analysis, we carry out Yarrpbox based TCP SYN scans over port 80 and 443 to BGP-announced prefixes in IPv6 (100 random IP addresses per prefix) and to all the routable /24s (one random IP per /24) from IPv4. This balances measurement scale with feasibility and aligns with prior work [34]. We use port 80 and 443 as these are two widely accepted, less likely to be blocked and commonly reachable ports thus allowing for maximizing the possibility of traversing deep into the destination networks. Additionally, prior work [20] showed that the vast majority of path-impairing middlebox interferences occur on these ports. Our TCP SYN probes carry four TCP options—MSS, SACK Permitted, MP Capable and Timestamp. We perform our measurements in the first week of March 2024 (towards port 80) and the third week of September 2024 (toward port 443). We identify the targets affected by path-impairing middleboxes and map them to BGP prefixes and ASes using Routeviews data [11] from the date of our scans.

Table 2 provides an overview of our dataset. We test nearly thrice more paths than prior work [27,34], with 251.6M IPv6 and 156.9M IPv4 paths, and see on-path router addresses across ten times (29k vs 2.9k) more ASes [27]. About 0.2% of the IPv6 targets are in known aliased prefixes [30,69]. The lower numbers for IPv4 result from fewer IPv4 targets.

For IPv6, we find 778 path-impairing middleboxes across 241 ASes, with location accuracy up to the AS level, and 756 for which identify the IP address. For IPv4, these numbers are 5,806 and 4,229, respectively, present across 1,757 ASes. The jump between the path-impairing middlebox numbers obtained by the two metrics is higher for IPv4 due to the partial-packet quoting by some IPv4 routers [57] which exacerbates the impairing device location uncertainty. In fact, over 60% of the observed IPv4 routers demonstrate this behavior [34].

4.2 Are IPv6 Paths, Prefixes, and ASes More (or Less) Impaired Than IPv4?

Of the 251.4M IPv6 measured paths, 41.6M (16.5%) cross some type of middlebox: 16.2% cross a benign middlebox, 0.11% cross a path-impairing middlebox and 0.35% face inconclusive interferences. For IPv4, of the 156.9M tested paths, 31.1M (19.8%) of the paths cross some type of middlebox: 19.5% cross a benign middlebox, 0.24% cross a path-impairing one, while 0.06% see inconclusive interferences. About 86% of the impaired IPv6 and 87.4% of the impaired IPv4 paths have MP Capable strippings. The path-breaking sole Payload Length modification is seen on 8% of the impaired IPv6 paths whereas less than 1% of the paths have the corresponding alteration for IPv4. Overall, we see over two times more IPv4 paths with MP Capable and SACK Permitted strippings and hindrance to ECN negotiation, whereas four times more IPv6 paths have the sole length field alteration.

To provide a perspective other than affected paths, we map the targets of those paths to their BGP-announced prefixes. We say a prefix is affected if a path from any VP to at least one target within it is affected. We discuss the view of different VPs in Sect. 4.5. For IPv6, 1,808 prefixes are affected, representing 0.9% of all announced IPv6 prefixes (see Table 3). These prefixes map to 339 ASes, representing 1% of the ASes announcing IPv6 prefixes. None of the affected IPv6 targets map to known aliased prefixes. For IPv4, we observe over 6 times more affected prefixes with 11,423 (1.1%) in 4,565 ASes (6.1%). In Sect. 7, we investigate the location of path-impairing middleboxes, finding that most are in the same networks as the targets.

A total of 4,763 ASes have at least one prefix with traffic to it impaired over IPv4 or IPv6, 141 ASes are affected over both, and 198 and 4,424 only over IPv6 and IPv4, respectively. Of the ASes which only see IPv4 prefixes affected, about 37.3% announce IPv6 prefixes. For ASes with only IPv6 prefixes affected, 91.4% also announce IPv4 prefixes. This implies that at least from our VPs, it could be possible for traffic to reach these ASes unimpaired over at least one IP protocol.

Takeaway:*Paths, prefixes, and ASes, are potentially relatively less impaired in IPv6 than in IPv4 highlighting IPv6 as a likely less ossified environment for transport-layer innovation.*

4.3 When an AS Is Impaired, Are All of Its Prefixes Impaired?

In order to quantify the impact of path-impairing middleboxes on individual affected ASes, we analyze how many prefixes are affected for an AS that has at least one prefix affected by a path-impairing middlebox (Fig. 1). For IPv6, 25% of affected ASes have less than 5% of their prefixes affected, and 40% of the ASes have all their prefixes affected, although 30% of the affected ASes announce a single prefix. For IPv4, just over 15% of the ASes have less than 5% affected prefixes, whereas 21% of ASes have all of their prefixes impaired albeit 18% of all affected ASes again announce only one prefix. This fraction of ASes which see all of their prefixes affected is still higher for IPv6 and could partially be explained by the middlebox position in the AS. Looking at the position of the path-impairing middleboxes for which the IP address is known (Sect. 7), we see that for IPv4 nearly 58% of these are present at the AS borders whereas for IPv6 the same is true for a much larger 85%.

As we observe that for most affected ASes, over either address family, not all of the prefixes are affected, we investigate the underlying causes further. To this end, we turn to affected ASes where the path-impairing middlebox is within the same AS. When we focus on affected prefixes for ASes which contain the path-impairing middleboxes themselves, we still see partial prefix affectedness. After ignoring ASes announcing a single prefix, less than 30% of the path-impairing middlebox containing ASes for both IPv6 and IPv4, have more than 50% of their prefixes affected. This low prefix affectedness could be down to a number of different reasons, such as filtering policies/legacy devices (unfamiliar with TCP options like the MP Capable) on only some entry points into the announcing network, or that the path-impairing middlebox applies its filtering selectively. To investigate this, for each AS with not all prefixes affected, we look at whether the paths to the unaffected prefixes contain the middlebox seen on the path to AS's affected prefixes[1]. We find that 63% of the middlebox-containing affected IPv6 ASes and 86% of such IPv4 ASes, have paths to unaffected prefixes that see the middlebox IP address. This result shows the application of selective prefix-based filtering policies is a factor at play. The effect may also be contributed to by path-impairing middleboxes exhibiting short-term dynamics. However, we find that to be rare and instead find more evidence for destination-based filtering in Sect. 8.2.

Takeaway: *Only a small fraction of affected ASes with multiple announced prefixes, both in IPv4 (3%) and IPv6 (10%), have all of their prefixes impaired.*

4.4   What Types of ASes Are Impaired?

We next investigate the type of ASes which see traffic to them impaired, using CAIDA's AS Classification dataset [12] from 2021[2]. Since we find the dataset to offer the best coverage for our analysis and also because ASes are quite unlikely to change their types, we choose to perform our analysis with this dataset despite its age. We observe largely similar results for IPv6 and IPv4. For IPv6, access networks are the most affected whereas for IPv4 they come second to transit/access networks (see Table 4). We also see prefixes in content hosting ASes to be impaired, with <1% of such ASes for IPv6 and 7.4% for IPv4. We explore switching opportunities for top domains in Sect. 5.2. Finally, we also see prefixes in several Tier-1 prefixes to be affected albeit more over IPv4. In Sect. 7, we will show that not only are prefixes in Tier-1s affected but path-impairing middleboxes located in Tier-1 prefixes disable TCP extensions for traffic destined to

---

[1] To prevent any potential source-based filtering from affecting the analysis, we consider the point of view from a single VP.

[2] The updates to the dataset were discontinued in 2021.

other networks. We cross-validate our findings by classification with data from PeeringDB [56], finding similar results.

With a special focus on hypergiants (HGs) ASes, extracted from CAIDA's AS to Organization Mapping dataset [13] similar to other studies [31,35], we see a total of 4 affected IPv6 prefixes announced from Apple and Disney ASes only. The impairment is either MP Capable or the SACK Permitted removal and always happens within these HG ASes. For IPv4, we see 37 affected prefixes across 10 different HGs. Most of the impairments are SACK Permitted or MP Capable strippings within the HG AS, although for 20–30% the impairments (range across the studied HGs) occur outside the HG AS. Google, Cloudflare and Akamai owned affected prefixes collectively contribute 20% and suffer similar impairments predominantly inside but occasionally outside their own networks as well.

Upon delving into path-impairing middleboxes and the type of ASes path-impairing middleboxes are themselves in, we see the same trend as for the affected ASes. The majority of path-impairing middleboxes are present across access networks. While we do not have VPs in access networks and as such it is also difficult to get access to a VP in every existing access network[3], our measurements to BGP-announced prefixes provide a means to uncover path-impairing middlebox presence in access networks. Moreover, we also find 12.7% of the ASes with IPv6 path-impairing middleboxes are enterprise (18.6% for IPv4) and another 6.3% (6.3% for IPv4) are content networks.

Takeaway: *Impairments are not confined to a particular class of network. All AS types are affected by path-impairing middleboxes, with IPv6 AS types again being an order of magnitude less affected than IPv4 AS types relative to AS count.*

4.5   Is There a VP Dependence for Observing Traffic Impairments?

To further understand the VP dependence for observing traffic impairments, we investigate how many prefixes are affected from what fraction of VPs. We see that 36% of all IPv6 prefixes found to be affected have traffic impaired from only singular VPs. However, nearly 45% are affected at more than 50% of our VPs, with 25% of the affected prefixes seeing traffic to them impaired from about 80% of the VPs. For IPv4, we see a sharp contrast to the IPv6 results. A much smaller 8%, compared to 36% in IPv6, are affected at only one VP whereas a substantially larger 64.7% see traffic subjected to impairments from more than 50% of the VPs. However, our university VP does not deviate drastically from AWS VPs neither in IPv4 nor in IPv6 (see Appendix A). We also follow these Yarrpbox-based traceroutes with traceroutes from the RIPE Atlas platform [59] to further investigate this VP dependence. Our findings are consistent with prior work [34] and we provide more details in Appendix A.

These fluctuations per VP could potentially stem either from path diversity or through the application of source-based policies by path-impairing middle-

---

[3] Platforms with such VPs like the NLNOG ring [54] and Atlas [59] do not support path-impairment detection measurements.

Table 5. The total number of Tranco targets (fraction of all scanned targets) that experience impaired traffic, and affected domains (fraction of domains available over each address family). Substantially fewer domains and targets are affected over IPv6 opening up the opportunity to switch to IPv6 to benefit from TCP extensions.

Address Family	Affected Targets (%)	Affected Domains (%)
IPv6	125 (0.03%)	150 (0.05%)
IPv4	7,599 (1.1%)	8,853 (1%)

boxes. To investigate this, we pick affected prefixes from our university VP that meet the criteria that (a) we know the IP address of the path-impairing middlebox, (b) the prefixes are unaffected from our AWS VPs. We then check if these IP addresses appear on-path to them from our AWS VPs. We find that for up to 97.1% of such IPv6 prefixes and 99.7% such IPv4 prefixes the path-impairing middlebox IP address does not appear on paths from the AWS VP, showing that the VP dependence is almost always related to path diversity. However, the small fraction of remaining unaffected prefixes that see the path-impairing address may be unaffected owing to potential source-based policies being also at play. To investigate source-based policies, we pick IP addresses we confirm to be path-impairing, from one VP and investigate if they also behave similarly for other VPs. When comparing our university VP to each AWS VP with at least 50 HCMB IPs in common, we find that nearly 85%-94.4% of IPv6 addresses that interfere in the university VP and appear in the AWS VP also interfere in the AWS VP. For IPv4 this ranges from 93.6% to 96.1%. When comparing different AWS VPs which have at least 50 HCMB IPs in common, we see the stat to range from 96.3% to 97.4% for IPv6 and 90.4% to 96.6% for IPv4. We also investigate potential source-based filtering on path-impairing middleboxes seen on-path to popular domains (Sect. 5.1). We find similar results when comparing the university VP to AWS. Additionally, we perform the same measurements from a European ISP and compare our findings to our university and AWS VPs. Besides finding similar numbers (as our university and AWS VPs) for path-impairing middlebox addresses, affected domains and targets, we see that 92%-96% of path-impairing middleboxes again interfere independently of the source. This seems to suggest that while an overwhelming majority of the path-impairing middleboxes impair independent of the connection source, source-based policies may sparingly exist in the wild. Note that the effect may also be contributed to in part by short-term middlebox inactivity, although we find that rare (Sect. 8.2).

Takeaway: *We see a VP dependence for affected prefixes and ASes. However, this seems to stem predominantly from path diversity rather than source-based policies.*

5   How Are Popular Domains Affected?

In addition to our Internet-scale study for IPv6 and IPv4, we investigate traffic impairments to top domains. With this analysis, we stand to answer other research questions, such as whether paths to popular targets carrying a lot of traffic are more or less affected than others, or whether there are opportunities for domains to prioritize impairment free paths over IPv4 or IPv6 if only one family is affected. Additionally, understanding how highly ranked the impacted domains are provides another perspective on the influence of path-impairing devices on the Internet.

5.1   Dataset

We perform Yarrpbox-based TCP SYN scans to targets found by resolving the Tranco Top 1M [66]. For each of our VPs, we first resolve the domains from the Tranco list using massDNS [10]. After extracting the A and AAAA records, we run Yarrpbox to the unique server IP addresses on ports 80 and 443. Across our VPs, we find a total of 423.6k unique IPv6 and 667.6k unique IPv4 server IP addresses. These measurements are performed during the last week of July (to port 80) and the first week of September 2024 (to port 443). Our dataset has 16.7M responses from 91.5k IPv6 router IP addresses across 3k ASes compared to 72.9M replies from 284.9k IPv4 router IPs in 13.3k ASes. The tested paths range from 1.6M in IPv6 to about 3.1M for IPv4.

About 15% of the domains on the Tranco top 1M are hosted in the AWS network where we also have our VPs. Although we find the majority of the path-impairing middleboxes present in hosting networks, we find no path-impairing middlebox address in the AWS network. Even our university VP does not report any AWS hosted domains to be affected.

Table 6. Impairment statistics for IPv6 and IPv4 prefixes (percentages are rounded off after 3 decimal places). DF stands for Disabled Feature, ND is Negotiation Disruption, DT is Disrupted Traffic, and PB is Potential for Traffic Block. DF behavior dominates led by MP Capable removals applied through NOP overwriting.

Impairment	IPv6			IPv4			MB Behavior
	Number	% Responses	% Paths	Number	% Responses	% Paths	
TCP::NOP	580,042	0.019%	0.097%	1,075,372	0.059%	0.227%	DF
TCP::MP Capable	492,832	0.016%	0.094%	948,852	0.052%	0.210%	DF
TCP::Sequence Number	167,699	0.005%	0.005%	129,860	0.007%	0.007%	DT
TCP::Timestamp	139,581	0.005%	0.004%	26,987	0.001%	-	DF
TCP::Sack Permitted	138,407	0.004%	0.003%	6,460	-	0.002%	DF, ND
TCP::ECN.00	25,954	0.001%	0.001%	5,134	-	0.002%	DF
TCP::MP Capable Sender Key	9	-	-	1	-	-	ND
IP::Payload Length Flip	59,431	0.002%	0.009%	-	-	-	PB
IP::Total Length Flip	-	-	-	7,901	-	0.002%	PB
TCP::MSS	4	-	-	843	-	-	DF
TCP::Rcv Window	4	-	-	-	-	-	DT

5.2 Are There Opportunities To Switch Between IPv6 and IPv4 To Evade Impairments?

The affected popular domains follow the same trend as the affected BGP prefixes (Sect. 4.2) with IPv6 showing lower impairment. Out of a total of 423.6k (Table 5) IPv6 targets that we scan collectively from our VPs, only 125 (0.03%) are affected and serve 150 domains. These affected domains make only 0.05% of the 307.5k domains for which we find AAAA records. On the IPv4 side, 7,599 targets, 1.1% of all scanned IPv4 targets, serving 8,853 domains (59 times more than IPv6) experience traffic impairments. We see a total of 8,953 domains affected over IPv4 or IPv6 and only 50 affected over both. Out of the 150 domains affected over IPv6, 66.6% are only affected over IPv6. Similarly, out of the 8,853 domains affected over IPv4, a much larger 99.4% are only affected over IPv4. However, 544 (6.1%) domains of these 8,803 IPv4 only affected domains have AAAA records. In fact, about 4% of these also have the same AS level paths and for 32% the path-impairing IPv4 middlebox is in the hosting network itself. This implies that over IPv6 these might be free of impairments observed over IPv4 paths and thus stand to benefit from TCP extensions. This is confirmed by Aschenbrenner et al. [5] who found worse performance on metrics such as handshake time and website load time for 30% of the cases when using MPTCP compared to standard TCP, towards destinations affected by MPTCP tamperings.

In terms of the rankings of the domains which see traffic to them impaired, 5.3% of all domains affected over IPv6 fall in the top 10k whereas 35.3% are in the top 100k. For IPv4, less than 2% fall in the top 10k and nearly 20% belong to the top 100k. For the aforementioned domains where the switching to IPv6 could allow for impairment free paths, we find 3.9% to be in the Tranco Top 10k whereas 28.9% lie in the Tranco Top 100k.

In terms of paths, 3.4% of the 1.6M cross a middlebox in IPv6. However, only 0.07% have a path-impairing middlebox with nearly 90% of these having a MP Capable stripping one. Other TCP options like the SACK Permitted, and the ECN negotiation are impacted on 0.0006% and 0.0003% of the paths respectively. For IPv4, a much higher 12.7% of the 3.1M paths cross a middlebox, and 1% where it impairs traffic, over 14 times more than for IPv6. The MP Capable is again altered on most of these paths. However compared to IPv6, MP Capable impairing paths over IPv4 are 13 times higher, those for SACK Permitted removals and ECN negotiation disruption are 14 and 67 times higher, respectively. Overall, impaired paths to popular domains over IPv4 appear to be substantially higher than IPv6. This further suggests that switching to IPv6 for the popular domains could improve the possibility of benefiting from MPTCP, SACK Permitted and ECN. Compared to our large-scale measurements to announced prefixes (Sect. 4.2), the fraction of impaired paths towards popular domains is marginally lower for IPv6 (0.11% vs 0.07%) but over four times larger for IPv4 (0.24% vs 1%).

Takeaway: *Especially for a fraction of domains (6.1%) that are affected in IPv4 and have an IPv6 counterpart, switching over to IPv6 could help evade path-impairing middleboxes.*

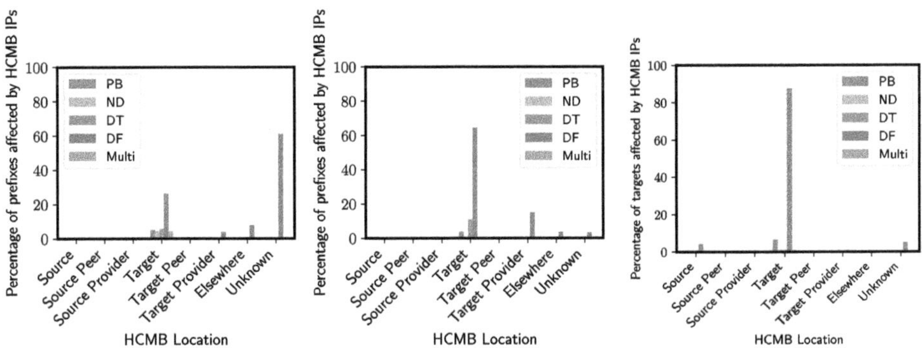

Fig. 2. On-path location where path-impairing middlebox behavior is applied for IPv6 (left) and IPv4 (middle) prefixes and IPv6 Tranco Top 1M (right).

6 Which Path-Impairing Middlebox Behaviors Do We Observe?

For our analysis in this section, we use the datasets from Sect. 4.1 and Sect. 5.1. Table 6 shows the number of responses with signs of interference, the percentage they make of all responses and the percentage of paths affected by each interference towards BGP prefixes, alongside the classification (Sect. 3.2). DF impaired paths make about 88% and 95% of all path-impairing middlebox affected paths towards IPv6 and IPv4 announced prefixes, respectively. While DT paths come second for IPv4 with about 3%, nearly 9% is contributed by PB paths for IPv6 (1.5% for IPv4).

Similarly, Table 9 in Appendix B details the impairments to popular domains: 97% of the 1,194 affected IPv6 paths again see DF behavior, whereas PB behavior affects 4%. Of the much higher 30.6k paths affected over IPv4, DF dominates with 98%, while DT and ND together contribute for 2%, and PB is negligible. These findings point to the application of similar path-impairing behaviors towards announced prefixes and servers hosting popular domains. They also show there could be relatively more middleboxes unexpectedly altering packet lengths and potentially setting the traffic up for drops along the path in IPv6.

For all path-impairing behaviors, the affected AS types follow the same distribution as seen in Sect. 4.4 for all path-impairing behaviors.

Translating affected paths into affected prefixes and domains, we find similar results, with DF dominating, and MP Capable being the major contributor.

Takeaway: *Whatever granularity we look at (paths, prefixes, ASes, domains, IPv6, IPv4), the most prevalent path-impairing middlebox behavior is DF dominated by MP Capable strippings.*

7 Where on Path Are the Path-Impairing Middlebox Behaviors Applied?

For measurements to affected prefixes, we can pinpoint path-impairing middlebox's position up to the AS level (Sect. 3.1), for 55.4% of the cases for IPv6 and 45.1% for IPv4, and we investigate where the impairments from different categories are applied on-path. The lower fraction for IPv4 could result from the partial quoting of the TTL exceeded packets by on-path IPv4 routers. RFC 792 recommends IPv4 routers return/quote only the first 64 bytes from the offending expiring TTL packet inside the ICMP Time-Exceeded response. As per previous work [34], over 60% of the tested IPv4 routers adhere to RFC 792 despite the updated recommendations in RFC 1812 [7], which—similar to ICMPv6—recommends to quote as much as possible from the original packet.

For the topological location of the path-impairing middlebox we consider the source network, the source's peers and providers, the target network, and the target's peers and providers, extracted from CAIDA's AS Relationship dataset [45]. If the path-impairing middlebox is in none of these, we consider it to be "Elsewhere". If we cannot map the path-impairing middlebox address to any AS, the prefix is considered to be affected in an indeterminate or "Unknown" position.

In Fig. 2, we observe that for the majority of the considered prefixes (*e.g.,* 26% of DF affected IPv6 prefixes and 65% of DF affected IPv4 prefixes, but this is also true for other behaviors), the path-impairing middlebox is in the target AS. Outside the target AS, for IPv6 the DF behavior is also visible "Elsewhere", or close to the target where it is predominantly observed in the provider networks for the target network. Further, the path-impairing middleboxes in these two topological positions collectively only impact about 10% of the prefixes. As a sharp contrast to IPv4, over IPv6 for about 60% of the considered prefixes, the middlebox AS cannot be determined. However, these IPv6 HCMB IPs make up only 25% of all identified ones. For IPv4, such instances are rarer with 15% of the affected prefixes having HCMB found in the providers of the target AS.

For popular domains, for nearly 97% of IPv6 affected Tranco targets and about 40% of IPv4 ones, we can determine the AS or exact IP address of the impairing device. For IPv6, we also see a huge drop in the share of impaired destinations (less than 5%) for which the path-impairing middlebox location is indeterminate (Fig. 2). Again, the dominant behavior is applied within the target AS, with 90% of DF impairments occurring within the target AS. For IPv4, impairments are even more concentrated in the target AS.

Since we see TCP feature disabling for traffic to prefixes even outside the announcing AS, we investigate if large ASes such as Tier-1 s could be contributing to this. We find that for IPv6, 28 (20%) of 140 HCMB IP addresses that apply DF behavior outside the target AS are in Tier-1 prefixes, whereas this number is 3.6 times higher (but 15%) for IPv4. For instance, Cogent, (AS 174), is the largest network which has IPv4 and IPv6 path-impairing middleboxes. We also find the results to be consistent with whois data. Further, in order to rule out the possibility that these IP addresses are in prefixes leased by Tier-1 s to stub networks, we examine whether multiple different ASes show up in our traces after the hops with path-impairing middlebox addresses. We find that for about 92% for IPv6 and 80% for IPv4 that is indeed the case showing that feature disabling also exists in large ASes, such as Tier-1 s, for transiting traffic.

We find no DF middleboxes in Tier-1 s on our IPv6 paths to servers hosting popular domains. However, of the 224 IPv4 addresses which disable features outside the target AS, about 16% are in Tier-1 s. This shows that DF towards popular domains in large transits could be stronger over IPv4.

In terms of AS type, affected AS types largely follow the same distribution as seen in Sect. 4.4 for each type of path-impairing behavior when it is observed in any topological location. Notably, while content networks also predominantly see feature disabling within the network itself, 5.6% and 1.6% of affected content networks over IPv4 have disabling of features applied in transit providers and elsewhere, respectively. For IPv6, we this is only seen for a singular content AS.

Takeaway:*Path-impairing middleboxes are mostly found in destination networks, confirming prior work [34]. However, a small fraction are in transit ASes (e.g., Tier 1 s), which affect traffic to other ASes.*

8   How Dynamic Are Path-Impairing Middleboxes?

High speed probing middlebox identification techniques allow us to look at short scale dynamics of path-impairing middleboxes over hours (Sect. 8.2). In addition, we investigate more long-term behavior, comparing how the state of path-impairing middleboxes has evolved since 2022 [34] basing our analysis on prefix affectedness, impaired paths and detected path-impairing middleboxes.

8.1   Dataset

Short-Term Dynamics: To study if path-impairing middleboxes exhibit transience, we use the data from running Yarrpbox to BGP prefixes (Sect. 4.1) and run five back to back IPv4 and IPv6 scans to them. Each IPv6 scan runs for up to 14 h and the IPv4 scans finish in about 3 h.

Long-Term Behavior: In order to investigate long-term dynamics for path-impairing middleboxes at Internet-scale, we require historical Internet-scale path-impairment data. We use publicly available data from 2022 [47] released by prior work [34]. For sound comparison, we replicate the measurements, again sending TCP SYNs carrying the same TCP options to BGP-announced prefixes using Yarrpbox in March 2024, from the same VPs. We use the same seed for generating targets from BGP prefixes, however, the number of targets vary, especially for IPv6, as more BGP prefixes are announced since 2022.

For IPv6, the number of on-path replying hop IPs shows a large increase of 65.3% increasing from 602.7k across 8.5k ASes in 2022 to 996.4k across 13.3k ASes. The increase follows the large rise in the number of announced IPv6 prefixes which go from 155.8k announced from 28.5k ASes to 208k (+33%) in 32.7k

ASes (+14.7%). For IPv4, the collected traces and replying hop IPs do not change as substantially as for IPv6. The number of traces collected in 2024 are also similar with 107.1M vs 107.6M in 2022. Finally, about 1M replying hop IPs are seen in both scans and are scattered across nearly 27k ASes. Compared to IPv6, the growth for the announced prefixes is less drastic with the number growing from 965.7k (in 72.8k ASes) to 990.1k (in 75.2k ASes).

8.2 Are Path-Impairing Middleboxes Always On?

To understand whether middleboxes always interfere with the traffic or if they occasionally do not apply their impairments in a short timescale, we look at how often a path-impairing middlebox applies the interference when it appears on the path towards different destinations in a single scan, and how this holds when we repeat the scans.

To prevent potential source address based impairment policies from biasing our results, we use the scans from a single VP initially picking our university VP. For IPv6, we find that nearly 80% of these devices seem to always be active, i.e., interfere with the traffic to all targets for which they appear on-path. However, 16% of the devices apply interferences towards less than 25% of targets for which they show up on-path. This could either be down to a failure on the devices' part to apply the impairment or some may be configured with traffic destination specific impairment policies. Looking at the type of impairments these occasionally inactive devices make, we find they apply MP Capable stripping in 73% of the cases and TCP Sequence Number alterations in 23% of the cases. For IPv4, nearly 96% of these devices are always found to be active during the course of the scanning duration, and 73% of the occasionally inactive devices again remove the MP Capable or alter the Sequence Number, however around 30% intermittently set incorrect length field values. We see similar results from our AWS VPs.

When we repeat scans, the results across all snapshots are consistent with above for both IPv6 and IPv4, showing that middlebox stability even persists beyond hours across snapshots collectively lasting 2-3 days.

We also investigate if destination-based filtering policies are being classified as inactivity. We utilize our repeated measurements, conducted from the same VP, for this analysis. We pick HCMB IP addresses from scan 1 that show inactivity and also appear in all four of the next scans. We look at how many of these do not interfere, although they appear on path, towards the same set of targets in all five scans. Not interfering towards the same targets consistently across multiple scans each lasting 3–14 hours could be indicative of destination-specific policies. For IPv6, considering HCMB IPs which appear in all five of our scans, 50% of the inactive IPv6 HCMB IP (1 out of 2) addresses and 91.6% inactive IPv4 (22 of 24) ones exhibit this behavior. This demonstrates that short-term inactivity is rare in the wild and destination-based filtering policies exist.

Takeaway: *Overall, the majority of path-impairing devices are active even in the short-term.*

Table 7. ASes (percentage of announcing ASes) that see traffic impaired and affected prefixes in them (percentage of all announced). Both affected IPv6 prefixes and ASes see a marked increase over the two year period while for IPv4 growth is less aggressive.

	2022		2024	
Scan	Affected ASes (%)	Affected Prefixes (%)	Affected ASes (%)	Affected Prefixes (%)
IPv6	160 (0.5%)	462 (0.2%)	239 (0.7%)	1,682 (0.8%)
IPv4	3,843 (5.1%)	9,122 (0.9%)	3,916 (6.1%)	10,012 (1%)

8.3 How Has the Fraction of Affected Paths, Prefixes and ASes Evolved Since 2022?

For IPv6, 60.5k (0.07%) of the 86.7M paths were impaired in 2022, whereas it is 186.5k (0.15%) of 127.6M paths in 2024, thus doubling relative to the number of tested paths. However, we only see 14.3% of the paths from 2022 to be still impaired. Since we use the same seed for selecting our targets as the 2022 study, we can compare the affected targets. Athough the path-level overlap is low, the affected target overlap is much higher at 51.2%. This points to a change in paths towards the targets over a two year period. The DF impaired paths, dominated by the MP Capable removal, contribute nearly 95% to the total impaired paths. However, they also follow the general increase going from 57.5k to 176.1k. The DT and ND impaired paths are roughly the same in terms of numbers. However, the paths broken by the dangerous PB behavior increase by nearly 8 times.

For IPv4, 173.4k (0.19%) of the 87.8M paths were impaired in 2022, whereas it is 177.6k (0.20%) in 2024, so it is relatively stable. We only find 0.1% of the paths from 2022 that still see impairment. Therefore, we again look at overlap for the affected targets and similar to IPv6 find it to be much higher with nearly 70% of the 2022 targets still affected. While DF is the most dominant on IPv4 impaired paths like IPv6, we do not see a major jump for any of the behaviors.

For affected prefixes, the IPv6 number rises by over three times from 462 (in 160 ASes) in 2022 to 1,682 (in 239 ASes) in 2024 (see Table 7). This increase exceeds the 33.4% rise in the announced IPv6 prefixes in the Routeviews data and cannot be solely due to the growth of the IPv6 routing table. Although the rise is steep, the affected prefixes as a fraction of all announced prefixes is still small, with 0.8% in 2024 compared to 0.2% in 2022. Interestingly, of the 1,682 prefixes affected in 2024, 1,363 were not affected in 2022, and 40% of the 1,363 prefixes were already announced in 2022.

For IPv4, the rise is not as drastic as the affected prefixes increase by 8.8% while the announced rise by 2.5%, but the fraction relative to the announced prefix number is stable (+0.1%). The affected ASes go from 3,813 (5.1% of all) to 3,916 (5.4% of all). Of 10,012 affected IPv4 prefixes, about 3.4k were not affected in 2022. Like IPv6, we see a shift as 82.5% of the 3.4k were announced in 2022.

Nearly 30% of the prefixes over IPv4 and IPv6 affected in 2022 stopped being affected. Of these prefixes, 30% are still announced for both IPv6 and IPv4, indicating a path-impairing middlebox is not encountered anymore or, if it appears, it no longer applies the impairment. We perform a more detailed analysis on the path-impairing middlebox IPs that no longer interfere in Sect. 8.5.

Takeaway:*Fraction of affected IPv6 paths, prefixes and ASes sees a strong increase, IPv4 is stable.*

8.4 How Has Path-Impairing Middlebox Behavior Evolved Since 2022?

Table 10 shows how IPv6 impairments have changed since 2022 to our measurements in 2024. For IPv6, we see that the MP Capable removal is still the most prevalent having gone up from 33.2% to 38.3% out of all impairments. On a positive note, interferences to the TCP Sequence number, and the removal of other TCP extensions including the Timestamp and Sack Permitted halved over the last two years. However, other critical instances of impairments, such as sole payload length modifications have doubled.

For IPv4, MP Capable tolerance shows a similar trend to IPv6 as the removal of the option has increased by roughly 10% (see Table 11). On the other hand, the TCP Sequence Number altering and Timestamp removal shows a marginal decrease whereas the tolerance to the SACK Permitted option seems to have improved as its stripping nearly halves. Finally, the path-breaking sole IP Total length modification seems to be largely stable.

Takeaway:*MP capable removal is rather stable, whereas other option impairments have either halved or doubled, and their numbers remain very low.*

8.5 Are the Path-Impairing Middleboxes From 2022 Still Interfering With Traffic?

Table 8 shows the number of potential MB and HCMB addresses between 2022 and 2024. For IPv6, the number of HCMB IP addresses nearly triples between 2022 and 2024 going from 231 to 602, with 72.7% present at both times. Filtering out the non replying (absent) IP addresses in 2024, the overlap increases to 91%. For the remaining HCMB IP addresses in 2022 and still replying in 2024 but not identified as HC, we find that 30% of those are still potential MB IP addresses. As a result, there are only 12 (5.2% of those in 2022) IP addresses from 2022 which no longer engage in path-impairing behavior but could also simply be inactive with regard to filtering during the course of the whole scan, although we find that to be rare (Sect. 8.2). These potentially fixed addresses are across 8 ASes and 50% of these used to strip the MP Capable in 2022. The rest of these used to remove the SACK Permitted or Timestamp among other interferences.

For IPv4, the path-impairing middlebox numbers only slightly increase, from 2608 to 2818 for HCMB IP addresses, with a lower overlap than for IPv6 of 43%. Removing the HCMB IP addresses seen in 2022 but absent in 2024 results in the overlap increasing to 75.5%. Looking at the HCMB IP addresses from 2022 still replying in 2024 but not classified as HC in 2024, we observe that

66.3% are still at least potential MB IP addresses, meaning the missing replies in traces prevent them from jumping to the HC set. Thus, the remaining 136 IP addresses, across 82 ASes, seem to have potentially discontinued impairments. Nearly 42% of the potentially fixed addresses, across 44 ASes, used to strip the MP Capable in 2022. Another 30% used to make Sequence Number or sole IP Total Length changes. In fact, 60% of those now potentially fixed addresses that used to make sole length changes are in Tier-1s like AS 3320 as reported by prior work [34].

Takeaway: *Path-impairing middleboxes numbers follow the increase of affected prefixes in IPv6 and remain stable for IPv4. Also, most of the ones identified in 2022 still interfere as of 2024.*

9   How Can We Engage With Network Operators to Aid De-ossification?

To confront our observations with the perspectives of network operators, we carry out a survey with operators on RIPE and NANOG mailing-lists in May 2025. In Sect. 6, we find the disabling of features to be the most common path-impairing middlebox behavior for TCP traffic. We therefore ask network operators about their opinions on new, and standardized TCP options and features (SACK Permitted, MP Capable, ECN), and if they configure policies for filtering TCP options in their networks. We receive 11 responses and the participants operate a diverse set of network types that include eyeballs (55%), content/hosting/CDN (36%), academic/research (27%), transit (18%), tier-1 (9%), IXP (9%) and others (9%). 73% of the participating operators support IPv6.

All of the responding operators, point to their networks being *"transparent"* to TCP options which some also deem to be *"essential for good performance"*. In fact, none claim to configure any explicit filtering policy over either family.

While none of the surveyed operators reported filtering, our measurements reveal evidence of explicit policies (Sects. 4.3 and 8.2). We interpret this as a reflection of the small size of the surveyed sample. Additionally, while none of the operators claim to deploy any filtering policies, for one operator, we find some IPv4 addresses filtering the MP Capable. We reached out to the operator to confirm the finding but at the time of writing, we have not heard back. This finding suggests that some operators may not be aware of path-impairing middleboxes in their networks. This could be owing to devices installed in their default configurations which might be overly restrictive towards TCP options, especially the more recently standardized ones that pertain to MPTCP. Therefore, in order to support operators, we deploy a web service where network operators could look up impairing IP addresses and the impairments they apply to TCP traffic in their networks in a bid to fix them from our measurements that we plan to refresh frequently. The service is available at:

path-impairments.mpi-inf.mpg.de

Table 8. Path-impairing middlebox numbers in 2022 and 2024.

Scan	2022		2024	
	HCMB IP addresses	Potential MB IP addresses	HCMB IP addresses	Potential MB IP
IPv6	231	432	602	1,126
IPv4	2,606	9,038	2,818	9126

10 Could Default Configurations Be One of the Causes Of Path-Impairments?

Our engagement with operators reveals that some operators may not be aware of impairments in their networks. This raises the question whether some of the impairments we observe are unintentional and potentially caused by default configurations. To explore this, we consider the MPTCP's MP Capable as a case study, since it represents the most common impairment in our data (Sect. 6).

We examine documentation for major vendors to identify the default behavior regarding how this option is handled. Many firewall vendors provide the ability to configure policies that filter out specific or undesirable TCP options, including MPTCP [18,51,52]. Notably, documentation from Cisco, Citrix, and Palo Alto explicitly states that the default behavior of their firewalls is to remove or replace unsupported TCP options, including MPTCP, with NOPs [17,52,61]. This behavior is also consistent with our findings. In such cases, an explicit policy is required to allow MPTCP traffic.

To gauge the plausibility of default configurations as the cause of MPTCP impairments, we attempt to identify the vendors of middleboxes in our dataset using a combination of widely used methods, including Nmap scanning and banner grabbing (via Censys and SNMPv3 datasets) [1,2,24,36]. In total, we identify 58 different vendors for 2,033 middleboxes (48% of the total). For 722 middleboxes, we obtain only a generic Linux fingerprint, which can not be mapped to a specific vendor (we discuss this further in Sect. 12). The next three most common vendors are Cisco (447), Palo Alto (329), and Check Point(166).

Since these vendors' products indeed impair MPTCP by default [15,17,52], this could potentially explain some of the impairments we observe. While this behavior can also result from explicit policies, validation is challenging without ground truth or direct access to network policy configurations. Further analysis of explicit filtering policies and vendor-specific behaviors is needed to fully understand the intentions and underlying causes of these impairments. We plan to investigate this further in future work.

Takeaway: *Default configurations are potentially one of the (unintended) causes of path-impairments.*

11   Ethical Considerations

Before performing Yarrpbox measurements, we incorporate proposals by Partridge and Allman [55] and Kenneally and Dittrich [41]. We adhere to best measurement practices [25] by limiting our probing rate, using a well-established blocklist, and making use of dedicated servers and AWS instances as measurement vantage points. These measurement servers communicate the scientific nature of our measurements with an informing rDNS name, a website providing more information, and contact details to reach out to us in case of issues. For our ISP scans, we again limit the probing rate, use a dedicated blocklist and also leave the purpose of our measurements and our contact information in the payload and only perform the domain-based ones to minimize the generated traffic. During our measurements, we did not receive any complaints or requests asking for being included on our blocklist. We conduct the survey via our institutionally hosted platform that ensures no data is shared with third parties. We collect no personally identifiable information (PII); only the operator's ASN and email (both optional) for follow-ups. Participation is voluntary and consent explicitly obtained. The survey was also approved by our university's ethics review board.

12   Discussion

Our study reinforces widely accepted guidance, e.g., for protocol designers, taking middleboxes into account (even for IPv6) when designing new protocols and providing robust fallbacks; for operators, prefer stripping features (if necessary) rather than packet drops to allow silent fall-backs and hence not degrade performance. Our study also enables more specific recommendations.

Recommendations for Protocol Designers: Despite nearly a decade since MPTCP's introduction, over 87% of impairments involve it. This points to the Internet's reluctance to adopt extensions deemed unessential. While IPv6 is not impairment-free, our findings suggest it still offers a less ossified environment. We recommend protocol designers and application developers to deploy innovative features over IPv6 first, while continuing to refine fallback behavior for IPv4. Additionally, for 6.1% of domains (Sect. 5.2), we found switching to IPv6 could allow for impairment-free paths. While latency should remain the primary signal for address-family selection (per the Happy Eyeballs), protocol stacks could also opportunistically favor the path that retains desired transport features when both families are viable.

Recommendations for Operators: Operators should audit and update their devices as some interferences seem to stem from default configurations (Sect. 10), especially true for providers (e.g., Tier-1 s) which could inadvertently affect a lot of traffic (Sect. 7). However, we believe operators might not always be aware of path-impairing middleboxes in their networks. Therefore, in order to support operators, we will deploy a web service as discussed in Sect. 9.

Limitations: While we test three times more paths than prior work [27,34], observe ten times more on-path networks [27] and our VPs span six continents–including cloud, academic and ISP networks–this provides broad but not exhaustive visibility. Although most impairments are close or in the destination networks, we acknowledge VP dependence for impairments. However, given the scale and diversity of Internet paths, no finite set of VPs can capture all instances of path-impairing behavior. Indeed, without VPs in each source network, some middleboxes may go undetected, although we do our best by probing to BGP prefixes and diversifying our VPs by also probing from our University and a European ISP. Although our set of VPs is limited, our measurements still allow us to identify impairments further along paths such as when network core affects traffic not destined to it or close or within the hosting network itself. This provides valuable insights into the systemic impact of ossification as the path-impairing middleboxes in these positions stand to impact a wide range of clients and VPs.

13   Related Work

The term "middlebox" refers to any intermediary device on a packet path that deviates from the standard functionality of an IP router. Such devices can offer a wide range of capabilities such as network address translation, load balancing, firewall, and proxy services. An extensive taxonomy of middleboxes is described in RFC 3234 [14], which also highlights that middleboxes can violate the End-to-End principle. Today, middleboxes are a major component of the Internet and evaluating their effects and unforeseen interactions on established and future protocols and extensions is a challenging task. Medina et al. made an early attempt [48,49] with the TCP Behavior Inference Tool (TBIT), which they use to measure the interaction between middleboxes and a set of protocol mechanisms such as ECN, PMTUD and TCP options on paths to web servers. By sending a sequence of TCP packets with different IP and TCP options and analyzing the responses, TBIT is able to detect the middlebox presence but not its location.

Craven et al. [20] put forth TCP HICCUPS, a TCP extension designed to detect on-path middleboxes albeit requiring modifications to the TCP stack, while Honda et al. [38] achieve a similar objective by introducing a client-server application with a custom TCP stack. However, these approaches require control over both ends of a connection limiting the feasibility for large-scale studies.

Delta et al. [23], introduce Tracebox and use it to investigate transport layer ossification while also measuring the prevalence of different types of middlebox interferences on network paths [27]. While this work similarly focuses on impairments applied towards domains from the Alexa Top 1M over IPv4, we extend its contributions by conducting Internet-scale measurements and investigating transport layer ossification over IPv6 and IPv4. We cannot perform an apple-to-apple comparison, as PlanetLab VPs were used, and have been decommissioned since. However, we provide a discussion related to this work in Appendix C.

Although Tracebox improves upon prior work, it is not suitable for Internet-scale census due to its stateful and thus slow operation. To address this, Hilal and Gasser introduce Yarrpbox [33], a stateless middlebox detector inspired by Yarrp [8]. The authors perform Internet-scale measurements accurately locating middleboxes in 35–55% of the cases, characterizing their ASes, and providing high-level numbers on observed interferences. However, the study primarily contributed a new tool to enable Internet-scale measurement and performed an initial middlebox census, offering preliminary insights into path-impairments. In contrast, our work deliberately builds on that foundation to provide a comprehensive and systematic study. We move beyond demonstrating feasibility to tackle broader research questions: quantifying impairments across IPv4 and IPv6 at Internet-scale and to popular domains, analyzing impact on ASes and prefixes, exploring both short-term and multi-year dynamics, investigating root causes, and complementing measurements with operator perspectives (Table 1).

14   Conclusion

We presented a multi-dimensional study about path-impairing middleboxes, characterizing how paths, prefixes, ASes, and domains are affected, for both IPv4 and IPv6, finding that IPv6 offers a potentially less impaired environment overall. We measured opportunities to switch to IPv6 to evade path-impairing middleboxes finding that for a non-negligible fraction of domains this could allow for impairment-free paths enabling the connection to benefit from TCP extensions like MPTCP. In addition, we explored path-impairing middlebox dynamics highlighting the stability of path-impairing middlebox behaviors, at both short and long time scales. Finally, in order to contrast our observations with network operator perspectives, we engaged with network operators. We observed that some operators might be unaware of impairments applied to traffic in their networks. Motivated by this, we investigated potential causes and observed that default device configurations could plausibly contribute to some of the behaviors we measure. Thus, in order to support operators and help fix unintentional impairments, we set up a service where network operators can look up IP addresses from their networks filtering TCP options.

A   Vantage Point Dependence

At a per VP level, the traffic to the fewest IPv6 prefixes (306) is impaired from the Swede VP, whereas the highest from the VP in Brazil (1.1k). Looking at the on-path location where the impairment is applied, we find that for the Swede VP the highest number of prefixes (169) for which the path-impairing middlebox's location is known are located in the target networks. Although we see a similar number (170) of prefixes affected in the target networks for the Brazil VP, for nearly 70% of the HCMB affected prefixes, path-impairing middlebox's IP does not map to any AS. On average, about 791 prefixes are affected at each VP. Our university VP shows similar results to the Swede VP reporting about 309 IPv6 prefixes as impaired. For IPv4, the VP on the west coast in the US reports the highest numbers with 8.7k affected prefixes and the lowest number at the

South African VP with 5.2k, an average of about 7,038 prefixes found to be impaired from each VP. The fraction of prefixes affected by HCMB IPs for which the AS can not be mapped is similar for both VPs and at about 3% is also substantially lower compared to IPv6. Most prefixes at both VPs are affected in the same networks as the prefixes. Finally, again the university VP does not deviate drastically (about 7.6k affected prefixes). However, these results demonstrate a clear VP dependence for traffic impairments despite the path-impairing middlebox being present in the same AS as the target most of the time.

For another perspective on the VP dependence, we follow Yarrpbox-based traceroutes with traceroutes from RIPE Atlas [59]. We pick affected prefixes for which we identify the HCMB IPs and traceroute to them from probes from 200 ASes selected using Metis [4, 39]. We intend to investigate if the affected prefixes also see the path-impairing middlebox IPs from VPs outside ours. We consider a prefix to be affected if it sees either the path-inpairing middlebox IP again or one of its aliases. To maximize the coverage of discovered aliases, we utilize multiple datasets [1, 3, 42, 46] However, less than 12% of the path-impairing middlebox IPs could be mapped to alias sets over either address family. For IPv6, we find about 39% of the prefixes to not see the expected path-impairing middlebox or its aliases from any VP whereas another 30% are still affected at more than one-fourth of the VPs. Only about 3% are affected at more than 75% of the RIPE Atlas VPs. On the IPv4 side, the numbers are even lower, as we find about 67% of the prefixes to not see the path-impairing middleboxes or their aliases. Although about one-fourth are affected from more than half the VPs. However, these numbers should be treated as lower bounds. Due to the limited coverage of alias resolution techniques, it is possible that undiscovered aliases of middlebox IPs show up on paths towards some prefixes (found here to be unaffected) from the RIPE probes instead of the IPs we find from our VPs.

Table 9. Impairment statistics for IPv6 and IPv4 Tranco Top-1M domains (percentages rounded to three decimals). DF dominates via MP Capable in both families, while IPv6 shows noticeably better SACK and ECN tolerance.

Impairment	IPv6			IPv4			MB Behavior
	Number	% of Responses	% of Paths	Number	% of Responses	% of Paths	
TCP::NOP	1,660	0.010%	0.071%	92,482	0.127%	0.096%	DF
TCP::MP Capable	1,440	0.009%	0.069%	90,627	0.124%	0.091%	DF
TCP::Timestamp	272	0.001%	0.005%	6,166	0.008%	0.031	DF
TCP::Sequence Number	210	0.001%	-	4,725	0.006%	0.0014%	DT
TCP::Sack Permitted	199	0.001%	-	4,328	0.006%	0.0010%	DF, ND
IP::Payload Length Flip	56	-	0.003%	-	-	-	PB
TCP::ECN.00	7	-	-	2,138	0.003%	0.002%	DF
TCP::MSS	-	-	-	3,731	0.005%	0.007%	DF
IP::Total Length Flip	-	-	-	15	-	-%	PB

B   Impairments to Popular domains

Table 9 depicts impairments towards Tranco top 1M domains (see Sect. 6).

C   Can We Identify Reasons for Drop in IPv4 impairments?

Our impaired path fraction is lower than Edeline and Donnet [26], who collected data in 2016, and reported about 6.5% of IPv4 paths as impaired to Alexa Top 1M domains. We investigate potential reasons for the difference. Firstly, comparing individual interferences, we see a large drop in some alterations. For instance, 17.7M (76.5%) of their responses with impairments have the TCP Sequence Number altered whereas it is 3% for us. Such sequence randomization was historically used by middleboxes to mitigate predictable initial sequence numbers, but OSes have implemented these protections for decades. It is plausible that this on-path behavior has diminished, reducing the number of affected paths.

Edeline and Donnet report similar removal counts for SACK Permitted and MP Capable (2.2M vs. 2.9M). In contrast, we observe substantially fewer SACK Permitted removals, 21 times fewer than MP Capable, and half the interference reported in 2022 [34] (Sect. 8.4). Moreover, while the authors find over 30K TCP MSS removals, we see 10 times fewer. Thirdly, the set of VPs used is different, where Edeline and Donnet use 89 PlanetLab nodes, located in more ASes than our setup which has two networks (AWS and our university). This implies that a path-impairing middlebox present in their source network is likely to affect several paths that their packets take from the network. In fact, their results show a minor presence of middleboxes in their probing networks. Finally, it is plausible that the hosting of domains changed since 2016. In fact, while they use Alexa in 2016, we use Tranco, as the former was since discontinued, and find that about 15% of the domains to be hosted in the AWS network. Although our findings, and also prior work [26,34], show that most path-impairing middleboxes are in destination/hosting networks, we find none in AWS. Still, we reiterate that our numbers on impaired paths should be treated as lower bounds.

Table 10. Impairment statistics for IPv6 prefix-based port-80 scans in 2024 vs. 2022 (Hilal and Gasser). MP Capable filtering doubles, while SACK Permitted halves.

Impairment	2022 (Hilal and Gasser)			2024 (our work)			MB Behavior
	Number	% of Responses	% of Paths	Number	% of Responses	% of Paths	
TCP::NOP	190,260	0.016%	0.066%	410,239	0.026%	0.137%	DF
TCP::MP Capable	155,836	0.013%	0.062%	358,309	0.023%	0.136%	DF
TCP::Sequence Number	103,704	0.009%	0.009%	112,364	0.007%	0.006%	DT
TCP::Timestamp	93,544	0.008%	0.008%	95,125	0.006%	0.004%	DF
TCP::Sack Permitted	92,591	0.008%	0.008%	94,668	0.006%	0.004%	DF, ND
IP::Payload Length Flip	5,359	0.0005%	0.001%	23,385	0.001%	0.006%	PB
TCP::MP Capable Sender Key	7	-	-	6	-	-	ND
TCP::MSS	1	-	-	2	-	-	DF
TCP::Rcv Window	1	-	-	1	-	-	DT

Table 11. Impairment statistics for IPv4 prefix-based port-80 scans in 2024 vs. 2022 (Hilal and Gasser).Impaired path fraction remains largely stable for all most all interferences.

Impairment	2022 (Hilal and Gasser)			2024 (our work)			MB Behavior
	Number	% of Responses	% of Paths	Number	% of Responses	% of Paths	
TCP::NOP	435,367	0.037%	0.203%	537,761	0.046%	0.217%	DF
TCP::MP Capable	397,167	0.034%	0.189%	477,587	0.041%	0.200%	DF
TCP::Sequence Number	59,448	0.005%	0.007%	66,396	0.006%	0.007%	DT
TCP::Timestamp	13,912	0.001%	0.003%	11,833	0.001%	0.005%	DF
TCP::Sack Permitted	7,523	0.001%	0.002%	4,065	-	0.002%	DF, ND
IP::Total Length Flip	3,311	-	0.002%	4,006	-	0.002%	PB
TCP::MSS	227	-	-	207	-	-	DF
TCP::MP Capable Sender Key	2	-	-	-	-	-	ND

References

1. Albakour, T., Gasser, O., Beverly, R., Smaragdakis, G.: Third time's not a charm: exploiting snmpv3 for router fingerprinting. In: Proceedings of the 21st ACM Internet Measurement Conference, pp. 150–164 (2021)
2. Albakour, T., Gasser, O., Beverly, R., Smaragdakis, G.: Illuminating router vendor diversity within providers and along network paths. In: Proceedings of the 2023 ACM on Internet Measurement Conference (2023)
3. Albakour, T., Gasser, O., Smaragdakis, G.: Pushing Alias Resolution to the Limit. In: Proceedings of ACM Internet Measurement Conference (IMC) 2023. Montreal, QC, Canada (October 2023)
4. Appel, M., Aben, E., Fontugne, R.: Metis: Better atlas vantage point selection for everyone. In: TMA (2022)
5. Aschenbrenner, F., Shreedhar, T., Gasser, O., Mohan, N., Ott, J.: From single lane to highways: analyzing the adoption of multipath TCP in the Internet. In: IFIP Networking Conference 2021 (Jun 2021)
6. Augustin, B., et al.: Avoiding traceroute anomalies with Paris traceroute. In: Proceedings of the 6th ACM SIGCOMM Conference on Internet Measurement, pp. 153–158 (2006)
7. Baker (Ed.), F.: Requirements for IP Version 4 Routers. RFC 1812 (Proposed Standard) (June 1995). https://doi.org/10.17487/RFC1812, https://www.rfc-editor.org/rfc/rfc1812.txt, updated by RFCs 2644, 6633

8. Beverly, R.: Yarrp'ing the Internet: randomized high-speed active topology discovery. In: Proceedings of the 2016 Internet Measurement Conference, pp. 413–420 (2016)

9. BGP.Tools: Bgp.tools. https://bgp.tools/ (2025). Accessed 23 May 2025

10. Blechschmidt, S.: MassDNS (2024). https://github.com/blechschmidt/massdns

11. CAIDA: Routeviews prefix to as mappings dataset (pfx2as) for ipv4 and ipv6. https://www.caida.org/catalog/datasets/routeviews-prefix2as/ (2024)

12. CAIDA, Center for Applied Internet Data Analysis: AS Classification Dataset (2024). https://www.caida.org/catalog/datasets/as-classification/

13. CAIDA, Center for Applied Internet Data Analysis: AS Organizations Dataset (2024). https://www.caida.org/data/as_organizations/

14. Carpenter, B., Brim, S.: Middleboxes: Taxonomy and Issues. RFC 3234 (Informational) (Feb 2002). https://doi.org/10.17487/RFC3234, https://www.rfc-editor.org/rfc/rfc3234.txt

15. Center, S.: sk114666 - How does Check Point Security Gateway handle Multipath TCP Connection (MPTCP) ? — support.checkpoint.com. https://support.checkpoint.com/results/sk/sk114666 (2016). Accessed 12 Oct 2025

16. Chaudhary, S., Sachdeva, P., Mondal, A., Chakraborty, S., Maity, M.: YouTube over Google's QUIC vs Internet Middleboxes: A Tug of War between Protocol Sustainability and Application QoE. arXiv preprint arXiv:2203.11977 (2022)

17. Cisco: MPTCP and Product Support Overview — cisco.com. https://www.cisco.com/c/en/us/support/docs/ip/transmission-control-protocol-tcp/116519-technote-mptcp-00.html (2001)

18. Cisco: ASDM Book 2: Cisco ASA Series Firewall ASDM Configuration Guide, 7.8 - Connection Settings [Cisco ASA 5500-X Series Firewalls] — cisco.com. https://www.cisco.com/c/en/us/td/docs/security/asa/asa98/asdm78/firewall/asdm-78-firewall-config/conns-connlimits.html (2025). Accessed 29 May 2025

19. Conta, A., Deering, S., Gupta (Ed.), M.: Internet Control Message Protocol (ICMPv6) for the Internet Protocol Version 6 (IPv6) Specification. RFC 4443 (Internet Standard) (Mar 2006). https://doi.org/10.17487/RFC4443, https://www.rfc-editor.org/rfc/rfc4443.txt, updated by RFC 4884

20. Craven, R., Beverly, R., Allman, M.: A middlebox-cooperative TCP for a non end-to-end internet. ACM SIGCOMM Comput. Commun. Rev. **44**(4), 151–162 (2014)

21. De Coninck, Q., et al.: Pluginizing QUIC. In: Proceedings of the ACM Special Interest Group on Data Communication, pp. 59–74 (2019)

22. Deering, S., Hinden, R.: Internet Protocol, Version 6 (IPv6) Specification. RFC 8200 (Internet Standard) (July 2017). https://doi.org/10.17487/RFC8200, https://www.rfc-editor.org/rfc/rfc8200.txt

23. Detal, G., Hesmans, B., Bonaventure, O., Vanaubel, Y., Donnet, B.: Revealing middlebox interference with tracebox. In: Proceedings of the 2013 Conference on Internet Measurement Conference, pp. 1–8 (2013)

24. Durumeric, Z., Adrian, D., Mirian, A., Bailey, M., Halderman, J.A.: A search engine backed by Internet-wide scanning. In: 22nd ACM Conference on Computer and Communications Security (2015)

25. Durumeric, Z., Wustrow, E., Halderman, J.A.: ZMap: fast internet-wide scanning and its security applications. In: 22nd USENIX Security Symposium (USENIX Security 13), pp. 605–620 (2013)

26. Edeline, K., Donnet, B.: A first look at the prevalence and persistence of middleboxes in the wild. In: 2017 29th International Teletraffic Congress (ITC 29), vol. 1, pp. 161–168. IEEE (2017)

27. Edeline, K., Donnet, B.: A bottom-up investigation of the transport-layer ossification. In: 2019 Network Traffic Measurement and Analysis Conference (TMA), pp. 169–176. IEEE (2019)
28. Ford, A., Raiciu, C., Handley, M., Bonaventure, O.: TCP Extensions for Multipath Operation with Multiple Addresses. RFC 6824 (Experimental) (Jan 2013). https://doi.org/10.17487/RFC6824, https://www.rfc-editor.org/rfc/rfc6824.txt, obsoleted by RFC 8684
29. Ford, A., Raiciu, C., Handley, M., Bonaventure, O., Paasch, C.: TCP Extensions for Multipath Operation with Multiple Addresses. RFC 8684 (Proposed Standard) (Mar 2020). https://doi.org/10.17487/RFC8684, https://www.rfc-editor.org/rfc/rfc8684.txt
30. Gasser, O., et al.: Clusters in the expanse: understanding and unbiasing IPv6 hitlists. In: Proceedings of the Internet Measurement Conference 2018, pp. 364–378 (2018)
31. Gigis, P., et al.: Seven years in the life of hypergiants' off-nets. In: Proceedings of the 2021 ACM SIGCOMM 2021 Conference, pp. 516–533 (2021)
32. Hesmans, B., Duchene, F., Paasch, C., Detal, G., Bonaventure, O.: Are tcp extensions middlebox-proof? In: Proceedings of the 2013 Workshop On Hot Topics In Middleboxes And Network Function Virtualization, pp. 37–42 (2013)
33. Hilal, F., Gasser, O.: Yarrpbox. https://github.com/yarrpbox/yarrpbox (2023)
34. Hilal, F., Gasser, O.: Yarrpbox: detecting middleboxes at internet-scale. Proc. ACM Network. **1**(CoNEXT1), 1–23 (2023)
35. Hilal, F., Sattler, P., Vermeulen, K., Gasser, O.: A first look at ipv6 hypergiant infrastructure. Proc. ACM Network. **2**(CoNEXT2), 1–25 (2024)
36. Holland, J., et al.: Classifying network vendors at internet scale. arXiv preprint arXiv:2006.13086 (2020)
37. Holz, R., et al.: Tracking the deployment of TLS 1.3 on the Web: a story of experimentation and centralization. ACM SIGCOMM Comput. Commun. Rev. **50**(3), 3–15 (2020)
38. Honda, M., Nishida, Y., Raiciu, C., Greenhalgh, A., Handley, M., Tokuda, H.: Is it still possible to extend TCP? In: Proceedings of the 2011 ACM SIGCOMM Conference on Internet Measurement Conference, pp. 181–194 (2011)
39. IIJ Research Laboratory: Metis: Internet Health Report (2024). https://ihr.iijlab.net/ihr/en-us/metis/selection
40. Iyengar (Ed.), J., Thomson (Ed.), M.: QUIC: A UDP-Based Multiplexed and Secure Transport. RFC 9000 (Proposed Standard) (May 2021). https://doi.org/10.17487/RFC9000, https://www.rfc-editor.org/rfc/rfc9000.txt
41. Kenneally, E., Dittrich, D.: The Menlo Report: Ethical Principles Guiding Information and Communication Technology Research. Available at SSRN 2445102 (2012)
42. Keys, K., Hyun, Y., Luckie, M., Claffy, K.: Internet-scale ipv4 alias resolution with midar. IEEE/ACM Trans. Network. **21**(2), 383–399 (2012)
43. Kohler, E., Handley, M., Floyd, S.: Datagram congestion control protocol (dccp). Tech. rep. (2006)
44. Lee, H., Kim, D., Kwon, Y.: TLS 1.3 in Practice: How TLS 1.3 Contributes to the Internet. In: Proceedings of the Web Conference 2021, pp. 70–79 (2021)
45. Luckie, M., Huffaker, B., claffy, k., Dhamdhere, A., Giotsas, V.: AS relationships, customer cones, and validation. In: ACM Internet Measurement Conference (IMC), pp. 243–256 (Oct 2013). https://doi.org/10.1145/2504730.2504735
46. Luckie, M., Beverly, R., Brinkmeyer, W., claffy, k.: Speedtrap: internet-scale ipv6 alias resolution. In: Proceedings of the 2013 Conference on Internet Measurement Conference, pp. 119–126 (2013)

47. Max Planck Society: Dataset on Edmond by Max Planck Society (2024). https://edmond.mpg.de/dataset.xhtml?persistentId=doi%3A10.17617%2F3.EVDWIT
48. Medina, A., Allman, M., Floyd, S.: Measuring interactions between transport protocols and middleboxes. In: Proceedings of the 4th ACM SIGCOMM Conference on Internet Measurement, pp. 336–341 (2004)
49. Medina, A., Allman, M., Floyd, S.: Measuring the evolution of transport protocols in the internet. ACM SIGCOMM Comput. Commun. Rev. **35**(2), 37–52 (2005)
50. Mehani, O., Holz, R., Ferlin, S., Boreli, R.: An early look at multipath TCP deployment in the wild. In: Proceedings of the 6th International Workshop on Hot Topics in Planet-scale Measurement, pp. 7–12 (2015)
51. Juniper Networks: tcp-options (Security Policies) — Junos OS — Juniper Networks — juniper.net. https://www.juniper.net/documentation/us/en/software/junos/cli-reference/topics/ref/statement/security-edit-tcp-options.html   (2025), [Accessed 29-05-2025]
52. Networks, P.A.: TCP Settings — docs.paloaltonetworks.com. https://docs.paloaltonetworks.com/pan-os/11-2/pan-os-web-interface-help/device/device-setup-session/tcp-settings (2025). Accessed 29 May 2025
53. Nichols, K., Blake, S., Baker, F., Black, D.: Definition of the Differentiated Services Field (DS Field) in the IPv4 and IPv6 Headers. RFC 2474 (Proposed Standard) (Dec 1998). https://doi.org/10.17487/RFC2474, https://www.rfc-editor.org/rfc/rfc2474.txt, updated by RFCs 3168, 3260, 8436
54. NLNOG: NLNOG RING (2024). https://ring.nlnog.net/
55. Partridge, C., Allman, M.: Ethical considerations in network measurement papers. Commun. ACM **59**(10), 58–64 (2016)
56. PeeringDB: PeeringDB (2024). https://www.peeringdb.com/
57. Postel, J.: Internet Control Message Protocol. RFC 792 (Internet Standard) (Sep 1981). https://doi.org/10.17487/RFC0792, https://www.rfc-editor.org/rfc/rfc792.txt, updated by RFCs 950, 4884, 6633, 6918
58. Rescorla, E.: The Transport Layer Security (TLS) Protocol Version 1.3. RFC 8446 (Proposed Standard) (Aug 2018). https://doi.org/10.17487/RFC8446, https://www.rfc-editor.org/rfc/rfc8446.txt
59. RIPE NCC: RIPE Atlas (2024). https://atlas.ripe.net/
60. Rüth, J., Poese, I., Dietzel, C., Hohlfeld, O.: A first look at QUIC in the wild. In: Beverly, R., Smaragdakis, G., Feldmann, A. (eds.) PAM 2018. LNCS, vol. 10771, pp. 255–268. Springer, Cham (2018). https://doi.org/10.1007/978-3-319-76481-8_19
61. Citrix Customer Service: Citrix Customer Service — support.citrix.com. https://support.citrix.com/s/article/CTX461232-tcp-option-lost-when-traffic-go-through-tcp-type-load-balancelb-vserver?language=en_US (2025). Accessed 29 May 2025
62. Sherry, J., Hasan, S., Scott, C., Krishnamurthy, A., Ratnasamy, S., Sekar, V.: Making middleboxes someone else's problem: network processing as a cloud service. ACM SIGCOMM Comput. Commun. Rev. **42**(4), 13–24 (2012)
63. Stewart, R., Xie, Q., Tuexen, M., Maruyama, S., Kozuka, M.: Rfc 5061: Stream control transmission protocol (sctp) dynamic address reconfiguration (2007)
64. Sullivan, N.: Why TLS 1.3 isn't in browsers yet. https://blog.cloudflare.com/why-tls-1-3-isnt-in-browsers-yet/ (2017)
65. Thirion, V., Edeline, K., Donnet, B.: Tracking middleboxes in the mobile world with traceboxandroid. In: International Workshop on Traffic Monitoring and Analysis, pp. 79–91. Springer (2015)

66. Tranco: Tranco: A Research-Oriented Top Sites Ranking (2024). https://tranco-list.eu/
67. Wang, Z., Qian, Z., Xu, Q., Mao, Z., Zhang, M.: An untold story of middleboxes in cellular networks. ACM SIGCOMM Comput. Commun. Rev. **41**(4), 374–385 (2011)
68. Zirngibl, J., Buschmann, P., Sattler, P., Jaeger, B., Aulbach, J., Carle, G.: It's Over 9000: analyzing early QUIC deployments with the standardization on the horizon. In: Proceedings of the 21st ACM Internet Measurement Conference, pp. 261–275 (2021)
69. Zirngibl, J., Steger, L., Sattler, P., Gasser, O., Carle, G.: Rusty clusters? dusting an ipv6 research foundation. In: Proceedings of the 22nd ACM Internet Measurement Conference, pp. 395–409 (2022)

Applications and Congestion

WikIPedia: Unearthing a 20-Year History of IPv6 Client Addressing

Erik Rye[1,2]($\boxtimes$) and Dave Levin[2]

[1] Johns Hopkins University, Baltimore, USA
`rye@jhu.edu`
[2] University of Maryland, College Park, USA

Abstract. Due to their article editing policies, Wikimedia sites like Wikipedia have become inadvertent time capsules for IPv6 addresses. When Wikimedia users make edits without signing into an account, their IP addresses are used in lieu of a username. Wikimedia site dumps therefore provide researchers with over two decades worth of timestamped client IPv6 addresses to understand address assignments and how they have changed over time and space.

In this work, we extract 19M unique IPv6 addresses from Wikimedia sites like Wikipedia that were used by editors from 2003 to 2024. We use these addresses to understand the prevalence of IPv6 in countries corresponding to Wikimedia site languages, how IPv6 adoption has grown over time, and the prevalence of EUI-64 addressing on client devices like desktops, laptops, and mobile phones.

1 Introduction

In the 1993 film *Jurassic Park*, the eccentric billionaire John Hammond resurrects long-extinct fauna by extracting infinitesimal amounts of their DNA from mosquitoes trapped in amber. The DNA in these mosquitoes serves as a historical blueprint for reverse engineering myriad dinosaur species, which eventually populate his eponymous theme park.

In the field of network measurement, Wikimedia sites may well be the analog of mosquito-entrapping amber. When Wikipedians—as editors of the sites are known—make edits to pages without logging in, their public IP address is used in lieu of a username. Thus, the sites (which preserve all historical edits, even those later reversed) and its 24 year history unintentionally function as an archive for historical Internet data. The IP addresses logged-out Wikipedians used are, in essence, frozen in amber along with the timestamp when they were used.

This type of longitudinal data is rare. Few other datasets match the wide timespan over which it was collected; its earliest entries predate most social media and many other mainstays of today's web experience. And datasets that do match its prodigious timeline do not typically include its type of data. Routeviews' Border Gateway Protocol (BGP) data archives [24], for instance, match the timespan of Wikimedia's existence. However, Autonomous Systems

S. Ferlin-Reiter et al. (Eds.): PAM 2026, LNCS 16477, pp. 137–151, 2026.
https://doi.org/10.1007/978-3-032-18268-5_6

(ASes) may advertise large swathes of unused address space, particularly in IPv6, and simply knowing which prefixes were historically advertised obscures the rich detail present in understanding real address assignments.

IPv6 research benefits significantly from knowing active IPv6 addresses. For instance, the IPv6 Hitlist [3,13] regularly provides researchers with lists of known-active addresses to use as targets of active measurement campaigns or as training data for Target Generation Algorithms (TGAs) [8–10,15,20,28–31,42,43]. Similarly, the IPv6 Observatory [26] releases the /48 prefixes of NTP clients that visit its servers on a weekly basis.

In this work, we use archival Wikimedia data to extract the client IP addresses of editors from 2001 through December 2024. We find almost 19 million unique IPv6 addresses, compared to 107 million IPv4 addresses, that are used in lieu of Wikipedia usernames. Our IP address data spans the gamut of sites under the Wikimedia ægis: from the popular primary "encyclopedia" sites for dozens of languages, to crowd-sourced textbooks, dictionaries, and quotes, as well.

In mining this rich vein of historical IPv6 addresses, this work makes the following primary contributions:

1. We analyze global Wikimedia IPv6 statistics, including i) differences between various Wikimedia sites and languages, ii) temporal aspects of Wikimedia IPv6 client addressing, and iii) changes in Wikimedia IPv6 data corresponding with major network events.
2. We examine EUI-64 IPv6 addresses in Wikimedia data and discover that this obsolescent type of address is actually undergoing a modern revival.
3. We compare our Wikimedia IPv6 corpus with the IPv6 Hitlist to understand the information gained from this unique dataset.

2   Background and Related Work

2.1   Wikimedia

The Wikimedia Foundation [32] supports a wide variety of free knowledge projects, including Wikipedia, Wikibooks, Wiktionary, Wikiquote, and others, that allow users to freely access, contribute, and verify its content. These projects are available in a wide variety of languages; Wikipedia, for instance, is available in over 300 languages.

Most users of Wikimedia sites do not contribute information to these wikis in the form of new articles or edits to existing ones. However, some users do; these contributors are encouraged to register an account to which their edit history will be attached. In early 2025, for instance, the English Wikipedia reports over 49M registered users with about a third (15M) having committed at least one edit [41].

However, Wikimedia sites also allow users to contribute edits without logging in. When contributors submit edits without logging in, a warning (Fig. 1) alerts them that their IP address will be used in lieu of a username and will be publicly visible.

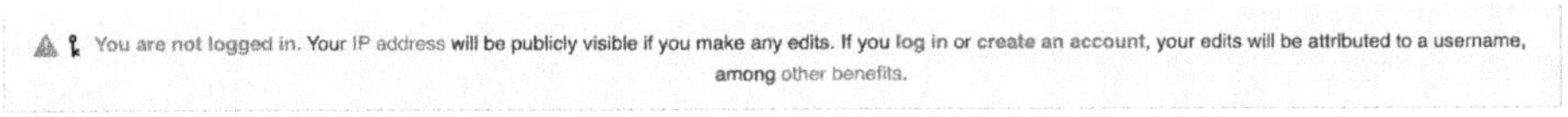

Fig. 1. Wikipedia warns logged-out users that their IP address will be publicly visible.

Wikimedia periodically publishes "dumps" of all of its constituent sites [33]. Each constituent site and language combination is available separately, so that consumers of this data can differentiate between English Wikipedia and Mandarin Chinese Wikiquote entries, for instance. Importantly, these archives contain both current and *historical* data, including edits that were made long ago and have since been overwritten, as well as edits that were later reverted.

2.2 Related Work

Studies of Wikimedia This work uses Wikimedia sites as a source of active client IPv6 addresses over time. It builds on several studies that measure Wikipedia generally, and make use of IP addresses found in Wikipedia edits specifically.

A significant body of work has studied Wikipedia content. Voss authored an early measurement of Wikipedia, counting the number of articles, authors, and edits across multiple language versions of the site [37]. Unlike these prior studies, our work does not focus on the wikis' *content*, but rather the IP addresses of those who help curate it.

Wikipedians' IP addresses have been studied in the context of Wikipedia vandalism—that is, removing accurate information from articles, removing articles entirely, inserting inaccurate information into articles, or otherwise making "unproductive" edits [16,38]. Others have used Wikimedia address edit history to filter for Tor exit nodes [34]. By contrast, we are interested in *all* edits recorded by IPv6 addresses in the Wikimedia dumps.

Almeida et al. performed a broad study of how user behavior on Wikipedia had evolved from 2001 to 2006 [4]. As part of this larger study, they reported finding 3.8M unique IP addresses in Wikipedia edits over this nearly six-year span. By contrast, our work spans over two decades, and examines primarily IPv6 addresses, which were not widely logged by Wikimedia sites until after 2012 (§4).

Finally, Zander et al. extracted IPv4 addresses from Wikipedia edit logs over the three-year period from 2011 to 2014 [44]. They used the IPv4 addresses they obtained to improve insights into IPv4 address space exhaustion beyond the visibility achieved through active measurement campaigns. We focus exclusively on IPv6 in this work, and our study spans over two decades (2003–2024).

Gathering IPv6 Addresses. This work seeks to gather a large corpus of IPv6 addresses, which has been the focus of many recent studies [3,8,13,20,26,30,42, 43]. These rely on a range of passive and active measurements, and have resulted in datasets orders of magnitude larger than we are able to obtain by looking only at Wikimedia sites. However, these prior efforts seek to obtain IPv6 addresses that are live and in active use *right now* (primarily to guide future scanning efforts); in contrast, our work provides a *historical* view of IPv6 addresses.

3   Data Collection Methodology

Wikipedia Historical Data. We obtain IPv6 addresses from edits to Wikipedia and other Wikimedia sites. Wikimedia publishes "dumps" of their sites' content: every article's text, links to every picture, and—critically—all edit metadata going back to the sites' inception in 2001. We obtained the December 2024 dumps for all available content sites.

The most common site type from the December 2024 dumps is Wikipedia, the flagship encyclopedia site. There are 394 individual Wikipedia sites that span both languages (e.g., enwiki and dewiki, for the English and German versions of Wikipedia, respectively[1]) and special events (e.g., Wikimania, Wikipedia's annual conference, had its own public wiki from 2005–2018). Wikitionaries, which are user-editable dictionaries, are the second-most common site type, with 195 individual Wiktionary sites spanning many languages. Table 1 in the Appendix lists the number of individual sites per category.

Extracting IP Addresses. After downloading this corpus from Wikimedia, we parse the historical edit data to obtain edits that were authored by an unregistered user. Because Wikimedia's policy is to log and use the IP address of unregistered users, this is equivalent to filtering edits for those authored by an IP address. This process is highly unlikely to result in false positives, as Wikipedia specifically prohibits usernames that are (or even look like) an IP address [40]. We separate these by IP version. In this work, we are primarily interested in IPv6 addresses due to the challenges of obtaining large-scale client IPv6 addresses, but retain IPv4 addresses for comparison purposes in §4.

Contemporaneous as Data. Finally, we also used Routeviews' IPv6 BGP RIB dumps [24]. In order to determine what AS a historical IP address was in at the time that it was logged, we need to be able to look up these IP addresses in BGP data contemporaneous to their appearance in a Wikimedia site. After obtaining the Routeviews data, we looked each IPv6 address in our dataset up in the chronologically closest Routeviews IPv6 RIB dump to obtain an ASN. As Routeviews produces BGP dumps every two hours, the time delta between an IP address's collection and its AS BGP lookup is rarely more than an hour.

Limitations. Our Wikimedia dataset offers a unique view into the history of client IPv6 addresses, but it is not without limitations. First, it is limited to client devices; the IPv6 addresses we extract from the Wikimedia dumps are associated with the user who was submitting the edits to the wiki. It is therefore highly unlikely that our data comprises addresses of web servers, routers, and

---

[1] Wikimedia uses ISO-639 2-letter language codes as prefixes and the site type as suffixes for the full Wikipedia site identifier.

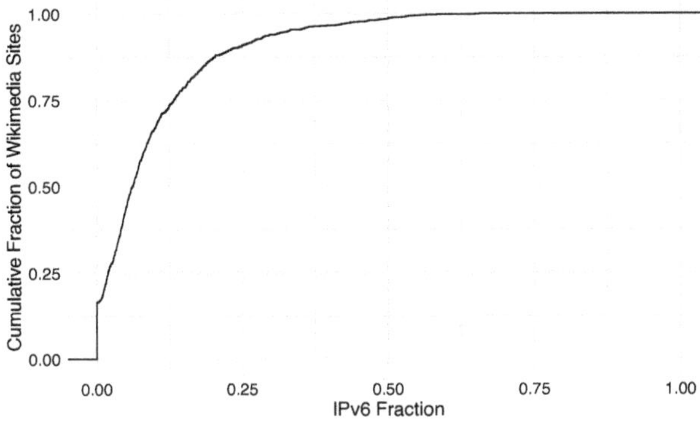

Fig. 2. Fraction of IPv6 addresses of the total number of IP addresses logged per Wikimedia site.

so on. Further, relatively few users make edits to Wikimedia pages, and even fewer make edits without logging into an account. Second, while it has broad reach, Wikipedia is not ubiquitous; several countries block access to Wikipedia (notably, China). This naturally creates bias in our dataset toward regions where Wikipedia is more accessible and popular, as populations without access or desire to visit Wikimedia sites will do less editing. Finally, it is difficult to reason about how representative the dumps' IP addresses are of the entirety of the IPv6 space. However, it is encouraging that the Wikimedia dumps contain hundreds of different language-specific sites, as they likely capture users from the regions that speak those languages.

4   Results

In this section, we analyze the IPv6 client addresses we obtained from the dumps of 1,005 Wikimedia sites, and compare this dataset to other contemporaneous data.

4.1   IPv6 Address Frequency

In parsing the Wikimedia site data dumps and extracting IPv6 addresses from them, we obtained 19,292,487 unique IPv6 addresses. This is approximately $0.18\times$ the number of unique IPv4 addresses used as user identifiers over the same period (107,371,338). The fraction of IPv6 addresses of all IP addresses logged per Wikimedia site varies between 0 and 0.66, though the median value is 0.06. Figure 2 shows the fraction of IPv6 addresses as a CDF of Wikimedia site.

Interestingly, because some Wikimedia sites are highly regional, their proportion of IPv6 addresses indicates regional adoption rates of IPv6. In the tail of the distribution are several sites with only a small number of total addresses,

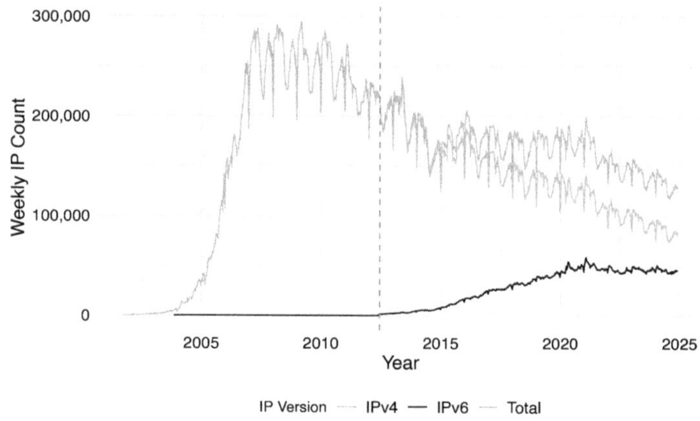

Fig. 3. Unique IP addresses per week by protocol version. Red dashed line is World IPv6 Launch day. (Color figure online)

such as the Assamese Wikiquote site, which has the highest IPv6 fraction of 0.66 (12 IPv4 and 23 IPv6 addresses). However, the Hindi Wikipedia site contains both a large number of total unique IP addresses, with 297,741, and a large fraction of IPv6 addresses, with 0.57 (168,703). The Serbian Wikipedia has an approximately equal number of total IP addresses logged, with 267,377. Conversely, however, it has an extremely low fraction of IPv6 addresses to total IP addresses, at 0.03 (259,118 IPv4 to 8,259).

The significant variation in the proportion of IPv6 addresses across different Wikimedia sites is likely due to the adoption rate of IPv6 in the countries the language-specific wikis are spoken in. RIPE reports an IPv6 adoption rate of 77% in India, where Hindi is primarily spoken, compared with an IPv6 adoption rate of 7% in Serbia, where Serbian is primarily spoken [23].

Not all Wikimedia sites have logged IPv6 addresses. Of the 1,005 Wikimedia for which we have data, only 828 (82%) have at least one IPv6 address logged. There is at least one IPv4 address logged as a user identifier for 993 (99%) Wikimedia sites. The English Wikipedia site contributes half of the total number of unique logged IPv6 addresses; the German, French, Japanese, and Spanish Wikipedia sites contribute more than 5%. Table 2 in the Appendix lists the top Wikimedia sites.

4.2 Temporal Characteristics

IPv6 addresses used as edit identifiers in Wikimedia sites appear between November 2003 to December 2024, the month that we obtained the Wikimedia data. However, IPv6 addresses as edit identifiers remained relatively sparse from Wikimedia's inception through the mid-2010s.

Figure 3 displays the number of unique weekly IP addresses logged by the 1,005 Wikimedia sites since 2001 across both versions of IP. While IPv6 addresses

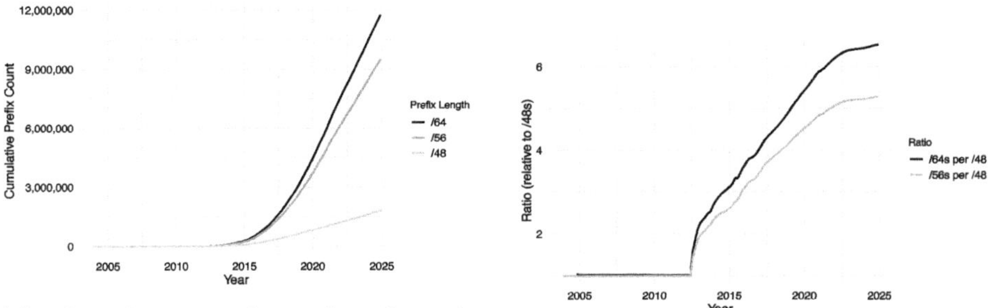

(a)   Cumulative numbers of prefixes observed in the Wikimedia corpus ($N = 19{,}292{,}487$ /128s).

(b) /56 and /64 ratio per /48 over time.

Fig. 4. Prefix observations in the Wikimedia corpus.

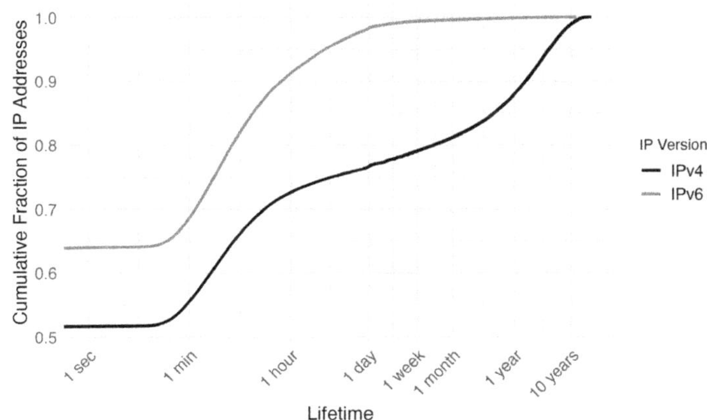

Fig. 5. Lifetimes of the IP addresses logged in the Wikimedia dataset by IP protocol version.

first appear in 2003, IPv4 addresses are first logged in 2001 and dominate throughout the first decade of Wikimedia's existence. IPv6 addresses start to increase shortly after World IPv6 Launch day, which occurred on 6 June 2012 and Wikimedia participated in [11], and is annotated in Fig. 3 as a red, vertical dashed line. At the end of 2024, roughly twice as many IPv4 addresses appeared as IPv6 addresses.

Figure 4(a) depicts the number of cumulative /48, /56, and /64 prefixes observed in the Wikimedia IPv6 corpus over time. While best practice recommends /48 and /56 as prefix delegation sizes to customer end sites, in practice, ISPs may assign /48, /52, /56, /60 and /64 [22]. This helps us estimate the number of unique clients with IPv6 addresses logged in the Wikimedia corpus. While the number of total /48 s is relatively low ($\sim$1.8M), the number of /64 s is approximately 60% of the total number of unique /128 s. This indicates that 40% of Wikimedia IPv6 addresses come from the same /64 networks, which strongly suggests edits were made by users that are part of the same home or campus network, if not the same individuals themselves. Figure 4(b) shows that the number of /56 s and /64 s per /48 increased rapidly through 2022. However, the number of observed subnets per /48 has flattened from 2023 onward, indicating relatively stable number of observed /56 and /64 subnets per /48.

Finally, Fig. 5 displays the length of time between the first and last observations of each IP address in the Wikimedia dataset. Most addresses ($\sim$52% of IPv4 and $\sim$64% of IPv6) are only observed once in the Wikimedia dump, which manifests as a lifetime of 0. Because best practice recommends that IPv6 client addresses be both random and ephemeral [21], IPv6 address lifetimes are significantly shorter than IPv4 address lifetimes. Further, IPv4 addresses may have *many* clients behind a device performing Network Address Translation (NAT), whereas NAT is extraordinarily rare in IPv6, and most IPv6 addresses correspond to a single host.

4.3 AS Contributions

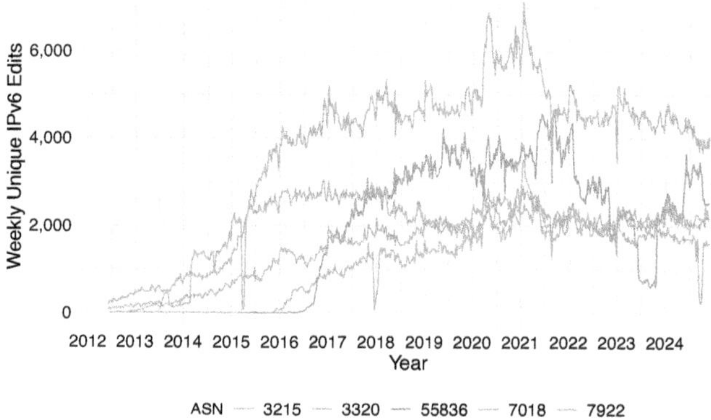

Fig. 6. Number of unique IPv6 addresses per week for the top 5 ASes.

Next, we examine the number of IPv6 addresses from Wikimedia edits according to their AS. Because the AS to which an IPv6 address belongs may change over time as address blocks are reallocated and reassigned, we use contemporaneous BGP RIB data from Routeviews to look up the AS of an IP address in the chronologically-closest RIB dump.

Figure 6 displays the number of unique weekly IPv6 addresses per week observed in the Wikimedia site dumps for each of the top five ASes. While Comcast (AS7922), AT&T (AS7018), and Deutsche Telekom (AS3320) have had IPv6 addresses in the Wikimedia corpus since 2012, other ASes did not deploy IPv6 until later. This is reflected in Fig. 6. For instance, Reliance Jio (AS55836), an Indian telecom provider, did not deploy IPv6 widely until September 2016 [19].

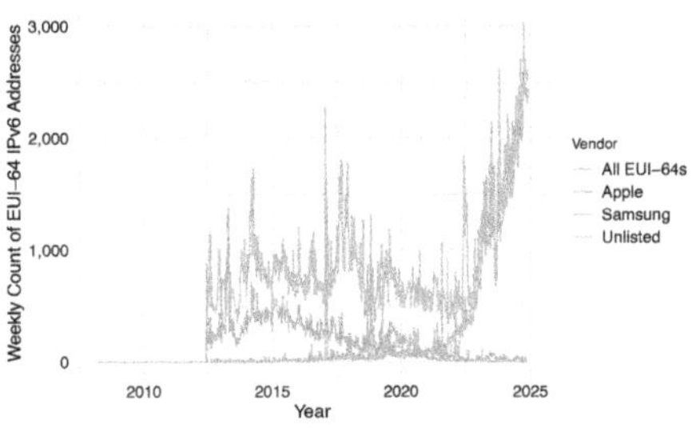

(a) Number of EUI-64 IPv6 addresses per week.

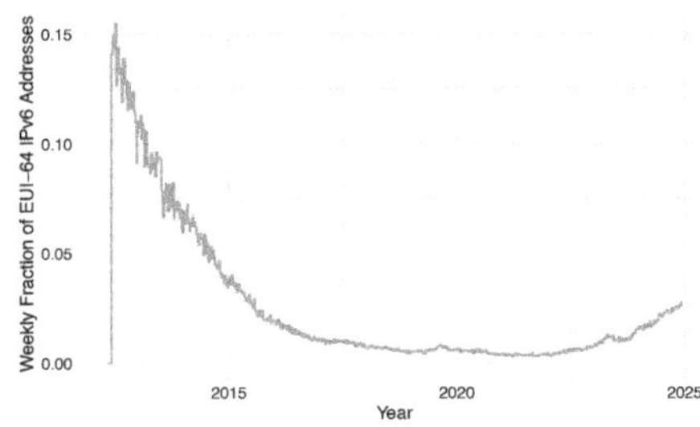

(b) The fraction of EUI-64 IPv6 addresses of all IPv6 addresses per week.

Fig. 7. EUI-64 addresses in the Wikimedia corpus.

This deployment date tracks with AS55836's curve in Fig. 6, and correlates with contemporaneous IPv6 availability measurements, e.g. from APNIC [6].

Finally, note that the Fig. 6 displays sharp decreases for many of the ASes. For instance, Comcast (AS7922) exhibited a large decrease in IPv6 addresses logged in early 2015, while Reliance Jio (AS55836) had an extended dip in IPv6 edits over a three-month period in 2023. While we were unable to definitively link these to publicized network events, we speculate that these decreases in IPv6 edits occurred due to changes in IPv6 address assignment policies or routing by these networks.

4.4 EUI-64 Addresses

Next, we turn to an analysis of the devices manufacturers of the logged Wikimedia IPv6 addresses. To do this, we filter for the subset of IPv6 addresses that are EUI-64. EUI-64 addresses embed the Media Access Control (MAC) address of the device's interface into the lower 64 bits of the IPv6 address[2]; because MAC addresses frequently encode the manufacturer of the device in the MAC address's upper three bytes, we can determine the type of devices unregistered Wikimedia users were using for this subset.

Of the 19M total IPv6 addresses logged, 167,417 (0.87%) of are EUI-64. These EUI-64 IPv6 addresses contain 145,832 unique MAC addresses. Table 3 in the Appendix lists the number of unique MAC addresses by the manufacturer derived from looking up the upper three bytes (the Organizationally Unique Identifier (OUI)) of each MAC address in the public list of IEEE OUI assignments [1]. While prior work has found large numbers of EUI 64 addresses assigned to routers [25] and IoT devices [26,27], EUI-64 addresses in the Wikimedia dataset largely belong to mobile, laptop, and desktop clients. For instance, Apple is the most commonly resolved OUI vendor, along with HP, Intel, ASUS,

---

[2] The MAC address is extended to 64 bits by inserting the bytes `0xfffe` between its third and fourth bytes; the second-least significant bit of the most significant byte of the MAC address (the Universal/Local (U/L) bit) is typically also inverted.

and Samsung. However, more than half (56%) of the EUI-64-derived MAC addresses did not resolve to an IEEE-assigned OUI, a phenomenon also observed by other recent work [26]. This suggests that some devices may be using EUI-64 IPv6 addresses in conjunction with randomized MAC addresses, a common privacy protection employed by mobile devices [12,17,18,35,36].

EUI-64 addresses are well-known to present a privacy risk to users, as they allow long-term tracking of a static identifier [21]. Surprisingly, the number of edits coming from EUI-64 addresses has *increased* over time. Figure 7a depicts the number of EUI-64 IPv6 addresses making edits per week. This is due in large part to the "Unlisted" MAC addresses, whose OUIs are not in the IEEE OUI database. Figure 7a also shows that while Apple historically employed EUI-64 addressing in the mid-2010s, it has largely phased out these types of addresses. However, the prevalence of "Unlisted" MAC addresses has dramatically increased since 2021. The privacy ramifications of using random MAC addresses to form EUI-64 IPv6 addresses are less severe than embedding a device's true hardware MAC address, as random MAC addresses obscure the device manufacturer. Nonetheless, if the random MAC address used in the EUI-64 IPv6 address is sufficiently long-lived (e.g., Android and iOS use a stable, random MAC address on a per-network basis for most Wi-Fi networks [5,7]) the longitudinal tracking threat of EUI-64 IPv6 addresses remains.

Not only have the raw number of EUI-64 IPv6 addresses increased over time, but the *fraction* of IPv6 addresses that are EUI-64 has simultaneously increased. Figure 7b shows that while EUI-64 IPv6 addresses represented less than 1% of the total number of IPv6 addresses seen weekly between 2017 and 2023 (down from a high of ~15%), they have become increasingly prevalent once again, comprising nearly 3% of IPv6 addresses in December 2024.

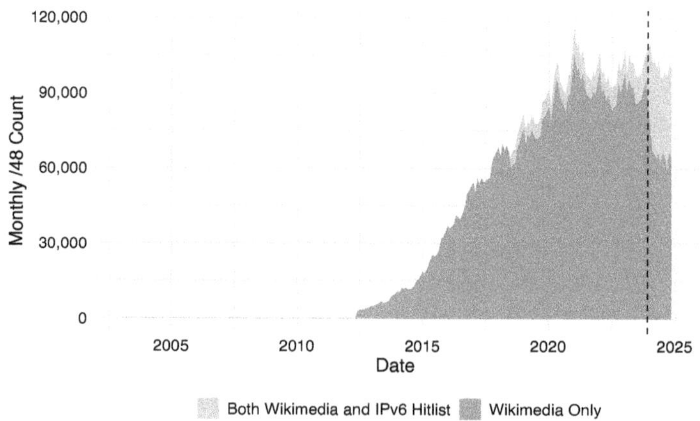

Fig. 8. Number of unique /48 s in the Wikimedia dumps and overlap with the IPv6 Hitlist. The red dashed line at December 2023 is when the IPv6 Hitlist began incorporating data from IPinfo.

4.5   Comparison with the IPv6 Hitlist

Finally, we compare the IPv6 addresses in the Wikimedia corpus to the IPv6 Hitlist's [3, 13, 14] ICMPv6-responsive addresses over the lifetime of the Hitlist. Figure 8 displays the number of unique /48 prefixes contained in the Wikimedia dumps, as well as overlapping /48 s with the IPv6 Hitlist (IPv6 Hitlist-only /48 s omitted for clarity) binned by month. The number of /48 s seen monthly in Wikimedia data reaches ~100k by about 2020. The overlap with the IPv6 Hitlist remains relatively low (~5–10%) until December 2023, when the IPv6 Hitlist began incorporating addresses from IPinfo [2]. From this point forward, the amount of overlap with the IPv6 Hitlist is approximately one-third, indicating that the /48 s coming from IPinfo are likely from customer networks.

This demonstrates that the Wikimedia IPv6 corpus provides a unique source of IPv6 address data that is difficult to obtain from either active measurements or without the broad reach than Wikimedia provides. For applications that rely on obtaining active IPv6 addresses (e.g., IPv6 TGAs), the Wikimedia corpus provides another data source currently missing from state-of-the-art hitlists.

5   Conclusion

Currently, the network measurement community is focused on collecting as many active, in-use IPv6 addresses as possible [3, 8, 26], so as to enable the future of Internet-wide scanning. In this paper, we have instead opted to peer into the past. By using IPv6 addresses encased in the "amber" of decades of edits to Wikipedia and other Wikimedia websites, we showed it is possible to reason about significant changes in IPv6 adoption and policy over decades.

Toward that end, we extracted 19M unique IPv6 addresses over 2003–2024, spanning multiple languages, and ASes around the world. Our historical view of IPv6 shows how critical the World IPv6 Launch Day truly was for IPv6 adoption: prior to it, IPv6 was an almost nonexistent novelty among client devices.

We find that IPv6 addresses tend to have shorter lifetimes than their IPv4 peers. The majority (~64%) of the IPv6 addresses that are logged in Wikimedia edits appear only once. This is likely an artifact of the IPv6 client addressing best practice to choose client addresses randomly and to change them periodically.

We observe IPv6 roll-outs occurring by ASes. When IPv6 service is deployed to customers by ASes, steep upticks in logged IPv6 addresses from those ASes occur. This allows us to retroactively detect when IPv6 is *deployed*, rather than simply *announced* by the AS using BGP.

Finally, our analyses showed how EUI-64 IPv6 addresses—largely considered a privacy violation [26]—had been getting phased out, but have recently started to see a resurgence. This points to randomized MAC addresses being used to build EUI-64 addresses, and confirms trends detected in other recent work.

Acknowledgments. This work was supported by NSF grant CNS-2323193.

Appendix A: Ethical Considerations

Users that wish to make an edit to a Wikimedia site page, but do not wish to create or log into an account, are warned with text that reads "You are not logged in. Your IP address will be publicly visible if you make any edits" (see Fig. 1). Continuing to submit an edit constitutes the consent of the user. Consistent with this statement, Wikimedia site dumps that contain user addresses are publicly available [32].

Due to these facts, the collection of the IP addresses logged by Wikimedia sites does not itself raise ethical issues. As of July 2025, Wikimedia is phasing out the collection of IP addresses from logged-out users due to GDPR and other privacy concerns [39]; as such, we will not release the set of IP addresses we extracted from these dumps separately.

Appendix B: Wikimedia Sites

Table 1. Number of Wikimedia sites by wiki type

Wiki Type	Site Count	Wiki Type	Site Count
Wikipedia	394	Wikimedia	37
Wiktionary	195	Wikinews	36
Wikibooks	121	Wikivoyage	27
Wikiquote	97	Wikiversity	18
Wikisource	80	**Total**	**1,005**

Table 1 lists the number of Wikimedia sites by category; within each category, most of the individual sites are language-specific variations of the site type, although others are for special events or uses (e.g., wikis for the Wikipedia "Wikimania" event.)

Appendix C: IPv6 Addresses by Wikimedia Site

Table 2 lists the top Wikimedia sites by number of unique IPv6 addresses logged in their site's dump.

Table 2. Number of unique logged IPv6 addresses per Wikimedia site; some addresses appear in the logs of multiple sites.

Wiki Site	#IPv6 Addresses	% of All IPv6
English Wikipedia	9,638,421	50
German Wikipedia	1,518,286	7.9
French Wikipedia	1,457,954	7.6
Japanese Wikipedia	1,173,841	6.1
Spanish Wikipedia	1,061,633	5.5
1,000 other	5,123,867	26.6
Total	**19,292,487**	**100**

Table 3. Number of distinct devices per manufacturer as determined from EUI-64 IPv6 address-embedded MAC addresses.

Manufacturer	Count	Manufacturer	Count
Unlisted	82,244	ASUSTek	2,962
Apple	23,168	HP	1,662
Samsung	5,367	Hon Hai Precision	1,246
Intel	4,393	1,141 other	21,631
Dell	3,159	**Total**	**145,832**

Appendix D: EUI-64 IPv6 Addresses

Table 3 lists the number of distinct MAC addresses observed in EUI-64 IPv6 addresses in the Wikimedia data. We use the IEEE OUI database [1] to resolve the MAC addresses to manufacturers. Surprisingly, the most commonly observed manufacturer is "unlisted", meaning that the OUIs did not resolve to any manufacturer.

References

1. IEEE OUI database (2025). http://standards-oui.ieee.org/oui.txt
2. IPInfo.io (2025). https://www.ipinfo.io
3. IPv6 Hitlist Service (2025). https://ipv6hitlist.github.io/
4. Almeida, R.B., Mozafari, B., Cho, J.: On the Evolution of Wikipedia (2007)
5. Android: MAC randomization behavior (2025). https://source.android.com/docs/core/connect/wifi-mac-randomization-behavior
6. APNIC: IPv6 per-country deployment for AS55836: RELIANCEJIO-IN Reliance Jio Infocomm Limited, India (IN) (2025). https://stats.labs.apnic.net/ipv6/AS55836?c=IN&p=1&v=1&w=30&x=1
7. Apple: use private Wi-Fi addresses on Apple devices (2025). https://support.apple.com/en-us/102509

8. Beverly, R., Durairajan, R., Plonka, D., Rohrer, J.P.: In the IP of the beholder: strategies for active IPv6 topology discovery. In: ACM Internet Measurement Conference (IMC) (2018)
9. Cui, T., Gou, G., Xiong, G.: 6GCVAE: gated convolutional variational autoencoder for IPv6 target generation. In: Lauw, H.W., Wong, R.C.-W., Ntoulas, A., Lim, E.-P., Ng, S.-K., Pan, S.J. (eds.) PAKDD 2020. LNCS (LNAI), vol. 12084, pp. 609–622. Springer, Cham (2020). https://doi.org/10.1007/978-3-030-47426-3_47
10. Cui, T., Xiong, G., Gou, G., Shi, J., Xia, W.: 6VecLM: language modeling in vector space for IPv6 target generation. In: European Conference on Machine Learning and Principles and Practice of Knowledge Discovery in Databases (ECML PKDD) (2020)
11. Erik Möller: IPv6 initiative/2012 IPv6 day announcement (2012). https://meta.wikimedia.org/wiki/IPv6_initiative/2012_IPv6_Day_announcement
12. Fenske, E., Brown, D., Martin, J., Mayberry, T., Ryan, P., Rye, E.C.: Three Years Later: a study of MAC address randomization in mobile devices and when it succeeds. In: Privacy Enhancing Technologies Symposium (PETS) (2021)
13. Gasser, O., et al.: Clusters in the expanse: understanding and unbiasing IPv6 hitlists. In: ACM Internet Measurement Conference (IMC) (2018)
14. Gasser, O., Scheitle, Q., Gebhard, S., Carle, G.: Scanning the IPv6 Internet: towards a comprehensive hitlist. CoRR **abs/1607.05179** (2016). http://arxiv.org/abs/1607.05179
15. Hou, B., Cai, Z., Wu, K., Yang, T., Zhou, T.: 6Scan: A High-Efficiency Dynamic Internet-Wide IPv6 Scanner With Regional Encoding. Networking, IEEE/ACM Transactions on (2023)
16. Kiesel, J., Potthast, M., Hagen, M., Stein, B.: Spatio-Temporal Analysis of Reverted Wikipedia Edits (2017)
17. Martin, J., et al.: A study of MAC address randomization in mobile devices and when it fails (2017)
18. Matte, C., Cunche, M., Rousseau, F., Vanhoef, M.: Defeating MAC address randomization through timing attacks. In: ACM Conference on Security and Privacy in Wireless and Mobile Networks (WiSec) (2016)
19. Molay Ghosh: Reliance Jio boosts India past 20% IPv6 capability (2017). https://blog.apnic.net/2017/02/07/reliance-jio-boosts-india-past-20-ipv6-capability/
20. Murdock, A., Li, F., Bramsen, P., Durumeric, Z., Paxson, V.: Target generation for internet-wide IPv6 scanning. In: ACM Internet Measurement Conference (IMC) (2017)
21. Narten, T., Draves, R., Krishnan, S.: Privacy Extensions for stateless address autoconfiguration in IPv6. RFC 4941 (Draft Standard) (2007). https://doi.org/10.17487/RFC4941, https://www.rfc-editor.org/rfc/rfc4941.txt
22. RIPE: best current operational practice for operators: IPv6 prefix assignment for end-users - persistent vs non-persistent, and what size to choose (2017). https://www.ripe.net/publications/docs/ripe-690
23. RIPE: Use of IPv6 for World (2025). https://stats.labs.apnic.net/ipv6/XA
24. Routeviews: university of Oregon route views project (2025). https://www.routeviews.org/routeviews/
25. Rye, E., Beverly, R., claffy, k.: Follow the scent: defeating IPv6 prefix rotation privacy. In: ACM Internet Measurement Conference (IMC) (2021)
26. Rye, E., Levin, D.: IPv6 hitlists at scale: be careful what you wish For. In: ACM SIGCOMM (2023)
27. Saidi, S.J., Gasser, O., Smaragdakis, G.: One bad apple can spoil your IPv6 privacy (2022)

28. Shen, Z., Chen, P., Xie, Y., Chen, C., Zhang, Y., Yang, G.: 6Trace: an effective method for active IPv6 topology discovery. MDPI Electr. (2025)
29. Song, G., et al.: DET: Enabling Efficient Probing of IPv6 Active Addresses. Networking, IEEE/ACM Transactions on (2022)
30. Steger, L., Kuang, L., Zirngibl, J., Carle, G., Gasser, O.: Target Acquired? Evaluating target generation algorithms for IPv6 (2023)
31. Sun, X., Dang, F., Yang, Z., Jin, X., Li, J., Liu, Y.: 6Loda: pattern filtering and ensemble learning for IPv6 target generation and scanning. In: IEEE Conference on Computer Communications (INFOCOM) (2025)
32. The Wikimedia Foundation: Wikimedia (2025). https://www.wikimedia.org/
33. The Wikimedia Foundation: Wikimedia Downloads (2025). https://dumps. wikimedia.org/
34. Tran, C., Champion, K., Forte, A., Hill, B.M., Greenstadt, R.: Are Anonymity-Seekers Just Like Everybody Else? IEEE Symposium on Security and Privacy, An analysis of contributions to Wikipedia from Tor. In (2020)
35. Uras, M., Ferrara, E., Cossu, R., Liotta, A., Atzori, L.: MAC address de-randomization for WIFI device counting: combining temporal-and content-based fingerprints. Comput. Netw. (2022)
36. Vanhoef, M., Matte, C., Cunche, M., Cardoso, L.S., Piessens, F.: Why MAC Address Randomization is not Enough: an Analysis of Wi-Fi Network Discovery Mechanisms (2016)
37. Voss, J.: Measuring Wikipedia. In: International Conference of the International Society for Scientometrics and Informetrics (ISSI) (2005)
38. West, A.G., Kannan, S., Lee, I.: Detecting Wikipedia vandalism via Spatio-temporal analysis of revision metadata? In: European Workshop on Systems Security (2010)
39. Wikipedia: trust and safety product/temporary accounts (2025). https://www. mediawiki.org/wiki/Trust_and_Safety_Product/Temporary_Accounts
40. Wikipedia: Username policy (2025). https://en.wikipedia.org/wiki/Wikipedia: Username_policy
41. Wikipedia: The Free Encyclopedia: Wikipedia:Wikipedians (2025). https://en. wikipedia.org/wiki/Wikipedia:Wikipedians
42. Williams, G., et al.: 6Sense: Internet-wide Ipv6 scanning and its security applications. In: USENIX Security Symposium (2024)
43. Williams, G., Pearce, P.: Seeds of Scanning: exploring the effects of datasets, methods, and metrics on Ipv6 internet scanning. In: ACM Internet Measurement Conference (IMC) (2024)
44. Zander, S., Andrew, L.L., Armitage, G.: Capturing ghosts: predicting the used IPv4 space by inferring unobserved addresses. In: ACM Internet Measurement Conference (IMC) (2014)

A Microscopic View of Congestion Control Behavior in Video Conferencing Applications

Nathaniel Cherian[ID], Akhil Prasad[ID], and Sonia Fahmy[✉][ID]

Purdue University, West Lafayette, IN, USA
{cheriann,prasad67,fahmy}@purdue.edu

Abstract. Video Conferencing Applications (VCAs) employ real-time congestion (rate) control algorithms on top of UDP. In this paper, we take an in-depth look at the congestion control behavior of four proprietary VCAs: Zoom, Microsoft Teams, Google Meet, and Cisco Webex. We compare their startup phases, bandwidth probing behaviors, and reactions to packet delays and drops. We uncover previously-unknown bandwidth estimation strategies, and tradeoffs in how quickly they react to available bandwidth changes. Our study is based on over 130 h of VCA traffic data collected under diverse network conditions and two buffer sizes, and annotated with sending rate, buffer occupancy, packet drop, and several user Quality of Experience (QoE) metrics. Our dataset is publicly available to support further research in understanding VCA performance (https://www.cs.purdue.edu/homes/fahmy/datasets/VCAPurdue/).

1 Introduction

Video Conferencing Applications (VCAs) have become key communication methods, with Zoom, Teams, Meet, and Webex being some of the most popular. Understanding these applications in depth is important for application designers, researchers, operators, and policy makers. VCAs use a real-time rate (congestion) controller, media encoder, and packet pacer on top of UDP. The congestion controller monitors network conditions to set a target bitrate for the video encoder. This rate is calculated to optimize user Quality of Experience (QoE) without negatively impacting other traffic sharing the network.

While there has been significant prior work showing differences in the way VCAs consume bandwidth [18,32], react to changing network conditions [17,25], and compete with other applications [18], that work primarily takes a macroscopic view. In this work, we investigate the *microscopic* behavior of congestion control of popular proprietary VCAs from multiple dimensions (startup phase, probing for available bandwidth, reaction to packet delay and loss) to demystify their designs and evaluate their efficacy. We aim to understand differences

N. Cherian and A. Prasad—Equal contribution.

© The Author(s), under exclusive license to Springer Nature Switzerland AG 2026
S. Ferlin-Reiter et al. (Eds.): PAM 2026, LNCS 16477, pp. 152–167, 2026.
https://doi.org/10.1007/978-3-032-18268-5_7

among VCA congestion control behaviors, which are due to intentional design choices and insights gained through iterative closed-source development.

Our primary focus is on investigating the reaction of a VCA congestion controller to available bandwidth changes. The two primary triggers for the congestion controller are packet delay and loss. Unlike prior work which uses delay and loss emulation, e.g., [17,18], and inspired by prior work on TCP congestion control fingerprinting [20,30], we precisely control and observe a queue (switch buffer) on the path between the VCA sender and receiver, in order to understand reactions to packet delay and loss at a microscopic level. A large buffer allows "bufferbloat" [8] and increases delay, whereas a small buffer triggers packet drops/loss. While our experiments may not always reflect real-world (in the wild) conditions, *our aim is to investigate the way that proprietary VCAs implement congestion control.* This is most effectively accomplished in a partially controlled setting where we create conditions that enable us to isolate the ways in which VCAs respond to specific events.

VCAs will undoubtedly evolve over time, but our goal is to aid researchers, designers, and operators in explaining behaviors of VCAs, and learning how network policies, such as the choice of buffer size, may impact the QoE of a particular VCA, e.g., because of the manner in which it probes for bandwidth or reacts to packet loss. Our ultimate goal is to aid designers of new algorithms that control real-time media transmission, especially in nascent fields such as eXtended Reality (XR) with stringent latency demands and severe consequences for QoE degradation (e.g., cyber sickness) [7].

The contribution of this paper is two-fold: **(1)** We compare four popular VCAs and explain aspects of their congestion control behavior and QoE. Specifically, we consider their startup phases (§4.1), reactions to bandwidth increase (§4.2), and reactions to latency and packet loss events (§4.3) under different scenarios of buffer sizes, bandwidth changes, and background traffic (§3), and **(2)** We uncover previously unknown VCA strategies, including bandwidth estimation and tradeoffs in responsiveness to changes. For instance, we find that Teams and Meet quickly react to changes but can over-correct. Teams may exhibit oscillations, whereas Zoom's reaction is threshold-based. To the best of our knowledge, our findings (summarized in Table 1) have not been previously reported in the literature, except for Zoom probing for bandwidth increase (findings Z2 and Z3) [6,9].

2   Related Work

A number of studies aim to understand and/or reverse engineer VCAs, starting with studies of Skype conducted back in 2004 [1]. This topic gained renewed attention after the COVID-19 pandemic [4,5,9,10,17–19,25].

Perhaps the closest to our work among these studies is the work by MacMillan et al. [18] and by Lee et al. [17]. MacMillan et al. [18] measured three popular VCAs (Zoom, Meet, Teams) to understand their resource requirements and fairness to other applications in different network settings and user modalities. They

Table 1. Summary of key findings. Table 3 as well as the section (and figure/table) noted in the last column below give supporting evidence.

VCA	Scenario	Finding	Refer to
Zoom	Startup	(Z1) Packets with no useful content sent before media transfer.	§4.1
	Probing	(Z2) Canary packets simulate higher rate.	§4.2
	Probing	(Z3) Staircase pattern while probing.	§4.2
	Reaction to Delay	(Z4) Waits for delay threshold; stops video.	§4.3, Fig. 3
	Reaction to Loss	(Z5) Loss increases sending rate; triggers on/off cycling.	§4.3, Fig. 3
Teams	Startup	(T1) Media transfer starts immediately.	§4.1
	Constant Bandwidth	(T2) Oscillations lead to freezing; no packet pacing.	§4.3, Fig. 2, Tab. 4
	Reaction to Delay	(T3) Reacts promptly; temporary over-correction.	§4.3, Fig. 3
Meet	Startup	(M1) Uses packet bursts for bandwidth estimation.	§4.1
	Reaction to Delay	(M2) Reacts promptly; temporary over-correction.	§4.3, Fig. 3
	Contention with TCP	(M3) Performs poorly with CUBIC background.	§4.3, Fig. 2
Webex	Startup	(W1) Media transfer starts immediately.	§4.1
	Constant Bandwidth	(W2) Consistently begins sending at 5 Mbps.	§4.1

attribute differences among bandwidth utilization to differences in proprietary congestion control algorithms, but do not investigate congestion control in depth. They only consider QoE for Meet and Teams (browser). Lee et al. [17] infer rate control and video quality adaptation mechanisms of commercial VCAs. They estimate parameters for WebRTC that could mimic a target VCA.

These prior studies emulated network conditions such as increased delay and random loss using tools such as netem [11]. However, we posit that this is not ideal for studying VCA behavior *at the microscopic level*. Precise control over and monitoring of a bottleneck queue enables uncovering new findings such as those listed in Table 1, with 11 out of the 13 key findings not previously reported in the literature to the best of our knowledge.

A number of studies explore other aspects of VCAs and are orthogonal to our work. Sander et al. [25] study Zoom's reaction to queue management and fairness with TCP. Michel et al. [19] infer Zoom's performance from packet traces. He et al. [9] show that congestion and video controllers used in proprietary VCAs make it difficult to estimate QoE. He et al. [10] propose new QoE metrics for VCAs that prioritize interactivity. Zhang et al. [32] investigate how Meet, Zoom, and Webex allocate bandwidth among media sources. Although related, these studies do not specifically focus on the details of VCA congestion control nor control and observe a bottleneck buffer size and link capacity.

3   Goals and Methodology

Goals: Limiting packet loss and reducing delay are important for user QoE. We treat closed-source VCA congestion control as a black-box where the input signals are the observed loss and delay and the output is a change in sending rate. We control both input signals by modifying a bottleneck buffer size. A large buffer size (e.g., 1024 packets) allows bufferbloat and high end-to-end delay.

Conversely, a small buffer size (e.g., 16 packets) implies that a change in VCA sending rate is likely due to packet loss as a consequence of buffer overflow. Observing VCAs and buffer occupancy in these two different environments (small buffer, large buffer) isolates the triggers for changing the sending rate of VCAs and aids us in characterizing how VCAs react to queuing delays and packet loss.

Experimental Setup: We conducted our experiments with the Windows 11 versions of four VCAs: Cisco Webex, Google Meet, Microsoft Teams, and Zoom. We use Zoom Version: 6.4.3 (63669), Microsoft Teams Version: 25072.1611.3570. 1995, Cisco Webex Version: 45.4.0.3215, and Chrome Version: 135.0.7049.115.

Our experimental setup is shown in Fig. 1 with settings listed in Table 2. We use two testbeds with nearly identical hardware (to collect experimental data concurrently). Both the VCA senders and receivers are connected to our campus network, but we confirmed that none of the VCAs used peer-to-peer transmission between the sender and receiver by examining packet traces. The receiver is configured to route the VCA traffic through a switch that we control. To clearly understand and isolate VCA reactions, we use the simplest scenario where we only measure unidirectional traffic from the VCA client. Also for simplicity, all devices in our testbed use wired connections, and we do not emulate additional propagation delays. We synchronize all our devices with NTP servers to mitigate clock drift. We automated our experiments with PyAutoGUI [23].

We use a BESS software switch [2] with a specified buffer size to study the effect of packet delay and loss on congestion control. We observe the BESS buffer occupancy, packet drops, sending rate (throughput), and packet inter-arrival times by capturing traffic before queuing. These metrics, combined with the Quality of Experience (QoE) measurement described in Sect. 3, capture VCA reactions to changes in network conditions. We measure network and VCA data at every packet enqueue event.

As discussed earlier, our goal is *not* to recreate realistic network conditions, but to isolate key characteristics of congestion control algorithms. We therefore use BESS to create five types of network conditions: constant bandwidth (link

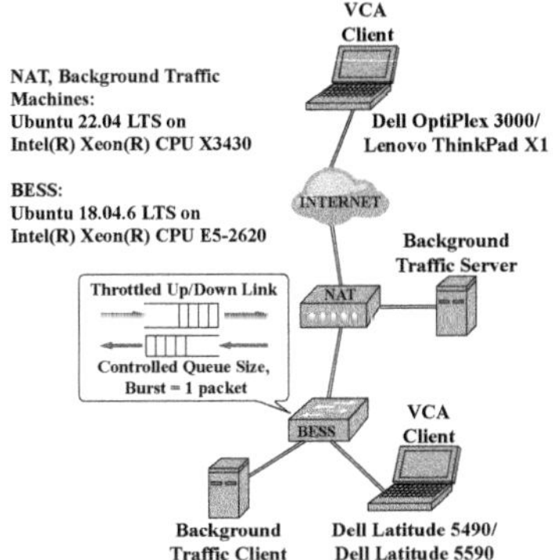

Fig. 1. Experimental testbed.

Table 2. Experimental settings.

Component	Settings
Buffer size	16, 64, 128, 1024 packets
Constant bandwidth (link rate)	0.25, 0.5 − 1.5 (100 Kbps intervals), 2.0, 2.5, 5, 10 Mbps for ∼150s
Bandwidth increase	0.5 → 2.5, 5 and 1 → 5, 10 Mbps
Bandwidth decrease	2.5, 5 → 0.5 and 5, 10 → 1 Mbps
Background UDP	3, 4, 5, 10 Mbps with 2.5, 5, 10, 15, 30, 60, 60, 100 s bursts
Background TCP	1, 4 MB TCP CUBIC, BBR starts after 2 minutes

rate or capacity), increasing bandwidth, decreasing bandwidth, and constant bandwidth with UDP or with TCP background traffic (Table 2). Our parameter choices are based on the bandwidth utilization values observed by MacMillan et al. [18]. We experimented with several different buffer sizes, but show results with buffer sizes of 16 packets and 1024 packets to highlight contrasting effects where small buffers induce packet drops and large buffers lead to high delay. We run each VCA with a particular link bandwidth (i.e., link rate or capacity) value for 120 s before changing it in the increasing and decreasing bandwidth experiments. We repeat each configuration five times. Our experiments spanned 21 days in March and April 2025, with data collection occurring continuously throughout the day and night, yielding approximately 2400 experiments, and totaling over 130 h of annotated data.

Estimating QoE Metrics: We adopt existing techniques for estimating QoE metrics [17] by placing a QR code occupying $300{\times}300$ pixels of the screen space ($1920{\times}1080$ pixels) that indicates the frame number of a talking head video [31] using a virtual camera on our sender device. We use a second QR code on the sender's virtual camera that contains the real time. On the receiver side, we pin and maximize the sender's video and take a screen recording at full 1920×1080 resolution at 60 frames per second. In addition to the frame number and sender timestamp QR code that are being recorded, we introduce a third QR code at this recording that contains the receiver's real time.

We estimate the frames-per-second (FPS), resolution, and end-to-end latency. We first extract the frame-number QR code from each frame of the receiver's screen recording. We count the number of unique frame numbers in each second to be the FPS. We compute the VIF score [27] of each frame to assess frame quality. VIF is a component of the VMAF metric that we found to highly correlate with SSIM (with a Pearson coefficient of 0.99). We do not use VMAF because the video is continuously looped at the VCA client and lacks a reference video for comparison. We edited our videos to black-out extraneous figures in the recording such as the QR codes or other buttons/pop-ups that the VCA introduces. To ensure fair comparison, we normalize our raw VIF scores using the 5th and 95th percentile VIF scores across *all* our experiments. Finally, we estimate the end-to-end latency by taking the difference between the value of the sender and receiver timestamp QR code. We synchronize our devices with campus timeservers every 30 min to mitigate the consequences of clock drift among the sender and receiver.

We note that Chrome provides tools to monitor the QoE of WebRTC streams. We did not use these tools because our method of taking a recording of the screen captures the QoE as seen by the user. Additionally, our method also applies to non-browser versions.

4   Results

We organize our results around three key areas: startup, active probing for available bandwidth increase, and reactions to congestion events. Tables 3 and 4 give our overall numerical results.

In Table 3, we compute reaction times T_i and T_d by observing the sending rates post a bandwidth increase/decrease event. We calculate a threshold defined as the 90th percentile of the gradient (positive for T_i, negative for T_d). We then find the first instance where the magnitude of the gradient exceeds this threshold. Similarly, we find how long a VCA took to stabilize after a bandwidth reduction to compute $T_{s,16}$ and $T_{s,1024}$. We first estimate the stable sending rate by taking the mean of the rate 60 s after a bandwidth reduction. We then identify (over a rolling window) the first two-second period where 90% of the sending rate samples in 100 ms bins are within a standard deviation of the previously calculated stable sending rate. All values in the tables represent the mean and standard deviation across experiments after excluding data points lying more than two standard deviations from the mean (removing $\sim 5\%$ of the data).

In the remainder of this section, we discuss our most interesting observations, but we have released the dataset from the complete set of experimental scenarios described in Sect. 3. Additional discussion is given in the Appendix.

Table 3. D = Bytes sent between first packet and first video packet. B = Bandwidth estimation accuracy (difference between rate in first 200 ms and 1 s) for constant bandwidth experiments. T_i = Time to react to bandwidth increase. R = Rate of increase of sending rate until peak. COV = Coefficient of Variation ($\frac{\sigma}{\mu}$) of normalized sending rate for constant bandwidth cases. T_d = Time to react to bandwidth decrease (1024-packet buffer). $T_{s,1024}$ = Time to stabilization (1024-packet buffer). $T_{s,16}$ = Time to stabilization in (16-packet buffer).

	Startup		Probing		Const. Bw. COV	Congestion		
VCA	$\mathbf{D}$ (KB)	$\mathbf{B}$ (Mbps)	$\mathbf{T_i}$ (s)	$\mathbf{R}$ (Kbps/s)		$\mathbf{T_d}$ (s)	$\mathbf{T_{s,16}}$ (s)	$\mathbf{T_{s,1024}}$ (s)
Zoom	1137.92 ± 97.68	0.36 ± 0.23	102.31 ± 27.06	33.04 ± 10.24	0.39 ± 0.06	11.72 ± 6.10	28.46 ± 2.30	94.25 ± 22.42
Teams	29.62 ± 2.73	1.39 ± 0.92	11.31 ± 18.25	64.69 ± 44.39	0.92 ± 0.11	0.67 ± 0.30	7.69 ± 4.03	17.81 ± 7.48
Meet	102.26 ± 41.67	0.48 ± 0.43	13.32 ± 12.21	11.39 ± 14.69	0.56 ± 0.03	0.60 ± 0.25	8.98 ± 3.52	20.36 ± 8.68
Webex	49.34 ± 16.70	3.13 ± 0.86	64.10 ± 29.01	41.60 ± 33.31	1.28 ± 0.24	8.29 ± 5.15	10.74 ± 1.77	12.37 ± 5.95

4.1   Startup

Findings Z1, T1, M1, W1, W2: We observe key differences in the startup behaviors of VCAs. Meet and Zoom use a pre-startup data stream to (presumably) estimate bandwidth or other network conditions. In contrast, Teams and Webex begin sending data at a fixed rate. This observation is based on Table 3 Column D. The column shows the number of bytes that are sent by each VCA

Table 4. Coefficient of Variation (COV) of VCA sending rate, number of freeze events per min., freeze duration in sec./min. (based on WebRTC standard for a freeze [29]), frames per sec., and frame ViF score in the constant bandwidth case for buffer sizes of 16 and 1024 packets. Best values are green, worst red.

Size	Metric	Zoom	Teams	Meet	Webex
16	COV	0.35±0.09	0.92±0.10	0.57±0.03	1.52±0.17
	# Freezes / Min	3.13±4.39	7.39±4.39	1.68±3.96	6.36±4.87
	Freeze Time / Min	2.33±6.25	3.47±2.91	0.66±2.06	11.66±10.92
	FPS	21.13±4.70	19.73±3.37	27.40±1.46	8.16±3.92
	ViF	0.75±0.05	0.56±0.06	0.57±0.07	0.72±0.05
1024	COV	0.41±0.05	0.93±0.12	0.56±0.3	1.04±0.33
	# Freezes / Min	2.87±3.72	13.93±7.77	1.35±3.85	5.64±3.68
	Freeze Time / Min	1.31±2.29	5.72±3.43	0.49±1.80	14.55±11.13
	FPS	19.92±4.45	18.96±4.23	27.44±1.47	8.07±3.99
	ViF	0.74±0.05	0.59±0.05	0.57±0.07	0.73±0.04

before the first video packet. We see that Teams and Webex each send less than 50 KB whereas Zoom sends over 1 MB of data.

A burst of small packets is always sent by Meet upon joining a meeting. These are RTP packets that have a unique type and a consistent synchronization source (SSRC) of 0x0. They are sent in bursts with under $\sim 15\mu s$ inter-arrival time. The number of bursts increases with growing link bandwidth. Upon completion, there is a 1.57±0.45 s pause before the data frames are observed. We suspect that this is an indication that Meet uses a variation of one of the available bandwidth estimation techniques, e.g., [13, 24, 28]. These techniques send a sequence of probes, such as packet pairs [16], packet trains [14], or "chirps" [24], and monitor packet inter-arrival times at the receiver.

Compared to Meet, which sends a burst of a few packets before starting data transmission, Zoom begins by sending a large number of packets that contain a single repeated character at a fixed bitrate. We observe that the average bitrate of this startup probe is 1.146 ± 0.032 Mbps over an interval of 0.704 ± 0.40 seconds. After this initial probe, the data flow is silent for an average of 1.13 seconds before resuming data transmission. Zoom does not reduce this probing sending rate in low link bandwidth conditions. This leads to 3× higher latency at the beginning of the video stream from bufferbloat at low link bandwidths.

We examine the difference between the sending rate of Zoom and Meet over the first 200 ms and the average sending rate over the first second (Table 3, Column B). We see that Zoom and Meet begin sending frames close to their target sending rates whereas Teams and Webex are further off, especially Webex. We observe that Webex consistently begins sending at a fixed rate of 5 Mbps (illustrated in Fig. 6 in the appendix). This confirms that Zoom and Meet are likely estimating available bandwidth, allowing them to fully utilize the link from the beginning of the video transmission without costly disruptions to QoE.

4.2   Probing for Bandwidth Increase

Findings Z2, Z3: We explore how VCAs probe for newly available bandwidth, and observe that both Zoom and Meet exhibit probing-like behavior throughout a VCA session. Probing strategies include (1) using "canary" packets to simulate a higher sending rate, and (2) using a short burst of packets to estimate bandwidth [13,21].

Zoom probes by increasing the sending rate of its control flow in steps. As it does during the startup phase, Zoom sends large packets of repeated characters through a separate flow to increase the sending rate for a period of time. If the higher sending rate of this flow does not lead to congestion, the system simultaneously increases the data flow and reduces the probing flow to make use of the available bandwidth. This adjustment also occurs at the beginning of a meeting to achieve the target sending rate. If successful, Zoom continues to probe creating a staircase pattern, as also observed in prior work [10]. The technique is effective in estimating available bandwidth, but when the probe exceeds available bandwidth, it may have negative consequences on QoE, e.g., causing a freeze. More details are given in Appendix B.

In contrast, Meet employs RTP packets (of type 99) for periodic probing. Each probe includes multiple bursts. A burst comprises 2–4 packets separated by $\sim 10\mu s$.

We now study reactions to available bandwidth increase. Table 3 Column T_i shows the average time elapsed after a bandwidth increase before a VCA reacts. We see that Teams and Meet react much faster than Zoom and Webex which take significantly longer to react. We also list the rate at which VCAs increase their sending rates upon reacting until the sending rate peaks in Table 3 Column R. We observe that Meet has the most conservative increase in sending rate, potentially underutilizing the link, whereas Teams increases its sending rate almost $6\times$ as fast. We note that prior work [22] has examined a similar parameter that controls additive increase in the case of GCC [3].

4.3   Reaction to Congestion

We now examine performance in three scenarios (constant bandwidth, high delay, packet loss) to understand the reaction of VCAs to congestion.

Constant Bandwidth (Finding T2): We first examine the constant bandwidth case. Figure 2 (left) shows the distributions of buffer utilization and packet drops. Teams exhibits frequent buffer saturation and packet drops, indicative of persistent link overuse, whereas Meet rarely experiences queue buildup or packet loss. Frequent buffer overuse may be the result of Team's bursty packet transmission. When a frame is packetized, there is no pacing in the transmission as the frame's packets are sent back to back. We observe that 87.06% of Team's packets had inter-arrival times (IATs) below 0.1 ms in contrast to only 11.77% for Meet. This burstiness risks triggering packet drops with small buffers, and can interfere with time-sensitive audio packets in large queue settings. Further discussion is given in Appendix C.

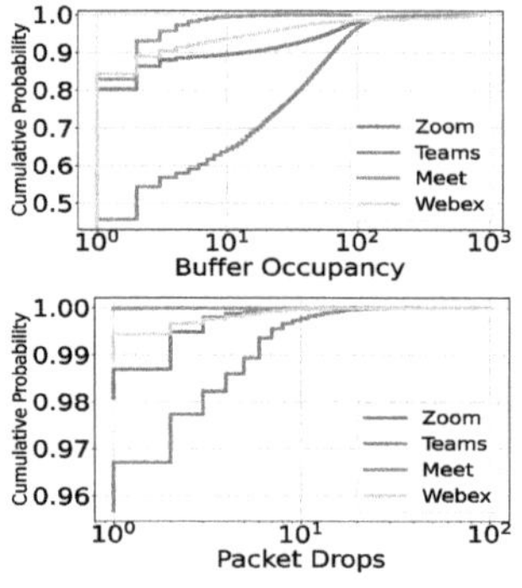

VCA	Size	None	C	B	U (C)	U (B)
Zoom	16	23.55	19.54	14.12	54.47 *	39.06
	1024	23.16	17.84	21.77	35.55	42.79
Teams	16	20.72	0.68	5.23	15.43	36.10
	1024	21.24	11.33	16.60	37.48	52.58 *
Meet	16	26.03	21.95	22.76	44.08	36.76
	1024	26.52	15.42	25.63	27.70	41.11
Webex	16	11.31	0.60	0.95	11.41	23.71
	1024	11.39	8.06	2.75	39.51 *	43.91 *

Fig. 2. (left) CDFs of buffer occupancy and packet drops for constant bandwidth scenarios. (right) Frames per second with and without TCP CUBIC (C) and BBR (B) background traffic for buffer sizes of 16 and 1024 packets. Also shown is the percentage link utilization (U) of VCA traffic. * means a variance > 15%.

A closer inspection of Teams shows that it oscillates around its target sending rate. We quantify the variability using the Coefficient of Variation (COV) of the sending rate. Table 3 indicates that Teams exhibits a higher COV than Zoom and Meet. Teams oscillations manifest as intermittent video freezes caused by packet delay or loss, which we identify following the WebRTC standard [29]: a freeze occurs when the interval between two rendered frames exceeds $max(3 \times AFD, 150\ ms + AFD)$ where AFD is the average frame duration. For each VCA, we compute both the number of freeze events per minute and the total time spent in a frozen state in seconds during each minute. As shown in Table 4, Teams has both a high COV and the highest freeze rate. In large-queue conditions, this gap increases as Teams experiences more than twice as many freezes as other VCAs. Although Teams freezes more frequently than Webex, the duration of freezes in Webex is almost three times longer. Meet maintains low COV values and has the fewest freezes. We also note that the variance in our freeze estimates is relatively high because results were aggregated across all bandwidth conditions (0.5 – 2.5 Mbps). Since all VCAs are evaluated consistently, this does not bias comparisons. Similar oscillatory sending-rate behavior in GCC has been documented by Carlucci et al. [3], but their work is for GCC and does not examine QoE implications.

Reaction to Queuing Delay (Findings T3, M2): We evaluate reaction to queuing delay by configuring a large queue and then reducing the link capacity after two minutes to induce bufferbloat and force VCAs to react to increasing delay without packet drop. Figure 3 gives an example.

Table 3 Column T_d shows the time elapsed between the capacity reduction and the VCA reaction. We observe that delay-gradient based VCAs [3], which Meet appears to be, respond promptly to this increasing delay (under 2 s). This strong reaction to delay also leads to an over-correction in the sending rate in large queue settings. Before stabilizing to the target rate, Meet's sending rate dips 73.03% below its stable target rate. Teams also dips below 51.85% of its stable target rate. Despite these dips, we see that this quick reaction results in the sending rate stabilizing in less than 9 s on average for Meet and Teams (Table 3 Column $T_{s,16}$).

Finding Z4: Zoom takes almost 4× as long to react: it maintains its sending rate until the end-to-end delay hits 2.16 ± 0.55 s before reacting. Therefore, Zoom appears not to react to transient delay increases unless they grow beyond a threshold. To compensate for its delayed reaction, Zoom is forced to drop its sending rate well below the target rate to allow time for the queue to drain. Zoom thus takes almost 3× longer for the sending rate to stabilize compared to Meet and Teams (Table 3, Column $T_{s,1024}$).

Finding M3: Meet's reaction to delay reduces its QoE when competing for bandwidth with loss-based TCP congestion-control that relies on packet drops to begin a multiplicative decrease. We examine how short-lived TCP background traffic competes with each VCA to simulate a real-world example where someone may be browsing the Internet and participating in a video call simultaneously. Figure 2 (right) reports the mean FPS QoE metric under different buffer sizes, and compares scenarios with and without TCP CUBIC and BBR, in order to assess the impact on playback quality. We find that Meet suffers significantly when paired with TCP CUBIC background traffic, with FPS reduced by almost 50% and the lowest link utilization when paired with CUBIC. Further discussion of TCP background traffic can be found in Appendix D.

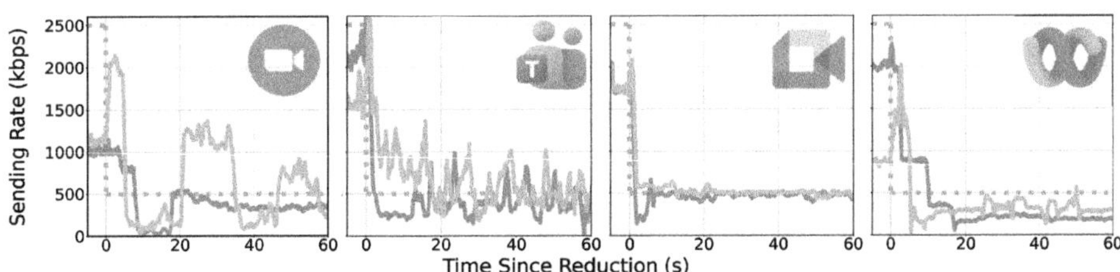

Fig. 3. Reactions to bandwidth reduction from 2.5 Mbps to 0.5 Mbps under a queue of 1024 packets (orange line) and a **queue of 16 packets (blue line)**. Dotted line is the link capacity. Left to right: Zoom, Teams, Meet, Webex. (Color figure online)

Reaction to Packet Drops (Finding Z5): We evaluate reaction to packet drops by reducing the link capacity and using a small queue configuration. Table 3 Column $T_{s,16}$ shows the time between capacity reduction and sending rate stabilization for a queue size of 16 packets. We observe that this time is $2 - 3\times$ greater than the case of a large queue (Column $T_{s,1024}$).

Interestingly, Zoom responds to packet loss with an on/off cycling behavior (Fig. 3). After an initial drop, it increases its sending rate, resulting in further loss. It then sharply reduces the rate below 100 Kbps, effectively "turning off" the flow. Upon resuming, Zoom transmits at approximately half the previous rate and repeats this pattern until convergence. Some packet loss still occurs during each subsequent "on" phase, though less than previously observed. Despite visual artifacts such as screen tearing, Zoom consistently preserved audio continuity, which we manually verified.

5   Conclusions, Limitations, and Future Work

In this paper, we have uncovered contrasting VCA startup and probing behaviors, and key tradeoffs in how VCAs react to available bandwidth changes. Our experimental testbed allows us to study both standalone and in-browser VCAs. We mitigate the impact of changes in network conditions by running each experiment a number of times over the span of multiple weeks. While we tune network parameters to induce a low capacity link – inspired by work on TCP congestion control fingerprinting [20, 30] – we acknowledge that our testbed is not fully controlled since the traffic between the VCA clients traverses a Selective Forwarding Unit (SFU). Consequently, if a congestion event occurs on the sender-SFU or receiver-SFU path, our testbed link may not be the bottleneck.

Since our goal was to understand the rate control of proprietary VCAs, we decided to use the simplest possible setup of a two-party meeting with unidirectional traffic and no induced delay. This simplifies attributing observations to bandwidth changes, rather than interference from reverse traffic or other factors. However, we acknowledge that we cannot generalize observed behaviors to other settings. In our future work, we will study additional scenarios including wireless networks and different client locations. We also plan to study the audio stream, and to correlate sending rates with QoE. With emerging applications such as eXtended Reality having stringent QoE requirements, we believe that real-time congestion control design and evaluation merit further investigation.

Acknowledgments. This work has been supported in part by NSF grant 2212200. We sincerely thank our shepherd Alessandro Finamore and the anonymous reviewers for their insightful feedback, and Adithya Abraham Philip for help with BESS.

A   Ethical Considerations

This work does not raise any ethical issues. We generate a dataset synthetically for the work by conducting our own experiments with commercial VCAs.

B   Zoom Probing

The average sending rate of the probe used by Zoom for experiments with different constant bandwidths is illustrated in Fig. 4. We observe that the size of the buffer influences the probing rate, resulting in increased probing with larger buffer sizes. Zoom probes every 56.63±15.50 s when the buffer size is 16, and 36.97±25.12 s when the buffer size is 1024. This indicates that Zoom is sensitive to packet loss, exhibiting reduced probing frequency and rate with a buffer size of 16 packets.

Figure 5 illustrates how Zoom behaves when the bandwidth is increased from 0.5 Mbps to 2.5 Mbps. We observe a staircase pattern, where the peaks are elevated for a larger buffer size.

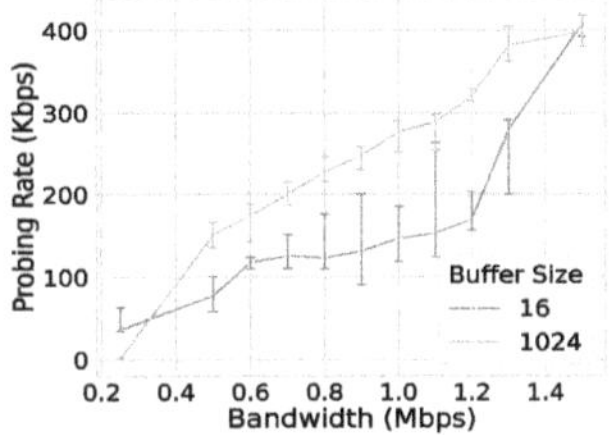
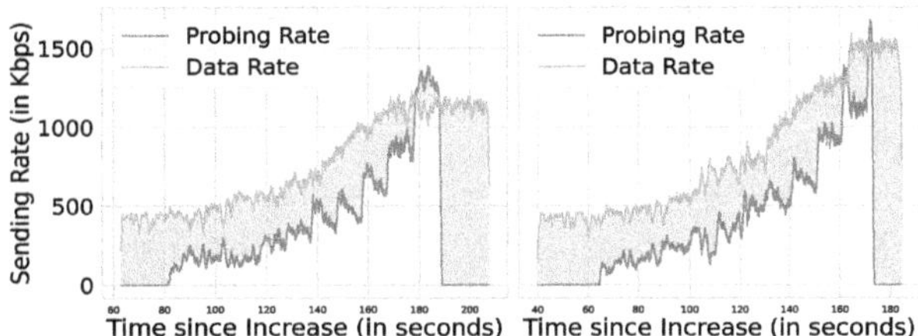

Fig. 4. Sending rate of the probe used by Zoom in constant bandwidth scenarios.

Fig. 5. Zoom probing pattern when bandwidth is increased from 0.5 Mbps to 2.5 Mbps when buffer size is 16 packets (left) and 1024 packets (right).

C   Sending Rate at Different Link Bandwidths

Figure 6 depicts the 90th percentile of the sending rate during the first 20 s of each VCA. The bandwidth of the link we control is varied between 0.25 Mbps and 10 Mbps as given on the x-axis. A VCA that fully utilizes the bandwidth of that link would follow the dashed line, which represents the link bandwidth. From this figure, we observe that Teams may send above the bandwidth of the link we control over the first 20 s. This corroborates our previous observations in Fig. 2 where we see that Teams exhibits higher buffer occupancy and higher packet drops. In contrast, Meet rarely crosses the link bandwidth threshold. Webex maintains a nearly constant sending rate throughout the first 20 s, independent of link capacity. We observe divergence between Zoom with buffer sizes of 16 and 1024. The smaller buffer allows Zoom to more closely match the available bandwidth, whereas the larger buffer leads to undershooting. We attribute this to Zoom's tendency to initially transmit at a fixed rate, which causes high delays under limited link capacities. The resulting queue buildup leads Zoom to reduce its sending rate well below the link capacity until the buffer drains.

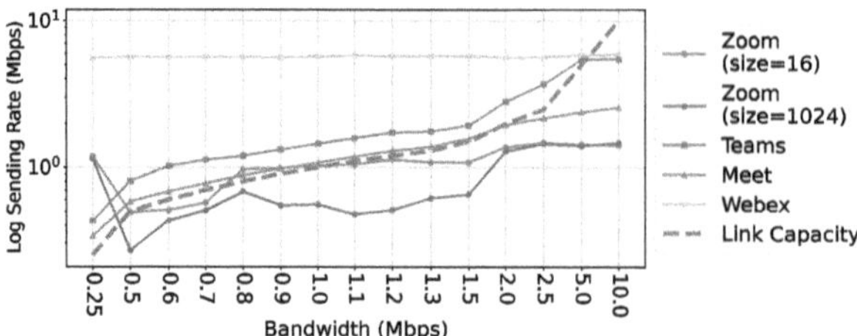 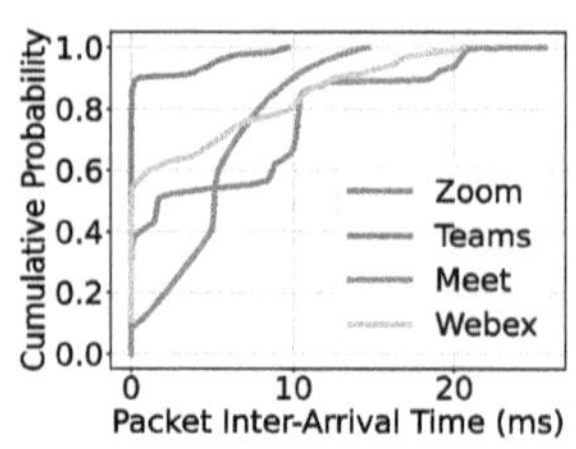

Fig. 6. The 90th percentile of the sending rate (throughput) during the first 20 s of a VCA session, for experiments conducted with different link bandwidths (dashed line).

Fig. 7. CDF of packet inter-arrival times.

Figure 7 depicts a cumulative distribution function of the interarrival times of the packets for each of the VCAs under constant bandwidth conditions. Teams deviates from other VCAs, having most packets arrive within a fraction of a millisecond of each other. This creates queuing delays even in high-bandwidth (10 Mbps) scenarios, despite the 50 ms-binned sending rates remaining below 5 Mbps. Recent work [12] has highlighted the impact of bursty frame transmissions on QoE and proposed measures to mitigate it. SCReAM [15] and GCC [3] both explicitly recommend packet pacing.

D   TCP Background Traffic

Several prior studies [3, 25, 26] have examined the effects of concurrent short-lived TCP background traffic on real-time applications. Figure 2 (right) reports the FPS QoE metric under different buffer sizes, comparing scenarios with and without TCP CUBIC and BBR traffic to assess the impact on playback quality.

In the case of Meet, the minimum FPS occurs with CUBIC background with buffer size 1024. We attribute this to CUBIC's buffer dominance during the slow-start phase until a packet drop occurs. Meet promptly attempts to mitigate this by progressively lowering its transmission rate, yet CUBIC continues sending until a packet drop. For CUBIC with a small buffer size, the FPS remains comparable to other scenarios as packet drop occurs quickly.

For Teams, the lowest FPS cases are at small buffer sizes, contrary to any expectation that a large buffer would introduce queuing delay and force Teams to reduce its sending rate. At small buffer sizes, Teams experiences many drops, leading to frequent video freezes. Teams' difficulty in maintaining a minimal buffer presence is confirmed by the left side of Fig. 2.

Finally, although not listed in the right side of Fig. 2, there exists a 4.66 FPS difference between the 4 MB and 1 MB experiments for Zoom. The corresponding difference for Teams, Webex, and Meet is 3.62, 1.81, and 0.00, respectively, indicating that Zoom is less impacted by small TCP traffic bursts compared to Meet, partially due to Zoom's higher tolerance to queue buildup before reacting.

This echoes the earlier tradeoff discussion regarding immediate reaction to queue buildup versus waiting for a delay threshold to be met.

In small buffer settings with TCP CUBIC, the penultimate rightmost column in the table (right side of Fig. 2) shows that Zoom achieves the highest link utilization among VCAs, with a high variance of 21.82%. Further examination reveals that in low link bandwidth scenarios, characterized by frequent packet drops, Zoom exhibits the on/off cycling behavior described in finding Z5. This behavior is aggressive and chokes out the TCP flow. When the bandwidth is below 2.5 Mbps, Zoom's link utilization jumps to 78.33 ± 9.65.

References

1. Baset, S., Schulzrinne, H.: An analysis of the skype peer-to-peer internet telephony protocol. CoRR, abs/cs/0412017 (2004)
2. BESS. BESS: A Software Switch (2025). https://github.com/NetSys/bess
3. Carlucci, G., De Cicco, L., Holmer, S., Mascolo, S.: Analysis and design of the google congestion control for web real-time communication (webrtc). In: Proceedings of the 7th International Conference on Multimedia Systems, pp. 1–12 (2016)
4. Carofiglio, G., Grassi, G., Loparco, E., Muscariello, L., Papalini, M., Samain, J.: Characterizing the relationship between application QoE and network QoS for real-time services. In: Proceedings of the ACM SIGCOMM 2021 Workshop on Network-Application Integration, NAI'21, pp. 20–25, New York, NY, USA, 2021. Association for Computing Machinery
5. Chang, H., Varvello, M., Hao, F., Mukherjee, S.: Can you see me now? A measurement study of zoom, webex, and meet. In: Proceedings of the 21st ACM Internet Measurement Conference, pp. 216–228 (2021)
6. Chen, P., Qiu, P., Lambda. Liu, Z.: Protocol compliance in popular RTC applications. In: Proceedings of the 2025 ACM Internet Measurement Conference, pp. 294–307 (2025)
7. Cheng, R., Wu, N., Varvello, M., Chai, E., Chen, S., Han, B.: A first look at immersive telepresence on apple vision pro. In: Proceedings of the 2024 ACM on Internet Measurement Conference, pp. 555–562 (2024)
8. Gettys, J., Nichols, K.: Bufferbloat: Dark buffers in the internet: Networks without effective AQM may again be vulnerable to congestion collapse. Queue **9**(11), 40–54 (2011)
9. He, J., Ammar, M., Zegura, E.: A measurement-derived functional model for the interaction between congestion control and QoE in video conferencing. In: Brunstrom, A., Flores, M., Fiore, M. (eds.) Passive and Active Measurement. pp, pp. 129–159. Springer Nature Switzerland, Cham (2023)
10. He, J., Ammar, M., Zegura, E., Halepovic, E., Karagioules, T.: QoE metrics for interactivity in video conferencing applications: definition and evaluation methodology. In: Proceedings of the 15th ACM Multimedia Systems Conference, MMSys '24, page 178–189, New York, NY, USA, 2024. Association for Computing Machinery
11. Hemminger, S.: Network emulation with NetEm. In: Proceedings of the 6th Australia's National Linux Conference (LCA2005) (2005)
12. Huang, X., et al.: Ace: sending burstiness control for high-quality real-time communication. In: Proceedings of the ACM SIGCOMM 2025 Conference, pp. 1182–1198 (2025)

13. Jain, M., Dovrolis, C.: End-to-end available bandwidth: measurement methodology, dynamics, and relation with TCP throughput. IEEE/ACM Trans. Networking **11**(4), 537–549 (2003)
14. Jain, R., Routhier, S.: Packet trains-measurements and a new model for computer network traffic. IEEE J. Sel. A. Commun. **4**(6), 986–995 (2006)
15. Johansson, I.: Self-clocked rate adaptation for conversational video in LTE. In: Proceedings of the 2014 ACM SIGCOMM Workshop on Capacity Sharing Workshop, CSWS '14, pp. 51–56, New York, NY, USA, 2014. Association for Computing Machinery
16. Keshav, S.: A control-theoretic approach to flow control. SIGCOMM Comput. Commun. Rev. **21**(4), 3–15 (1991)
17. Lee, I., Lee, J., Lee, K., Grunwald, D., Ha, S.: Demystifying commercial video conferencing applications. In: Proceedings of the 29th ACM International Conference on Multimedia, MM '21, pp. 3583–3591, New York, NY, USA, (2021). Association for Computing Machinery
18. MacMillan, K., Mangla, T., Saxon, J., Feamster, N.: Measuring the performance and network utilization of popular video conferencing applications. In: Proceedings of the 21st ACM Internet Measurement Conference, IMC '21, pp. 229–244, New York, NY, USA, (2021). Association for Computing Machinery
19. Michel, O., Sengupta, S., Kim, H., Netravali, R., Rexford, J.: Enabling passive measurement of zoom performance in production networks. In: Proceedings of the 22nd ACM Internet Measurement Conference, pp. 244–260 (2022)
20. Mishra, A., Rastogi, L., Joshi, R., Leong, B.: Keeping an eye on congestion control in the wild with nebby. In: Proceedings of the ACM SIGCOMM 2024 Conference, ACM SIGCOMM '24, pp. 136–150, New York, NY, USA, (2024). Association for Computing Machinery
21. Nagy, M., Singh, V., Ott, J., Eggert, L.: Congestion control using FEC for conversational multimedia communication. In: Proceedings of the 5th ACM Multimedia Systems Conference, pp. 191–202 (2014)
22. Prasad, A., Cherian, N., Fahmy, S.: Poster: a case for modeling video conferencing applications. In: Proceedings of the 2025 ACM Internet Measurement Conference, IMC '25, page 1066–1067, New York, NY, USA, (2025). Association for Computing Machinery
23. Python. PyAutoGUI. https://pypi.org/project/PyAutoGUI/
24. Ribeiro, V.J., Riedi, R.H., Baraniuk, R.G., Navratil, J., Cottrell, L.: Pathchirp: efficient available bandwidth estimation for network paths. In: Passive and Active Measurement Workshop (2003)
25. Sander, C., Kunze, I., Wehrle, K., Rüth, J.: Video conferencing and flow-rate fairness: a first look at zoom and the impact of flow-queuing AQM. In: Hohlfeld, O., Lutu, A., Levin, D. (eds.) PAM 2021. LNCS, vol. 12671, pp. 3–19. Springer, Cham (2021). https://doi.org/10.1007/978-3-030-72582-2_1
26. Schlomer, A., Philip, A.A., Sherry, J., Meng, Z.: Poster: user-controllable congestion mitigation for low-latency applications. In: Proceedings of the ACM SIGCOMM 2024 Conference: Posters and Demos, pp. 54–56 (2024)
27. Sheikh, H., Bovik, A.: Image information and visual quality. IEEE Trans. Image Process. **15**(2), 430–444 (2006)
28. Strauss, J., Katabi, D., Kaashoek, F.: A measurement study of available bandwidth estimation tools. In: Proceedings of the 3rd ACM SIGCOMM Conference on Internet Measurement, IMC '03, page 39–44, New York, NY, USA, (2003). Association for Computing Machinery

29. W3C. Webrtc statistics API: `RTCInboundRtpStreamStats.freezeCount`. https://w3c.github.io/webrtc-stats/#dom-rtcinboundrtpstreamstats-freezecount. Accessed: 30-11-2025

30. Ware, R., Philip, A.A., Hungria, N., Kothari, Y., Sherry, J., Seshan, S.: CCAnalyzer: an efficient and nearly-passive congestion control classifier. In: Proceedings of the ACM SIGCOMM 2024 Conference, ACM SIGCOMM '24, page 181–196, New York, NY, USA, (2024). Association for Computing Machinery

31. YouTube. Talking-head Video. https://www.youtube.com/watch?v=hWTT4J_xNwY

32. Zhang, Z., Zhu, X., Zhang, A., Qian, F.: An in-depth study of bandwidth allocation across media sources in video conferencing. In: Proceedings of the 32nd ACM International Conference on Multimedia, MM '24, page 7696–7704, New York, NY, USA, (2024). Association for Computing Machinery

Measuring Low Latency at Scale: A Field Study of L4S in Residential Broadband

Ayoub Ben-Ameur[1(✉)], Francesco Bronzino[1,2,3], Paul Schmitt[1,4],
and Nick Feamster[1,5]

[1] NetMicroscope Inc., Chicago, IL 60637, USA
{ayoub.ben-ameur,francesco.bronzino,paul.schmitt,
nick.feamster}@netmicroscope.com
[2] École Normale Supérieure de Lyon, 69007 Lyon, France
[3] Institut Universitaire de France, 75005 Paris, France
[4] California Polytechnic State University, San Luis Obispo, CA 93407, USA
[5] University of Chicago, Chicago, IL 60637, USA

Abstract. The Low Latency, Low Loss, Scalable Throughput (L4S) architecture promises to reduce queuing delay while sustaining high throughput. Prior work has largely evaluated L4S in synthetic environments or controlled testbeds, leaving its real-world performance underexplored. In this study, we measure L4S performance specifically on **Apple services delivered over Comcast residential networks**. We deploy 83 Raspberry Pi devices across Comcast subscriber households and conduct over 120000 controlled experiments comparing L4S to traditional congestion control. Our results show that L4S reduces tail latency by up to 25% for interactive applications and for bulk downloads from Apple's CDN, while providing minimal gains for iCloud. Gains are most pronounced during peak usage hours when networks are congested, highlighting the situational benefit of L4S in a single ISP ecosystem.

1 Introduction

The Internet is undergoing a fundamental shift in performance priorities. For decades, throughput was the primary bottleneck, driving innovations in link capacity, backbone infrastructure, and content distribution. Today, with widespread gigabit access and abundant bandwidth, latency has emerged as the critical performance metric. Modern interactive applications (*e.g.*, video conferencing, cloud gaming, remote collaboration, and real-time communication) are increasingly constrained not by available bandwidth, but by end-to-end delay and its variability.

This shift poses a fundamental challenge for Internet congestion control, which has historically optimized for throughput and fairness. Traditional Active Queue Management (AQM) schemes and congestion signaling techniques struggle to maintain low queuing delay under load, often forcing a tradeoff between latency and link utilization. The result is persistent bufferbloat [6] and unpredictable latency, even on high-capacity access links.

© The Author(s), under exclusive license to Springer Nature Switzerland AG 2026
S. Ferlin-Reiter et al. (Eds.): PAM 2026, LNCS 16477, pp. 168–181, 2026.
https://doi.org/10.1007/978-3-032-18268-5_8

To address this, the Internet Engineering Task Force (IETF) has proposed the Low Latency, Low Loss, Scalable Throughput (L4S) architecture [4,12], which reimagines congestion control by enabling ultra-low queuing delay through scalable Explicit Congestion Notification (ECN) marking and new transport behaviors. L4S introduces dual-queue AQMs (such as DualPI2 [13]) and transport algorithms that respond more aggressively to ECN signals, aiming to keep queues short while maximizing link utilization.

While L4S has been evaluated extensively in controlled testbeds and simulations [3,7,9,14], its real-world performance remains largely unmeasured. This gap is particularly critical as L4S transitions from research prototype to production deployment. Recently, several major Internet players have begun enabling L4S: Apple has integrated L4S support into iOS and macOS [1] for Facetime, iCloud, and CDN downloads; NVIDIA has deployed L4S in its GeForce NOW cloud gaming platform [11]; and Comcast has started provisioning residential customers with L4S-capable dual-queue routers [5]. This emerging deployment creates an unprecedented opportunity to measure L4S performance at scale in production networks, under real traffic conditions, with actual applications— measurements that are impossible to replicate in controlled environments.

In this paper, we present the first large-scale, in situ measurement study of L4S in a single production network. We deploy 83 Raspberry Pi measurement nodes across Comcast residential broadband networks in the United States, conducting over 120000 controlled experiments comparing L4S-enabled Apple services (FaceTime, iCloud, and Apple CDN downloads) against their traditional congestion control baselines. Our measurement methodology combines active probing, packet-level instrumentation, and application-layer metrics to quantify L4S impact on latency, throughput, packet loss, and application responsiveness within Comcast s access network and under its real-world operating conditions.

Our key contributions are as follows:

- We design and deploy a large-scale measurement infrastructure spanning 83 residential networks to measure L4S performance in production, conducting over 60,000 controlled experiments across diverse ISPs, access technologies, and network conditions.
- We demonstrate that L4S benefits are highly context-dependent: tail latency reductions of up to 25% for interactive applications occur primarily during peak congestion hours, while benefits are minimal during off-peak periods and for certain application types (e.g., iCloud sync).
- We identify both the benefits and limitations of L4S in real-world deployments, including deployment challenges and coexistence concerns.

Our findings reveal that L4S delivers measurable latency improvements in production, but its benefits are concentrated in specific contexts (*e.g.*, congested networks, peak hours, and latency-sensitive applications). These results provide the first empirical evidence of L4S effectiveness at scale and highlight both the promise and practical limitations of deploying low-latency congestion control in the Internet.

2 Related Work

While L4S has received considerable attention in both academic and standardization communities, most evaluations to date have been confined to testbeds or simulations. This study complements prior work by providing an empirical analysis of L4S performance in production networks with real-world traffic.

Controlled Testbed Evaluations. Early empirical validation of L4S [3] focused on fairness between scalable and classic congestion controls under controlled experiments, demonstrating substantial queuing delay reductions while identifying coexistence challenges when flows share bottlenecks. Graff *et al.* [7] evaluate L4S in a custom platform that imitates cloud gaming, implementing the Self-Clocked Rate Adaptation for Multimedia (SCReAM) algorithm under emulated cellular conditions. Their work examines fairness and Quality of Service (QoS) for synthetic traffic, comparing L4S with class-based queuing. Monteiro *et al.* [8] examine L4S in a private 5G industrial setting for real-time video streaming, measuring latency, throughput, and video quality. They show significant queuing delay reductions under certain traffic loads within their controlled network. While these studies provide valuable insights into L4S behavior under specific conditions, they rely on synthetic traffic patterns and controlled environments.

Network-Specific Contexts. Srivastava *et al.* [14] investigate low-latency congestion control protocols—TCP BBR and TCP Prague—over mmWave links, which experience frequent capacity drops due to blockage and rapid variations. Their results show that while these protocols reduce queueing delay under many conditions, fairness issues emerge (some flows starve), and frequent capacity disruption limits achievable latency improvements. This work highlights how specific link characteristics constrain L4S benefits, though in controlled rather than production settings.

Architectural and Instrumentation Perspectives. Complementary work has explored L4S from architectural and measurement perspectives. Szilveszter *et al.* [9] challenge the tight coupling between L4S and specific scalable congestion control algorithms, introducing a scheduler that delivers low-latency service regardless of sender congestion control. Their primarily algorithmic work, evaluated in controlled settings, demonstrates the feasibility of decoupling architectural benefits from end-host adoption. Nguyen *et al.* [10] leverage programmable data planes to observe and validate L4S flow behavior in fine-grained detail, building a P4-based framework with in-band network telemetry that captures per-packet latency and congestion signals. Their focus on data plane instrumentation provides valuable tools for debugging and validation.

Our Contribution. In contrast to these controlled and instrumentation-focused studies, we provide large-scale, in-situ measurements of L4S across residential broadband deployments. We quantify end-to-end performance that end-users experience with L4S-enabled commercial Apple services over Comcast networks, using live traffic from geographically distributed devices. This empirical analysis reveals how L4S performs under real-world conditions, including varying congestion levels, diverse service types, and partial deployment scenarios.

3   Methodology

We design a measurement campaign to assess L4S performance in real-world environments across representative application scenarios. Our study systematically compares traffic using L4S-enabled congestion control against traditional queueing. We focus on three categories of Apple services that span latency-sensitive and throughput-oriented applications: (i) Apple CDN downloads, (ii) iCloud, and (iii) FaceTime. These services were selected because Apple has recently enabled native L4S support across its application stack and content delivery infrastructure, providing a rare opportunity to evaluate L4S in production conditions with unmodified end systems. Moreover, they collectively represent distinct transport behaviors: Apple CDN downloads produce long-lived, high-throughput transfers that reveal how L4S handles sustained congestion; iCloud downloads exhibit short, bursty synchronization flows typical of background traffic; and FaceTime calls generate continuous, interactive streams that stress low-latency performance.

3.1   Experimental Design

For each service, we define reproducible test procedures executed periodically under two network configurations:

1. **L4S-enabled:** ECN with ECT(1) marking and Dual Queue support on the access link, enabling scalable congestion control.
2. **Non-L4S:** Conventional congestion control without ECN or with classic ECN (ECT(0)).

We employ a paired testing approach where L4S and non-L4S measurements execute in immediate succession (*i.e.*, within 60 s) to minimize temporal variability. This design controls for time-of-day effects, transient congestion, and routing changes that could confound comparisons. Each paired test alternates the order (L4S-first vs. non-L4S-first) to account for potential ordering effects.

3.2   Measurement Procedures

We instrument each service type to collect network and application-layer metrics:

Apple CDN Download Tests. We download large media files (480 MB) hosted on Apple CDN infrastructure using HTTP/2 over TCP or HTTP/3 over QUIC. We measure time-to-first-byte (TTFB), total transfer time, achieved throughput, and path-level RTT. This workload represents high-throughput, non-interactive usage.

Fig. 1. Geographical distribution of deployed devices across the United States

iCloud tests. We trigger downloads of 500 MB files through a headless iCloud client session, ensuring repeatable transfer sizes. We log application-layer throughput and TCP RTT. Network-layer measurements include congestion window evolution and ECN activity (ECT/CE markings).

FaceTime tests. We establish automated two-party video calls and use passive packet capture (tcpdump) to measure call establishment time, ECN markings, and packet loss. These metrics quantify the impact of queue management and congestion control on real-time interactive performance.

3.3   Measurement Infrastructure

We deploy a distributed measurement infrastructure consisting of 83 Raspberry Pi devices in volunteer residential homes across the United States (Fig. 1). We manage the fleet remotely using the openBalena [2] platform, enabling over-the-air software updates, configuration management, and centralized logging without requiring on-site intervention.

All volunteer homes subscribe to Comcast Xfinity residential broadband service with advertised speeds up to 1 Gbps downstream and 300 Mbps upstream. Critically, Comcast has deployed routers with dual-queue AQM support in these homes, satisfying the infrastructure requirements for L4S operation. Each device connects via Ethernet to the home router, ensuring stable connectivity and minimizing wireless interference in measurements.

Devices are geographically distributed across multiple US regions to capture diverse network conditions including varying ISP peering relationships, regional congestion patterns, and path characteristics. Each device executes the measurement procedures described in Sect. 3, alternating between L4S-enabled and non-L4S configurations. Measurements run autonomously 24/7, capturing diurnal traffic patterns and congestion dynamics.

3.4   Final Dataset

Tests execute every 3 h across a 48-week measurement period, yielding approximately 2688 paired measurements per service type per deployment site.[1] We schedule tests to capture diurnal patterns. Each test cycle generates structured logs containing: timestamps, ECN counters, flow-level statistics, and application metrics. We aggregate measurements centrally for post-processing and analysis. Table 1 summarizes the key characteristics and statistical properties of the resulting dataset.

Table 1. Summary of the dataset.

Collection period	Nov. 1st 2024 – Sep. 30th 2025
Country	United States of America
Number of homes	83
Experiments per service per day	8
Total experiments per service	Apple CDN (50000); iCloud (35000); FaceTime (35000)
Collected metrics	Latency (ms); Throughput (Mbps); ECN marking

3.5   Limitations

Our measurement methodology has several limitations that constrain the generality of our findings. First, our deployment covers only a single ISP (Comcast) and uses L4S-capable home routers provisioned by the operator; thus, our observations reflect Comcast's access-network configuration and may not generalize to other ISPs. Second, we measure only Apple services, whose L4S and congestion-control behaviors are specific to Apple's ecosystem and may differ from other applications. Third, we cannot directly verify dual-queue AQM across the entire path; instead, we infer queue behavior from ECN markings and end-host congestion-control signals. Although end devices connect via Ethernet to the home router, bottlenecks may still arise upstream in the access or aggregation network, and our methodology cannot always isolate their location. Fourth, volunteer access-link speeds exceed those of many broadband users, reducing the likelihood of persistent queueing and limiting opportunities for L4S mechanisms to engage. Finally, we do not introduce controlled cross-traffic or engineered coexistence scenarios; results therefore reflect real-world but uncontrolled residential traffic mixes. These constraints do not invalidate our findings but do bound their applicability, and we make these assumptions explicit to guide interpretation.

---

[1] Data collection was progressively activated across devices and services; consequently, not all nodes or applications contributed measurements during the exact same time intervals.

Ethical Considerations. This work does not raise ethical concerns. Volunteers provided informed consent, and we collect only anonymized network measurements via triggered tests, not user application data or any personally identifiable information. All data is stored securely, and volunteers can withdraw from the study at any time.

4 Results

We present empirical results from our deployment, analyzing over 60,000 paired measurements across 83 residential sites to assess L4S performance in production. We focus on tail latency (99th percentile) as the primary metric, given its importance for interactive applications and user-perceived quality. We examine how L4S benefits vary across service types, time of day, and network conditions. We introduce the shorthand notation $\Delta = p_{99}(\text{L4S}) - p_{99}(\text{Classic Queue})$ as the difference in 99th-percentile latencies between L4S and classic queue.

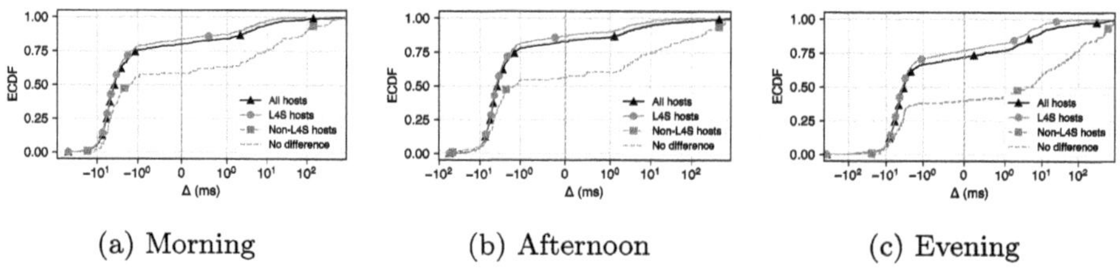

(a) Morning	(b) Afternoon	(c) Evening

Fig. 2. ECDFs of differences in 99th-percentile latency for Apple CDN download by time of day. Negative values indicate L4S reduces tail latency compared to classic congestion control. (50000 datapoints)

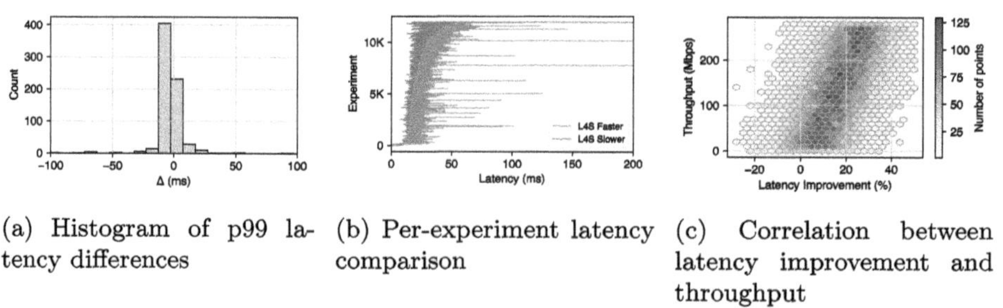

(a) Histogram of p99 latency differences (b) Per-experiment latency comparison (c) Correlation between latency improvement and throughput

Fig. 3. Apple CDN download per-experiment analysis showing tight distribution of improvements and consistent L4S advantage (blue lines indicate L4S reduces latency). (Color figure online)

4.1   Apple CDN Download: Bulk Transfer Performance

We begin with Apple CDN download tests to evaluate how L4S performs under sustained, throughput-oriented traffic, where long-lived flows are most likely to experience queue buildup and benefit from dual-queue scheduling. Grouping the data by time of day allows us to capture diurnal variations in access-network congestion, revealing whether L4S advantages persist across both lightly and heavily loaded periods.

Aggregate Latency Improvements Across Time Periods. Figure 2 shows the empirical cumulative distribution of p99 latency differences for Apple CDN downloads across three time periods. Negative values indicate L4S reduces tail latency. L4S-enabled hosts (blue) consistently achieve lower p99 latency, with distributions shifted left of zero across all periods. During morning and after-noon, approximately 80% of L4S hosts experience latency reductions. Non-L4S hosts (green) show flatter distributions centered near zero, indicating negligible improvement. The aggregate across all hosts (black) follows the L4S trend, con-firming benefits stem primarily from L4S-capable endpoints. Importantly, these improvements are not confined to a few favorable sites: similar left-shifted dis-tributions are observed across the majority of deployment locations, suggesting that the latency improvements are robust and broadly consistent rather than driven by outliers or site-specific network conditions. During evening peak hours (06:00pm - 00:00am), absolute L4S improvements decrease slightly but remain substantial. Critically, the separation between L4S and non-L4S hosts widens considerably: the gap between blue and green curves increases on average from 8 ms (afternoon) to 20 ms (evening). This suggests that while absolute gains diminish under heavy load, L4S maintains a significant advantage over classic congestion control precisely when networks are most congested.

Consistency and Throughput Correlation. To validate the aggregate trends, we examine per-experiment variability through histograms of p99 latency differences and comparison plots summarizing the direction and magnitude of change across all experiments. These views reveal consistency and outlier behav-ior across our measurement campaign. The histogram (Fig. 3a) shows a tight distribution centered just below zero, with most samples clustered between -10 ms and 0 ms. The pairwise plot (Fig. 3b) confirms this with blue lines (L4S reduces latency) dominating across all sites and time periods. This consistency suggests that bulk download traffic reliably triggers queue buildup where L4S excels. Figure 3c shows that these latency improvements are not achieved at the expense of throughput. The scatter distribution shows no negative corre-lation between latency reduction and achieved throughput: experiments with strong latency gains sustain similar or even slightly higher throughput levels. This demonstrates that L4S achieves lower delay without compromising bulk-transfer efficiency, underscoring its effectiveness in balancing throughput and responsiveness under real-world conditions.

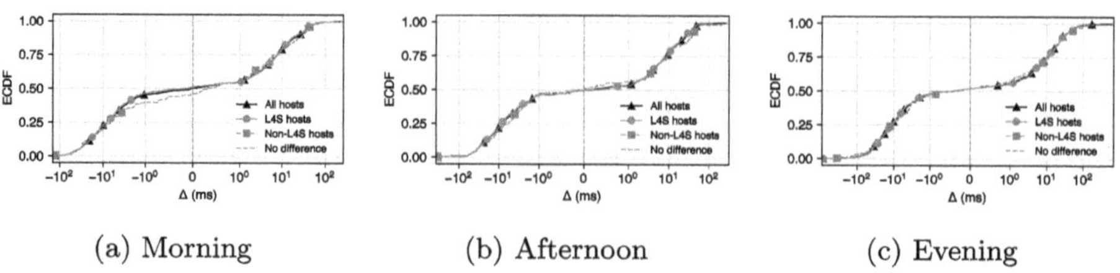

(a) Morning   (b) Afternoon   (c) Evening

Fig. 4. ECDFs of differences in 99th-percentile latency for iCloud download by time of day. L4S and non-L4S distributions largely overlap. (35000 datapoints)

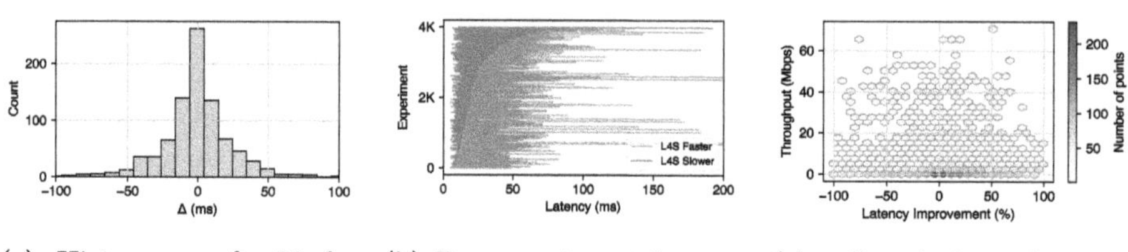

(a) Histogram of p99 latency differences

(b) Per-experiment latency comparison

(c) Correlation between latency improvement and throughput

Fig. 5. iCloud download per-experiment analysis showing symmetric distribution and mixed results (balanced blue/red lines indicate no systematic L4S benefit). (Color figure online)

4.2   iCloud Download: Bursty Transfer Performance

We next analyze iCloud download to assess how L4S behaves for short flows that differ fundamentally from sustained bulk transfers.

Aggregate Latency Improvements Across Time Periods. In contrast to Apple CDN downloads, iCloud traffic shows minimal L4S benefit (Fig. 4). The L4S (blue) and non-L4S (green) distributions overlap substantially across all time periods, with both centered near zero difference. During afternoon and evening, the curves nearly coincide, with median change near 1 ms. This negligible improvement suggests that L4S provides little advantage for services that are tuned for synchronization. We attribute this to iCloud's traffic characteristics. Unlike sustained bulk transfers, iCloud is synchronization-oriented that consists of bursty, chunked uploads/downloads with application-layer rate limiting. These short bursts may not build sufficient queue depth for L4S's precise congestion signaling to yield measurable benefits. Additionally, iCloud traffic may use background priority classes that avoid saturating links, further limiting opportunities for queue buildup. The lack of time-of-day variation (similar performance during peak and off-peak hours) supports this interpretation; iCloud traffic does not stress the network enough to benefit from improved queue management.

Consistency and Throughput Correlation. The histogram (Fig. 5a) exhibits a wider, symmetric distribution centered near 0 ms for iCloud. Both improvements (negative) and degradations (positive) appear with roughly equal probability. The pairwise plot (Fig. 5b) shows balanced blue and red lines, confirming no systematic L4S advantage. The high variability suggests that iCloud performance depends on factors orthogonal to queue management, *i.e.*, application-layer behavior and traffic patterns. Figure 5c reveals no consistent correlation between throughput and latency improvement, indicating that L4S effects are largely independent of bulk-transfer rate. Unlike Apple CDN downloads, where latency gains align with sustained throughput, iCloud experiments show a highly scattered pattern: several tests even display positive latency differences (i.e., higher latency under L4S) at moderate throughputs. This dispersion suggests that the short-lived, bursty nature of iCloud traffic prevents L4S from establishing stable dual-queue dynamics, limiting its ability to realize queueing-delay reductions. Overall, the absence of a clear trend reinforces that L4S benefits are workload dependent—effective for steady, congestion-prone flows but less impactful for sporadic, background exchanges.

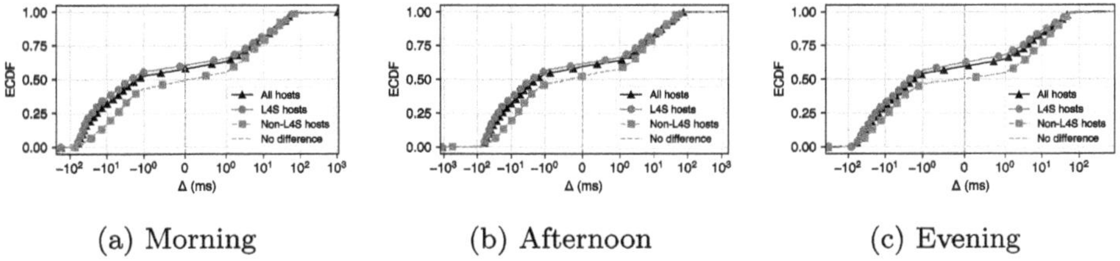

(a) Morning   (b) Afternoon   (c) Evening

Fig. 6. ECDFs of differences in 99th-percentile call establishment time for FaceTime by time of day. L4S consistently reduces latency, especially during peak hours. (35000 datapoints)

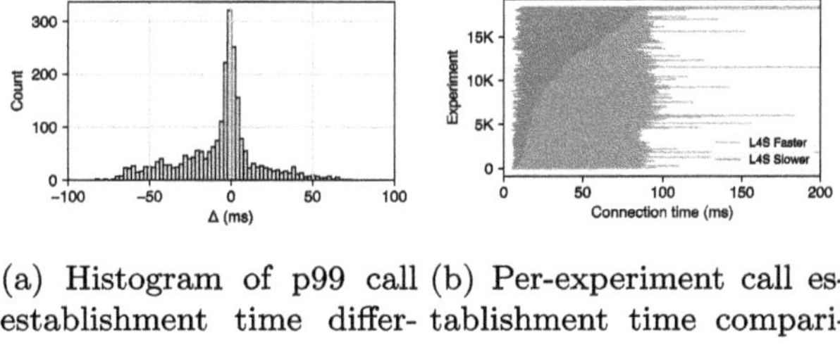

(a) Histogram of p99 call establishment time differences   (b) Per-experiment call establishment time comparison

Fig. 7. FaceTime per-experiment analysis showing broader distribution with heavy left tail and strong L4S advantage during peak periods

4.3   FaceTime: Real-Time Interactive Performance

Having examined L4S behavior for throughput-oriented services, we now turn to FaceTime, a latency-critical application. FaceTime's performance is dominated by real-time delay sensitivity, making it an ideal test case to assess L4S benefits under human-perceptible latency constraints.

Aggregate Latency Improvements Across Time Periods. Figure 6 shows consistent L4S benefits across all time periods. The effect is relatively stable across morning, afternoon, and evening, with improvements of roughly 8 ms compared to classic, suggesting the service benefits from L4S even under moderate load. Non-L4S hosts (green) show substantially worse performance, particularly during afternoon and evening periods where distributions shift rightward (indicating latency increases). The separation between L4S and non-L4S curves widens during peak hours, reaching 10 ms in the evening. This pattern suggests that interactive real-time applications derive greater relative benefit from L4S under congestion—precisely when low latency is most critical for user experience.

Consistency and Per-experiment Validation. Figure 7a displays a broader distribution with heavy left tail extending to −50 ms, indicating substantial improvements for a subset of experiments. Figure 7b shows a clear dominance of blue lines, indicating that L4S consistently improves connection setup latency across most experiments. Improvements are concentrated around the lower latency range (below 100 ms), consistent with FaceTime's real-time nature and short flow durations. The limited number of red outliers suggests that L4S rarely degrades performance, and when it does, the magnitude of regression is small. Overall, the results confirm that L4S provides reliable latency reduction for interactive, delay-sensitive traffic, validating its suitability for real-time applications like video conferencing.

> *Main takeaways: Across all analyses, our findings reveal that L4S effectiveness strongly depends on the traffic characteristics of each service. For Apple CDN downloads, L4S consistently lowers tail latency for bulk transfers, confirming that dual-queue mechanisms are most effective when flows sustain congestion long enough for ECN signaling to stabilize. For iCloud downloads, however, the impact remains negligible, as short, bursty synchronization flows seldom trigger persistent queue buildup. Finally, FaceTime demonstrates meaningful latency reductions, particularly during peak hours, validating L4S's value for interactive, real-time communication. Overall, these results show that L4S delivers tangible benefits where persistent congestion or latency sensitivity dominate performance, but offers limited gains for transient, low-volume traffic.*

5   Conclusion

We present the first large-scale, in situ measurement study of L4S in production residential broadband networks. Deploying 83 devices across US Comcast networks and conducting over 60,000 paired experiments, we quantify L4S performance for three representative Apple services: Apple CDN, iCloud and FaceTime.

Our key findings reveal substantial but service-dependent L4S benefits. FaceTime and CDN downloads experience consistent tail latency reductions up to 25%, with advantages most pronounced during evening peak hours (20 ms for CDN, 10 ms for FaceTime) when non-L4S performance degrades. In stark contrast, iCloud shows negligible benefit, with L4S and non-L4S distributions overlapping across all periods. This disparity reveals a critical insight: L4S effectiveness requires sustained queue buildup; while bursty, application-paced traffic cannot benefit from improved queue management. The widening performance gap during congestion suggests L4S successfully isolates latency-sensitive flows from the effects that degrade classic congestion control.

Our results provide evidence of L4S's practical value for interactive and bulk transfer workloads, while identifying deployment contexts where benefits may not materialize. As L4S adoption expands in commercial services and ISP infrastructure, our measurement methodology and empirical findings offer guidance for operators and application developers assessing L4S deployment value.

A   Controlled Vs Inferred Assumptions

This appendix summarizes which aspects of our ECN/L4S measurement methodology are *controlled* (i.e., known with certainty based on our deployment and instrumentation) and which aspects are *inferred* from observable traffic characteristics. These apply uniformly across all three workloads (Apple CDN, iCloud, and FaceTime).

A.1   Controlled Aspects

- **L4S-capable home routers.** Comcast provides an up to date list of volunteers provisioned with home routers that are L4S-capable.
- **L4S-capable measurement device.** All experiments run on Raspberry Pi devices whose Linux kernel includes L4S-capable congestion control and ECN support.
- **Explicit enable/disable control for L4S.** Our measurement client controls whether L4S is enabled or disabled at the end device. This configuration is set deterministically by our code for each experiment.
- **Apple services implement L4S.** The Apple CDN, iCloud, and FaceTime services we measure implement L4S semantics and set ECT(1) for L4S-capable flows.

A.2   Inferred Aspects

- **End-to-end L4S support.** We do not know whether all intermediate hops between Apple servers and our Raspberry Pi devices support or preserve L4S behavior.

- **Queue behavior and AQM configuration.** We infer queueing behavior—including possible dual-queue operation—indirectly from ECN codepoints observed in received packets and from endpoint TCP state.
- **Bottleneck.** Congestion may arise upstream in the access or aggregation network, and we cannot always isolate the precise bottleneck.

B Summary Statistics and Baseline Distributions

Table 2. Baseline summary statistics (ms).

Service	Configuration	Mean	Median	p90	IQR	StdDev
Apple CDN	Classic Queue	25.47	22.66	38.40	9.52	10.40
	L4S	24.65	18.97	35.92	10.20	39.99
iCloud	Classic Queue	27.46	18.34	47.98	14.92	58.89
	L4S	24.47	18.64	45.57	13.83	34.68
FaceTime	Classic Queue	39.28	31.98	76.87	42.36	31.57
	L4S	33.66	24.3	71.86	28.39	28.84

To complement our tail-latency analysis and provide baseline context, we report descriptive statistics for each service under both L4S and Classic configurations. These values summarize typical latency levels and their variability. In Table 2, we present the mean, median, p90, interquartile range (IQR), and standard deviation (StdDev) for Apple CDN downloads, iCloud, and FaceTime call establishment time. These baseline statistics contextualize the tail behavior discussed earlier in Sect. 4 and help quantify how representative the tail differences are relative to the overall distribution.

References

1. Apple Inc.: Testing and Debugging L4S in Your App. https://developer.apple.com/documentation/network/testing-and-debugging-l4s-in-your-app
2. balena: OpenBalena. https://open-balena-docs.balena.io/
3. BoruOljira, D., Grinnemo, K.J., Brunstrom, A., Taheri, J.: Validating the sharing behavior and latency characteristics of the l4s architecture. SIGCOMM Comput. Commun. Rev. 37–44 (2020)
4. Briscoe, B., Schepper, K.D., Bagnulo, M., White, G.: Low Latency, Low Loss, and Scalable Throughput (L4S) Internet Service: Architecture. RFC 9330 (Jan 2023). https://doi.org/10.17487/RFC9330, https://www.rfc-editor.org/info/rfc9330
5. Comcast: What is Latency. https://corporate.comcast.com/stories/latency-speed-explainer
6. Gettys, J., Nichols, K.: Bufferbloat: dark buffers in the internet. Commun. ACM **55**(1), 57–65 (2012)

7. Graff, P., Marchal, X., Cholez, T., Mathieu, B., Tuffin, S., Festor, O.: Improving Cloud Gaming traffic QoS: a comparison between class-based queuing policy and L4S. In: 2024 8th Network Traffic Measurement and Analysis Conference (TMA), pp. 1–10. IEEE (2024)
8. Monteiro, L.V., Simão, V.S., Lira, R.d.B., de Almeida, L.C., Gomes, R.D., Ditarso Maciel, P.: L4s in private 5g industrial networks: A case study for real-time video transmission in programmable networks. In: 2024 IEEE Conference on Network Function Virtualization and Software Defined Networks (NFV-SDN), pp. 1–4 (2024). https://doi.org/10.1109/NFV-SDN61811.2024.10807467
9. Nádas, S., Gombos, G., Fejes, F., Laki, S.: A congestion control independent l4s scheduler. In: Proceedings of the 2020 Applied Networking Research Workshop, pp. 45–51 (2020). https://doi.org/10.1145/3404868.3406669
10. Nguyen, H.N., Mathieu, B., Letourneau, M., Doyen, G., Tuffin, S., Oca, E.M.d.: A comprehensive p4-based monitoring framework for l4s leveraging in-band network telemetry. In: NOMS 2023-2023 IEEE/IFIP Network Operations and Management Symposium, pp. 1–6 (2023). https://doi.org/10.1109/NOMS56928.2023.10154331
11. Nvidia: What is the L4S setting in the GeForce NOW streaming quality menu. https://nvidia.custhelp.com/app/answers/detail/a_id/5522
12. Schepper, K.D., Briscoe, B.: The Explicit Congestion Notification (ECN) Protocol for Low Latency, Low Loss, and Scalable Throughput (L4S). RFC 9331 (Jan 2023). https://doi.org/10.17487/RFC9331, https://www.rfc-editor.org/info/rfc9331
13. Schepper, K.D., Briscoe, B., White, G.: Dual-Queue Coupled Active Queue Management (AQM) for Low Latency, Low Loss, and Scalable Throughput (L4S). RFC 9332 (Jan 2023). https://doi.org/10.17487/RFC9332, https://www.rfc-editor.org/info/rfc9332
14. Srivastava, A., Fund, F., Panwar, S.S.: An experimental evaluation of low latency congestion control for mmwave links. In: IEEE INFOCOM 2020 - IEEE Conference on Computer Communications Workshops (INFOCOM WKSHPS), pp. 352–357 (2020). https://doi.org/10.1109/INFOCOMWKSHPS50562.2020.9162881

DNS

Black Holes and Prisoners: Understanding AS112 Deployment Characteristics

Elizabeth Boswell[1(✉)] [iD], Xinyan Xian[1] [iD], Mingshu Wang[1] [iD],
Stephen McQuistin[2] [iD], and Colin Perkins[1] [iD]

[1] University of Glasgow, Glasgow, UK
`{e.boswell.2,x.xian.1}@research.gla.ac.uk, mingshu.wang@glasgow.ac.uk,`
`csp@csperkins.org`
[2] University of St Andrews, St Andrews, UK
`sm@smcquistin.uk`

Abstract. AS112 is a distributed, volunteer-run, anycast DNS service that acts as a sink for leaked DNS queries for local resources, preventing them from overloading core DNS infrastructure. AS112 helps protect important parts of the Internet infrastructure, but there has been no comprehensive study of who runs the AS112 servers, where they are located, and whether they effectively capture leaked queries. Using RIPE Atlas and 33646 open recursive resolvers, we detect 469 AS112 sites, run by 97 operators, and compare the response time and query distances of AS112 to root server queries. AS112 performs well, with 23.21% lower median response times and 36.11% lower median distances than the root. However, AS112 is largely dependent on few large operators (one operator serves 41.71% of probes in our study), limiting its resilience.

1 Introduction

Misconfigured hosts can leak DNS queries for local resources, such as reverse DNS queries for local addresses [6,39] and queries for the `home.arpa` [45] and `service.arpa` domains [35], into the public Internet. This is a concern because such queries place a burden on critical infrastructure (e.g., Cloudflare receives ~100k of these requests per second [22]), and because they can leak private information about those local resources [14].

The AS112 project (https://www.as112.net) is a worldwide, distributed, volunteer-run effort to respond to such leaked DNS queries, diverting load from the `in-addr.arpa` [6] and `arpa` nameservers [35,45]. Anyone can run an AS112 server and respond to queries via anycast IP [6]. This lack of central governance facilitates wide deployment, but it is not clear who runs the AS112 servers, where they are located, from where they are accessed, and whether they effectively distribute the load. AS112 protects critical infrastructure, but we do not know how well it works, or how its unplanned, volunteer-led infrastructure compares to more carefully planned infrastructure deployments, such as the DNS root servers.

S. Ferlin-Reiter et al. (Eds.): PAM 2026, LNCS 16477, pp. 185–201, 2026.
https://doi.org/10.1007/978-3-032-18268-5_9

In this paper, we present the first large-scale measurement of the deployment characteristics of AS112 using vantage points worldwide. We find that:

- AS112 is dependent on a small number of large operators (§2.1), with one operator serving 41.71% of the vantage points in our study. We identify 469 AS112 sites, run by 97 operators, of which only 57 appear on the self-reported list of operators published by the AS112 project.
- AS112 is connected to at least 235 ASes, and is widely deployed in Europe, North America, and Oceania. However, geographic (§2.2) and network (§2.3) diversity could be improved to increase resilience [50], as only 5% of our vantage points reach an AS112 site in a neighbouring AS.
- Queries sent to AS112 see 23.21% lower response times and 36.11% lower query distances than queries to the root servers, but only 22.24% of vantage points query their closest AS112 site. 31.94% of AS112 queries in our measurements are sent across national borders, compared to 50.88% of root queries (§3).

While prior studies used AS112 to study anycast characteristics [10,29] or analysed AS112 query logs [12,13], ours is, to the best of our knowledge, the first study of AS112 deployment. We conduct large-scale measurements, using 11973 RIPE Atlas probes and 33646 open recursive resolvers, to illustrate the geographical reach and performance of AS112, and compare this unplanned network with the more carefully planned anycast root server deployments. We show that the AS112 network is widely distributed, with better performance than the root servers, but increasing geographical diversity and decreasing its reliance on a small group of operators would improve resilience.

2   Understanding AS112 Deployment

AS112 is a set of anycast DNS servers that capture leaked reverse DNS queries for private and link local addresses [6] and leaked queries for `home.arpa` [45] and `service.arpa` [35]. The `blackhole-1.iana.org` and `blackhole-2.iana.org` nameservers respond to these queries with `NXDOMAIN` [6]. A third nameserver, `prisoner.iana.org`, handles erroneous dynamic updates [6,13]. In addition, DNAME redirection for AS112, introduced in 2015 to redirect arbitrary queries to AS112 [5,49], uses the nameserver `blackhole.as112.arpa`. When deployed following RFC 7534 [6], a single multi-homed server acts as all four nameservers.

Anyone can run an AS112 INSTANCE by announcing the AS112 anycast prefixes via BGP [6]. A SITE [23] contains one or more co-located INSTANCES [29]. An anycast DEPLOYMENT [34,54] is the set of SITES run by one operator.

AS112 nameservers respond to TXT queries for `hostname.as112.arpa` and `hostname.as112.net` with information about the location and operator of the SITE (e.g., 'RIPE NCC, Amsterdam, The Netherlands. See http://www.as112. net/ for more information.') [6]. The format of the responses is not consistent.

To find the geographical locations and operators of AS112 SITES, we use RIPE Atlas to send TXT queries for `hostname.as112.arpa` and `hostname.as112.net`

Table 1. The AS112 DNS query datasets (excl. recursive RIPE Atlas queries). Valid answers specify are used in further analysis, invalid answers were not used.

Measurement	Version	VPs	Valid Answer	No Answer Section	Invalid Answer Unknown Location/Operator	GPDNS in NSID	Sites
`hostname.as112.arpa` (RIPE Atlas)	IPv4	11540	44270	2221	98	1	310
	IPv6	3671	12603	568	66	0	120
`hostname.as112.net` (RIPE Atlas)	IPv4	11302	44532	2804	224	16	331
	IPv6	3486	13095	1359	138	0	130
`hostname.as112.arpa` (open resolvers)	IPv4	26267	26267	5495	834	n/a	306
`hostname.as112.net` (open resolvers)	IPv4	26635	26635	5619	701	n/a	326

to `blackhole-1.iana.org`, `blackhole-2.iana.org`, `prisoner.iana.org` and `blackhole.as112.arpa`, in IPv4 and IPv6 (similar to studies [8,29]). These are *non-recursive* queries, sent directly from the probes to the nameservers, allowing us to analyse distances and response times between probes and SITES (§3.1). This also ensures the response will contain any NSID set by the AS112 INSTANCE (NSID is lost in recursive queries [9]). To verify that recursive queries yield similar results, we sent *recursive* `hostname.as112.arpa` and `hostname.as112.net` queries (in IPv4 and IPv6) using 891 randomly distributed RIPE Atlas probes.

Most RIPE Atlas probes are in Europe and North America [47]. To reduce bias, we sent TXT queries for `hostname.as112.arpa` and `hostname.as112.net` to 33646 open IPv4 recursive resolvers from a Censys scan [27] (similar to [8,29]), located in 6055 ASes and 18708 BGP prefixes (compared to 3829 ASes for RIPE Atlas). We used *recursive* resolvers, not DNS forwarders, to ensure they queried AS112 directly [51], and only used IPv4 resolvers, as Censys does "not conduct comprehensive IPv6 scans" [28]. The resolvers were probed from one vantage point; multiple vantage points are unlikely to detect more SITES, as the LACeS anycast census [31] only found 14 resolvers be anycast with high confidence.

All measurements were performed in September 2025. Ethical considerations relating to the measurements are discussed in Appendix A. The data gathering and analysis code is available at https://doi.org/10.5281/zenodo.17863954.

We used a semi-automated process to extract SITE locations and operators from the responses. Most responses specified a city, in which case we determined its geographic coordinates using Google, or an airport code, which we geolocated using online information [1]. If the information was ambiguous, we manually searched to determine the location. If no location was given in the TXT record, we checked whether the NSID (9.52% of responses) or reverse DNS records of unicast

IP addresses given the TXT record (1.87% of responses) encoded a location. SITES were geolocated with city-level granularity.

We excluded responses with no answer section (9.63% of responses), answers with no location or identifying information (1.10%), and answers with GPDNS in the NSID (0.01% – they were likely intercepted and sent to the Google Public DNS resolver [44]). For 2.11% of (non-recursive) RIPE Atlas responses and 0.01% of open resolver responses, the geolocation violates speed-of-light constraints (200km/ms), based on the response time. We do *not* exclude these responses, as we cannot tell whether it is due to inaccurate geolocation of the probe or the SITE, and because the bias introduced by these measurements is likely counteracted by geolocation inaccuracies that *decrease* the distance. 11973 RIPE Atlas probes and 30208 resolvers received valid responses that were *not* excluded. Table 1 summarises our datasets. We refer to the RIPE Atlas probes and resolvers collectively as Vantage Points (VPs). Figure 2a shows the locations of the resolvers.

We assume that responses that are identical, except for the strings 'hostname.as112.arpa' and 'hostname.as112.net', that come from the same location are from the same SITE. This distinguishes SITES that only encode the location in the NSID. We don't distinguish SITES based on the NSID because some operators use different NSIDs for different INSTANCES in the same SITE.

Some VPs don't consistently query the same SITE. For 31.36% of probes in IPv4 (40.94% IPv6) and 26.83% of resolvers, responses to hostname.as112.arpa and hostname.as112.net come from, or appear to come from, different SITES, mainly due to inconsistent formatting and variation in internal routing (Appendix B). For 848 IPv4 probes (265 IPv6), queries to the four nameservers reach different SITES due to inconsistent routing and lack of DNAME support (Appendix C).

2.1   AS112 Operators

Sites and Features—Our non-recursive RIPE Atlas measurements found 416 AS112 SITES, of which 405 responded to IPv4 (194 IPv6; 183 both). The recursive open resolver queries found 388 SITES, of which 342 were found by RIPE Atlas. Recursive RIPE Atlas measurements found 7 additional SITES. In total, we found 469 SITES, significantly more than the 72 [8] and 65 [29] SITES found in 2012 and 2013. That the recursive resolvers did not find more SITES than RIPE Atlas indicates that this is close to the true number of SITES. 389 of the 416 SITES found through non-recursive RIPE Atlas measurements respond to queries sent to blackhole.as112.arpa, indicating DNAME support. This is a lower bound, as not all SITES received this query (Appendices B, C). We do not consider the recursive RIPE Atlas queries in the following (except in Fig. 2b and Table 2), as we cannot conclusively determine which/how many resolvers queried each SITE, and most of the analysis relies on associating VPs with the SITES they query.

Operators— DNS-OARC maintain an AS112 operator listing [7] based on *"voluntary submissions [...] and ad-hoc surveys"* and detection at IXPs, noting it is likely that some SITES are missing and some inactive. In September 2025,

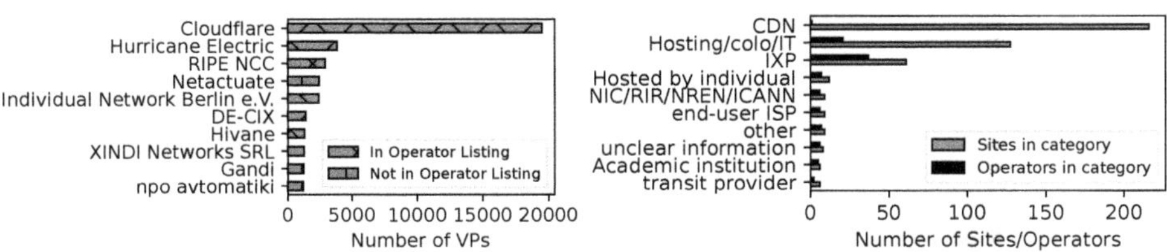

(a) Top 10 AS112 operators, based on number of VPs whose queries they answered

(b) Categories of AS112 operators

Fig. 1. AS112 Operators

this included 189 operators: 107 manually reported at 135 SITES, and 139 automatically detected IXP SITES run by 96 operators (14 of which were manually reported).

We found 97 operators, of which 40 are not present on the AS112 operator list, including three of the most queried operators (Fig. 1a). Similarly, Fan et al. [29] in 2013 found 64 SITES, of which 35 were not on the published list at that time. Using the TXT records and online information (e.g. operators' websites), we categorise the operators (Fig. 1b; note that all "CDN" SITES belong to Cloudflare). 37 IXP operators host SITES, as suggested in [6].

Our measurements did not find 132 of the 189 operators on the published AS112 operator list, possibly because queries are drawn to more well-connected networks (e.g., Cloudflare). However, only 73 of these operators appear to be active: 3 of the 58 operators that listed a transit AS were neighbours of AS112 according to RIPE Stat [48], 69 operators at IXPs peered with AS112, according to PeeringDB [15], and another operator responded to `hostname.as112.arpa` queries on a unicast address listed on the website. We don't consider these operators in the following as we cannot confirm they are reachable by *any* clients.

The discrepancy between the SITES and operators found by us, and those listed by DNS-OARC on the AS112 website is likely because the list relies on manual effort: only SITES at IXPs are detected automatically. DNS-OARC could periodically run measurements to update the list, as discussed in [8], though this would require manual effort to parse and classify the TXT records.

Deployment sizes—AS112 DEPLOYMENTS differ in size. Cloudflare joined in 2022, using the platform of the Cloudflare public resolver [18], greatly increasing the number of SITES [8,29]. It is by far the largest DEPLOYMENT, with 216 discovered SITES, of which at least 177 contain multiple INSTANCES. Other DEPLOYMENTS are smaller, and many don't appear to have load-balanced SITES, as they never return the same answer with different NSIDs. As a result, the number of VPs that query each operator is unbalanced (Fig. 1a): Cloudflare is queried by 41.71% of VPs. The Gini coefficient [30] of the share of VPs that query each operator is 0.78, indicating high inequality. While there are many operators, this inequality is a concern as they contribute on a volunteer basis. The exit of a large operator could shift the load in an unpredictable manner, leading to cascading failure of smaller operators who can't deal with the load.

2.2 Geographic Distribution of AS112 Sites

In a volunteer-based system like AS112, SITES could cluster in regions where the project is well-known, skewing the geographic impact of localised failures. Additionally, AS112 queries originating in regions with low coverage might travel via international links, increasing network load and costs [33]. While AS112 queries are not generally latency sensitive, poorly-written applications may block waiting for the NXDOMAIN responses and would benefit from proximity to AS112.

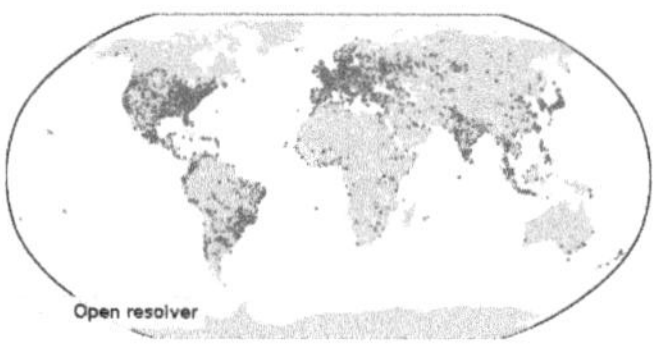

(a) Location of open resolvers

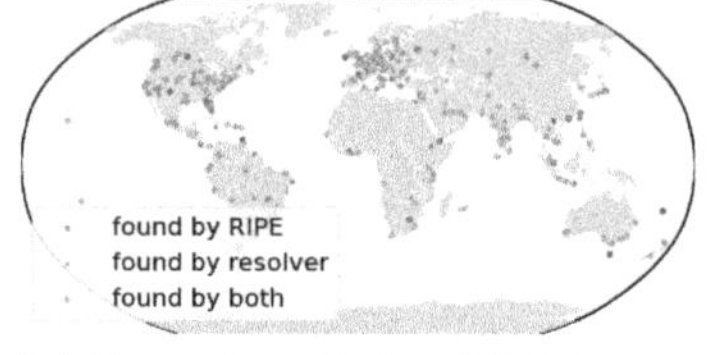

(b) Location of the AS112 SITES

Fig. 2. Location of open resolvers and AS112 SITES

Table 2. AS112 SITES per 1M inhabitants

UN Sub-Region	SITES/1M	UN Sub-Region	SITES/1M
Polynesia	3.56	Central Asia	0.11
Melanesia	3.45	Latin America and the Caribbean	0.10
Australia and New Zealand	0.50	Western Asia	0.09
Northern America	0.31	Sub-Saharan Africa	0.05
Western Europe	0.28	South-eastern Asia	0.03
Northern Europe	0.22	Northern Africa	0.02
Southern Europe	0.19	Southern Asia	0.01
Eastern Europe	0.14	Eastern Asia	0.01

AS112 SITES are mainly located in Europe and North America (Fig. 2b). To assess deployment density we count the number of SITES per 1M inhabitants in each UN subregion [4] (Table 2). Population is an imperfect approximation of AS112 demand, but we were unable to access representative AS112 query logs to determine sources of AS112 traffic, and leave this for future work. Apart from high rates in Polynesia and Melanesia (caused by two Cloudflare SITES), Australia/New Zealand, North America and Europe have the highest rates. Other regions would benefit from additional SITES, especially because queries in these regions are often sent across borders (§3.1) suggesting poor locality.

These results could be skewed by the placement of the VPs. The number of VPs in a country and its population [55] is only weakly correlated (Pearson correlation coefficient 0.15 for RIPE Atlas and 0.34 for open resolvers), and the number of SITES found in a country is more strongly correlated with the number of VPs than its population (correlation between population and number of SITES is 0.22 for RIPE Atlas and 0.38 for open resolvers, correlation between number of VPs and SITES is 0.78 for RIPE Atlas and 0.80 for open resolvers). There may be regions with undetected SITES because no VPs are close enough to query them.

RIPE Atlas probe locations may correlate with AS112 SITES because both attract the same type of volunteer operator. The uneven distribution of SITES found by resolvers is partly because some regions received many invalid responses: many resolvers in Africa and India received DNS errors or empty answers and most resolvers in China queried SITES whose answers were discarded because they encode the SITE location in the NSID, which is lost in recursive queries [9].

2.3 Network Distribution of AS112 Sites

Apart from geographical diversity (§2.2), AS112 must be well-connected for resilience and to ensure sensitive queries [14] are resolved locally. We count ASes directly connected to AS112, VPs in neighbouring ASes, and routing inefficiencies.

For some SITES, the AS112 website lists *host ASes* (final transit AS on the path to an AS112 SITE). To find more host ASes, we traceroute to `blackhole-1.iana.org`, using RIPE Atlas probes that only reached one SITE when querying `blackhole-1.iana.org`, to ensure traceroutes go to the same SITE. The host AS is the AS of the hop before `blackhole-1.iana.org`, determined by RIPE Stat.

We found 235 host ASes for 337 SITES: the website gave 33 host ASes for 289 SITES, and the traceroutes found 204 host ASes for another 48 SITES. For 37 of the 50 SITES for which we found a host AS using both methods, the host ASes were different; in this case we used the host AS given on the AS112 website. A total of 13.35% of SITES have several host ASes, with one DE-CIX SITE having 72 host ASes. CLOUDFLARENET hosts the most SITES (216), followed by MISAKA-ANYCAST (24 SITES). Most SITES aren't directly accessible to clients within their own AS: of the 36194 VPs that query a SITE with a known host AS, only 8.47% are in the host AS of any SITE, and only 5% also query that SITE.

The median SITE is queried from VPs in 8.0 ASes, but some SITES are queried from hundreds of ASes (Table 3). A log-log complementary cumulative distribution plot, omitted due to space constraints, is suggestive of a heavy-tailed popularity distribution but available data is insufficient to confirm [26].

To measure geographic spread of the VPs querying SITES and the extent queries come from widely distributed networks, we consider the *convex hull*. For the 80.52% of SITES queried from >2 locations we project VP coordinates onto an Azimuthal Equidistant Projection, centred on their mean coordinate, determine which VPs bound their convex hull, and calculate the area of the hull on the globe (Appendix D). While the hull area could be skewed by outlier VPs, we don't know the true distribution of clients in the hull, so we use it to approximate client spread. Most convex hulls are small, with a median area similar to Germany [55]. The smallest hull is $0.08km^2$; the largest, for a Hurricane Electric SITE, covers 98.78% of Earth [41] (Fig. 3a). The SITES that are queried by the most ASes have large hulls (Table 3), which is indicative of routing inefficiency, and possible anycast polarisation [43]. These SITES draw in many clients (correlation between hull size and number of VPs querying a SITE is 0.77), diverting them from more local AS112 SITES, leading to instability if the large AS112 SITE fails. Large hulls don't appear to increase response time: convex hull area and average response time (measured by RIPE Atlas) per SITE are only weakly correlated (Pearson correlation coefficient 0.46). However, SITES with large hulls are in areas with many VPs, so many VPs in the hull are close to the SITE (Table 3), and the number of clients on the geographic periphery of the hull may be larger.

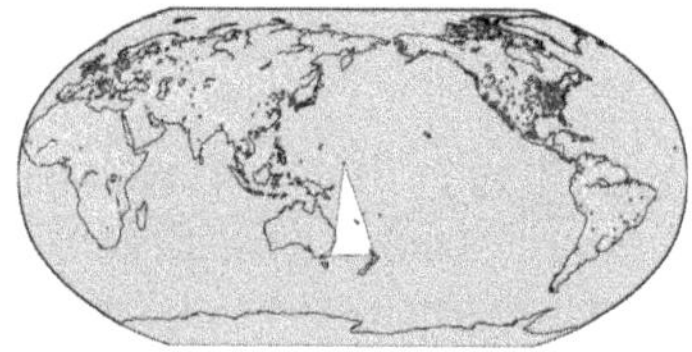

(a) Largest convex hull (shaded)   (b) AS Path Length Distribution

Fig. 3. Largest convex hull and AS path length distribution

Table 3. Top 10 SITES, by number of VP ASes

Operator & Country	ASes	Hull (km^2)	% Earth	Distance (km)		
				Mean	Median	90%-ile
Hurricane Electric, US	872	503.75M	98.78	6274.44	4138.50	11822.00
Hurricane Electric, US	713	503.75M	98.77	6077.09	4084.00	11822.00
RIPE NCC, NL	635	383.44M	75.18	2066.38	649.00	8578.00
Hurricane Electric, US	439	192.86M	37.82	4955.63	6174.00	7540.90
Hurricane Electric, US	435	192.86M	37.82	4953.53	6180.50	7542.80
Individual Network Berlin e.V., DE	410	323.90M	63.51	1518.59	538.00	3342.00
DE-CIX, DE	317	261.62M	51.30	1632.32	198.00	8734.00
npo avtomatiki, RU	303	300.64M	58.95	3806.39	1787.00	9399.00
npo avtomatiki, RU	293	304.60M	59.73	3947.63	1790.00	9399.00
Hivane, FR	293	310.89M	60.96	2791.67	462.00	9647.00

Finally, we consider the AS path length. Using RIPE Stat, we determine the AS of each traceroute hop, counting repeated ASes as one (i.e., B B * C * C → B * C with path length 3). The average length is 3.48 ASes, but some paths are noticeably longer (Fig. 3b); those ASes could benefit from AS112 deployment.

3 Comparing AS112 and the Root

The DNS root servers are run by 12 independent organisations, some of which (e.g. K-root [2] and F-root [32]) allow volunteers to apply to run a SITE. However, while the placement of some DNS root servers is known to be sub-optimal [34], it is more coordinated than the placement of AS112 SITES, which are run by an unlimited number of organisations that might not be aware of each other. In the following, we compare the placement of AS112 SITES and the 13 DNS root server DEPLOYMENTS, considering distance, response time, amount of queries sent across borders (§3.1), and distance inflation (§3.2). While AS112 mainly diverts queries from the `in-addr.arpa` servers, it also prevents queries for `home.arpa` and `service.arpa` from reaching the `arpa` nameservers, which are currently served by 12 of the 13 root letters (note that initial queries will still reach the root/`arpa` servers to retrieve the parent NS records, but subsequent queries will only go to AS112). Additionally, comparing AS112 to the more carefully planned root provides an insight into the effectiveness of unplanned anycast deployments.

Table 4. Number of queries and SITES in the root dataset

	Probes	Answers	SITES	A	B	C	D	E	F	G	H	I	J	K	**L**	M
IPv4	10274	133562	1076	27	6	12	164	225	239	6	12	77	101	100	88	19
IPv6	3345	43485	740	25	6	12	106	146	145	5	12	57	84	74	55	13

Every four minutes, RIPE Atlas probes send `CHAOS TXT hostname.bind` queries directly to the 13 root servers [46]. Root server operators encode the SITE location in their responses using airport codes (e.g., `c01.prg.eroot` for a E-root SITE in Prague) or a custom mapping [3,53], enabling us to geolocate the SITE.

We consider IPv4 and IPv6 `hostname.bind` queries to the root servers sent in the same hour as RIPE Atlas `hostname.as112.arpa` queries, from probes that sent `hostname.as112.arpa` or `hostname.as112.net` queries in the same address family (one response per address family, probe and root letter, excluding probes receiving errors or abnormal responses [44]). We assume responses from the same root letter encoding the same location come from the same SITE. As in §2, we do not exclude the 0.70% of root responses whose geolocation violates speed-of-light constraints. Table 4 summarises the root dataset.

3.1   Distance, Response Time, and Geographic Reach

Root server deployments are planned but may be resource constrained, AS112 deployment is uncoordinated but potentially larger in scope. We compare the distance and response time from our VPs to the AS112 and root SITES. Distance, also considered in similar studies [17,36,38,50], gives a lower bound on latency (due to the speed of light [50]) and shows how the VPs are distributed relative to the SITES. AS112 queries are not generally latency sensitive, but comparing response times lets us compare the real-world performance of AS112 to the root.

We count each {VP, SITE} pair once, and only use response times from RIPE Atlas (open resolver response times are inflated since they include the path from the measurement host to the resolver). Most probes sent multiple queries to the same SITE (§2), and we take the average of those response times.

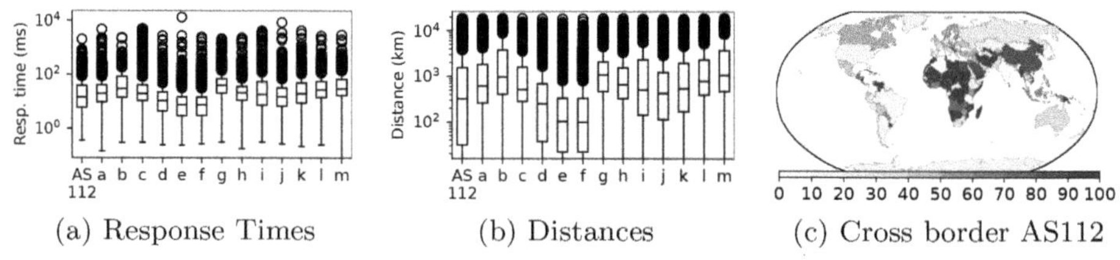

(a) Response Times   (b) Distances   (c) Cross border AS112

Fig. 4. Distances, response time, and country boundaries

AS112 has *lower* median response times and distances than the root servers. The median response time to the root is 18.66ms, for AS112 it is 14.33ms (23.21% lower). The median distance between RIPE Atlas probes and the root is 504.0km, the median distance between VPs and AS112 is 322.0km (36.11% difference). Response times (Fig. 4a) and distances (Fig. 4b) vary between root letters: F and E-root have lower median response time (7.57ms, 7.58ms) and distance (100.00km, 101.00km) than AS112. The better AS112 performance is partly due to the prevalence of Cloudflare; non-Cloudflare SITES have lower median response time (16.73ms) but higher median distance (684.00km) than the root. As of 2023, 76% of F-root SITES are hosted by Cloudflare [11], which explains its performance. Still, this shows that uncoordinated deployment *at scale* performs well.

Queries that leak to AS112 may contain sensitive device names or configuration details [14]. Failing to handle these locally, particularly sending them across borders, could present a privacy issue. We find 31.94% of AS112 queries were sent across borders, compared to 50.88% of root queries, showing AS112 is more effective at handling queries locally. However, AS112 has more SITES than F-root (the largest root letter we found), and only 12.20% of F-root queries cross borders, so the number of AS112 queries crossing borders is high. Queries cross borders more in areas with low coverage (Fig. 4c, §2.2), though this may be skewed by low data availability in, e.g., China (§2.2). These areas could benefit from more AS112

SITES, particularly as only 28.24% of queries that cross borders are answered in a neighbouring country (only 31.33% in the same UN subregion).

3.2   Distance Inflation

To determine how well-placed the AS112 and root SITES are relative to each probe, we consider the distances between each RIPE Atlas probe and the AS112 and root SITES it queries. We define the *Normalised Distance Score* ($\overline{D}$) as:

$$\overline{D} = \frac{(D_{\text{AS112}} - D_{\text{Root}\Downarrow})}{(D_{\text{Root}\Uparrow} - D_{\text{Root}\Downarrow})} \tag{1}$$

where D_{AS112} is the distance to the furthest AS112 SITE queried by the probe, and $D_{\text{root}\Uparrow}$ and $D_{\text{root}\Downarrow}$ are the distance to the furthest and closest queried root SITE. This sets the distance to the closest and furthest root to 0 and 1, and maps the distance to AS112 into that interval. We consider the furthest AS112 SITE as 60.04% of probes only queried one SITE, for the others this is the maximum $\overline{D}$.

Most AS112 SITES are well placed: for 22.65% of probes, the distance to AS112 is less than, or equal to, the minimum distance to the root, while for another 71.71%, it is not more than the distance to the furthest root SITE (Fig. 5a). Many cases where AS112 is further away than any root server ($\overline{D} > 1$) occur when routing to AS112 doesn't choose the closest SITE. If the probes with $\overline{D} > 1$ queried the closest AS112 SITE, they would have an average $\overline{D}$ of -0.05.

We define *distance inflation* as the difference between the distance to the SITE queried by a VP and the closest SITE (similar to [38,50]). Unlike [10,23,34,36,37, 50], we consider distance and not latency inflation: measuring latency inflation requires the unicast addresses of the SITES (to measure the latencies to specific SITES), which are not always known. AS112 has a median distance inflation of 199km, for the root it varies [34,36,38] from 474km (L-root) to 0km (B, C, E, F, G, H, and M-root) (Fig. 5b). The distance to AS112 could be decreased: only 22.24% of VPs query the closest AS112 SITE, compared to 30.37% for L-Root and 83.60% for B-Root. If every VP queried the closest AS112 SITE, the median *distance* would be 23.00km. Despite the more systematic deployment of the root, 12.33% of RIPE Atlas probes are closer to an AS112 SITE than to any root SITE.

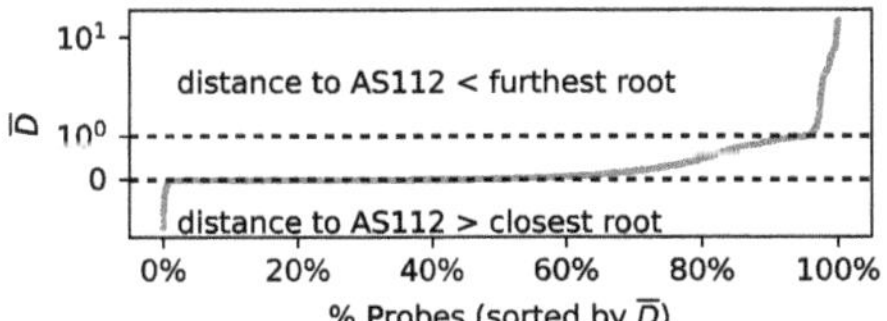

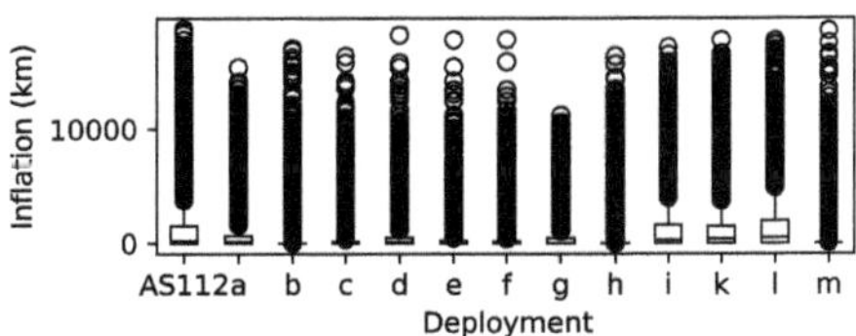

(a) Normalised Distance Score for all probes   (b) Distance inflation for AS112 and root

Fig. 5. Normalised Distance Score and distance inflation

Smaller anycast networks often have lower distance inflation because queries are less likely to go to suboptimal SITES [23,34,36,50]; AS112 might have higher distance inflation because it has more SITES (469) than any root letter (Table 4). Inflation also varies between AS112 operators: for 15.46% there is no distance inflation; 20.62% of operators have mean distance inflation > 1000km. Thus, while AS112 SITES are well placed, compared to the root, providing access to the geographically closest SITE would further decrease distances.

4   Related Work

Fan et al. [29] compared `CHAOS TXT` query accuracy (§3) with `hostname.as112.arpa`, while Ballini et al. [10] compared anycast characteristics of F-root, J-root and AS112. Unlike our work, these studies don't consider AS112 deployment characteristics such as operators and location. Others studied dynamic updates sent to AS112 [12,13], or sensitive information in AS112 queries [14]. An informal measurement by the AS112 project in 2012 also counted the number of SITES[8].

Anycast characteristics of root servers, e.g., catchments [38], latency [23,37, 50], stability [50,54] and inflation [34,36,50], are frequently studied. Other targets include CDNs [17,34,40], cloud providers [42], TLD servers [37,50] and public resolvers [25]. Like our work, [16] studies client and server locations, but for a non-anycast CDN. We use DNS queries to find SITES, other anycast measurements use ping [19–21], TCP logs [43], or use SITES as measurement hosts [24,52].

5   Conclusions

We studied the deployment of AS112, finding 469 SITES, significantly more than past studies [8,29]. While these SITES are run by 97 operators (§2.1), one operator is queried by 41.71% of VPs. The median distance that AS112 queries travel is 36.11% lower than root queries, with 23.21% lower response times (§3.1). Still, geographic and network diversity could be improved: AS112 is mainly deployed in Europe, North America and Oceania, only 8.47% of VPs are in an AS that is connected to AS112, and 31.94% of AS112 queries are sent to different countries. Future work will study differences in IPv4 and IPv6 AS112 queries; determine the quantity and source of AS112 queries (similar to [12,13]), and query privacy.

Acknowledgements. This research was partly funded by the University of Glasgow School of Computing Science Minerva Scholarship.

Disclosure of Interests. The authors have no competing interests to declare that are relevant to the content of this article.

A   Ethical Considerations

We use the RIPE Atlas measurement platform to collect DNS responses from, and latency measurements to, publicly available servers. In some cases the information in the TXT records returned in response to queries for `hostname.as112.arpa` and `hostname.as112.net` contains personal information (e.g., the name of a contact person for the SITE). While this data has been made publicly available by the SITE operator, we treat it as confidential.

We also make queries to a list of open recursive resolvers, derived from a Censys scan [27]. While these queries were made without prior approval from the resolver operator, we minimised any potential impact that the additional traffic might have. Queries were strictly rate-limited, to one query per second, and were spread evenly over time to avoid traffic spikes. The additional traffic that our study has generated toward these open resolvers is negligible, and we do not expect it to have any operational impact.

Advice was sought about this study from our institution's research ethics committee, who stated that approval was not required.

B   Comparing `.arpa` and `.net` Responses

As discussed in §2, 3487 probes in IPv4 (1373 IPv6) received different responses for `hostname.as112.arpa` and `hostname.as112.net` queries to the same nameserver. 10182/12546 such IPv4 responses (3726/4389 IPv6) encode the same operator and location, with formatting differences. Another 1264 IPv4 responses (393 IPv6) come from the same operator in a different location, or a related operator (i.e., NIX.CZ and NIX.SK), possibly due internal routing decisions.

To determine whether the remaining 1100 IPv4 queries (270 IPv6) go to different SITES due to anycast flaps, we re-ran the IPv4 `hostname.as112.arpa` and `hostname.as112.net` queries on the 479 probes in this set, twice, ~90min apart. Of the 427 probes that participated, 310 no longer received inconsistent responses from the nameservers that previously gave inconsistent results (for 64 probes the result differs depending on the nameserver). Here the difference could be caused by anycast flaps or unstable routing. We leave explaining why the remaining 53 probes consistently received different responses for future work.

C   Nameserver Impact on AS112 Site Choice

Queries to `blackhole-1,2.iana.org`, `prisoner.iana.org` and `blackhole. as112.arpa` are mostly routed to the same SITE (94.40% for IPv4 and 93.27% for IPv6 queries, see §2). Of the probes whose queries for `hostname.as112.arpa` reach multiple SITES in IPv4, 85.92% reach SITES run by different operators (96.95% in IPv6), indicating the query is not being load balanced between SITES run by the same operator. Rather, the cause seems to be a lack of DNAME adoption, anycast flaps/routing instability, or differing BGP announcements.

Note that this section only considers `hostname.as112.arpa` queries, sent by probes that successfully queried all four nameservers.

DNAME adoption— 69 IPv4 probes (16 IPv6) reach the same SITE when querying `blackhole-1.iana.org`, `blackhole-2.iana.org` and `prisoner.iana.org` (the *direct delegation nameservers*), but a different SITE when querying `blackhole.as112.arpa`, because the SITE they query for the direct delegation nameservers doesn't support DNAME [5]. If a SITE doesn't announce the prefix for `blackhole.as112.arpa`, then these queries will go to a different SITE. We assume a SITE supports DNAME if it responds to `hostname.as112.arpa` or `hostname.as112.net` queries sent to `blackhole.as112.arpa`, in IPv4 or IPv6.

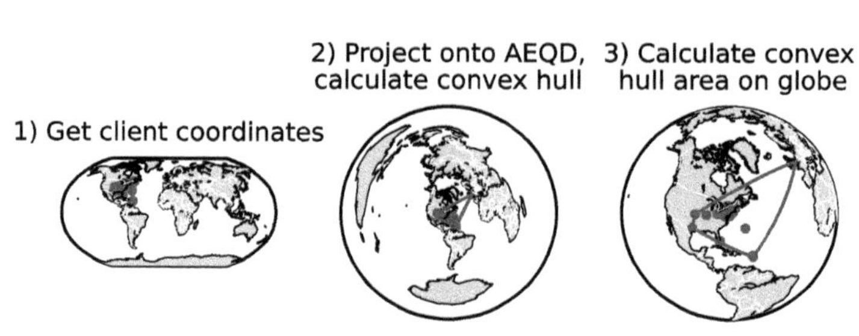

Fig. 6. Process to calculate the convex hull area.

Anycast flaps—The remaining 499 IPv4 probes (115 IPv6) queried at least one DNAME SITE when querying direct delegation nameservers. To determine if they query multiple SITES due to anycast flaps or routing instability, we repeat the IPv4 and IPv6 `hostname.as112.arpa` measurements for these probes after 1-3 days. 492 IPv4 and 115 IPv6 probes participated in these measurements. In IPv4, 63 probes no longer queried multiple SITES (11 in IPv6). Of the 429 IPv4 probes that still queried multiple SITES, 295 queried a different set of SITES than before (44 of 104 probes in IPv6). Thus, for 358 probes in IPv4 and 55 probes in IPv6, the difference is likely due to anycast flaps or other routing instability.

BGP Announcements— Some probes consistently queried one SITE for the direct delegation nameservers and another for `blackhole.as112.arpa`, but not due to DNAME or anycast flaps. The direct delegation nameservers use a different anycast prefix than `blackhole.as112.arpa`, so the probes' ASes might receive the announcements for the two prefixes from different ASes. We run traceroutes to all four nameservers, using 52 IPv4 probes (51 IPv6) that fit this category. We determine the last AS before AS112 (final AS for unsuccessful traceroutes) using RIPE Stat [48]. For 41/52 IPv4 probes (17/51 IPv6), this AS is the same in paths to the direct delegation nameservers, but different for `blackhole.as112.arpa`, suggesting the prefix for `blackhole.as112.arpa` is announced by a different AS.

D   Convex Hull Calculation

As shown in Fig. 6, to determine the convex hull (§2.3) we project the VP coordinates onto an Azimuthal Equidistant Projection, centred on their mean coordinate, determine which VPs bound the convex hull, and calculate the area of the hull on Earth (modelling Earth as a perfect sphere).

References

1. https://github.com/ip2location/ip2location-iata-icao/blob/3efa68a77f36de52035a87a666581b712a823c7e/iata-icao.csv
2. K-root. https://www.ripe.net/analyse/dns/k-root/
3. Root Server Technical Operations Association. https://root-servers.org/
4. UNSD Methodology. https://unstats.un.org/unsd/methodology/m49/overview
5. Abley, J., Dickson, B., Kumari, W.A., Michaelson, G.G.: AS112 Redirection Using DNAME. Tech. Rep. RFC 7535, IETF (May 2015). https://doi.org/10.17487/RFC7535
6. Abley, J., Maton, W.F.: AS112 Nameserver Operations. Tech. Rep. RFC 7534, IETF (May 2015). https://doi.org/10.17487/RFC7534
7. AS112 Project: AS112 Operator Listing. https://www.as112.net/ops-listing/
8. AS112 Project: How many public AS112 nodes are there as of March 31, 2012? https://web.archive.org/web/20120618101627/https://public.as112.net/node/30 (Jun 2012)
9. Austein, R.: DNS Name Server Identifier (NSID) Option. Tech. Rep. RFC 5001, IETF (Aug 2007). https://doi.org/10.17487/RFC5001
10. Ballani, H., Francis, P., Ratnasamy, S.: A measurement-based deployment proposal for IP anycast. In: Proceedings IMC. ACM, Rio de Janeriro Brazil (Oct 2006). https://doi.org/10.1145/1177080.1177109
11. Bellis, R.: The State of F-Root. https://www.isc.org/blogs/2023-f-root-update/ (Feb 2023)
12. Broido, A., Nemeth, E., claffy, k.: Spectroscopy of private DNS update sources. In: Proceedings the Third IEEE Workshop on Internet Applications. WIAPP 2003 (Jun 2003). https://doi.org/10.1109/WIAPP.2003.1210282
13. Broido, A., Shang, H., Fomenkov, M., Hyun, Y., Claffy, K.C.: The Windows of Private DNS Updates. SIGCOMM CCR **36**(3) (2006)
14. Bromirski, L.: Bezpieczeństwo sieci w kontekście usług DNS. https://lukasz.bromirski.net/docs/prezos/plnog2024/dns-as112-update.pdf (May 2024)
15. CAIDA: PeeringDB. https://www.caida.org/catalog/datasets/peeringdb/
16. Calder, M., Fan, X., Hu, Z., Katz-Bassett, E., Heidemann, J., Govindan, R.: Mapping the expansion of Google's serving infrastructure. In: Proceedings IMC. ACM (Oct 2013). https://doi.org/10.1145/2504730.2504754
17. Calder, M., Flavel, A., Katz-Bassett, E., Mahajan, R., Padhye, J.. Analyzing the Performance of an Anycast CDN. In: Proceedings IMC. ACM (Oct 2015). https://doi.org/10.1145/2815675.2815717
18. Chen, H.: Cloudflare is joining the AS112 project to help the Internet deal with misdirected DNS queries. https://cfl.re/3W2fFjg (Dec 2022)
19. Cicalese, D., Augé, J., Joumblatt, D., Friedman, T., Rossi, D.: Characterizing IPv4 anycast adoption and deployment. In: Proceedings CoNEXT. ACM (Dec 2015). https://doi.org/10.1145/2716281.2836101

20. Cicalese, D., Joumblatt, D., Rossi, D., Buob, M.O., Augé, J., Friedman, T.: A fistful of pings: Accurate and lightweight anycast enumeration and geolocation. In: Proceedings Infocom. IEEE (Apr 2015). https://doi.org/10.1109/INFOCOM.2015.7218670

21. Cicalese, D., Rossi, D.: A longitudinal study of IP Anycast. SIGCOMM Comput. Commun. Rev. **48**(1) (Apr 2018). https://doi.org/10.1145/3211852.3211855

22. Cloudflare Radar: AS112. https://radar.cloudflare.com/as112

23. de Oliveira Schmidt, R., Heidemann, J., Kuipers, J.H.: Anycast Latency: How Many Sites Are Enough? In: Passive and Active Measurement (2017). https://doi.org/10.1007/978-3-319-54328-4_14

24. de Vries, W.B., de O. Schmidt, R., Hardaker, W., Heidemann, J., de Boer, P.T., Pras, A.: Broad and load-aware anycast mapping with verfploeter. In: Proceedings IMC. ACM (Nov 2017). https://doi.org/10.1145/3131365.3131371

25. De Vries, W.B., Van Rijswijk-Deij, R., De Boer, P.T., Pras, A.: Passive Observations of a Large DNS Service: 2.5 Years in the Life of Google. In: 2018 Network Traffic Measurement and Analysis Conference (TMA). IEEE, Vienna (Jun 2018). https://doi.org/10.23919/TMA.2018.8506536

26. Downey, A.: Lognormal and Pareto distributions in the Internet. Comput. Commun. (2005). https://doi.org/10.1016/j.comcom.2004.11.001

27. Durumeric, Z., Adrian, D., Mirian, A., Bailey, M., Halderman, J.A.: A search engine backed by internet-wide scanning. In: Proceedings CCS. ACM (Oct 2015). https://doi.org/10.1145/2810103.2813703

28. Durumeric, Z., Clark, H., Cody, J., Cubit, E., Ellison, M., Izhikevich, L., Mirian, A.: Censys: a map of internet hosts and services. In: Proceedings of the ACM SIGCOMM 2025 Conference. pp. 147–163. SIGCOMM '25, ACM, New York, NY, USA (Aug 2025). https://doi.org/10.1145/3718958.3754344

29. Fan, X., Heidemann, J., Govindan, R.: Evaluating anycast in the domain name system. In: 2013 Proceedings IEEE INFOCOM (Apr 2013). https://doi.org/10.1109/INFCOM.2013.6566965

30. Hasell, J.: Measuring inequality: What is the Gini coefficient? https://ourworldindata.org/what-is-the-gini-coefficient (Jun 2023)

31. Hendriks, R., Luckie, M., Jonker, M., Sommese, R., van Rijswijk-Deij, R.: Laces: an open, fast, responsible and efficient longitudinal anycast census system. In: Proceedings of the 2025 ACM Internet Measurement Conference, pp. 445–461. IMC '25, ACM, New York, NY, USA (2025). https://doi.org/10.1145/3730567.3764484

32. ISC: Hosting an F-Root Node. https://www.isc.org/froot-process/ (Dec 2023)

33. Kende, M., Rose, K.: Promoting Local Content Hosting to Develop the Internet Ecosystem. Internet Society (Jan, Tech. rep. (2015)

34. Koch, T., Katz-Bassett, E., Heidemann, J., Calder, M., Ardi, C., Li, K.: Anycast in context: a tale of two systems. In: Proceedings SIGCOMM. ACM (Aug 2021). https://doi.org/10.1145/3452296.3472891

35. Lemon, T., Cheshire, S.: Service Registration Protocol for DNS-Based Service Discovery. Internet Draft draft-ietf-dnssd-srp-27, IETF (Feb 2025)

36. Li, Z., Levin, D., Spring, N., Bhattacharjee, B.: Internet anycast: Performance, problems, & potential. In: Proceedings SIGCOMM. ACM (Aug 2018). https://doi.org/10.1145/3230543.3230547

37. Liang, J., Jiang, J., Duan, H., Li, K., Wu, J.: Measuring query latency of top level DNS servers. In: Passive and Active Measurement (2013). https://doi.org/10.1007/978-3-642-36516-4_15

38. Liu, Z., Huffaker, B., Fomenkov, M., Brownlee, N., claffy, k.: Two days in the life of the DNS anycast root servers. In: Passive and Active Network Measurement (2007). https://doi.org/10.1007/978-3-540-71617-4_13
39. Maton, W.F., Abley, J.: I'm Being Attacked by PRISONER.IANA.ORG! Tech. Rep. RFC 6305, IETF (Jul 2011). https://doi.org/10.17487/RFC6305
40. McQuistin, S., Uppu, S.P., Flores, M.: Taming Anycast in the Wild Internet. In: Proceedings IMC. ACM (Oct 2019). https://doi.org/10.1145/3355369.3355573
41. Milo, R., Jorgensen, P., Moran, U., Weber, G., Springer, M.: BioNumbers—the database of key numbers in molecular and cell biology. Nucleic Acids Research **38**(Database issue) (Jan 2010). https://doi.org/10.1093/nar/gkp889
42. Moura, G.C.M., Castro, S., Hardaker, W., Wullink, M., Hesselman, C.: Clouding up the Internet: How centralized is DNS traffic becoming? In: Proceedings IMC. ACM (Oct 2020). https://doi.org/10.1145/3419394.3423625
43. Moura, G.C.M., et al.: Old but gold: prospecting TCP to engineer and live monitor DNS anycast. In: Passive and Active Measurement (2022). https://doi.org/10.1007/978-3-030-98785-5_12
44. Nosyk, Y., et al.: Intercept and Inject: DNS Response Manipulation in the Wild. In: Passive and Active Measurement (2023). https://doi.org/10.1007/978-3-031-28486-1_19
45. Pfister, P., Lemon, T.: Special-Use Domain 'home.arpa.'. Tech. Rep. RFC 8375, IETF (May 2018). https://doi.org/10.17487/RFC8375
46. RIPE Atlas: Built-in measurements. https://atlas.ripe.net/docs/getting-started/built-in-measurements
47. RIPE NCC: RIPE Atlas. https://atlas.ripe.net/statistics/coverage
48. RIPE NCC: RIPEstat. https://stat.ripe.net/
49. Rose, S., Wijngaards, W.: DNAME Redirection in the DNS. Tech. Rep. RFC 6672, IETF (Jun 2012). https://doi.org/10.17487/RFC6672
50. Sarat, S., Pappas, V., Terzis, A.: On the use of anycast in DNS. In: Proceedings of 15th International Conference on Computer Communications and Networks (Oct 2006). https://doi.org/10.1109/ICCCN.2006.286248
51. Schomp, K., Callahan, T., Rabinovich, M., Allman, M.: On measuring the client-side DNS infrastructure. In: Proceedings IMC. ACM, Barcelona Spain (Oct 2013). https://doi.org/10.1145/2504730.2504734
52. Sommese, R., et al.: MAnycast2: using anycast to measure anycast. In: Proceedings IMC. ACM (Oct 2020). https://doi.org/10.1145/3419394.3423646
53. Steurer, F., Wagner, D., Lachos, D., Feldmann, A., Fiebig, T.: The Roots Go Deep: Measuring '.' Under Change. In: Proceedings IMC. ACM (2024). https://doi.org/10.1145/3646547.3689008
54. Wei, L., Heidemann, J.: Does anycast hang up on you (UDP and TCP)? IEEE Trans. Netw. Serv. Manage. **15**(2) (Jun 2018). https://doi.org/10.1109/TNSM.2018.2804884
55. World Bank: Open data. https://data.worldbank.org

The Future of DNS Privacy: A Comparison of DNS over QUIC and DNS over HTTP/3

Philipp Bielefeld, Felix Hoffmann[(✉)], Steffen Sassalla, vasilis ververis[(✉)], and Vaibhav Bajpai[(✉)]

Hasso Plattner Institute, University of Potsdam, Potsdam, Germany
`felix.hoffmann@student.hpi.uni-potsdam.de`,
`{vasilis.ververis,vaibhav.bajpai}@hpi.de`

Abstract. This study presents a large-scale empirical analysis of DNSover-Encryption (DoE) protocols, focusing on the adoption, protocol feature support, and impact on webpage loading performance. We conducted measurements across over three thousand DoE resolvers, characterizing their support for features such as session resumption and 0-Round-trip Time (RTT) in DNS-over-QUIC (DoQ) and DNS-over-HTTP/3 (DoH/3). Despite broader feature adoption by DoQ, major browsers currently favor DoH/3. Our extensive latency measurements demonstrate that both protocols perform comparably, with DoQ slightly outperforming on average. Complementary experiments with the top one million websites show negligible overall page load time penalties when using DoQ or DoH/3 compared to traditional DNS-over-UDP (Do53), even under low-latency conditions.

Further, our analysis explores the relationship between webpage complexity, quantified via metrics including number of objects, queried servers, and `MIME` type diversity, and the performance impact of DoE. We find no statistically significant correlation, indicating that DoEs performance effects are consistent across a range of website architectures. The study also addresses limitations in current client support for key protocol enhancements and validates effective 0-0-RTT resumption using proxy resolvers. Our findings alleviate prevalent concerns about DoE-induced performance degradation, supporting broader adoption of encrypted Domain Name System (DNS) protocols without sacrificing user experience. We release our datasets, source code, and analysis scripts to facilitate reproducibility and foster further research into encrypted DNS ecosystems.

1 Introduction

Initially, Internet development prioritized data transport over encryption. However, as critical systems increasingly rely on Internet communication, security concerns necessitated encryption. Today, most Internet traffic is encrypted, though components like DNS [37] still depend on unencrypted communication.

S. Ferlin-Reiter et al. (Eds.): PAM 2026, LNCS 16477, pp. 202–228, 2026.
https://doi.org/10.1007/978-3-032-18268-5_10

The DNS protocol is vital for domain resolution, traffic balancing, and Content Delivery Networks (CDNs) [33]. The rise of cloud providers has democratized access to these services, supporting diverse applications. While DNS traffic may seem less sensitive, it can disclose significant information, such as requested domains, requestor IP addresses, and query timestamps. Users typically remember domain names rather than numerical IP addresses, while machines operate on address-based systems. Although dynamic IP addresses complicate long-term tracking, behavioral patterns in DNS queries can still reveal user interests [35], highlighting the need for encrypted DNS traffic. To enhance privacy, DNS-over-TLS (DoT) was introduced in 2016 to encrypt DNS requests, but its adoption was limited due to performance concerns compared to Do53 [27]. For any encrypted DNS protocol to gain widespread use, it must balance privacy and performance. Recently standardized DoQ and DoH/3 offer reduced performance overhead, utilizing QUIC for improved speed and reliability. However, DoQ directly carries DNS queries, while DoH/3 encapsulates them within HTTP/3, complicating user decision-making. Given that domain resolution is crucial for web browsing, with numerous DNS requests per visit, any latency from encryption can hinder page load times. Users expect pages to load within two seconds [48], yet frequently visited sites generate at least 20 background DNS queries [6]. While existing research often compares RTT between DNS and newer protocols, there is limited evidence linking these metrics to real-world user experiences. Evaluations should prioritize user-perceived performance over network metrics. In light of these considerations, we address the following Research Questions (RQs):

RQ1: What percentage of resolvers support performance enhancement features such as session resumption and 0-RTT for DoQ and DoH/3?

RQ2: What is the performance penalty of DoE protocols such as DoQ and DoH/3 on website loading speed?

RQ3: Do certain website categories experience greater or lesser impacts from DoE resolvers, and what factors influence these variations?

To answer these RQs, we take a user-centric approach to evaluate encrypted DNS's impact on browsing, comparing features and performance costs across millions of websites. Our **research contributions** are:

1. Nearly all DoQ resolvers we measured support session resumption. Two thirds of DoQ resolvers also support 0-RTT. Only 65 % of DoH/3 resolvers support session resumption (see Sect. 4).
2. While DoQ and DoH/3 offer comparable speeds, DoQ has a slight edge due to DoH/3's absence of 0-RTT support. Interestingly, major browsers prefer DoH/3. Resolvers supporting all DoE protocols show superior performance, and DoQ's response times in this subset even outperform the average Do53 speeds (see Sect. 5).
3. There is no significant penalty for using DoQ or DoH/3 over Do53 in low-latency conditions. Average page load differences between DoQ, DoH/3, and

Do53 are $\leq 1\%$. There is no substantial correlation between the number of DNS requests made to load a website (i.e., web complexity) and its First Contentful Paint (FCP) performance (see Subsect. 5.1 and Subsect. 5.2).

We observe that nearly all DoQ resolvers support session resumption, with approximately two-thirds also enabling 0-RTT. In contrast, only 65% of DoH/3 resolvers offer session resumption. Despite the more extensive feature adoption by DoQ, DoH/3 remains the preferred protocol in major web browsers. Performance comparisons indicate both protocols achieve similar speeds, with DoQ demonstrating a slight average advantage. Additionally, our assessment of DoE effects on page load times across the top one million websites reveals no significant performance penalty for using DoQ or DoH/3 compared to traditional Do53 under low-latency network conditions, with average webpage load time differences ranging between -2 ms to 16 ms.

Reproducibility. In order to promote reproducibility and encourage further research, we have released our research artifacts, including the source code and analysis scripts, as well as the measurement study data [25]. Detailed documentation is provided to guide users on how to reproduce our results.

2   Background and Foundations

This section provides background on how unencrypted DNS enables user tracking—a privacy concern that modern encrypted protocols address. Although early encryption attempts were slow, newer protocols such as DoQ and DoH/3 leverage QUIC to improve both performance and privacy. Our study evaluates these claims by comparing DoQ and DoH/3.

2.1   DNS over Encryption Protocols

DoE protocols leverage existing connection protocols to securely transmit DNS queries and responses over encrypted channels, ensuring both the authenticity and integrity of the transmitted data. Although initially introduced to secure *stub-to-recursive* communication, technically they can also be used to secure *recursive-to-authoritative* communication [22]. Three such protocols have been standardized: DoT in May 2016 [28], DNS-over-HTTPS (DoH) in October 2018 [24], and DoQ in April 2024 [29]. To provide their security characteristics, they rely on Transport Layer Security (TLS) and its Public Key Infrastructure (PKI) based on X.509 certificates [11]. In the case of the QUIC protocol [31], the QUIC 1.3 handshake is integrated directly into the protocol itself [66].

2.2   Transport Layer Security

TLS is designed to create a secure communication channel between two endpoints over an insecure network, ensuring confidentiality, integrity, and authenticity. Currently, TLS 1.2 [14] and TLS 1.3 [57] are the most widely deployed

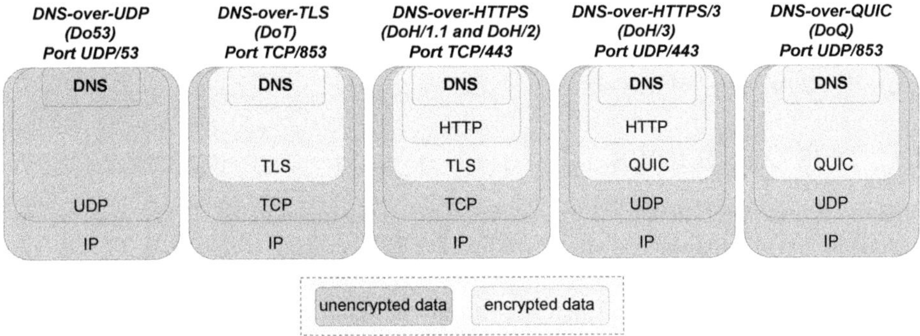

Fig. 1. The structure of the packet layers starting from the IP layer.

versions [53], with one of its primary applications being HTTPS [56] on the web. However, TLS is a versatile protocol used in various Internet applications. TLS consists of two main components: the record protocol and the handshake protocol. The record protocol is responsible for the integrity-protected and encrypted transmission of data using symmetric session keys. Meanwhile, the handshake protocol handles server (and client) authentication and establishes the session key for the record protocol.

To ensure authenticity of the server and optionally the client in the handshake phase, TLS relies on the X.509 PKI [11]. This PKI establishes authentication chains through a hierarchical structure (similar to DNS Security Extensions (DNSSEC)), where trust is anchored in a root Certificate Authority (CA) and cascades down through intermediate CAs, enabling secure verification of digital certificates across a network. This hierarchical model ensures that each entity's identity is authenticated by a trusted authority, creating a chain of trust from the root CA to the end user. Thus, a client can validate the identity and authenticity of a server's response, for example.

2.3 DNS over TLS

DoT is a DoE protocol designed to securely transmit DNS queries and responses over a TLS-encrypted channel, ensuring privacy and integrity of the exchanged data [28]. While initially defined for *stub-to-recursive* communication, DoT can also be extended to secure *recursive-to-authoritative* server connections. By default, DNS servers that run DoT should use port TCP/853 unless an alternative arrangement is negotiated between both parties [28]. Clients are responsible for maintaining knowledge of which DNS servers support TLS and must be capable of handling connections with both encrypted and unencrypted resolvers. When establishing a connection, clients are expected to follow the TLS protocol, including the proper verification of the server's certificate chain in accordance to best practices for secure communication [64].

Once the TLS handshake is completed, DNS queries and responses are exchanged over the TLS channel via the DNS wire format [46], a byte-level representation of DNS messages. This ensures that while the underlying data remains consistent with existing DNS standards, the communication is protected against eavesdropping and tampering.

2.4 DNS over HTTPS

DoH is a protocol designed to secure the transmission of DNS queries and responses by encapsulating them within HTTPS traffic, leveraging TLS to provide both authenticity and encryption [24]. In contrast to DoT, which operates DNS directly over TLS, DoH utilizes the intermediate layer HTTP between DNS and TLS (see Fig. 1). This architectural difference allows DoH to take advantage of various HTTP features, such as redirection, proxying, client authentication, compression, and response format negotiation. Furthermore, DoH allows HTTP clients such as web applications to interact with the DNS ecosystem seamlessly via standard Application Programming Interfaces (APIs). However, a challenge with DoH lies in the potential ambiguity surrounding caching mechanisms and error codes, since both HTTP and DNS natively implement these features. DoH can operate on Transmission Control Protocol (TCP) and TLS with HTTP/1.1 (legacy) and HTTP/2. In addition, it also supports HTTP/3, which operates over User Datagram Protocol (UDP) and uses QUIC as its transport layer, similar to DoQ. By default, HTTPS traffic runs on port 443 [56].

Unlike DoT and DoQ where clients only need to know the resolver and the port to exchange DNS information, DoH requires additional configuration. Specifically, DoH clients must be aware of the specific Uniform Resource Identifier (URI) path where the DNS queries are processed. For instance, Google's DoH resolver accepts queries at https://dns.google/dns-query. Additionally, DoH supports both HTTP GET and HTTP POST methods for transmitting DNS queries. When using HTTP POST, the DNS query is encoded in its wire format and embedded in the body of the HTTP request. For HTTP GET, the query is base64url [32] encoded and appended to the URI as a query parameter. For example, a GET request to Google's resolver would appear as https://dns.google/dns-query?dns=⟨b64-dns-query⟩. Although the DoH standardization specifies a URI path `dns-query` and parameter `dns`, it allows resolvers to use different configurations.

2.5 DNS over QUIC

QUIC is a secure transport protocol built on top of UDP, designed to minimize latency through features like 0-RTT resumption, advanced loss recovery, and multiplexing data streams to avoid head-of-line blocking [29,31]. Unlike TCP, QUIC implements reliability and ordering at the transport layer and integrates the TLS 1.3 handshake directly, ensuring encrypted and authenticated communication [66]. DoQ encapsulates DNS traffic within QUIC, providing equivalent security guarantees to DoT with performance benefits [29]. By default, DoQ servers listen on UDP port 853. Each DNS query is sent over a separate

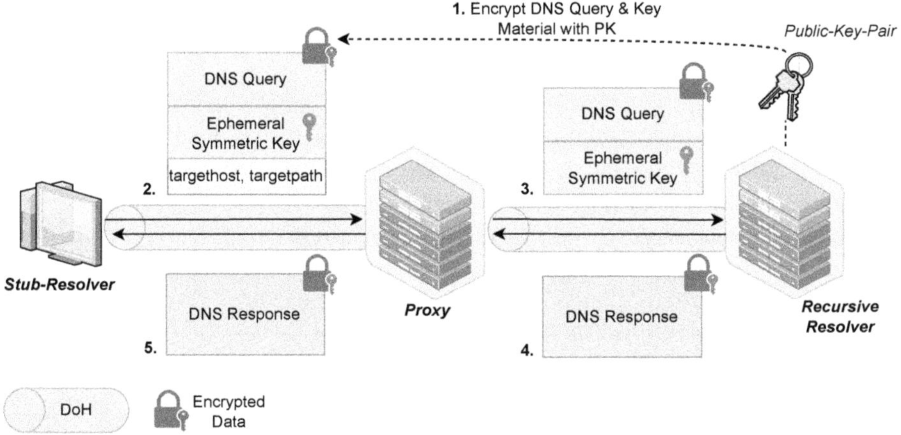

Fig. 2. Simplified illustration of the oDoH protocol. Green tunnels indicate DoH connections. Blue boxes show data encrypted with the resolver's public key; red boxes show data encrypted with the client's ephemeral symmetric key.

QUIC stream, enabling concurrent requests without TCP's head-of-line blocking, improving throughput and responsiveness. Queries and responses use the standard DNS wire format [45]. DoQ also defines new transport-specific error codes, such as `DOQ_EXCESSIVE_LOAD`, to signal server resource constraints and enhance error handling.

2.6 Oblivious DNS Over HTTPS

While DoE protocols encrypt DNS queries between stub resolvers and Recursive Resolver (RR), the RR still learns the client's IP address, enabling user tracking similar to unencrypted Do53. To enhance privacy, Oblivious DNS-over-HTTPS (oDoH) was standardized in 2022 [34] as an extension of DoH that adds a proxy to prevent any single server from seeing both client identity and DNS query contents. As illustrated in Fig. 2, the client encrypts its DNS query and an ephemeral symmetric key with the resolver's public key using Hybrid Public Key Encryption (HPKE), and sends this to a proxy over DoH (see Subsect. 2.4). The proxy forwards the encrypted query to the resolver but cannot decrypt it. Only the resolver, possessing the private key, can decrypt and answer the query, encrypting its response with the ephemeral symmetric key using an Authenticated Encryption with Associated Data (AEAD) scheme to ensure confidentiality and integrity. The proxy then relays the encrypted response back to the client, which decrypts it with the previously generated symmetric key.

This design ensures that the resolver cannot link client IPs to query contents, and the proxy cannot access query details. Even if routing information (`targethost`, `targetpath`) is tampered with, only the resolver can decrypt and respond correctly, preserving response integrity.

2.7   Security and Privacy Considerations

All DoE protocols inherit the security properties of the underlying TLS version, providing confidentiality, integrity, and authentication [63]. However, privacy risks arise during resolver discovery: clients typically probe the default DoE port (e.g., TCP/853 for DoT) to establish connections [13]. Such probing can be targeted by attackers performing downgrade or redirect attacks by blocking probes, forcing the client to fall back to unencrypted Do53.

RFC 8310 [13] defines two privacy usage profiles to mitigate this risk: *Opportunistic Privacy*, where clients prefer encryption but do not strictly authenticate resolvers, allowing use of potentially untrusted servers (e.g., discovered via DHCP). This profile protects against passive eavesdropping but remains vulnerable to active attacks. *Strict Privacy* requires pre-established trust, often implemented by pinning the resolver's public key fingerprint [18]. This prevents downgrades and ensures resolver authenticity but may lead to denial-of-service if connections fail or are blocked. These profiles, initially defined for DoT, apply conceptually to all DoE protocols, balancing privacy guarantees against availability and deployment complexity.

2.8   DNS Resolution Impact on Webpage Load Time

DNS resolution is a critical step in the webpage loading process, as the browser must resolve domain names to IP addresses before fetching any content. DNS lookups typically take between a few milliseconds and several hundred milliseconds, depending on factors such as server proximity, caching effectiveness, network congestion, and resolver performance. Since modern webpages often load resources from multiple distinct domains—including images, scripts, stylesheets, and third-party services—multiple DNS queries are triggered. Each additional lookup adds latency cumulatively, which can substantially prolong total page load time, especially on slower networks or mobile devices.

To mitigate this impact, techniques such as DNS prefetching allow browsers to proactively resolve domain names before they are actually needed, while preconnect can further reduce delays by initiating TCP and TLS handshakes early. CDN-based resolver distribution, anycast routing, and optimized TTL configurations also contribute to minimizing DNS-related latency. Effective DNS performance directly benefits user experience by reducing time to first byte and accelerating the loading sequence, thereby supporting improved search rankings, lower bounce rates, and higher user engagement. Our experiments incorporate DoE protocols to evaluate such latency effects within the broader webpage load timeline described in Sect. 2.8.

Loading a Webpage. Loading a webpage follows well-defined steps common to modern browsers like Chrome and Edge, both based on the Chromium engine [65]. Figure 3 illustrates the sequence of key events aligned with the *Navigation Timing* interface implemented in major browsers [61,68,69].

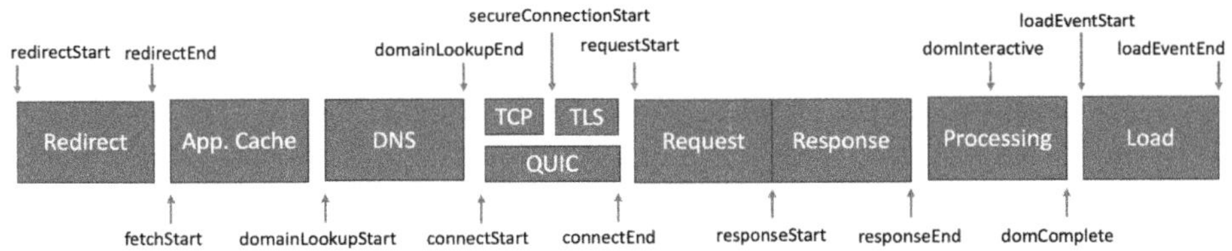

Fig. 3. Timeline of webpage loading highlighting key browser events captured in our experiments.

The process begins with a user-initiated request, minimizing redirects and disabling application caching to ensure consistent measurements. The browser first performs DNS resolution, influenced by the chosen DoE protocol. Next, it establishes the connection using TCP/TLS or QUIC, marked by `connectStart` and `connectEnd` during the TLS handshake. The HTTP `GET` request follows, with `responseStart` and `responseEnd` indicating receipt of the HTML document. As content streams in, the browser builds the Document Object Model (DOM). The `domInteractive` event marks when the DOM is ready for interaction, allowing non-blocking scripts to execute. Subsequent resource loading and script execution conclude with `loadEventStart` and `loadEventEnd`, although asynchronous loading often continues beyond these points.

Page Performance and Relevancy. Webpage performance critically impacts user satisfaction and business metrics [2,55]. In competitive domains like e-commerce, improved responsiveness can be a key differentiator [19,65]. Users typically expect answers within two seconds for simple queries [48], highlighting the importance of efficient DNS resolution. While search rankings are sensitive to page speed, the direct influence of DoE protocols on rankings remains unclear [61]. Variability in DNS performance across sites may partly explain ranking differences, motivating our analysis in Sect. 5.

Page Complexity. Modern webpages often have complex architectures, employing techniques like Single Page Applications (SPAs) that increase script usage and interactivity. This complexity affects the relative impact of DNS performance on overall load times. Key technical complexity factors include the `number of loaded objects` (total resources such as images, scripts, and stylesheets), the `total downloaded bytes` (larger payloads can reduce the proportional impact of DNS latency), the `distinct MIME types` (indicating content diversity and complexity), the `distinct queried servers` (reflecting microservices or third-party content distribution), the `non-origin queried servers` (often related to advertising and analytics domains), the `DNS request count` (higher request counts increase DNS protocol influence), and the `objects and bytes per MIME type` (providing deeper insight into how content types affect load times).

For example, `facebook.com` loads over 70 resources, including numerous JavaScript files, whereas `google.com` loads approximately 34 resources (see Fig. 4). This illustrates the wide range of complexity that can impact load behavior [5,67].

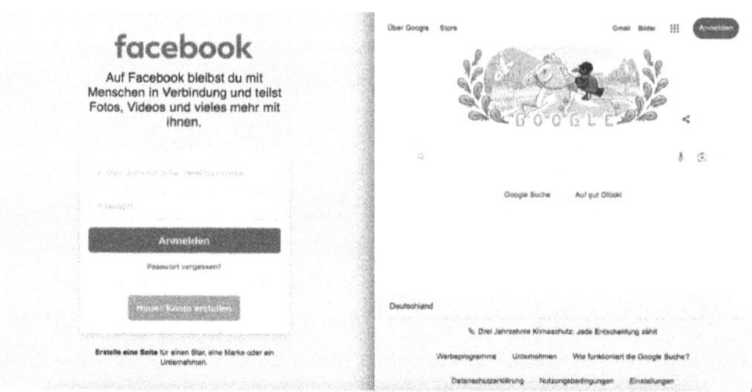

Fig. 4. Complexity comparison: Facebook (left) with 70+ objects versus Google (right) with fewer objects. Both display a simple interface but vary in underlying complexity.

2.9   Related Work

The effectiveness of any DNS protocol relies on resolver support. User adoption of DoQ has been limited by inadequate browser and DNS provider support. Early analyses [59] showed minimal QUIC adoption before standardization, with few hosts offering valid X.509 certificates. Despite this, QUIC's performance advantages over HTTP/2 [10] suggest potential benefits for DNS. Studies [43] found no DoQ resolvers prior to its 2019 standardization. However, DoE usage has increased in censorship-heavy regions, with DoH being less detectable than DoT. While DoE support has grown, actual usage remains low [20], with DoT dominating. Recent research [36] indicates a rise in DoQ resolvers, though many are experimental. A significant increase [40] in DoQ servers and improved certificate validity rates suggest growing productive use [42].

Existing DNS measurements [36] focus on latency, noting that misconfigured traffic amplification can inflate handshake times. Comparisons [6] show significant latency in DoT and DNS-over-HTTP/1.1 (DoH/1.1) compared to plain UDP, especially under TLS head-of-line blocking. Persistent connections are crucial for minimizing encryption overhead [43]. Performance comparisons indicate DoQ can outperform Do53 over short distances due to optimized hardware handling. Provider influence is significant, with response time disparities across DNS services [9]. When connection setups are minimized [26], median response times between Do53 and DoT become comparable.

Studies emphasize the impact of DNS resolvers on page load times. Research [37] suggests DoQ can delay time to first contentful paint, influenced by site-specific factors. QUIC's resilience in high-loss environments [10,37] correlates

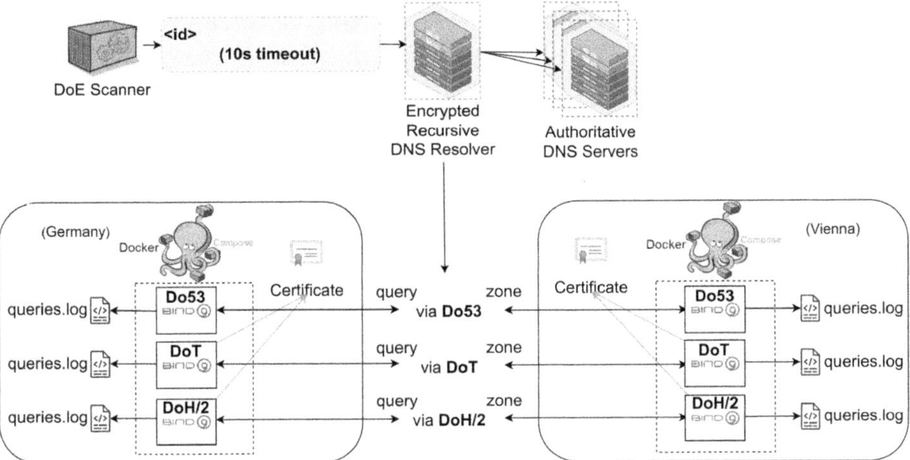

Fig. 5. Architecture of our authoritative DNS servers deployed in separate Docker containers to support multiple protocols and enable independent logging, with encrypted communication via DoT and DoH/2.

with improved performance. Studies [62] link DoQ and DNS-over-HTTP/2 (DoH/2) page load times to access technology, reporting significant latency increases, especially on mobile devices. This contrasts with earlier findings [67] that DNS lookups contribute modestly to critical path delays. Optimizing DNS loading times through persistent connection improvements remains essential. While earlier DoE protocols have been investigated, a comparative evaluation of the latest DoQ and DoH/3 is still needed, highlighting a research gap that our study addresses.

3   Methodology

This section describes the experimental framework used to evaluate DNS resolver capabilities, web performance impacts, and the relationship between webpage complexity and DoE protocols. We designed and implemented three complementary measurement experiments focused on DNS performance, website loading behavior, and site complexity analysis. Figure 6 provides a visual overview of these experimental setups.

3.1   Authoritative DNS Server Setup

To analyze the adoption of encrypted *recursive-to-authoritative* DNS communication, standardized in RFC 9539 [22], we query all discovered DoE resolvers with uniquely crafted Query Names (QNAMEs) targeting A records in our controlled DNS zone. Each QNAME follows a unique pattern `<id>.measurement.example`, with a wildcard `*.measurement.example` pointing to an IPv4 address hosting our measurement infrastructure (see Subsect. 3.6). This approach ensures that every query is resolvable and identifiable, permitting detailed observation of DoE resolver recursive behaviors and revealing whether encrypted channels are used in recursive-to-authoritative communications.

Our authoritative name servers, located in Germany and Austria, run *bind9* [30], which natively supports DoT and DoH/2. Since *bind9* logs do not differentiate query transport protocols, we deploy separate Docker containers for each protocol, all sharing the same zone file (see Fig. 5). These containers are based on Canonical's official *bind9* Ubuntu images [7]. Valid TLS certificates for DoT and DoH/2 are obtained via *certbot* using Let's Encrypt [16,17].

3.2   Discovery of IPv4 and IPv6 DNS Resolvers

We perform large-scale discovery of IPv4 DNS resolvers by executing frequent scans from a single vantage point using *ZMap* [15]. The scanner probes IPv4 addresses on UDP port 53 by requesting the A record for www.google.com[1], to maximize hits through cached responses due to the domain's high popularity [41] (see Fig. 5). We filter the resulting IPv4 addresses against a comprehensive blocklist of private and reserved address spaces [12,54] and abuse-reported ranges supplied by the *MassDNS* project [4], to respect network operators' requests and avoid scanning inappropriate targets.

Due to the infeasibility of IPv6 exhaustive scans, we leverage the *IPv6 Hitlist Service* [21,60] which curates responsive IPv6 UDP/53 addresses, updated weekly. Though this introduces a minor time lag that may bias results due to address churn [51], it remains the most practical approach. To automate retrieval, the system daily fetches updates from the IPv6 Hitlist Service. Our scan producer coordinates the scanning workflow by consuming IP outputs from *ZMap* via named pipes.

To avoid backpressure and blocking caused by limited pipe buffers [50], we implemented a large internal buffer and concurrent go routines to continuously read and schedule scan tasks to *Apache Kafka*. This design ensures robust, scalable handling of scanning pipelines without data loss or process interruptions. The scan producer's parsing logic requires minimal knowledge of scanner output formats, supporting seamless integration of new scanning tool versions and immediate follow-up scanning to mitigate the effects of IP churn [38,44,58].

3.3   Evaluating DNS Performance

The DNS performance experiment (see Fig. 6a) is managed by a Python script that merges resolver lists, removes duplicates, configures RouteDNS proxies for DoQ and DoH/3 (including fallbacks), and verifies resolver reachability with ping. It dispatches queries to test protocol support, warms resolver caches, measures round-trip times, session resumption, and 0-RTT. Results with resolver metadata and protocol support are stored in a database.

---

[1] A single query per IP is sufficient, given marginal gains from multiple probes.

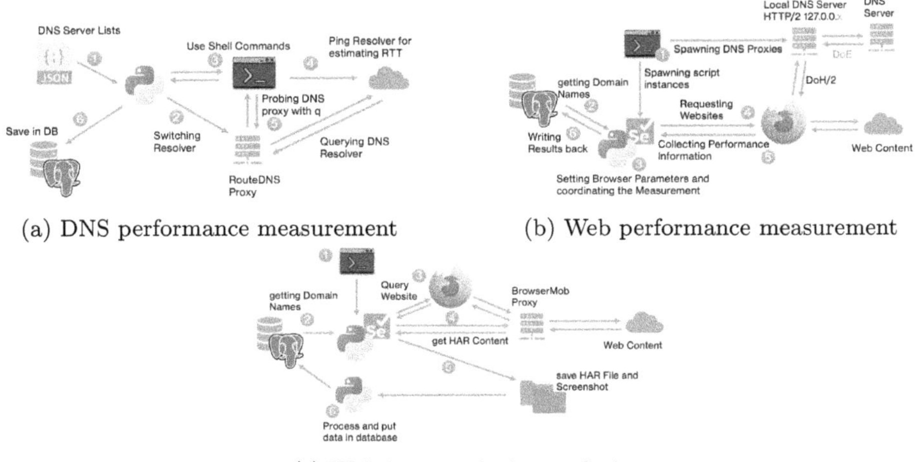

(a) DNS performance measurement   (b) Web performance measurement

(c) Website complexity analysis

Fig. 6. Architectures of the three experimental setups: DNS performance testing, controlled web performance evaluation, and web complexity assessment.

3.4 Assessing Website Performance

We evaluate web performance using the metrics established in [37]: FCP, Largest Contentful Paint (LCP), and Page Load Time (PLT). Testing the Tranco top 1M sites [52] with Firefox (for TLS 1.3 0-RTT support [3,47]), we use a local DNS proxy resolving via UDP, QUIC, or HTTP/3. Unlike prior methods [37], we assign the proxy's IP directly to the Selenium WebDriver for scalability.

The procedure, shown in Fig. 6b, comprises: 1. Starting DNS proxies and Python scripts with configuration parameters, 2. Obtaining domain sets from the database filtered by complexity, 3. Configuring WebDriver DNS to use the local proxy, 4. Performing warm-up requests to refresh upstream caches, 5. Executing measurement navigation upon successful warm-up; logging failures, 6. Recording all browser performance metrics in the database.

3.5 Measuring Web Complexity

The web complexity experiment (see Fig. 6c) quantifies site structure effects on DNS protocol performance via parallel Python scripts collecting network traffic. Steps include: 1. Running multiple Python instances for parallel queries, 2. One query per website, with error detection, 3. Capturing HAR-format network traffic on page load via BrowserMob Proxy, 4. Storing HAR files and screenshots for verification, 5. Processing HARs to extract metrics (e.g., object counts, MIME types, queried servers) saved to a database. This structured approach enables thorough, scalable analysis of DNS and webpage performance interdependencies.

3.6   Ethical Considerations

We follow established best practices and ethical guidelines [1,8,23,39,49] to ensure responsible measurement. No user-related or personally identifiable data is collected; only publicly available information on DNS servers' and DoE configurations is analyzed. We do not exploit or probe insecure systems. To minimize network impact, DNS server discovery is limited to twice weekly, with caching to avoid redundant queries. Scans use *ZMap* [15] and the *IPv6 Hitlist Service* [21,60], which employ randomization to prevent network overload.

3.7   Global and AS-Level Distribution

We enriched our resolver discovery with geographical and Autonomous System (AS) location data, observing deployments in over 70 countries. The United States and several European countries accounted for a substantial proportion of advertised resolvers. Protocols like DoQ and DoH/2 showed the greatest diversity, with resolvers spanning hundreds of ASes, suggesting widespread but fragmented deployment, sometimes driven by smaller operators. In contrast, DoH/3 and DoT were hosted in a limited subset of ASes, often within large service providers such as AdGuard. This uneven distribution could have implications for the ecosystem's resilience and accessibility (Fig. 7).

3.8   Performance

Latency measurements were collected for 28,792 successful DoE queries from a vantage point in Berlin, Germany. Figure 8a presents the Cumulative Distribution Function (CDF) of RTTs across all resolved queries, comparing performance of the five major DoE protocols. While DoQ and DoH/3 both use QUIC, latency results differed: DoH/3 showed the fastest median RTT, followed closely by DoH/2 and DoQ with comparable values. Interestingly, DoT exhibited the lowest average latency overall, with median RTT around 60 ms. These results suggest that although transport choice influences latency, factors including resolver location, network paths, and provider infrastructure significantly affect observed performance.

Figure 8b zooms in on resolvers operated by entities supporting multiple protocols (e.g., AdGuard and Control D). Here, the median RTTs for DoQ, DoH/2, and DoH/3 range narrowly between 115 ms to 123 ms, indicating that network locality and operational environment are major determinants of performance, potentially more so than specific protocol overheads.

3.9   Errors and Reliability

Across more than 75,000 encrypted DNS requests, we identified and categorized connection failures, TLS errors, HTTP-layer problems (for DoH/2 and DoH/3), DNS errors, and responses with non-zero RCODEs. Connection problems such as unreachable endpoints and timeouts dominated, particularly among DoQ and

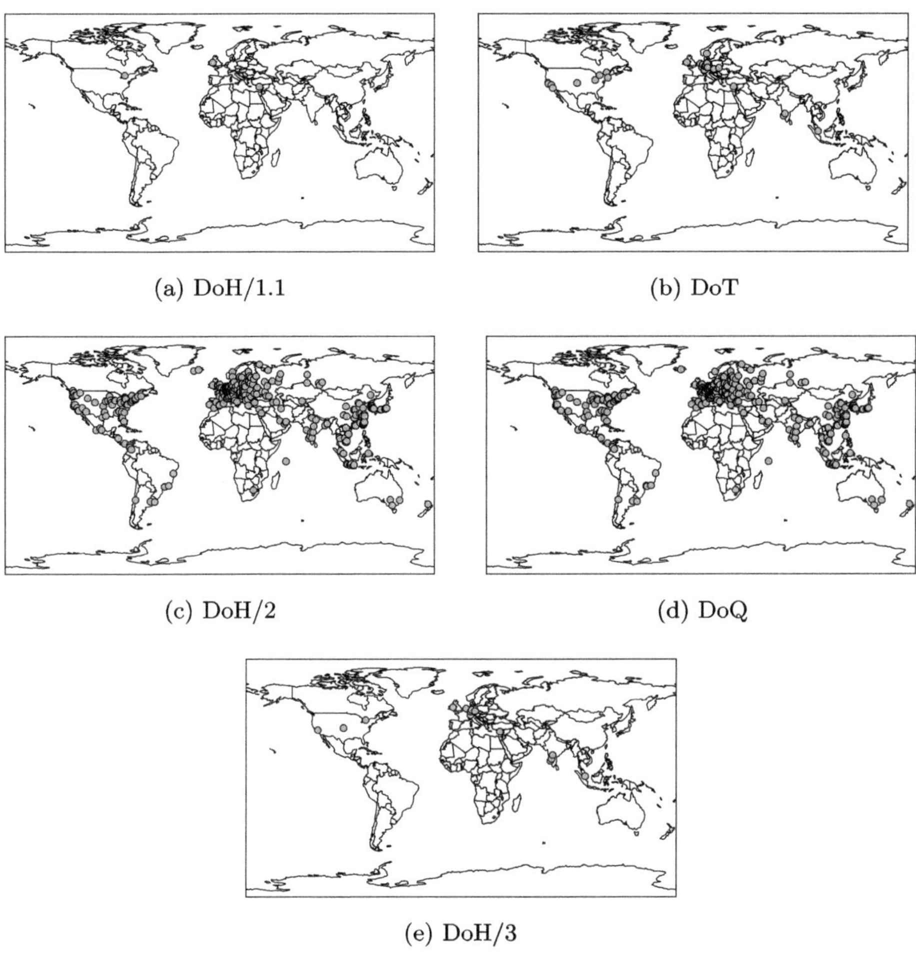

(a) DoH/1.1

(b) DoT

(c) DoH/2

(d) DoQ

(e) DoH/3

Fig. 7. Global distribution of unique DNS over Encryption (DoE) resolvers per protocol. Each dot represents the approximate location of a distinct DoE resolver. As a single resolver may support multiple DoE protocols, dots can coincide across multiple protocol-specific maps. This visualizes the geographical spread and overlap of resolver deployments across different encrypted DNS protocols.

DoH/2, while TLS certificate issues accounted for a significant share of failures, often due to expired certificates or unknown authorities. HTTP errors frequently resulted from invalid resource paths or non-compliant endpoints. Notably, a high percentage of non-zero RCODEs consisted of REFUSED responses, indicative of mismatches between advertising and actual resolver capabilities. A comparative view across protocols showed that DoH/1.1, DoH/3, and DoT achieved the highest rates of successful DNS responses.

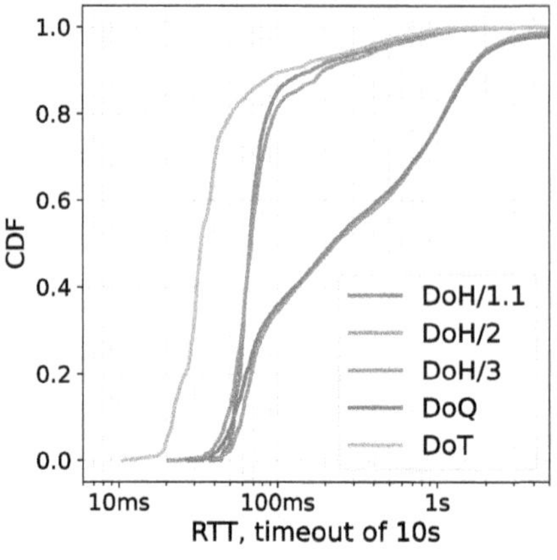

(a) Cumulative distribution function (CDF) of round-trip times (RTTs) for all successful DoE probes.

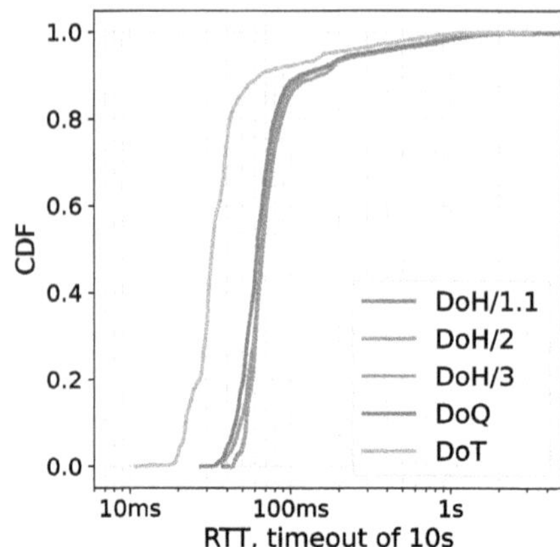

(b) CDF of RTTs for DoE probes specifically targeting resolvers within the *AdGuard* and *Control D* ASes.

Fig. 8. Latency distributions of discovered DoE resolvers during the probing phase. The left panel shows the overall RTT distribution for all probes that successfully returned a DNS response. The right panel focuses on RTTs measured solely from probes sent to resolvers operated by major providers supporting multiple DoE protocols. These CDFs provide insight into the variability and typical latency experienced across protocols and operators.

3.10   TLS Security Properties

All observed DoE resolvers negotiated either TLS 1.2 or TLS 1.3, with 99% preferring TLS 1.3, especially for QUIC-backed protocols. The dominant cipher suite was `TLS_AES_128_GCM_SHA256`, utilized in well over 90% of connections; secondary suites included `TLS_AES_256_GCM_SHA384` and `TLS_CHACHA20_POLY1305_SHA256`. Diffie-Hellman key exchange was universal, ensuring ephemeral session keys. No weak or deprecated configurations were identified, supporting a robust security posture among active resolvers.

3.11   Recursive Resolving Behavior

Using authoritative server-side logs, we observed repeated query behaviors: out of 75,299 tagged DNS queries sent to discovered DoE resolvers, roughly 22% were replayed, sometimes with delays of up to several weeks. Such replay patterns were concentrated in a handful of ASes, predominantly in China, aligning with prior descriptions of "traffic shadowing" or "DNS zombies" in literature. Additional anomalies included 142 instances where resolvers returned invalid IPv4 addresses, like 0.0.0.0, mainly from U.S. and South Korean networks—signaling partial misconfiguration or deviation from standard DNS practices. Importantly, despite offering encrypted recursive-to-authoritative endpoints, no

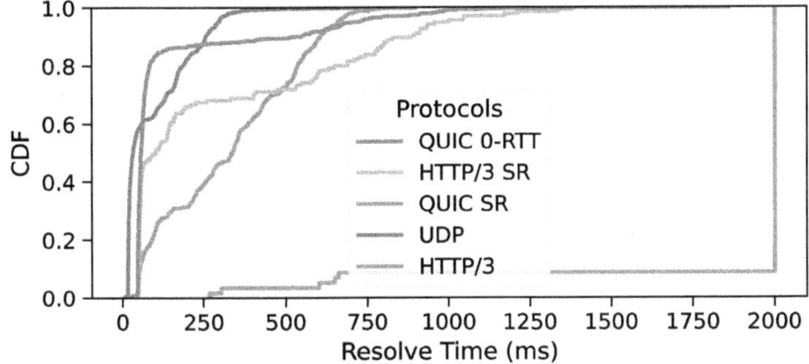

Fig. 9. CDF of DNS resolve times comparing resolvers with and without 0-RTT and session resumption.

Table 1. Performance comparison of DNS resolvers across HTTP/3, QUIC, and UDP, including session-resumption behavior, 0-RTT capabilities, request success rates, and response-time characteristics. The numbers in parentheses indicate results obtained during the third measurement run.

	HTTP/3	QUIC	UDP
Total Requests	554	1091	1529
Completed Requests	202	1112	1526
Failed Requests	391 (401)	3 (6)	3 (9)
Session Resumption	131	1039	–
0-RTT Support	0	733	–
0-RTT Error	554 (N/A)	6 (11)	–
Median Response Time (ms)	883 (2000)	88 (71)	33 (32)
Fastest Response (ms)	55 (46)	37 (23)	5 (4)
Slowest Response (ms)	2002 (2001)	1313 (1861)	1093 (800)

resolvers made use of these protocols, relying instead on traditional unencrypted recursion—likely a decision to minimize computational and operational overhead.

4   Session Resumption and 0-RTT

We performed two additional measurement campaigns to validate our findings and address a 0-RTT detection issue, which showed highly consistent results with only minor deviations. Table 1 displays the session resumption and 0-RTT support features, along with their corresponding response times.

Notably, nearly all DoQ resolvers (1039/1112) and 65 % of DoH/3 resolvers (131/202) supported session resumption, indicating improved DoE efficiency compared to previous findings [37]. However, DoH/3 showed no 0-RTT support. DoQ exhibited a significantly lower median response time (88 ms) than

Table 2. Fastest resolvers across all evaluated DNS protocols.

Rank	Host	Avg. Time	DoHTime	Do53Time	DoQTime
1.	2f07i9strpu.dns.controld.com.	46 ms	59 ms	20 ms	59 ms
52.	ams.core.access.zznet.fun.	66 ms	100 ms	21 ms	78 ms
53.	resolver64.dns4all.eu.	72 ms	93 ms	29 ms	92 ms
54.	nue2.moderateinfra.net.	76 ms	109 ms	20 ms	100 ms
55.	adguard.marcosbl.com.	96 ms	177 ms	29 ms	82 ms

DoH/3 (883 ms), likely due to DoH/3's lack of 0-RTT. Performance outliers, such as consistently slow AdGuard DNS resolvers, further skewed DoH/3's median. Table 1 also highlights DoH/3's high unreliability, with 391 out of 401 resolvers failing measurements. This issue was not related to the implemented fallback mechanism. Despite these protocol differences, resolver selection is crucial to user experience. The fastest UDP resolver (5 ms) significantly outperformed the fastest DoQ (37 ms) and DoH/3 (55 ms) resolvers. This UDP advantage may be attributed to resolver proximity, reflecting the distance between our measurement point and the closest resolver. While DoH/3 optimization remains a challenge, DoQ resolvers are increasingly embracing 0-RTT support, as shown by these findings.

While Do53 requires only one round trip, DoH/3 and DoQ initially need three. However, session resumption and 0-RTT allow DoQ and DoH/3 to achieve Do53's round-trip efficiency. Figure 9 presents the CDF of resolve times, where DoH/3 shows a distinctive step pattern mainly due to the `adguard-dns.com` resolvers (covering approximately 85 % of the dataset). Their consistent response times suggest potential geographical or infrastructure limitations, which warrants further investigation. Resolvers supporting 0-RTT show lower average latency, but their fastest responses aren't quicker than non-0-RTT resolvers. This can be attributed to our fiber-optic vantage point, which reduces latency by minimizing propagation delays. After removing slow `adguard-dns.com` resolvers, nearly half of the DoH/3 resolvers with session resumption match DoQ's performance. Nonetheless, DoH/3 remains the least performant overall, possibly due to a larger proportion of experimental resolvers given its recent standardization.

5   DNS Performance

Table 2 displays the fastest resolvers across all tested protocols. Unlike the previous analysis, this selection accounts for the resolver's proximity to our measurement point, which is crucial for accurate web performance assessments. To minimize distance-related variations, we identified resolvers supporting all three protocols (Do53, DoQ, DoH/3). Although IP addresses may resolve to load balancers, potentially affecting routing, this approach ensured consistency. We selected resolvers that completed all protocol measurements and calculated their mean response time. Table 2 highlights the top performers. The highest-ranked

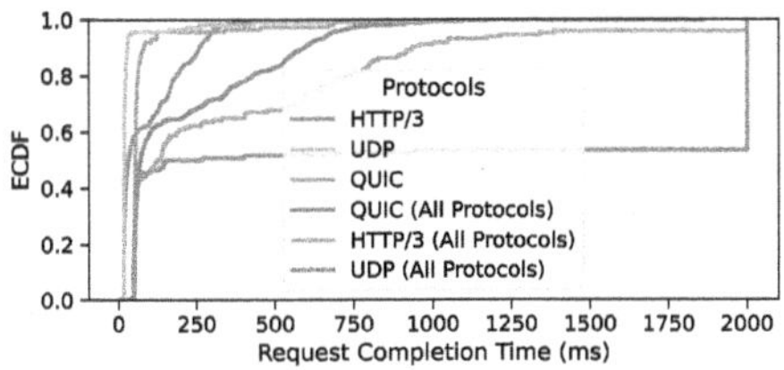

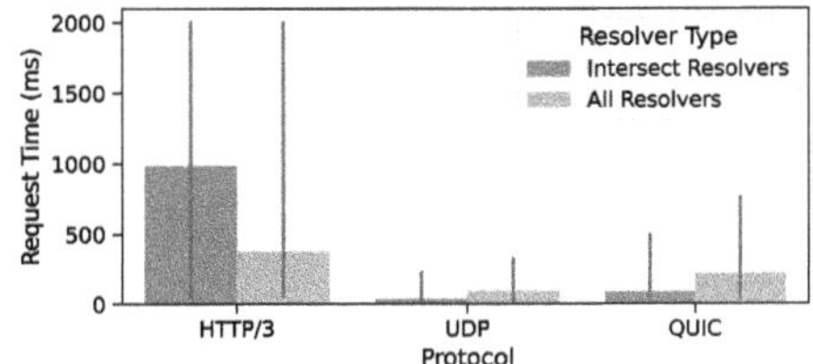

(a) CDF of DNS resolution times

(b) Mean and 95th percentile of resolution times

Fig. 10. Comparison of DNS resolve times between the subset of resolvers supporting all DoE protocols and the complete resolver set.

resolver lacked 0-RTT support for DoQ, resulting in similar response times across all protocols. Since web performance measurements disabled 0-RTT, we prioritized resolvers with minimal DoH/3 and DoQ response time differences. Initial tests with the top resolver showed promise, but large-scale experiments revealed frequent timeouts. Therefore, the 53rd-ranked resolver, known for its stability, was ultimately chosen for the study.

Figure 10 compares response times for resolvers supporting all protocols against the full dataset. The subset generally exhibits lower response times, except for DoH/3, which is significantly influenced by **adguard-dns.com** outliers, as seen in the CDF. The bar plot presents average response times. While median Do53 resolvers outperform DoQ and DoH/3, subset DoQ resolvers surpass the overall Do53 average. The CDF reveals approximately 95 % of subset Do53 resolvers respond within 30 ms, with peak resolvers outperforming other protocols. Protocol-specific patterns emerge: Do53 shows a sharp initial response (approximately 60 % within 50 ms) before tapering off over 250 ms. DoQ and DoH/3 gradually increase response time distribution, with DoQ exhibiting a longer tail (approximately 1000 ms convergence). This indicates a minority of slow DoQ resolvers, while Do53 maintains a more uniform distribution. Overall, resolvers supporting all protocols perform better on average and occupy faster percentiles. The subset's 95th percentile response time is lower, driven by a consistently fast core group. The performance gap between DoH/3 and DoQ is due to DoH/3's lack of 0-RTT support. With approximately 65 % of DoQ resolvers supporting 0-RTT, their average RTT is significantly reduced. Both DoH/3 and DoQ suffer from longer tails due to a few slow resolvers, a trend absent in the Do53 CDF.

5.1 Impact of DNS on Website Performance

This section examines how various DNS protocols affect website loading times. Measurements were conducted from October 22 to 31, 2024, using three DNS stub resolver instances. To ensure consistent resolver distance, `resolver64.dns4all.eu` was used for all protocols. We probed 719,281 websites per DNS pro-

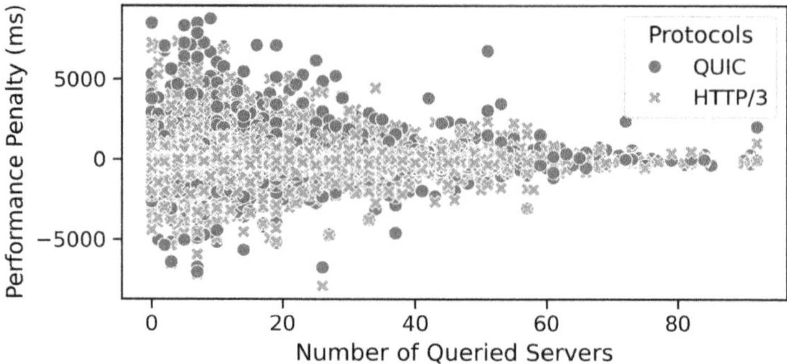

Fig. 11. Impact of the number of DNS queries on webpage FCP experience.

tocol, with each successful warm-up request followed by a measurement request. Ideally, this would yield 4,315,686 measurements. However, only 1,869,105 successful page loads were recorded, indicating significant website loading failures. Given that unsuccessful warm-up requests prevented measurements, and the complexity measurement only successfully loaded 572,367 websites, we obtained measurements for approximately half of the intended dataset.

Our results indicate similar error counts across all DNS protocols for measurement queries. Despite these errors, the dataset, with nearly 700k completed measurements, remains robust for analysis. We applied the following filtering criteria to ensure data consistency and reliability: (a) Removed measurements with any recorded errors. (b) Excluded instances where the `loadEventEnd` was zero, but the FCP was not. (c) Focused solely on measurement requests, excluding warm-up requests. (d) Retained only websites with successful measurements across all protocols, reducing the dataset to 46,440 domains from the initial 455,677. This refined dataset guarantees that all per-protocol metrics and visualizations are based on the same set of websites, providing a fair and accurate assessment of how DNS protocols affect website performance.

We calculate the DNS loading times using $T_{\mathrm{DNS}} =$ `domainLookupEnd` − `domainLookupStart` and website loading time using $T_{\mathrm{Load}} =$ `loadEventEnd` − `fetchStart` . We also measure FCP for user experience, especially on ad-supported websites.

Figure 11 reveals no substantial correlation between the number of queried servers and FCP performance. Performance penalties remain close to zero, suggesting that complex websites with numerous DNS requests effectively parallelize other tasks, thus minimizing impact. DoH/3 shows fewer outliers near zero penalty, while DoQ exhibits more extreme values. Although most users experience negligible differences, certain websites encounter delays exceeding 2.5 s, which are noticeable and potentially disruptive. Therefore, given its lower incidence of extreme delays, DoH/3 may offer a better user experience.

Figure 12a compares performance differences and overall loading times (Fig. 12b) for each protocol. Figure 12b shows minimal average loading time

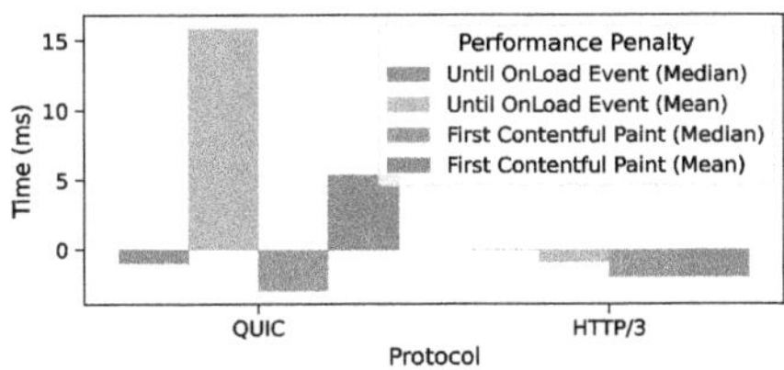 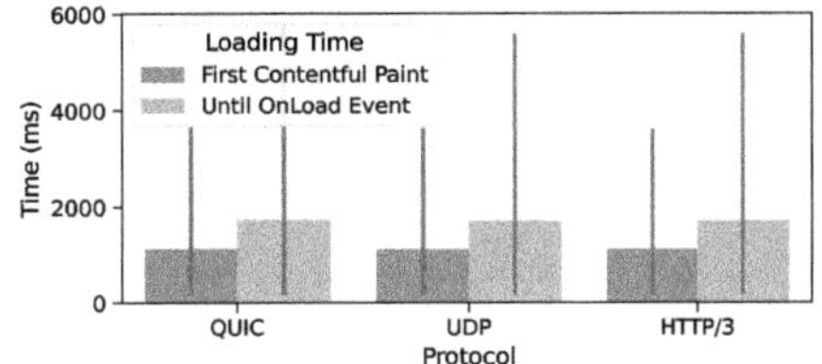

(a) Performance penalty in milliseconds per protocol   (b) Overall page loading times per protocol

Fig. 12. Website performance metrics for successfully measured cases across all protocols.

differences across DNS protocols, with similar 95th percentile intervals. The FCP to `onLoad` time gap remains consistent. The left bar chart confirms performance differences within $\pm 1\%$ of total load time, which is imperceptible to users. Since FCP contributes to `onLoad`, a shorter FCP implies reduced total loading time. While DoH/3 follows this trend, DoQ shows a larger `onLoad` average time spike, likely due to a few outlier websites with significantly longer load times (as shown in Fig. 11). This delay occurs post-FCP, potentially due to inconsistent loading elements like advertisements. Surprisingly, websites using DoQ or DoH/3 load slightly faster than Do53, resulting in negative performance penalties. This contradicts earlier findings indicating that DoQ and DoH/3 have response times more than 200 % longer times than Do53. This suggests either enhanced packet loss recovery compensates for delays (unlikely in low-loss environments) or DNS response time doesn't strongly correlate with website load time within the observed range. The following section will examine website characteristics and their correlation with performance penalties to identify sensitivities to DNS protocol variations.

5.2 Impact of Website Complexity

Building on our prior analysis of DoQ and DoH/3 performance, this section examines why some websites experience greater performance impacts than others and why performance penalties tend to stabilize around zero as the number of DNS requests increases. Furthermore, we analyze potential correlations between webpage characteristics and performance variations across different DNS protocols.

The web complexity experiment, probed 1 million domains and identified 719,281 active websites. In a follow-up analysis, only 572,345 of these websites were accessible. This discrepancy suggests that many sites experienced temporary failures, maintenance issues, or permanent takedowns, especially among gambling, adult content, and streaming websites, which may face legal concerns. We found that a median webpage required downloading 1.2 MB across 42 resources, involving seven different servers. This results in seven DNS resolutions, with five typically being external to the domain owner. The median load

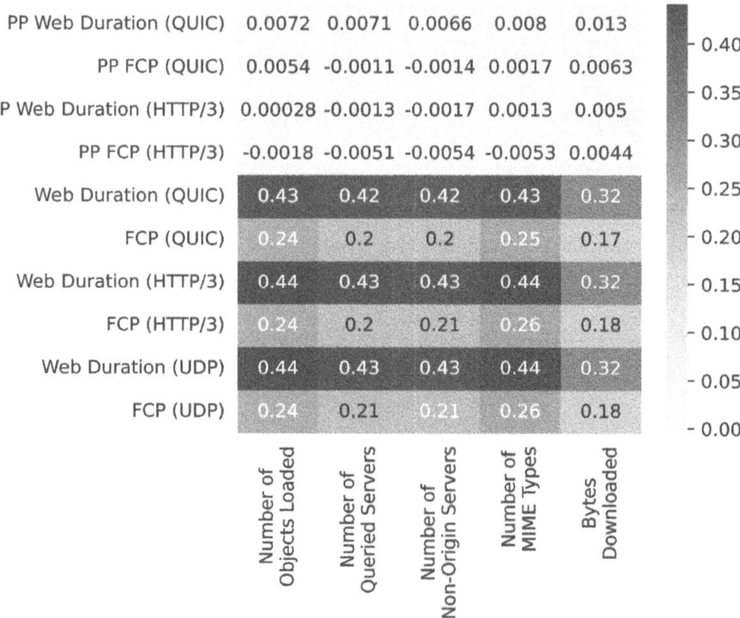

Fig. 13. Heatmap of the correlation between website complexity and performance across different DNS protocols.

time for all DNS protocols was approximately 0.9 s. To understand the relationship between website complexity and performance penalties, we calculated correlation coefficients and visualized them in heatmaps (Fig. 13). We found weak correlations (≤ 0.45) between complexity features and performance penalties. This suggests that complexity attributes do not significantly influence DoH/3 or DoQ performance penalties for either FCP or `onLoad`, likely due to efficient parallelization of DNS query durations (25 ms to 93 ms) within browser tasks. However, a positive correlation exists between complexity metrics and total load time (`fetchStart` to `onLoad`). This indicates increased loaded objects, queried servers, and resource types extend page load times. Interestingly, total website size has a minor impact. While FCP remains unaffected mainly, total load time increases as more resources are fetched before the `onLoad` event. Furthermore, the correlation remains consistent across different DNS protocols, suggesting minimal DNS impact in low-latency environments.

Impact of MIME Types. Our findings show that performance penalties do not depend on the number of MIME types, we now examine the relationship between specific MIME types and their impact on performance penalties and loading times, as illustrated in Fig. 14. We focused on MIME types appearing over 100 times, resulting in 82 valid types, and analyzed the correlation among the 40 most frequent ones. The correlation scale ranged from -0.2 to 0.4, indi-

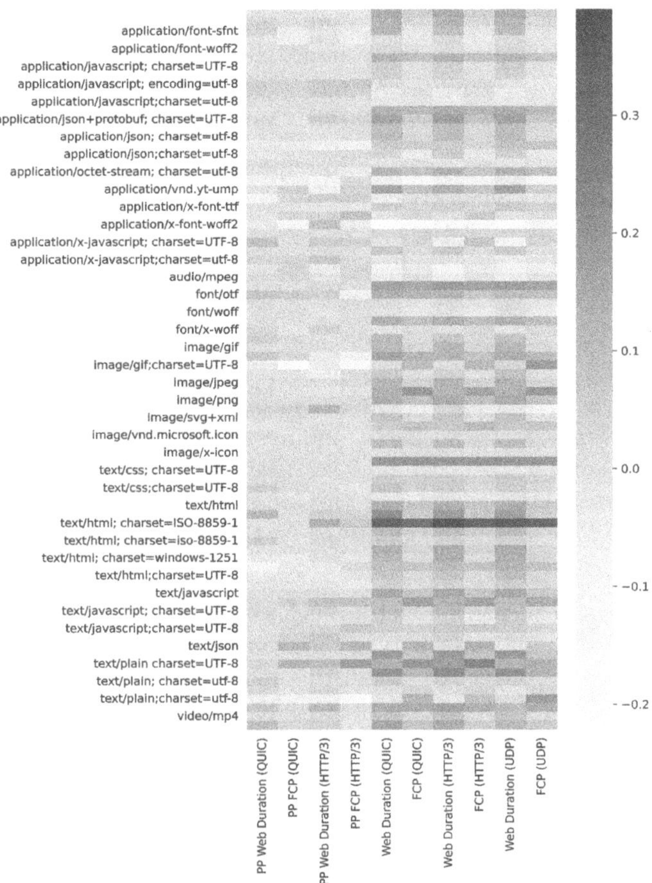

Fig. 14. Heatmap of the correlation between MIME types, DNS performance, and website loading times (*PP* stands for performance penalty).

cating generally weak correlations. Specifically, the performance-related rows showed correlation coefficients between −0.2 and 0.3, lacking consistency across different performance metrics.

6   Conclusion

This study conducted three integral measurements to evaluate the adoption and performance implications of DNS protocols. First, we assessed the prevalence of resolvers supporting QUIC, which significantly enhances the performance of DoQ and DoH/3. Second, we examined how different DNS protocols influence query times and, consequently, webpage load speeds. Third, we analyzed the relationship between webpage characteristics and performance effects when applying DoE protocols. While DoE introduces a measurable "performance penalty" in terms of DNS response times, our results indicate that the overall impact on web performance is negligible on average. This suggests that initial concerns regarding DoE usage may be overstated when considering end-to-end webpage load metrics. We conclude by summarizing our research questions (see Sect. 1):

RQ1: Nearly all DoQ resolvers (93 %) support session resumption, with two-thirds also endorsing 0-RTT. By comparison, only 65 % of DoH/3 resolvers support session resumption. Although we could not fully assess 0-RTT support for DoH/3 due to stub resolver limitations, the observed 66 % support in DoQ resolvers reflects a substantial adoption of QUIC features since 2022 [37].

RQ2: Despite DoE protocols significantly lengthening DNS query times, this increase typically does not translate into slower overall website loading. DoH/3 exhibits more consistent loading times than DoQ, performing better on both median and average metrics. These findings imply that DNS queries operate largely concurrently with other browser activities. However, the impact may differ in high-latency or packet-loss environments, and our evaluation did not incorporate 0-RTT, session resumption, or DNS caching, which could further affect results.

RQ3: Our analysis considering factors such as number of loaded objects, queried servers, website size, and MIME type distributions found no significant correlation between these webpage characteristics and the performance penalty induced by DoE. Our results demonstrate that while encrypted DNS protocols impose some overhead on DNS response times, they do not meaningfully degrade overall webpage load performance under typical conditions. This supports the broader adoption of privacy-enhancing DoE protocols without sacrificing user experience.

References

1. Allman, M., Paxson, V.: Issues and etiquette concerning use of shared measurement data. In: Dovrolis, C., Roughan, M. (eds.) Proceedings of the 7th ACM SIGCOMM Internet Measurement Conference, IMC 2007, San Diego, California, USA, October 24–26, 2007, pp. 135–140. ACM (2007). https://doi.org/10.1145/1298306.1298327
2. Basalla, M., Schneider, J., Luksik, M., Jaakonmäki, R., Vom Brocke, J.: On latency of e-commerce platforms. J. Organ. Comput. Electron. Commer. **31**(1), 1–17 (2021)
3. Benjamin, D.: TLS 1.3 0-RTT (2022). https://chromestatus.com/feature/5447945241493504
4. Blechschmidt, B.: GitHub — blechschmidt/massdns: a high-performance DNS stub resolver for bulk lookups and reconnaissance (subdomain enumeration) (2016). https://github.com/blechschmidt/massdns/
5. Butkiewicz, M., Madhyastha, H.V., Sekar, V.: Understanding website complexity: measurements, metrics, and implications. In: Proceedings of the 2011 ACM SIGCOMM Conference on Internet Measurement Conference, pp. 313–328 (2011)
6. Böttger, T., et al.: An Empirical Study of the Cost of DNS-over-HTTPS. In: Proceedings of the Internet Measurement Conference, pp. 15–21. ACM, Amsterdam Netherlands (2019). https://doi.org/10.1145/3355369.3355575, https://dl.acm.org/doi/10.1145/3355369.3355575

7. Canonical: dockerhub - ubuntu/bind9. https://hub.docker.com/r/ubuntu/bind9/
8. Cerf, V.G.: Guidelines for internet measurement activities. RFC **1262**, 1–3 (1991). https://doi.org/10.17487/RFC1262
9. Chhabra, R., Murley, P., Kumar, D., Bailey, M., Wang, G.: Measuring DNS-over-HTTPS performance around the world. In: Proceedings of the 21st ACM Internet Measurement Conference, pp. 351–365. ACM, Virtual Event (2021). https://doi.org/10.1145/3487552.3487849, https://dl.acm.org/doi/10.1145/3487552.3487849
10. Cook, S., Mathieu, B., Truong, P., Hamchaoui, I.: QUIC: better for what and for whom? In: 2017 IEEE International Conference on Communications (ICC), Paris, France, pp. 1–6. IEEE (2017). https://doi.org/10.1109/ICC.2017.7997281, http://ieeexplore.ieee.org/document/7997281/
11. Cooper, D., Santesson, S., Farrell, S., Boeyen, S., Housley, R., Polk, W.T.: Internet X.509 public key infrastructure certificate and certificate revocation list (CRL) profile. RFC **5280**, 1–151 (2008). https://doi.org/10.17487/RFC5280
12. Cotton, M., Vegoda, L.: Special use ipv4 addresses. RFC **5735**, 1–10 (2010). https://doi.org/10.17487/RFC5735
13. Dickinson, S., Gillmor, D.K., Reddy, T.: Usage profiles for DNS over TLS and DNS over DTLS. RFC **8310**, 1–27 (2018). https://doi.org/10.17487/RFC8310
14. Dierks, T., Rescorla, E.: The transport layer security (TLS) protocol version 1.2. RFC **5246**, 1–104 (2008). https://doi.org/10.17487/RFC5246
15. Durumeric, Z., Wustrow, E., Halderman, J.A.: Zmap: Fast internet-wide scanning and its security applications. In: King, S.T. (ed.) Proceedings of the 22th USENIX Security Symposium, Washington, DC, USA, August 14–16, 2013, pp. 605–620. USENIX Association (2013). https://www.usenix.org/conference/usenixsecurity13/technical-sessions/paper/durumeric
16. Electronic Frontier Foundation: Certbot. https://certbot.eff.org/
17. Encrypt, L.: Free ssl/tls certificates. https://letsencrypt.org/de/
18. Evans, C., Palmer, C., Sleevi, R.: Public key pinning extension for HTTP. RFC **7469**, 1–28 (2015). https://doi.org/10.17487/RFC7469
19. Fariselli, P., Oughton, C., Picory, C., Sugden, R.: Electronic commerce and the future for SMEs in a global market-place: networking and public policies. Small Bus. Econ. **12**, 261–275 (1999)
20. García, S., Hynek, K., Vekshin, D., Čejka, T., Wasicek, A.: Large Scale Measurement on the Adoption of Encrypted DNS (2021). https://doi.org/10.48550/ARXIV.2107.04436, https://arxiv.org/abs/2107.04436, version Number: 1
21. Gasser, O., Scheitle, Q., Gebhard, S., Carle, G.: Scanning the ipv6 internet: towards a comprehensive hitlist. In: Botta, A., Sadre, R., Bustamante, F.E. (eds.) Traffic Monitoring and Analysis - 8th International Workshop, TMA 2016, Louvain la Neuve, Belgium, April 7–8, 2016. IFIP (2016). http://dl.ifip.org/db/conf/tma/tma2016/tma2016-final51.pdf
22. Gillmor, D.K., Salazar, J., Hoffman, P.: Unilateral opportunistic deployment of encrypted recursive-to-authoritative DNS. RFC **9539**, 1–24 (2024). https://doi.org/10.17487/RFC9539
23. van der Ham, J.: Ethics and internet measurements. In: 2017 IEEE Security and Privacy Workshops, SP Workshops 2017, San Jose, CA, USA, May 25, 2017, pp. 247–251. IEEE Computer Society (2017). https://doi.org/10.1109/SPW.2017.17
24. Hoffman, P.E., McManus, P.: DNS queries over HTTPS (doh). RFC **8484**, 1–21 (2018). https://doi.org/10.17487/RFC8484
25. Hoffmann, F., Bajpai, V., Ververis, V.: The future of DNS privacy: a comparison of DNS over QUIC and DNS over http/3 (2025). https://doi.org/10.5281/zenodo.17860118

26. Hounsel, A., Schmitt, P., Borgolte, K., Feamster, N.: Can encrypted DNS be fast? In: Hohlfeld, O., Lutu, A., Levin, D. (eds.) PAM 2021. LNCS, vol. 12671, pp. 444–459. Springer, Cham (2021). https://doi.org/10.1007/978-3-030-72582-2_26

27. Hu, Z., Zhu, L., Heidemann, J., Mankin, A., Wessels, D., Hoffman, P.E.: Specification for DNS over Transport Layer Security (TLS). Request for Comments RFC 7858, Internet Engineering Task Force (2016). https://doi.org/10.17487/RFC7858, https://datatracker.ietf.org/doc/rfc7858, num Pages: 19

28. Hu, Z., Zhu, L., Heidemann, J.S., Mankin, A., Wessels, D., Hoffman, P.E.: Specification for DNS over transport layer security (TLS). RFC **7858**, 1–19 (2016). https://doi.org/10.17487/RFC7858

29. Huitema, C., Dickinson, S., Mankin, A.: DNS over dedicated QUIC connections. RFC **9250**, 1–27 (2022). https://doi.org/10.17487/RFC9250

30. Internet Systems Consortium Inc.: Bind 9 - isc.org. https://www.isc.org/bind/

31. Iyengar, J., Thomson, M.: QUIC: a UDP-based multiplexed and secure transport. RFC **9000**, 1–151 (2021). https://doi.org/10.17487/RFC9000

32. Josefsson, S.: The base16, base32, and base64 data encodings. RFC **4648**, 1–18 (2006). https://doi.org/10.17487/RFC4648

33. Kim, D.W., Zhang, J.: You are how you query: deriving behavioral fingerprints from DNS traffic. In: Thuraisingham, B., Wang, X.F., Yegneswaran, V. (eds.) SecureComm 2015. LNICST, vol. 164, pp. 348–366. Springer, Cham (2015). https://doi.org/10.1007/978-3-319-28865-9_19

34. Kinnear, E., McManus, P., Pauly, T., Verma, T., Wood, C.A.: Oblivious DNS over HTTPS. RFC **9230**, 1–19 (2022). https://doi.org/10.17487/RFC9230

35. Kirchler, M., Herrmann, D., Lindemann, J., Kloft, M.: Tracked without a trace: linking sessions of users by unsupervised learning of patterns in their DNS traffic. In: Proceedings of the 2016 ACM Workshop on Artificial Intelligence and Security, Vienna Austria, pp. 23–34. ACM (2016). https://doi.org/10.1145/2996758.2996770, https://dl.acm.org/doi/10.1145/2996758.2996770

36. Kosek, M., Doan, T.V., Granderath, M., Bajpai, V.: One to rule them all? A first look at DNS over QUIC. In: Hohlfeld, O., Moura, G., Pelsser, C. (eds.) Passive and Active Measurement. LNCS, vol. 13210, pp. 537–551. Springer, Cham (2022). https://doi.org/10.1007/978-3-030-98785-5_24

37. Kosek, M., Schumann, L., Marx, R., Doan, T.V., Bajpai, V.: DNS privacy with speed?: evaluating DNS over QUIC and its impact on web performance. In: Proceedings of the 22nd ACM Internet Measurement Conference, Nice France, pp. 44–50. ACM (2022). https://doi.org/10.1145/3517745.3561445

38. Kührer, M., Hupperich, T., Bushart, J., Rossow, C., Holz, T.: Going wild: large-scale classification of open DNS resolvers. In: Cho, K., Fukuda, K., Pai, V.S., Spring, N. (eds.) Proceedings of the 2015 ACM Internet Measurement Conference, IMC 2015, Tokyo, Japan, October 28-30, 2015, pp. 355–368. ACM (2015). https://doi.org/10.1145/2815675.2815683

39. Learmonth, I.R., Knodel, M., Grover, G.: Guidelines for Performing Safe Measurement on the Internet. Internet-Draft draft-irtf-pearg-safe-internet-measurement-10, Internet Engineering Task Force (2024). https://datatracker.ietf.org/doc/draft-irtf-pearg-safe-internet-measurement/10/, work in Progress

40. Li, R., Liu, B., Lu, C., Duan, H., Shao, J.: A worldwide view on the reachability of encrypted DNS services. In: Proceedings of the ACM Web Conference 2024, Singapore, pp. 1193–1202. ACM (2024). https://doi.org/10.1145/3589334.3645539, https://dl.acm.org/doi/10.1145/3589334.3645539

41. LTD, S.: Top websites ranking (2024). https://www.similarweb.com/top-websites/

42. Lu, C., Liu, B., Duan, H., Xing, Y., Li, R., Sun, J.: Open Encrypted DNS Servers (2024). https://port-53.info/data/open-encrypted-dns-servers/
43. Lu, C., et al.: An end-to-end, large-scale measurement of DNS-over-encryption: how far have we come? In: Proceedings of the Internet Measurement Conference, pp. 22–35. ACM, Amsterdam Netherlands (2019). https://doi.org/10.1145/3355369.3355580, https://dl.acm.org/doi/10.1145/3355369.3355580
44. Mao, J., Rabinovich, M., Schomp, K.: Assessing support for DNS-over-TCP in the wild. In: Hohlfeld, O., Moura, G.C.M., Pelsser, C. (eds.) Passive and Active Measurement - 23rd International Conference, PAM 2022, Virtual Event, March 28-30, 2022, Proceedings. Lecture Notes in Computer Science, vol. 13210, pp. 487–517. Springer (2022). https://doi.org/10.1007/978-3-030-98785-5_22
45. Mockapetris, P.V.: Domain names - concepts and facilities. RFC **1034**, 1–55 (1987). https://doi.org/10.17487/RFC1034
46. Mockapetris, P.V.: Domain names - implementation and specification. RFC **1035**, 1–55 (1987). https://doi.org/10.17487/RFC1035
47. Mozilla: Early-Data - HTTP (2024). https://developer.mozilla.org/en-US/docs/Web/HTTP/Headers/Early-Data
48. Nah, F.F.H.: A study on tolerable waiting time: how long are web users willing to wait? Behav. Inf. Technol. **23**(3), 153–163 (2004). publisher: Taylor & Francis
49. Narayanan, A., Zevenbergen, B.: No encore for encore? Ethical questions for webbased censorship measurement. SSRN Electron. J. (2015). https://doi.org/10.2139/ssrn.2665148
50. Pages, L.M.: pipe(7) (2024). https://man7.org/linux/man-pages/man7/pipe.7.html
51. Plonka, D., Berger, A.W.: Temporal and spatial classification of active ipv6 addresses. In: Cho, K., Fukuda, K., Pai, V.S., Spring, N. (eds.) Proceedings of the 2015 ACM Internet Measurement Conference, IMC 2015, Tokyo, Japan, October 28–30, 2015, pp. 509–522. ACM (2015). https://doi.org/10.1145/2815675.2815678
52. Pochat, V.L., Goethem, T.V., Tajalizadehkhoob, S., Korczynski, M., Joosen, W.: Tranco: a research-oriented top sites ranking hardened against manipulation. In: 26th Annual Network and Distributed System Security Symposium, NDSS 2019, San Diego, California, USA, February 24-27, 2019. The Internet Society (2019). https://www.ndss-symposium.org/ndss-paper/tranco-a-research-oriented-top-sites-ranking-hardened-against-manipulation/
53. Qualys, Inc.: Qualys SSL labs - SSL pulse. https://www.ssllabs.com/ssl-pulse/
54. Rekhter, Y., Moskowitz, B.G., Karrenberg, D., de Groot, G.J., Lear, E.: Address allocation for private internets. RFC **1918**, 1–9 (1996). https://doi.org/10.17487/RFC1918, https://doi.org/10.17487/RFC1918
55. Rempel, G.: Defining standards for web page performance in business applications. In: Proceedings of the 6th ACM/SPEC International Conference on Performance Engineering, pp. 245–252 (2015)
56. Rescorla, E.: HTTP over TLS. RFC **2818**, 1–7 (2000). https://doi.org/10.17487/RFC2818
57. Rescorla, E.: The transport layer security (TLS) protocol version 1.3. RFC **8446**, 1–160 (2018). https://doi.org/10.17487/RFC8446
58. Richter, P., Smaragdakis, G., Plonka, D., Berger, A.W.: Beyond counting: new perspectives on the active ipv4 address space. In: Gill, P., Heidemann, J.S., Byers, J.W., Govindan, R. (eds.) Proceedings of the 2016 ACM on Internet Measurement Conference, IMC 2016, Santa Monica, CA, USA, November 14-16, 2016, pp. 135–149. ACM (2016). http://dl.acm.org/citation.cfm?id=2987473

59. Rüth, J., Poese, I., Dietzel, C., Hohlfeld, O.: A first look at QUIC in the wild. In: Beverly, R., Smaragdakis, G., Feldmann, A. (eds.) PAM 2018. LNCS, vol. 10771, pp. 255–268. Springer, Cham (2018). https://doi.org/10.1007/978-3-319-76481-8_19

60. Scheitle, Q., et al.: A long way to the top: Significance, structure, and stability of internet top lists. In: Proceedings of the Internet Measurement Conference 2018, IMC 2018, Boston, MA, USA, October 31 - November 02, 2018, pp. 478–493. ACM (2018). https://dl.acm.org/citation.cfm?id=3278574

61. Schumann, L.: A Regional Analysis of DNS over QUIC and its Impact on Applications. Ma.S. thesis, Technical University of Munich (2022)

62. Sengupta, J., Kosek, M., Fries, J., Dikshit, P., Bajpai, V.: Web privacy by design: evaluating cross-layer interactions of QUIC, DNS and H/3. In: 2023 IFIP Networking Conference (IFIP Networking), Barcelona, Spain, pp. 1–9. IEEE (2023). https://doi.org/10.23919/IFIPNetworking57963.2023.10186362, https://ieeexplore.ieee.org/document/10186362/

63. Sheffer, Y., Holz, R., Saint-Andre, P.: Summarizing known attacks on transport layer security (TLS) and datagram TLS (DTLS). RFC **7457**, 1–13 (2015). https://doi.org/10.17487/RFC7457, https://doi.org/10.17487/RFC7457

64. Sheffer, Y., Saint-Andre, P., Fossati, T.: Recommendations for secure use of transport layer security (TLS) and datagram transport layer security (DTLS). RFC **9325**, 1–34 (2022). https://doi.org/10.17487/RFC9325, https://doi.org/10.17487/RFC9325

65. StatCounter: Internet browser market share 2012-2024 (2024). https://www.statista.com/statistics/268254/market-share-of-internet-browsers-worldwide-since-2009/

66. Thomson, M., Turner, S.: Using TLS to secure QUIC. RFC **9001**, 1–52 (2021). https://doi.org/10.17487/RFC9001, https://doi.org/10.17487/RFC9001

67. Wang, X.S., Balasubramanian, A., Krishnamurthy, A., Wetherall, D.: Demystifying page load performance with WProf. In: Proceedings of the 10th USENIX Conference on Networked Systems Design and Implementation. NSDI'13, USA, pp. 473–486. USENIX Association (2013). event-place: Lombard, IL

68. Weiss, Y., et al.: Navigation and resource Timing (2024). https://developer.mozilla.org/en-US/docs/Web/Performance/Navigation_and_resource_timings

69. World Wide Web Consortium: Resource timing (2025). https://www.w3.org/TR/resource-timing/. candidate Recommendation Draft

Wireless and Mobile

Different Policies for Different NodeBs: Comparing Downlink Schedulers in Cellular Base Stations

Zesen Zhang[1(✉)], Jon Larrea[2], Jarrett Huddleston[3], Haoran Wan[4], Ricky K. P. Mok[1,5], Bradley Huffaker[1,5], KC Claffy[1,5], Kyle Jamieson[4], Alexander Marder[3], and Aaron Schulman[1]

[1] University of California,California, USA
zez003@ucsd.edu
[2] The University of Edinburgh,Edinburgh, UK
[3] Johns Hopkins University,Baltimore, USA
[4] Princeton University,Princeton, USA
[5] CAIDA,La Jolla, USA

Abstract. Cellular base stations rely on proprietary downlink scheduling algorithms that vendors independently develop to fairly and efficiently schedules traffic to competing users. Schedulers from different vendors can make different scheduling decisions depending on channel conditions, buffer status, fairness, and capability. This work is the first to show the significant scheduling policy differences in a head-to-head comparison of the behavior of downlink schedulers across four base station vendors (Ericsson, Samsung, Nokia and Huawei) running on four cellular providers (AT&T, Verizon, T-Mobile and Vodafone). The evaluation is based on 500Gbytes of downlink transfers across 20 base stations in five cities during semi-controlled network and signal conditions. In particular, we observe different strategies for allocating radio resources, for rate control, and for handling users with asymmetric channel quality. These results challenge the assumptions made about downlink scheduler uniformity in prior cellular performance measurement studies.

1 Introduction

The 3GPP standards [7] provide flexibility for base station vendors to provide their own proprietary downlink scheduling policies. For example, although the 3GPP suggests a certain data rate in a particular channel condition, it does not specify the relationship between these two variables [7]. The 3GPP also only recommends base station scheduler designers to balance between user demands and their equipment's capabilities, while simultaneously maintaining fairness. It does not define a strategy for doing so, as with other mobile protocols [1]. Therefore, each of the four primary base station vendors in the world (Ericsson, Nokia, Samsung, and Huawei) implements their own proprietary scheduling policies. These policies are the primary "secret sauce" that differentiates base station performance across vendors.

S. Ferlin-Reiter et al. (Eds.): PAM 2026, LNCS 16477, pp. 231–246, 2026.
https://doi.org/10.1007/978-3-032-18268-5_11

Since all LTE base stations are 3GPP standards compliant, and compounded by the lack of visibility into what vendor base station a device is using, there has been an assumption of homogeneous behavior across different vendors' schedulers. However, prior studies have yielded contradictory observations about LTE base station scheduling behavior. Several studies have found bursty patterns in resource allocation across time slots, [4,5,27], while others have found equal sharing of resources across UEs in every time slot [25,26]. This apparent contradiction implies that cellular performance monitoring assessments may require tailoring to a variety of base station scheduling policies.

In this study, we provide the first preliminary evaluation of differences in resource scheduling policies across the top four base station vendors: Ericsson, Samsung, Huawei and Nokia. Ascertaining differences between downlink scheduling policies is challenging because: (1) Cellular modems have no built-in method to determine the vendor of a base station. (2) Observing the scheduling policy of a base station requires a controlled environment, namely an idle base station with two controlled users contending for resources. (3) Base stations may behave differently based on configuration parameters or deployment locations, although operators tend to deploy a single vendor's equipment within a region.

We identified a base station's vendor through a combination of directly viewing the logo on the base station itself, and using a proprietary dataset of vendor fingerprints collected by Revelare Networks [16] We achieved a semi-controlled setting by performing experiments overnight in non-residential areas; we validated that the base stations were idle by checking if one UE could be allocated all resources of the base station. To evaluate a variety of vendors, we collected data from 20 different base stations, with different configurations, in five cities, across two countries, and across deployments of four major mobile carriers (Verizon, AT&T, T-Mobile, Vodafone). We compared scheduler behavior from the four most popular base station vendors, with two competing users, in a range of conditions including differing buffer status, channel quality, and traffic sources (i.e., application and transport protocol). Our contributions are:

1. We found different, but consistent, *radio resource allocation policies* for competing users across base station vendors, providers, and channel conditions.
2. We found differing *rate adaptation* algorithms in use. We found that some base station vendors aggressively pick data rates, while others opt for a linear data rate mapping to channel quality. The aggressive strategy resulted in higher end-to-end throughput in high quality channel conditions.
3. We found that when competing users have different channel qualities, different vendors in different deployments prioritize users differently. Some allocate resources unequally, while others evenly shared radio resources.

2   Background and Related Work

We focus on evaluating LTE base station behavior, as 4G/LTE remains the primary mobile data network in use today. Many 5G services still depend on 4G infrastructure via NSA mode, where 5G radio access is anchored by a 4G core [8]. We confirmed this in our experiments: among the four providers we examined, only T-Mobile operated 5G in SA mode, and only at two base stations.

Because the scheduling algorithm is largely determined by the core network, we configured phones to stay in LTE/4G mode, focusing on 4G scheduling behavior to avoid distortions caused by UEs switching between 5G and 4G bands, which complicates observation of base station scheduling. We discuss 5G results separately to motivate and frame future directions (Sect. 5). For context, we describe two key processes not directly defined by the 3GPP— radio resource scheduling (2.1) and link adaptation (2.2)—leaving their implementation and associated network performance implications as vendor-specific characteristics.

2.1 Radio Resource Scheduling

The scheduler is the process through which the base station distributes available Physical Resource Blocks (PRBs) across the UEs. The base station scheduler manages radio resource allocation for both uplink and downlink directions. Given the dominance of downlink traffic, we focus on downlink scheduling.

During our experiments, we found that a single UE receives all base station resources when it is the only UE downloading traffic. Therefore, we focus on base station scheduling strategies in competing UE scenarios. The scheduler makes a scheduling decision, i.e., distributes available PRBs across contending UEs, every Transmission Time Interval (TTI), which is 1 ms. In general, scheduler decisions consider multiple sources of information from UEs (KPIs), as well as radio measurements collected by the base station, combined with historic allocation data. Relevant KPIs commonly used across schedulers include the number of UEs, UEs' CQI reports, buffer status reports, and QoS rank [2,22].

The literature defines several theoretical scheduling algorithms, including Round Robin, Maximum CQI, and Proportional Fair [12]. Most commercial base stations implement a custom variant of Proportional Fair that leverages the aforementioned KPIs, among others. This approach balances throughput and fairness by prioritizing UEs that meet custom criteria (e.g., those that have not recently received resources or that have substantial traffic to send) [5,6].

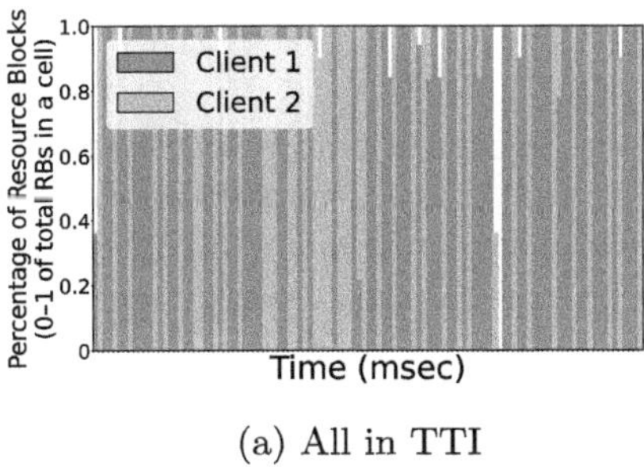

(a) All in TTI

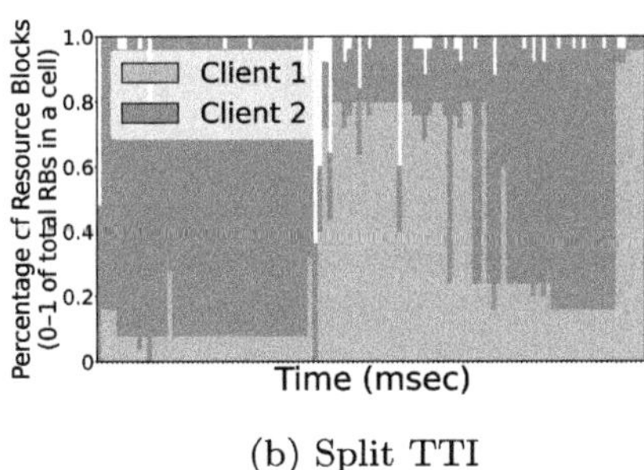

(b) Split TTI

Fig. 1. Allocated PRBs over time for two different possible base station schedulers.

Researchers have used observations of a specific commercial base station behavior to infer the assumptions that scheduling protocols make [4,5,26]. For example, some authors [4,27] suggest that the base station scheduler assigns all PRBs to a single UE within one TTI, effectively generating a traffic burst (Fig. 1 a). Note in this figure how in each TTI the base station tends to assign resources to only one of the two UEs. Other studies [25,26] have observed different resource allocation behaviors, such as in Fig. 1 b, where the base station usually shares resources of one TTI between two competing UEs. This difference in scheduling behavior can limit the benefits offered by proposed optimizations, e.g., BurstTracker [4] would trigger false positives in the case shown in Fig. 1 b.

2.2   Link Adaptation Policy

Link Adaptation is the process by which the base station dynamically adjusts the Modulation and Coding Scheme (MCS) to encode channel quality information in each PRB, to maximize data rates and minimize loss. MCS selection and adaptation is vendor-specific; the 3GPP provides only recommendations. In practice, base stations generally rely on a combination of the Channel Quality Indicator (CQI) periodically sent by the UE and other radio KPIs measured at the base station. In general, higher CQI values enable the use of more advanced modulation schemes, such as 64-QAM, whereas lower CQI values trigger more robust coding and simpler modulation techniques, like QPSK.

As suggested in WiFi research, rate control algorithms can greatly affect network throughput and power consumption [9,11,17,18]. How base station link adaptation is implemented, and how it impacts network performance, has been discussed in previous work [3,14,15]. However, those studies were either simulation-based or limited to a single vendor. None of them identified that CQI-related MCS selection strategies can vary across different vendors.

3   Methodology and Instrumentation

We describe our experimental environment and methodology, and demonstrate its efficacy for data acquisition and analysis of idle base stations.

3.1   Experimental Setup

Our goal is to delineate the differences between base station downlink schedulers implemented by different vendors. We performed all measurements with idle base stations, and generated downlink traffic by downloading from a controlled server to our UEs. Figure 2 illustrates our setup, with three distinct components.

Server Configuration. A server running Ubuntu 22.04 LTS with Linux kernel 5.15 LTS was deployed within the same geographic region as the base stations to ensure a round-trip time (RTT) under 40 milliseconds, thereby reducing the impact of end-to-end latency. The server was provisioned with sufficient egress

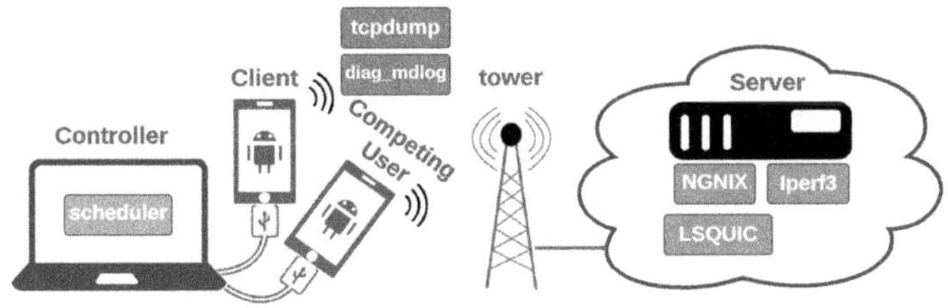

Fig. 2. Experimental setup for data collection.

bandwidth to avoid becoming a bottleneck. We generated network traffic using `iperf3 version 3.9` for TCP and UDP, `LSQUIC version 4.0.8` for QUIC, and `NGINX version 1.26.1` for HTTPS. We used the BBR congestion control algorithm for both TCP and QUIC in our tests.

Client Configuration. The client side consisted of two mobile phones (OnePlus Nord N30) running Android 14. The two phones competed for downlink resources by generating traffic using `iperf3`, `lsquic`, and `curl`. The connection between the phones and a laptop was maintained via USB, used solely for synchronization during code execution. To capture the base station's behavior at the Physical (PHY) layer, Qualcomm Modem Diagnostic Log (QMDL) files were recorded using `diag_mdlog` [13] and decoded with QXDM software [19,23]. Additionally, `tcpdump` was employed to monitor and later analyze network traffic at the transport layer on the mobile devices.

Controller Functionality. The synchronization of the two phones was managed via a laptop by using thread barrier to guarantee a competitive scenario. We also release our code base on github [28].

3.2 Base Station Scheduler Analysis

Table 1. Details about the 20 diverse base stations we observed from 4 vendors

Downlink Config.	Ericsson Macro						Ericsson Micro				Samsung Macro				Samsung Micro		Huawei Macro			Nokia Macro
Provider	A	A	T	T	T	A	A	A	A	A	VZ	VZ	VZ	VZ	VZ	VZ	VO	VO	VO	A
Bandwidth	50	50	35	40	35	20	40	40	35	40	60	50	60	50	20	20	30	30	25	40
MIMO	2	2	4	4	4	4	2	2	2	2	2	4	4	4	4	4	2	2	2	4
Carrier Agg.	4	4	2	3	3	1	3	3	2	3	4	4	4	4	2	3	2	2	2	2

A=AT&T   **T**=T-Mobile   **VZ**=Verizon   **VO**=Vodafone

To understand the base station's scheduling behavior, we examine how it allocates bandwidth resources. This requires identifying an idle base station so that we can monitor all downlink traffic. An idle base station also allows us to reconstruct its behavior by aggregating the PHY-layer activity across all UEs.

To find idle base stations, we selected those located in non-residential areas during nocturnal hours to ensure a controlled environment. Most people remain at home during late night hours and typically use Wi-Fi even if they are awake accessing the Internet. The primary interference comes from passing pedestrians or drivers who briefly connect to the base station. To mitigate this risk, we performed an initial 5-second UDP download at the beginning of each experimental phase as metadata. When idle, all idle cells we tested allocated 98.8% of RBs to our single UE. We assume the remaining 1.2% of unallocated RBs were mostly reserved for control messages such as MIBs or SIBs, since they appear in subframes 0 and 5 [20]. We repeated each experiment multiple times (at least 3) to reduce the likelihood of interference from transient users.

During the experiments, we ensured that both phones were registered to the same Cell ID using NetMonster [21] before proceeding. We forced UEs to operate in LTE-only mode to observe LTE scheduling behavior, and enabled 5G mode when gathering 5G results. To study how vendors schedule heavy downlink traffic, we saturated the base station buffer for both User Equipments (UEs) by having each phone generate four parallel threads of 1 Gbps downlink UDP traffic from the server. By using UDP without congestion control and tolerating high packet loss rates, we ensured the base station buffer remained full for each UE throughout the experiment. Additionally, we used prepaid SIM cards to ensure consistent QoS and traffic conditions. In this way, we controlled as many factors as possible to observe vendor-specific scheduling differences.

Under high traffic load, carrier aggregation was triggered by the network. We identified cases during our experiments as carrier aggregation rather than dual connectivity by comparing physical cell IDs, RSSI, and frame number synchronization. The presence of consistent frame number and identical physical cell IDs indicated that multiple component carriers originated from the same base station (eNB) rather than from separate cells. Therefore, we treated these cases as carrier aggregation events and conducted our analysis across all aggregated carriers, under the assumption that they were managed by a single eNB with a common scheduler.

3.3 Data Overview

We collected downlink scheduler traces from 20 base stations across four of the top cellular vendors: Ericsson, Samsung, Nokia, and Huawei (Table 1), deployed by four major carriers: AT&T, T-Mobile, Verizon Wireless, and Vodafone. Our dataset includes 5 Ericsson Macro Cells, 4 Ericsson Micro Cells, 4 Samsung Macro Cells, 2 Samsung Micro Cells, 3 Huawei Macro Cells, and 1 Nokia Macro Cell. Operators typically deploy a vendor's equipment homogeneously within a given region (e.g., a city or state). To capture vendor diversity, we collected data from four U.S. cities—three on the west coast and one on the east coast. and from one city in Spain. Our data set represents most of the commonly deployed base stations worldwide, but is not exhaustive. In this preliminary study, we use this diverse collection of base stations to highlight differences in downlink schedulers, with the goal of emphasizing the need to account for such variation.

4   Results

We observed many differences in downlink scheduler behavior across vendors and base station types. Specifically, we identified significant differences along three dimensions of base station scheduling behavior: (1) the number of radio Resource Blocks (RBs) allocated to competing UEs per scheduling interval (TTI), (2) the link adaptation algorithm (i.e., how CQI is mapped to MCS), and (3) the behavior of UEs with diverse channel quality relative to the base station. We also provide a preliminary view of scheduling differences on 5G NR base stations.

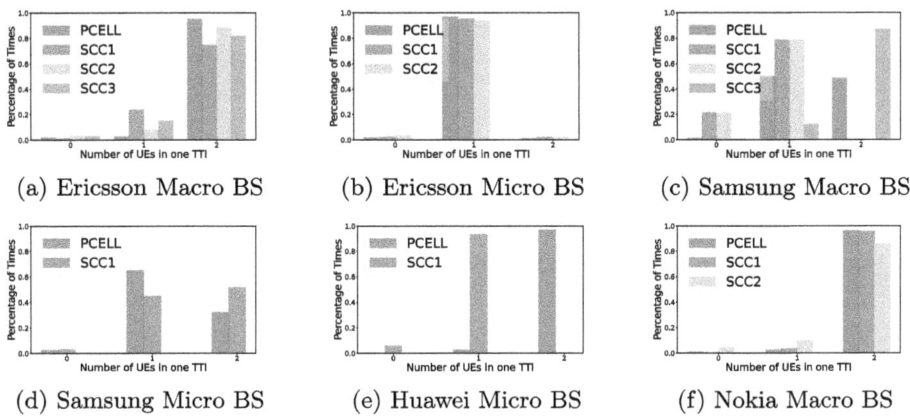

(a) Ericsson Macro BS   (b) Ericsson Micro BS   (c) Samsung Macro BS

(d) Samsung Micro BS   (e) Huawei Micro BS   (f) Nokia Macro BS

Fig. 3. BS stands for Base Station. Base station schedulers across different vendors as well as macro and micro cell configurations.

4.1   Radio Resource Allocation Policy

Figure 3 shows how often more than one of the two competing UEs are scheduled within a single TTI. Resources allocated to competing users varied across base station vendors, and even within each vendor's macro and micro cells. The differences between macro and micro base station reside in base station's power coverage. It can be easily differentiated by counting the number of sectors in one base station. Micro base stations are usually on the street lamp, while macro base stations can be found in base station towers. The behavior was consistent within each vendor and base station type, regardless of carrier. Therefore, We selected the most representative base stations to illustrate the behavior of those base stations in Fig. 3 and we provide the remaining base station's result in Appendix.

Ericsson and Nokia. *macro* base stations (Fig. 3 a), across all three carriers, consistently allocated resources to both UEs in every TTI. Three aggregated carriers transmitted traffic to the UEs simultaneously, including one primary and two secondary carriers. Within each carrier, resources were consistently distributed between the two competing phones. Resources were allocated in varying proportions each TTI, with ratios alternating every 5–6 TTIs. It is possible that *Nokia* base stations (Fig. 3 f) behave similarly to Ericsson's, as they are deployed by the same providers in different regions [10]. In contrast, Ericsson *micro* base stations (Fig. 3 b) generally allocated all RBs to a single UE per TTI, resulting in bursty resource distribution. However, across all aggregated carriers on the base station, both UEs received resources from at least one carrier 80% of the time. This suggests that Ericsson *micro* base stations primarily divide resources by assigning them to different users.

Samsung. *macro* base stations (Fig. 3 c) displayed a different resource allocation pattern: 50% of the time, all RBs were assigned to one UE per TTI, while the other 50% of the time, both UEs shared resources within the same TTI on each carrier. Samsung *micro* base stations (Fig. 3d) exhibited hybrid behavior, combining aspects of Ericsson's macro and micro cells. They frequently shared resources among UEs within the same TTI, like the macro cells, but occasionally allocated full RBs to one UE on each carrier, similar to the micro cells.

Huawei. *micro* base stations (Fig. 3 e) behaved differently from Ericsson and Samsung, primarily in its use of carrier aggregation. The primary carrier consistently allocated resources to both UEs in each TTI, while the secondary carrier allocated all resources to only one UE per TTI. However, the secondary carrier alternated its allocations between the two UEs across TTIs, ensuring fairness.

Finally, we validated our UDP probing method by observing that similar scheduling policies emerged when using TCP downloads via iperf, as well as HTTPS and QUIC traffic (Sect. 5).

4.2 Link Adaptation Policy

Figure 4 shows the distribution of MCS rate control across various CQI levels (i.e., link adaptation). *Ericsson* is generally aggressive, assigning high MCS levels at high CQI. *Samsung* and *Huawei* exhibit a more cautious approach, with MCS allocation showing a linear decline in median MCS as CQI decreases, though *Huawei* generally assigns higher MCS values than *Samsung*. *Nokia* is as aggressive as *Ericsson* at high CQI but is more conservative at low CQI.

These observed differences reflect distinct vendor-specific strategies. Ericsson appears to prioritize speed and throughput under favorable signal conditions, potentially improving performance in high-CQI scenarios. By contrast, Samsung and Huawei's strategies appear more balanced, possibly to mitigate rapid throughput degradation under fluctuating signal strengths.

These results indicate that when a UE has high CQI, it will achieve higher end-to-end throughput from an Ericsson than from a Samsung base station. We validated this by testing the same UE in locations close to both Samsung and

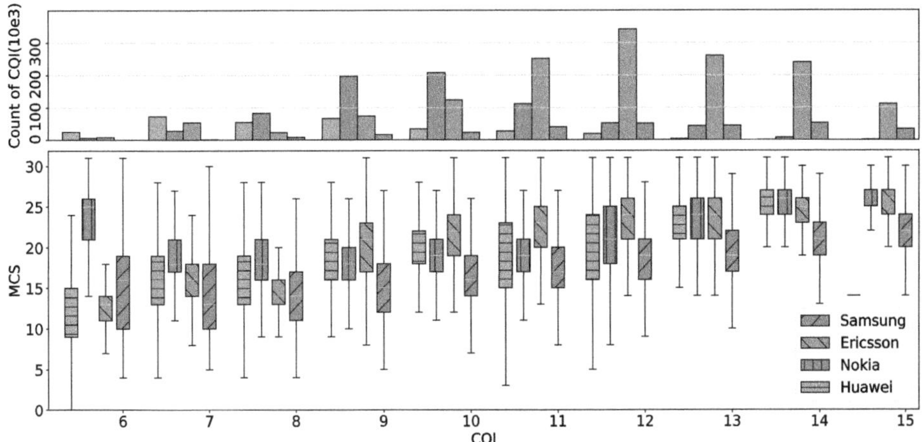

Fig. 4. Box-and-histogram plot showing MCS allocations by vendors across different CQI levels. The box plot indicates the range of MCS values observed for each CQI. The histogram shows the number of samples per CQI. *Note:* Results for CQI=6, particularly for Nokia, are based on limited data and should be interpreted with caution, as we rarely observed low-CQI scenarios (CQI 0–6). Such conditions likely triggered cell handoffs when better nearby cells were available.

Ericsson base stations. We positioned the UE as close as possible to each base station and ensured that its CQI remained between 12–15 during the experiments (conducted at night when the base stations were idle). Using an iperf UDP flood, we measured bandwidth-normalized throughput of 8.75 bits/sec/Hz for Ericsson and 4.25 bits/sec/Hz for Samsung (both using 4×4 MIMO). This confirms that, under similar radio conditions, Ericsson base stations provided higher throughput. However, this performance gap likely narrowsin mid-range CQI levels, as Ericsson's aggressive strategy may lead to increased loss and retransmissions.

4.3 Policy for Diverse Channel Quality

Next, we compared the resource allocation policies of macro base stations under varying network conditions. The focus was on observing how base stations from two vendors allocated resources to User Equipments (UEs) competing for the same radio resources when one UE had a much higher CQI than the other (e.g., when one was closer to the base station). We limited this experiment to *Ericsson* and *Samsung* to examine whether the divergent behaviors they demonstrated in earlier experiments also applied in this scenario (Fig. 5).

We compared the fraction of RBs allocated to each UE in each TTI, normalized by the total number of RBs available at the base station (i.e., its bandwidth). We discovered distinct vendor-specific allocation policies:

Ericsson: Ericsson exhibited resource distribution that varied according to signal quality differences between UEs:

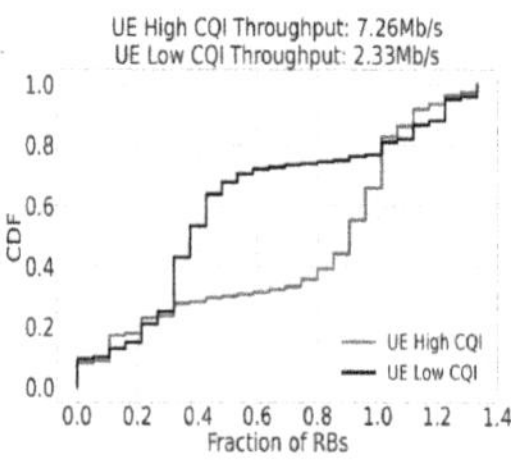 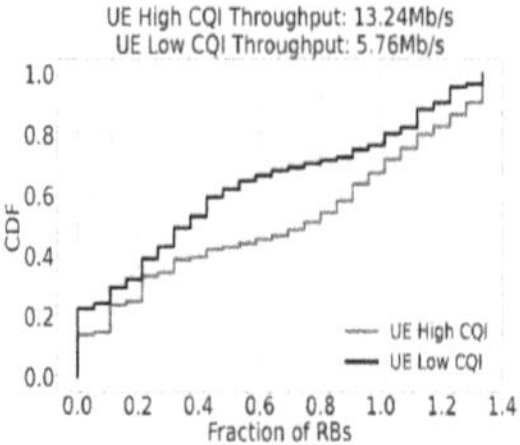 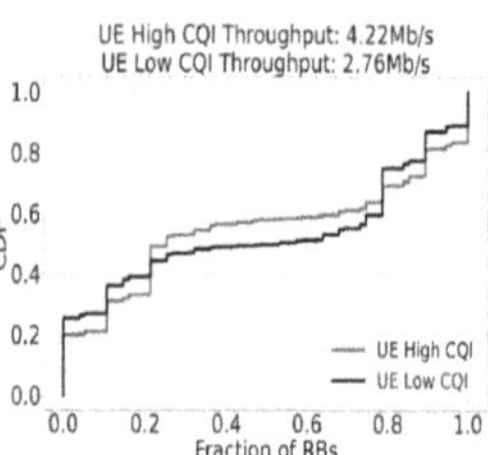

(a) Ericsson base station on campus.

(b) Ericsson base station in crowd area.

(c) Samsung base station.

Fig. 5. CDF of PRB usage for UEs with different CQIs contending for the same base station's downlink resources.

- *Campus scenario (Fig. 5 a):* The UE closer to the base station had an average CQI of 11.7, while the more distant UE averaged 6.9. Surprisingly, the base station allocated more resources to the UE with poorer connectivity.

- *Crowd scenario (Fig. 5 b):* The closer UE averaged a CQI of 12.37, while the farther UE averaged 8.69. In this case, the base station allocated more resources to the UE with better channel quality.

Samsung: Samsung adopted a more balanced resource allocation strategy (Fig. 5 c); its macro base stations distributed RBs nearly equally between UEs, even when their channel qualities differed significantly. For the UE near the base station, the average CQI was 14.7, while the more distant UE averaged 7.19.

These divergent strategies highlight how Ericsson and Samsung base stations implement different approaches to resource management. In future work, we plan to extend this analysis to additional vendors.

5   Discussion

5.1   Scheduling Policy Diversity in 5G

This work focused on 4G LTE downlink scheduler differences, given its dominant deployment. However, we also compared radio resource scheduling on 5G base stations from Ericsson, Samsung, and Huawei. We conducted tests on AT&T, Verizon, and Vodafone who uses 5G NSA, and on T-Mobile, who use 5G Standalone. AT&T and T-Mobile use Ericsson base stations, Verizon uses Samsung, and Vodafone uses Huawei. Figure 6 displays the frequency of the number of UEs appearing per TTI. AT&T, Verizon, and Vodafone transmitted packets through both 5G NR and LTE radios simultaneously, as they use an NSA core network. AT&T and Vodafone scheduled one UE via the 5G radio and another via the LTE radio, which made it appear as though the 5G radio scheduled only one UE per TTI. However, synchronization between 5G and LTE transmissions is challenging because 5G uses Time Division Duplexing (TDD), whereas LTE uses Frequency Division Duplexing (FDD) in the regions where we collected data. Another issue is that 5G packet transmission is sensitive to CQI, since higher

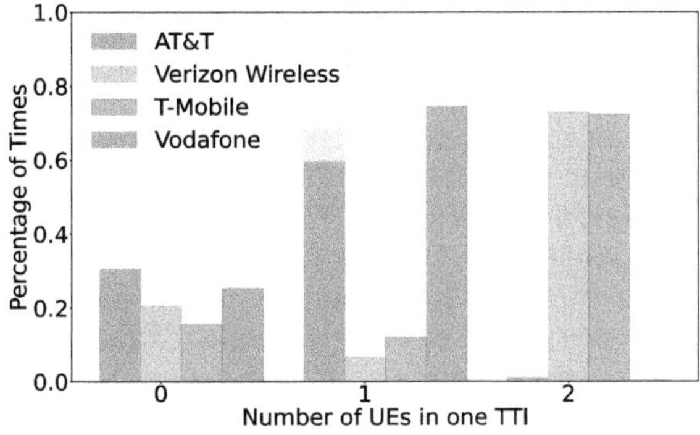

Fig. 6. UEs per TTI for 5G base station schedulers.

radio frequencies are more easily affected by noise. This makes observing behavior pattern between LTE and 5G harder. Conversely, T-Mobile, which operates on a 5G SA network, transmitted packets solely through 5G NR, and its base stations tend to share resources among UEs within the same TTI.

5.2 Policy Effects on Congestion Control

Besides UDP tests, we conducted iperf TCP tests and file downloads via HTTPS and QUIC protocols with curl and lsquic to generate network traffic. We observed similar scheduling patterns as when downloading packets with UDP in each cell. Unfortunately, we are not able to provide further meaningful comparison between protocols, as the channel qualities between experiments are not under control.

We analyzed throughput fairness between UEs by evaluating 66 experiments conducted with two UEs located in the same position. We found that the throughput difference between the two UEs was less than 20% for over 85% of the time, indicating fair congestion management across all vendors despite differences in their scheduling algorithms. For the remaining 15% of cases, further investigation revealed two categories of anomalies. In five of these cases, the two UEs exhibited an average CQI difference greater than 2. We believe this may be related to the fact that even UEs placed in the same location can still experience slight channel differences. The next five cases were more interesting. In two of them—both involving Huawei base stations—we observed differences regarding how much each UE was using carrier aggregation. This raises questions about how base stations make carrier-aggregation decisions, which we plan to explore in future work. In the remaining three cases, one UE consistently received more than 25% additional resource blocks compared to the other. We also plan to investigate these cases further to determine whether they are caused by congestion-control algorithms or other underlying factors.

Our findings warrant reconsideration of previous studies that assume all base station scheduling behaves consistently. For example, BurstTracker [4] assumes that a base station schedules one UE in each TTI when managing traffic across competing UEs. Our experiments reveal this assumption is likely valid only for Ericsson Micro base stations. Applying the same assumption to Ericsson Macro base stations or Samsung or Nokia base stations would yield false positive detections of burst boundaries. In contrast, PBE-CC [26] assumes that resources are shared equally among multiple UEs within the same subframe or short runs of subframes. This model fits Ericsson Macro and Nokia base stations, where resources are shared among UEs for each carrier. However, Ericsson Micro base stations and occasionally Samsung base stations may allocate all RBs in a carrier to a single UE, which may limit the effectiveness of PBE-CC when implemented with these vendors. Deeper evaluation of these issues using tools such as NG-Scope [25] and NR-Scope [24] is a subject of ongoing work.

Overall, our findings highlight the importance of considering vendor-specific scheduling algorithms when evaluating or designing measurement and optimization tools for cellular networks. Ignoring these differences risks the integrity and generalizibility of research outcomes.

6   Conclusion

We analyzed downlink scheduling algorithms used by four base station vendors, Ericsson, Samsung, Huawei and Nokia, across five cities. Our experiments revealed vendor-specific strategies in resource allocation. Our findings also revealed significant differences in how these vendors allocate resources in LTE networks with contending users. Ericsson base stations tended to favor high MCS levels to users with better channel conditions, optimizing throughput in scenarios where signal quality was favorable. Samsung's approach was more conservative, maintaining a balance across varying signal conditions, which might help stabilize the user experience during fluctuating network quality. We hope these detailed insights into scheduling behavior and MCS allocation strategies will enhance future research on cellular network performance measurement and improvement (Figs. 7, 8, 9 and 10).

Acknowledgements. We thank our shepherd and the anonymous reviewers for their insightful comments. This work was supported in part by National Science Foundation grants CNS-2223556, AST-2232457, OAC-2429485, ITE-2226460, ITE-2326928 and CNS-2213688. The views should not be interpreted as necessarily representing the official policies or endorsements, either expressed or implied, of NSF.

A   Ethical Considerations

This study was conducted using researcher-owned devices on publicly deployed commercial cellular networks under non-invasive, observational conditions. All experiments were performed with our own SIM cards and equipment during low-traffic hours to avoid affecting normal users. No privileged network access, user data collection, or packet injection was involved, and only anonymized radio-level metadata and throughput statistics were analyzed. The work complies with institutional ethical standards and the ACM Code of Ethics, ensuring that all measurements respected user privacy and did not disrupt network operations or third parties.

B   All the Base Stations' Radio Allocation Behavior

In the following paragraph, we present all the other base stations' behaviors we have examined. Overall, for two phones downloading UDP packets at the same location at the same time, we conducted experiments on 16 base stations. Besides the 6 listed in Fig. 3, we list the remaining 10 in this appendix for reference.

B.1   Ericsson Macro Base Stations

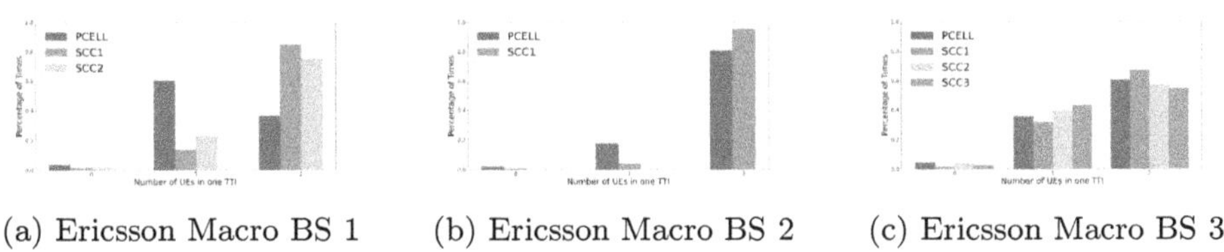

(a) Ericsson Macro BS 1   (b) Ericsson Macro BS 2   (c) Ericsson Macro BS 3

Fig. 7. Radio allocation for Ericsson macro base stations.

B.2   Ericsson Micro Base Stations

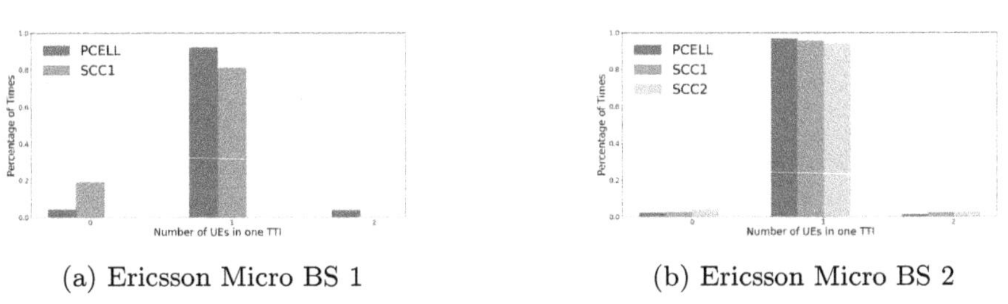

(a) Ericsson Micro BS 1   (b) Ericsson Micro BS 2

Fig. 8. Radio allocation for Ericsson micro base stations.

B.3   Samsung Base Stations

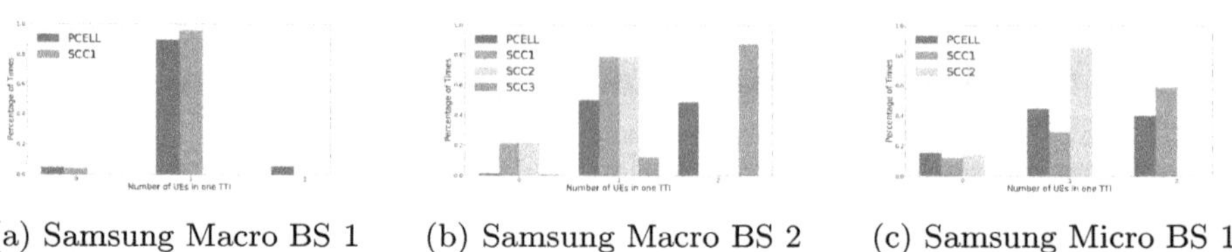

(a) Samsung Macro BS 1   (b) Samsung Macro BS 2   (c) Samsung Micro BS 1

Fig. 9. Radio allocation for Samsung base stations.

B.4   Huawei Micro Base Stations

(a) Huawei Macro BS 1

(b) Huawei Macro BS 2

Fig. 10. Radio allocation for Huawei micro base stations.

References

1. 3GPP: 5G NR Medium Access Control (MAC) protocol specification. https://www.etsi.org/deliver/etsi_ts/138300_138399/138321/15.03.00_60/ts_138321v150300p.pdf
2. 3rd Generation Partnership Project (3GPP): Scheduling. https://www.3gpp.org/technologies/scheduling
3. Arshad, K.: LTE system level performance in the presence of CQI feedback uplink delay and mobility. In: 2015 International Conference on Communications, Signal Processing, and their Applications (ICCSPA'15), pp. 1–5 (2015). https://doi.org/10.1109/ICCSPA.2015.7081294
4. Balasingam, A., Bansal, M., Misra, R., Nagaraj, K., Tandra, R., Katti, S., Schulman, A.: Detecting if LTE is the bottleneck with bursttracker. In: The 25th Annual International Conference on Mobile Computing and Networking. MobiCom '19, Association for Computing Machinery, New York (2019). https://doi.org/10.1145/3300061.3300140

5. Baranasuriya, N., Navda, V., Padmanabhan, V.N., Gilbert, S.: Qprobe: locating the bottleneck in cellular communication. In: Proceedings of the 11th ACM Conference on Emerging Networking Experiments and Technologies. CoNEXT '15, Association for Computing Machinery, New York (2015). https://doi.org/10.1145/2716281.2836118

6. Biernacki, A., Tutschku, K.: Comparative performance study of lte downlink schedulers. Wireless Pers. Commun. **74**, 585–599 (2014)

7. European Telecommunications Standards Institute: LTE; Evolved Universal Terrestrial Radio Access (E-UTRA); Physical layer procedures (3GPP TS 36.213 version 12.3.0 Release 12). Technical Specification TS 136 213 V12.3.0, ETSI, Sophia Antipolis (2014). https://www.etsi.org/

8. Ginsberg, M.: 4g shutdown timeline: When LTE will end and how to future-proof with 5g and redcap. https://5gstore.com/blog/2025/06/25/4g-shutdown/ (2025), Accessed 06 Oct 2025

9. Gupta, V., Gutterman, C., Bejerano, Y., Zussman, G.: Experimental evaluation of large scale wifi multicast rate control. IEEE Trans. Wireless Commun. **17**(4), 2319–2332 (2018)

10. Hossain, B.: Case study: at&t's nokia-to-ericsson equipment swap in the u.s. https://www.linkedin.com/pulse/case-study-atts-nokia-to-ericsson-equipment-swap-us-bellal-hossain-hquve (2023), Accessed 05 Oct 2025

11. Huehn, T., Sengul, C.: Practical power and rate control for wifi. In: 2012 21st International Conference on Computer Communications and Networks (ICCCN), pp. 1–7. IEEE (2012)

12. Kumar, S., Sarkar, A., Sriram, S., Sur, A.: A three level LTE downlink scheduling framework for rt VBR traffic. Comput. Netw. **91**, 654–674 (2015). https://doi.org/10.1016/j.comnet.2015.08.027, https://www.sciencedirect.com/science/article/pii/S138912861500287X

13. Larrea, J., Shreedhar, T., Marina, M.K.: Biscay: practical radio KPI driven congestion control for mobile networks. arXiv preprint arXiv:2509.02806 (2025)

14. Lu, F., Du, H., Jain, A., Voelker, G.M., Snoeren, A.C., Terzis, A.: CQIC: revisiting cross-layer congestion control for cellular networks. In: Proceedings of the 16th International Workshop on Mobile Computing Systems and Applications, pp. 45–50. HotMobile '15, Association for Computing Machinery, New York (2015). https://doi.org/10.1145/2699343.2699345

15. Maattanen, H.L., Huovinen, T., Koivisto, T., Enescu, M., Tirkkonen, O., Valkama, M.: Performance evaluations for multiuser CQI enhancements for LTE-advanced. In: 2011 IEEE 73rd Vehicular Technology Conference (VTC Spring), pp. 1–5 (2011). https://doi.org/10.1109/VETECS.2011.5956693

16. Marder, A., et al.: Reveal: real-time evaluation and verification of external adversarial links. In: MILCOM 2024-2024 IEEE Military Communications Conference (MILCOM), pp. 1106–1111. IEEE (2024)

17. Murray, D., Koziniec, T., Dixon, M., Lee, K.: Measuring the reliability of 802.11 wifi networks. In: 2015 Internet Technologies and Applications (ITA), pp. 233–238. IEEE (2015)

18. Pal, S., Kundu, S.R., Basu, K., Das, S.K.: IEEE 802.11 rate control algorithms: experimentation and performance evaluation in infrastructure mode. In: Passive and Active Measurement Conference. Citeseer (2006)

19. Qualcomm: eXtensible Diagnostic Monitor. https://tinyurl.com/yc4e9dcy

20. ShareTechnote: Sib scheduling. https://www.sharetechnote.com/html/BasicProcedure_LTE_SIB_Scheduling.html (2024)

21. Team, N.: Netmonster – advanced signal discovery. https://netmonster.app/ (2024)
22. Tech LTE World: LTE mac scheduler. https://techlteworld.com/lte-mac-scheduler
23. Vallina-Rodriguez, N., Auçinas, A., Almeida, M., Grunenberger, Y., Papagiannaki, K., Crowcroft, J.: Rilanalyzer: a comprehensive 3g monitor on your phone. In: Proceedings of the 2013 Conference on Internet Measurement Conference, pp. 257–264. IMC '13, Association for Computing Machinery, New York (2013). https://doi.org/10.1145/2504730.2504764
24. Wan, H., Cao, X., Marder, A., Jamieson, K.: Nr-scope: a practical 5g standalone telemetry tool. In: Proceedings of the 20th International Conference on Emerging Networking EXperiments and Technologies, pp. 73–80. CoNEXT '24, Association for Computing Machinery, New York (2024). https://doi.org/10.1145/3680121.3697808
25. Xie, Y., Jamieson, K.: Ng-scope: fine-grained telemetry for nextg cellular networks. Proc. ACM Meas. Anal. Comput. Syst. **6**(1) (2022). https://doi.org/10.1145/3508032
26. Xie, Y., Yi, F., Jamieson, K.: PBE-CC: congestion control via endpoint-centric, physical-layer bandwidth measurements. In: Proceedings of the Annual Conference of the ACM Special Interest Group on Data Communication on the Applications, Technologies, Architectures, and Protocols for Computer Communication, pp. 451–464. SIGCOMM '20, Association for Computing Machinery, New York (2020). https://doi.org/10.1145/3387514.3405880
27. Xu, Y., Wang, Z., Leong, W.K., Leong, B.: An end-to-end measurement study of modern cellular data networks. In: Proceedings of the 15th International Conference on Passive and Active Measurement - vol. 8362, pp. 34–45. PAM 2014, Springer-Verlag, Berlin, Heidelberg (2014). https://doi.org/10.1007/978-3-319-04918-2_4
28. Zhang, Z.: Basestation scheduling test. https://github.com/ZSenZhang/Basestation_scheduling_test, gitHub repository

Disentangling the Throughput Contributions of MIMO and Carrier Aggregation in 5G Networks

Yufei Feng[1]([✉])[iD], Phuc Dinh[1][iD], Moinak Ghosal[1][iD], Omar Basit[2][iD], Sizhe Wang[1][iD], Y. Charlie Hu[2][iD], and Dimitrios Koutsonikolas[1][iD]

[1] Northeastern University, Boston, MA, USA
{feng.yuf,dinh.p,ghoshal.m,wang.sizh,d.koutsonikolas}@northeastern.edu
[2] Purdue University, West Lafayette, IN, USA
{obasit,ychu}@purdue.edu

Abstract. Multiple-input multiple-output (MIMO) and carrier aggregation (CA) are two key MAC/PHY layer technologies employed by both user equipment and base stations to boost data throughput in 5G networks; yet, their respective contributions on real-world throughput improvements remain largely unexplored. Although both approaches conceptually rely on parallel transmissions, they differ fundamentally in their implementations: MIMO exploits spatial diversity through multiple data streams within a band, while CA aggregates spectrum across multiple bands. In this work, we present the first comparative study of MIMO and CA throughput gains in operational 5G networks. Using extensive measurements with commercial smartphones over all three major US cellular operators during a cross-country trip (from LA to Boston, 5700km+), we first present the current state of deployment of both technologies in today's 5G networks. We then disentangle their combined effects on throughput, quantifying the relative contribution of each technology to overall performance. Finally, we analyze how throughput scales across higher-order configurations of each technology, considering different MIMO transmission ranks and numbers of aggregated carriers, providing insights for future 5G deployments.

1 Introduction

The deployment of 5G networks has been driven largely by the promise of higher data rates. While 5G promises multi-gigabit rates, the actual improvements over 4G can be inconsistent, depending on spectrum availability, deployment configurations, and device capabilities. Two physical layer techniques are central to these throughput gains: multiple-input multiple-output (MIMO) communication and carrier aggregation (CA). Although both were first introduced in 4G, their role has expanded in 5G, where the availability of new spectrum bands and more advanced device capabilities make them key enablers of high throughput.

MIMO and CA, however, represent fundamentally different throughput enhancing approaches with distinct trade-offs. CA improves throughput by

S. Ferlin-Reiter et al. (Eds.): PAM 2026, LNCS 16477, pp. 247–273, 2026.
https://doi.org/10.1007/978-3-032-18268-5_12

expanding the aggregate communication bandwidth, but requires access to licensed spectrum, which is scarce and tightly regulated, with limited availability, driving up the cost to mobile operators. In contrast, MIMO increases capacity by transmitting multiple independent data streams over the same frequency band, exploiting differences in wireless propagation paths along with advanced signal processing. Its gains, however, depend on sophisticated hardware at both the base station and the user equipment (UE), as well as favorable propagation conditions.

Consequently, operators face spectrum costs when scaling throughput with CA, while vendors face higher design complexity and manufacturing cost when scaling throughput with MIMO. Moreover, while in theory throughput scales linearly with the MIMO rank (i.e., the number of independent data streams) and the aggregate channel bandwidth, the benefits can quickly saturate in practice and may even reverse under unfavorable conditions. Ultimately, these trade-offs impose costs on different stakeholders, raising the question of whether the throughput gains of the two technologies justify their respective economic and technical burdens.

Understanding the individual impact of each of the two technologies on end user throughput, however, is challenging. In operational networks, MIMO and CA are often used jointly and the throughput observed by end users reflects their combined effects, as well as the impact of other factors, such as frequency band, channel quality, modulation and coding scheme (MCS), or overall cell load. Previous works [28–30,36,42,47] have often focused on improving MIMO and CA in isolation, developing models and algorithms that advance the performance of one of the two technologies in terms of physical layer metrics rather than the overall end user throughput in operational networks. In contrast, previous measurement studies [10,18–20,34,40] report only aggregate end user performance results from operational networks, where the gains of MIMO and CA are entangled. To our best knowledge, no previous work has attempted to *disentangle* the contributions of MIMO and CA to the overall end user throughput, to determine which technology contributes more and under what conditions, and to analyze how throughput scales with higher order MIMO or CA configurations in operational networks. Answering these questions is essential for operators and vendors to inform spectrum acquisition decisions, hardware design choices, and future deployment and configuration decisions.

To fill this gap, in this paper, we present the first large-scale comparative study of the individual throughput gains from MIMO and CA in operational 5G networks, using a large dataset collected through a cross-country driving trip (Los Angeles to Boston, 5700+ km). Our dataset spans all three major US operators (AT&T, Verizon, T-Mobile), multiple frequency bands (5G-low, 5G-mid, and 5G-high/mmWave), and both 5G deployment modes (non-standalone/NSA and standalone/SA). Our study makes the following contributions: (1) We characterize the current state of deployment of MIMO and CA across 5G low, mid, and mmWave bands. (2) We disentangle their combined effects and quantify the relative throughput gains attributable to each technology. (3) We analyze throughput scaling with higher-order configurations, including different transmission ranks and numbers of aggregated carriers. (4) To facilitate reproducibility and further research, we make our dataset publicly available [3].

The main findings of our study are summarized as follows:

- **Deployment–standard gap.** Halfway through the 5G life cycle, commercial deployments remain far from 3GPP-specified capabilities. While NR supports up to 8×8 downlink MIMO, 4×4 uplink MIMO, and 16 aggregated carriers, we observe at most 4×4/2×2 MIMO in the downlink/uplink direction and up to 8 CA in 5G-high bands, only half of the standardized limit, and even fewer carriers in 5G-low and 5G-mid bands.
- **Operator-specific priorities.** Throughput scaling patterns reveal clear differences in operator priorities and deployment strategies. AT&T achieves most gains through MIMO enhancements in the mid band, T-Mobile leverages broader mid band CA for consistent throughput growth, and Verizon's mmWave focused strategy yields extreme peak rates but limited coverage.
- **Technology scaling limits.** MIMO performance exhibits diminishing returns beyond two to three layers, with higher ranks often reducing throughput due to practical channel limitations, while CA generally delivers steadier, typically superlinear throughput growth with the number of aggregated carriers across bands but remains disproportionate to the aggregate bandwidth. Together, these trends indicate that scaling in commercial networks is ultimately constrained by real-time operating conditions rather than merely using higher-order configurations of these technologies.

2   Background

This section provides a brief background on CA and MIMO and their implementation details specified by 3GPP standards.

2.1   MIMO

MIMO uses multiple transmit and receive antennas to improve both the capacity and reliability of a wireless link. It operates primarily in two modes. Spatial multiplexing increases throughput by transmitting multiple independent data streams simultaneously, each over a distinct spatial channel. Spatial diversity, in contrast, transmits redundant copies of the same signal across antennas to improve reception reliability under fading. The number of spatial streams that can be transmitted at once depends on the rank of the channel, which reflects how many of those spatial paths are effectively independent. High-rank channels arise in rich scattering environments with low correlation, enabling true multiplexing gain, while highly correlated channels have fewer independent paths, limiting the number of spatial streams. As the number of transmitted streams approaches the effective rank of the channel, inter-stream interference grows, leading to diminishing returns from higher-order multiplexing.

The transmitter continuously estimates or receives channel state information (CSI) feedback from the receiver to adapt its transmission strategy. This process forms a closed-loop control system: the receiver measures the downlink channel, quantizes and reports channel state information feedback such as preferred precoding matrices, rank indicators (RI), and channel quality indicators (CQI), and the transmitter updates its precoder accordingly. The precoding matrix linearly combines the data streams across antennas to align them with the strongest and most independent spatial paths of the channel. This alignment reduces interference between layers and helps the receiver separate the signals more effectively. In high-mobility environments, feedback delay causes the transmitter to base its precoding on outdated CSI, reducing the accuracy with which it can match its transmission to the true channel and leading to performance degradation.

3GPP Release 15 established the baseline MIMO framework for 5G NR, defining support for up to 8 spatial data streams in the downlink and up to 4 in the uplink [1], although in commercial networks these numbers are typically lower. Measurement and diagnostic interfaces, including XCAL and Qualcomm logs, report two MIMO-related quantities, *MIMO mode* and *MIMO layers*. The *MIMO mode* specifies the physical antenna configuration, such as 2×2, 4×4, or 8×8, representing the number of available transmit and receive antennas. The number of *MIMO layers* (or transmission rank) indicates the number of independent data streams actually transmitted at a given time, which depends on the instantaneous channel conditions and scheduling decisions.

2.2   Carrier Aggregation

CA enables a user equipment (UE) to transmit and receive data over multiple component carriers (CCs) or cells[1] at the same time. Since each CC provides its own independent channel resource, combining them effectively increases the total bandwidth available to the link, which directly translates into higher potential throughput. In theory, the maximum achievable throughput grows proportionally to the aggregate bandwidth, as a wider channel allows more symbols to be conveyed per unit time under similar channel conditions. However, in practice, the realized gains can be lower due to scheduling inefficiencies, coordination overhead between carriers, differences in channel propagation properties among different bands, and the choice of modulation and coding schemes (MCS) and number of MIMO layers in each carrier.

---

[1] The two terms are used interchangeably.

In CA, one carrier is designated as the Primary Cell (PCell), which serves as the anchor for control signaling and may also carry user data, while the additional Secondary Cells (SCells) provide extra bandwidth for data transmission and can be activated or released as needed.[2] CA can be *intra-band*, where the CCs belong to the same 3GPP-defined frequency band (e.g., n41+n41, with both CCs belonging to the mid band n41 at 2.5 GHz) or *inter-band*, where the CCs belong to different bands (e.g., n71+n41, with the PCell belonging to the low band n71 at 600 MHz and the SCell belonging to the mid band n41 at 2.5 GHz). Different CCs can have different bandwidths and, in the case of inter-band CA, different subcarrier spacing (SCS) and different transmission mode (TDD vs. FDD). While inter-band CA allows for a more flexible use of resources by enabling operators to utilize scattered spectrum chunks, it also introduces design complexity for the RF hardware and requires interference-aware scheduling, along with additional signaling overhead.

3GPP Release 15, finalized in 2019, was the first complete 5G NR specification and established the foundation for CA capabilities in NR [1]. 5G NR, by standardization, may support up to 16 CCs in each direction. Each carrier must be at least 5 MHz wide. In the sub-6 GHz (low and mid) frequency bands (FR1), a single CC can be as wide as 100 MHz, while in the mmWave bands (FR2) it can be as wide as 400 MHz. This gives a theoretical maximum of 1.6 GHz total downlink or uplink bandwidth in FR1 and 6.4 GHz in FR2. In practice, commercial deployments are far more limited. Most networks activate only a few carriers in parallel, with total aggregate bandwidth usually in the range of a few tens to a few hundreds of MHz. Later releases (16–18) refined signaling, expanded uplink aggregation options, and added efficiency improvements, but did not alter the fundamental limits introduced in Release 15.

Summary. Both MIMO and CA conceptually rely on parallel transmissions, but they expand capacity along different resource dimensions of the system. MIMO increases spectral efficiency by transmitting multiple data streams within the same bandwidth, while CA increases throughput by combining additional spectrum resources. In practice, MIMO is limited by propagation conditions and hardware, while CA is limited primarily by spectrum availability and coordination overhead.

3 Methodology

Driving Route. We drove 5700+ km from Los Angeles, CA to Boston, MA covering all major cities in between (Las Vegas, Salt Lake City, Denver, Omaha,

---

[2] In this work, CA refers to the aggregation of different 5G cells. In this context, one of the 5G CCs, over which the 5G RRC signalling messages are transmitted along with user data, is marked as PCell, while other CCs (SCells) are added or removed dynamically for data transmission only. We do not consider CA with respect to 5G NSA Dual Connectivity, where the 5G connection acts as a secondary cell (SCell) by anchoring over a 4G LTE primary Cell (PCell).

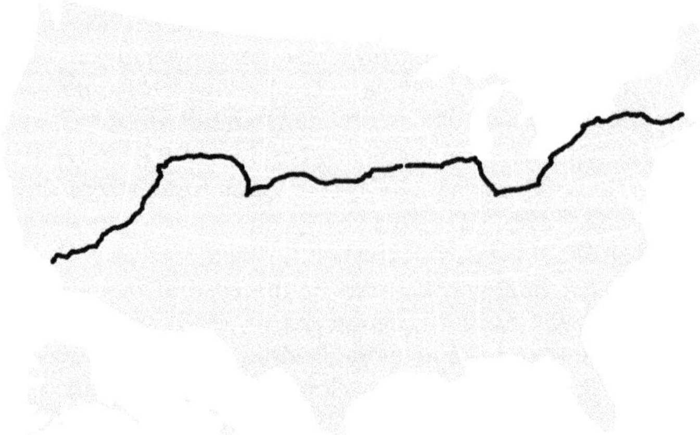

Fig. 1. Driving route.

Table 1. Bands and number of measurement samples in our dataset.

	Band(frequency/mode)	AT&T	Verizon	T-Mobile
		Number of samples		
Low	n5(850 MHz/FDD)	192,243	7,947	–
	n71(600 MHz/FDD)	–	–	226,829
Mid	n77(3.7 GHz/TDD)	210,235	531,237	–
	n2(1.9 GHz/FDD)	9,585	1,208	–
	n66(1.7/2.1 GHz/FDD)	7,084	–	209
	n41(2.5 GHz/TDD)	–	–	766,978
	n25(1.9 GHz/FDD)	–	–	206,990
High	n260(39 GHz/TDD)	21,149	1,990	37
	n261(28 GHz/TDD)	–	100,895	–

Chicago, Indianapolis, Cleveland, Rochester) over 8 days – November 1–8, 2024. The route is shown in Fig. 1. Our measurement data were collected on interstate highways, in suburban areas, and within city limits. Additional measurements were conducted within several major cities encountered along the routes. The vehicle speed ranged from 5 miles per hour in cities to 90 miles per hour on interstate highways.

5G Carriers, UE, and Servers. We obtained multiple unlimited data plans from the three major US cellular operators – Verizon, T-Mobile, and AT&T – to conduct our experiments. All three operators offer substantial 5G coverage along the driving route (AT&T: 44%, Verizon: 49%, T-Mobile: 94% of the driving route). T-Mobile is the only US carrier currently offering both NSA and SA services, with 5G SA covering 60% of the driving route. The other two operators offer only 5G NSA service. AT&T and Verizon offer service in the low, mid and high bands, while T-Mobile offers service primarily in the low and mid bands. Table 1 summarizes the different bands for each operator and the number of measurement samples collected in each band. In our analysis, we do not consider bands n66 and n260 for T-Mobile, due to the very small number of measurements over these two bands.

We used Samsung Galaxy S24 smartphones as our UEs, featuring the Snapdragon X75 modem. The phone supports downlink/uplink CA of up to 4/2 CCs in the low- and mid-bands and up to 8/4 CCs in the mmWave bands. All our experiments were conducted with 3 UEs, each connected to a different operator, to *concurrently* measure the performance over the three operators. Since commercial off-the-shelf smartphones do not provide access to low-level KPIs (MIMO, CA, MCS, etc.), we used Accuver XCAL Solo [2] devices, which tap into the Qualcomm diagnostic (diag) interface to capture signaling messages exchanged between the UE and the base station and extract these KPIs. For server-side infrastructure, we deployed two AWS EC2 cloud servers in California and Ohio for tests done with all three operators, and AWS EC2 Wavelength edge servers in Los Angeles, Las Vegas, Denver, Chicago, and Boston for tests done only with Verizon in those cities.

Experimental Methodology. We conducted backlogged downlink and uplink throughput tests using nuttcp [37] in a round robin fashion throughout the driving trip. The nuttcp tests lasted for 2 min each. Throughput samples were logged at intervals of 500 ms. Lower layer metrics (CA and MIMO information, MAC throughput per carrier, bandwidth, MCS, RSRP, CQI, etc.) are logged by XCAL at a granularity of 100 ms. Since higher-order MIMO and CA are typically activated only under heavy traffic to conserve energy and spectrum, we only use the data collected during download/upload tests for our downlink/uplink analysis, respectively. In the case of inter-band CA, different CCs belong to different bands, as we noted in Sect. 2; in our CA analysis, we classify each CA sample as 5G-low, 5G-mid, or 5G-mmWave based on the PCell. In contrast, in our MIMO analysis, we consider each cell separately, regardless of whether it is a PCell or an SCell.

4   Deployment Statistics

Even though 5G NR specifications define an ambitious PHY layer design, supporting up to 8 MIMO layers and 16 CCs within a single link, the extent to which these capabilities have materialized in real deployments remains unclear. In principle, such configurations would deliver multi-Gbps rates and unprecedented spectral efficiency. In practice, however, feature adoption often lags behind standardization: network rollouts are incremental, hardware support evolves across device generations, and operator policies often favor stability over aggressive feature extension. As 5G is passing the midpoint of its deployment cycle, it is timely to ask how close commercial networks have come to realizing the standard's full promise. In this section, we examine the real-world deployments of the three major US operators, analyzing the distributions of MIMO modes, MIMO layers, and CA configurations across frequency bands and link directions.

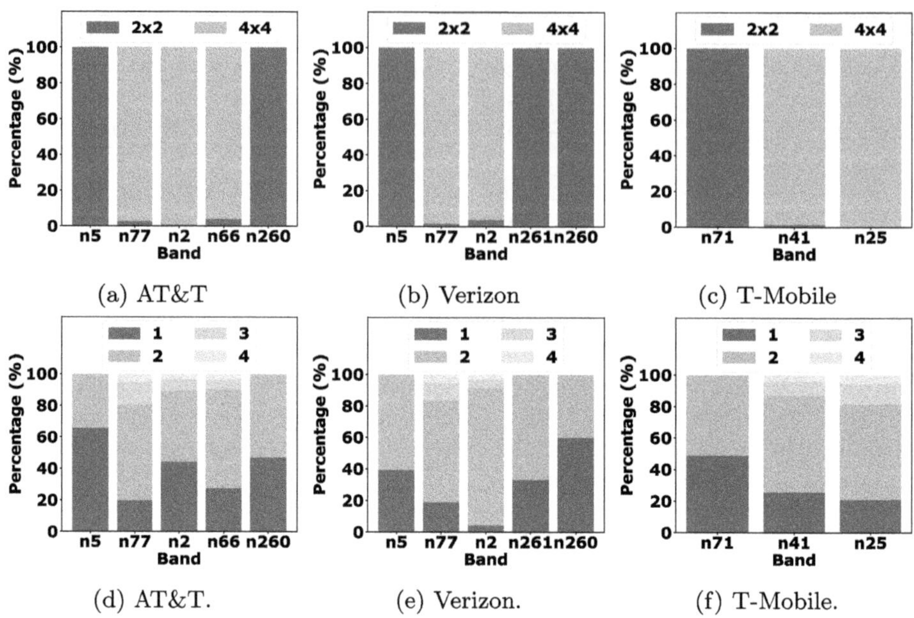

(a) AT&T   (b) Verizon   (c) T-Mobile

(d) AT&T.   (e) Verizon.   (f) T-Mobile.

Fig. 2. Distribution of MIMO modes and layers for different operators (DL).

4.1 MIMO Deployment Statistics

Figures 2a -2c show the distribution of downlink MIMO modes across operators and frequency bands during downlink throughput tests. Our first observation is a clear standard–deployment gap. Although NR permits up to 8 downlink layers, we observe no 8×8 configurations; the highest mode seen in practice is 4×4. Deployment is also strongly frequency dependent: mid-band cells operate predominantly in 4×4 mode (minimum 96% in the n2/n66 bands for AT&T, n2 band Verizon, and n41/n25 bands for T-Mobile), whereas all observed low-band and mmWave cells use exclusively 2×2 MIMO. This band-dependent behavior aligns with physical realities. The low band is provisioned for coverage and control rather than peak throughput, and hence, higher spatial multiplexing is not prioritized. On the other hand, mmWave radios face higher path loss and strong spatial correlation due to directional transmissions [16,17], which limit the gains of higher order MIMO. The mid band thus emerges as the practical middle ground for higher-order downlink MIMO.

While MIMO mode expresses the provisioned hardware configuration of a cell, MIMO layers report the number of spatial streams actually scheduled at transmission time, thus reflecting real utilization rather than configuration. The difference between the two arises from rank adaptation to instantaneous channel conditions (e.g., mobility, blockage) and scheduler policies. The layer distributions in Figs. 2 d-2 f show that scheduled rank is typically below the provisioned mode. In the low bands, where 2×2 MIMO is always available, AT&T uses

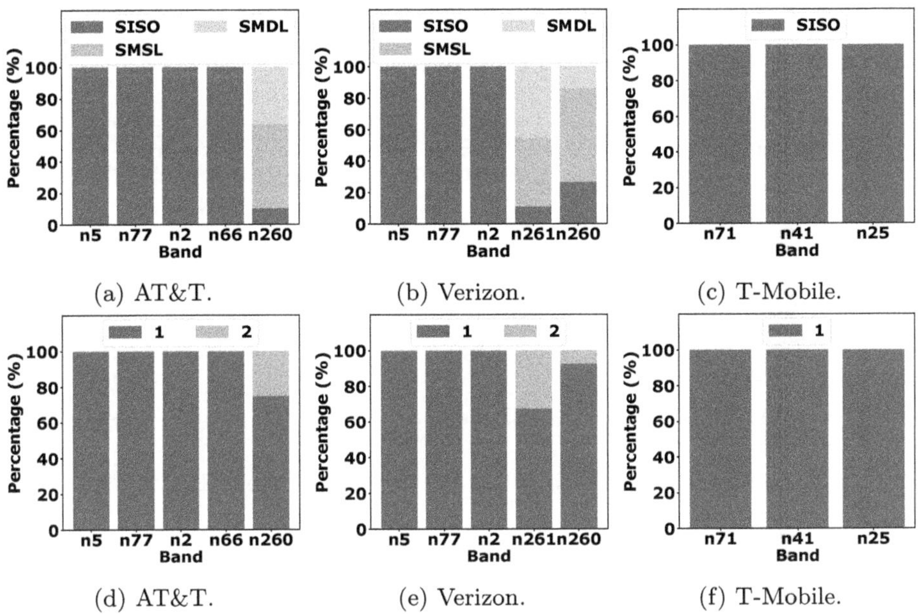

(a) AT&T.   (b) Verizon.   (c) T-Mobile.

(d) AT&T.   (e) Verizon.   (f) T-Mobile.

Fig. 3. Distribution of MIMO modes and layers for different operators (UL).

two layers only about 34% of the time (n5), Verizon about 61% (n5), and T-Mobile about 51% of the time (n71). In the mid bands, where 4×4 MIMO is almost always available, we observe a similar trend. Two-layer operation dominates (roughly 60–90%) while three layers are used only 6–15% of the time and four layers only 3–5% of the time for different bands. Finally, in the mmWave bands, where, similar to low bands, 2×2 MIMO is always available, two-layer operation ranges from 40% (Verizon n260) to 67% (Verizon n261). Overall, our results show that actual layer usage remains conservative in practice, even when high order MIMO configurations are provisioned.

Figures 3 a-3 c show that uplink MIMO configurations are far more conservative than downlink configurations. No 4×4 configurations are observed, and all FR1 bands across all three operators are exclusively SISO (single-input single output). MIMO is used only in the mmWave bands and is limited to 2×2 mode. Further, in contrast to downlink transmissions, here only a small fraction of the MIMO configurations actually support two different data streams (SMDL, two layers): around 45% in n261 for Verizon and roughly 15/35% in n260 for Verizon/AT&T. Most of the configurations support only one data stream (SMSL, one layer), which is transmitted over both antennas for diversity.

Uplink MIMO layer utilization also shows even more conservative configurations compare to downlink that mirror the distributions of uplink MIMO modes. Figures 3 d-3 f show that in FR1, all operators use a single layer 100% of the time. Only mmWave occasionally schedules two layers (either two different data streams or a single stream duplicated over both antennas) as a minority share: 25% for AT&T n260, 32% for Verizon n261, 7.5% for Verizon n260.

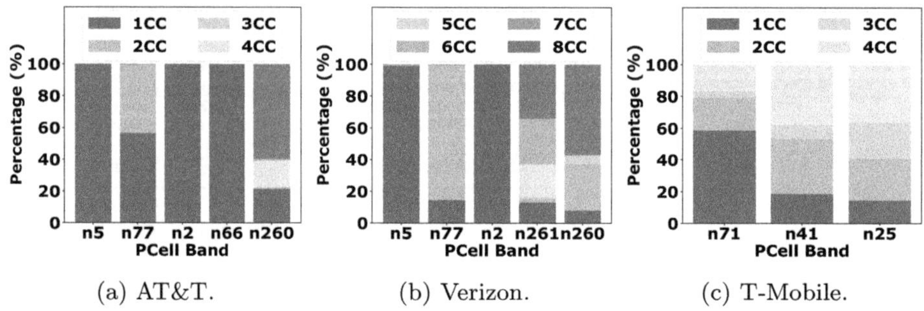

(a) AT&T. (b) Verizon. (c) T-Mobile.

Fig. 4. Distribution of CA for different operators (DL).

4.2 CA Deployment Statistics

Figure 4 summarizes the distribution of downlink CA. The highest level we observe is 8CC, appearing exclusively in the mmWave bands. Both AT&T n260 and Verizon n260 use 8CC most often (about 59% and 57%, respectively), while n261, operated exclusively by Verizon, shows a more balanced distribution among 8CC, 6CC, and 4CC. We also observe that in the mmWave bands, all three operators show preference to certain CA configurations, while other configurations are rarely used or not used at all. AT&T uses only 1CC, 4CC, and 8 CC. Verizon uses primarily 1CC, 2CC, and 8CC in n260 and rarely 5CC while in n261 it uses primarily 1CC, 4CC, 6CC, and 8CC, and rarely 2CC.

In contrast, in FR1 the maximum CA level is 4CA. AT&T and Verizon make little use of CA in low and mid bands, where most samples show use only 1 CC (i.e., no CA). The only notable exception is their mid band n77, where AT&T uses 2CC about 43% of the time and Verizon about 86% of the time. T-Mobile, which does not deploy mmWave, but is the only operator that uses 5G SA, relies more heavily on sub-6 CA. In the mid bands n41 and n25, 3CC and 4CC (observed exclusively in SA mode [18]) account for a large share (for example, 4CC alone appears 37.5% in n41 and 36% in n25). These patterns reflect operator-specific preferences for downlink CA deployment: Verizon invests most heavily in mmWave, operating two FR2 bands with frequent high-order CA, whereas T-Mobile focuses on the mid bands, where the SA mode enables 3CC and 4CC configurations in contrast to AT&T and Verizon, which operate exclusively in NSA mode and use at most 2CC.

We also found that T-Mobile relies heavily on inter-band CA (56% of the samples), aggregating cells from up to 3 different bands. A similar observation was made in [18,45]. In contrast, Verizon uses inter-band CA less than 0.02% of the time in FR1 but never in FR2 and AT&T uses only intra-band CA.

Figure 5 shows uplink CA deployment statistics. Overall, uplink CA is limited compared to downlink CA. The highest CA level we observe is 4CC in the mmWave bands: AT&T n260 uses 4CC 41% of the time, Verizon n260 uses 4CC 3% of the time, and Verizon n261 uses 4CC 35% of the time. In FR1, AT&T and Verizon use no CA in the uplink, and T-Mobile shows only a modest 2CC share in n41 (37%), and a tiny 2CC share (3%) in n71 and n25.

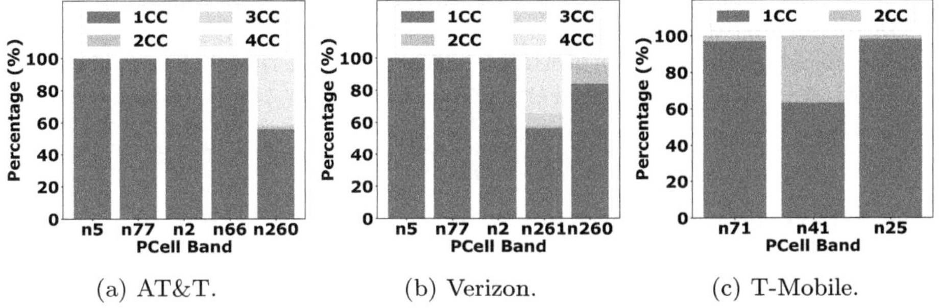

(a) AT&T.   (b) Verizon.   (c) T-Mobile.

Fig. 5. Distribution of CA for different operators (UL).

Summary. In summary, we observe a consistent standard–deployment gap. While NR allows up to 8 downlink MIMO layers, 4 uplink MIMO layers, and 16 CCs, we see at most 4×4 MIMO in the downlink and 2×2 MIMO in the uplink, and high-order CA (up to 8) appears only in the mmWave bands while FR1 CA remains modest, especially for Verizon and AT&T, which rely only on NSA. MIMO utilization is also limited: downlink transmissions rarely use more than two layers, whereas uplink transmissions use a single layer most of the time, even if higher order MIMO modes are supported. Deployment configurations also show clear asymmetry between the downlink and uplink directions, reflecting design choices driven by practical power constraints on the UE versus the base station side.

5 Disentangling Throughput Contributions of MIMO and CA

In this section, we dissect how much of the observed 5G throughput contribution originates from MIMO vs CA. In commercial networks, both technologies operate simultaneously, and their effects are intertwined at runtime. Each active CC contributes its own throughput based on its allocated bandwidth; each active CC may also independently employ a different number of MIMO layers as the wireless channel response varies across frequencies. This coupling makes it challenging to attribute the total throughput contribution to a single technology to evaluate their effectiveness. As such, to disentangle the individual contributions of the two technologies to the overall throughput, we decompose each throughput measurement sample into four distinct components, each capturing a specific contribution of the underlying technologies, as follows.

Let $T_i, L_i, i \in \{0, 1, \ldots, N\}$ denote the MAC throughput and the number of MIMO layers of CC i, respectively; $i = 0$ indexes the primary cell, and $i > 0$ indexes the $i - th$ secondary cell (recall from Sect. 4 that $N = 1$ in FR1 for AT&T and Verizon, $N = 3$ for T-Mobile in FR1, and $N = 7$ for AT&T and Verizon in FR2). We then define:

- **Baseline throughput ($\mathbf{T}_{\text{BASE}}$):** the throughput of the primary cell only, normalized by the number of MIMO layers active at runtime. It captures the contribution of a single spatial stream on the primary cell, without accounting for CA.

$$T_{\text{BASE}} = \frac{T_0}{L_0} \tag{1}$$

- **MIMO throughput ($\mathbf{T}_{\text{MIMO}}$):** the throughput under MIMO-enabled operation on the primary cell, reflecting the spatial multiplexing gain from transmitting multiple layers simultaneously.

$$T_{\text{MIMO}} = T_0 \tag{2}$$

- **CA throughput ($\mathbf{T}_{\text{CA}}$):** the throughput when CA is active, representing the combined throughput across all active CCs. The contribution of each CC is calculated as the normalized per-layer throughput to remove the impact of MIMO.

$$T_{\text{CA}} = \sum_{i=0}^{N} \frac{T_i}{L_i} \tag{3}$$

- **Total throughput ($\mathbf{T}_{\text{TOTAL}}$):** the measured MAC-layer throughput, reflecting the combined effect of MIMO and CA.

$$T_{\text{TOTAL}} = \sum_{i=0}^{N} T_i \tag{4}$$

By comparing these quantities across frequency ranges (low, mid, and mmWave) and across operators, we assess how each mechanism contributes to throughput performance in real deployments.

For a more comprehensive view, we show in the following three types of cumulative distribution functions (CDFs) when analyzing each band. First, we show the CDFs of $\mathbf{T}_{\text{BASE}}$, $\mathbf{T}_{\text{MIMO}}$, $\mathbf{T}_{\text{CA}}$, and $\mathbf{T}_{\text{TOTAL}}$. Second, we include the CDFs of throughput ratios, $\mathbf{T}_{\text{MIMO}}/\mathbf{T}_{\text{BASE}}$, $\mathbf{T}_{\text{CA}}/\mathbf{T}_{\text{BASE}}$, and $\mathbf{T}_{\text{TOTAL}}/\mathbf{T}_{\text{BASE}}$, to better visualize the direct throughput enhancement effects contributed by MIMO, CA, and combination of the two technologies, respectively. Finally, we show the CDFs of the aggregate-to-primary-carrier bandwidth ratio to reveal how much spectrum is actually used under CA operation.

Since both MIMO and CA are used sparsely or not at all in the uplink direction (Figs. 3, 5), in the rest of this section and the next section, we limit our analysis to the downlink direction only.

5.1   Low Bands

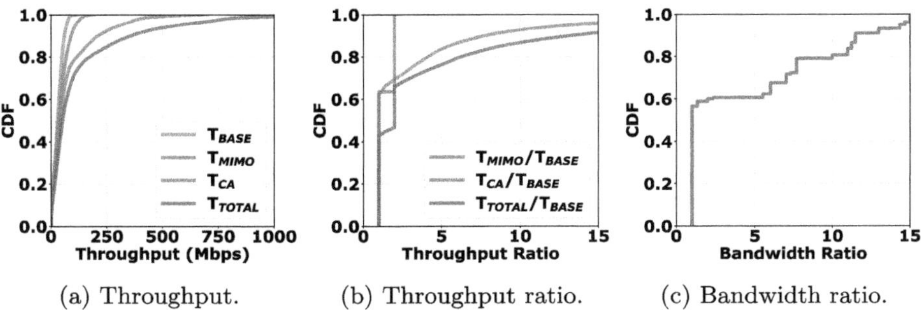

(a) Throughput.   (b) Throughput ratio.   (c) Bandwidth ratio.

Fig. 6. Low band throughput, throughput ratio, and bandwidth ratio (T-Mobile).

Figure 6 shows the CDFs of throughput, throughput ratio, and bandwidth ratio for T-Mobile in the low bands. Recall that T-Mobile is the only operator that employs CA in the low bands.

Figure 6 a shows that the throughput enhancement from MIMO and CA are limited in the lower percentile range. For example, the 25-th percentiles for T_{MIMO} and T_{CA} are 15.7 Mbps and 19.6 Mbps, respectively, vs. 12.8 Mbps for T_{BASE}. Even in the median case, the improvement remains modest – 29.4 Mbps for T_{BASE}, 35.4 Mbps for T_{MIMO}, and 42.8 Mbps for T_{CA}. The gap widens only at higher percentiles; e.g., the 90-th percentiles for T_{BASE}, T_{MIMO}, and T_{CA} are 60.4 Mbps, 90.6 Mbps, and 210.9 Mbps, respectively.

These trends reflect the sparse use of high-order MIMO and CA configurations at low frequencies: all low-band cells operate in 2×2 MIMO mode (Fig. 2 c) with only a single layer being active about half the time (Fig. 2 f), and about 60% of samples show no CA (Fig. 4 c). The ratio plots in Fig. 6 (b) mirror this behavior: T_{MIMO}/T_{BASE} is limited to 1–2, reflecting the capped number of spatial layers in deployment, while T_{CA}/T_{BASE} exhibits a much broader spread.

The broader spread of T_{CA}/T_{BASE} in Fig. 6 (b) reflects the flexibility of CA in real-world deployments. Unlike MIMO, whose gain is capped by the configured number of spatial layers, CA can exploit additional spectrum with varying bandwidth per added cell. T-Mobile often aggregates low band PCells with mid band SCells, leveraging wider bandwidth from higher-frequency bands while maintaining robust coverage on the low band. Figure 6 c hows the CDF of the total-to-primary bandwidth ratio: when aggregation is active, the effective bandwidth ratio ranges from 2× to 15×, with roughly 40% of samples exceeding 5×. This variability demonstrates the higher flexibility of CA in improving throughput whenever there is available spectrum, while MIMO focuses on maximizing spectral efficiency within a given bandwidth.

5.2 Mid Bands

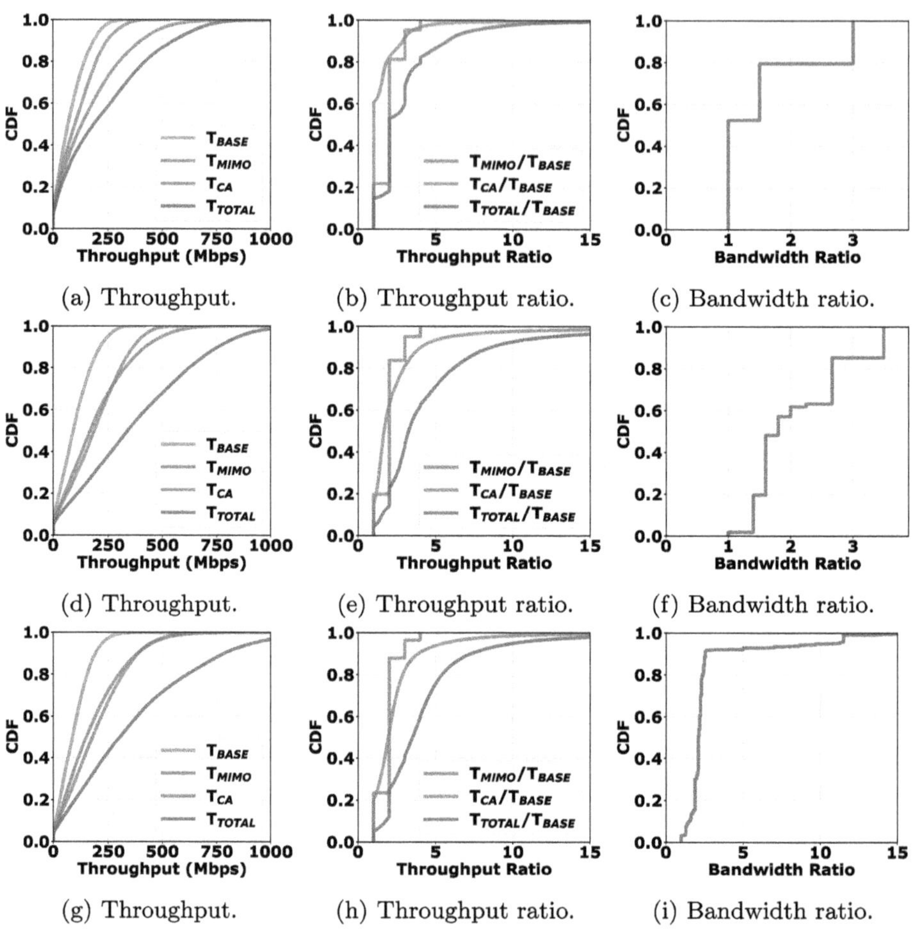

(a) Throughput.　　(b) Throughput ratio.　　(c) Bandwidth ratio.

(d) Throughput.　　(e) Throughput ratio.　　(f) Bandwidth ratio.

(g) Throughput.　　(h) Throughput ratio.　　(i) Bandwidth ratio.

Fig. 7. Mid band throughput, throughput ratio, and bandwidth ratio for AT&T (a)-(c), Verizon (d)-(f), T-Mobile (g)-(i).

Figures 7 a-7 c, 7 d -7 f, 7 g-7 i show the CDFs of throughput, throughput ratio, and bandwidth ratio for AT&T, Verizon, and T-Mobile, respectively, in the mid band deployments. The three operators exhibit noticeably different preferences for enhancing throughput via MIMO and CA.

For AT&T, throughput enhancement is primarily driven by MIMO rather than CA (Fig. 7 a). This trend aligns with the limited CA deployment previously shown in Fig. 4 a. In the median case, throughput increases from 68.0 Mbps for $\mathbf{T}_{\text{BASE}}$ to 131.7 Mbps for $\mathbf{T}_{\text{MIMO}}$, while $\mathbf{T}_{\text{CA}}$ only reaches 99.6 Mbps. Similarly, at the 90th percentile, $\mathbf{T}_{\text{MIMO}}$ (402.8 Mbps) remains higher than

$\mathbf{T}_{CA}$ (245.8 Mbps). The corresponding median throughput ratios (Fig. 7 b), $\mathbf{T}_{MIMO}/\mathbf{T}_{BASE} = 2.0$ and $\mathbf{T}_{CA}/\mathbf{T}_{BASE} = 1.0$, further highlight MIMO's dominant role in AT&T's mid-band performance. This imbalance stems from the restricted CA scaling flexibility seen in Fig. 7 c: the bandwidth ratio takes only three values ($1\times$, $2\times$, $3\times$), its median value is 1x, and it reaches its maximum value ($3\times$) only at the 80-th percentile.

In contrast, the throughput enhancement contributions from MIMO and CA are much more balanced for Verizon and T-Mobile, as shown in Figs. 7 d, 7 g, respectively. For Verizon, the median throughput rises from 91.2 Mbps to 168.7 Mbps with MIMO and to 187.3 Mbps with CA, while for T-Mobile, the corresponding values are 87.2 Mbps, 150.3 Mbps, and 178.6 Mbps. The median throughput ratios (Figs 7 e, 7 h) reinforce this pattern: $\mathbf{T}_{CA}/\mathbf{T}_{BASE}$ equals 1.7 for Verizon and 1.9 for T-Mobile, compared to only 1.0 for AT&T. These gains align with their more flexible CA configurations— Fig. 7 i and Fig. 7 f show significantly more fine-grained bandwidth ratio distributions than AT & T's, which has only three discrete levels ($1\times$, $2\times$, $3\times$). The smoother CDF slopes for T-Mobile and Verizon reflect a larger number of unique aggregation configurations with varying total aggregated bandwidths, enabling more flexible spectrum use. This is particularly true for T-Mobile, due to its inter-band CA. Interestingly, the bandwidth ratio for T-Mobile can exceed $10\times$, thanks to the operator's 3CC and 4CC configurations, which are not supported by AT&T and Verizon. However, the 90-th percentile of the bandwidth ratio for T-Mobile is lower than for Verizon (2.5x vs. $3.5\times$), as most 3CC and 4CC configuration include low-bandwidth SCells for robustness instead of high-bandwidth cells for throughput enhancement.

5.3   MmWave Bands

Figures 8 a-8 c, 8 d-8 f show the CDFs of throughput, throughput ratio, and bandwidth ratio for AT&T and Verizon, respectively, in mmWave deployments. Unlike in the lower bands, here both operators rely almost entirely on CA for throughput enhancement, while MIMO plays a secondary role.

For AT&T (Fig. 8 a), the median throughput increases from 96.7 Mbps for $\mathbf{T}_{BASE}$ to 137.6 Mbps with MIMO and to 542.2 Mbps with CA. Similarly, at the 90th percentile, $\mathbf{T}_{CA}$ (1151.3 Mbps) far exceeds $\mathbf{T}_{MIMO}$ (236.3 Mbps). The corresponding median throughput ratios (Fig. 8 b) can reach up to 15x for CA but are limited to $2\times$ for MIMO. Verizon follows a similar trend, but with slightly higher overall performance and more heterogeneity across CA deployments (compare Figs. 8 f vs. 8 c). The median throughput for Verizon ((Fig. 8 d)) increases from 118.5 Mbps to 201.8 Mbps with MIMO and to 639.0 Mbps with CA, reaching 1348.9 Mbps at the 90th percentile. The throughput ratio (median $4.5\times$, 90-th percentile $8.5\times$) for CA (vs. $2\times$ for MIMO) aligns with its bandwidth ratio distribution (median $5.5\times$, 90th percentile $8\times$; Fig. 8 f), indicating a wider range of aggregated bandwidths across locations thanks to the higher diversity of CA configurations compared to AT&T (see Figs. 4 b vs. 4 a). Overall, the dominant role of CA in throughput enhancement in mmWave bands is expected, given the

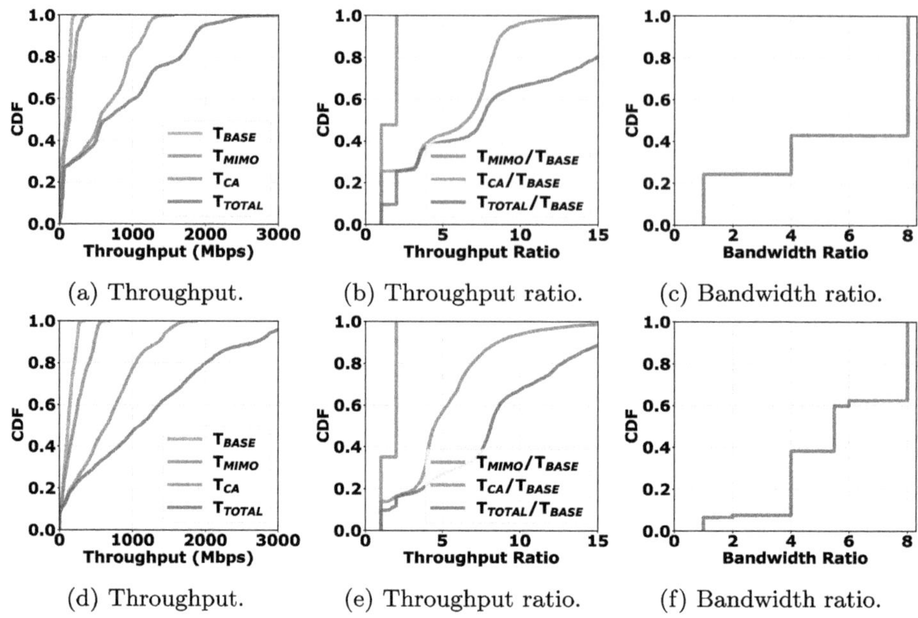

(a) Throughput.   (b) Throughput ratio.   (c) Bandwidth ratio.

(d) Throughput.   (e) Throughput ratio.   (f) Bandwidth ratio.

Fig. 8. mmWave throughput, throughput ratio, and bandwidth ratio for AT&T (a)-(c) and Verizon (d)-(f).

abundant spectrum available in these bands and the propagation characteristics of mmWave frequencies – highly directional links, strong path loss, and limited multipath richness, which restrict MIMO spatial multiplexing gains.

Summary. Overall, we observe clear operator-specific differences in how throughput scales with MIMO and CA across frequency bands. (1) In the low bands (for T-Mobile only), throughput gains are modest because advanced configurations are rarely used: MIMO operation is typically limited to 2×2 and single-layer operation is often preferred. CA contributes mainly in the upper tail, where inter-band aggregation provides additional bandwidth. (2) In the mid bands, operator strategies diverge: AT&T's improvements are largely driven by MIMO, with CA constrained to a few discrete bandwidth ratios, whereas T-Mobile and Verizon achieve greater improvements from CA, reflecting more diverse aggregation settings and larger aggregate bandwidths. (3) In the mmWave bands, CA dominates as a throughput enhancing factor for both operators, combining multiple carriers to reach multi-Gbps rates, while MIMO gains remain bounded (at most $2\times$) due to limited multipath and highly directional propagation, which prevent deployments of higher-order MIMO modes.

6   Scaling Analysis

In this section, we evaluate the impact of higher-order configurations on throughput distributions in commercial 5G deployments. We observe how throughput evolves with increasing numbers of MIMO layers or CCs across frequency bands and operators to understand how spatial and spectral parallelism manifest in practice. This analysis provides an empirical view of how effectively 5G networks realize the theoretical scaling promised by high-rank MIMO and multi-carrier aggregation, and where those gains begin to saturate.

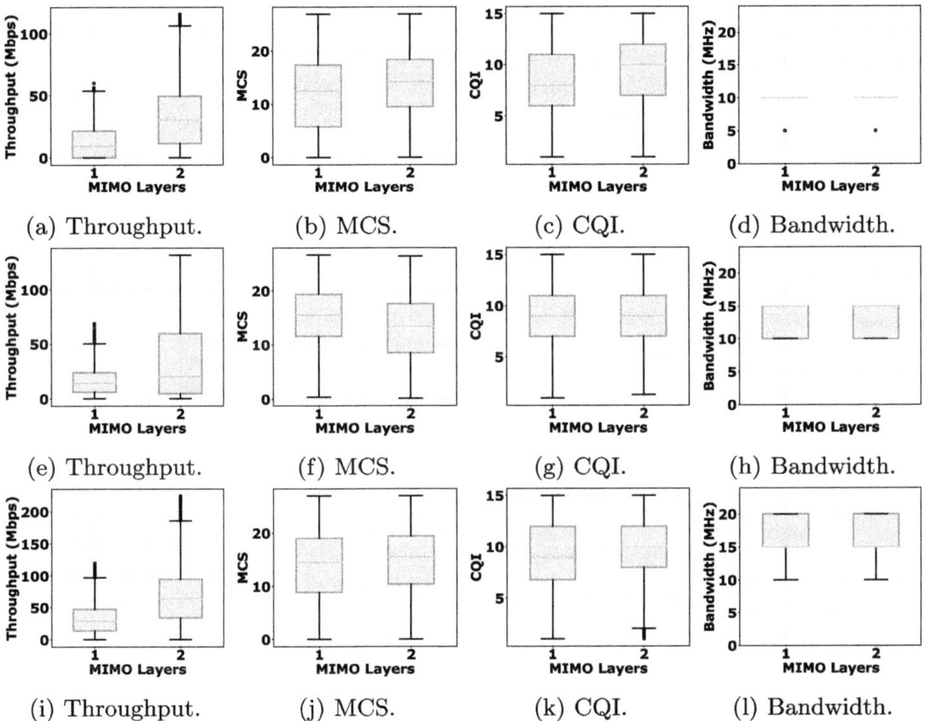

(a) Throughput.   (b) MCS.   (c) CQI.   (d) Bandwidth.

(e) Throughput.   (f) MCS.   (g) CQI.   (h) Bandwidth.

(i) Throughput.   (j) MCS.   (k) CQI.   (l) Bandwidth.

Fig. 9. MIMO scaling analysis in the low bands for AT&T (a)-(d), Verizon (e)-(h), T-Mobile (i)-(l).

6.1   MIMO Scaling Analysis

Low Bands. Figures 9 a, 9 e, 9 i show that two-layer MIMO substantially improves throughput across all operators. The median throughput rises from 9.4 to 30.2 Mbps for AT &T, 14.3 to 20.2 Mbps for Verizon, and 29.0 to 63.7 Mbps for T-Mobile, with corresponding maximum values of 59.9 to 115.5 Mbps, 68.5 to 131.5 Mbps, and 119.9 to 224.2 Mbps, respectively. Interestingly, while the gains at the maximum throughput values are close to the theoretical value of 2× for all three operators (1.87 for T-Mobile, 1.92 for AT&T and Verizon), the gains in the median case vary significantly: 1.4× for Verizon (much lower than the theoretical gain), 2.2× for T-Mobile (slightly higher than the theoretical gain), and 3.2x for AT&T (much higher than the theoretical gain).

Figures 9 d, 9 h, 9 l show that the cell bandwidth distributions are very similar for 1- and 2-layer configurations for all three operators, suggesting that they do not contribute to the differences in the observed throughput gains. However, Figs. 9 c, 9 g, 9 k show that the median channel quality indicator (CQI) is higher for 2-layer configurations compared to 1-layer configurations for AT&T and T-Mobile, but slightly lower for Verizon. In other words, AT&T and T-Mobile conservatively activate spatial multiplexing for high-quality links, while Verizon is more aggressive activating spatial multiplexing even for links of lower channel quality (see also Figs. 2 d, 2 f vs. Figure 2 e). As a result, the median MCS (modulation and coding schemes) is lower for 2-layer configurations compared to 1-layer configurations in the case of Verizon (Fig. 9 f vs. Figures 9 b, 9 j), canceling out part of the multiplexing gains, which explains the lower gains from MIMO in the case of Verizon.

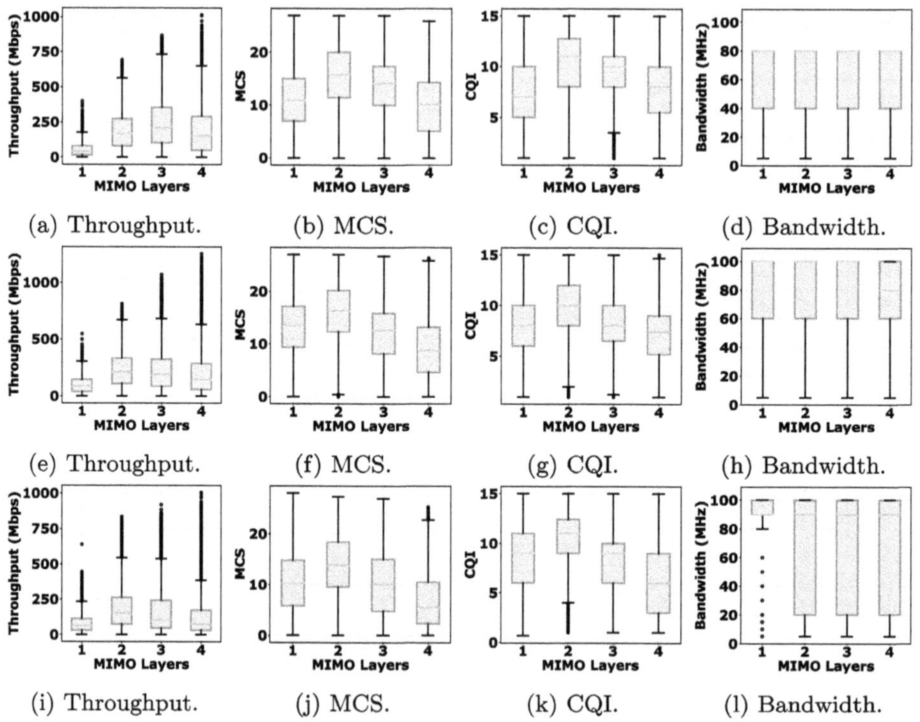

(a) Throughput.   (b) MCS.   (c) CQI.   (d) Bandwidth.

(e) Throughput.   (f) MCS.   (g) CQI.   (h) Bandwidth.

(i) Throughput.   (j) MCS.   (k) CQI.   (l) Bandwidth.

Fig. 10. MIMO scaling analysis in the mid bands for AT&T (a)-(d), Verizon (e)-(h), T-Mobile (i)-(l).

Mid Bands. Figures 10 a, 10 e, 10 i show that, in the mid bands, the throughput increases with the number of layers for up to 3 layers with AT&T and up to 2 layers with the other two operators, but decreases with higher layer configurations. The median throughput changes from 41 to 167 to 209 to 155 Mbps for AT&T as the number of layers changes from 1 to 4, from and 85 to 211 to 188 to 145 Mbps for Verizon, and from 63 to 151 to 103 to 74 Mbps for T-Mobile. The largest gains occur between one and two layers (4.1×, 2.48×, 2.4× in the median case for AT&T, Verizon, and T-Mobile, respectively, higher or much higher – for AT&T – than the theoretical value of 2x), with AT&T showing slight additional improvement at three layers (1.25x over 2 layers in the median case, lower than the theoretical value of 1.5×).

Figures 10 d, 10 h, 10 l show that the cell bandwidth distributions remain essentially similar across ranks (except for T-Mobile's one-layer cases that generally use higher bandwidth), confirming that the gains still primarily arise from spatial multiplexing rather than additional spectrum. Figures 10 c, 10 g, 10 k and Figs. 10 b, 10 f, 10 j show that CQI and MCS exhibit a similar peak at two layers across all operators, but start dropping at higher-order configurations, explaining the reduced gains at those configurations. Together the low band and mid band results suggest that two-layer MIMO represents a practical sweet spot for today's FR1 deployments; higher ranks tend to yield diminishing or negative returns, likely due to limited spatial separation and inter-layer interference under real-world conditions.

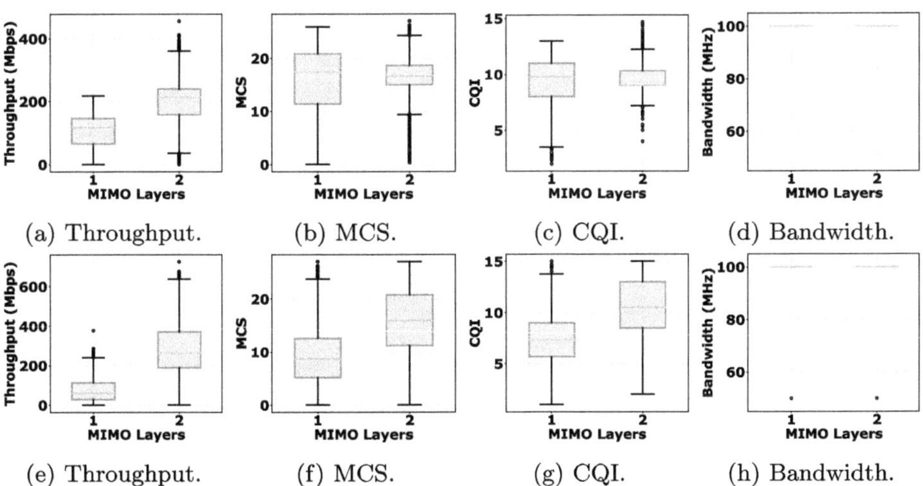

(a) Throughput. (b) MCS. (c) CQI. (d) Bandwidth.

(e) Throughput. (f) MCS. (g) CQI. (h) Bandwidth.

Fig. 11. MIMO scaling analysis in the mmWave bands for AT&T (a)-(d), Verizon (e)-(h).

MmWave Bands. Figures 11 a, 11 e show that mmWave throughput scales strongly with the number of MIMO layers for both operators. The median throughput increases from 116 to 213 Mbps (1.8x) for AT&T and from 60 to 264 Mbps (4.4×) for Verizon, while the maximum throughput roughly doubles (218 → 455 Mbps, 2.1x for AT&T and 377 → 724 Mbps, 1.9× for Verizon). The cell bandwidth remains constant at 100 MHz (Figs. 11 d, 11 h), isolating the observations from bandwidth scaling effects and indicating that the observed gain primarily arises from spatial multiplexing. However, AT&T's median CQI and MCS are similar under 1-layer and 2-layer configurations (Figs. 11 c, 11 b), indicating that its scheduler enables 2-layer transmission broadly, even without particularly favorable channel conditions. Verizon, in contrast, activates two layers mainly under high-CQI states (Fig. 11 g), combining multiplexing gains with favorable channel conditions that support high MCS values (Fig. 11 b) and reinforce throughput growth far beyond 3×. Overall, even without CQI improvement, AT&T's near-2× scaling demonstrates that spatial multiplexing at mmWave remains effective, though slightly weaker than in FR1, while Verizon's stronger scaling reflects the combined effects of beam alignment and selective rank scheduling.

6.2 CA Scaling Analysis

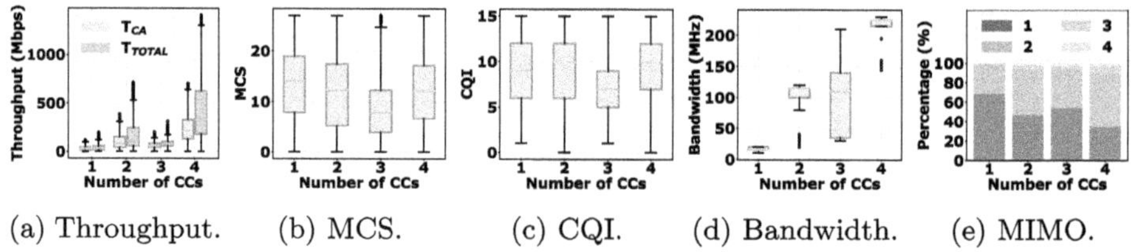

(a) Throughput.   (b) MCS.   (c) CQI.   (d) Bandwidth.   (e) MIMO.

Fig. 12. CA scaling analysis in the low bands for T-Mobile.

Low Bands. Figure 12 summarizes low-band CA scaling for T-Mobile. We focus on 1CC, 2CC, and 4CC configurations, as the 3CC case (only about 500 samples observed compared to more than 5000 for other configurations) appears to be a transient rather than a steady network state. Figure 12 a shows that the median throughput increases from 33.1 to 111.1 (3.6× gain) to 333.2 (10× gain) Mbps as CA expands from 1 to 2 to 4 CCs, i.e., it scales *superlinearly* with the number of carriers, driven by a corresponding aggregate bandwidth increase from 15 MHz to 115 MHz and 225 MHz (Fig. 12 e) and by an increase to the fraction of higher-layer MIMO configurations (Fig. 12 e). This is because secondary cells are often mid-band cells with much higher bandwidth and higher MIMO support than the low-band PCell. However, the throughput gain does not scale linearly with the aggregated bandwidth. When the CA level increases from 1CC to 2CC, the bandwidth gain is 7.7×, but the throughput gain is only 3.6× in the median case. One possible reason for this is the lower MCS in 2CC configurations (Fig. 12 b) despite the higher CQI (Fig. 12 c). On the other hand, when the CA level increases from 2CC to 4CC, the bandwidth gain is 1.96×, but the throughput gain is 3× in the median case, possibly due to higher MCS (at the 25-th percentile) and a higher fraction of 2 MIMO layers at 4CC configurations. To remove the effect of MIMO, we also plot $\mathbf{T}_{CA}$ (see Sect. 5 in Fig. 12 a). The $\mathbf{T}_{CA}$ gains at 2CC vs. 1CC and at 4CC vs. 2CC are 2.8× and 2.6×, respectively, lower than the corresponding throughput gains.

Mid Bands. Figs. 13 a-13 e, 13 f-13 j, 13 k-13 o summarize mid band CA scaling for AT&T, Verizon, and T-Mobile, respectively. Similar to the low band, throughput scales again superlinearly with the number of CCs for all three operators. For AT&T and Verizon, the median throughput increases from 105 Mbps (1CC) to 329 Mbps (2CC) and from 21 Mbps (1CA) to 401 Mbps (2CA), respectively, when the bandwidth increases for 80 MHz to 120 MHz and from 100 MHz to 160 MHz, respectively. Similarly, for T-Mobile, the throughput rises from 61 Mbps (1CC) to 257 Mbps (2CC), 364 Mbps (3CC), and 501 Mbps (4CC), while the aggregate bandwidth changes from 100 MHz to 190 MHz, 140 MHz, and 220 MHz, respectively. We observe that the throughput scales much faster than the bandwidth for all three operators; in fact, notice that, in the case of T-Mobile, the median aggregate bandwidth is lower at 3CC configurations compared to 2CC configurations and yet, the throughput is higher. The $\mathbf{T}_{CA}$ gains as the CA level increases from 1CC to 2CC for AT&T and Verizon and from 1CC to 4CC for T-Mobile are very similar to the corresponding throughput gains (e.g., 4.25× vs. 4.21×, 1.4× vs. 1.3×, and 1.37× vs. 1.4× for T-Mobile), suggesting that MIMO is not a contributing factor to the throughput scaling. For Verizon and T-Mobile, Figs. 13 g , 13 l show much higher MCS values at higher CA levels, which explain the superlinear throughput increase. In contrast, for AT & T, the MCS is already high at 1CC and only slightly increases at 2CC (Fig. 13 b); this explains the lower throughput gains for AT&T compared to the other two operators as the CA levels rises from 1CC to 2CC.

MmWave Bands. Figs. 14 a–14 e, 14 f–14 j summarize mmWave CA scaling for AT&T and Verizon, respectively. Here, almost all carriers have the same bandwidth (100 MHz, Figs. 14 d, 14 f), and hence, the aggregate bandwidth scales linearly with the CA level. Figures 14 a, 14 f show that throughput scales superlinearly with the number of CCs for both operators, similar to the low and mid bands. For AT&T, the median throughput increases from 46.6 Mbps at 1CC to 499.1 Mbps at 4CC and 1252.5 Mbps at 8CC; for Verizon, the median total throughput increases from 4.2 Mbps at 1CC to 920.1 Mbps at 4CC, 1315.4 Mbps at 6CC, and 1713.5 Mbps at 8CC. For ATT, we observe a higher CQI (Fig. 14 c) and a much higher MCS (Fig. 14 b) for configurations that employ CA (4CC and 8CC) compared to single-carrier configurations (1CC). This explains the large

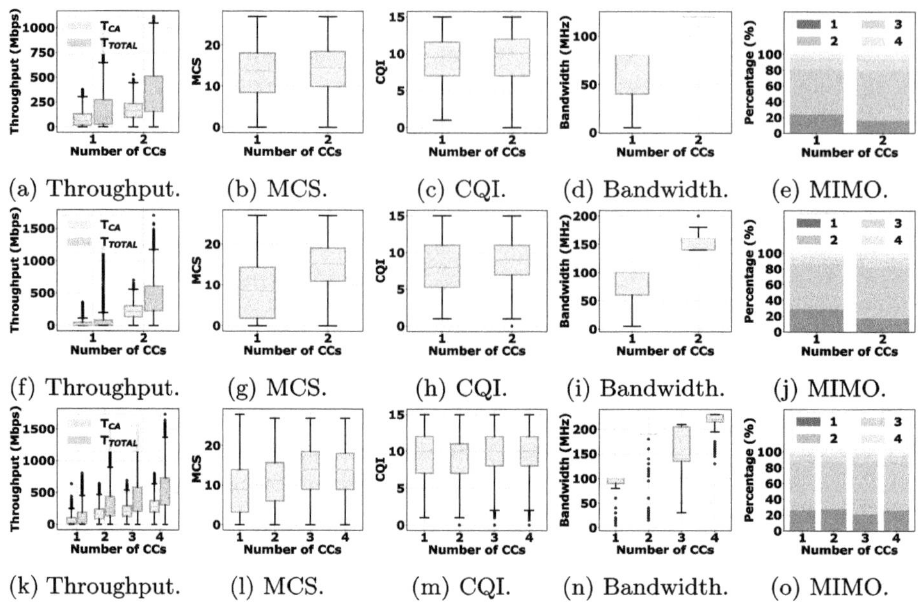

(a) Throughput.   (b) MCS.   (c) CQI.   (d) Bandwidth.   (e) MIMO.

(f) Throughput.   (g) MCS.   (h) CQI.   (i) Bandwidth.   (j) MIMO.

(k) Throughput.   (l) MCS.   (m) CQI.   (n) Bandwidth.   (o) MIMO.

Fig. 13. CA scaling analysis in the mid bands for AT & T (a)-(e), Verizon (f)-(j), T-Mobile (k)-(o).

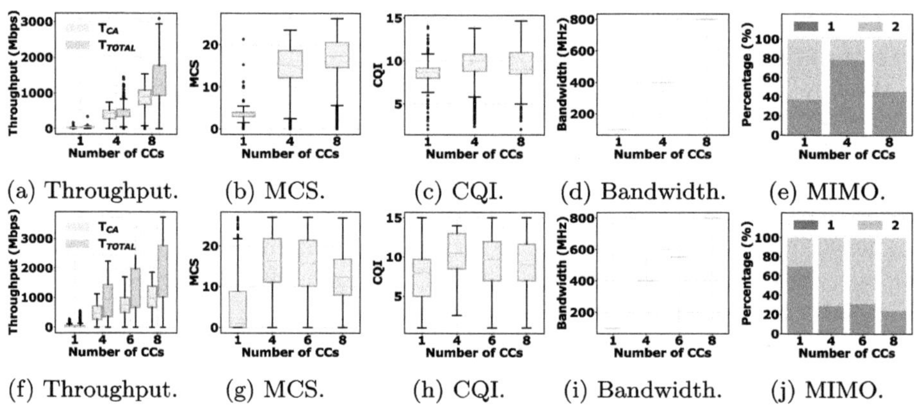

(a) Throughput.   (b) MCS.   (c) CQI.   (d) Bandwidth.   (e) MIMO.

(f) Throughput.   (g) MCS.   (h) CQI.   (i) Bandwidth.   (j) MIMO.

Fig. 14. CA scaling analysis in the mmWave bands for AT & T (a)-(e) and Verizon (f)-(j).

throughput improvements at 4CC and 8CC despite the fact that the fraction of 2-layer configurations drops drastically at 4CC (Fig. 14 e). For Verizon, CQI, MCS, and the fraction of 2-layer configurations are all much higher at 4CC-8CC compared to 1CC (Figs. 14 c, 14 b, 14 e), which again explain the superlinear throughput increase with the number of CCs. However, in contrast to AT & T, the MCS for Verizon plateaus at 4CC and drops at 8CC; this explains the lower scaling rate for Verizon with higher CA levels (the throughput gain at 8CC over 4CC is 2.5× for AT & T but 1.86× for Verizon).

Summary. Throughput scaling varies substantially across operators and between MIMO and carrier aggregation. For MIMO, FR1 deployments show consistent gains up to two layers and, in some cases, moderate improvement at three layers, after which CQI and MCS degradation degradation lead to diminishing returns. In contrast, FR2 (mmWave) deployments exhibit strong but more variable scaling: AT&T enables higher-layer transmission broadly, yielding near-2× gains even without CQI improvement, whereas Verizon schedules additional layers selectively under high-CQI conditions, where multiplexing gains are combined with favorable channels to produce 4× throughput increases. For CA, throughput increases monotonically across all bands, typically superlinearly when higher-order CCs coincide with improved CQI and MCS, but rarely in direct proportion to aggregate bandwidth.

7   Related Work

5G Measurements. Since its initial roll-out in 2019, numerous studies have evaluated various aspects of 5G networks including performance [4,6,7,12,18–21,24,26,27,31,32,35,38,39,41,43,44,46], latency [13], handovers [15,22,23], resource allocation [9], power consumption [35], impact on application QoE [6,25,35], beamforming [10,34], roaming [6,14], multi-carrier access [8], and throughput prediction [5,33,45]. Among them, the works in [4,11,18–20,22,41] followed a methodology similar to ours, collecting datasets through cross-country drives, using multiple phones connected to different cellular networks and XCAL to log lower layer data. While some of these works briefly review CA [10,18,19,34] and MIMO [19] deployments in operational 5G networks, none of them has attempted to systematically disentangle the relative throughput contributions of these two technologies in commercial 5G deployments.

CA and MIMO Studies. The two works closest to our study are those in [40, 45]. Rochman et al. [40] use a dataset collected in 2022/2023 (when only T-Mobile supported CA in the low-/mid-bands) in Chicago and Minneapolis to study the factors that contribute to 5G performance improvements over 4G in low- and mid-bands, including channel bandwidths, CA, MIMO, and higher-order MCS. Their analysis shows that much of 5G's observed throughput gains over 4G stems from wider channel bandwidths, both over single and aggregated channels, rather than from PHY techniques, such as MIMO or higher-order MCS, alone. Ye et al. [45] focus exclusively on CA, characterizing its deployment in operational networks in two cities and developing a CA-aware predictor that improves throughput estimation. Both these studies provide valuable insights into CA behavior and MIMO deployments, although in a limited geographic area, but none of them quantifies the relative contributions of MIMO and CA to the overall 5G throughput or studies how throughput scales with each of these two factors. *Our work addresses precisely this gap by systematically comparing* *their throughput gains and scaling behavior across all three frequency bands via a large dataset obtained from a cross-country drive covering large urban centers as well as suburban and rural areas.*

Complementary to measurement studies, foundational theoretical and simulation based research has modeled the expected performance of MIMO and CA under idealized conditions. For MIMO, representative analytical works have characterized capacity scaling, spatial diversity, and antenna selection tradeoffs in multi-antenna systems [29, 30, 36]. For CA, system-level models have examined load balancing, packet scheduling, and capacity or admission control across aggregated carriers [42, 47]. These studies establish theoretical bounds and design principles under simplified assumptions such as perfect channel knowledge and stationary propagation conditions, but they do not capture the variability and constraints of commercial deployments that our measurement-driven analysis quantifies at scale. Different from these works, the work in [28] identifies experimentally limitations of the sequential, cell-by-cell CA operations employed by today's 5G networks and proposes PHY layer enhancements to enable inferring the channel quality of multiple carriers by measuring only one carrier. However, it neither considers MIMO nor does it explore the contribution of CA to the overall end user throughput.

8 Conclusion

We presented, to our best knowledge, the first quantitative comparison of the throughput gains attributable to MIMO and carrier aggregation (CA) in operational 5G networks. Our large-scale measurements show that real-world performance diverges largely from theoretical expectations. While both technologies enhance end user throughput, their scaling behaviors and deployment priorities differ. MIMO's spatial multiplexing gains often plateau and can even degrade beyond two to three layers as channel correlation and CQI loss offset the benefits of additional spatial streams. In contrast, CA yields steadier, often superlinear throughput growth across frequency bands, though the gains typically scale nonlinearly with aggregated bandwidth. Together, these findings expose two persistent gaps in today's 5G landscape: a theory–operation gap, where empirical scaling falls short of analytical models, and a deployment-standard gap, where commercial networks implement only a subset of 3GPP capabilities. These gaps, along with distinct operator strategies in balancing spectral expansion against hardware and signaling complexity, underscore the importance of understanding these trade-offs to guide spectrum policy, base station design, and the transition toward 6G.

Acknowledgement. We thank the anonymous reviewers for their helpful comments. This work is supported in part by NSF grants 2312834 and 2340283.

References

1. 3GPP: Release 15 Description; Summary of Rel-15 Work Items (TR 21.915) (2019). https://www.3gpp.org/DynaReport/21915.htm, 3rd Generation Partnership Project (3GPP)
2. XCAL Solo. https://accuver.com/sub/products/view.php?idx=11;
3. Dataset: Disentangling the Throughput Contributions of MIMO and Carrier Aggregation in 5G Networks (2025). https://github.com/NUWiNS/pam25-mimo-ca-dataset
4. Baena, E., et al.: Root cause analysis of cellular network throughput degradations under vehicular mobility. In: Proc. of IEEE MASS (2025)
5. Basit, O., et al.: On the predictability of fine-grained cellular network throughput using machine learning models. In: Proc. of IEEE MASS (2024)
6. Caso, G., et al.: The chronicles of 5G non-standalone: an empirical analysis of performance and service evolution. IEEE Open J. Commun. Soc. **5**, 7380–7399 (2024)
7. Caso, G., et al.: An initial look into the performance evolution of 5G non-standalone networks. In: Proc. of IFIP/IEEE TMA (2023)
8. Chen, F., et al.: A large-scale study of the potential of multi-carrier access in the 5G Era. In: Proc. of PAM (2025)
9. Dinh, P., Ghoshal, M., Han, Y., Feng, Y., Koutsonikolas, D., Widmer, J.: Demystifying resource allocation policies in operational 5g mmwave networks. IEEE Trans. Netw. **33**(2), 1–16 (2024)
10. Feng, Y., Dinh, P., Ghoshal, M., Baena, E., Bouchebbah, H., Koutsonikolas, D.: Vivisecting beam management in operational 5G mmWave networks. In: Proc. of ACM CoNEXT (2025)
11. Fezeu, R., et al.: Unveiling the 5G mid-band landscape: from network deployment to performance and application QoE. In: Proc. of ACM SIGCOMM (2024)
12. Fezeu, R., et al.: Unveiling the 5G mid-band landscape: from network deployment to performance and application QoE. In: Proc. of ACM SIGCOMM 2024 (2024)
13. Fezeu, R., et al.: An in-depth measurement analysis of 5G mmWave PHY latency and its impact on end-to-end delay. In: Proc. of PAM (2023)
14. Fezeu, R.A.K., et al.: Roaming across the European union in the 5G era: performance, challenges, and opportunities. In: Proc. of IEEE INFOCOM (2024)
15. Fiandrino, C., Juárez Martínez-Villanueva, D., Widmer, J.: Uncovering 5G performance on public transit systems with an app-based measurement study. In: Proc. of ACM MSWiM (2022)
16. Ghasempour, Y., Haider, M.K., Cordeiro, C., Koutsonikolas, D., Knightly, E.: Multi-stream beam-training for mmWave MIMO networks. In: Proc. of ACM MobiCom (2018)
17. Ghasempour, Y., Knightly, E.: Decoupling beam steering and user selection for scaling multi-user 60 GHz WLANs. In: Proc. of ACM MobiHoc (2018)
18. Ghoshal, M., et al.: A first large-scale study of operational 5g standalone networks. In: Proc. of ACM CoNEXT (2025)
19. Ghoshal, M., et al.: Replication: performance of cellular networks on the wheels. In: Proc. of ACM IMC (2025)
20. Ghoshal, M., Khan, I., Kong, Z.J., Dinh, P., Meng, J., Hu, Y.C., Koutsonikolas, D.: Performance of cellular networks on the wheels. In: Proc. of ACM IMC (2023)
21. Ghoshal, M., et al.: An in-depth study of uplink performance of 5G mmWave networks. In: Proc. of the ACM SIGCOMM 5G-MeMU Workshop (2022)

22. Hassan, A., et al.: Vivisecting mobility management in 5G cellular networks. In: Proc. of ACM SIGCOMM (2022)
23. Kalntis, M., et al.: Through the telco lens: a countrywide empirical study of cellular handovers. In: Proc. of ACM IMC (2024)
24. Khan, I., et al.: How mature is 5g deployment? a cross-sectional, year-long study of 5g uplink performance. In: Proceedings of the IFIP/IEEE Networking 2024 Conference (2024)
25. Khan, I., Tran, T.X., Hiltunen, M., Karagioules, T., Koutsonikolas, D.: An experimental study of low-latency video streaming over 5G. In: Proc. of IEEE MeditCom (2024)
26. Kousias, K., et al.: Coverage and performance analysis of 5G non-standalone deployments. In: Proc. of ACM WiNTECH (2022)
27. Kousias, K., et al.: Empirical performance analysis and ML-based modeling of 5G non-standalone networks. Elsevier Comput. Netw. **241**(C) (2024)
28. Li, Q., Zhang, Z., Liu, Y., Tan, Z., Peng, C., Lu, S.: CA++: enhancing carrier aggregation beyond 5G. In: Proc. of ACM MobiCom (2023)
29. Liu, Z., Dai, L.: A comparative study of downlink mimo cellular networks with co-located and distributed base-station antennas. IEEE Trans. Wireless Commun. **13**(11), 6259–6274 (2014)
30. Molisch, A.F., Win, M.Z., Choi, Y.S., Winters, J.H.: Capacity of mimo systems with antenna selection. IEEE Trans. Wireless Commun. **4**(4), 1759–1772 (2005)
31. Moreno, J., Contini, M., Aguiar, A.: 5G NSA performance: a measurement study. In: Proc. of IFIP WONS (2024)
32. Narayanan, A., et al.: A first look at commercial 5G performance on smartphones. In: Proc. of ACM WWW (2020)
33. Narayanan, A., et al.: Lumos5G: mapping and predicting commercial mmWave 5G throughput. In: Proc. of ACM IMC (2020)
34. Narayanan, A., et al.: A comparative measurement study of commercial 5G mmWave deployments. In: In Proc. of IEEE INFOCOM (2022)
35. Narayanan, A., et al.: A variegated look at 5G in the wild: performance, power, and QoE implications. In: Proc. of ACM SIGCOMM (2021)
36. Ngo, H.Q., Larsson, E.G., Marzetta, T.L.: Energy and spectral efficiency of very large multiuser mimo systems. IEEE Trans. Commun. **61**(4), 1436–1449 (2013)
37. NUTTCP - Network Performance Measurement Tool. https://www.nuttcp.net
38. Parastar, P., Alay, A.L.O.O., Caso, G., Perino, D.: Spotlight on 5G: performance, device evolution and challenges from a mobile operator perspective. In: Proc. of IEEE INFOCOM (2023)
39. Rochman, M.I., et al.: A comprehensive analysis of the coverage and performance of 4G and 5G deployments. Comput. Netw. **237** (2023)
40. Rochman, M.I., Ye, W., Zhang, Z.L., Ghosh, M.: A comprehensive real-world evaluation of 5G improvements over 4G in low- and mid-bands. IEEE Trans. Cogn. Commun. Netw. **11**(3), 1427–1440 (2025)
41. Wang, S., et al.: A first large-scale study of operational 5g standalone networks. In: Proc. of ACM SIGMETRICS (2026)
42. Wang, Y., Pedersen, K.I., Sørensen, T.B., Mogensen, P.E.: Carrier load balancing and packet scheduling for multi-carrier systems. IEEE Trans. Wireless Commun. **9**(5), 1780–1789 (2010)
43. Xu, D., et al.: Understanding operational 5G: a first measurement study on its coverage, performance and energy consumption. In: Proc. of ACM SIGCOMM (2020)

44. Ye, W., Carpenter, J., Zhang, Z., Fezeu, R.A.K., Qian, F., Zhang, Z.L.: A closer look at stand-alone 5g deployments from the UE perspective. In: Proc. of IEEE MeditCom (2023)
45. Ye, W., et al.: Dissecting carrier aggregation in 5G networks: measurement, QoE implications and prediction. In: Proc. of ACM SIGCOMM (2024)
46. Yuan, X., et al.: Understanding 5G performance for real-world services: a content provider's perspective. In: Proc. of ACM SIGCOMM (2022)
47. Zhang, R., Zheng, Z., Wang, M., Shen, X., Xie, L.L.: Equivalent capacity in carrier aggregation-based LTE-a systems: a probabilistic analysis. IEEE Trans. Wireless Commun. **13**(11), 6444–6460 (2014)

Security and Privacy

A Measurement of Genuine Tor Traces for Realistic Website Fingerprinting

Rob Jansen[1], Ryan Wails[2], and Aaron Johnson[1(✉)]

[1] U.S. Naval Research Laboratory, Washington, D.C., USA
`{robert.g.jansen7.civ,aaron.m.johnson213.civ}@us.navy.mil`
[2] Georgetown University, Washington, D.C., USA
`rsw66@georgetown.edu`

Abstract. Website fingerprinting (WF) enables an adversary to predict the website a user is visiting, despite the use of encryption or Tor. Previous work almost exclusively uses *synthetic* datasets to evaluate the success of WF attacks. We present GTT23, the first dataset of *genuine* Tor traces, intended especially for WF analysis. We obtain it through a measurement of the Tor network, and, with 1.4×10^7 traces, it is larger than any existing WF dataset by an order of magnitude. We survey 28 WF datasets published since 2008 and compare them to GTT23, discovering common deficiencies of synthetic datasets for drawing conclusions about WF effectiveness. We have made GTT23 available to other researchers.

Keywords: website fingerprinting · traffic analysis · anonymity network

1 Introduction

Website fingerprinting (WF) is a dangerous attack on web privacy because it enables an adversary that can observe a user's outgoing connections to predict the website the user is visiting [6,18,19,26,47], even if those connections are protected with encryption, virtual private networks (VPNs), or anonymizing networks such as Tor [15]. WF attacks are particularly serious against Tor because they can break Tor's anonymity [5,9–11,13,17,21,32–35,38–41,43,44,52,53,55]. In WF on Tor, an adversary guesses the user's destinations from a vantage point that observes the user. The state-of-the-art WF attacks use machine learning (ML), where a classifier is trained using labeled traffic traces to identify the destination. In WF research, labeled data is thus useful for evaluating attack accuracy, both for training and testing.

Through a survey of 28 WF datasets published since 2008 (see Sect. 4), we find that all but a *single* prior study consider an adversary that collects labeled traces using an automated browser that programmatically fetches a set of selected webpages through Tor [2]. Such *synthetic* datasets have been criticized

S. Ferlin-Reiter et al. (Eds.): PAM 2026, LNCS 16477, pp. 277–293, 2026.
https://doi.org/10.1007/978-3-032-18268-5_13

as unrepresentative of genuine Tor traffic along numerous axes [21,25,36,40], and their use has led WF research to fall victim to several common ML evaluation pitfalls such as the base rate fallacy [3,10,25].

In an effort to address the serious limitations of synthetic WF datasets, a recent study by Cherubin et al. [10] considers a WF strategy in which the adversary uses a Tor exit relay to collect *genuine* traces, which can be observed and labeled by a relay in the exit position. Genuine traces exhibit the real-world diversity in all factors that might influence classifier performance, and they enable researchers to more accurately evaluate the WF performance that we expect an adversary might realistically attain. Unfortunately, this prior study was done in a *fully online* setting in order to avoid persistently storing genuine data or trained WF classifiers. As a result, it is impossible to replicate their results, and it is difficult to build on the methodology. Indeed, many later works have continued to study WF using synthetically generated datasets [4,13,21,27,29,41].

In this paper we present GTT23, the first dataset of labeled *genuine Tor traces*. We describe a large-scale Tor relay measurement plan that we designed to prioritize safety and privacy, which we developed through consultation with our organization's Institutional Review Board and with the Tor Research Safety Board [50] (details on the safety measures appear in App. A of the full version of this paper [22]). We executed our reviewed measurement process to safely measure 13,900,621 circuits to 1,142,115 unique destination domains and 68 unique destination server ports during a 13-week measurement period. We analyze GTT23 and find that 96% of the measured circuits use ports 80, 8080, or 443 to first connect to a destination, that most of the measured circuits carry fewer than 25 cells (<10.5 KB), and that just a single circuit was measured for over 80% of the measured domains. Our analysis of GTT23 helps demonstrate the high degree of traffic diversity with which a WF adversary must contend when launching WF attacks in the real world.

We further evaluate GTT23 to compare its genuine characteristics to those of existing synthetic WF datasets. First, we survey 28 WF datasets published since 2008 and identify several common deficiencies of synthetic datasets. We find that synthetic datasets are composed of a single traffic type (web) using simplistic user models and static software tools while focusing on website *index pages* at uninformed base rates. Second, we conduct a detailed analysis of the statistical disparities between GTT23 and two recent synthetic datasets that are specifically designed for more complex *website* fingerprinting wherein a website contains multiple accessible webpages. We find that the circuit-length variation and website base rates are still not reflected well in the synthetic datasets despite the improved modeling.

We conclude that, because GTT23 contains genuine traces of websites accessed by real Tor users at natural base rates, it is more realistic than any existing synthetic dataset, and thus enables WF evaluations that more accurately estimate real-world WF performance. We also note that, while GTT23 was designed to facilitate WF research, it may be useful for other research on Tor traffic analysis, such as correlation attacks [31] or malware detection [16].

This dataset has been available to researchers upon request since 2024 [23]. This report contains details and analyses of the data to further the understanding and use of GTT23 and to promote the development of similar datasets. A full version of this paper is available with additional details [22].

2   Methodology

2.1   Background

Tor [15] uses onion routing to anonymize TCP connections on the Internet. The Tor network consists of a globally distributed set of *relays*. Each connection through Tor to an outside server is sent through a three-hop *circuit*. This design is intended to prevent an adversary observing any single relay, or one observing either the client or destination but not both, from being able to identify both the source and destination of a connection. In the Tor network today, there are currently over 8,500 relays and over 3 million daily users [49].

To use Tor, a client builds circuits, each passing through an *entry*, a *middle*, and an *exit* relay. A circuit supports multiplexing multiple *streams* of end-to-end TCP communication with internet services. When a new TCP connection to a service is requested by an application (e.g., Tor Browser), the Tor client will use fixed-size application-layer control messages called *cells* to instruct the exit relay to (1) resolve the service's domain name, and (2) make a TCP connection to the service. Each of a circuit's TCP byte-streams is subsequently forwarded bidirectionally through the circuit in data cells. Circuit traffic observed from a single network location can be represented as a time-ordered sequence of (direction, time) pairs (one for each cell sent through a circuit), called a *cell trace*.

A TCP stream may be assigned to any circuit with an exit relay that allows connection to the destination's IP address and port; if no such circuit exists, a new one is built after choosing an exit independently at random from among those with conforming exit policies and weighted by relay bandwidth to balance load. However, Tor Browser employs additional stream assignment rules. When loading a webpage URL, Tor Browser computes the URL's first-party domain name (FPDN) and instructs the Tor client to assign all streams created to load that URL (including those to third-party domains to load embedded objects) on a circuit uniquely associated with the FPDN and isolated from other streams.

Browsing to a page of a new website in Tor Browser will result in a unique FPDN and a new circuit that first resolves a DNS query for the FPDN and then loads the page, while subsequent subpages of that website will be loaded through the same circuit. Cherubin et al. [10] recognized that (1) the FPDN in the circuit's first DNS query can be used to *label* the website of a circuit's cell trace, and (2) an adversary running exit relays can observe *genuine* cell traces and their domain name labels, which can be used to train WF classifiers and produce more realistic estimates of WF performance. (Non-exit relays can observe cell traces but not domain names due to onion routing [48].) Unfortunately, their study considered an online setting to avoid persistently storing sensitive data or classifiers; thus a new measurement is needed to build on the methodology.

In website fingerprinting, an adversary uses the volume and timing of traffic to infer which website is being visited [25]. This attack is suited to breaking the privacy of traffic sent through VPNs or Tor because their traffic plaintext and destination are unobservable. In a WF attack, the adversary observes the client and its traffic. Typical WF attacks use machine-learning classifiers trained on traffic traces labeled with the destination website (e.g., [11,41,43]). The classifiers are applied to traffic traces from the target client to identify the destination website. In the Tor setting, unlike for VPN traffic, WF classifiers are typically only given when a cell appears and in which direction because of Tor's fixed-size cells, which can either be recorded directly by a malicious Tor relay or reconstructed from TCP packet payloads by a network observer.

2.2   Measurement Process

We designed a measurement process that employs one or more Tor exit relays to safely measure genuine Tor cell traces and FPDN labels. The traces and labels are collected into a *dataset* for subsequent analysis. Each participating relay runs a patched version of Tor that we modified to support our measurement as follows.

Circuit Selection. When a relay observes a new circuit, it rejects any non-exit type circuit (i.e., onion-service and internal circuits) from measurement. Additionally, the relay applies a probabilistic sampling procedure such that 80% of exit-type circuits are rejected during *high-volume* measurement intervals, and 98% of exit-type circuits are rejected during *low-volume* measurement intervals. Sampling helps us limit the total amount of data collected and provides plausible deniability: any individual circuit created through a participating relay is unlikely to exist in the dataset. Non-rejected circuits are selected for further measurement.

Circuit Measurement. A relay internally stores circuit metadata and cell traces during operation for the randomly selected exit-type circuits. To protect some of this metadata, we use the encoding function

$$H(x) = \text{base64encode}(\text{sha256}(x \| salt)) \tag{1}$$

where *salt* is chosen uniformly at random, fixed on all measurement relays for the duration of the measurement period, and then destroyed. The relay iteratively constructs a circuit metadata record for each selected circuit (applying $H(\cdot)$ to domain names) until either the circuit closes or N cells have been observed, whichever occurs first.[1] The metadata record is then exported via Tor's control interface to an external process that compresses it, encrypts it with a public-key encryption scheme,[2] and writes it to persistent storage.

---

[1] We use $N = 5,000$ cells to remain consistent with previous work.

[2] We encrypt to an offline secret key to prevent on-device decryption.

Each metadata record includes the following: (1) *day*: an integer number of days that have elapsed since the start of the measurement; (2) *domain*: $H(d)$ where d is the domain name of the circuit's first exit stream;[3] (3) *shortest_ private_ suffix*: $H(s)$ where s is the shortest private suffix of the pre-image of *domain* computed using Mozilla's public suffix list and `libpsl` [7]; (4) *port*: the server port used when connecting the circuit's first exit stream to its destination; and (5) *cells*: a list of at most N cell metadata items. Each cell metadata item is a 4-tuple containing the time the cell was observed relative to the circuit's creation time, an integer encoding the cell's direction, and two integers encoding the cell and relay command, respectively [14].

3   Measurement and Analysis

3.1   Measurement Details

We execute a large-scale Tor measurement study following our methodology from Sect. 2. First, we run a total of eight exit relays, four on each of two identical machines hosted by the Calyx Institute (a nonprofit research and education organization located in NY, USA). Each machine is equipped with 2 Intel Xeon E5-2695 v2 12-core CPUs (48 hyper-threads in total) and connected to an unmetered 1 Gbit/s symmetric network access link. Second, we run a measurement over a 13 week period in 2023; we assign weeks 1, 7, and 13 as high-volume intervals, and the remaining 10 weeks as low-volume intervals. We combined all recorded circuit metadata records into a single dataset which we call GTT23[4] [23].

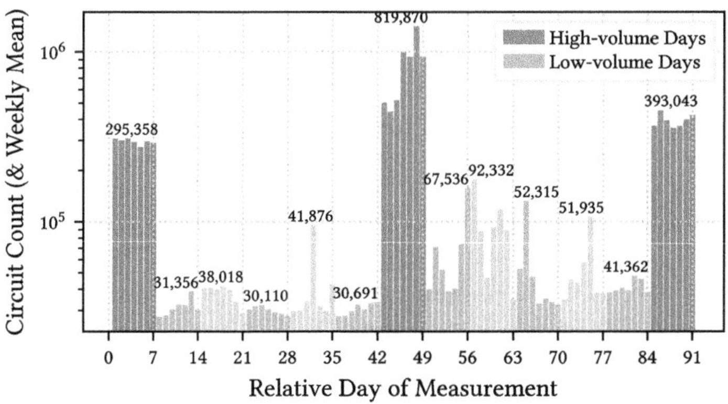

Fig. 1. The daily total (bars) and weekly mean (text) number of circuits during our 13 week measurement.

---

[3] Circuits for which the first exit stream connects to the destination with an IP address instead of a domain name are rejected from measurement.

[4] GTT: an acronym for "Genuine Tor Traces"; 2023: the year of measurement.

3.2 Data Analysis

In total, GTT23 contains 13,900,621 circuits, 10,557,898 of which were observed during the high-volume weeks (1, 7, and 13) and 3,342,723 of which were observed during the remaining 10 low-volume weeks.

The daily total and weekly mean number of GTT23 circuits are shown in Fig. 1; the daily mean during high-volume weeks is 502,757 and the daily mean during low-volume weeks is 47,753. We observe a slight increase in circuit counts during the latter half of the measurement period which we attribute to natural fluctuation in network usage and the load-balancing weights used for relay selection.

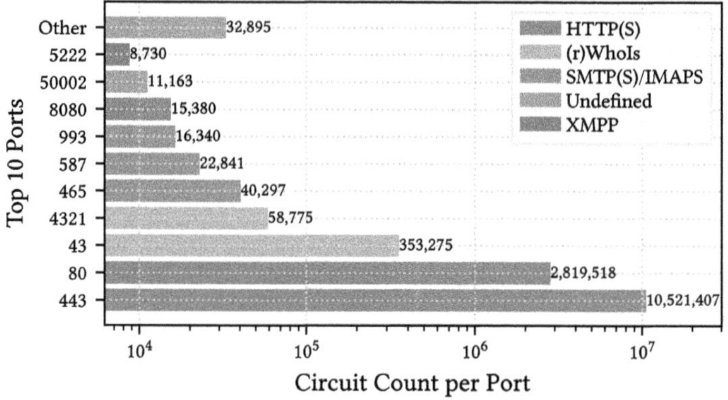

Fig. 2. The total number of GTT23 circuits by server port, with IANA-assigned service names [51].

GTT23 contains circuits measured across 68 unique destination server ports. The distribution of the number of measured circuits across the top-ten most-popular service ports is shown in Fig. 2 (with a logarithmic x-axis, and the IANA-assigned service names shown in the legend). We observe that 13,356,305 circuits (96%) use ports 80, 8080, or 443 to connect their first stream to a destination service; these ports are assigned to HTTP and HTTPS by the IANA [51]. The vast majority of the remaining circuits use port 43 or 4321, which are respectively assigned to WhoIs and Remote WhoIs services by the IANA. Frequent connections to these ports have been observed in prior studies of Tor exit traffic [45,46]: Sonntag observed that they corresponded to a large number of reverse DNS lookups scanning several large networks [45].

The cumulative distribution of the number of observed cells per GTT23 circuit is shown in Fig. 3. We were surprised to find that most circuits are extremely short: the median number of cells over all circuits is just 25, which would support at most 10.5 KB of application payload after accounting for control cells and cell-header overhead. For comparison, we also plot in Fig. 3 the circuit length distribution for the subsets of circuits containing at least 25, 100, and 1,000 cells, respectively corresponding to 10.5, 47.8, and 496 KB of application payload. For reference, the HTTP Archive reports that over 90% of webpages have a transfer size greater than 450 KB across samples of 12 and 16 million desktop and mobile URLs, respectively. Thus, we believe that most GTT23 circuits did not carry full webpage transfers.

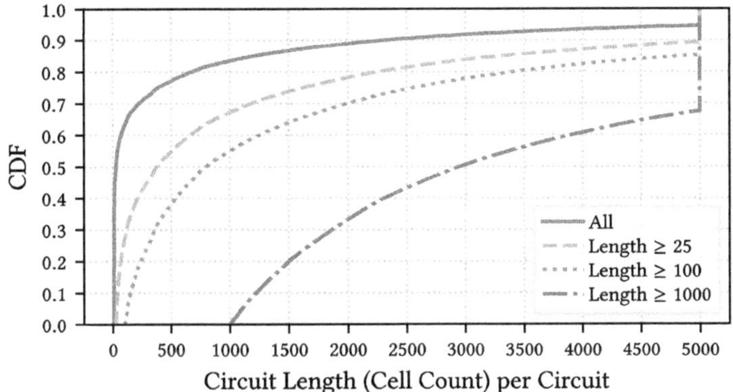

Fig. 3. Cumulative distribution of the number of cells per circuit over subsets of GTT23 circuits.

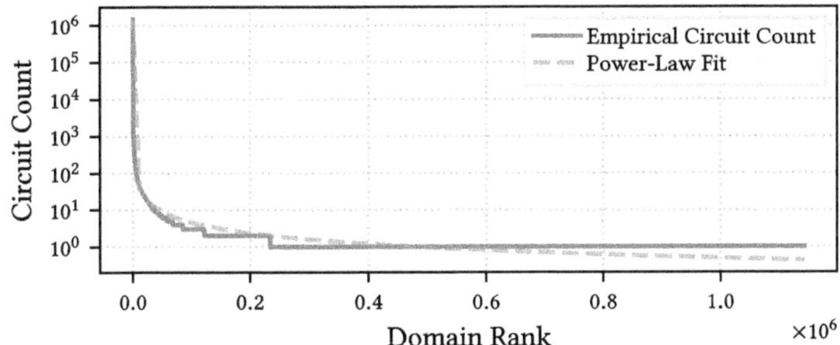

Fig. 4. The number of GTT23 circuits per domain; we observe a close fit to a power-law distribution.

GTT23 contains circuits measured across 1,142,115 unique destination domains. The distribution of the number of measured circuits per domain is plotted in Fig. 4. We observe a close fit to a power-law distribution (shape = 0.023, loc = 0.769, scale = 1,495,234), where few popular domains dominate the measurement while a long tail exists with just a single circuit measured for 908,422 (80%) of the domains.

Note that obtaining realistic base rates for the domains visited by Tor users is a major advantage of GTT23 over synthetic datasets. In open-world binary classification, the negative class is composed of traces to all sites other than the monitored ones. Thus, the false-positive rate, which is crucial for estimating precision [52], depends on the base rates in the negative class. Similarly, in a multiclass setting (open or closed world), overall WF accuracy depends on the base rates of each class.

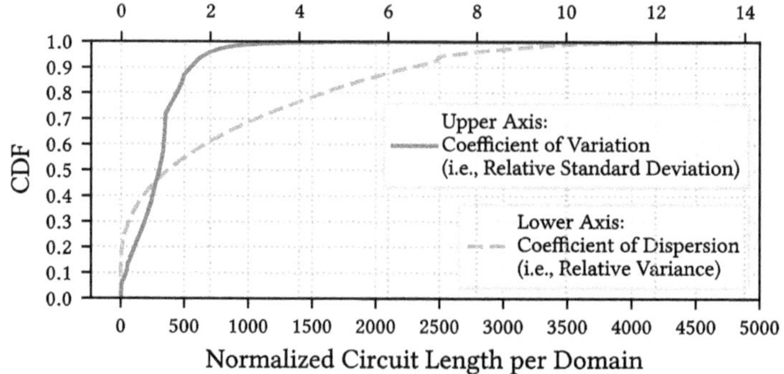

Fig. 5. Cumulative distribution of circuit length variation across domains with at least two GTT23 circuits.

Figure 5 shows the cumulative distribution of two measures of circuit length variability for each domain with more than one GTT23 circuit. The median Coefficient of Variation (i.e., the standard deviation divided by the mean) shows that more than half of the domains have a circuit length standard deviation greater than the mean, while the Coefficient of Dispersion (i.e., the variance divided by the mean) shows that most domains have a relative variance in circuit lengths of multiple hundreds of cells. The high variability in circuit lengths is consistent with our prior observation that most of the measurement circuits are short, and suggests that many Tor circuits may completely or prematurely fail.

4   Evaluation

In this section, we compare GTT23 and synthetic datasets to understand how well the synthetic datasets model some of the genuine data characteristics that are important for WF.

4.1   Deficiencies of Synthetic Datasets

We survey 28 datasets proposed for WF tasks covering the years 2008–2025. In Table 1 we provide an overview of the properties of a subset of the surveyed datasets selected for their size, complexity, and frequency with which they are used to evaluate later attacks. See Table 2 in Appendix A for the full comparison.

Like GTT23, these datasets also consist of Tor traffic traces labeled with a destination domain, and they record traffic that actually transited the Tor network and connected to some third-party server. However, we find that every dataset exhibited similar deficiencies: (1) they consist of only web traffic; (2) they are collected using simplistic user models and static software tools, almost exclusively at the client position; (3) they primarily focus on fetching popular webpages; and (4) they do not contain informed base rates. In contrast, real Tor clients use a wide variety of software and software versions, interact with non-web services, and do more than just non-interactively fetch selected webpages. These deficiencies make it difficult to use existing datasets to draw meaningful conclusions about the effectiveness of a WF attack directed at real Tor users [10, 25].

In comparison, GTT23 is the only dataset with traces sampled from genuine traffic created by real Tor users interacting with real internet services at natural base rates. GTT23 is not limited to only web traffic: it contains traces of different types of internet activity and supports the evaluation of WF attacks and defenses based on websites' first-party domain names (see Sect. 2.1). These traces better represent the WF problem, where an adversary observes undifferentiated traffic from real users and cannot assume that the traffic is just to index web pages or is even to a website at all. Thus, GTT23 can serve to more accurately evaluate the threat posed by a real-world WF adversary. Moreover, GTT23 is larger than the previous largest dataset (the AWF dataset [40]) by an order of magnitude which is important to assess modern deep learning attacks requiring many training examples. Extended results and analysis from our dataset survey appear in App. A.

Table 1. Select WF Datasets (full details in Table 2)

Dataset	Year	Size	Description[†]
k-NN [53]	2014	1.4×10^4	Web, top index pages
AWF CW_{900} [40]	2017	2.3×10^6	Web, top index pages
AWF Open [40]	2017	8×10^5	Web, top index pages
DF [43]	2018	1.4×10^5	Web, top index pages
GoodEnough [37]	2020	2×10^4	Web, top index pages + subpages
BigEnough [29]	2021	3.8×10^4	Web, top index pages + subpages
Multi-tab [13]	2022	5.7×10^5	Web, top index pages, multiple tabs
GTT23	2023	1.4×10^7	Genuine traffic, real user behavior, visited services, natural base rates

† All but GTT23 synthetically fetch webpages using automated tools.

4.2   Genuine and Synthetic Disparities

We analyze the statistical disparities between GTT23 and synthetic datasets to understand dataset quality. We place particular emphasis on the trace features found in prior work [17] to be informative for WF. We focus our analysis on two popular synthetic datasets, BigEnough [29] and GoodEnough [37], that were specifically designed to model web*site* fingerprinting; both datasets contain at

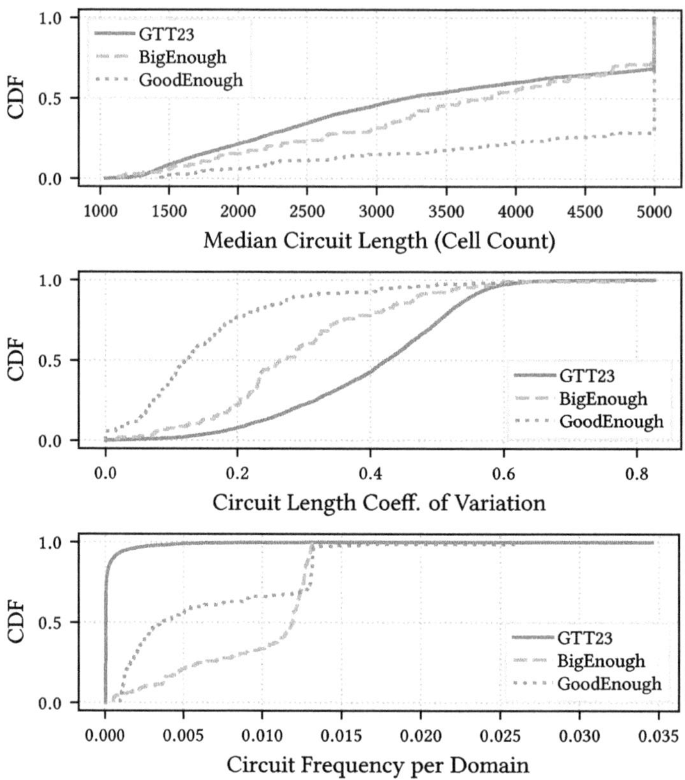

Fig. 6. Per-domain statistics computed from the GTT23, BigEnough [29], and Good-Enough [37] datasets. For statistical rigor, here we consider traces with at least 1,000 cells and, among those, domains with at least 30 traces.

least ten pages per website, and so they represent among the highest website diversity of the datasets surveyed.

Dataset Composition. The GTT23 dataset contains traces generated from real users interacting with any services accessible via the internet (including non-web services), whereas synthetic datasets such as BigEnough and GoodEnough contain traces generated from automated visits to small number of popular websites. Empirical data from this work and previous work suggests that Tor users do not just visit popular websites. First, Fig. 2 shows that a long tail ($\approx$4%) of GTT23 traces are generated from interactions with hosts not running on known web ports such as 80, 443, or 8080. Second, a privacy-preserving measurement of the Tor network performed in 2018 [28] determined that over 20% of web streams exiting the Tor network access a host not in the Alexa Top 1 Million list. This long tail of activity is not reflected in the synthetic datasets and is likely to make the WF classification task more difficult [34].

Data Modeling. Even simple features computed from the synthetic datasets do not accurately model genuine Tor traces. Consider, for example, overall trace length, a feature shown in prior work to be informative in the WF task [17]. The top plot in Fig. 6 shows, for all 3 datasets, the distribution of each domain's median circuit length (cell count) for circuit traces with at least 1,000 cells and among those, domains with at least 30 traces. The plot shows that GTT23 traces tend to be shorter than synthetic dataset traces. GoodEnough traces, in partic-ular, tend to be much longer than genuine traces: roughly 70% of GoodEnough domains have a median circuit length of 5,000 cells (the capture limit), whereas this is true of only 32% of domains in the GTT23 dataset. Inaccurate data modeling makes it difficult to draw meaningful conclusions from the synthetic datasets [3].

Intra-class Variance. Genuine user traces contain a much richer set of activity than is generated by synthetic, automated crawls to webpages. Gen-uine traces may be generated from various unpredictable user-initiated behaviors and processes and may reflect complex, interactive sessions with internet hosts, whereas synthetic traces are usually generated by a single, fixed crawling appli-cation such as tor-browser-selenium [2] and are limited to simple page accesses. The middle plot in Fig. 6 shows the distribution of the coefficient of variation of trace length—that is, the ratio of the trace length's standard deviation to the mean—for each dataset's domains. At nearly every percentile, the coefficient is higher for GTT23 domains than it is for BigEnough and GoodEnough domains, suggesting that GTT23 traces exhibit higher variation. The higher variance for each domain suggests that WF is more difficult on genuine than synthetic traces.

Base Rates. Recall that the frequency of website occurrence in the GTT23 dataset is characterized by a few heavy hitters and a long tail of rarely accessed sites (see Fig. 4). In contrast, the bottom plot of Fig. 6 shows that most domains in the synthetic datasets occur with much higher frequency. For example, the median domain occurs with frequency 5×10^{-4} in GTT23. In comparison, the median domain in the BigEnough and GoodEnough dataset occur with frequen-cies that are orders-of-magnitude greater, 1×10^{-2} and 4×10^{-3}. Base rate real-ism is an important aspect of evaluating WF attacks because increasingly low false positive rates are needed to maintain precision at low base rates of occur-rence [8,25,52]. Precisely fingerprinting most websites in GTT23 requires orders-of-magnitude lower false positives rates compared to BigEnough and GoodE-nough.

5   Conclusion

The GTT23 dataset represents the first available collection of genuine Tor cell traces for research in traffic analysis. It has been available to researchers upon request since 2004 since [23], and it has already been used to improve our under-standing of WF on Tor. Jansen et al. [24], develop the Retracer methodology for performing WF analysis on Tor trace datasets that, like GTT23 are collected at the exit relay. Retracer modifies the traffic traces to appear more as they would to an adversary observing the client. The results indicate that a WF adversary is likely to obtain much lower accuracy than synthetic datasets have indicated. Jansen [20] further develops this methodology. Similarly, Deng et al. [12] use GTT23 to perform a WF analysis where the adversary is detecting connections to a monitored set of sites. Their results indicate that the Var-CNN classifier obtains higher accuracy than the DF classifier used by Jansen et al.

GTT23 also motivates future work to handle the realities of genuine traces. The appearance of many circuits with few cells requires a WF adversary to consider how much trace data is sufficient to make a confident claim about the destination. The existence of non-trivial amounts of non-Web traffic may motivate new methods to identify the subset of traffic that is to a website at all before applying WF. Accurate base rates may require a WF adversary to choose between training for high accuracy averaged over distinct labels or over traces.

Acknowledgments. This work was supported by the Office of Naval Research (ONR).

Appendix

A   Survey of Existing WF Datasets

We surveyed prior work related to website fingerprinting attacks in order to better understand the datasets used to quantify attack effectiveness. We evaluated each dataset among a number of different dimensions, as follows.

Year: the time the dataset was collected;
Activity: the kind of user behavior contained in the dataset;
User model: the way in which users perform the activity;
Trace generation software: the tools used in activity creation;
Size: the number of classes and traces in the dataset;
Availability: the accessibility of the dataset to others;
Attacks: the WF attacks originally evaluated on the dataset.

We also noted how each dataset was recorded (that is, the software used and trace observation point, if provided).

The summary of results is shown in Table 2. All datasets surveyed were composed of primarily web activity. Most datasets assume users interact with popular websites, usually those present in the now-discontinued "Alexa Internet" top websites ranking. A few works consider more sophisticated user behaviors: Herrmann et al. [18] collect URLs obtained from monitoring an academic proxy server they had access to; Juárez et al. [25] collect URLs obtained from volunteers browsing the Internet; Panchenko et al. [34] considered URLs obtained from observing Tor HTTP exit traffic, as well as from interacting with popular Internet services such as Twitter and Google; and Deng et al. [13] collected URLs from volunteers browsing the Internet.

The task designated for each dataset may vary. For example, RND-WWW [34], Juárez et al. [25], GDLF-25 [32], GoodEnough [37], BigEnough [29],

Table 2. Summary of website fingerprinting datasets curated over the past 15 years. The '$\perp$' symbol is used to indicate a dataset is unnamed, and the '-' symbol is used when a cell's contents are identical to the above cell. When the year of data collection is not mentioned, we assume it is around ("ca.") the associated article's publication date. Not all datasets describe their trace generation software with the same specificity. N, N_C, N_I, N_{Bg} are the total number of traces in the dataset, the number of positive classes, the number of instances per positive class, and the number of background traces. The "Attacks" column shows a list of WF attack papers evaluated on the dataset.

Ref.	Name	Year	Activity	Activity Detailed	User Model	Trace Gen. Software	N	N_C	N_I	N_{Bg}	Available	Attacks
[18]	$\perp$ (Hermann)	2008	Web	Links from real-world academic proxy server	Index page	Autofox	8.5×10^3	775	≈ 10		Dead link ⧉	[18]
[9]	$\perp$ (Cai)	Ca. 2012	Web	Alexa top sites	Index page	tor 0.2.1/2	3.2×10^4	800	≈ 40		No	[9]
[54]	levdata2	Ca. 2013	Web	Alexa top sites	Index page	tor 0.2.4.7; TBB 2.4.7	4×10^3	100	40		Online ⧉	[34,54]
-	levdata3	-	-	Popular blocked sites, Alexa top sites	-	-	9×10^2	4	10	8.6×10^2	-	-
[53]	k-NN	Ca. 2014	Web	Sensitive sites, Alexa top sites	Index page	TBB 3.5.1; iMacros 8.6.0	1.4×10^4	100	90	5×10^3	Online ⧉	[1,33,34,44,53–55]
[25]	$\perp$ (Juárez)	Ca. 2014	Web	Alexa top sites, volunteer browsing	Index page, visited pages	TBB (2/3.X); Selenium	4.3×10^4	200	≈ 40	3.5×10^4	On request	[25]
[55]	$\perp$ (Wang)	2014	Web	Sensitive sites, Alexa top sites	Index page	tor 0.3.6.4; TBB 3.6.4	9×10^3	100	40	5×10^3	No	[55]
[34]	RND-WWW	Ca. 2016	Web	Twitter, Alexa one-click, Google Trends, Google Random, censored sites	Random subpage	TBB 3.6.1; Chickenfoot; iMacros; Scriptish	2.1×10^5	1125	40	2.1×10^5	Dead link ⧉	[34]
-	TOR-Exit	-	-	HTTP requests of real Tor users	Visited page	-	2.1×10^5			2.1×10^5	-	-
-	WEBSITES	-	-	Popular websites	Index page, random subpage	-	5.3×10^3	50	105		-	-
[17]	DS_{Tor}	Ca. 2016	Web	Alexa top sites, popular .onion sites	Index page	TBB; Selenium	1.1×10^5	85	≈ 90	1×10^5	Dead link ⧉	[17,33]
[40]	AWF CW_{900}	2017	Web	Alexa top sites	Index page	tor 0.2.8.11; TBB 6.5; Selenium	2.3×10^6	900	2500		Online ⧉	[5,32,33,40,44]
-	AWF Recollect	-	-	-	-	-	1×10^5	200	500		-	-
-	AWF Open	-	-	-	-	-	8×10^5	200	2000	4×10^5	-	-
[43]	DF	Ca. 2018	Web	Alexa top sites	Index page	tor-browser-selenium	1.4×10^5	95	1000	4.1×10^4	Online ⧉	[32,39,43,44]
[33]	WTT-time	2018	Web	Alexa top sites	Index page	tor 0.4.0.8; tor-browser-crawler	8×10^4	100	300	5×10^4	On request	[33]
[37]	Good Enough	2020	Web	Alexa top pages, random subpage	Index page	TBB 9.0.2	2×10^4	500	20	1×10^4	Online ⧉	-
[52]	$\perp$ (Wang)	2019	Web	Alexa top sites	Index page	tor 0.4.0.1; TBB 8.5a7	1×10^5	100	200	8×10^4	Partially Online ⧉	[52]
-	Wikipedia	-	-	Wikipedia browsing	Random subpage	-	2×10^4	100	100	1×10^4	-	-
[32]	GDLF-25	Ca. 2021	Web	Alexa top sites	Random subpage	tor-browser-crawler	9.4×10^4	2400	39		On request	[32]
-	GDLF-OW	-	-	Links from Rimmer et al. [40]	Random subpage	-	7×10^4			7×10^4	-	-
[29]	BigEnough	2021	Web	Open PageRank top pages	Index page	TBB	3.8×10^4	950	20	1.9×10^4	On request	
[13]	Multi-tab	2022	Web	Alexa top pages	Index page (multi-tab)	TBB; Selenium	5.7×10^5				Online ⧉	[13]
[21]	D(tbs, tor)	2022	Web	Wikipedia browsing	Random subpage	tor-browser-selenium	2×10^4	98	200		Online ⧉	
[4]	Drift	Ca. 2023	Web	Popular websites, links from Rimmer et al. [40]	Index page	TBB 11.0.10; tor-browser-selenium 0.6.3	1.5×10^4	90	≈ 110	5×10^3	Online ⧉	[4]
	GTT23	2023	Any	Real Tor usage	Visited service	Real client software	1.4×10^7	$\langle 1.1 \times 10^6$ domains $\rangle$			On request	
[30]	ALEXA-WSC-FG/BG	Ca. 2024	Web	Alexa top sites, random subpage	Random subpage	TBB 7.5.6	8.6×10^5	9000	90	4.5×10^4	No	[30]
[56]	CW/OW	Ca. 2024	Web	Alexa top sites, random subpage	Random subpage (multi-tab)	TBB	8.1×10^4	1000	10	9.3×10^3	Online ⧉	[56]
[42]	D1–D7	2024	Web	Tranco top sites	Index page	TBB 10.5; Chrome 112.0	7.4×10^5	100	700	4.00×10^3	Online ⧉	[42]

ALEXA-WSC-FG/BG [30], and CW/OW [56] are designed to incorporate multiple pages for each of many websites. AWF Recollect [40] and WTT-Time [33] are designed to explore aspects of concept drift. DS_{Tor} contains .onion sites in addition to ordinary websites. Multi-tab [13,56] contain browsing behavior occurring simultaneously in several browser tabs.

All extant datasets are collected synthetically with an automated crawl, often using a single set of software to generate flows (Juárez et al. [25] and Deng et al. [13] both consider the effect that varying versions of Tor Browser Bundle (TBB) may have on attacks). Additionally, nearly every work uses `tcpdump` to collect packet traces on the *client* generation machine. Only Good-Enough, BigEnough, and $D(\text{tbs},\text{tor})$ [21] collect cell traces using the `tor` process directly; GoodEnough and BigEnough are collected at the client position, whereas $D(\text{tbs},\text{tor})$ is collected at the guard position.

Inconsistent purposes, over-simplified user models, and static collection software make it difficult to draw meaningful conclusions about the effectiveness of a WF attack directed at real Tor users. Real Tor clients use a wide variety of software (most network applications supporting SOCKS5 can be used with Tor), interact with non-web services, and do more than just non-interactively fetch random pages on the web. In contrast, *GTT23 is the only dataset addressing these weaknesses*—it contains traces from real Tor client interacting with real internet services. Moreover, GTT23 is larger than the previous largest dataset by an order of magnitude (AWF CW_{900} [40]) and is larger than most other existing datasets by multiples orders of magnitude; this volume of data is important when training modern deep learning models which may require millions of examples to be effective.

References

1. Abe, K., Goto, S.: Fingerprinting attack on Tor anonymity using deep learning. APAN, 42 (2016)
2. Acar, G., Juarez, M., individual contributors. tor-browser-selenium - Tor browser automation with Selenium. https://github.com/webfp/tor-browser-selenium (2023)
3. Arp, D., et al.: Dos and don'ts of machine learning in computer security. In: Butler, K.R.B., Thomas, K. (eds.) USENIX Security 2022, pp. 3971–3988. USENIX Association, August 2022
4. Bahramali, A., Bozorgi, A., Houmansadr, A.: Realistic website fingerprinting by augmenting network traces. In: ACM CCS 2023. ACM Press (2023). https://doi.org/10.1145/3576915.3616639
5. Bhat, S., Lu, D., Kwon, A., Devadas, S.: Var-CNN: A data-efficient website fingerprinting attack based on deep learning. PoPETs 2019(4) (2019). https://doi.org/10.2478/popets-2019-0070
6. Bissias, G.D., Liberatore, M., Jensen, D.D., Levine, B.N.: Privacy vulnerabilities in encrypted HTTP streams. In: PET 2005, vol. 3856, May 2005. https://doi.org/10.1007/11767831_1
7. C library for the public suffix list. https://github.com/rockdaboot/libpsl (2023). https://publicsuffix.org

8. Cai, X., Nithyanand, R., Wang, T., Johnson, R., Goldberg, I.: A systematic approach to developing and evaluating website fingerprinting defenses. In: Ahn, G.-J., Yung, M., Li, N. (eds). ACM CCS 2014, pp. 227–238. ACM Press (2014). https://doi.org/10.1145/2660267.2660362

9. Cai, X., Zhang, X.C., Joshi, B., Johnson, R.: Touching from a distance: website fingerprinting attacks and defenses. In: ACM CCS 2012 (2012). https://doi.org/10.1145/2382196.2382260

10. Cherubin, G., Jansen, R., Troncoso, C.: Online website fingerprinting: Evaluating website fingerprinting attacks on Tor in the real world. In: USENIX Security 2022, August 2022

11. Deng, X., Zhao, R., Wang, Y., Zhan, M., Xue, Z., Wang, Y.: Countmamba: a generalized website fingerprinting attack via coarse-grained representation and fine-grained prediction. In: 2025 IEEE Symposium on Security and Privacy, pp. 1419–1437 (2025a)

12. Deng, X., et al.: Beyond a single perspective: towards a realistic evaluation of website fingerprinting attacks. Tsinghua Science and Technology (2025b)

13. Deng, X., et al.: Robust multi-tab website fingerprinting attacks in the wild. In: 2023 IEEE Symposium on Security and Privacy, pp. 1005–1022. IEEE Computer Society Press (2023). https://doi.org/10.1109/SP46215.2023.10179464

14. Dingledine, R., Mathewson, N.: The Tor protocol specification (2003). https://gitlab.torproject.org/tpo/core/torspec/-/blob/main/tor-spec.txt.   Accessed: September 30, 2023

15. Dingledine, R., Mathewson, N., Syverson, P.F.: Tor: the second-generation onion router. In: USENIX Security 2004, August 2004

16. Dodia, P., AlSabah, M., Alrawi, O., Wang, T.: Exposing the rat in the tunnel: Using traffic analysis for tor-based malware detection. In: Yin, H., Stavrou, A., Cremers, C., Shi, E. (eds.) ACM CCS 2022, pp. 875–889. ACM Press (2022)

17. Hayes, J., Danezis, G.: k-fingerprinting: a robust scalable website fingerprinting technique. In: USENIX Security 2016, August 2016

18. Herrmann, D., Wendolsky, R., Federrath, H.: Website fingerprinting: attacking popular privacy enhancing technologies with the multinomial naïve-bayes classifier. In: The Workshop on Cloud Computing Security (2009)

19. Hintz, A.: Fingerprinting websites using traffic analysis. In: PET 2002, vol. 2482, April 2002. https://doi.org/10.1007/3-540-36467-6_13

20. Jansen, R.: Cellshift: Rtt-aware trace transduction for real-world website fingerprinting. In: NDSS 2026 (2026). https://doi.org/10.14722/ndss.2026.231004

21. Jansen, J., Wails, R.: Data-explainable website fingerprinting with network simulation. PoPETs, 2023(4), July 2023. https://doi.org/10.56553/popets-2023-0125

22. Jansen, R., Wails, R., Johnson, A.: A measurement of genuine tor traces for realistic website fingerprinting (2024). arXiv: 2404.07892 [cs.CR]

23. Jansen, R., Wails, R., Johnson, A.: Gtt23: a 2023 dataset of genuine tor traces, February 2024b. https://doi.org/10.5281/zenodo.10620520

24. Jansen, R., Wails, R., Johnson, A.: Repositioning real-world website fingerprinting on tor. In: WPES 2023, pp. 124–140 (2023)

25. Juárez, M., Afroz, S., Acar, G., Díaz, C., Greenstadt, R.: A critical evaluation of website fingerprinting attacks. In: ACM CCS 2014, pp. 263–274 (2014). https://doi.org/10.1145/2660267.2660368

26. Liberatore, M., Levine, B.N.: Inferring the source of encrypted HTTP connections. In: ACM CCS 2006 (2006). https://doi.org/10.1145/1180405.1180437

27. Limam, N., et al.: A first look at generating website fingerprinting attacks via neural architecture search. In: WPES 2023 (2023)

28. Mani, A., Wilson-Brown, T, Jansen, R., Johnson, A., Sherr, M.: Understanding Tor usage with privacy-preserving measurement. In: ACM IMC 2018 (2018)
29. Mathews, N., et al.: SoK: a critical evaluation of efficient website fingerprinting defenses. In: 2023 IEEE Symposium on Security and Privacy, pp. 969–986. IEEE Computer Society Press (2023). https://doi.org/10.1109/SP46215.2023.10179289
30. Mitseva, A., Panchenko, A.: Stop, don't click here anymore: boosting website fingerprinting by considering sets of subpages. In: USENIX Security 2024, pp. 4139–4156 (2024)
31. Nasr, M., Bahramali, A., Houmansadr, A.: DeepCorr: strong flow correlation attacks on tor using deep learning. In: Lie, D., Mannan, M., Backes, M., Wang, X. (eds.) ACM CCS 2018, pp. 1962–1976. ACM Press (2018)
32. Oh, S.E., Mathews, N., Rahman, M.S., Wright, M., Hopper, N.: GANDaLF: GAN for data-limited fingerprinting. PoPETs, 2021(2) (2021). https://doi.org/10.2478/popets-2021-0029
33. Oh, S.E., Sunkam, S., Hopper, N.: p-FP: extraction, classification, and prediction of website fingerprints with deep learning. PoPETs 2019(3) (2019). https://doi.org/10.2478/popets-2019-0043
34. Panchenko, A., et al.: Website fingerprinting at internet scale. In: NDSS 2016 (2016)
35. Panchenko, A., Niessen, L., Zinnen, A., Engel, T.: Website fingerprinting in onion routing based anonymization networks. In: WPES 2011 (2011)
36. Perry, M.: A critique of website traffic fingerprinting attacks (2013). https://blog.torproject.org/blog/critique-website-traffic-fingerprinting-attacks
37. Pulls, T.: Towards effective and efficient padding machines for tor (2020). arXiv:2011.13471 [cs.CR]
38. Tobias Pulls and Rasmus Dahlberg. Website fingerprinting with website oracles. PoPETs, 2020(1) (2020). https://doi.org/10.2478/popets-2020-0013
39. Rahman, M.S., Sirinam, P., Mathews, N., Gangadhara, K.G., Wright, M.: Tik-Tok: the utility of packet timing in website fingerprinting attacks. PoPETs, 2020(3) (2020). https://doi.org/10.2478/popets-2020-0043
40. Rimmer, V., Preuveneers, D., Juárez, M., van Goethem, T., Joosen, W.: Automated website fingerprinting through deep learning. In: NDSS 2018 (2018)
41. Shen, M., Ji, K., Gao, Z., Li, Q., Zhu, L., Xu, K.: Subverting website fingerprinting defenses with robust traffic representation. In: USENIX Security 2023, pp. 607–624. USENIX Association (2023)
42. Shen, M., Wu, J., Ai, J., Li, Q., Ren, C., Xu, K., Zhu, L.: Swallow: A transfer-robust website fingerprinting attack via consistent feature learning. In: ACM CCS 2025. ACM Press (2025)
43. Sirinam, P., Imani, M., Juárez, M., Wright, M.: Deep fingerprinting: undermining website fingerprinting defenses with deep learning. In: ACM CCS 2018 (2018). https://doi.org/10.1145/3243734.3243768
44. Sirinam, P., Mathews, N., Rahman, M.S., Wright, M.: Triplet fingerprinting: More practical and portable website fingerprinting with N-shot learning. In: ACM CCS 2019 (2019). https://doi.org/10.1145/3319535.3354217
45. Sonntag, M.: Malicious DNS traffic in Tor: analysis and countermeasures. In: ICISSP, pp. 536–543 (2019)
46. Sonntag, M., Mayrhofer, R.: Traffic statistics of a high-bandwidth Tor exit node. In: ICISSP, pp. 270–277 (2017)
47. Sun, Q., Simon, D.R., Wang, Y.-M., Russell, W., Padmanabhan, V.N., Qiu, L.: Statistical identification of encrypted web browsing traffic. In: 2002 IEEE Symposium on Security and Privacy (2002). https://doi.org/10.1109/SECPRI.2002.1004359

48. Syverson, P.F., Goldschlag, D.M., Reed, M.G.: Anonymous connections and onion routing. In: 1997 IEEE Symposium on Security and Privacy (1997). https://doi.org/10.1109/SECPRI.1997.601314
49. The Tor Metrics Portal (2023). https://metrics.torproject.org
50. The Tor research safety board (2023). https://research.torproject.org/safetyboard
51. Touch, J., et al.: Service name and transport protocol port number registry (2023). https://www.iana.org/assignments/service-names-port-numbers/service-names-port-numbers.txt
52. Wang, T.: High precision open-world website fingerprinting. In: 2020 IEEE Symposium on Security and Privacy (2020). https://doi.org/10.1109/SP40000.2020.00015
53. Wang, T., Cai, X., Nithyanand, R., Johnson, R., Goldberg, I.: Effective attacks and provable defenses for website fingerprinting. In: USENIX Security 2014 (2014)
54. Wang, T., Goldberg, I.: Improved website fingerprinting on Tor. In: WPES 2013, pp. 201–212 (2013). https://doi.org/10.1145/2517840.2517851
55. Wang, T., Goldberg, I.: On realistically attacking tor with website fingerprinting. PoPETs 2016(4) (2016). https://doi.org/10.1515/popets-2016-0027
56. Zhao, X., Deng, X., Li, Q., Liu, Y., Liu, Z., Sun, K., Ke, X.: Towards fine-grained webpage fingerprinting at scale. In: ACM CCS 2024, pp. 423–436 (2024)

Through a Smaller Lens: Revisiting Opportunistic Analysis Using Network Telescopes

Bernhard Degen[1(✉)], Nils Kempen[2], K. C. Claffy[3], Ricky K. P. Mok[3], Ralph Holz[1,2], Roland van Rijswijk-Deij[1], Raffaele Sommese[1], and Mattijs Jonker[1]

[1] University of Twente, Enschede, The Netherlands
b.j.degen@utwente.nl
[2] University of Münster, Münster, Germany
[3] CAIDA/UC San Diego, La Jolla, CA, USA

Abstract. Unsolicited network traffic observed to the addresses monitored by a network telescope enables, among other things, tracking of Internet outages, botnets and DDoS attacks. We examine how a decrease in available address space affects what we can learn about the phenomena we study with telescopes. We conduct a targeted replication of a seminal study conducted 10 years ago. Since then, IPv4 scarcity and rising operational costs have placed increased pressure on operators to maximize use of their allocated space, which has resulted in a reduction of address space available to major telescopes. As a first step, we characterize traffic to three network telescopes that differ in size, spatial distribution, and prominence. We find that most address blocks within each telescope observe a similar number of source IP addresses, and that smaller telescopes offer higher visibility per monitored address. We also find that sources target the IPv4 address space pervasively, with 37.0% of them targeting a /16 block in each of the three telescopes within an hour. As a case study, we examine the sensitivity of randomly-spoofed DoS attack inference to the size of the address space under observation and find that larger telescopes detect many attacks missed by smaller ones, although smaller telescopes observe disproportionately many relative to their address space size. Our study provides a framework to quantify the effects of reduced telescope address space and outlines future directions for telescope research.

1 Introduction

Network telescopes (also called *darknets*) are routed but unused address ranges. The unsolicited traffic they receive, referred to as Internet background radiation (IBR), has proved instrumental in identifying scans that probe for vulnerabilities [1,2,13,14,25,36], inferring Internet-wide randomly-spoofed denialof-service (RSDoS) attack activity [21,24], and detecting Internet outages [3,11]. Operators can also use them to infer scanning activity targeting their networks [6,16].

S. Ferlin-Reiter et al. (Eds.): PAM 2026, LNCS 16477, pp. 294–318, 2026.
https://doi.org/10.1007/978-3-032-18268-5_14

In contrast to honeypots, which are designed to respond to probes, network telescopes are intentionally silent. As they consist of unused addresses, they attract activity from misconfigured hosts, backscatter resulting from RSDoS attacks, and scans that indiscriminately target a sufficiently large part of the IPv4 address space.

In recent years, we have seen a confluence of issues that threaten to affect the use of telescopes as a tool to study Internet phenomena. First, a growing body of work shows that scanners target different parts of the Internet differently [20,29].

Second, the scarcity of IPv4 address blocks [27] has put pressure on operators to maximize use of their allocated space. In the last 10 years, operators of two major network telescopes (UCSD-NT and MERIT-NT) have seen significant reductions of their address space. Such reductions may limit the effectiveness in observing Internet phenomena such as outages and security threats.

Third, over the past two decades, the volume of traffic captured by large telescopes has grown considerably [15], placing increasing demands on IBR archival and analysis infrastructure. These challenges hinder researchers' ability to extract meaningful insights from IBR, providing additional motivation to investigate how telescope size and placement affect visibility of Internet-wide activity.

These challenges make it imperative to understand 1) how representative IBR observed in a network telescope is of IBR destined to the entire address space, and 2) how a telescope's capacity to capture global events depends on the size of its address space.

This paper revisits Benson et al. [4], a seminal work published in 2015 on analyzing IBR, to assess the validity of the findings in today's traffic dynamics and telescope deployments. Specifically, we address the following research questions: How many sources are observed over time (§6.1)? How frequently do sources contact telescopes (§6.2)? How large are the observed autonomous systems (ASes), based on their advertised address space (§6.3)? How does the visibility of telescopes depend on their sizes (§6.4)? To what extent do sources target[1] specific parts of a telescope's address space (§6.5)? To what extent are sources observed across telescopes (§6.6) and how does IP/port concentration differ (§6.7)? In addition, we perform a case study where we examine the sensitivity of RSDoS inference to the size of the address space (§6.8). We use data from the same two large, but downsized network telescopes (UCSD-NT and MERIT-NT) and from one additional, smaller telescope in a topologically and geographically different location (SURF-NT), and re-examine the question of how telescope size and position influence visibility. Our findings are largely consistent with those of the original study. While we observe higher data volumes and packet rates, network telescopes continue to provide a valuable lens for Internet-wide analysis. Our contributions are as follows:

---

[1] We use "target" to indicate that traffic is directed toward the telescope and do not imply any intent by the source.

1. We provide an empirical comparison of three network telescopes varying in size, distribution, and prominence, identifying differences in the volume and patterns of sources targeting them.
2. We find that many sources target the IPv4 address space indiscriminately: 37.0% of source IP addresses targeted a /16 block across three network telescopes within one hour.
3. We conduct a case study on the inference of RSDoS attacks and find that while larger address blocks captured more targets, a smaller telescope identified a disproportionally high share of them.
4. We discuss challenges faced by telescope operators and the efficacy of alternative deployment strategies in overcoming these.

2   Background

2.1   Network Telescopes

Network telescopes are collections of routed but unused address space that passively collect traffic. Since they do not host any services, they capture Internet background radiation (IBR): persistent, unsolicited traffic. This includes errant packets from misconfigured hosts, backscatter from RSDoS attacks, and scanning activity. This traffic provides academia and industry with a valuable resource for collecting cyber threat intelligence (CTI). Telescopes can be *centralized*, with all monitored addresses in a single block, or *distributed*, spanning multiple non-contiguous blocks, possibly in diverse topological or geographical regions. These deployment choices influence the type and volume of traffic they attract [20,29].

With increased global scanning and attack activity, the volume of IBR has surged. At the same time, IPv4 scarcity limits the address space available for telescopes. Despite reductions in telescope address space, between 2002 and 2022 IBR captured by UCSD-NT has increased by three orders of magnitude [15], significantly raising the challenges of storing, processing, and analyzing telescope data.

Apart from IPv4, telescopes can also be deployed on unused IPv6 address space. However, exhaustively scanning the entire IPv6 address space is infeasible. Therefore, these telescopes attract a different class of scanners; those that use public data sources to select prefixes to scan [33].

2.2   RSDoS Inference

Network telescopes offer a valuable tool for inferring ongoing randomly-spoofed denial-of-service (RSDoS) attacks. In an RSDoS attack, an attacker sends traffic with randomly spoofed source addresses to its target, aiming to overwhelm it. Spoofing the source addresses can enable the attacker to circumvent traffic filters or thwart intervention. This type of attack is visible to telescopes via *backscatter*: reply packets from the target to a spoofed address. The UCSD-NT covers approximately 0.254% of the IPv4 address space, and assuming source addresses are spoofed uniformly at random, there is an equal likelihood of 0.254% that a reply packet will be directed to an address within the telescope's range. The probability of observing at least one backscatter packet is

$$1 - \left(1 - \frac{n}{2^{32}}\right)^m$$

where n is the number of addresses monitored by the telescope and m the number of packets sent by the attacker. For example, a modest attack of 1,000 packets per second (pps) lasting one minute would be observed in a /16 telescope with a probability of approximately 60% and in UCSD-NT's entire /9 and /10 address blocks with nearly 100% probability.

By grouping reply packets by target IP address and recording when the first packet was observed, it is possible to estimate the duration and intensity of an attack [24]. Applying thresholds on the number of packets, rate, and duration can remove noise and small attacks with negligible impact.

3   Related Work

We group prior research along three dimensions: visibility across telescopes, scanner strategies, and efforts to collect IBR using fewer addresses. We build on these studies by revisiting a 10-year-old study under current conditions.

3.1   Visibility Across Network Telescopes

Early works [2, 25, 36] characterized IBR in several /8 prefixes, noting differences in the ports targeted and the locality of the traffic. Several studies have shown that the geographical location of observation influences the IBR it received [17, 32]. Like these studies, we evaluate visibility from multiple vantage points. In light of ongoing address space contraction, we further analyze intra-telescope visibility to assess the effectiveness of smaller telescopes.

3.2   Scanning Strategies

The characteristics of IBR can vary across different parts of the address space. Although the introduction of Internet-wide scanning tools has lowered the barrier to probing the entire IPv4 address space, scanners may still selectively target certain portions of it. One study [14] found that between January 1, 2013 and May 1, 2014, 68% of scans targeted at least 10% of the IPv4 address space, and another [29] analyzed server firewall logs from a content distribution network (CDN) in November 2014 and found that 30% of the scans were localized. Izhikevich et al. [20] studied how scanners discriminate between MERIT-NT, two educational networks, and honeypots hosted in five cloud environments during July 1–7, 2021, and found that networks with legitimate services attract more scanners. While these studies focused on scanner strategies and their biases toward certain network types, our study centers on how targeting behavior varies across different network telescopes.

3.3   Reducing Address Space Footprint

Traditional large-scale network telescopes passively monitor vast swaths of unused address space. Several alternative approaches have been proposed to reduce the address space footprint while maintaining or improving visibility. One approach is to employ partially unused network resources, such as *greynet* addresses [16] or ports [29]. A related approach is to deploy sensors in cloud networks [5,20,26]. While these may draw scanners that do not appear in telescopes, the traffic a virtual machine (VM) receives can be influenced by the prior usage of its address. It is also possible to monitor IBR without owning the address space targeted, using Internet exchange points (IXPs) as vantage points [35]. However, this method's visibility is limited to traffic traversing the IXP and may inadvertently capture production traffic.

Similar to our work, several studies have explored the effect of downsizing existing telescopes. Chindipha et al. [9] used error metrics to compare /27–/30 samples to their covering /24 telescope in February 2018 and March 2019, demonstrating the viability of smaller sensors. Camargo et al. [6] analyzed /19 telescopes in Brazil (December 2023) and Japan (October 2018), showing that halving each still captured 80% of source addresses. It is unclear whether these studies filtered spoofed packets, which can heavily skew results (§5.2).

3.4   Leveraging Internet Background Radiation for Opportunistic Network Analysis

Benson et al. [4] compared the utility of IBR for opportunistic network analysis in two network telescopes, UCSD-NT and MERIT-NT. They analyzed UCSD-NT for two one-month periods—one in 2012 and the other in 2013—and MERIT-NT for the coinciding one-month period in 2013. Their work quantified sources, analyzed IBR components, and characterized temporal IBR patterns. They found an overlap of 84% in observed source /24 blocks in both telescopes, but noted substantial variation across UCSD-NT /16 blocks. Ten years later, the UCSD-NT and MERIT-NT have shrunk by 34% and 96%, respectively. We revisit the utility of these network telescopes for Internet-wide analysis using updated data as part of a targeted replication of their work, and we include one additional, smaller network telescope (§4). Motivated by the persistent threat of distributed denialof-service (DDoS) attacks and the use of telescopes to study them [18,31], we benchmark RSDoS inference as a case study.

4   Datasets

We utilize three network telescopes and two additional datasets.

UCSD-NT A major network telescope composed of a /9 and an adjacent /10 subnet, interspersed with assigned subnets. 13.2% of the addresses belong to these assigned subnets and are therefore excluded from our dataset, leaving 10.9 M monitored addresses.

Table 1. Starting times (UTC) and packet counts of random one-hour samples.

| Sample | | Packet count | | |
Date	Time	UCSD-NT	MERIT-NT	SURF-NT
2025-04-05	03:00	3,545,835,110	209,260,789	25,210,194
2025-04-06	11:00	3,409,739,023	200,977,859	29,848,213
2025-04-07	16:00	3,314,010,076	179,474,838	21,243,581
2025-04-08	22:00	4,434,768,231	176,348,784	19,603,466
2025-04-09	05:00	4,030,952,660	187,660,477	22,591,846
2025-04-10	14:00	3,457,389,678	202,179,146	26,560,589
2025-04-11	02:00	3,356,122,335	211,108,787	28,547,691

MERIT-NT A network telescope composed of various /14–/23 subnets, some of which are contiguous, totaling 476 k addresses.

SURF-NT A network telescope composed of one /16 and three /24 non-contiguous subnets, totaling 66.3 k addresses.

BGP RIB We use a Border Gateway Protocol (BGP) routing information base (RIB) to resolve the AS originating an IP address and to count advertised prefixes by their size. Specifically, we use the RIB from collector routeviews2.routeviews.org [30] captured on April 5, 2025 at 00:00 UTC, corresponding to the start of our observation period.

RIR allocation statistics We use allocation statistics published by each regional Internet registry (RIR) on April 5, 2025 [34] to count allocations by prefix size.

The telescope datasets span seven days, starting on April 5 at midnight UTC. The total gzip-compressed size of the pcaps is 20.4 TB, 2.25 TB, and 121 GB for UCSD-NT, MERIT-NT, and SURF-NT, respectively. While our observation period is shorter and the telescopes are smaller than in the original study [4], we process 4–5.1× and 1.5× more data for UCSD-NT and MERIT-NT, respectively. Due to gaps in the availability of UCSD-NT pcap files within the observation period and constraints on processing and storage resources, we use seven random (but consistent throughout the study) 60-minute samples, one from each day. This sampling strategy was designed to maximize the amount of data we could process within our budget and available cluster resources. Inevitably, this choice sacrifices some visibility into longer-term trends, underscoring the trade-offs that researchers must make when analyzing large-scale network telescope data. For experiments where capturing the complete timespan is required (§6.1–6.3), we use flow data containing the necessary information for the full seven-day period[2].

---

[2] UCSD-NT captures were unavailable during 2025-04-11 18:00–23:59. Where this gap affects our analysis, we note it explicitly.

Table 1 lists the times and packet counts for each random sample. The packet count per destination address is largely stable across both samples and telescopes. To capture the average pattern over time, we report the *mean* across time samples. To reflect the typical case while minimizing the influence of outliers (e.g., due to filtered telescope addresses), we report the *median* across address blocks. Although our results show consistent trends across samples, supporting the representativeness of our sampling method, we cannot rule out the possibility of anomalies or transient behaviors within the observation period.

5   Methodology

In this section we outline our methodology. We first explain how we preprocess packet captures (§5.1). Then, we explain how we correct for spoofed traffic targeting the network telescope itself, as such traffic can heavily skew the results of any analysis performed on captured traffic (§5.2).

5.1   Preprocessing Packet Traces

Each of the three telescopes provides raw packet traces in pcap format. MERIT-NT data is also available in the form of aggregated *events* [22], such as periods of scanning and backscatter. UCSD-NT data is additionally distributed as flows in the *FlowTuple* [7] format. Our study does not require payloads, as payload-based traffic classification is non-trivial and lies beyond its scope.

To obtain one unified data representation for all telescopes, we used Corsaro 3 [10] to convert raw traces to FlowTuples while preserving the destination IP address. For UCSD-NT analyses spanning the entire observation period, we used the provided FlowTuples with flows aggregated by destination /16 subnet to overcome storage and processing constraints. This granularity matches the requirements of our analyses.

5.2   Filtering Spoofed Source Addresses

For our analysis, we are not interested in traffic that is spoofed directly toward a network telescope. Unlike RSDoS attack traffic—which is spoofed toward a target, with the target's replies potentially reaching a telescope—this spoofed traffic is directed to a telescope itself. In this section, we describe how we mitigated the impact of such spoofed traffic on our results.

While it may be impossible to accurately detect spoofed traffic without conducting active measurements, previous work [10,12] empirically derived a set of heuristics to identify spoofed packets passively. These heuristics were based on commonalities in spoofed traffic captured in 2012. We tested them but found them unsuitable for our purposes for several reasons. First, some heuristics filtered out valuable IBR components because they exclude packets sent to UDP port 80, which presently is one of the ports assigned to HTTP over QUIC [19]. Second, we observed that the heuristics did not reliably identify spoofed packets during short-lived spoofing events. Although they flagged some sources above the baseline as spoofed, noticeable spikes in source addresses remained after filtering, indicating that the heuristics did not account for the full deviations. Given these limitations, we decided not to apply these heuristics.

Instead, we devised a statistics-based method to remove surges of spoofed traffic from our datasets, focusing only on short-lived, high-rate events that disproportionately skew our results. By targeting only these bursts, we minimize the risk of excluding legitimate data throughout the observation period. To identify such events, we manually inspected the time series of unique source addresses and empirically derived a threshold of twice the mean number of sources. We computed the mean number of unique source addresses per 5-minute interval, the FlowTuple aggregation interval, and identified two high-rate spoofing events in UCSD-NT, along with several smaller ones. These events peaked at $79.0\times$ and $18.0\times$ the mean number of sources observed in each (excluding the events themselves). Both events occurred outside the one-hour samples listed in Table 1 and thus could only affect analyses based on data from the entire observation period (§6.1–6.3). For each event, we derived a signature based on the 5-minute time intervals in which it occurred, along with the targeted telescope addresses, ports, and protocols. After excluding these two high-rate spoofing events, only modest spikes (less than twice the mean number of sources) remained. While any residual spoofed traffic may slightly affect our results, removing these smaller deviations could come at the cost of removing legitimate IBR. We also inspected MERIT-NT and SURF-NT time series, but these datasets did not contain any intervals where the source address count exceeded the threshold; hence, we did not exclude any events. A possible explanation is that these telescopes are much smaller and therefore less likely to attract spoofed traffic than UCSD-NT.

More generally, there is an inherent risk that some persistent, low-rate spoofing remains undetected. Such residual spoofed traffic could lead to an overestimation of visibility in terms of sources observed, although this effect is limited relative to the excluded high-rate events.

6 Results

We first study how analyzing network telescopes over different time intervals impacts visibility, i.e., how many IBR sources it observes (§6.1). This helps us understand the trade-off between expending computational resources on longer analyses against the utility of the outcomes. Next, we analyze how frequently sources contact the three telescopes in our study (§6.2), which informs the predictability of IBR. We then analyze the source ASes observed by each telescope (§6.3) to estimate the coverage of the routed address space. We also investigate how visibility varies with the size (§6.4) and position (§6.5) of telescope address blocks, providing insight into the marginal gain in visibility and the similarity between blocks. Following that, we assess the locality of IBR to the blocks under observation (§6.6). This provides insight into how distributed traffic sources are over the IPv4 address space. After that, we analyze how probing

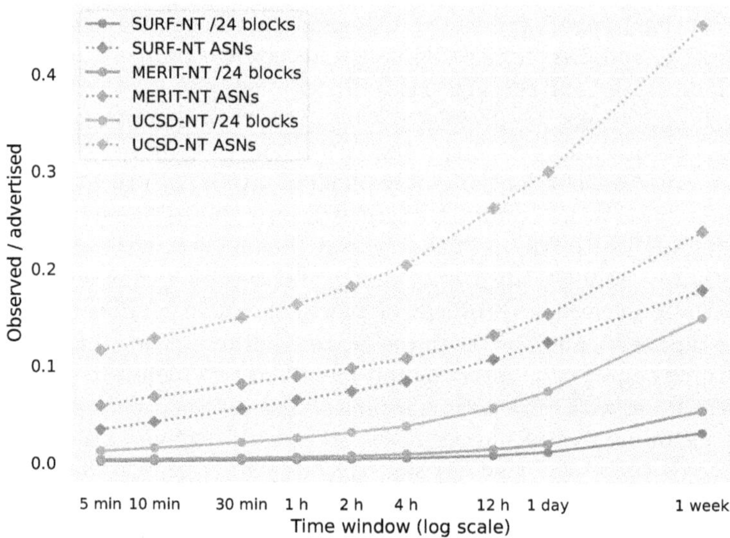

Fig. 1. Median autonomous system numbers (ASNs) and /24 blocks observed across time windows during the observation period. The observation counts increase for longer windows. The fractions are relative to the total number of advertised ASNs and /24 blocks. The faster-than-logarithmic growth suggests that longer observation periods capture more source diversity.

patterns differ by telescope (§6.7) to better understand what draws traffic to specific regions of the address space. Finally, we conclude this section with a case study on RSDoS inference across blocks of varying sizes (§6.8), demonstrating the practical utility of different telescope configurations.

6.1   Effect of Observation Duration

To quantify the sources each network telescope attracts over time at different levels of granularity, we used two metrics: the number of observed source /24 blocks and ASNs. For each telescope, we calculated the median of these values across varying time windows. As shown in Fig. 1, extending the observation period resulted in an increase in both /24 blocks and ASNs. Consistent with the study by Benson et al. [4], the number of sources observed grew sublinearly as we lengthened the time windows, due to sources repeatedly contacting a telescopes. As they also observed, however, the curves continued to rise near the longest window of one week, suggesting that even longer observation periods would yield additional sources. This trend was consistent across telescopes. Observations during one-week windows were between 3.51× (MERIT-NT) and 4.23× (SURF-NT) those of five-minute windows for ASNs, and between 9.91× (UCSD-NT) and 15.5× (SURF-NT) for /24 blocks. To illustrate, achieving a coverage of at least 10% of routed ASNs would necessitate observing traffic for at least 5 min in UCSD-NT,

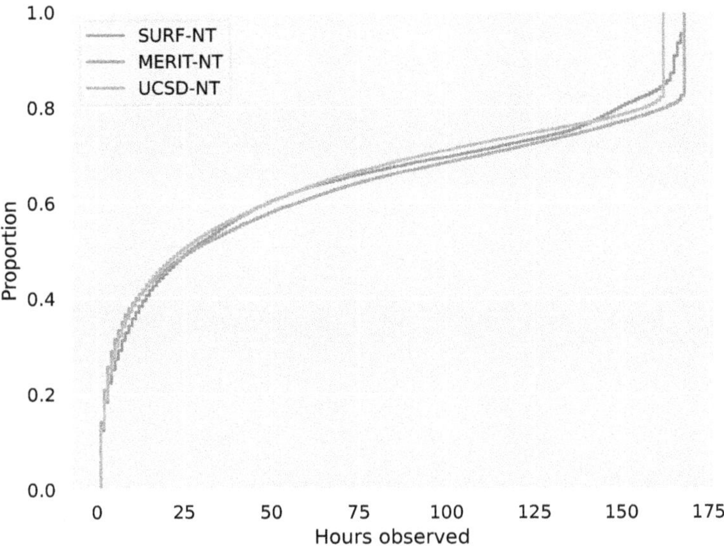

Fig. 2. ECDF of one-hour bins that ASNs were observed in. Approximately 18% of ASes contacted a telescopes every hour or more frequently, supporting longitudinal studies.

2 h in `MERIT-NT`, and 12 h in `SURF-NT`. This shows that telescopes with smaller address spaces can achieve high source visibility over time.

6.2   Contact Frequency of IBR Sources

The incessant nature of IBR has enabled longitudinal studies, such as network outage detection [3,11]. The accuracy of such inferences depends on the stability and frequency with which remote systems send traffic to network telescopes. To measure this, we counted the number of hours sources were observed and calculated the median time between these observations.

The FlowTuples used in this section contain packet counts per five-minute flow. To approximate packet timing within each flow, we assumed a uniform distribution of packet arrival times. The steps at multiples and simple fractions of 300 s in Fig. 3 arise from this assumption.

Autonomous System Stability. Repeated ASes observations enable longitudinal studies. Figure 2 shows the eCDF of the number of one-hour bins in which ASNs were observed over the one-week observation period. `UCSD-NT` was missing data for six hours; this gap is reflected in the lower maximum value. The tail of the distributions indicates that approximately 18% of ASes sent traffic at least hourly, making these ASes suitable for analyses that require regular observations. In contrast, /24 blocks are less reliable for longitudinal analysis,

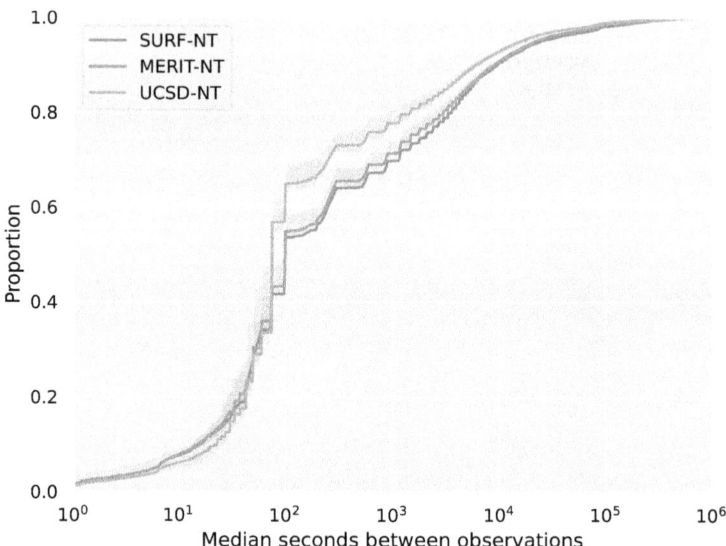

Fig. 3. ECDF of the median IAT per source /24 block in each /16 telescope block. The lines represent the median value across blocks, and the shaded regions indicate the minimum and maximum IATs. /24 blocks sent traffic to UCSD-NT at a higher rate than to SURF-NT and MERIT-NT. Nearly a third of /24 sources sent traffic with median IATs of one minute, supporting analysis that requires short intervals.

since we found only 2% of these active every hour. These findings align with the original study [4] and indicate that only a few sources exhibit sufficient stability to support longitudinal analysis requiring hourly observations. Alternatively, aggregation can be performed on longer time bins to trade precision for broader coverage.

Packet Rate. Inferences may additionally benefit from short intervals between observations. Figure 3 shows the eCDF of the median inter-arrival times (IATs) of source /24 blocks. To account for the size difference of the three telescopes in our study, we calculated the IATs of packets destined to each /16 block fully covered by the respective telescope throughout the observation period (83 blocks for UCSD-NT, 7 for MERIT-NT, and 1 for SURF-NT). Between 27.6% and 30.2% of /24 blocks and 35.7% and 37.5% of ASes sent traffic with a median IAT of one minute or less. Although the original study [4] analyzed the entire UCSD-NT, which was 256× larger than the /16 s we used, we consistently observed higher per-source packet rates.

In our datasets, UCSD-NT/16 blocks received traffic at higher rates than the /16 s of the other two telescopes did. To analyze this difference, we examined the packet size distributions, since smaller packets can be transmitted at higher rates. While UCSD-NT observed approximately 10% more of the smallest packets (smaller than 44 bytes) relative to the other telescopes, we found that it received

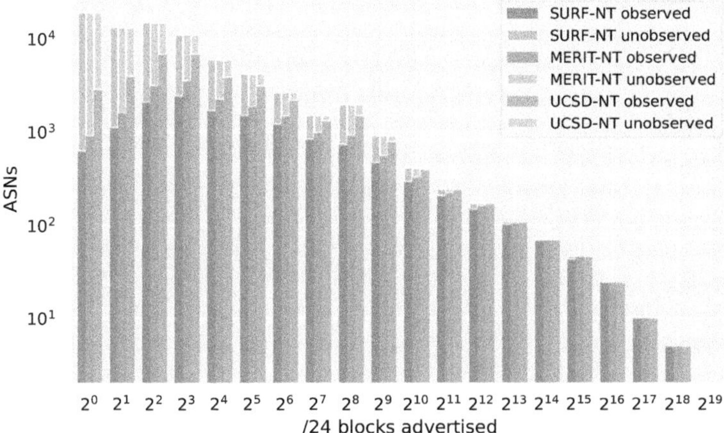

Fig. 4. ASes observed transmitting to network telescopes over the full observation period, grouped by number of originated IP address blocks, expressed in /24 equivalents. The solid and faded bars together indicate the number of ASes in that size class in the global routing table. `UCSD-NT` saw the most ASNs and `SURF-NT` the least. ASes originating many IP addresses were more likely to send traffic to the telescopes.

approximately 15% *fewer* medium-sized packets (44 to 60 bytes), which may underlie the difference in IATs. At the AS granularity, telescopes exhibited more consistency with 80% of the ASes having a median IAT of at most 50, 45, and 45 min across `SURF-NT`, `MERIT-NT`, and `UCSD-NT` blocks, respectively.

In conclusion, only a small fraction of sources consistently sent traffic to a telescope every hour, whereas most sources exhibited median IATs on the order of minutes. This pattern suggests that IBR sources typically generate traffic in bursts, and that longitudinal inferences should be drawn with caution, especially at /24 or finer source granularity.

6.3 Autonomous System Visibility

To better understand how much of the routed address space is observable in each network telescope, we calculated the number of source ASNs, grouped by the size of their originated address space. Figure 4 shows the number of ASNs sending traffic to the three telescopes during one week. The size of the originated address space is expressed in powers of two of /24 blocks, rounded down. For example, an AS originating two /15 s and another AS originating a /14 and a non-overlapping /15 are both counted as originating 2^{10} /24 blocks.

Differences among telescopes were most evident for ASes that originate relatively few addresses. During the one-week observation period, `UCSD-NT` captured traffic from at least half of the ASes originating address space equivalent to a /21 prefix or larger. `MERIT-NT` and `SURF-NT` observed many fewer small ASes; each captured at least half of the ASes originating address space equivalent to a

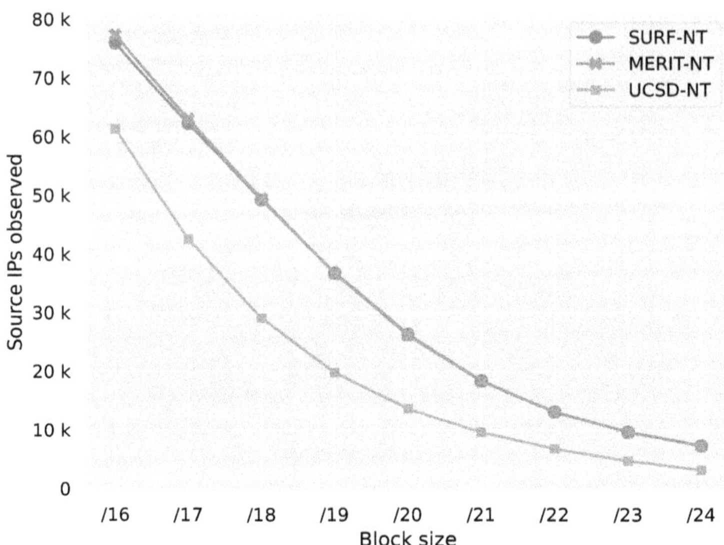

Fig. 5. Median IP addresses observed per hour across all /16–/24 network telescope blocks. The observation counts decrease for larger blocks. The rate of decrease slows with increasing x (halvings of the address space), indicating diminishing returns.

/15 or larger. All network telescopes received traffic from the largest ASes, those originating address space equivalent to a /8 or larger.

Consistent with the original study [4], we found a relatively low visibility of ASes announcing an equivalent of a /16 (2^8 /24 blocks). This effect may stem from a concentration of legacy address space in this size class, which tends to exhibit lower active use. To investigate this further, we analyzed RIR allocation statistics and found that across all RIRs, there were 3.13× more /16 than /17 allocations, and 5.71× more /16 than /15 allocations. This may account for the increase of ASes in the /16 size class that we observed. Moreover, the RIR statistics reported a higher proportion of legacy address space among /16 allocations. Legacy allocations predate the existence of the RIRs and are often address blocks allocated to academic institutions and other early adopters of the Internet. This means that these allocations are likely generous in comparison to more recent allocations and as such see less dense utilization [28], providing an explanation for the relatively low visibility in the /16 size class.

6.4   Effect of Telescope Size

Existing network telescopes vary greatly in size [6]. Larger telescopes potentially capture a broader set of network activity, enabling more comprehensive insights. To estimate the effect of size, we counted the source IP addresses observed in each telescope for all telescope block sizes from /16 to /24, using daily one-hour samples. For consistency, we only included /16 telescope blocks fully covered by the respective telescope. Given that the number of data points varies across block sizes and telescopes, we present only the median value for each block size in our analysis.

Figure 5 shows the results of this experiment. While the address space of each telescope is halved at each step, the number of sources did not decline as quickly. As also observed by Benson et al. in 2015 [4], we found that the number of sources scales as a power-law with the size of the address space.

To normalize for block size, we report the ratio of source addresses observed to destination addresses within the block. For MERIT-NT and SURF-NT, a destination address in a /24 block observed a median of 28.5 and 28.6 source addresses per hour, respectively, whereas an address in a /16 block saw only a median of 1.2 source addresses per hour for both telescopes. UCSD-NT destination addresses observed fewer sources than the other two telescopes: addresses in /24 and /16 blocks saw a median of 12.5 and 0.9 source addresses per hour, respectively. These findings indicate that increasing the monitored address space leads to diminishing marginal returns.

Additionally, we found that UCSD-NT observed fewer sources than the other two telescopes across all block sizes. The median number of source addresses observed per destination address was at least 19.9% lower compared to the same block sizes of the other two telescopes, suggesting that some IBR sources do not target the UCSD-NT address space.

6.5 Effect of Position in Address Space

To isolate the effect of position in the global IPv4 address space on observed sources, we divided the first MERIT-NT /16 block and the sole SURF-NT /16 block address space into smaller /24 blocks, counted the sources addresses observed in each /24 block, and calculated the mean over the seven daily one-hour samples. We repeated this procedure for UCSD-NT by dividing its covering /8 into /16 blocks. Several blocks were in assigned and therefore excluded from our dataset, resulting in fewer observed packets. Figure 6 shows the three resulting Hilbert curves. The number of source addresses was rather consistent across blocks, with only a few exceptions.

Figures 6a and 6b show /24 blocks within the first /16 s of MERIT-NT and SURF-NT. It shows that, for both telescopes, the −.−.255/24 block observed fewer source addresses than the other /24 blocks. In addition to /24 blocks shown in the figure, we examined all /24 blocks with a third octet of 255 within MERIT-NT and SURF-NT, and found that these blocks received 1.70–3.06% fewer sources relative to the median number of sources in /24 blocks in MERIT-NT across samples, and between 4.74% fewer and 0.45% more in SURF-NT. In contrast, this trend did not hold for UCSD-NT, whose −.−.255/24 blocks saw a slight increase in source counts, between 0.46% and 1.75% across samples.

A few other blocks stood out. In MERIT-NT, the −.−.102/24 block within the first /16 block received 5.32–13.3% more sources than the median across all /24 blocks in that /16, although other /24 hotspots appeared in different /16 s. In UCSD-NT, the −.44/16 block observed 32.8–92.2% more sources than the

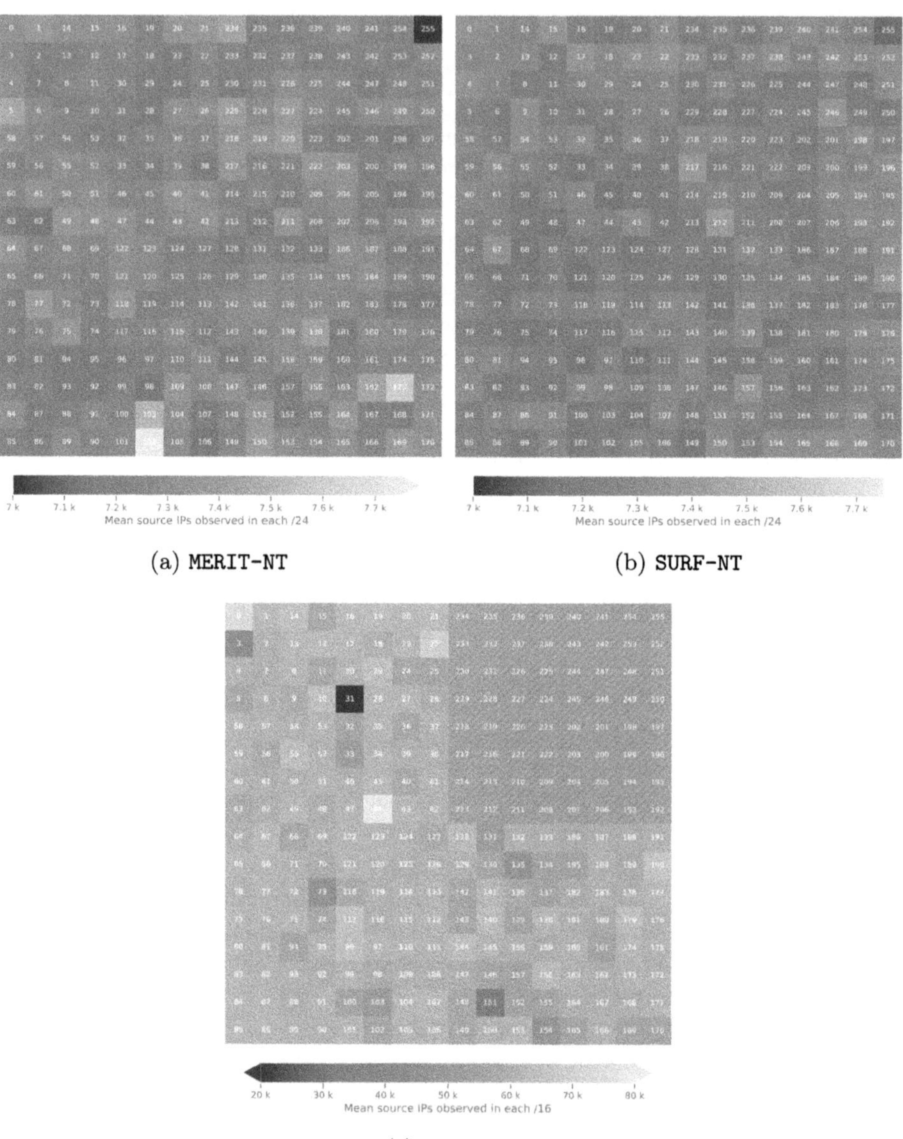

Fig. 6. Number of source IP addresses observed per destination IP address block. Each cell represents a /24 block for MERIT-NT and SURF-NT, and a /16 block for UCSD-NT, labeled with the third and second octet of the block, respectively. Gray blocks indicate that no packets were observed (i.e., the subnet is assigned and therefore excluded), while the hatched region indicates the /10 prefix no longer part of UCSD-NT. An arrow at either end of a color bar indicates that values extend beyond the scale. Most blocks in each plot observed similar numbers of unique source addresses.

median across samples, whereas the $-.31/16$ block saw a substantial decrease, with 91.4–93.2% fewer sources than the median. The decreased sources observed in $-.31/16$ can be attributed to 99.2% of the address block being assigned and excluded from our dataset throughout the observation period. We no longer observed elevated source counts caused by BitTorrent and Conficker in the first /9 of UCSD-NT described in the original study [4].

IP Address Structure. IBR sources may target addresses ending in .0 or .255 differently, as they may assume these addresses to be reserved network and broadcast addresses [23]. This is an important consideration when deploying telescopes on small address ranges. We counted the unique source addresses observed per last octet across all fully covered /24 telescope blocks.

We found that telescope addresses ending in .255 were generally targeted less than addresses with another final octet. In MERIT-NT, such addresses received between 0.18% more and 5.45% fewer sources than the median across samples. In SURF-NT, they were 4.30–7.71% less likely to be targeted, while in UCSD-NT they were 4.17–10.87% less likely. Earlier work [20] reported a similar pattern in MERIT-NT, although with large variations by port.

Addresses ending in .0 showed a less consistent pattern. In MERIT-NT and SURF-NT, such addresses observed 3.53–4.22% and 1.76–3.37% fewer sources addresses than the median across samples, respectively. In UCSD-NT, the trend was opposite with addresses with a last octet of 0 being targeted by 14.8–59.9% *more* sources. The previously identified anomalous $-.44/16$ block was the largest contributor to this effect. Even after excluding this block, UCSD-NT destination addresses ending in .0 remained 2.94–30.1% more likely to be targeted.

This discrepancy may stem from the mixed usage of the UCSD-NT space. The three UCSD-NT/16 blocks contributing most source addresses all contained assigned subnets in the 12 months prior to the observation period, suggesting potential local scanning activity or a memory effect.

6.6   Traffic Locality

As established in Sect. 6.1, telescope blocks of the same size generally observed similar numbers of source addresses. We investigated the extent to which IBR is specific to each telescope. The authors of the original study [4] compared traffic to MERIT-NT and UCSD-NT addresses with overlapping second, third, and fourth octets. However, because the three telescopes in our study do not share a common second octet (nor first octet), we randomly selected /16 blocks with different second octets[3] for the comparison to avoid inflated overlap caused by IBR bias toward specific octets. We ensured that the UCSD-NT/16 block was not assigned and thus completely covered by the telescope. Figure 7 shows the overlap in source addresses for the first one-hour sample of the three telescopes. Across the samples we tested, the proportion of addresses observed in all three telescopes ranged from 35.1% to 39.4%.

---

[3] 83, 65, and 95 for UCSD-NT, MERIT-NT, and SURF-NT, respectively.

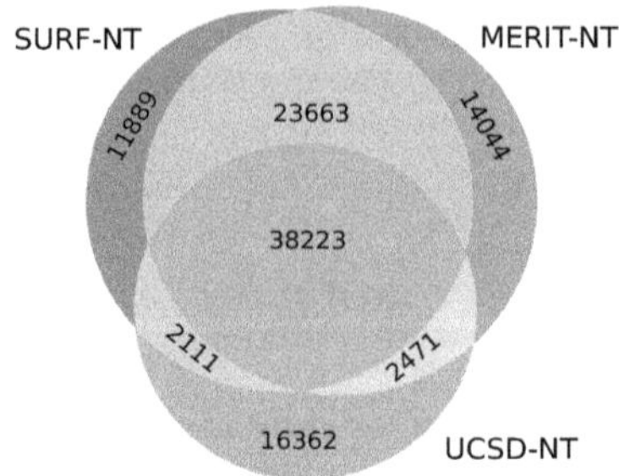

Fig. 7. Overlap in source IP addresses observed in /16 blocks across the three telescopes on April 5, 2025 at 3:00–4:00 UTC. The overlap between SURF-NT and MERIT-NT was consistently higher than that between either of them and UCSD-NT, while the overlap among all three telescopes was the consistently highest across samples.

In addition to the selected /16 blocks, we computed a Jaccard similarity matrix for all possible /16 combinations. We observed that the overlap between MERIT-NT and SURF-NT was consistently higher than that between UCSD-NT and either MERIT-NT or SURF-NT. This suggests that some IBR sources tend to not target UCSD-NT or specifically target both MERIT-NT and SURF-NT. Furthermore, the overall high overlap across all telescopes suggests that individual IBR sources were ubiquitous throughout the address space, indiscriminately transmitting at a sufficiently high rate to be observed in one-hour samples across three distributed /16 s. Specifically, assuming uniformly random probing of the IPv4 address space, a Poisson approximation shows that a probing rate of at least 74.2 pps is required to reach all three /16 s with 95% probability.

6.7   IP Vs. Port Concentration

In addition to the analyses presented in the original study [4], we assess the number of destination addresses and ports sources targeted by IBR sources. We counted the destinations observed in the three /16 blocks of the three telescopes, using the same second octets that we analyzed in §6.6. Figure 8 shows the distribution of the number of destination addresses and port/protocol combinations contacted per source address. For the MERIT-NT and SURF-NT /16 s, approximately 30.1% and 30.3% of sources contacted only one address of the telescope, and 57.1% and 57.6% contacted only one port. In contrast, the IBR observed in the UCSD-NT /16 showed a reversed pattern: 58.4% of sources contacted only one address, while just 36.8% contacted a single port. We found that this pattern was consistent across all fully covered /16 s of each telescope. A possible explanation for this difference is UCSD-NT's much larger address space, which may cause scanners to adapt their probing strategies. Understanding this difference in targeting behavior warrants additional study.

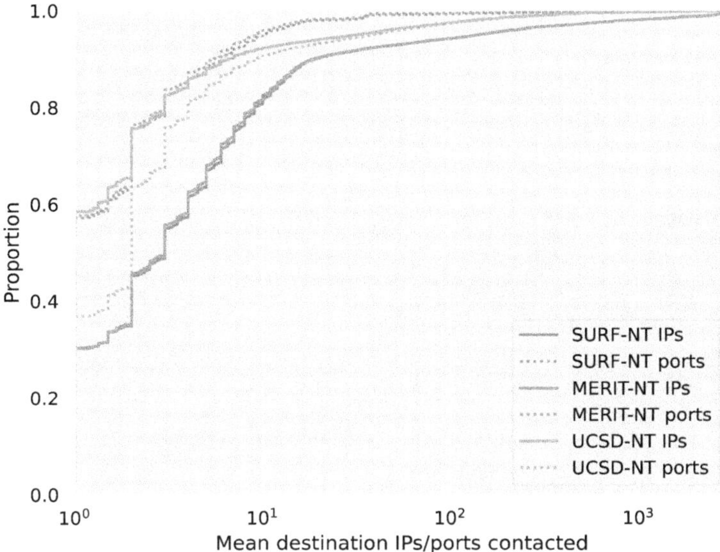

Fig. 8. ECDF of the mean destination addresses and protocol/ports combinations contacted per source address within /16 blocks across one-hour samples. Sources to SURF-NT and MERIT-NT contact more addresses than ports, whereas the opposite holds for UCSD-NT.

6.8 RSDoS Detection

As a practical illustration of how the size of telescope impacts its utility, we considered its ability to infer RSDoS attacks. To this end, we follow the methodology of Moore et al. [24] (§2.2) on increasingly smaller portions of the UCSD-NT address space. We set the same parameters to the values that CAIDA uses to generate the RSDoS attack metadata feed [8]: at least 30 pps calculated over a 60-second sliding window, targeting 25 or more telescope addresses. We started by calculating the number of inferred RSDoS targets from the entire UCSD-NT address space (/9+/10), then removed the /10 block, and subsequently step-wise halved the telescope block size until we arrived at /16 blocks.

Figure 9 shows the median RSDoS targets inferred from one-hour samples per address block size. As the address space shrinks, the number of targets declines logarithmically. However, there is substantial variation in the number of targets inferred at the block level. For each block size and sample, we calculated the coefficient of variation (CV) of the inferred target counts across blocks. The CVs ranged from 0.26 to 1.65, suggesting that spoofed source addresses are not uniformly random. Further investigation is required to confirm this observation.

Next, we compared the largest consecutive prefixes in each telescope, UCSD-NT (/9), MERIT-NT (/14), and SURF-NT (/16). A mean of 95.4% of RSDoS targets observed in the MERIT-NT block during one-hour samples were also detected in the UCSD-NT block during the same period, which aligns with findings from prior research [18]. Conversely, a mean of 13.2% of targets seen in UCSD-NT were also

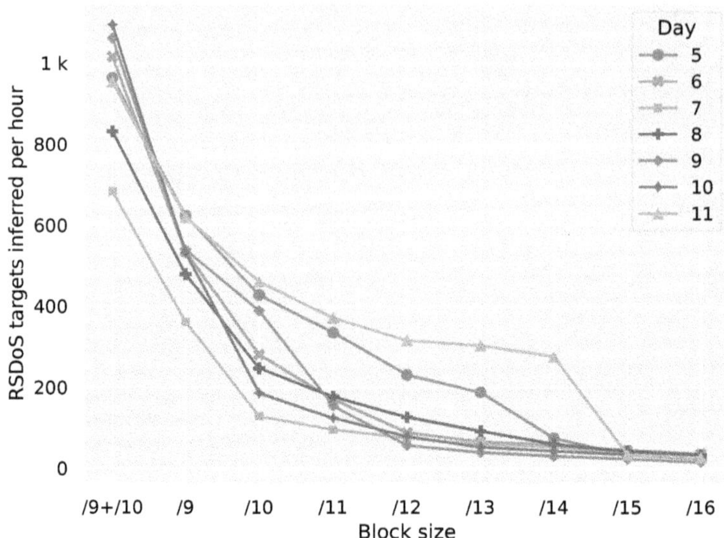

Fig. 9. Median RSDoS targets inferred from one-hour UCSD-NT samples. The observation counts decrease for larger IP address blocks. RSDoS target visibility decreased logarithmically with the size of the address space.

seen in MERIT-NT, although the latter comprised only 3.28%[4] of the address space of the former. Similarly, 93.9% of targets observed in SURF-NT were also detected in UCSD-NT, while 13.1% of targets seen in SURF-NT were also seen in UCSD-NT. However, in terms of the number of addresses, the SURF-NT block comprises only 0.8% of the UCSD-NT block. The relatively high overlap can be attributed to the randomly spoofed nature of such attacks and the fact that they rely on high packet rates to be effective. In general, using a distributed telescope makes it more difficult for attackers to evade all its address blocks.

Figure 10 compares the attacks that were observed in both UCSD-NT and MERIT-NT. The diagonal line indicates the proportional difference in monitored address space. We found that the number of packets inferred to be part of RSDoS attacks closely follows this line. Additionally, we found that some targets sent over five orders of magnitude more backscatter than others. The number of packets enables inference of a lower bound—packets may be dropped at or on the path to or from the target—on the packet rate of the attack.

One notable outlier is the cluster of targets demarcated by the rectangle. Upon inspection, 105 (76.1%) of these targets were inferred on April 5, 3:00–4:00 UTC. All of these 105 target addresses were targeted within this hour, they all fell within the same /24 subnet of an Argentinian game hosting provider. Furthermore, the drift of this cluster to the left of the diagonal indicates a skew

---

[4] Only considering addresses within the /9 block that are monitored by UCSD-NT.

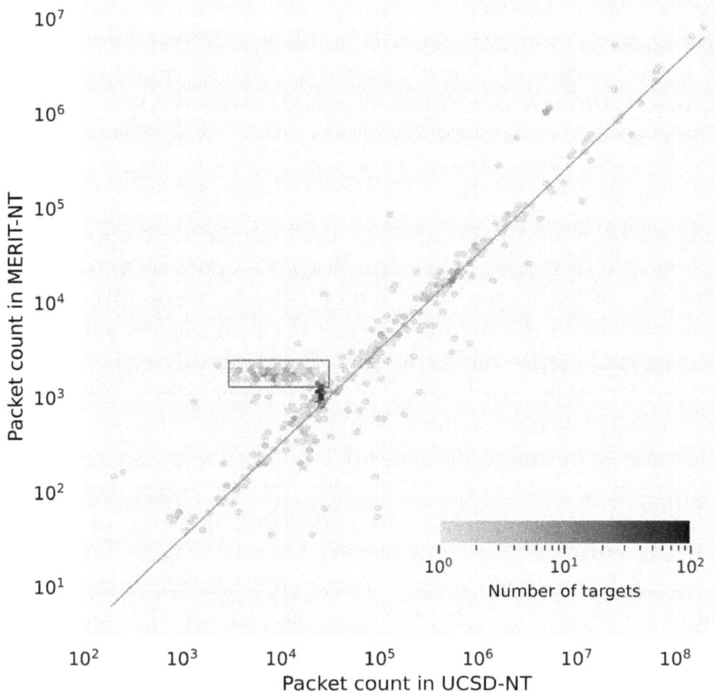

Fig. 10. Targets observed in MERIT-NT and UCSD-NT with corresponding backscatter packet counts. The color gradient indicates the number of targets observed for each packet count. The diagonal line represents the expected packet count based on the relative sizes of the telescopes. The majority of points within the rectangle belong to a clustered attack on a /24 subnet during a one-hour sample.

in spoofed source addresses, which could be the result of a random number generator biased toward MERIT-NT addresses.

7   Discussion

Growing IPv4 shortage and rising operational costs prompt operators of network telescopes to reconsider their darknet deployments. Prior work [5,16,20,26,29, 35] has proposed alternative approaches. These developments raise a central question: are large network telescopes still necessary as a data source for Internet-wide measurements?

Smaller, fragmented telescopes can provide viable alternatives. When measured over longer periods, smaller telescopes still achieve high visibility, i.e., the number of sources observed (§6.1), and their marginal visibility tends to be higher (§6.4, §6.6). Moreover, the generally even distribution of sources over blocks within large and smaller telescopes (§6.5) suggests that even limited portions of address space can capture representative IBR.

Nevertheless, large telescopes continue to provide a unique perspective. Our analysis showed that IBR sources exhibited different targeting patterns toward the larger telescope in our study (§6.2, §6.7). Furthermore, having a larger monitored address space enhances observation of ASes originating fewer addresses (§6.3) and lower-rate RSDoS attacks (§6.8). These results indicate that large-scale telescopes can observe events that smaller telescopes would likely miss.

The trade-off between operating large and smaller telescopes leaves operators with a practical dilemma: to downsize or not. Apart from the availability of address space, dimensioning decisions should consider the computation and storage requirements. Given the pressure to use IPv4 allocations efficiently, we recommend aligning telescope configurations with the study objectives. For example, research investigating topological scanning behavior would benefit from a telescope composed of many fragmented address blocks, whereas a study focusing on RSDoS attacks is better served by a telescope encompassing a large address space, regardless of its contiguity. While sub-/24 telescopes may suffice for certain studies, our observations show that addresses differing in their last octet are targeted differently, which can introduce bias if the selection is too narrow.

A collection of fragmented address blocks thus provide a cost-effective alternative to large, contiguous telescope ranges due to their high marginal visibility and potentially topological diversity. Analogous to radio astronomy, where distributed arrays provide a broader field of view, distributed network telescopes can monitor diverse segments of the global address space. Nevertheless, the increased management and synchronization complexity of such distributed deployments should also be taken into account.

7.1   Future Work

Filtering Spoofed Traffic. While we made a best-effort attempt to filter bursty spoofing activity, we acknowledge that lower-rate spoofing activity may remain. Failing to filter such traffic could lead researchers to overestimate the number of sources observed and derived metrics, such as /24 blocks and ASNs. Another concern is that short-term spoofing activity effectively constitutes a denial-of-service attack on the telescope infrastructure and may create gaps in the captured packet traces. Future work should explore automatic derivation of heuristics to reliably and durably identify spoofed packets directly targeting a telescope.

Ephemeral Telescopes. Leased address blocks and on-demand cloud-based sensors could increase geographical and topological coverage, with the additional benefit of being more difficult for malicious actors to avoid. However, their data may be biased by traffic intended for a previous tenant of the address space and thus requires novel filtering strategies [26].

8   Conclusions

The work by Benson et al. [4] examined how unsolicited traffic (called IBR) can be used to study a variety of Internet phenomena. We revisited their seminal work 10 years later, amid IPv4 address scarcity and surging IBR levels, and found overall consistent results. Our findings show that IBR continues to be a useful data source of Internet-wide measurements, despite being collected from telescopes covering a substantially smaller address space.

We also showed that although visibility increases with telescope size, it exhibits diminishing returns. This pattern held consistently throughout our study: the IBR sources, their originating ASes, and RSDoS targets all grew sublinearly with the size of the monitored space. Furthermore, we observed ubiquitous presence of IBR sources across telescopes, suggesting pervasive Internet-wide probing. Nevertheless, the largest telescope in our study, `UCSD-NT`, observed more sources in absolute terms and detected RSDoS events missed by the other two telescopes.

Operators can apply our methodology to guide telescope dimensioning decisions. Our findings suggest that distributed telescope deployments may provide a cost-effective alternative for maintaining broad visibility. Further research is needed to better understand spoofed traffic and environment-specific targeting behavior, as both factors can substantially influence what a telescope observes.

Acknowledgements. We thank our shepherd and the anonymous reviewers for their insightful comments. We also extend our gratitude to Merit and SURF for providing the telescope data used in this study.

This material is based on research sponsored by the National Science Foundation (NSF) grants CNS-2120399, CNS-2450552, OAC-2319959, OAC-2531134, by the European Commission under the GN5-2 project, by the Dutch Research Council (NWO) CATRIN project (NWA.1215.18.003), and by the Netherlands Enterprise Agency (RVO) MISD project under the 8ra initiative (IPCEI-CIS). The views and conclusions contained herein are those of the authors and should not be interpreted as necessarily representing the official policies or endorsements, either expressed or implied, of the funding agencies.

Ethical Considerations. This work does not raise ethical concerns.

References

1. Antonakakis, M., et al.: Understanding the Mirai Botnet. In: 26th USENIX Security Symposium (USENIX Security 17), pp. 1093–1110 (2017). https://www.usenix.org/conference/usenixsecurity17/technical-sessions/presentation/antonakakis
2. Bailey, M., Cooke, E., Jahanian, F., Nazario, J., Watson, D.: The internet motion sensor: a distributed blackhole monitoring system. In: NDSS Symposium 2005 (2005). https://www.ndss-symposium.org/ndss2005/internet-motion-sensor-distributed-blackhole-monitoring-system/

3. Benson, K., Dainotti, A., Claffy, KC., Aben, E.: Gaining insight into AS-level outages through analysis of Internet Background Radiation. In: 2013 IEEE Conference on Computer Communications Workshops (INFOCOM WKSHPS), pp. 447–452 (2013). https://doi.org/10.1109/INFCOMW.2013.6562915
4. Benson, K., Dainotti, A., Claffy, K., Snoeren, A.C., Kallitsis, M.: Leveraging Internet Background Radiation for Opportunistic Network Analysis. In: Proceedings of the 2015 Internet Measurement Conference, pp. 423–436. IMC 2015, Association for Computing Machinery, New York, NY, USA (2015). https://doi.org/10.1145/2815675.2815702
5. Bortoluzzi, F., Irwin, B., Beiler, L.S., Westphall, C.M.: Cloud telescope: a distributed architecture for capturing internet background radiation. In: 2023 IEEE 12th International Conference on Cloud Networking (CloudNet), pp. 77–85 (2023). https://doi.org/10.1109/CloudNet59005.2023.10490018
6. Camargo, A.V.C., Granville, L., Bertholdo, L.M.: Beyond size: investigating the impact of scaled-down network telescopes on threat detection. Int. J. Netw. Manage 35(3), e70014 (2025). https://doi.org/10.1002/nem.70014
7. Center for Applied Internet Data Analysis (CAIDA): FlowTuple - STARDUST (2021). https://www.caida.org/projects/stardust/docs/data/flowtuple/
8. Center for Applied Internet Data Analysis (CAIDA): Randomly and Uniformly Spoofed Denial-of-Service (RSDoS) Attack Metadata (2025). https://www.caida.org/catalog/datasets/rsdos-targets/
9. Chindipha, S.D., Irwin, B., Herbert, A.: Quantifying the accuracy of small subnet-equivalent sampling of IPv4 internet background radiation datasets. In: Proceedings of the South African Institute of Computer Scientists and Information Technologists 2019, pp. 1–8. SAICSIT 2019, Association for Computing Machinery, New York, NY, USA (2019). https://doi.org/10.1145/3351108.3351129
10. corsaro3 contributors: CAIDA/corsaro3. CAIDA (2025). https://github.com/CAIDA/corsaro3
11. Dainotti, A., Amman, R., Aben, E., Claffy, K.C.: Extracting benefit from harm: using malware pollution to analyze the impact of political and geophysical events on the internet. ACM SIGCOMM Comput. Commun. Rev. 42(1), 31–39 (2012). https://doi.org/10.1145/2096149.2096154
12. Dainotti, A., et al.: Estimating internet address space usage through passive measurements. ACM SIGCOMM Comput. Commun. Rev. 44(1), 42–49 (2014). https://doi.org/10.1145/2567561.2567568
13. Dainotti, A., King, A., Claffy, K., Papale, F., Pescapè, A.: Analysis of a "/" stealth scan from a botnet. In: Proceedings of the 2012 Internet Measurement Conference, pp. 1–14. IMC 2012, Association for Computing Machinery, New York, NY, USA (2012). https://doi.org/10.1145/2398776.2398778
14. Durumeric, Z., Bailey, M., Halderman, J.A.: An internet-wide view of internet-wide scanning. In: 23rd USENIX Security Symposium (USENIX Security 14), pp. 65–78 (2014). https://www.usenix.org/node/184494
15. Gao, M., Mok, R., Carisimo, E., Li, E., Kulkarni, S., Claffy, K.: DarkSim: A similarity-based time-series analytic framework for darknet traffic. In: Proceedings of the 2024 ACM on Internet Measurement Conference, pp. 241–258. IMC 2024, Association for Computing Machinery, New York, NY, USA (2024). https://doi.org/10.1145/3646547.3688426
16. Harrop, W., Armitage, G.: Defining and evaluating Greynets (sparse darknets). In: The IEEE Conference on Local Computer Networks 30th Anniversary (LCN 2005), pp. 344–350 (2005). https://doi.org/10.1109/LCN.2005.46

17. Hiesgen, R.: SPOKI: Unveiling a new wave of scanners through a reactive network telescope. In: 31st USENIX Security Symposium (USENIX Security 22) (2022). https://www.usenix.org/conference/usenixsecurity22/presentation/hiesgen
18. Hiesgen, R., et al.: The age of DDoScovery: an empirical comparison of industry and academic DDoS assessments. In: Proceedings of the 2024 ACM on Internet Measurement Conference, pp. 259–279. IMC 2024, Association for Computing Machinery, New York, NY, USA (2024). https://doi.org/10.1145/3646547.3688451
19. Internet Assigned Numbers Authority (IANA): Service name and transport protocol port number registry (2025). https://www.iana.org/assignments/service-names-port-numbers/service-names-port-numbers.xhtml
20. Izhikevich, L., Tran, M., Kallitsis, M., Fass, A., Durumeric, Z.: Cloud watching: understanding attacks against cloud-hosted services. In: Proceedings of the 2023 ACM on Internet Measurement Conference, pp. 313–327. IMC 2023, Association for Computing Machinery, New York, NY, USA (2023). https://doi.org/10.1145/3618257.3624818
21. Jonker, M., King, A., Krupp, J., Rossow, C., Sperotto, A., Dainotti, A.: Millions of targets under attack: A macroscopic characterization of the DoS ecosystem. In: Proceedings of the 2017 Internet Measurement Conference, pp. 100–113. IMC 2017, Association for Computing Machinery, New York, NY, USA (2017). https://doi.org/10.1145/3131365.3131383
22. Merit: Orion network telescope (2025). https://www.merit.edu/research/projects/orion-network-telescope/
23. Mogul, J., Postel, J.: Internet standard subnetting procedure. RFC 950, IETF (1985). http://tools.ietf.org/rfc/rfc950.txt
24. Moore, D., Shannon, C., Brown, D.J., Voelker, G.M., Savage, S.: Inferring internet denial-of-service activity. ACM Trans. Comput. Syst. **24**(2), 115–139 (2006). https://doi.org/10.1145/1132026.1132027
25. Pang, R., Yegneswaran, V., Barford, P., Paxson, V., Peterson, L.: Characteristics of internet background radiation. In: Proceedings of the 4th ACM SIGCOMM Conference on Internet Measurement, pp. 27–40. IMC 2004, Association for Computing Machinery, New York, NY, USA (2004). https://doi.org/10.1145/1028788.1028794
26. Pauley, E., Barford, P., McDaniel, P.: DScope: a cloud-native internet telescope. In: 32nd USENIX Security Symposium (USENIX Security 23), pp. 5989–6006 (2023). https://www.usenix.org/conference/usenixsecurity23/presentation/pauley
27. Prehn, L., Lichtblau, F., Feldmann, A.: When wells run dry: the 2020 IPv4 address market. In: Proceedings of the 16th International Conference on Emerging Networking EXperiments and Technologies, pp. 46–54. CoNEXT 2020, Association for Computing Machinery, New York, NY, USA (2020). https://doi.org/10.1145/3386367.3431301
28. Richter, P., Allman, M., Bush, R., Paxson, V.: A primer on IPv4 scarcity. ACM SIGCOMM Comput. Commun. Rev. **45**(2), 21–31 (2015). https://doi.org/10.1145/2766330.2766335
29. Richter, P., Berger, A.: Scanning the scanners: sensing the internet from a massively distributed network telescope. In: Proceedings of the Internet Measurement Conference, pp. 144–157. IMC 2019, Association for Computing Machinery, New York, NY, USA (2019). https://doi.org/10.1145/3355369.3355595
30. RouteViews: University of Oregon RouteViews Project (2025). https://www.routeviews.org/routeviews/

31. Sommese, R., et al.: Investigating the impact of DDoS attacks on DNS infrastructure. In: Proceedings of the 22nd ACM Internet Measurement Conference, pp. 51–64. IMC 2022, Association for Computing Machinery, New York, NY, USA (2022). https://doi.org/10.1145/3517745.3561458
32. Soro, F., Drago, I., Trevisan, M., Mellia, M., Ceron, J., Santanna, J.J.: Are darknets all the same? On darknet visibility for security monitoring. In: 2019 IEEE International Symposium on Local and Metropolitan Area Networks (LANMAN), pp. 1–6 (2019). https://doi.org/10.1109/LANMAN.2019.8847113
33. Tanveer, H.B., et al.: Unveiling IPv6 scanning dynamics: a longitudinal study using large scale proactive and passive IPv6 telescopes (2025). https://doi.org/10.48550/arXiv.2508.07506
34. The number resource organization: RIR statistics (2025). https://www.nro.net/about/rirs/statistics/
35. Wagner, D., et al.: How to operate a meta-telescope in your spare time. In: Proceedings of the 2023 ACM on Internet Measurement Conference, pp. 328–343. IMC 2023, Association for Computing Machinery, New York, NY, USA (2023). https://doi.org/10.1145/3618257.3624831
36. Wustrow, E., Karir, M., Bailey, M., Jahanian, F., Huston, G.: Internet background radiation revisited. In: Proceedings of the 10th ACM SIGCOMM Conference on Internet Measurement, pp. 62–74. IMC 2010, Association for Computing Machinery, New York, NY, USA (2010). https://doi.org/10.1145/1879141.1879149

State of Passkey Authentication in the Wild: A Census of the Top 100K Sites

Prince Bhardwaj[(✉)] and Nishanth Sastry

University of Surrey, Guildford, UK
`{p.pawankumarsharma,n.sastry}@surrey.ac.uk`

Abstract. Passkeys – discoverable WebAuthn credentials synchronized across devices are widely promoted as the future of passwordless authentication. Built on the FIDO2 standard, they eliminate shared secrets and resist phishing while offering usability through platform credential managers. Since their introduction in 2022, major vendors have integrated passkeys into operating systems and browsers, and prominent websites have announced support. Yet the true extent of adoption across the broader web remains unknown.

Measuring this is challenging because websites implement passkeys in heterogeneous ways. Some expose explicit "Sign in with passkey" buttons, others hide options under multi-step flows or rely on conditional mediation, and many adopt external mechanisms such as JavaScript libraries or OAuth-based identity providers. There is no standardized discovery endpoint, and dynamic, JavaScript-heavy pages complicate automated detection.

This paper makes two contributions. First, we present *Fidentikit*, a browser-based crawler implementing 43 heuristics across five categories – UI elements, DOM structures, WebAuthn API calls, network patterns, and library detection developed through iterative refinement over manual examination of 1,500 sites. Second, we apply Fidentikit to the top 100,000 Tranco-ranked domains, producing the first large-scale census of passkey adoption. Our results show adoption strongly correlates with site popularity and often depends on external identity providers rather than native implementations.

Keywords: passkeys · WebAuthn · FIDO2 · passwordless · large-scale measurement · authentication

1 Introduction

Passwords remain the dominant form of web authentication, yet they are inherently insecure. Users frequently reuse passwords across services, enabling credential stuffing attacks. Even unique passwords are vulnerable when websites fail to store them securely, exposing plaintext or weakly hashed credentials in

S. Ferlin-Reiter et al. (Eds.): PAM 2026, LNCS 16477, pp. 319–347, 2026.
https://doi.org/10.1007/978-3-032-18268-5_15

breaches. Worse, a stolen password can be replayed indefinitely unless detected and revoked. These weaknesses have driven the search for a "holy grail" of passwordless authentication [33]: mechanisms that eliminate shared secrets, resist phishing, and reduce reliance on human memory.

Passkeys represent the most promising realization of this vision. A passkey is a discoverable WebAuthn credential synchronized across a user's devices via encrypted cloud storage, enabling seamless multi-device login without passwords. Built on the FIDO2 standard, passkeys inherit the phishing resistance of public-key cryptography: private keys never leave the authenticator, and signatures are origin-bound, preventing replay on lookalike domains. Unlike device-bound FIDO credentials tied to a single hardware token, passkeys leverage platform credential managers such as Apple iCloud Keychain, Google Password Manager, and Microsoft Authenticator to provide ubiquity and convenience. Introduced in 2022 by the FIDO Alliance [12], passkeys have since been championed by major vendors and integrated into mainstream operating systems and browsers. Industry announcements tout rapid adoption [25], yet these claims remain anecdotal and skewed toward high-profile brands. The true extent of passkey deployment across the broader web ecosystem is unknown.

Passkeys have matured beyond early prototypes: platform support is stable, major websites have rolled out passkey login options, and developer tooling has improved. At the same time, the ecosystem faces fragmentation. Unlike OAuth or OpenID Connect, which expose standardized discovery endpoints, WebAuthn lacks machine-readable metadata for passkey support. A site may implement passkeys without advertising this capability in any predictable URL or API. Consequently, automated detection is non-trivial. Websites differ in how they surface passkey options: some display explicit "Sign in with a passkey" buttons, others embed them under "More sign-in options," and still others rely on conditional mediation, where the browser reveals passkey choices only after user interaction. Non-English sites introduce further variability with localized terminology. Beyond UI heterogeneity, technical signals vary: some sites invoke WebAuthn APIs immediately on page load, others defer calls until after multi-step flows. These challenges render naïve crawling ineffective.

Our goal in this paper is twofold. First, we present a robust, reproducible methodology for detecting passkey support at scale. We developed a browser-based crawler, **Fidentikit**, equipped with heuristics that capture the diverse ways websites implement passkeys. Our system combines five classes of heuristics: (1) UI text and ARIA labels, (2) DOM attributes and form structures, (3) JavaScript WebAuthn API invocations, (4) network request patterns, and (5) known WebAuthn library filenames. These heuristics were derived through an iterative, semi-automated process. Starting with manual inspection of the top 100 Tranco-ranked sites, we encoded observed patterns into detection rules, validated them on progressively larger sets (ranks 101–500, then 501–1,000, and so on), and refined the rules whenever false negatives emerged. After examining over 1,500 sites, the marginal discovery rate fell below 2%, yielding a primary set of 43 heuristics which we group into five classes described above. This system forms our first contribution: an open-source crawler and passkey detection framework hosted at https://netsys.surrey.ac.uk/softwares/fidentikit/ and Dashboard shown in Fig. 10 of Appendix A, enabling researchers and practitioners to verify passkey support and identify the heuristic that triggered detection.

Second, we apply this crawler to conduct the first large-scale census of passkey adoption in the wild. Using the Tranco list, we measured passkey support across the top 100,000 websites. Our analysis reveals several key findings. First, adoption is strongly correlated with site popularity: top-ranked domains exhibit substantially higher passkey support than lower ranked sites. Second, many sites do not implement passkeys natively but rely on external mechanisms. Two dominant patterns emerge: (a) integration of JavaScript libraries such as `fido-lib`, `webauthn-framework`, and `passwordless.id`, and (b) offering OAuth-based login via identity providers like Google, which themselves support passkeys. In the latter case, a user can authenticate to the site using OAuth and complete the login with a passkey at the identity provider, effectively extending passkey benefits without direct implementation by the relying party. We also find that passkey adoption varies by geographic region, with sites hosted in the USA, Europe and Russia having the highest passkey adoption rates, followed by countries like Australia and India.

In summary, this paper makes the following contributions:

1. **Fidentikit**, a scalable tool consisting of a crawler and heuristics-based detection framework implementing 43 heuristics across five categories, enabling reliable identification of passkey support on modern, JavaScript-heavy websites.
2. A comprehensive census of passkey adoption across the top 100K Tranco-ranked domains, providing empirical insight into deployment trends, implementation strategies, and reliance on external identity providers.

Our results offer a grounded perspective on the state of passwordless authentication on the web, complementing prior usability and protocol-level studies with quantitative evidence from the field. By illuminating where and how passkeys are deployed, we aim to inform both researchers and practitioners seeking to accelerate the transition toward a passwordless future.

Scope and Limitations. We emphasise that this work focuses on measuring passkey *deployment*, whether websites offer passkey authentication as an option rather than measuring actual *user adoption* of passkeys. Understanding user-side adoption would require access to authentication telemetry or user surveys, which is beyond the scope of this measurement study. Nevertheless, quantifying service-side availability is a prerequisite for understanding adoption barriers: users cannot adopt passkeys if websites do not offer them. Our findings reveal that whilst major service providers have adopted passkeys, they are predominantly offered as an *additional* authentication method alongside passwords and traditional MFA, rather than as a replacement. This observation suggests that the "passwordless future" remains aspirational, with passkeys currently serving as a supplementary security enhancement rather than the primary authentication mechanism.

2 Background: Passkey Login Flow

2.1 WebAuthn and FIDO2 Fundamentals

The W3C Web Authentication API (WebAuthn) [36] defines a standard interface for public-key-based authentication in web browsers. WebAuthn is the browser-facing component of the FIDO2 specification [12], which combines WebAuthn with the Client-to-Authenticator Protocol (CTAP). Three entities participate: the *Relying Party* (RP, the web server), the *client* (browser), and the *authenticator*.

Authenticator Types. FIDO2 supports multiple authenticator categories: (1) *Platform authenticators* embedded in the user's device (e.g., Touch ID on iPhone, Windows Hello on laptops, biometric sensors on Android phones); (2) *Hardware authenticators* like USB security keys (YubiKey, Google Titan) that connect via USB, NFC, or Bluetooth; (3) *Credential managers* (iCloud Keychain, Google Password Manager, 1Password) that store and sync passkeys across devices via encrypted cloud storage. For cross-device authentication, the user scans a QR code displayed on the login page with their smartphone, which then uses CTAP over Bluetooth Low Energy (BLE) to complete authentication.

Registration and Authentication Flows. During registration, the Relying Party (RP, e.g., google.com) initiates credential creation by calling `navigator.credentials.create()` with a challenge and relying party identifier. The browser issues an HTTP POST request to the RP's server (e.g., `/webauthn/register`) to obtain the challenge payload containing `publicKey` parameters. The authenticator generates a public-private key pair, stores the private key securely, and returns the public key plus attestation data to the RP via a subsequent HTTP POST to `/webauthn/register/complete`. During authentication, the RP calls `navigator.credentials.get()`, triggering an HTTP request to fetch the authentication challenge. The authenticator signs the challenge with the stored private key, and the signed assertion is posted back to the RP's verification endpoint (e.g., `/webauthn/authenticate`). This challenge-response protocol ensures credentials cannot be phished: the private key never leaves the authenticator, and signatures are cryptographically bound to the RP's origin domain. Unlike passwords (shared secrets vulnerable to breaches and reuse), WebAuthn credentials are asymmetric and origin-bound, fundamentally mitigating phishing, man-in-the-middle attacks, and database leaks [7]. The origin binding means that even if a user visits a lookalike phishing domain (`g00gle.com` instead of `google.com`), the authenticator will refuse to sign challenges for the incorrect origin.

2.2 Passkey Authentication Flow

The term *passkey* refers to a specific instantiation of WebAuthn credentials that are *discoverable* (also known as resident credentials) and are synchronized across devices via cloud services. Introduced in 2022 by the FIDO Alliance, passkeys are designed to provide a seamless, multi-device authentication experience [4,15]. Unlike device-bound FIDO credentials, which reside on a single hardware token, passkeys leverage platform-specific credential managers (e.g., Apple iCloud Keychain, Google Password Manager, Microsoft Authenticator) to synchronize credentials across a user's ecosystem.

Figure 1 shows a simplified passkey authentication login flow in which a user wants to log into a website, (e.g., github.com). The user visits the website's login page and clicks on the "Sign in with Passkey" button to initiate the passkey login flow. The website calls `navigator.credentials.get()`, the browser prompts the user to select a passkey and verify their identity (via biometric or PIN), the authenticator signs the challenge, and the website verifies the signature to establish the session.

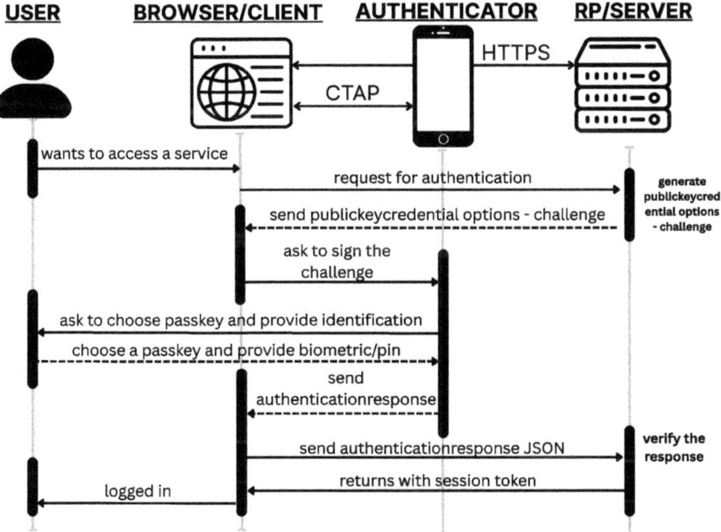

Fig. 1. Simplified passkey authentication flow. The user initiates login, the relying party requests authentication via `navigator.credentials.get()`, the authenticator prompts for user verification (biometric/PIN), signs the challenge, and returns the signed assertion to the relying party for verification.

This flow eliminates the need for users to remember or type passwords promising the combination of the phishing-resistance of FIDO2 with the convenience and ubiquity expected by mainstream users.

2.3   Passkey: The Current State

Industry Claims. Major technology companies have invested heavily in passkey infrastructure. Google announced support for passkeys across Android and

Chrome in May 2022 [15], and by mid-2023, reported that "hundreds of millions" of Google accounts had enabled passkey login. Apple integrated passkeys into iOS 16, iPadOS 16, and macOS Ventura in September 2022 [4], marketing them as the future of secure sign-in. Microsoft followed suit, adding passkey support to Windows 11 and Microsoft Authenticator, and encouraging developers to adopt passwordless authentication by default [24]. Beyond the platform vendors, a growing number of high-profile websites have announced passkey support. Today, Amazon, PayPal, Best Buy, eBay, and several major financial institutions (including Bank of America and Chase) have rolled out passkey login options [14]. The FIDO Alliance maintains an official Passkeys Directory listing prominent adopters, which as of October 2025 included over 200 websites and applications. Industry advocates claim that passkey adoption is accelerating, with predictions that passwordless authentication will become the default within the next few years. These claims are difficult to verify independently. The official directory relies on voluntary submissions and omits smaller sites, regional services, and deployments hidden behind gated authentication flows. Community maintained indices such as Passkeys directory [2], Dashlane's Passkeys Directory [10], and the 2FA Directory's passkey section [3] provide additional coverage but exhibit significant overlap and frequent staleness. The true extent of passkey deployment particularly among the long tail of websites outside the top-tier brands remains unknown. *This paper is an attempt to understand the current state of passkey support, and to develop tooling that can be run at regular intervals to create a full picture of passkey support across the top websites – a **census**.*

Why Existing Directories Fall Short. Manual curation of passkey directories faces inherent scalability and completeness challenges. First, *submission bias* skews coverage toward high-visibility brands that actively promote their passwordless offerings. Smaller e-commerce sites, regional banks, and niche SaaS platforms are unlikely to submit to multiple directories, leading to systematic under-representation. Second, *staleness* is pervasive: websites add or remove authentication options over time, but directories are infrequently updated. Directories typically rely on users to report changes rather than actively monitoring sites. For instance, `passkeys.directory` depends on community pull requests to GitHub [2], introducing delays between deployment and listing. Third, *hidden deployments* escape manual detection. Some sites offer passkey authentication only after a user enable or create a passkey from user settings (e.g., `intuit.com` requires users to navigate to Security Settings > Two-Factor Authentication > Add Passkey). Static directory entries cannot capture this conditional availability. Fourth, Finally, manual directories provide no quantitative insight into *deployment trends*. How rapidly is passkey adoption growing? Which industry verticals are leading? How do adoption rates vary by website popularity or geographic region? Answering these questions requires pragmatic, large-scale, and longitudinal measurement, an undertaking that manual curation cannot achieve.

3   Measurement Challenges

Although a census of whether a list of websites adopts a certain standard (such as Passkeys) should in principle be straightforward, there can be numerous challenges in practice. Below, we list some of the main difficulties we observed:

1. **Partial Adoption of Standardized Endpoints.** In August 2025, the W3C published the first public working draft of "A Well-Known URL for Relying Party Passkey Endpoints" [37], defining `.well-known/passkey-endpoints` as a standardized mechanism for sites to advertise passkey support and provide direct URLs for creation (`enroll`) and management (`manage`) pages (e.g.,`adobe.com`).

    While this specification promises to simplify passkey discovery, adoption remains minimal. In our measurement of 100,000 domains, we found that only 12 sites ($<$0.02%) exposed `.well-known/passkey-endpoints`. Most sites supporting passkeys do not advertise this capability in a machine-readable format, necessitating alternative detection strategies. Consequently, detection requires examining the login page itself—assuming the login page can be located. Modern web applications increasingly rely on client-side JavaScript frameworks (React, Vue, Angular) that render content dynamically. A static HTTP request to a homepage may return minimal HTML with a loading spinner, while the actual login UI is constructed asynchronously after page load. Traditional web scrapers that fetch and parse raw HTML miss this dynamically injected content. For example, many single-page applications load the passkey login button only after executing several hundred kilobytes of JavaScript and fetching additional resources via AJAX. Detecting passkeys therefore necessitates *browser-based crawling*, which executes JavaScript and waits for the page to stabilize before analysis.

2. **Conditional Mediation and Hidden UI.** WebAuthn's conditional mediation feature [22,29,36] allows RPs to present passkey options inline with traditional login forms, typically in the browser's autofill dropdown. In this mode, the passkey affordance may not be visible as a standalone button or link. Instead, clicking into a username field triggers the browser to display "Use a passkey" in the autofill menu. A crawler that merely inspects visible DOM elements will miss this hidden affordance. For instance, `google.com` invokes `navigator.credentials.get({mediation:'conditional'})` on page load, but the passkey option appears only when users interact with the email input field. Similarly, some sites progressively disclose authentication options: a user enters an email address, and only after clicking "Next" or "Continue" does the page display available authentication options. For example, `intuit.com` uses identifier-first flow, revealing passkey options only after email submission. Static snapshots of the initial login page fail to capture these multi-step flows.

3. **Detection Heterogeneity.** No canonical passkey user interface exists across the web ecosystem. Sites display varying labels: "Sign in with a passkey," "Use Touch ID," "Windows Hello," "Biometric login," or platform-specific branding. Some embed passkey options in dropdown menus labeled "More sign-in

options." (e.g., `microsoft.com`). Others rely entirely on conditional mediation with no explicit visible button. Non-English sites use localized terminology (German: Passkey-Anmeldung, Spanish: clave de acceso). Even when visible UI elements exist, the actual `navigator.credentials.get()` API call may be deferred until user interaction. A passive crawler loading the page without simulating clicks will never observe the WebAuthn API invocation.

4 Fidentikit: Crawler Architecture and Detection Heuristics

For large-scale web measurements, researchers implemented various techniques to identify login pages and SSO buttons [6,16,38]. Unfortunately, the unique challenges of passkey detection (Sect. 3) render existing approaches insufficient. In this section, we present Fidentikit, a distributed browser-based crawler with novel passkey detection heuristics designed to address the above discussed challenges.

4.1 System Architecture

Fidentikit follows a distributed task-queue architecture optimized for scalability and fault tolerance (Fig. 2).

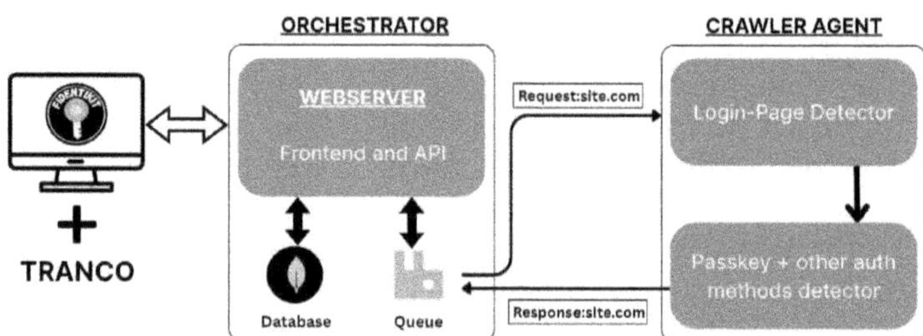

Fig. 2. Fidentikit's Design and Architecture. The Orchestrator coordinates continuous archiving, connects to long-term storage, and provides snapshots. Multiple crawlers retrieve requests from the queue to analyze specific domains.

Distributed Pipeline. The system employs RabbitMQ [1] as the central message broker, configured with durable queues to persist tasks across service restarts. A *dispatcher* service reads target domains from the Tranco list, performs initial DNS resolution (attempting HTTPS first, falling back to HTTP for sites without TLS), and enqueues scan tasks containing the target domain and configuration parameters. Each task is JSON-serialized and published to a dedicated queue (`passkey_landscape_analysis`) with delivery confirmations enabled. Multiple independent *worker* processes consume tasks from the queue using a prefetch count of 1, ensuring fair distribution across workers. Upon receiving a task, a worker spawns an isolated subprocess with a 3-hour timeout using Python's multiprocessing pool. Each worker executes the measurement pipeline: (1) resolve canonical URL, (2) discover login page candidates, (3) navigate to each candidate using headless browser, (4) apply passkey detection heuristics, (5) extract evidence artifacts (screenshots, HAR traces, API call logs), (6) serialize results to JSON, and (7) publish findings to a centralized PostgreSQL database via authenticated HTTP POST. Workers acknowledge task completion only after successfully storing results, ensuring no measurement loss during crashes. This decouples task generation from execution, enabling horizontal scaling: adding more worker VMs linearly increases throughput.

Browser Automation Stack. Each worker employs Playwright [23], a modern browser automation framework that controls Chromium via the Chrome DevTools Protocol (CDP). We selected Playwright over Selenium for three advantages: (1) native support for modern JavaScript APIs including WebAuthn, (2) automatic waiting for page stability (reducing race conditions), and (3) integrated network interception enabling HTTP Archive (HAR) capture without external proxies. Workers launch Chromium in headless mode with realistic user-agent strings (Chrome 120 on Linux), viewport 1920×1080, JavaScript enabled. To avoid bot detection, we randomize inter-action delays (200–500ms jitter) and scroll pages gradually. Workers run within Docker containers with resource limits (6 GB RAM, 4 CPU cores) and use tmpfs-backed temporary storage for browser profiles to minimize disk I/O overhead.

Fault Tolerance and Monitoring. RabbitMQ's durable queues persist tasks to disk, surviving broker restarts. Each task includes a unique idempotency key (SHA-256 hash of domain and timestamp); the database enforces uniqueness constraints preventing duplicate measurements. Workers checkpoint progress every 100 tasks to a shared Redis cache. Detailed telemetry (task latency, error rates, detection method distributions) flows to Prometheus [27] for real-time monitoring and alerting. Failed tasks are automatically re-queued with exponential backoff (initial 60s delay, max 5 retry attempts) to handle transient failures (network timeouts, CAPTCHA challenges).

Ethical Considerations and Crawling Practices. We acknowledge the ethical considerations surrounding web crawling, particularly regarding bot detection mechanisms. Our approach employs randomised interaction delays (200–500ms) to simulate realistic human browsing patterns, which could be perceived as circumventing bot detection. We clarify our ethical stance:

1. **Respect for `robots.txt`:** We strictly honour `robots.txt` directives. Any domain with a "no-crawling" directive for our user-agent or the relevant paths was excluded from our measurement (1,656 domains, 1.7% of the target set).
2. **Rate Limiting:** We enforce a conservative rate limit of one request per second per domain, with exponential backoff on HTTP 429 (Too Many Requests)

and 503 (Service Unavailable) responses. This minimises server load and respects site capacity.

3. **No Credential Submission:** We do not submit login forms, create accounts, or attempt authentication. Our measurement is confined to publicly accessible login page interfaces.

4. **No Sensitive Data Collection:** We collect only structural information (DOM elements, API call signatures, network patterns) necessary for passkey detection. No personally identifiable information or user credentials are captured.

5. **Research Intent:** Our crawling serves legitimate academic research purposes, quantifying passkey deployment to benefit the security community. The randomised delays are employed not to evade detection maliciously, but to avoid triggering rate limiters that would produce incomplete measurements.

4.2   Login Page Discovery

Following prior work on SSO measurement [6,38], we employ a multi-strategy approach to identify login pages. We adapt established methods and execute them in priority order, with candidates deduplicated and ranked by specificity.

Priority Assignment Rationale. The priority values (ranging from 70 to 98) were empirically derived through our iterative validation process on the top 1,500 sites. We observed that explicit authentication paths (e.g., `/login`, `/signin`) yielded the highest true positive rate (94.2%) for locating functional login pages, hence receiving priority 98. Homepage analysis with keyword matching achieved 89.7% accuracy, receiving priority 95. Interactive crawling (priority 85) and sitemap parsing (priority 80) showed progressively lower precision due to false positives from non-login pages containing authentication-related terms. Robots.txt analysis (priority 75) proved useful as a fallback but occasionally flagged administrative pages rather than user-facing login interfaces. These priorities determine candidate ranking when multiple strategies identify login pages for the same domain; higher-priority candidates are analysed first, and in 89% of detected passkey deployments, the passkey was found on the highest-priority candidate.

(1) **Homepage Analysis.** Workers navigate to the domain root (`e.g.`, https://github.com/), wait for page stability (500ms idle network), and parse hyperlinks. We inspect `href` attributes and link text for login keywords. We maintain curated keyword lists spanning multiple languages: English ("login," "log in," "sign in," "signin," "auth," "account"), Spanish ("iniciar sesión," "acceder"), German ("anmelden," "einloggen"), French ("connexion," "se connecter"). Links matching patterns receive priority 95. If the homepage contains login forms (`<form>` with `<input  type="password">`), we analyze it directly as a candidate.

(2) **Well-Known Paths.** We probe common authentication paths: `/login`, `/signin`, `/auth/login`, `/account/login`, `/user/login`, `/accounts`, `/profile`, `/my-account`. Priority: 98 (highest for explicit paths).

(3) Interactive Element Crawling. If the homepage and well-known paths yield no candidates, workers perform limited breadth-first crawl. We click elements matching login-related selectors (`button, a[href*="login"]`, elements with text containing "sign in") and capture resulting navigation. Constraints: max 50 pages per domain to control resource usage, exclude `/blog/`, `/support/`, `/help/` (likely documentation), prioritize `/account/`, `/auth/` paths. Priority: 85.

(4) Sitemap Parsing. We fetch and parse XML sitemaps at `/sitemap.xml` and `/sitemap_index.xml`, extracting URLs and filtering for login keywords. Sitemaps often list primary navigation pages, providing valuable ground truth. Priority: 80.

(5) Robots.txt Analysis. We parse `/robots.txt` for disallowed paths containing "login" or "account," hypothesizing that sites hide login pages from search engine indexing. Priority: 75.

We deduplicate candidates by URL normalization (ignoring query parameters and fragments except for SPA route indicators like `#/login`). We analyze the top 5 candidates per domain (ranked by priority) to balance coverage with measurement time. In validation (Sect. 5.2), 89% of passkey deployments occurred on the highest-priority candidate, justifying this limit.

4.3 Passkey Detection Heuristics

Building a ground truth allows us and other researchers to estimate the success rate and reliability of passkey detection techniques.

Methodology. Starting with manual inspection of the Tranco top 100 domains, we enumerated candidate signals across five categories: (1) UI text and ARIA labels, (2) DOM attributes and form structures, (3) JavaScript WebAuthn API invocations, (4) network endpoints and HTTP request/response patterns, and (5) known WebAuthn library filenames. We implemented these signals as automated checks, initially yielding 18 heuristics. We then evaluated them on a validation set of ranks 101–500 (400 domains), using Firefox and Chrome developer tools to manually inspect each site's login flow, looking for: visible passkey buttons, `navigator.credentials` calls (monitored via browser console instrumentation), WebAuthn-related network requests (captured via browser DevTools Network tab), and library filenames in loaded scripts. This manual review revealed 34 false negatives (known passkey sites that our initial heuristics missed) and 12 false positives (non-passkey sites incorrectly flagged). For each false negative, we analyzed the site to identify the overlooked signal. For example, we discovered that `yandex.ru` hides its passkey option in a dropdown menu with Russian text (biometrics), prompting us to add non-English keyword variants. The complete text keyword patterns are listed in Appendix B.3, Table 5. We added 9 new detection rules to address these gaps.

We repeated this process on progressively larger validation sets: ranks 501–1,000 (500 domains), ranks 1,001–1,500 (500 domains), manually reviewing detection outcomes after each iteration. Across five iterations, we identified and addressed 87 false negatives and 43 false positives, adding heuristics incrementally. By iteration 5, the marginal discovery rate fell below 2% (only 7 new heuristics added for 500 sites examined), indicating diminishing returns. The process yielded a final detection system with 43 core distinct heuristics grouped into five classes, which we describe below.

Extended Validation Beyond Top 1,500. To assess whether our heuristics generalise beyond the top 1,500 sites used for development, we conducted additional spot-check validation on a random sample of 200 sites from lower rank ranges: 50 sites each from ranks 5,000–10,000, 20,000–30,000, 50,000–60,000, and 80,000–90,000. Manual inspection of these 200 sites revealed 3 additional false negatives (sites with passkey support missed by our heuristics) and 2 false positives, yielding an estimated accuracy of 97.5% on lower-ranked sites. The false negatives involved: one site using an uncommon JavaScript bundler that obfuscated WebAuthn API calls, and two sites with passkey options accessible only after account creation. These findings suggest our heuristics remain effective across the full rank spectrum, though with slightly reduced coverage for sites employing aggressive code obfuscation or post-authentication passkey enablement.

Heuristic Stability Over Time. Our 43 heuristics target fundamental WebAuthn API patterns (e.g., `navigator.credentials.get/create`), standardised DOM structures (e.g., `<input type="password">`), and established JavaScript libraries. These signals are anchored in web standards and are unlikely to change frequently. However, new implementation patterns may emerge as: (a) new WebAuthn libraries gain popularity, (b) browser vendors introduce new UI affordances for passkeys, or (c) sites adopt novel conditional mediation patterns. We anticipate that periodic re-validation (e.g., quarterly manual review of 100–200 sites) would be sufficient to identify emerging patterns and maintain detection accuracy. The modular design of Fidentikit allows straightforward addition of new heuristics without disrupting existing detection logic.

1. **Class 1: UI Elements and ARIA Labels.** We search for buttons, links, and form labels containing passkey-related text using 7 distinct selector patterns (UI-1 through UI-7 in Appendix B.2, Table 4). We inspect ARIA labels (`aria-label`, `aria-describedby`) for hidden accessibility text, as some sites expose passkey options only via ARIA attributes for screen reader accessibility. To reduce false positives, we require matches within interactive elements (`<button>`, `<a>`, `<input type="button">`) or within 50 characters of a password field, excluding help documentation and footer links. Example: `bumble.com` (rank 2720) displays `<button aria-label="Quick Sign in">`.
2. **Class 2: WebAuthn API Instrumentation.** The most reliable signal is an actual call to `navigator.credentials.get()` or `navigator.credentials.create()`. We inject JavaScript shims before any page scripts execute (via Playwright's `addInitScript`), wrapping these methods to capture invocations. At page visit completion, we log captured parameters including user verification requirement, authenticator attachment preference, mediation mode, and allowed credentials list. We treat

API invocations as definitive evidence because they confirm functional WebAuthn implementation. Example: `twitter.com` (rank 14) calls `navigator.credentials.get({mediation:'conditional'})` immediately upon page load, before any user interaction.

3. **Class 3: Network Request Patterns.** Playwright's network interception captures all HTTP requests and responses via CDP. We flag sites that issue requests to endpoints matching WebAuthn patterns (URLs containing `webauthn`, `passkey`, `credential`, `auth`). Additionally, we inspect response bodies (limited to first 10 KB) for JSON fields indicating WebAuthn challenges: `"publicKey"`, `"challenge"`, `"allowCredentials"`, `"rpId"`, `"attestation"`. Our instrumentation shim also intercepts `fetch()` calls (Appendix B.4). We record the full HTTP Archive (HAR) entry for reproducibility. We treat network patterns as medium-strength evidence: they confirm backend WebAuthn infrastructure but may not indicate user-facing functionality.

4. **Class 4: Known WebAuthn Libraries.** We scan loaded JavaScript files for WebAuthn library signatures, including `@simplewebauthn/browser`, `webauthn-json`, `fido2-lib`, and `@github/webauthn-json`. Playwright captures all script sources via CDP, and we apply string matching against filenames and bundled source code. We also detect 11 JavaScript implementation patterns (JS-1 through JS-11 in Appendix B.1, Table 3). We treat library presence as weak evidence: it indicates developer intent but does not confirm the feature is live. Example: `wordpress.com` (rank 76) loads WebAuthn scripts, but passkey functionality is available only for Business or eCommerce plans.

5. **Class 5: Third-Party Identity Providers.** Sites delegating authentication to Google, Apple, Microsoft, or GitHub inherit passkey support transitively *if the user has enrolled passkeys with those providers.* We detect OAuth flows via network request interception matching provider-specific URL patterns and SDK signatures (Appendix B.5, Table 6).

We also detect SDK integrations by scanning loaded scripts for provider-specific signatures (e.g., `gapi.auth2`, `AppleID.auth`, `msal.js`). We treat Identity Provider (IdP)-delegated support as *conditional evidence*, contingent on the user's provider-side passkey enrollment. For example, many sites display "Continue with Google" buttons. If the user has enrolled a passkey with their Google account, Google's authentication flow offers passkey login, but this is invisible to the relying party. The RP receives only an OAuth token, with no knowledge of whether the user authenticated via password, passkey, TOTP, or SMS OTP at Google's side. In our results (Sect. 5), we report IdP-delegated support separately to avoid conflating native passkey implementations with transitive dependencies.

Fidentikit Availability. Fidentikit is publicly available as an open-source tool at https://netsys.surrey.ac.uk/softwares/fidentikit/. Researchers and practitioners can use the crawler off-the-shelf to scan individual domains one at a time through a web interface, enabling verification of passkey support on specific websites without requiring local installation or infrastructure setup. This accessibility facilitates independent validation of our findings and enables longitudinal studies of passkey adoption on specific sites of interest.

Table 1 summarises our five heuristic classes, providing examples of implemented detection techniques and their evidence types. The complete catalogue of 43 heuristics with regex patterns and code listings is provided in Appendix B.

Table 1. Summary of Fidentikit detection heuristics across five classes. Each class includes multiple specific techniques (43 core heuristics). Content Type indicates the primary data source analyzed. Detectable Methods lists the authentication mechanisms each class can identify.

Heuristic Class	Detection Technique	Content Type	Detectable Methods
UI Elements & ARIA Labels	Regex-based text matching, DOM inspection	HTML	Passkeys, FIDO2, WebAuthn
WebAuthn API Invocations	JavaScript instrumentation, API hooking	JavaScript	Passkeys, WebAuthn, U2F
Network Request Patterns	HTTP interception, payload analysis	Network	Passkeys, WebAuthn
Known Libraries	Script fingerprinting, filename matching	JavaScript	Passkeys, WebAuthn
Third-Party IdPs	OAuth flow detection, SDK identification	Network, JavaScript	Passkeys (transitive), SSO

5   Reproducible and Reliable Passkey Measurements

We conducted a large-scale measurement of passkey adoption across the Tranco [20] Top 100K list of websites, as of March 2025, when we started this study. In this section, we first present details of the dataset, discuss validation against ground truth based on other existing lists of passkey supported websites, and then move on to empirical findings and initial trends, which we further categorise by binning based on website ranks.

5.1   Dataset and Reachability Issues

To create a baseline understanding of how widely passkeys are adopted, we need a list of websites to check. We adopt the widely used Tranco list [20]. Driven by the hypothesis that more "high profile" or popular websites are more likely to adopt the latest best practices, and also because the most popular websites are visited by the highest numbers of users, and therefore more important for the overall web security, we focus on the top-ranked websites, and aim to investigate the adoption of passkey-based logins in the **Top 100K** websites. We acknowledge that the cut-off based on the Top 100K ranks is arbitrarily chosen, as this is a first

Table 2. Site Reachability Issues by Rank Bin

Rank Bin	Not Reachable	Crawler Missed	Process Timeout	Total
1-1K	302	8	2	312
1K-10K	2,227	117	25	2,369
10K-50K	10,737	606	82	11,425
50K-100K	7,440	190	66	7,696
Total	**20,706**	**921**	**175**	**21,802**

census. This decision was further justified as we found that adoption of passkeys becomes rare as we move down the ranks (Sect. 5.3). In future censuses, we aim to expand this by focussing on larger sets of websites (e.g., Top 1 Million).

Note that even in the Top 100K sites, we were unable to reach a fairly large proportion of websites. Table 2 summarises site reachability issues by rank bin. Not Reachable indicates DNS resolution failure or 404 Not Found. Crawler Missed indicates sites where login page discovery failed (no candidates found). Process Timeout indicates sites where browser automation exceeded the task timeout, typically due to infinite redirects or extremely slow page loads.

The results in the rest of this paper focus on the reachable subset of the Tranco Top 100K ranked list of websites.

5.2   Ground Truth Validation

To assess Fidentikit's detection accuracy, we first compared our measurements against two manually curated ground truth sources: the 2FA Directory [3] and the Passwordless Directory [2].

2FA Directory. The 2FA Directory is a community-maintained list of websites supporting two-factor authentication, including FIDO U2F and WebAuthn. We obtained a snapshot of 2FA directory as of Oct 2025, containing 2,886 domains from the Tranco Top 100K list with U2F/WebAuthn support (indicated by `u2f=true` in their dataset). Since U2F and WebAuthn are closely related (WebAuthn supersedes U2F [13]), sites supporting U2F often also support WebAuthn/passkeys. We cross-referenced these 2,886 domains with our Tranco Top 100K scan results and found 193 domains supporting passkeys.

Passwordless Directory. The Passwordless Directory (`passkeys.directory`) is a GitHub-hosted list specifically documenting passkey support, maintained through community contributions. We obtained a snapshot as of 2025, and found it contained 163 domains from the Tranco Top 100K list of sites that are explicitly listed as supporting passkeys. We cross-referenced these with our scan results.

Coverage Analysis. Of the 163 domains in the Passwordless Directory:

- **143 detected (87.7%):** Fidentikit successfully identified passkey support, matching the ground truth.

- **20 false negatives (12.3%):** Fidentikit failed to detect passkey support on 20 domains. Manual inspection revealed: 8 sites required account creation before exposing passkey enrollment (e.g., `dashlane.com` offers passkey features only within the password manager app after signup), 5 sites were temporarily unreachable during our scan window, 4 sites implemented passkeys exclusively in mobile apps with no web interface, and 3 sites (including `kayak.com`) use multi-step identifier-first flows where passkey options appear only after email submission, which our crawler's timeout did not capture.

Of the 2,886 domains in the 2FA Directory with U2F support:

- **2,104 detected (72.9%):** Fidentikit identified WebAuthn/passkey support.
- **782 not detected (27.1%):** These likely support only U2F (the predecessor to WebAuthn) without upgrading to WebAuthn/passkeys, or implement WebAuthn for hardware security keys but not discoverable passkeys. The 2FA Directory does not distinguish between U2F, WebAuthn with hardware keys, and passkeys, leading to this discrepancy.

The rank distribution reveals further insights. Manual directories exhibit strong bias toward high-visibility sites: 27.6% of Passkey Directory entries fall in the top 1K ranks, compared to only 1.9% of our detected sites. This reflects submission bias prominent brands actively promote their passwordless features and are more likely to be community-submitted to directories. Conversely, our automated detection finds the majority of passkey sites in the long tail: 47.8% reside in ranks 10K–50K, and 36.7% in ranks 50K–100K. These lower-ranked sites, which include regional banks, niche SaaS platforms, and small e-commerce stores, rarely appear in manually curated lists despite offering passkey authentication to their users.

The stacked bars in Fig. 3 illustrate that the two manual directories exhibit similar rank distributions, both skewed toward popular sites. The Passkey Directory shows slightly greater concentration in top ranks (51.5% in top 10K) compared to the 2FA Directory (59.1% in top 10K), but both vastly under-represent the long tail.

Reverse Comparison: To quantify directory incompleteness from the opposite perspective, we analysed how many sites in our dataset are *not* present in the manual directories. Of our 9,397 detected passkey sites: **9,234 (98.3%)** are absent from the Passwordless Directory (163 sites), and **9,204 (97.9%)** are absent from the 2FA Directory's U2F/WebAuthn subset (193 sites). Accounting for overlap between directories, **9,041 sites (96.2%)** detected by Fidentikit appear in neither directory. This demonstrates that manual curation captures less than 4% of actual passkey deployment, with the overwhelming majority of passkey-supporting sites particularly smaller e-commerce platforms, regional services, and niche SaaS applications remaining undocumented.

This validation demonstrates that whilst manual directories provide high-quality ground truth for well-known sites, they cannot capture the breadth of passkey deployment across the web ecosystem. Automated, large-scale measurement is essential for understanding adoption patterns, particularly among smaller sites that collectively serve millions of users but lack the visibility to attract directory submissions.

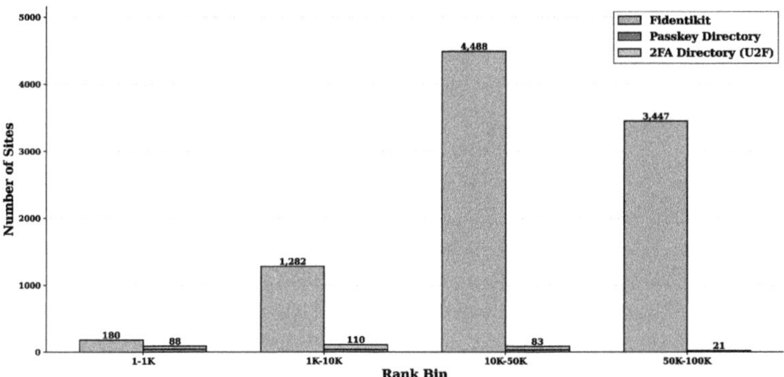

Fig. 3. Comparison of automated passkey detection versus manually curated directories, stratified by Tranco rank bins. The left bars show Fidentikit's automated detection (9,397 sites), while the right stacked bars combine two manual directories: Passkey Directory (163 sites, purple) and 2FA Directory with U2F support (193 sites, orange). Our automated approach detects 26.4× more passkey-supporting sites than manual curation. Manual directories exhibit strong bias toward high-ranked sites (27.6% in top 1K), while automated detection finds the majority of deployments in the long tail (84.5% beyond rank 10K). This validates that manual curation systematically underestimates passkey adoption, particularly among smaller sites that collectively serve substantial user populations.

5.3 Passkey Adoption by Website Rank: Empirical Census Findings

In the rest of this section, we focus on identifying trends in how passkeys are being adopted. We stratify these trends based on website ranks, with increasingly wider rank bins: top 1K, 1K-10K, 10K-50K and 50K-100K.

Figure 4 (left panel) shows the distribution of passkey-supporting versus non-supporting sites, stratified by Tranco rank. Adoption is strongly concentrated among high-traffic websites: 20% of the top 100 sites support passkeys, compared to only 6.9% of sites ranked 50K–100K—a nearly 3× difference. The right panel distinguishes between native passkey implementations and external identity provider integrations. Native implementations show relatively consistent prevalence across rank bins, while external Identity Provider (IdP)-delegated passkey support dominates, particularly in higher-ranked sites. This indicates that many sites do not implement WebAuthn directly but offer passkey authentication transitively through "Sign in with Google" or similar OAuth flows.

Figure 5 categorises sites *without* passkey support by whether they require user login. Sites classified as "No Login Required" showed no recognised identity providers or authentication UI elements on their landing pages (e.g., static content sites, news portals, search engines). It is understandable that a website

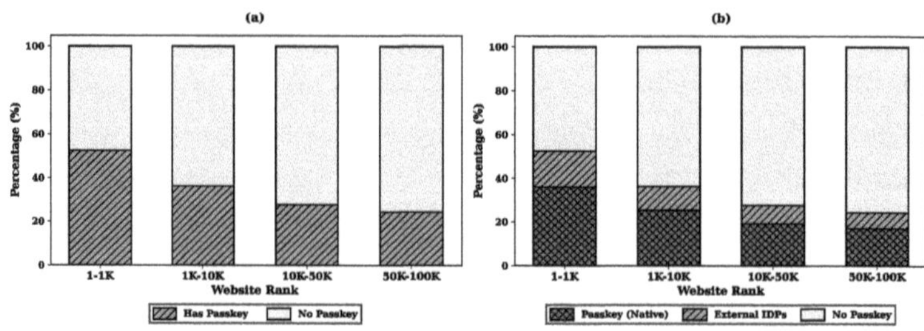

Fig. 4. Authentication landscape of websites across rank bins. (Left) Distribution of sites supporting passkeys versus those without passkey authentication, stratified by Tranco rank (1-1K, 1K-10K, 10-50K, 50-100K). (Right) Detailed breakdown of passkey-supporting sites, distinguishing between native passkey implementation and external identity provider. Higher-ranked sites demonstrate substantially greater passkey adoption, with the top 1,000 sites showing 4.2× higher adoption than sites ranked 50K-100K. Stacked bars represent percentage distribution within each rank bin.

which does not require logins (e.g., a university's homepage, or a popular site like Wikipedia which can be accessed without login), does not need to implement passkeys.

Among sites without passkey support, the proportion requiring login increases from 58% in the top 1K to 71% in ranks 50K–100K. This indicates that a substantial number of websites across all rank ranges have implemented user authentication systems but have not yet adopted passkey support. Combining this with Fig. 4, we observe that whilst high-traffic sites are more likely to support passkeys (20% in top 100 vs. 6.9% in 50K–100K), *many sites with login functionality still lack passkey support*, representing a significant opportunity for expanding passwordless authentication adoption.

Figure 6 shows the distribution of third-party authentication providers among passkey-supporting sites. Google dominates, appearing on approximately 70–75% of sites with external Identity Providers (IdPs) across all rank ranges, followed by Microsoft (15–18%), Apple (8–12%), and GitHub (5–8%). The consistency of these proportions across rank bins indicates standardised adoption patterns in external authentication systems. Notably, **75.2% of all passkey-supporting sites integrate Google SSO**, creating a transitive passkey dependency: users with Google-enrolled passkeys can authenticate to these sites via OAuth, yet the relying party has no visibility into the authentication method used at Google's side. *This indicates that the quickest path to passkey adoption in the wild might be through piggybacking on top of Google's support for passkey-based logins, and the popularity of the "Sign in with Google" option, which has been available for several years on many websites.*

GitHub as a Separate Entity. We present GitHub separately from Microsoft in Fig. 6 despite Microsoft's 2018 acquisition of GitHub, for two reasons: (1) GitHub maintains independent authentication infrastructure (https:// github.com/login/oauth) distinct from Microsoft's identity services (https://

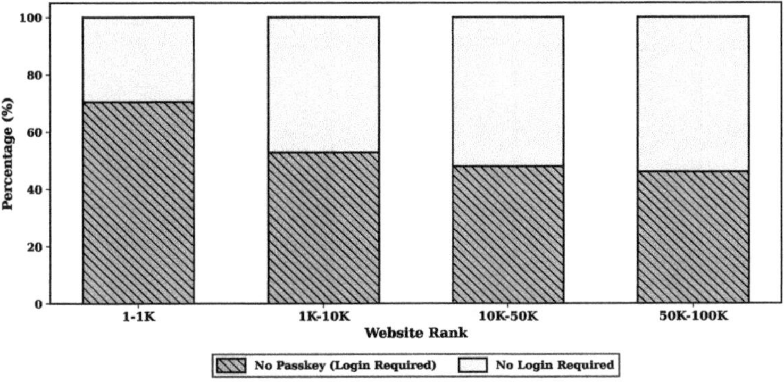

Fig. 5. Distribution of sites without passkey support, categorised by whether they require user login. Sites classified as "No Login Required" showed no recognised identity providers or authentication UI on their landing pages (e.g., content sites, news portals). Among non-passkey sites, the proportion with login functionality increases in lower rank bins, indicating that many sites have authentication systems but have not yet adopted passkeys.

login.microsoftonline.com, https://login.live.com), and (2) developer communities typically perceive and use GitHub OAuth as a distinct identity provider, particularly for technical platforms targeting software developers. Merging the two would obscure this important distinction in adoption patterns across different user demographics.

Figure 7 categorizes passkey-supporting sites by detection method. API Instrumentation (monitoring `navigator.credentials` calls) captured the most reliable implementations, detecting 82.3% of passkey sites across all rank bins. Login Page Analysis (button text and in-page keyword matching) detected 4.5% of sites, indicating that most passkey implementations do not expose visible UI elements. JavaScript Libraries detected 18.6%, OAuth Enterprise integrations (Microsoft/Google OAuth with WebAuthn support) detected 11.4%, and External IdPs (transitive passkey support via OAuth) detected 75.2% (note: categories overlap, as sites may trigger multiple heuristics). This demonstrates that **static HTML analysis is fundamentally insufficient** for passkey measurement: API instrumentation via browser automation is essential for reliable detection.

Figure 8 shows the geographic distribution of passkey-supporting websites based on geolocation.

Geolocation Methodology. We determine website location using a multi-step process: (1) we resolve the domain's authoritative DNS records to obtain IP addresses; (2) we query the WhoisXML API GeoIP service (https://ip-geolocation.whoisxmlapi.com/api) to map IP addresses to geographic locations; (3) for sites using Content Delivery Networks (CDNs), we attempt to identify the origin server by examining `X-Served-By`, `X-Cache`, and similar headers that reveal backend infrastructure, then geolocate the origin IP rather than edge server IPs. For sites employing anycast routing (where the same IP address is

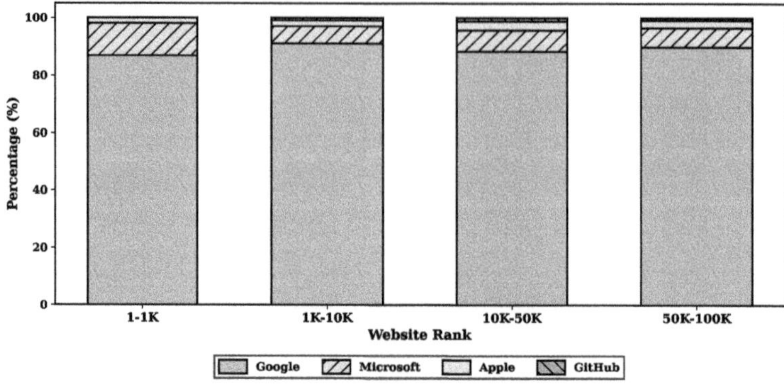

Fig. 6. External identity provider distribution among passkey-supporting sites. Breakdown of third-party authentication providers (Google, Microsoft, Apple, Github) detected on websites that offer passkey support alongside federated login options. Google dominates across all rank ranges, appearing on approx. *70-75%* of sites with external IDPs, followed by Microsoft *15-18%*, Apple *8-12%*, and Github *5-8%*. The consistency of these proportions across rank bins indicates standardized adoption pattern in the external authentication system.

announced from multiple geographic locations), we acknowledge this introduces potential bias, as anycast-enabled sites may be attributed to US locations. To mitigate this, we cross-referenced our geolocation data with WHOIS registration information where available, finding 94.2% agreement between IP geolocation and registration country for sites outside major CDNs.

The United States dominates with 5,133 sites (55.1% of geolocated passkey sites), followed by Canada (22.1%), Germany (3.6%), United Kingdom (2.8%), and France (2.1%). This geographic concentration reflects both internet infrastructure distribution and the regional dominance of U.S.-based web services. The logarithmic colour scale enables visualisation of countries with fewer sites, revealing global but highly uneven adoption patterns. Notably, passkey adoption in Asia-Pacific (excluding China, which has limited Tranco representation due to the Great Firewall) is lower than expected, with Japan (1.2%), India (0.9%), and Australia (1.4%) showing modest adoption despite large internet user populations.

To understand which sectors have embraced passkeys most readily, we analyzed the distribution of passkey-supporting sites across website categories. Using domain classification data from whoisxmlapi.com, we categorized each passkey-supporting site by its primary industry vertical. Figure 9 presents this distribution, revealing considerable concentration among certain sectors.

The results show that passkey adoption varies substantially across website categories, with a heavy tail distribution. The top three categories account for 69.5% of passkey-supporting sites: Business and Finance (26.5%), Shopping (22.0%), Technology & Computing (9.4%), Style & Fashion (6.9%), and Personal Finance (4.7%). Business and Finance leads adoption decisively, which aligns

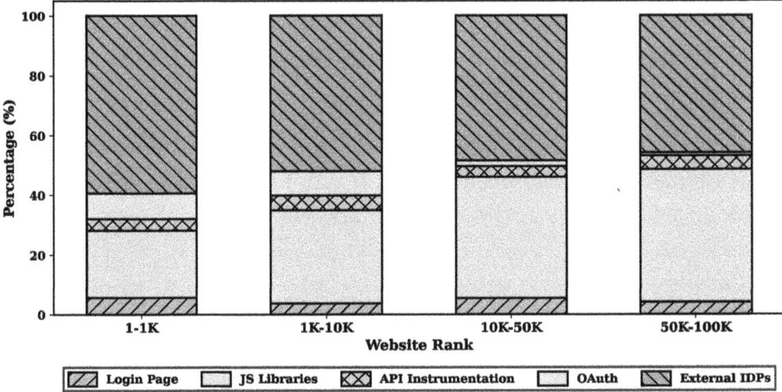

Fig. 7. Distribution of passkey-supporting sites categorized by detection method: Login Page analysis (Button, In-Page Text), JavaScript Libraries, API Instrumentation (navigator. credentials calls), OAuth Enterprise integrations, and External IDPs. API Instrumentation captured the most reliable implementations across all rank bins.

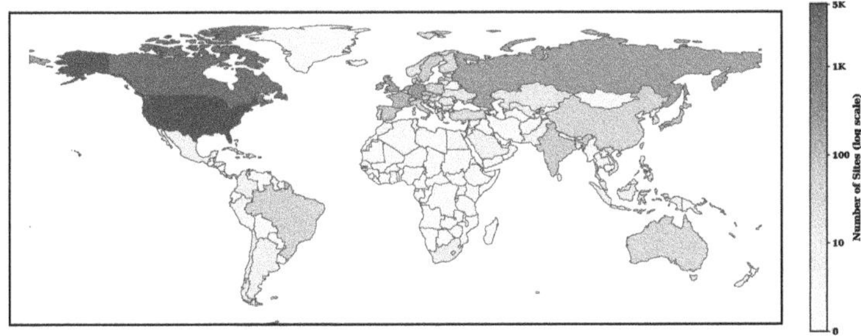

Fig. 8. Geographic distribution of passkey-supporting websites. World map heatmap showing the concentration of passkey adoption by country, derived from IP geolocation of domains supporting passkey authentication. The United States dominates with 5,133 sites (*55.1%* of geolocated passkey sites), followed by Canada (*22.1%*), and Germany (*3.6%*). This geographic concentration reflects both internet infrastructure distribution and the regional dominance of U.S.-based web services. The logarithmic colour scale enables visualization of countries with fewer sites, revealing global but highly uneven adoption patterns.

with this sector's higher security requirements and regulatory compliance. E-commerce sites (Shopping) follow closely. Technology companies, despite being early adopters of new authentication standards, represent a smaller proportion. Beyond the top five, adoption becomes sparse. Family and Relationships (4.3%), Travel (3.9%), Education (2.3%), and Community & Society (1.6%) show moderate uptake. Entertainment categories like video gaming, Streaming, and Books collectively represent less than 2% of categorised passkey sites.

Critical Services Analysis. From a security perspective, it is particularly important to understand passkey adoption in sectors handling sensitive data. Our analysis reveals:

- **Banking and Financial Services:** Within the Business and Finance category, we identified 847 banking and financial services sites. Of these, 312 (36.8%) support passkeys, the highest adoption rate among critical sectors. Major banks including Bank of America, Chase, and PayPal have implemented passkey support, though many regional and international banks remain without passwordless options.
- **Healthcare:** Healthcare and medical services sites show concerning under-representation, with only 89 sites (0.9% of passkey-supporting sites) in our dataset. Given the sensitivity of medical records and regulatory requirements (e.g., HIPAA in the US), this sector presents significant room for improvement.
- **E-commerce:** The Shopping category (22.0% of passkey sites) indicates strong adoption among online retailers, driven by fraud reduction incentives. Major platforms including Amazon, eBay, and Shopify have implemented passkeys.
- **Government Services:** Government and public sector sites account for only 1.1% of passkey-supporting sites (103 sites), despite handling sensitive citizen data. This represents a notable gap in passwordless adoption for critical infrastructure.

Overall, this pattern suggests that passkeys have primarily focused on sectors with immediate economic incentives (fraud reduction in finance and e-commerce), whilst healthcare, government, and educational services which arguably handle equally sensitive data lag behind.

6 Related Work

Authentication Mechanism Measurements. Password security weaknesses have been extensively documented. Bonneau [7] analyzed 70 million Yahoo passwords, revealing widespread use of weak, guessable passwords. Das et al. [8] demonstrated password reuse prevalence across services, enabling credential stuffing. These foundational studies established passwords as fundamentally insecure, motivating alternatives. Prior work measured MFA deployment. Reese et al. [28] conducted user surveys to understand adoption barriers for hardware security keys. Cristofaro et al. [11] analyzed Twitter's MFA, reporting fewer than 2% of accounts enabled any 2FA despite high-profile takeovers. Studies of SMS authentication highlighted vulnerabilities including SIM-swapping [30,32]. These findings motivated interest in phishing-resistant alternatives like FIDO2, but prior work did not systematically measure FIDO2/passkey deployment, a gap this work addresses. SSO measurement benefited from standardized discovery. Zhou and Evans [38] analyzed OAuth implementations on 96 sites, discovering widespread vulnerabilities. Sun and Beznosov [34] surveyed 500 Facebook

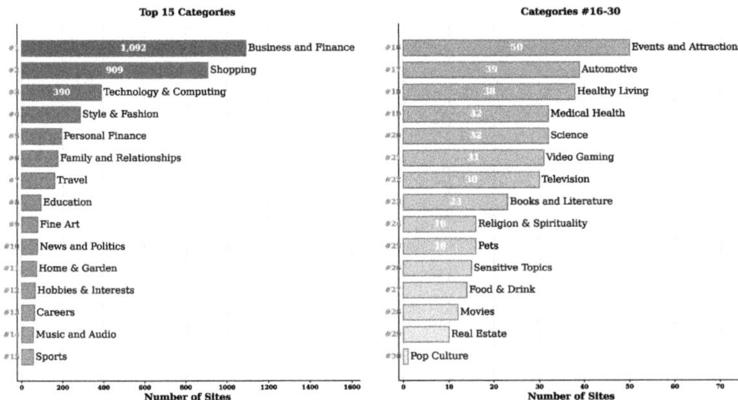

Fig. 9. Distribution of passkey-supporting sites by website category, the top five categories account for 69.5% of passkey adoption: Business and Finance (26.5%), Shopping (22.0%), Technology & Computing (9.4%), Style & Fashion (6.9%), and Personal Finance (4.7%). Business and Finance leads decisively, reflecting higher security requirements and economic incentives in financial sectors. Entertainment and content-focused categories show minimal adoption, suggesting passkey deployment is primarily driven by fraud reduction and regulatory compliance rather than technical enthusiasm alone.

Connect sites, identifying integration errors. OAuth's `.well-known` endpoints enabled automated detection. Passkeys lack such mechanisms, complicating our measurement task. We extend SSO methodologies to the passkey domain, developing novel heuristics.

WebAuthn and FIDO2 Studies. WebAuthn security properties have been rigorously analyzed. Barbosa et al. [5] provided formal proof of protocol security, demonstrating resistance to credential theft, phishing, and MitM attacks. Ulqinaku et al. [35] investigated real-time phishing (relaying challenges), showing traditional credential phishing is eliminated but session token theft post-authentication remains viable. Schwarz et al. [31] proposed FeIDo for recoverable FIDO2 credentials using eIDs. These protocol-level studies took deployment as given. Our work empirically tests that assumption. Usability research identified adoption barriers. Lyastani et al. [21] compared FIDO2 security keys with passwords/SMS 2FA, finding strong protection but setup complexity. Das et al. [9] studied security key adoption among Google employees, reporting friction during enrollment. Recently, Kunke et al. [17] showed users found passkeys more convenient than passwords but expressed confusion about synchronization. Lassak et al. [18] investigated user understanding, revealing misconceptions about biometric authentication and cloud storage. These usability studies provide valuable insights but rely on lab settings or surveys. Our measurement complements these by quantifying how many users actually encounter passkey options in the wild.

Web Crawling and Large-Scale Measurement. Traditional crawlers fetch raw HTML, failing on JavaScript-heavy modern websites. Lauinger et al. [19] highlighted this limitation when studying JavaScript library vulnerabilities, noting static scrapers missed dynamically loaded scripts. Nikiforakis et al. [26] demonstrated that client-side JavaScript often modifies the DOM post-load, rendering static analysis incomplete. Browser-based crawling addresses these issues but at higher computational cost. Bock [6] conducted a thesis measuring WebAuthn adoption using distributed browser automation, comparing Playwright with static scraping. He found browser methods increased detection by 47% but required 20× more resources. Our work builds on Bock's methodology, refining detection heuristics and scaling to larger datasets. Distributed crawling architectures are necessary for large-scale measurements. Our FIDENTIKIT adopts task queues and worker pools similar to prior systems, adapted to login page detection challenges. Le Pochat et al. [20] introduced Tranco, a domain ranking aggregating multiple sources with temporal stability filters, more robust than Alexa. We adopt Tranco for measurements, following best practices.

7   Conclusion

Passkeys represent a technically sound approach to eliminating password vulnerabilities, yet their adoption across the web remains far from the industry's aspirational vision of a passwordless future. This paper presented Fidentikit, the first comprehensive browser-based measurement framework for detecting passkey support at scale, and applied it to the Tranco Top 100K websites. Our key findings reveal that 11.3% of scanned sites support passkeys. This is 62× more sites than reported by the largest manually curated directory, which indicates an encouraging upward trajectory in usage of passkeys. However, adoption is heavily concentrated among popular (high-traffic) destinations and often depends on external identity providers rather than native WebAuthn implementations. We demonstrated that 82.3% of passkey deployments require JavaScript execution and API instrumentation to detect, rendering static HTML analysis fundamentally insufficient.

By releasing Fidentikit as open-source infrastructure along with our detection heuristics and measurement data, we enable the research community to conduct reproducible, longitudinal studies of passkey adoption. Our work provides a grounded, empirical foundation for understanding the current state of passwordless authentication on the web, informing both researchers studying authentication security and practitioners working to accelerate passkey deployment.

Source Code. Source Code. *Fidentikit* is available at https://netsys.surrey.ac.uk/softwares/fidentikit/ with a single-run feature (to scan individual domains) and webview interface with API endpoints for dataset download. The source code is available at https://github.com/socsys/fidentikit.

Appendix

A Dashboard View

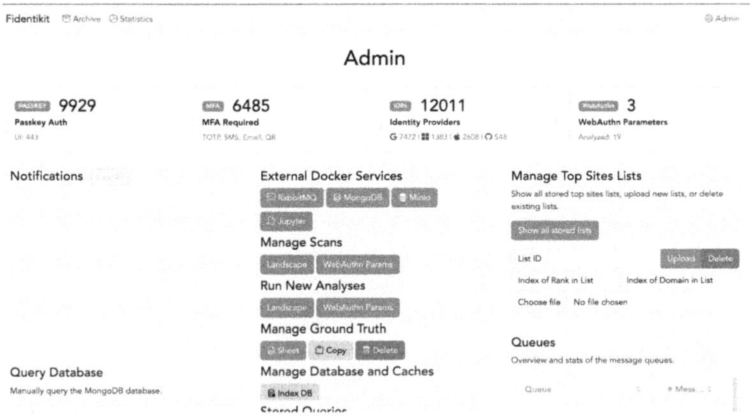

Fig. 10. Admin Dashboard.

B Detection Heuristics Catalogue

This appendix provides the complete specification of detection heuristics implemented in Fidentikit. We organise them by detection class.

B.1 JavaScript Pattern Detection

Table 3 lists the regular expressions used to detect WebAuthn implementation patterns in inline and external JavaScript. These patterns target actual passkey functionality rather than mere API availability.

B.2 UI Element Detection Patterns

Table 4 specifies CSS selectors and text patterns used for UI-based passkey detection. We filter social media icons to reduce false positives.

B.3 Text Keyword Patterns

Table 5 lists the keyword patterns used for text-based passkey detection, organised by confidence level.

Table 3. JavaScript WebAuthn Implementation Detection Patterns

ID	Confidence	Pattern/Description
JS-1	HIGH	`navigator\.credentials\.create\s*\(\s*\{[\s\S]*?publicKey\s*:` WebAuthn credential creation with publicKey options
JS-2	HIGH	`navigator\.credentials\.get\s*\(\s*\{[\s\S]*?publicKey\s*:` WebAuthn credential retrieval with publicKey options
JS-3	HIGH	`PublicKeyCredential\.isUserVerifyingPlatformAuthenticatorAvailable` Platform authenticator availability check
JS-4	HIGH	`PublicKeyCredential\.isConditionalMediationAvailable` Conditional mediation (autofill) support check
JS-5	MEDIUM	`\.getCredential\s*\(\s*\{[\s\S]*?type\s*:\s*['"]public-key['"]` Credential API with public-key type
JS-6	MEDIUM	`authenticatorAttachment\s*:\s*['"]platform['"]` Platform authenticator configuration
JS-7	MEDIUM	`authenticatorAttachment\s*:\s*['"]cross-platform['"]` Roaming authenticator (security key) configuration
JS-8	MEDIUM	`userVerification\s*:\s*['"]preferred|required['"]` User verification requirement configuration
JS-9	MEDIUM	`"challenge"\s*:\s*["'][A-Za-z0-9+/=]+["']` WebAuthn challenge data (Base64-encoded)
JS-10	MEDIUM	`"publicKey"\s*:\s*\{[\s\S]*?"challenge"\s*:` PublicKey credential options object
JS-11	MEDIUM	`residentKey\s*:\s*['"]required|preferred['"]` Discoverable credential (passkey) requirement

Table 4. UI Element Detection Selectors and Patterns

ID	Type	Selector/Pattern
UI-1	Button Text	`/(passkey|sign.in.with.passkey|continue.with.passkey|use.passkey)/i`
UI-2	Biometric Text	`/(fingerprint|face.?id|touch.?id|biometric|windows.?hello)/i` combined with `/(sign.?in|log.?in|login|continue)/i`
UI-3	Data Attributes	`[data-webauthn]`, `[data-passkey]`, `[data-credential]`
UI-4	Auth Method Attr	`[data-authentication-method="passkey"]`, `[data-auth-type="passkey"]`
UI-5	Credential Inputs	`input[autocomplete="webauthn"]`, `input[type="publickey"]`
UI-6	ARIA Labels	`button[aria-label*="passkey"]`, `[role="button"][aria-label*="security key"]`
UI-7	Images/Icons	`img[alt*="passkey"]`, `svg[aria-label*="fingerprint"]`

B.4　API Instrumentation Code

A JavaScript shim injected via Playwright's `addInitScript` to intercept WebAuthn API calls. The shim wraps `navigator.credentials.create()` and `navigator.credentials.get()`, capturing invocation parameters including challenge data, authenticator selection, and user verification requirements.

B.5　Third-Party Identity Provider Detection

Table 6 summarises the OAuth flow detection rules for major identity providers. Detection combines network request interception with SDK signature matching.

Table 5. Passkey Text Detection Keywords

ID	Confidence	Pattern
KW-1	HIGH	`sign\s+in\s+with\s+passkey`
KW-2	HIGH	`login\s+with\s+passkey`
KW-3	HIGH	`use\s+passkey`
KW-4	HIGH	`continue\s+with\s+passkey`
KW-5	HIGH	`passkey\s+authentication`
KW-6	MEDIUM	`passkey` (standalone)
KW-7	MEDIUM	`webauthn`
KW-8	LOW	`biometric\s+login`
KW-9	LOW	`passwordless\s+login`
KW-10	LOW	`login\s+without\s+password`

Table 6. Third-Party Identity Provider Detection Rules

Provider	Domain Pattern	Path Pattern	SDK Signatures
Google	`^accounts\.google\.com$`	`/gsi/select, /oauth2`	`gapi.auth2, google.accounts.id`
Apple	`^appleid\.apple\.com$`	`/auth/authorize`	`AppleID.auth`
Microsoft	`^login\.(live|microsoftonline)\.com$`	`/oauth`	`msal.js, @azure/msal-browser`
GitHub	`^github\.com$`	`/login/oauth`	`-`
Facebook	`facebook\.com$`	`/dialog/oauth`	`FB.login`

References

1. Rabbitmq (2025). https://www.rabbitmq.com/. Official project site and documentation. Accessed 16 Oct 2025
2. 1Password. Passkeys.directory: Community-driven index of passkey-supporting sites. Crowdsourced passkey listings (2025)
3. 2FA.directory. Passkey directory, 2024. Index of FIDO2/WebAuthn-enabled services
4. Apple Developer. Meet passkeys – wwdc 22 (2022). Accessed 2025 05 June
5. Barbosa, M., Boldyreva, A., Chen, S., Warinschi, B.: Provable security analysis of fido2. In: Proceedings of the 41st Annual International Cryptology Conference (2021), CRYPTO '21, Springer, pp. 125–156 (2021)
6. Bock, M.: Measuring adoption of phishing-resistant authentication methods on the web. Master's thesis, Stuttgart Media University, Stuttgart, Germany, June 2023
7. Bonneau, J., Herley, C., van Oorschot, P.C., Stajano, F.: The quest to replace passwords: A framework for comparative evaluation of web authentication schemes. Technical Report UCAM-CL-TR-817, University of Cambridge, Computer Laboratory, March 2012
8. Das, A., Bonneau, J., Caesar, M., Borisov, N., Wang, X.: The tangled web of password reuse. In: Proceedings of the 2014 Network and Distributed System Security Symposium, NDSS '14, The Internet Society (2014)

9. Das, S., Dingman, A., Camp, L.J.: Why johnny doesn't use two factor: a two-phase usability study of the fido u2f security key. In: Proceedings of the International Conference on Financial Cryptography and Data Security (2018), FC '18. Springer, pp. 160–179
10. Dashlane. Passkeys directory, 2025. User-submitted passkey site listings
11. De Cristofaro, E., Du, H., Freudiger, J., Norcie, G.: A comparative usability study of two-factor authentication. In: Proceedings of the Workshop on Usable Security (2019), USEC '19, Internet Society
12. FIDO Alliance. Fido2: Web authentication (webauthn) specification (2019)
13. FIDO Alliance. Fido u2f overview (2025). https://fidoalliance.org/specs/u2f-specs-master/fido-u2f-overview.html. Accessed 16 Oct 2025
14. FIDO Alliance. Passkeys directory. Interactive listing of known passkey deployments (2025)
15. Google Safety & Security Blog. The beginning of the end of the password, (2022). Accessed 05 June 2025
16. Jannett, L., Westers, M., Wich, T., Mainka, C., Mayer, A., Mladenov, V.: Sok: Sso-monitor - the current state and future research directions in single sign-on security measurements. In: 2024 IEEE 9th European Symposium on Security and Privacy (EuroS&P), pp. 173–192 (2024)
17. Kunke, J., Wiefling, S., Ullmann, M., Lo Iacono, L.: Evaluation of account recovery strategies with fido2-based passwordless authentication. In: Proceedings of the 18th International Conference on Availability, Reliability and Security, ARES '23. ACM (2023)
18. Lassak, L., Pan, E., Ur, B., Golla, M.: Why aren't we using passkeys? obstacles companies face deploying FIDO2 passwordless authentication. In: 33rd USENIX Security Symposium (USENIX Security 24), Philadelphia, PA. USENIX Association, pp. 7231–7248, August 2024
19. Lauinger, T., Chaabane, A., Arshad, S., Robertson, W., Wilson, C., Kirda, E.: Thou shalt not depend on me: Analysing the use of outdated javascript libraries on the web. In: Proceedings of the 2017 Network and Distributed System Security Symposium, NDSS '17, The Internet Society (2017)
20. Le Pochat, V., Van Goethem, T., Tajalizadehkhoob, S., Korczyński, M., Joosen, W.: Tranco: a research-oriented top sites ranking hardened against manipulation. In: 28th USENIX Security Symposium (USENIX Security 19) (2018)
21. Lyastani, S.G., Schilling, M., Neumayr, M., Backes, M., Bugiel, S.: Is fido2 the kingslayer of user authentication? a comparative usability study of fido2 passwordless authentication. In: Proceedings of the 2020 IEEE Symposium on Security and Privacy, SP '20, pp. 268–285. IEEE (2020)
22. MDN Web Docs. Credentialscontainer.get(), 2025. MDN reference for WebAuthn assertion API
23. Microsoft Playwright contributors. Playwright. https://playwright.dev/, 2025. Playwright – cross-browser web automation framework. Repository: https://github.com/microsoft/playwright Accessed 16 Oct 2025
24. Microsoft Security Blog. Pushing passkeys forward: Microsoft's latest updates for simpler, safer sign-ins (2025). Accessed 06 May 2025
25. National Cyber Security Centre (NCSC). Government to adopt passkey technology for digital services. https://www.ncsc.gov.uk/news/government-adopt-passkey-technology-digital-services (2025). Accessed 16 Oct 2025
26. Nikiforakis, N., et al.: You are what you include: Large-scale evaluation of remote javascript inclusions. In: Proceedings of the 2012 ACM Conference on Computer and Communications Security (2012), CCS '12. ACM, pp. 736–747

27. Prometheus Authors. Prometheus: Monitoring system and time series database (2025). https://prometheus.io/. Official project site and documentation. Accessed 16 Oct 2025
28. Reese, K., Smith, T., Dutson, J., Armknecht, J., Cameron, J.,Seamons, K.: A usability study of five two-factor authentication methods. In: Proceedings of the Fifteenth Symposium on Usable Privacy and Security, SOUPS '19, USENIX Association, pp. 357–370 (2019)
29. Satragno, N., Hodges, J.: Explainer: Webauthn conditional ui. W3C WebAuthn Wiki, October 2022. Accessed 13 Oct 2025
30. Schartner, P., Burger, S.: Attacking mtan-applications like e-banking and mobile signatures. Technical Report TR-syssec-11-01, University of Klagenfurt, December 2011
31. Schwarz, F., Do, K., Heide, G.: Feido: recoverable fido2 tokens using electronic ids. In: Proceedings of the 2022 ACM SIGSAC Conference on Computer and Communications Security (2022), CCS '22. ACM, pp. 2581–2594
32. Siadati, H., Saket, B., Tovanich, N., Memon, N.: Mind your smses: mitigating social engineering in second factor authentication. Comput. Secur. **65**, 14–28 (2017)
33. Stajano, F.: Pico: No more passwords! In: International Workshop on Security Protocols, pp. 49–81. Springer (2011)
34. Sun, S.-T., Beznosov, K.: The devil is in the (implementation) details: An empirical analysis of oauth sso systems. In: Proceedings of the 2012 ACM Conference on Computer and Communications Security, CCS '12, pp. 378–390. ACM (2012)
35. Ulqinaku, E., Lain, D., Capkun, S.: Is real-time phishing eliminated with fido? social engineering downgrade attacks against fido protocols. In: Proceedings of the 30th USENIX Security Symposium (2021), Security '21. USENIX Association, pp. 3811–3828
36. W3C. Web authentication: An api for accessing public key credentials – level 2 recommendation. W3C Recommendation, April 2021
37. World Wide Web Consortium (Web Application Security Working Group). A well-known url for relying party passkey endpoints. W3C First Public Working Draft, Aug. 2025. First Public Working Draft (21 August 2025). Accessed 16 Oct 2025
38. Zhou, Y., Evans, D.: Ssoscan: automated testing of web applications for single sign-on vulnerabilities. In: Proceedings of the 23rd USENIX Security Symposium, Security 2014. USENIX Association, pp. 495–510 (2014)

Efficient System Log Analysis via Quantized On-Device Anomaly Detection and Response

Qinxuan Shi, Zhanglong Yang, and Sicong Shao[✉]

School of Electrical Engineering and Computer Science, University of North Dakota, Grand Forks, ND 58202, USA
sicong.shao@und.edu

Abstract. The rapid expansion of the Internet of Things (IoT) and the growing interconnectivity of industrial systems have created an urgent need for log anomaly detection (LAD) to be performed locally on edge devices. However, a significant gap exists between the computational resources required by advanced deep learning models and the limited processing capacity of edge hardware, often forcing a trade-off between detection accuracy and deployment feasibility. To address this challenge, this paper makes two major contributions. First, we introduce EM-AT-based LAD by designing an unsupervised LAD method that extends the Transformer-based anomaly detection model via integrating the Expectation-Maximization (EM) algorithm for fully automated threshold determination. While EM-AT-based LAD achieves high detection accuracy, its computational requirement limits its direct applicability on power-constrained edge devices. Therefore, we introduce Lite-LADR, a framework that enables efficient system log analysis via quantized on-device anomaly detection and response. LiteLADR leverages TorchAO and ExecuTorch for model quantization and optimization, enabling both EM-AT and large language models (LLMs) to operate efficiently on resource-constrained edge nodes. Comprehensive evaluations on the HDFS and OpenStack datasets show that EM-AT outperforms leading methods, achieving F_1-scores of 98.90% and 99.61%, respectively. LiteLADR preserves strong detection performance (F_1-scores of 98.65% and 99.43%) while substantially reducing computational resource consumption.

Keywords: System Security · Software Security · IoT · Edge Inference · Anomaly Detection · LLM

1   Introduction

In recent decades, modern software and systems have become significantly more complex and scaled, resulting in the generation of large volumes of system log

S. Ferlin-Reiter et al. (Eds.): PAM 2026, LNCS 16477, pp. 348–373, 2026.
https://doi.org/10.1007/978-3-032-18268-5_16

data. These data are critical sources of runtime information, enabling the diagnosis of system anomalies, computer troubleshooting, and performance optimization [20,48]. With rapid technological advancements and widespread adoption of cloud and edge computing, automated log analysis has emerged as essential for ensuring system reliability and security [59]. However, the logging landscape in modern Internet of Things (IoT) ecosystems presents unique challenges distinct from traditional server environments. Heterogeneous devices, ranging from resource-constrained environmental sensors and microcontroller units (MCUs) to intelligent gateways, continuously generate diverse log streams. These logs often originate from embedded operating systems (e.g., FreeRTOS, Zephyr, or embedded Linux) and are transmitted via lightweight protocols such as MQTT or CoAP, creating a fragmented and high-volume data environment that traditional centralized analysis struggles to handle in real-time [24].

Conventional methods, such as manual inspections, rule-based, and traditional machine learning systems, are increasingly inadequate due to their inability to handle the growing complexity and sheer volume of log data effectively and efficiently [20,23]. Deep learning approaches for LAD have demonstrated high effectiveness by capturing intricate sequential patterns and adapting dynamically to complex log data. Notable examples such as DeepLog [12], HitAnomaly [22], and LogFiT [2] have shown outstanding detection performance on standard datasets. However, these methods typically involve substantial computational overhead and memory requirements, making their deployment particularly challenging on computational resource-constrained edge devices (e.g., single-board computers, sensors, and medical wearable devices).

Meanwhile, the rapid growth of the IoT and Cyber-Physical Systems (CPS), combined with increasing demand for real-time applications and distributed computing, has made edge devices integral to modern computing system architectures [57]. Edge computing enables processing, storage, and analysis near data sources, improving quality-of-experience (QoE) and quality-of-service (QoS) and mitigating cloud-side challenges such as latency, bandwidth, and privacy risks [32,50]. In IoT deployments, including sensors, embedded controllers, and mobile devices, logs are continuously generated by lightweight operating systems, middleware, and application services [4,9,21,24,26]. Current LAD pipelines typically collect these logs at the edge and transmit them to a centralized cloud server, where more complex machine learning models perform analysis. While effective in terms of accuracy, this architecture introduces substantial communication latency, increases bandwidth consumption, and exposes sensitive operational logs to security and privacy risks during transmission [34].

To address these limitations, LiteLADR enables the deployment of Transformer models and uses RAG-enhanced LLM responses for LAD at the edge, close to where logs are produced. In a modern IoT architecture, LiteLADR is designed to serve as an intelligent edge gateway. It aggregates raw logs from downstream sensors and embedded devices that lack sufficient onboard compute for heavy inference, processing data locally on the gateway level (e.g., a Raspberry Pi or NVIDIA Jetson-class device). It converts both the anomaly detection model and the integrated LLM-based response module into lightweight Execu-Torch programs [37], enabling efficient on-device anomaly detection and fault response without requiring cloud connectivity. As a result, LiteLADR offers a practical solution that enables IoT devices to perform local inference with minimal latency and high accuracy, preserves privacy by keeping logs on-device, and thus improves the reliability and security of modern systems.

To address the challenge of improving unsupervised anomaly-detection performance, we introduce the EM-AT model, a powerful unsupervised anomaly detection model that enhances the AT model by integrating the EM algorithm. Unlike AT, which relies on manually tuned thresholds, EM-AT adopts a data-driven EM-GMM-derived method to enable automated threshold determination. This design improves both the efficiency and effectiveness of the framework, particularly in edge environments where multiple devices operate simultaneously, making manual tuning for each model impractical and error-prone. In addition, we employ ExecuTorch to enable efficient operation of the EM-AT model on resource-constrained edge devices while preserving detection performance. The combination of EM-AT and ExecuTorch ensures our framework delivers robust detection results on resource-constrained edge devices without requiring human intervention.

The key contributions of this paper are as follows:

- We propose LiteLADR, a framework that enables efficient system log analysis via quantized on-device anomaly detection and response. LiteLADR leverages ExecuTorch [37] to convert deep learning models into ExecuTorch programs, enabling efficient execution on resource-constrained edge devices while maintaining performance comparable to the original models. In addition, Lite-LADR integrates an RAG-enhanced LLM-based response module, which is also optimized using ExecuTorch to support on-device inference and deliver context-aware responses for effective problem solving.
- We present EM-AT-based LAD as the core component of LiteLADR, where a highly effective unsupervised anomaly detection model that builds on the Anomaly Transformer (AT) architecture to enhance LAD performance. EM-AT replaces the K-Means-based Gap-Statistic threshold selection method in Anomaly Transformer with an EM-fitted Gaussian Mixture Model (GMM), with the number of clusters selected using the Bayesian Information Criterion (BIC). This approach fully automates the threshold calculation without human intervention, which was required in the original Anomaly Transformer model. In edge environments, where multiple devices typically operate simultaneously, a scalable, hands-free detection model is crucial for enhancing overall system efficiency.
- LiteLADR's performance was rigorously evaluated on the HDFS and Open-Stack datasets. Experimental results demonstrate that EM-AT surpasses the leading LAD methods, such as DeepLog [12] and MDFULog [27]. Furthermore, the LiteLADR preserves strong anomaly detection capability while reducing computational resource consumption.

The remainder of this paper is structured as follows. Section 2 presents a review of related work. Section 3 introduces the framework of LiteLADR and details its components. Experimental results are discussed in Sect. 4. Finally, Sect. 5 concludes the paper.

2   Related Work

2.1   Log Anomaly Detection (LAD)

LAD has been a foundational technique for monitoring system activities and uncovering potential security risks. Early techniques primarily relied on manual inspection or rule-based methods for LAD. For example, Hansen et al. [17] developed a configurable log file filter to help the system administrator monitor events on servers and workstations. Rouillard et al. [47] implemented a rule-based simple event correlator for log analysis. However, these traditional approaches often prove inefficient and inadequate when confronting modern, increasingly sophisticated cyberattacks. To overcome these limitations, machine learning techniques have been introduced to automatically identify patterns and anomalies in system logs. Liang et al. [29] extracted failure characteristics first and then predicted failures using the rule-based classifier, along with one SVM and two Nearest Neighbor classifiers. Xu et al. [56] utilized Principal Component Analysis (PCA) to create normal and abnormal spaces for the log event count matrix to detect anomalies. However, these traditional machine learning-based methods struggle to handle large-scale datasets and identify complex patterns in high-dimensional log data.

Deep learning methods have gained popularity in recent years for LAD due to their ability to efficiently process large datasets and automatically learn relevant features. For instance, Deeplog [12] leveraged Long Short-Term Memory (LSTM) to model a system log as a natural language sequence, while Guo et al. [16] introduced LogBERT based on the bidirectional encoder representations from BERT to capture data patterns of normal log sequences. Qi et al. [43] proposed LogEncoder, a semi-supervised anomaly detection framework that supports both offline and online detection. It employs a pretrained model to generate semantic vectors of log events. Additionally, Xiao et al. [53] proposed Loader, a semi-supervised LAD method built upon the Transformer architecture. Shi et al. [49] presented an Anomaly Transformer-based architecture for system log anomaly detection. However, these leading methods still face notable limitations despite their promising performance. They often struggle to detect rare or subtle anomalies and tend to suffer from high false positive rates. Moreover, most are tailored for high-performance computing environments, overlooking the practical constraints of real-world deployments where models must operate efficiently on resource-limited edge devices.

2.2   LAD at the Edge

As the IoT continues to grow, edge devices with constrained computational capabilities (e.g., actuators, microcontroller units, and single-board computers) are producing increasing amounts of data, including system logs, network traffic, and audio/video content. Traditionally, these data are transmitted to centralized servers or cloud platforms for analysis, decision-making, storage, or anomaly detection [34]. While effective, such centralized processing incurs latency that can hinder real-time applications such as health monitoring and industrial control, and increases security risks by exposing transmitted data to interception and cyberattacks. Performing data processing directly on resource-constrained edge devices mitigates these issues by enabling real-time monitoring and anomaly detection without reliance on external computing resources [1]. Furthermore, these devices can operate and detect anomalies even without network connectivity, ensuring dependable performance in remote or offline environments.

LAD methods for computational resource-constrained environments remain unexplored, with only limited research addressing this area. For example, Wang et al. [52] introduced LightLog, a log anomaly detection method built on Temporal Convolutional Networks (TCN). It applies PCA with post-processing algorithms to reduce the dimensionality of semantic vectors generated from log templates. Similarly, Chen et al. [7] proposed EdgeLog, which builds on a compressed TCN and introduces a tree-structured framework and deployment scheme for cloud-edge collaborative systems. In addition, Nguyen et al. [40] use a Word2Vec model combined with GRU and knowledge distillation to develop DistilLog, a lightweight approach for system log anomaly detection that reduces computational and storage overhead. However, existing approaches such as LightLog and EdgeLog primarily emphasize operational metrics (i.e., floating-point operations and parameter counts) while overlooking computational resource consumption. Although DistilLog reports peak CPU and memory usage, it still lacks a holistic analysis that jointly considers resource consumption and anomaly detection performance. In contrast, our framework provides a comprehensive evaluation by capturing a broader range of metrics and integrating an efficient RAG-enhanced LLM response module. This design enhances problem-solving efficiency and improves the framework's suitability for deployment on resource-constrained edge devices, thereby increasing system reliability and security.

3   Proposed Framework

3.1   Framework Overview

In this section, we introduce LiteLADR, a framework designed to enable efficient system log analysis via quantized on-device anomaly detection and response. As shown in Fig. 1, the framework consists of four key modules: data processing, a lightweight anomaly detector, an LLM-based response module, and edge deployment. Critically, LiteLADR is architected to support hierarchical IoT deployments. While ultra-low-power sensors and MCUs (e.g., actuators, temperature sensors) focus solely on data acquisition and basic logging, LiteLADR resides on the aggregation node or edge gateway. This gateway intercepts log streams from these downstream peripherals before they traverse the wide-area network. The

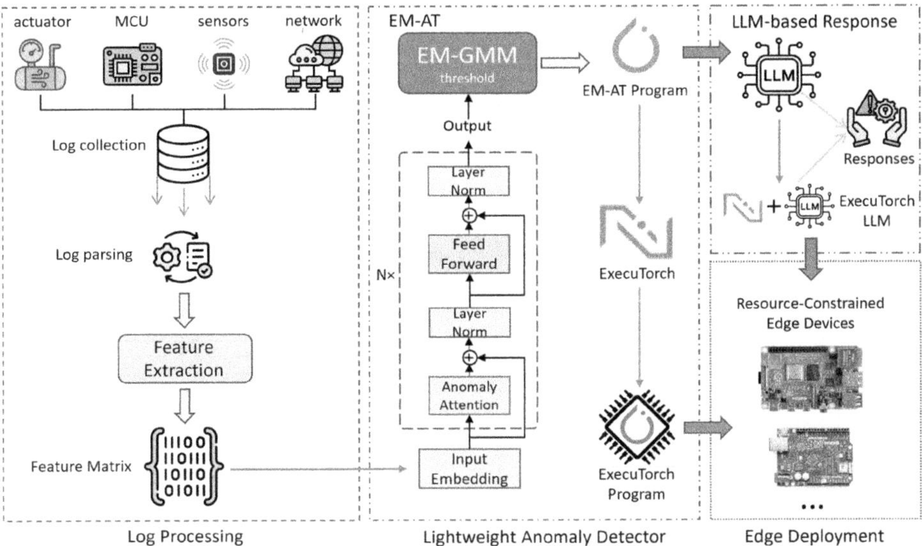

Fig. 1. The overall architecture of LiteLADR. The framework consists of four main modules: the log processing module transforms raw log data into a feature matrix; the lightweight anomaly detector, built on the EM-AT model and optimized using ExecuTorch for efficient inference; the LLM-based response module, which generates actionable responses and can also be optimized with ExecuTorch for on-device execution; and the edge deployment module, which runs the lightweight anomaly detector and LLM efficiently on computational resource constrained edge devices.

data processing component parses unstructured system logs received from various embedded endpoints into structured formats, applies feature extraction, and generates sequences that are transformed into feature vectors. The lightweight anomaly detector, built upon the proposed EM-AT model, is converted into an ExecuTorch program through model quantization and optimization using TorchAO and ExecuTorch. The LLM-based response module is similarly converted with ExecuTorch, enabling efficient on-device analysis of abnormal log messages and generation of actionable responses on resource-constrained edge devices. This local processing capability enables that critical alerts regarding sensor malfunctions or gateway operating system faults are handled immediately without the latency incurred by round-trip cloud communication. Finally, both the quantized anomaly detector and LLM are deployed on edge devices, achieving efficient system log analysis and response.

3.2   Log Data Processing

Large-scale systems routinely generate logs that capture system states and runtime behaviors, providing information relevant to diagnosability, maintenance, and performance [20]. A typical logging statement comprises three components:

Log Messages	

nova-compute.log.1.2017-05-16_13:55:31 2017-05-16 00:00:20.349 2931 INFO nova.virt.libvirt.imagecache [req-addc1839-2ed5-4778-b57e-5854eb7b8b09 - - - - -] Removing base or swap file: /var/lib/nova/instances/_base/a489c868f0c37da93b76227c91bb03908ac0e742
nova-api.log.1.2017-05-16_13:53:08 2017-05-16 00:00:21.067 25746 INFO nova.api.openstack.wsgi [req-0b851395-2895-44b9-8265-a27d0bb52910 f7b8d1f1d4d44643b07fa10ca7d021fb e9746973ac574c6b8a9e8857f56a7608 - - -] HTTP exception thrown: No instances found for any event
nova-api.log.1.2017-05-16_13:53:08 2017-05-16 00:00:21.069 25746 INFO nova.osapi_compute.wsgi.server [req-0b851395-2895-44b9-8265-a27d0bb52910 f7b8d1f1d4d44643b07fa10ca7d021fb e9746973ac574c6b8a9e8857f56a7608 - - -] 10.11.10.1 "POST /v2/e9746973ac574c6b8a9e8857f56a7608/os-server-external-events HTTP/1.1" status: 404 len: 296 time: 0.0793190

⇩

Parsed Logs				
Date	**Time**	**Level**	**Component**	**EventTemplate**
2017-05-16	00:00:20.349	INFO	nova.virt.libvirt.imagecache	Removing base or swap file: <*>
2017-05-16	00:00:21.067	INFO	nova.api.openstack.wsgi	HTTP exception thrown: No instances found for any event
2017-05-16	00:00:21.069	INFO	nova.osapi_compute.wsgi.server	<*> "POST <*>" status: <*> len: <*> time: <*>.<*>

Fig. 2. Examples of OpenStack log messages transformed into a structured format through log parsing.

verbosity level, static text, and dynamic content. The verbosity level indicates the importance or severity of the message; the static text is the fixed part of the log message to describe the event; and the dynamic content consists of the variables or values that are inserted into the log message. However, the resulting log messages are often unstructured or semi-structured, making manual analysis take considerable effort and time. To address this challenge and facilitate automated system log analysis, LiteLADR employs a data processing component to transform unstructured logs into a feature matrix. The data processing component of our framework handles the log data through three steps: log parsing, feature extraction, and sequence generation.

Log Parser. Log parsing is a critical initial step that extracts log templates and variables from log entries, converting them into a standardized format for further analysis. This transformation enables the construction of log sequences that facilitate anomaly detection. As illustrated in Fig. 2, log parsing extracts the event template, which captures the constant words in the log entry, and the placeholders <*> denote variable elements. Many log parsing techniques have been studied in academic literature, such as Drain [19], Spell [11], and Logram [8]. In this paper, we leverage Spell, a tool based on the longest common subsequence technique, to parse incoming logs and convert them into structured system logs. Spell outperforms other popular log parsers in both efficiency and effectiveness.

Feature Extractor. Partition and feature extraction are critical steps for converting textual log messages into numerical features suitable for machine learning algorithms. Common partition techniques include fixed partition, sliding partition, and identifier partition, which are widely used to group logs into sequences. These techniques effectively organize logs, such as those generated by concurrent processes, into distinct log sequences. Fixed partition and sliding partition are based on timestamps, while the identifier partition divides logs by log identifiers. After partition, log messages are represented by log keys extracted from the raw data. In this work, HDFS logs are partitioned using the identifier partition, while OpenStack logs are partitioned using the fixed partition. We then adopt a common strategy in deep learning-based methods for feature extraction, in which each log key's index corresponds to an individual element in the sequence.

Sequence Generator. Since the identifier partition is used to divide log messages into log sequences, the resulting sequences typically vary in length. Therefore, a sequence generator is needed to fit the data into the anomaly detection model and improve its performance. Specifically, we use a sliding window with a given window size j to extract context features for each log key. Here, we take the forward subsequence of each log key as its context. Assuming the dataset contains D distinct log keys, we assign an index $G \notin [1, D]$ to represent NO_EVENT, used for filling the sliding window when the available length of the forward subsequence is shorter than j. For example, given a numerical log key sequence $\{e_1, e_2, e_3, e_4, \dots\}$ and a sliding window size $j = 3$, the generated subsequences would be $\{G, G, G\}$, $\{G, G, e_1\}$, $\{G, e_1, e_2\}$, $\{e_1, e_2, e_3\}$, and so forth.

3.3   EM-AT for Unsupervised LAD

In the lightweight anomaly detector component, we first introduce the EM-AT model for unsupervised LAD. It extends the Anomaly Transformer [54] by integrating the EM algorithm to fully automate the threshold determination process. Instead of relying on manually tuned thresholds, EM-AT employs an EM-GMM-based, data-driven approach, thereby enhancing both reliability and efficiency in environments where numerous devices operate concurrently, particularly at the edge. The EM-AT model uses only the transformer's encoder structure and does not require abnormal data for training, making it well-suited for practical anomaly detection scenarios. In our implementation, we configure the EM-AT to include three identical layers ($N = 3$), where each layer contains two primary components: an Anomaly Attention layer and a feed-forward network. Besides, the multi-head self-attention layer in the original transformer is replaced with the Anomaly Attention layer in order to enhance anomaly detection performance. This layer consists of two branches, which enable it to calculate both the series association and prior association to get the global representations and adjacent data patterns from the log data simultaneously. By leveraging the Anomaly Attention mechanism, EM-AT enhances the distinction between normal and abnormal points, making log anomalies more identifiable and improving detection performance. With the integration of this model, LiteLADR can effectively handle complex LAD tasks while ensuring reliable and accurate detection results. In addition, the hidden channel dimension is set to 512, and the number of heads is set to 8. The Adam optimizer is employed with an initial learning rate of 10^{-4}.

The Anomaly Attention initialization in the n-th layer is defined as

$$\mathcal{K} = \mathcal{T}^{n-1}W_{\mathcal{K}}^n, \mathcal{Q} = \mathcal{T}^{n-1}W_{\mathcal{Q}}^n, \mathcal{V} = \mathcal{T}^{n-1}W_{\mathcal{V}}^n, \delta = \mathcal{T}^{n-1}W_{\delta}^n, \tag{1}$$

where $W_{\mathcal{Q}}^n, W_{\mathcal{K}}^n, W_{\mathcal{V}}^n, W_{\delta}^n$ are parameter matrices. The **prior association** in the Anomaly Attention mechanism is meant to build the associations from adjacent log keys. It leverages a learnable Gaussian kernel, making the prior association focus more on the adjacent data patterns. The prior-association in n-th layer $\mathcal{P}^n \in \mathbb{R}^{L \times L}$ is defined as

$$\mathcal{P}^n = \text{rescale}\left(\left[\frac{1}{\sqrt{2\pi}\delta_x}\exp\left(-\frac{|y-x|^2}{2\delta_x^2}\right)\right]_{x,y \in \{1,\cdots,L\}}\right). \tag{2}$$

Another branch of the Anomaly Attention mechanism, **series association**, is designed to capture global association patterns present in the data. The series association $\mathcal{S}^n \in \mathbb{R}^{L \times L}$ is computed as

$$\mathcal{S}^n = \text{softmax}\left(\frac{\mathcal{Q}\mathcal{K}^{\mathrm{T}}}{\sqrt{d_{\text{model}}}}\right). \tag{3}$$

The reconstruction in the n-th layer is computed as $\widehat{\mathcal{Z}}^n = \mathcal{S}^n\mathcal{V}$. To further capture the information gain between the series association and prior association, the association discrepancy is defined as the symmetrized Kullback-Leibler (KL) divergence between the two distributions:

$$\text{AssoD}(\mathcal{P}, \mathcal{S}; \mathcal{T}) = \left[\frac{1}{N}\sum_{n=1}^{N}\left(\text{KL}(\mathcal{P}_{x,:}^n\|\mathcal{S}_{x,:}^n) + \text{KL}(\mathcal{S}_{x,:}^n\|\mathcal{P}_{x,:}^n)\right)\right]_{x=1,\cdots,L}. \tag{4}$$

The model is optimized for an unsupervised task using the reconstruction loss, which also guides the model to understand the associations more accurately, and the loss function for EM-AT is defined as

$$\mathcal{L}_{\text{Total}}(\widehat{\mathcal{T}}, \mathcal{P}, \mathcal{S}, \mu; \mathcal{T}) = \|\mathcal{T} - \widehat{\mathcal{T}}\|_{\mathrm{F}}^2 - \mu \times \|\text{AssoD}(\mathcal{P}, \mathcal{S}; \mathcal{T})\|_1, \tag{5}$$

where $\widehat{\mathcal{T}}$ is used to represent the reconstruction of $\mathcal{T}$ and μ works as the loss weight. Moreover, a minimax strategy that involves trading off between two branches of the Anomaly Attention module is proposed. The minimax strategy contains two phases: the minimize phase and the maximize phase. In the minimize phase, the loss function is defined as $\mathcal{L}_{\text{Total}}(\widehat{\mathcal{T}}, \mathcal{P}, \mathcal{S}_{\text{detach}}, -\mu; \mathcal{T})$. While in the maximize phase, the loss function becomes $\mathcal{L}_{\text{Total}}(\widehat{\mathcal{T}}, \mathcal{P}_{\text{detach}}, \mathcal{S}, \mu; \mathcal{T})$.

In the end, the anomaly score that is used to classify anomaly is calculated as

$$\text{C}(\mathcal{T}) = \text{softmax}\left(-\text{AssoD}(\mathcal{P}, \mathcal{S}; \mathcal{T})\right) \odot \left[\|\mathcal{T}_{x,:} - \widehat{\mathcal{T}}_{x,:}\|_2^2\right]_{x=1,\cdots,L}, \tag{6}$$

where $\odot$ is the element-wise multiplication. The anomaly score uses both the temporal representation and identifiable association discrepancy, incorporating normalized association discrepancy into the reconstruction criterion. Higher anomaly scores are obtained when anomalies decrease the association discrepancy for a more precise reconstruction.

Rather than choosing a cutoff via K-Means based on manual inspection, to fully automate threshold determination and enhance anomaly detection accuracy, we model the distribution of anomaly scores using a GMM fitted via the EM algorithm. The GMM models the distribution using several multidimensional Gaussian distributions and is defined as

$$P(c_i) = \sum_{i=1}^{B} \varphi_i p_i(c_i), \tag{7}$$

where $P(c_i)$ denotes a component of the GMM, and φ_i indicates the coefficient of weight in the sum corresponding the $P(c_i)$, and B specifies the total number of GMM components. The parameters $P(c_i)$ is required to meet the following conditions:

$$p_i(c_i) = \frac{1}{(2\pi)^{\frac{D}{2}} |\sum_i|^2} \exp\left(-\frac{(c_i - \eta_i)^{\mathrm{T}} \sum_i^{-1} (c_i - \eta_i)}{2}\right), \tag{8}$$

and φ_i is satisfied by $\sum_{i=1}^{B} \varphi_i = 1$. From the analysis above, each GMM component $P(c_i)$ is described using its mean vector η_i and covariance matrix $\sum_i$. Therefore, the complete GMM model can be represented through the parameter set $\theta = \{\varphi_i, \eta_i, \sum_i\}_{i=1,\dots,B}$. Meanwhile, the probability density function of GMM is defined as $P(C \mid \theta) = \sum_i^{B} \varphi_i p_i(C \mid \theta_i)$.

To estimate GMM parameters using maximum likelihood estimation, the EM algorithm provides the optimal solution. Following the EM algorithm approach, the logarithmic likelihood function is formulated as

$$\log(\ell(\theta \mid C)) = \log \prod_{l=1}^{L} p(c_l \mid \theta) = \sum_{l=1}^{L} \log \left(\sum_{j=1}^{B} \varphi_j p_j(c_l \mid \theta_j)\right), \tag{9}$$

where L represents the total count of anomaly score points in C, and B indicates the quantity of Gaussian components within the GMM. After introducing the unobservational parameter H, the logarithmic likelihood function for the anomaly scores C can be written as:

$$\log(\ell(\theta \mid C, H)) = \log(P(C, H \mid \theta)) = \sum_{l=1}^{L} \log\left(\varphi_{hl} p_{hl}(c_l \mid \theta_{hl})\right). \tag{10}$$

In the Expectation step (E step), the expectation of the above likelihood function can be described in $\mathscr{Q}\left(\theta, \theta^E\right) = E[\log(\ell(\theta \mid C, H))]$. In the Maximization step (M step), we need to find the parameters that can maximize the likelihood function. By repeatedly alternating between the E-step and M-step processes, the best parameter set θ is achieved once the likelihood function reaches its peak value.

The optimal number of Gaussian components is selected based on the BIC [28]. After fitting, the components are sorted in ascending order of their means: $\eta_1 \leq \eta_2 \leq \cdots \leq \eta_B$, with corresponding weights $\varphi_1, \varphi_2, \ldots, \varphi_B$. Typically, in the common case, the lowest-mean component already contains a simple majority of the mass and is taken as the normal class; thus, the anomaly rate is the remaining mixture weight, and the decision threshold is the corresponding upper quantile of the score distribution. Although all experiment results in this study fall into the common case, the method also handles special cases where normal data might span across multiple low-mean components. In such scenarios, normal components are then identified by cumulatively combining the lowest-mean components until their collective mixture weight reaches or exceeds a majority threshold τ (e.g., 0.5 for ensuring a simple majority). This is done by finding the smallest m such that $\sum_{k=1}^{m} \varphi_k \geq \tau$. Once the normal components are identified, the anomaly proportion r is then set as $r = 1 - \sum_{k=1}^{m} \varphi_k$, and the threshold λ is set as the $(1-r)$-quantile of the anomaly scores. Furthermore, one advantage of this method is its ability to cluster different types of anomalies into different components, as distinct abnormal patterns may form separate Gaussian components; we leave this for future exploration.

3.4 Lightweight Anomaly Detector

Processing LAD at the edge reduces latency and bandwidth usage by enabling local data analysis without first collecting logs from edge devices and transferring them to a centralized server or cloud for processing. Additionally, local log processing enhances data privacy and is particularly crucial in sensitive environments, allowing engineers to promptly identify and address anomalies. Moreover, advancements in edge computing reduce the computational resource consumption for LAD. Leveraging the capabilities of edge devices, the edge-based strategy enables the deployment of the advanced EM-AT model and provides efficient detection of log anomalies. We employ ExecuTorch [37] to enable efficient edge-based deployment in environments with limited computational resources. The prepared PyTorch program is initially exported as a graph and then compiled into the lightweight ExecuTorch program, an executable format that enables execution on the edge. Additionally, we use TorchAO [33] for quantization during the program preparation phase, reducing the precision of the weights and activations to optimize both model size and computational complexity. Leveraging the strengths of ExecuTorch and the superior EM-AT model, the lightweight anomaly detector is designed to enable our framework to efficiently detect log anomalies on resource-constrained edge devices with high accuracy.

ExecuTorch for On-Device Inference. With the growing demand for anomaly detection on edge devices and the need to deploy machine learning models in environments with constrained computational resources, several frameworks have been developed for on-device AI. For instance, ExecuTorch, LiteRT [15] (formerly known as TensorFlow Lite), Core ML [3], and TensorRT [41]. However, Core ML is developed exclusively for Apple's ecosystem, while TensorRT requires NVIDIA GPU hardware and software dependencies such as CUDA or the TensorRT SDK. This makes it unsuitable for edge devices with limited computational resources, which are predominantly CPU-only. Compared with Core ML and TensorRT, ExecuTorch and LiteRT support multiple platforms. Both provide key features in terms of latency, privacy, connectivity, and size to address the problem of detecting log anomalies on edge devices.

However, compared to LiteRT, ExecuTorch, as part of the PyTorch edge ecosystem, is better suited to our LAD framework on resource-constrained edge devices. Firstly, ExecuTorch enables the customization of memory plans for the EM-AT model [35]. By customizing the regions of memory, we can utilize multiple memory locations and assign the outputs of specific nodes to designated locations. This custom memory allocation enhances real-time LAD performance and reduces overall memory consumption during execution [5]. As a result, Lite-LADR can achieve higher performance in memory-constrained environments, thereby improving the framework's overall performance. In addition, ExecuTorch can represent control flows and dynamic tensor shapes using the *torch.export*() function. The export phase specialization turns many dynamic behaviors into static plans, improving portability across backends and simplifying tuning. This reduces runtime overhead, enables static memory planning, and provides tighter, more stable latency on edge devices [37]. In contrast, LiteRT keeps control flow logic during inference and executes via subgraphs, which increases scheduling and memory pressure. Moreover, with respect to kernel libraries, in order to minimize dependencies for portability and execution efficiency of the program execution phase, ExecuTorch separates the operator signature from its implementation [36]. This design enables the ExecuTorch runtime to exclude standard ATen operator implementations, thus reducing core runtime components and improving execution efficiency. Given that the edge-based strategy is intended for LAD in environments with constrained computational resources, such efficiency is a critical requirement during inference. Additionally, ExecuTorch enables us to link against kernel libraries that contain implementations of the operators required by our ExecuTorch program. This flexibility enables us to select specific operator implementations tailored to our requirements, such as reducing the program's memory usage and battery usage. As a result, our framework can achieve further reductions in computational resource consumption, making it well-suited for deployment on resource-constrained edge devices. To leverage the aforementioned advantages for LAD at the edge, we incorporate **ExecuTorch** into LiteLADR. This enables the prepared program to be converted into a lightweight format, enabling efficient deployment and inference on computational resource-constrained edge devices.

As illustrated in Fig. 3, the overall workflow of ExecuTorch is divided into two key phases: **program preparation** and **program execution**. In the program preparation phase, the PyTorch model is transformed into an ExecuTorch program using the FlatBuffer format and compiled into a lightweight binary *.pte* file. The PyTorch program is first exported using the *torch.export*() function, generating an Export Intermediate Representation (EXIR) with the ATen Dialect. The EXIR serves as the foundation for subsequent steps, and the ATen

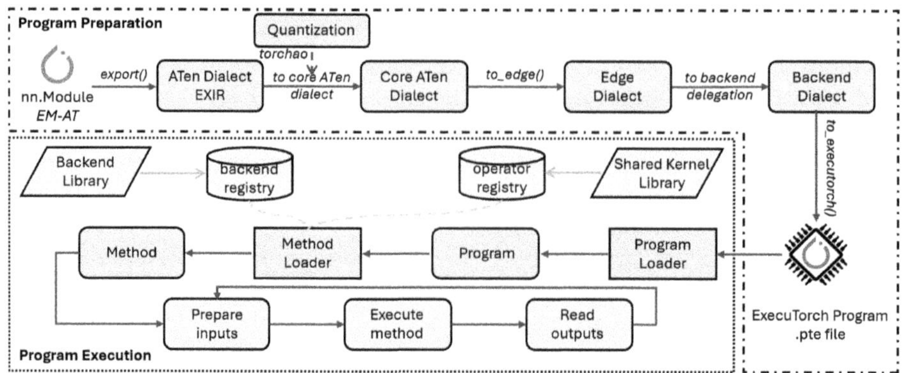

Fig. 3. ExecuTorch workflow consists of two main phases. In the program preparation phase, the EM-AT model is exported into a graph representation and then compiled to an ExecuTorch program. During program execution, the compiled program is loaded and executed on edge devices.

Dialect ensures efficient execution throughout the process. The ATen Dialect then decomposed into a Core ATen Dialect with a smaller operator set. Quantization can be applied during this process to reduce both the model size and computational cost. After that, the Core ATen Dialect is transformed into the Edge Dialect using the *to_ edge()* function. This transformation enables further lowering to the Backend Dialect, which includes metadata and nodes specific to the backend. Finally, the *to_ executorch()* function serializes the program to flatbuffer format and generates a binary `.pte` program file, which is efficiently loaded and executed during the program execution phase. The program execution phase loads the `.pte` file and executes it on the target edge device, enabling efficient anomaly detection in computational resource-constrained environments. During the program execution, the `.pte` file is first loaded by the program loader. Next, the method loader retrieves the runtime operations library, which includes kernel libraries and backend libraries, and loads the serialized program to prepare it for execution. After these steps, the executor carries out the method by preparing the input data, executing the loaded program, and producing the output results. This phase incurs low execution overhead and is lightweight and portable to operate directly in bare-metal embedded environments without an operating system, dynamic memory allocation, or multi-threading.

During the conversion of the EM-AT program to the ExecuTorch program, quantization can be integrated in the program preparation phase to reduce model size and lower computational resource consumption. It is particularly valuable for efficient anomaly detection on resource-constrained devices. In this work, we utilize **TorchAO** [33], a PyTorch library designed for data type customization and model optimization, which enables the quantization and sparsification of weights, gradients, optimizers, and activations. For the EM-AT model, we prefer post-training quantization, primarily due to the extensive computational demands associated with the fine-tuning required by QAT. Besides, since the

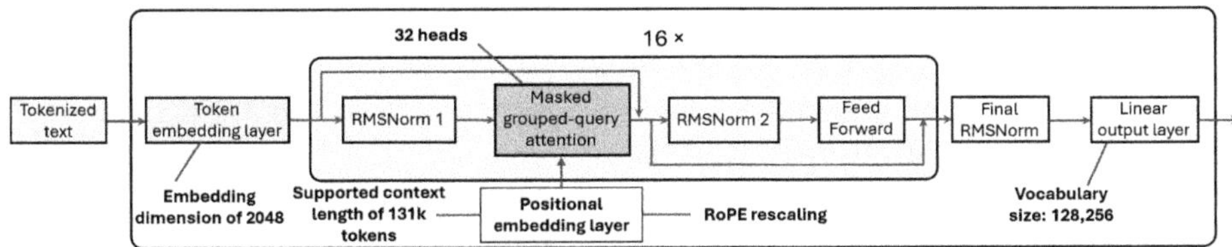

Fig. 4. The architecture of Meta-Llama-3.2-1B.

high dynamic activations of EM-AT are difficult to represent with a low-bit fixed-point format [6], applying the mixed-precision PTQ functions with higher activation precision can enhance the accuracy of the quantized model. In this work, we apply the PTQ function `int8_dynamic_activation_int4_weight()`, which quantizes activations to 8-bit integer values and weights to 4-bit integer values. This function enables the EM-AT model to be converted with a smaller file size, reducing memory usage without compromising accuracy [10].

3.5 LLM-Based Response

Although traditional machine learning models can automatically identify log anomalies, they lack the capability to interpret raw log messages and provide contextual information such as fault descriptions, severity, operational impact, or recommended corrective actions. Recent advances in LLMs help address this gap. Prior studies such as LogPrompt [30], DivLog [55], Llmelog [18], and LLM-LADE [58] demonstrate that LLMs can enhance log understanding and support anomaly analysis. LLMs' natural language processing capabilities enable them to analyze log messages, extract precise information across heterogeneous systems, and generate informative responses, including anomaly descriptions, detection insights, and possible mitigation, to assist engineers in problem-solving. It is important to clarify that this module is designed for fault response and decision support (e.g., mitigation and remediation advice) rather than direct attack response. Unlike an Intrusion Prevention System (IPS) which might automatically block network traffic in real-time, the LLM functions as an intelligent assistant, synthesizing complex log data into actionable human-readable guidance.

In the proposed LiteLADR, we integrate an LLM-based response module that generates context-aware responses tailored to abnormal log messages, thus enhancing system reliability and security. Regarding deployment feasibility, integrating an LLM on the edge involves a calculated trade-off. While necessary for interpreting unstructured logs where rigid rule-based parsers fail, it imposes significant memory demands compared to the lightweight detector. However, our experiments evaluation has shown that quantization via ExecuTorch renders this feasible on mid-range edge gateways (e.g., Raspberry Pi 5), effectively bridging the gap between high-level reasoning and resource-constrained environments. While this precludes deployment on extreme-edge microcontrollers, it provides a necessary capability for autonomous, disconnected fault diagnosis in local IoT networks.

To perform system log analysis and response, we adopt the Meta-Llama-3.2-1B model [51], a transformer-based large language model with 16 layers and 32-head grouped-query attention (GQA) for enhanced efficiency (as shown in Fig. 4). Each input token is mapped to a 2048-dimensional embedding, and the feedforward network expands it to 8192 dimensions before projecting back to 2048. The model supports a context length of up to 128K tokens and a vocabulary size of 128,256. Meta-Llama-3.2-1B replaces traditional LayerNorm with RMS normalization (RMSNorm) applied before and after each attention block and introduces scaled rotary positional embeddings (RoPE) for positional encoding. Within each feedforward block, a SiLU activation is applied between the projection layers. These architectural choices (16 layers, 32-head GQA, RMSNorm, RoPE, and SiLU MLP) collectively contribute to the model's high efficiency and scalability for long-context reasoning tasks. In addition, to enable local on-device inference with LLMs, ExecuTorch provides a comprehensive set of tools, including export APIs, acceleration backends, quantization libraries, and tokenizers compatible with Meta-Llama-3.2-1B. These components enable the model to be compacted, reducing computational and memory requirements and enabling efficient execution on resource-constrained edge devices while maintaining robust inference performance.

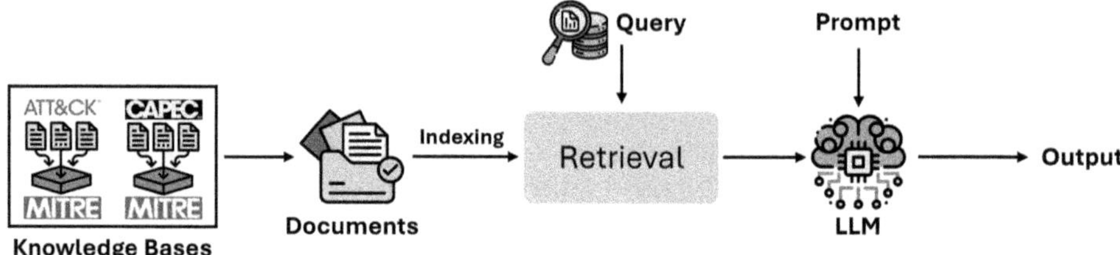

Fig. 5. RAG for LLM to analyze log messages.

Retrieval-Augmented Generation (RAG) enhances LLMs by retrieving semantically relevant document segments from external knowledge bases through semantic similarity calculation. By referencing external knowledge, RAG mitigates the risk of producing incorrect content [14]. In this work, we employ RAG to enable LLM-based analysis of software log sequences. For the abnormal sequences, the LLM describes the anomaly, analyzes potential consequences, and provides mitigations. As illustrated in Fig. 5, domain context information is obtained from offline versions of the MITRE ATT&CK and MITRE CAPEC knowledge bases and supplemented with additional web resources. MITRE ATT&CK is a globally-accessible knowledge base of adversary tactics and techniques based on real-world observations [39]. MITRE CAPEC (Common Attack Pattern Enumerations and Classifications) offers identification and understanding of cyber-attack patterns [38]. To enable retrieval, documents are indexed by segmenting them into chunks, encoding each into vectors, and storing them in a vector database. Then, the most semantically relevant chunks are retrieved and combined with the original log query, which is then input into the LLM to generate the final output.

4 Experiments

4.1 Dataset

We evaluate LiteLADR using two popular system log datasets: HDFS [56] and OpenStack [12]. The **HDFS** dataset contains 11,175,629 log messages collected from Hadoop-based tasks executed across more than 200 Amazon EC2 nodes. The dataset encompasses 31 failure types, including "namenode not updated after deleting," "write exception client give up," "write failed at beginning," "replica immediately deleted," "redundant addStoredBlock," "empty packet for block," "receive block exception," and other anomalies. Among the log sessions, 16,838 are classified as anomalous. Following [12], we use the first 4,855 normal sessions for training and the remaining sessions for testing. The **OpenStack** dataset was collected by deploying the OpenStack Mitaka release on Cloud-Lab [45], consisting of one control node, one network node, and eight compute nodes. To mimic realistic system faults, three types of anomalies were injected at different stages of operation: (1) neutron timeout during VM creation, (2) libvirt error while destroying a VM, and (3) libvirt error during cleanup after destroying a VM. The dataset contains 207,820 log messages, among which 18,434 are labeled as abnormal. We train the model using the first 52,312 normal log messages and evaluate it on the remaining portion. To ensure a fair comparison, we adopt the same training and testing configurations as those employed by the methods evaluated in this paper.

4.2 Evaluation Metrics

Precision, Recall, and F_1-score are evaluation metrics that are essential to comprehend the effectiveness of the suggested method in locating abnormalities in the system logs of large-scale systems [13]. Precision measures the proportion of true positive anomalies out of all detected anomalies. High precision indicates a low rate of false positives, which is vital in ensuring that the system does not raise unnecessary alarms. Precision is defined as

$$\text{Precision} = \frac{TP}{TP + FP}. \tag{11}$$

Recall measures the ability of the method to detect all actual anomalies. High recall values suggest that the method is thorough in identifying instances of anomalies, reducing the risk of missed detections. However, a high recall might come at the cost of lower precision if the method also tends to detect a large number of non-anomalies. Recall is defined as

$$\text{Recall} = \frac{TP}{TP + FN}. \tag{12}$$

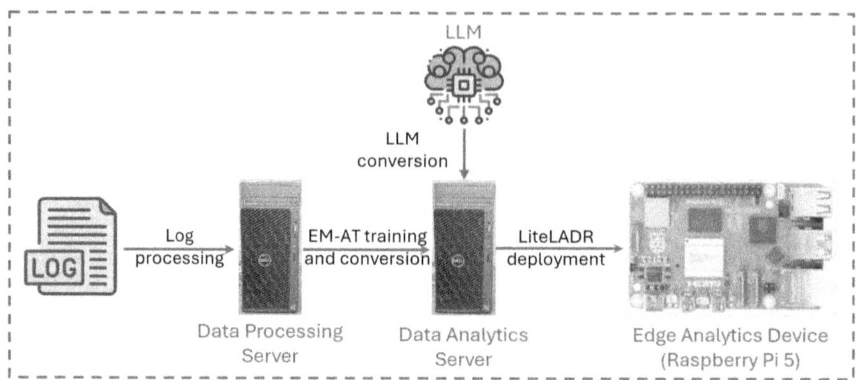

Fig. 6. The key data pipeline components of the testbed for the LiteLADR framework.

F_1-score is the harmonic mean of precision and recall, providing a single metric that balances the trade-off between these two aspects. A higher F_1-score indicates a method that effectively balances the detection of true anomalies while minimizing false positives. It is calculated as

$$\mathrm{F}_1\text{-score} = \frac{2 \cdot \mathrm{Precision} \cdot \mathrm{Recall}}{\mathrm{Precision} + \mathrm{Recall}}. \tag{13}$$

4.3 Experimental Setting

Figure 6 shows the key components of the LiteLADR testbed and its data pipeline. Both the data processing server and the data analytics server are equipped with an NVIDIA RTX 2000 Ada Generation GPU and an Intel Core i7-14700 processor, featuring 28 cores and 56 threads. The data processing server stores the log data and processes it, while the data analytics server provides sufficient computational resources for training the EM-AT model, hyperparameter tuning, and converting both the EM-AT and LLM models. To evaluate the framework's capability for efficient on-device anomaly detection and response, we deploy both EM-AT and LiteLADR on a Raspberry Pi 5, which serves as the edge analytics device. Detailed hardware specifications of the testbed are illustrated in Table 1.

Table 1. Hardware specifications of LiteLADR testbed.

Machine	CPU					GPU	RAM	Operating System
	Core	Thread	Processor	Base	Max			
Data Processing Server	28	56	Intel Core i7-14700	2.1GHz	5.4GHz	NVIDIA RTX 2000 Ada Generation	32 GB	Windows 11
Data Analytics Server	28	56	Intel Core i7-14700	2.1GHz	5.4GHz	NVIDIA RTX 2000 Ada Generation	32 GB	Ubuntu 24.04 LTS
Edge Analytics Device (Raspberry Pi 5)	4	4	ARM64 Cortex-A76	–	2.4GHz	–	8 GB	Ubuntu 20.04 LTS

We configure the EM-AT with three transformer encoder layers ($N = 3$). Following the settings in [54], we set the number of hidden channels to 512 and the number of heads to 8. A non-overlapped sliding window is adopted to obtain a set of sub-series. The Adam optimizer [25] is employed with an initial learning rate of 10^{-4}. All experiments are implemented in PyTorch [42]. For EM-AT hyperparameter tuning, we vary the loss weight within $\{1, 2, 3, 4, 5, 6\}$ and batch sizes within $\{32, 64, 96, 128, 160, 192\}$. To enable efficient execution on edge devices, both the EM-AT and Meta-Llama-3.2-1B models are optimized and quantized using the ExecuTorch framework. During model lowering, we adopt the `int8_dynamic_activation_int4_weight`() quantization function, which reduces compute and memory overhead while preserving accuracy [10]. In addition, we utilize the psutil library [46], a cross-platform tool for real-time system and process monitoring, to measure computational resource consumption, including CPU temperature, process-wide CPU utilization, and memory usage. All measurements are collected on resource-constrained edge devices under a controlled execution environment, where only the evaluated method (e.g., EM-AT or LiteLADR), psutil, and essential background services are active. The reported metrics represent average values computed over the entire evaluation period.

4.4   Previous Methods

We compared the results of our framework with five previous popular and leading LAD methods. The details of these methods are as follows:

- **PCA** [12, 56] constructs state ratio vector and message count vector from log sequences, then applies PCA combined with term-weighting techniques on both feature matrices for anomaly detection.
- **IM** [12, 31] builds the feature matrix using a message count vector and mines small invariants that are satisfied by the majority of vectors. Those vectors that violate these invariants are treated as anomalies.
- **DeepLog** [12] leverages LSTM networks to model system logs as natural language sequences, learning patterns from normal system behavior. Additionally, it introduces a mechanism to incrementally update the model to adapt to new log patterns over time.
- **Adanomaly** [44] utilizes BiGAN (bidirectional generative adversarial networks) to calculate reconstruction loss and discriminative loss as features and leverages ensemble learning to overcome the class imbalance problem.
- **MDFULog** [27] employs a log resolution method to suppress noise and an Informer-based classification model for detection. It effectively captures correlations among semantic information, time information, and sequence features to improve LAD.

4.5   Experiment Results

To comprehensively evaluate our proposed framework, we first assess the LAD performance of EM-AT on the HDFS and OpenStack datasets. We then examine the influence of different hyperparameter settings on EM-AT's performance. In

Table 2. Anomaly detection performance (in %) of EM-AT and LiteLADR on the HDFS and OpenStack datasets compared to the results of other methods sourced from their respective citations.

Dataset	HDFS			OpenStack		
Metric	Precision	Recall	F_1-score	Precision	Recall	F_1-score
PCA [12]	98	67	79	77	99	87
IM [12]	88	95	91	2	100	5
DeepLog [12]	95	96	96	96	100	98
Adanomaly [44]	98	98	98	-	-	-
MDFULog [27]	98	98	98	96	96	96
EM-AT	97.82	**100.00**	**98.90**	99.22	**100.00**	**99.61**
LiteLADR	**100.00**	97.33	98.65	**100.00**	98.86	99.43

addition, we analyze the computational resource consumption of both EM-AT and LiteLADR when deployed on resource-constrained edge devices. Finally, we present example responses generated by the LLM.

Table 2 compares the LAD performance of EM-AT and LiteLADR with previous methods on the HDFS and OpenStack datasets. On the HDFS dataset, all methods except PCA achieve strong results, likely due to high-quality log parsing that provides a reliable foundation for model training and anomaly detection. Deep learning methods achieve better performance, confirming their advantage for learning complex log patterns. EM-AT, benefiting from the transformer architecture and automated thresholding, achieves the best performance with an F_1-score of 98.90%, while LiteLADR attains a comparable F_1-score with only a 0.25% reduction. On the OpenStack dataset, IM performs poorly, achieving only 2% precision due to randomly generated logs that obscure the "stable small invariants" required for traditional anomaly detection. In contrast, EM-AT achieves the highest performance with an F_1-score of 99.61%. LiteLADR maintains competitive performance, exhibiting only a 0.18% decrease in F_1-score despite quantization, which inherently reduces activation and weight precision. This minimal degradation demonstrates the effectiveness of LiteLADR in anomaly detection, even operating on resource-constrained edge devices.

In addition, we evaluated the effect of two key hyperparameters, loss weight and batch size, on EM-AT's performance. As shown in Fig. 7, HDFS achieves its best performance with a loss weight of 2 and a batch size of 64. Larger batch sizes, particularly above 128, lead to lower F_1-scores, indicating that overly large batches weaken the model's ability to capture anomaly-related patterns. In Fig. 8, the OpenStack dataset shows much less sensitivity to these parameters. Its F_1-scores remain above 98% for most settings, suggesting that EM-AT is stable on this dataset across a wide range of configurations. These results indicate that the two datasets differ in their sensitivity to the loss weight and batch size, which is likely due to differences in their data patterns and intrinsic characteristics.

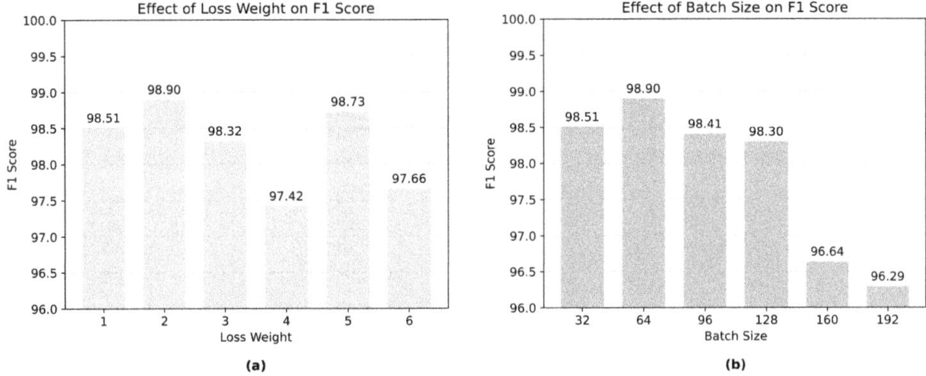

Fig. 7. Anomaly detection performance of EM-AT with different loss weight and batch size on HDFS.

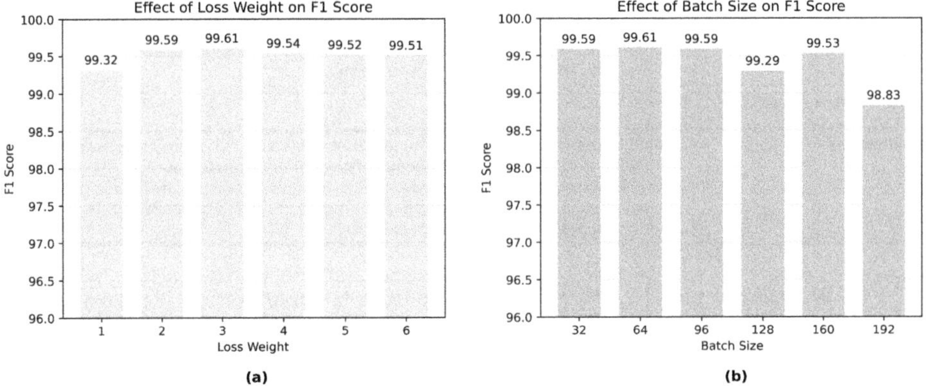

Fig. 8. Anomaly detection performance of EM-AT with different loss weight and batch size on OpenStack.

We further evaluated the computational resource consumption of DeepLog, EM-AT, quantized EM-AT, and LiteLADR on a Raspberry Pi 5 (Table 3). To provide a granular view of efficiency, we analyze the resource usage per component, contrasting the baseline DeepLog against the lightweight anomaly detector component of LiteLADR and the complete framework.

First, we observe that the baseline DeepLog places a heavy burden on edge resources regardless of the dataset. On the HDFS dataset, DeepLog consumes 91.39% CPU utilization and occupies over 2.8 GB of RAM. Similarly, on the OpenStack dataset, it maintains a critically high resource profile with 89.81% CPU utilization and approximately 2.3 GB of memory usage. This consistent resource exhaustion makes DeepLog prohibitive for battery-powered or multi-tenant edge devices.

Table 3. Computational resource consumption of EM-AT and LiteLADR on Raspberry Pi 5. Metrics are averaged over the entire evaluation period.

Dataset	Method	CPU Temperature (°C)	Process CPU Utilization (%)	Process Memory Usage (MB)	Model File Size (KB)
HDFS	DeepLog	69.05	91.39	2824.16	19620
	EM-AT	80.93	94.17	643.69	28660
	Quantized EM-AT	**66.15**	**24.34**	**43.42**	**19979**
	LiteLADR	66.75	74.92	1521.82	861481
OpenStack	DeepLog	66.15	89.81	2331.59	24904
	EM-AT	82.73	94.31	501.53	28628
	Quantized EM-AT	**64.86**	**23.82**	**51.30**	**20030**
	LiteLADR	65.55	65.69	1530.51	861538

⤷ Input	
Abnormal Log Message	nova-compute.log.1.2017-05-16_13:55:31 2017-05-16 00:00:20.345 2931 WARNING nova.virt.libvirt.imagecache [req-addc1839-2ed5-4778-b57e-5854eb7b8b09 - - - - -] Unknown base file: /var/lib/nova/instances/_base /a489c868f0c37da93b76227c91bb03908ac0e742

⤶ Output	
Description	The compute host reports that a VM "base image" in Nova's local image cache is present/missing in a way Nova doesn't recognize; it's likely orphaned, deleted, or tampered with, and Nova is flagging it for cleanup.
Typical Severity Level	Medium
Mitigations	• Stabilize service: Stop new VM launches that would use this base image; switch affected workloads to a known-good image while you investigate. • Verify the file: Check whether the file exists, compare its checksum to the trusted image, and restore the correct version from your image store if it differs or is missing. (… Additional outputs are omitted for brevity.)

Fig. 9. An example of LLM-generated responses to an abnormal log message.

In stark contrast, the anomaly detection component of LiteLADR (Quantized EM-AT) demonstrates superior efficiency on both datasets. On HDFS, it reduces CPU utilization to 24.34% and memory usage to just 43.42 MB. The OpenStack results mirror this massive efficiency gain, showing 23.82% CPU usage and 51.30 MB of memory. Across both testing environments, this represents a reduction of roughly 73% in CPU load and a negligible memory footprint compared to DeepLog's gigabyte-scale requirements.

When evaluating the full LiteLADR framework which adds the quantized Meta-Llama-3.2-1B, the system remains more efficient than the baseline. For HDFS, LiteLADR operates at 74.92% CPU and around 1.5 GB memory, while on OpenStack, it runs even more efficiently at 65.69% CPU with similar memory consumption. Crucially, for both HDFS and OpenStack, the full LiteLADR framework consumes significantly less memory (i.e., 1.5 GB vs. 2.3âĂŞ2.8 GB) and lower CPU resources than the standalone DeepLog baseline, despite providing the additional capability of LLM-based root cause analysis. While 65% utilization involves significant compute, it is achieved while running a Quantized Large Language Model (Llama-3.2-1B) alongside the anomaly detector, a workload that typically requires server-grade GPUs. Although DeepLog and EM-AT

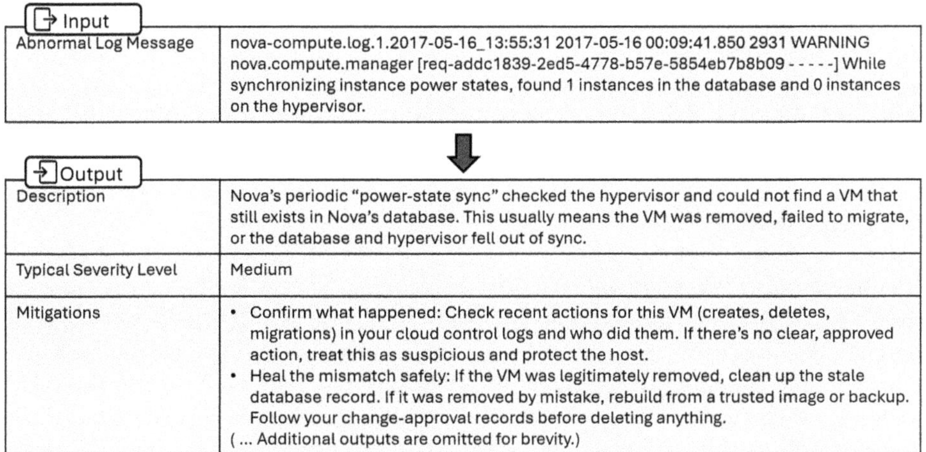

Fig. 10. Another example of LLM-generated responses to an abnormal log message.

can technically run on resource-constrained devices, their high CPU demand, large memory usage, and elevated operating temperatures make them unsuitable for long-term or multi-task workloads. In contrast, LiteLADR substantially reduces resource consumption across all metrics while preserving detection performance.

Based on these empirical resource profiles (e.g., approx. 1.5 GB RAM and moderate ARM64 compute load), we identify the minimal system requirements for LiteLADR as a device featuring at least 2 GB of RAM and a Quad-core Cortex-A72 class processor (or x86 equivalent).

Consequently, LiteLADR is not limited to the Raspberry Pi 5 used in this testbed. It is suitable for a broad grade of mid-range edge devices, including the Raspberry Pi 4 (4GB/8GB models), NVIDIA Jetson Nano, Orange Pi 5, and industrial-grade x86 IoT gateways.

After identifying the anomalies, the corresponding abnormal log messages are forwarded to the RAG-enhanced LLM for contextual analysis and response generation on resource-constrained edge devices. We employ a carefully designed prompt to guide the ExecuTorch Meta-Llama-3.2-1B: *"You will be given a system log message. Provide a clear description of the anomaly and present the typical severity level. Then suggest mitigation steps in plain language, avoiding technical jargon or abbreviations. Input: <LOG Message>."* As illustrated in Fig. 9, the model leverages both the prompt and offline domain knowledge from MITRE ATT&CK and MITRE CAPEC to interpret the abnormal log message. In this case, the model identifies the issue as related to File Manipulation (CAPEC-165), categorizes the severity level as medium, and proposes targeted mitigation steps such as stabilizing the service and verifying the affected base image. Similarly, Fig. 10 presents another example in which the model associates the anomaly with Incomplete Data Deletion in Multi-Tenant Environments (CAPEC-546).

The response assigns a medium severity level and provides corresponding resolutions to ensure database consistency and secure recovery. These examples demonstrate how the LLM combines its understanding of log semantics with security knowledge bases to generate practical insights that enhance the system's reliability.

5   Conclusion

In summary, this work introduces EM-AT-based LAD by designing an unsupervised LAD approach that extends the Anomaly Transformer model via integrating the EM algorithm. EM-AT achieves higher accuracy and consistency across diverse environments by enabling fully automated anomaly decision-making. Building on this foundation, we present LiteLADR, the core contribution of this study, which enables efficient and actionable analysis of system logs via quantized on-device anomaly detection and context-aware fault response. LiteLADR employs TorchAO for model quantization and ExecuTorch to convert both the EM-AT and Meta-Llama-3.2-1B models into lightweight formats optimized for deployment on resource-constrained edge gateways.

Our approach addresses a critical gap in modern cyber infrastructure, where massive volumes of logs from sensors, actuators, and embedded operating systems are often discarded or batched due to bandwidth constraints. By deploying LiteLADR directly at the network edge, organizations can achieve real-time observability over their IoT mesh networks without relying on continuous cloud connectivity. Our comprehensive evaluations on the HDFS and OpenStack datasets demonstrate that LiteLADR maintains leading LAD performance while significantly reducing computational resource consumption. Moreover, integrating LLM-based interpretation enhances system reliability by providing interpretable mitigation strategies.

However, we acknowledge certain limitations. First, our evaluation relied on two public log datasets; future work will explore a more diverse set of real-world logs, specifically targeting binary logs from safety-critical industrial domains. Second, despite aggressive quantization, the integrated LLM component still requires substantial device resources, preventing deployment on extreme-edge microcontrollers. Consequently, future development will investigate domain-specific, small language models (SLMs) that are more practical for highly constrained edge environments.

References

1. Abadade, Y., Temouden, A., Bamoumen, H., Benamar, N., Chtouki, Y., Hafid, A.S.: A comprehensive survey on TinyML. IEEE Access (2023)
2. Almodovar, C., Sabrina, F., Karimi, S., Azad, S.: LogFit: log anomaly detection using fine-tuned language models. IEEE Trans. Netw. Serv. Manage. **21**(2), 1715–1723 (2024)
3. Apple: an apple framework to integrate machine learning models into your app (2024). https://developer.apple.com/documentation/coreml. Accessed 19 Sep 2024

4. Aures, G., Lübben, C.: DDS vs. MQTT vs. VSL for IoT. Network **1**, 1–5 (2019)
5. Berger, E.D., Zorn, B.G., McKinley, K.S.: Reconsidering custom memory allocation. In: Proceedings of the 17th ACM SIGPLAN Conference on Object-Oriented Programming, Systems, Languages, and Applications, pp. 1–12 (2002)
6. Bondarenko, Y., Nagel, M., Blankevoort, T.: Understanding and overcoming the challenges of efficient transformer quantization. arXiv preprint arXiv:2109.12948 (2021)
7. Chen, J., Chong, W., Yu, S., Xu, Z., Tan, C., Chen, N.: TCN-based lightweight log anomaly detection in cloud-edge collaborative environment. In: 2022 Tenth International Conference on Advanced Cloud and Big Data (CBD), pp. 13–18. IEEE (2022)
8. Dai, H., Li, H., Chen, C.S., Shang, W., Chen, T.H.: LogRam: Efficient log parsing using n n-gram dictionaries. IEEE Trans. Software Eng. **48**(3), 879–892 (2020)
9. Dollinger, J.F., Bouhouch, K., Bouzarkouna, I.: Benchmarking OpenStack for edge computing applications. In: 2023 IEEE/ACIS 8th International Conference on Big Data, Cloud Computing, and Data Science (BCD), pp. 295–302. IEEE (2023)
10. Dong, P., et al.: EQ-Vit: algorithm-hardware co-design for end-to-end acceleration of real-time vision transformer inference on versal acap architecture. IEEE Trans. Comput. Aided Des. Integr. Circuits Syst. **43**(11), 3949–3960 (2024)
11. Du, M., Li, F.: Spell: online streaming parsing of large unstructured system logs. IEEE Trans. Knowl. Data Eng. **31**(11), 2213–2227 (2018)
12. Du, M., Li, F., Zheng, G., Srikumar, V.: DeepLog: anomaly detection and diagnosis from system logs through deep learning. In: Proceedings of the 2017 ACM SIGSAC Conference on Computer and Communications Security, pp. 1285–1298 (2017)
13. Elmrabit, N., Zhou, F., Li, F., Zhou, H.: Evaluation of machine learning algorithms for anomaly detection. In: 2020 International Conference on Cyber Security and Protection of Digital Services (Cyber Security), pp. 1–8. IEEE (2020)
14. Gao, Y., et al.: Retrieval-augmented generation for large language models: a survey. arXiv preprint arXiv:2312.10997 (2023)
15. Google: Google's high-performance runtime for on-device ai (2024). https://ai.google.dev/edge/litert. Accessed 19 Sep 2024
16. Guo, H., Yuan, S., Wu, X.: LogBert: log anomaly detection via BERT. In: 2021 International Joint Conference on Neural Networks (IJCNN), pp. 1–8. IEEE (2021)
17. Hansen, S.E., Atkins, E.T.: Automated system monitoring and notification with swatch. In: LISA, vol. 93, pp. 145–152. Monterey, CA (1993)
18. He, M., Jia, T., Duan, C., Cai, H., Li, Y., Huang, G.: LlmeLog: an approach for anomaly detection based on LLM-enriched log events. In: 2024 IEEE 35th International Symposium on Software Reliability Engineering (ISSRE), pp. 132–143. IEEE (2024)
19. He, P., Zhu, J., Zheng, Z., Lyu, M.R.: Drain: an online log parsing approach with fixed depth tree. In: 2017 IEEE International Conference on Web Services (ICWS), pp. 33–40. IEEE (2017)
20. He, S., He, P., Chen, Z., Yang, T., Su, Y., Lyu, M.R.: A survey on automated log analysis for reliability engineering. ACM Comput. Surv. (CSUR) **54**(6), 1–37 (2021)
21. Himler, P., Landauer, M., Skopik, F., Wurzenberger, M.: Anomaly detection in log-event sequences: a federated deep learning approach and open challenges. Mach. Learn. Appl. **16**, 100554 (2024)
22. Huang, S., et al.: Hitanomaly: hierarchical transformers for anomaly detection in system log. IEEE Trans. Netw. Serv. Manage. **17**(4), 2064–2076 (2020)

23. Jiang, W., Hu, C., Pasupathy, S., Kanevsky, A., Li, Z., Zhou, Y.: Understanding customer problem troubleshooting from storage system logs. In: Proceedings of the 7th Conference on File and Storage Technologies, pp. 43–56 (2009)
24. Kim, C., Kim, S.: Optimizing logging and monitoring in heterogeneous cloud environments for IoT and edge applications. IEEE Internet Things J. **10**(24), 22611–22622 (2023)
25. Kingma, D.P., Ba, J.: Adam: a method for stochastic optimization. arXiv preprint arXiv:1412.6980 (2014)
26. Lebre, A., Pastor, J., Simonet, A., Desprez, F.: Revising Openstack to operate fog/edge computing infrastructures. In: 2017 IEEE International Conference on Cloud Engineering (IC2E), pp. 138–148. IEEE (2017)
27. Li, M., Sun, M., Li, G., Han, D., Zhou, M.: MDFULOG: multi-feature deep fusion of unstable log anomaly detection model. Appl. Sci. **13**(4), 2237 (2023)
28. Li, X., Miller, D.J., Xiang, Z., Kesidis, G.: Bic-based mixture model defense against data poisoning attacks on classifiers: a comprehensive study. IEEE Trans. Knowl. Data Eng. **36**(8), 3697–3711 (2024)
29. Liang, Y., Zhang, Y., Xiong, H., Sahoo, R.: Failure prediction in IBM BLUE-GENE/l event logs. In: Seventh IEEE International Conference on Data Mining (ICDM 2007), pp. 583–588. IEEE (2007)
30. Liu, Y., Tao, S., Meng, W., Yao, F., Zhao, X., Yang, H.: LogPrompt: prompt engineering towards zero-shot and interpretable log analysis. In: Proceedings of the 2024 IEEE/ACM 46th International Conference on Software Engineering: Companion Proceedings, pp. 364–365 (2024)
31. Lou, J.G., Fu, Q., Yang, S., Xu, Y., Li, J.: Mining invariants from console logs for system problem detection. In: 2010 USENIX Annual Technical Conference (USENIX ATC 10) (2010)
32. Luo, Q., Hu, S., Li, C., Li, G., Shi, W.: Resource scheduling in edge computing: a survey. IEEE Commun. Surv. Tutorials **23**(4), 2131–2165 (2021)
33. torchao maintainers, contributors: Torchao: PyTorch native quantization and sparsity for training and inference (2024). https://github.com/pytorch/ao
34. Manokaran, J., Vairavel, G.: Smart anomaly detection using data-driven techniques in IoT edge: a survey. In: Proceedings of Third International Conference on Communication, Computing and Electronics Systems: ICCCES 2021, pp. 685–702. Springer (2022). https://doi.org/10.1007/978-981-16-8862-1_45
35. Meta: Executorch docs: memory planning (2024). https://pytorch.org/executorch/stable/compiler-memory-planning.html#memory-planning. Accessed 20 Sep 2024
36. Meta: Executorch docs: overview of executorch's kernel libraries (2024). https://pytorch.org/executorch/stable/kernel-library-overview.html#portable-kernel-library. Accessed 20 Sep 2024
37. Meta: on-device ai across mobile, embedded and edge for PyTorch (2024). https://github.com/pytorch/executorch. Accessed 19 Sep 2024
38. MITRE: Common attack pattern enumerations and classifications (2025). https://capec.mitre.org/index.html. Accessed 21 Aug 2025
39. MITRE: Mitre ATT&CK (2025). https://attack.mitre.org/. Accessed 21 Aug 2025
40. Nguyen, H.T., Nguyen, L.V., Le, V.H., Zhang, H., Le, M.T.: Efficient log-based anomaly detection with knowledge distillation. In: 2024 IEEE International Conference on Web Services (ICWS), pp. 578–589. IEEE (2024)
41. NVIDIA: An SDK for high-performance deep learning inference on NVIDIA GPUS (2024). https://github.com/NVIDIA/TensorRT. Accessed 19 Sep 2024
42. Paszke, A.: PyTorch: an imperative style, high-performance deep learning library. arXiv preprint arXiv:1912.01703 (2019)

43. Qi, J., et al.: LogenCoder: log-based contrastive representation learning for anomaly detection. IEEE Trans. Netw. Serv. Manage. **20**(2), 1378–1391 (2023)

44. Qi, J., et al.: Adanomaly: adaptive anomaly detection for system logs with adversarial learning. In: NOMS 2022-2022 IEEE/IFIP Network Operations and Management Symposium, pp. 1–5. IEEE (2022)

45. Robert, R., Eric, E., Team, T.C.: Introducing CloudLab: scientific infrastructure for advancing cloud architectures and applications (2014). https://www.usenix.org/publications/login/dec14/ricci

46. Rodola, G.: Cross-platform lib for process and system monitoring in python (2024). https://github.com/giampaolo/psutil. Accessed Oct 3 2024

47. Rouillard, J.P.: Real-time log file analysis using the simple event correlator (sec). In: LISA, vol. 4, pp. 133–150 (2004)

48. Shao, S., et al.: Multi-layer mapping of cyberspace for intrusion detection. In: 2021 IEEE 18th International Conference on Computer Systems and Applications, pp. 1–8. IEEE (2021)

49. Shi, Q., et al.: Anomaly transformer-based system log anomaly detection. In: 2024 Cyber Awareness and Research Symposium (CARS), pp. 1–6 (2024). https://doi.org/10.1109/CARS61786.2024.10778676

50. Singh, R., Gill, S.S.: Edge ai: a survey. Internet Things Cyber-Phys. Syst. **3**, 71–92 (2023)

51. Touvron, H., et al.: LLAMA: open and efficient foundation language models (2023). https://arxiv.org/abs/2302.13971

52. Wang, Z., Tian, J., Fang, H., Chen, L., Qin, J.: LightLog: a lightweight temporal convolutional network for log anomaly detection on the edge. Comput. Netw. **203**, 108616 (2022)

53. Xiao, T., et al.: Loader: a log anomaly detector based on transformer. IEEE Trans. Serv. Comput. **16**(5), 3479–3492 (2023)

54. Xu, J., Wu, H., Wang, J., Long, M.: Anomaly transformer: time series anomaly detection with association discrepancy. In: International Conference on Learning Representations (2022). https://openreview.net/forum?id=LzQQ89U1qm_

55. Xu, J., Yang, R., Huo, Y., Zhang, C., He, P.: DivLog: log parsing with prompt enhanced in-context learning. In: Proceedings of the IEEE/ACM 46th International Conference on Software Engineering, pp. 1–12 (2024)

56. Xu, W., Huang, L., Fox, A., Patterson, D., Jordan, M.I.: Detecting large-scale system problems by mining console logs. In: Proceedings of the ACM SIGOPS 22nd Symposium on Operating Systems Principles, pp. 117–132 (2009)

57. Yao, L., Shi, Q., Yang, Z., Shao, S., Hariri, S.: Development of an edge resilient ml ensemble to tolerate ICS adversarial attacks. arXiv preprint arXiv:2409.18244 (2024)

58. Zhang, Z., Li, S., Zhang, L., Ye, J., Hu, C., Yan, L.: LLM-lade: large language model-based log anomaly detection with explanation. Knowl. Based Syst. **326**, 114064 (2025)

59. Zhao, N., et al.: An empirical investigation of practical log anomaly detection for online service systems. In: Proceedings of the 29th ACM Joint Meeting on European Software Engineering Conference and Symposium on the Foundations of Software Engineering, pp. 1404–1415 (2021)

Virtualization

xPUBench: Scalable and Energy-Efficient GPU and DPU-Accelerated Network Functions

Maxime Vanliefde[1]([✉])(iD), Romain Van Hauwaert[1], Nikita Tyunyayev[1](iD), Clément Delzotti[1](iD), Elena Agostini[2], and Tom Barbette[1](iD)

[1] ICTEAM, UCLouvain, Louvain-la-Neuve, Belgium
{maxime.vanliefde,nikita.tyunyayev,clement.delzotti,
tom.barbette}@uclouvain.be
[2] NVIDIA, Santa Clara, USA
eagostini@nvidia.com

Abstract. The rapid increase in network speeds makes packet processing on general-purpose CPUs increasingly challenging. At 100 Gbps and beyond, CPUs struggle to sustain complex network functions without dedicated acceleration. This trend motivates the exploration and measurement of alternative compute platforms such as GPUs and embedded CPUs in Network Interface Cards (NICs). Modern NICs provide tighter integration with GPUs, with the ability to write received packets directly to GPU memory. SmartNICs, also known as Data Processing Units (DPUs), further feature embedded ARM or RISC-V cores capable of offloading NFV packet processing entirely.

In this work, we introduce xPUBench, a benchmarking environment that systematically measures the performance and energy efficiency of packet processing across CPUs, GPUs, and DPUs. We evaluate several (co-)processing models relevant to Network Function Virtualization, including CPU+GPU hybrid, DPU-only, and GPU-only approaches. Our measurements show that, for a computation-heavy workload, current CPU-only implementations manage to handle up to 50% of the 100 Gbps NIC rate. In contrast, GPU implementations can saturate it. We also show that the DPUs' most powerful embedded cores can replace the main CPU for some traditional packet processing, alleviating the load on the host, which can now be entirely dedicated to running applications. We finally propose a novel energy-efficiency dimension, showing that DPUs outperform traditional CPUs for low-throughput processing, requiring only 24 W to sustain 10 Gbps, and that GPUs outperform CPUs for high-throughput processing. Our findings emphasize the need to assess both performance and energy in heterogeneous packet-processing pipelines, given the growing diversity of "xPUs" in networked systems.

Keywords: NFV · GPU · DPU · DPA · Energy Efficiency · Packet Processing

© The Author(s), under exclusive license to Springer Nature Switzerland AG 2026
S. Ferlin-Reiter et al. (Eds.): PAM 2026, LNCS 16477, pp. 377–405, 2026.
https://doi.org/10.1007/978-3-032-18268-5_17

1   Introduction

With enterprises increasingly moving their infrastructure to the cloud, the emergence of high-bandwidth connectivity for end users, such as 5G and fiber-to-the-home, increases heavily the demand for high-speed network packet processing. Network Interface Cards (NICs) speeds have risen dramatically in the last decades. Interfaces offering up to 100 Gbps are now a commodity in datacenters [59], while cards with speeds of 400 Gbps can today be found on the consumer market [53]. Data centers also constantly improve their hardware to improve response times and reduce congestion [61].

Network functions such as firewalls, Network Address Translation (NAT), AI-enhanced malware detection, WAN optimizers, and even Radio Access Networks (RANs) have recently followed the approach of Network Function Virtualization (NFV), implemented primarily on software for flexibility and the ability to be offloaded on generic cloud machines [2,7,47].

With such high speeds, it can be difficult to keep up with the rate at which packets are received and processed on flexible and programmable platforms like Central Processing Units (CPUs). At 100 Gbps, processing a 64 B packet should happen as fast as 6.72 ns (i.e., 430 CPU cycles for a 16-cores 4 GHz CPU). Sustaining such a packet rate for even basic network functions already consumes much of today's CPU. Executing complex network functions at 100 Gbps is even beyond the capacity of current CPUs, as will be shown in Sect. 4.3.

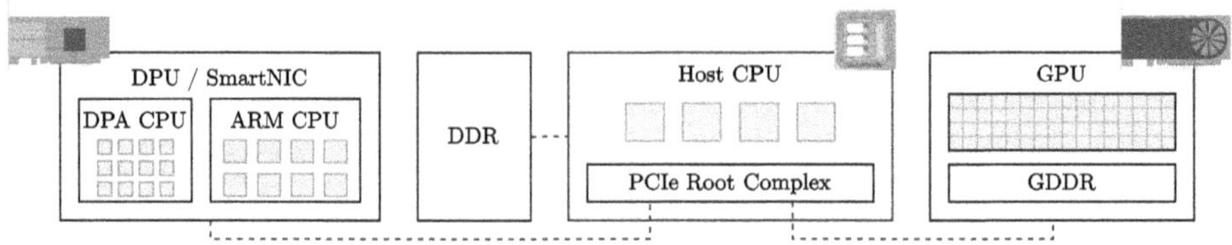

Fig. 1. Modern server architecture with multiple heterogeneous processing units

To keep up the pace, multiple previous works have been conducted to lighten the load on CPUs, by porting network packet processing to other hardware units like Graphics Processing Units (GPUs) and Data Processing Units (DPUs) as highlighted in Fig. 1.

GPUs can be used to offload some of the processing from the CPU. Their many-core parallel architecture and high-bandwidth memory make them well suited for parallel computations on numerous packets. The literature has mostly focused on GPU co-processing as GPUs were not able to manage the NIC on their own until recently [28,54]. PacketShader [22] was the first to use discrete GPUs to accelerate network processing; APUNet [19] reviewed the findings using integrated GPUs; GPU-Ether [28] finally allows running GPU-only applications by using GPU threads to perform the packet I/O, completely bypassing the CPU.

DPUs, also called SmartNICs, designate NICs with some on-NIC CPU cores. They have also been proposed as candidates to process traffic outside the CPU, following recent interest from the community [17,24,42,45]. They are becoming a part of today's datacenters and increase the computational power available on a single machine [26,31]. While it is common for SmartNICs to embed ARM cores running a full operating system, a recent trend also pushes for the integration of weaker but simpler RISC-V cores, such as the Data-Path Accelerator (DPA) on NVIDIA ConnectX-8 and BlueField-3 ASIC [56] or other FPGA-based architectures [12,23,33,58]. In this work, we consider DPUs general-purpose cores to offload network functions from the host. This allows for processing packets even before they reach the host, thereby reducing the load on the CPU and freeing up CPU cycles for other tasks. This model is relevant for datacenter operators, implementing network interposition in the SmartNIC they control, freeing up CPU cores for their tenants. In addition to complete offloading, DPUs enable a hybrid approach, offloading only some parts of the chain, more suitable for the less flexible NIC ASIC [42,43].

Nowadays, the interconnections between the NIC, the CPU and the GPU are much faster than in most of these previous works. In about 10 years, NIC speeds have multiplied by 40 [55] and PCIe speeds by 4 [57]. GPU memory bandwidth has doubled and is still much faster than both. With such increased speeds, GPUs and DPUs are poised to become more useful than ever for network processing.

Given these order-of-magnitude parameter changes, we ask the following question: *Are flexible (as in "easy to program") platforms like GPUs and CPU-based DPUs candidates to process packets at a rate of 100 Gbps?*

In this work, we present **xPUBench**, a benchmarking framework designed to evaluate and compare CPU-, GPU-, and DPU-based packet processing approaches in terms of throughput and energy efficiency. xPUBench is the first tool offering an environment that reproduces and measures the performance of a plethora of previously proposed (co-)processing models and of various devices, with a widely available baseline of 100 Gbps and similar applications. Based on a literature review on GPU network packet processing, xPUBench also integrates a novel processing model to enable harnessing the full potential of a GPU, resulting in a new, more scalable hybrid CPU-GPU framework. xPUBench is finally the first to propose the comparison of these (co-)processing models regarding energy efficiency. Notably, it explores how tuning the core and uncore CPU frequency and the core count is critical, even when the CPU is bypassed entirely. We open source xPUBench, so that the community can benefit from simple-to-use implementations and build upon our work.

Using xPUBench, we demonstrate that GPU-based methods provide higher throughput than CPU-only methods, particularly for heavy computational workloads; however, the optimal GPU processing model depends on the application to be run. The GPU-only approach (without CPU involvement) is the highest-performing implementation (up to $6.3\times$ the throughput of the CPU-only approach and $2.7\times$ that of the hybrid CPU-GPU approach). We also show that

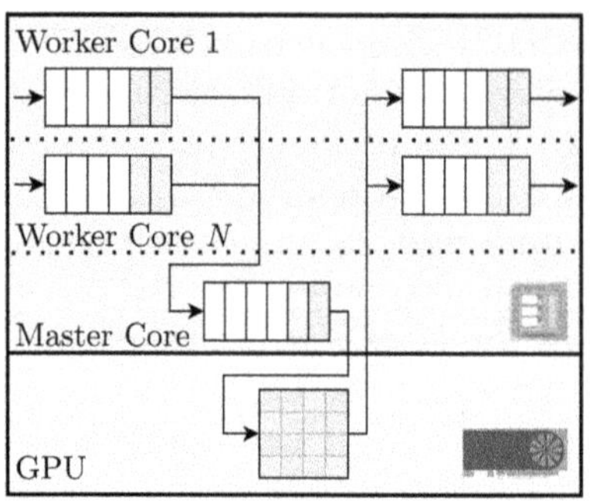

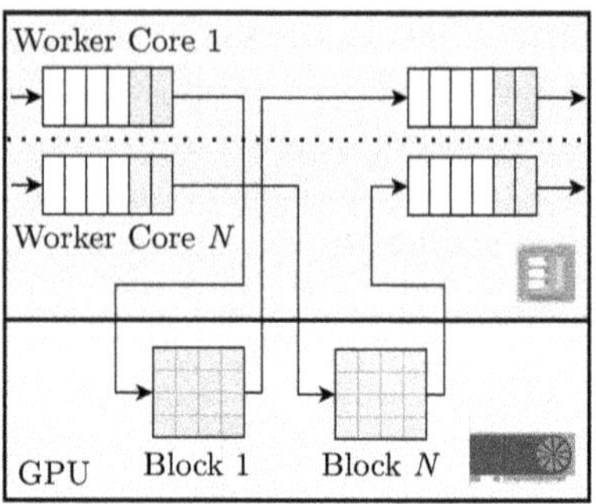

(a) Single-Master – Multiple-Workers, as in PacketShader [22] and APUNet [19]

(b) Parallel Workers, as in Snap [69]

Fig. 2. CPU-GPU processing models

DPU-based methods are able to sustain the line rate for basic network functions, while providing lower latency compared to a CPU-only implementation, and that they are the most energy efficient, drawing up to 3× less power than a CPU-only equivalent approach.

The rest of this paper is organized as follows. Section 2 presents the background on GPU and DPU (co-)processing models and related works. Section 3 provides the design and implementation of xPUBench. Section 4 measures and discusses the performance and energy consumption of a cross-combination of the "xPUs" and processing models. Finally, Sect. 5 summarizes the main findings of this work.

2   Background

In the following, we review existing models for packet processing with GPU, first the larger body of work on CPU-GPU co-processing, and then GPU-only models. We then review the DPU literature and, finally, the energy efficiency aspects of NFV on xPUs. We first present processing models and then summarize the state of the art.

2.1   CPU-GPU (Co-)Processing

Processing Models for CPU-GPU Co-processing. All hybrid implementations use shared queues to communicate between CPU and GPU. These queues reside in CPU memory, hold pointers to packets' payloads, and can be accessed by both the CPU and the GPU. Upon reception, packets are enqueued as batches.

Master-Worker Architecture. As shown in Fig. 2a, in the master-worker architecture proposed in PacketShader [22] and APUNet [19], workers are responsible for the packet I/O, while the master is the only thread communicating with the GPU. The master and workers are each associated with one CPU thread running on its own CPU core. In this model, GPU utilization is independent of the number of CPU cores used. Using more cores only helps to spread the load of received packets using Receive Side Scaling (RSS), but every packet will, in the end, transit through the same master core.

Parallel Workers Architecture. The parallel model, shown in Fig. 2b, supports multiprocessing by completely duplicating the processing pipeline per CPU core, as proposed by Snap [69] and NBA [34]. Each pipeline is processed by a different GPU block (group of GPU threads) with a one-to-one matching between a GPU thread and a packet in a batch. Multiple CPU cores are used to receive packets, and each packet is processed on the core that received it.

Memory Models for CPU-GPU Co-processing. In a naïve approach, packets can be received on CPU, then copied to GPU memory (Fig. 3 Ⓐ). This approach is simple to implement but can waste a lot of PCIe bandwidth, especially when only a portion of the packet is needed for processing.

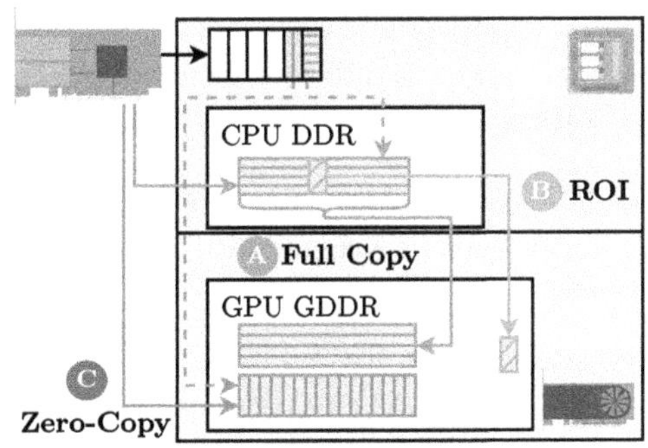

Fig. 3. GPUs can access packets' payloads using 3 different methods. A solid arrow indicates a data copy, and a dashed arrow indicates data access.

Region of Interest. A number of Virtual Network Functions (VNFs) only use a portion of the packet to process it. In particular, many only need a protocol header. For example, IP lookups only need the destination IP address, and Ethernet mirroring only needs the source and destination MAC addresses. Some previous work [22,69] proposed to only send the data that is actually needed to the GPU, as shown in Fig. 3 Ⓑ. The contiguous byte range of the packet that is used is called a Region of Interest (ROI). GPUs read from global memory by section of 32 B [50]. It is beneficial to coalesce Regions of Interest (ROIs) of packets if the ROI is smaller than the size of a single read. This way, multiple GPU threads can be served with a single GPU memory access. For example, for an IPv4 lookup whose ROI size is 4 B, one memory transaction would serve $32/4 = 8$ threads all in one.

Zero-Copy (Z-C). If packets are to be entirely processed on GPU, NICs can directly write the payloads to GPU memory, without passing them through CPU memory, as shown in Fig. 3 Ⓒ. The host still receives the packets' metadata

Table 1. Comparison of Related GPU Packet Processing Works.

	MW*	Parallel	ROI[†]	Z-C[‡] (CPU)	Z-C[‡] (GPU)	GPU-only	Max. Speed[§]	Available	Last Maintained
PacketShader	✓	✗	✓	✗	✗	✗	4*dual-10 Gbps	✗	Not Available
Snap	✗	✓	✓	✗	✗	✗	4*10 Gbps	✓	2014
APUNet	✓	✗	✗	~	~	✗	dual-40 Gbps	✗	Not Available
NBA	✗	✓	✗	✗	✗	✗	dual-40 Gbps	✗	Not Available
GASPP	✗	✓	✗	✓	✗	✗	2*dual-10 Gbps	✗	Not Available
GPU-Ether	N/A	N/A	N/A	N/A	✓	✓	10 Gbps	✗	Not Available
xPUBench	✓	✓	✓	✓	✓	✓	1*100 Gbps	✓	2025

*Single Master, Multiple Workers. [†]Region of Interest. [‡]Zero-Copy.
[§]Maximum speed achieved by the original work.

(including results of offloaded classification) to decide which application should be scheduled on the GPU. APUNet [19] alleviates the problem using the unified memory of APUs (combined CPU-GPU chips) to share memory between CPU and GPU. We do not consider APUs in this study as they are not common in servers. GASPP [71] calls zero-copy the idea that the GPU directly reads CPU memory, which is different from the zero-copy considered by our work, as well as by Romein, J. W. [64], where the packets are directly written to GPU memory by the NIC. Using CPU memory, the packet is actually copied *once more* from CPU to GPU memory, meaning it crosses the PCIe bus twice. To avoid ambiguity, we explicitly specify either Zero-Copy on CPU or on GPU.

Kernel Models for CPU-GPU Co-processing. When using the Zero-Copy memory model, we can also take advantage of persistent GPU thread execution, as shown in APUNet [19]. The use of explicit transfers between the CPU and GPU prohibits this approach, as we first initiate the copy request and then the kernel launch for each batch on a stream. Such a kernel defines the function executed in parallel by each GPU thread. Persistent GPU threads can reduce the latency of processing for lightweight applications whose processing is shorter than the kernel launch.

GPU-Only Bypassing CPU. GPU-Ether [28] introduces a framework designed to enable the development of GPU-only applications. As shown in Fig. 4, incoming packets are directly received in GPU memory, and GPU threads manage network traffic. It does not use any CPU core after initialization. This technique is now standard to NVIDIA NICs, commercially known as GPUNetIO [54].

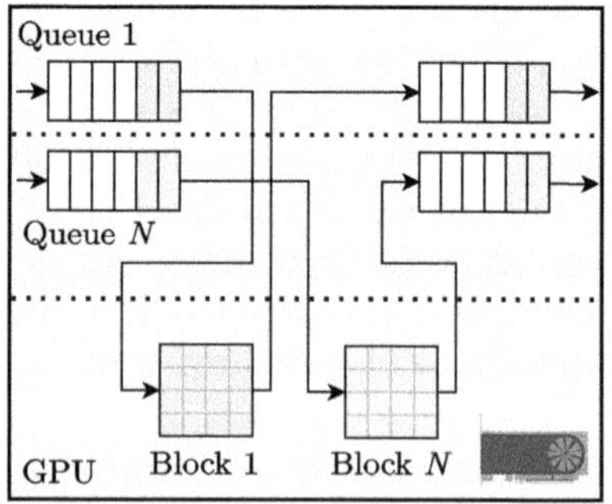

Fig. 4. GPU-Only, as in GPU-Ether [28]

Summary of Models in the Literature.
Previous work explored different combinations of those models to separate CPU processing from GPU processing in GPU-accelerated frameworks, as shown in Table 1. While all these works present working solutions, speeds delivered nowadays by network cards call for a revision of the processing models with a common baseline.

Batching. Batching is a technique whereby multiple packets are processed at once. Multiple packets are received from the NIC and processed as a batch on the CPU. Similarly, the GPU and CPU communicate packets in batches. Previous work has shown that batching is essential to achieve high performance in packet processing. On the I/O side, batching reduces the overhead of accessing the NIC [5,36,63]. On the GPU side, using batches makes better use of the parallelism offered by the GPU [34,69]. At the same time, batching increases average latency. Finding the optimal batching size thus involves a trade-off and depends on multiple factors, such as packet size, network bandwidth, and GPU processing power. Previous proposals [36,71] support a dynamic batch size, whereby the batch is processed after a certain amount of time even if it is not full.

2.2   Other GPU-Related Work

Some work focuses on specific packet processing algorithms tailored to GPU, such as for IP lookup [38,68], NDN lookup [74], Pattern Matching [72] or DPI [66], on alleviating the problem of divergence due to different packet sizes on GPU [41], or on algorithms for scheduling multiple NFV chains on a GPU [8]. GPUnet [67] proposes orthogonal work to ease the GPU abstraction for network programming, connecting the GPU through RDMA but without focusing on NFV workloads. These works are beyond the scope of this paper, which focuses mainly on communication patterns and not the acceleration of the GPU itself.

G-Opt [29] focuses on accelerating CPU-based packet processing inspired by GPU parallelism. Similar recent advances in high-speed NFV CPU processing [15,18,46] are also beyond the scope of communication patterns.

NBA [34] studies the load-balancing of packets between the CPU and the GPU for packet processing. It does not attempt to process batches larger than 64 packets, even when they are sent to the GPU for processing. 64 packets is not enough to achieve high-speed, as will be shown in Sect. 4.4. FlowShader [76] evaluates the balance of flows across CPU and GPU according to flow size, while G-NET [77] focuses on virtualizing the GPU and scheduling functions between multiple tenants. These works are orthogonal, as we focus on modeling performance for each system.

Romein, J. W. [64] processes a large amount of data from telescopes using a high-end NVIDIA integrated platform (NVIDIA Grace Hopper). In this work, we stick to commodity platforms and propose a systematic review of multiple use cases, across multiple approaches beyond the design of a single use-case. They also use a feature of modern NICs to split packets, sending a certain number of bytes to the CPU, and the rest to the GPU. We do not evaluate this possibility in this work, but it enables use cases where zero-copy can be used for most of the payload while the CPU handles the header of the packet.

2.3 DPU

Other works have explored the use of DPUs to free CPU cores from packet processing. DPUs can intercept network traffic and either process it independently, fully offloading tasks from the CPU, or preprocess packet traffic before forwarding it to the host. As GPUs, they can therefore be used as candidates for our study on flexible (co-)processors for NFV processing.

DPUs are heavily heterogeneous computing platforms. They embed accelerators tailored for network processing, like crypto engines or RegEx acceleration [52]. Lognic [20] accounts for this heterogeneity by modeling the performance of an offloaded program on the SmartNIC as a graph of computing units interconnected by a fabric. By specifying the performance of the accelerators and the fabric, as well as a traffic profile, Lognic can predict the latency and throughput of an application.

DPUs also feature rich programmable pipelines capable of high-rate packet processing (e.g., DPDK's `rte_flow` [13]). However, these pipelines are typically limited in flexibility [30]. In addition, as both DPUs and hosts share access to this common pipeline, we disregard it as a distinguishing factor. Instead, our analysis focuses on the performance of the general-purpose CPU cores within the DPU.

As opposed to packet processing on GPUs, we note that the body of work on packet processing on DPUs reflects the heterogeneity of the DPUs themselves. The techniques used vary from DPU to DPU, making it impractical to rerun all the ideas from the literature. Nonetheless, in this work, we propose a performance comparison of 3 different types of CPU cores present in 2 generations of NVIDIA BlueField cards: the BlueField-2 [52] and the BlueField-3 [53].

In addition to general-purpose CPU cores running a traditional operating system, the BlueField-3 [53] is equipped with a Data-Path Accelerator (DPA) [56]. It consists of 16 RISC-V cores, allowing up to 256 hardware threads. Those cores run a custom operating system that does not support DPDK. However, the DPA includes several architectural adaptations tailored for packet processing. Notably, its proximity to the ASIC can reduce latency. Chen *et al.* [9] benchmarked the BlueField-3 DPA and showed that its cores are considerably less powerful than the BlueField ARM cores and host CPU cores. In this work, in addition to the performance aspect addressed by their work, we benchmark those processors for energy efficiency.

2.4 Energy Efficiency

Previous work has looked at techniques to reduce the energy footprint of network functions on the CPU. They explore different power reduction mechanisms, such as Dynamic Voltage Frequency Scaling (DVFS) [39], sleeping time [14], core count reduction [60] and interrupts [48]. Because of the NFVs heavy reliance on packet polling, any effort for frequency autoscaling such as using *performance governors* [25] is annihilated by polling instructions filling CPUs to their maximal capacity.

Metronome [14] successfully reduced power consumption by implementing a *sleep&wake* method to reduce the impact of NIC polling. *ixcp* [60] progressively increases the core count then the frequency to scale the system's capacity to the workload. TUPE [39] reduces core frequency and inserts *napping* times following heuristics on CPU utilization. Natori et al. [48] takes advantage of a new CPU governor to control the C-states of a CPU core, allowing to go into deeper and energy-efficient C-states while ensuring short wake up delays upon packets arrival. Their work also takes advantage of hardware interrupts to lengthen the duration of stay in such deeper states. Additionally, other works [64] use DVFS directly on a GPU combined with frequency and core count reduction on the CPU to reduce power consumption. However, taking advantage of applying DVFS to the GPU requires a significant workload to fill GPUs' high capacity. Even at 100 Gbps, a GPU can remain at its idle-level energy consumption.

These solutions all induce an increase in latency, as packets are either not processed immediately when they arrive or because the CPU is slowed down. Sloth [11] allows reducing this latency increase by relying on previous observations of the workload. From these observations, Sloth identifies the least energy consuming cores-frequency combination which can sustain any specific latency.

Reducing power consumption is also possible by tuning the *uncore frequency*. Such terms, coined by Intel, designate the frequency at which every controller outside cores (e.g., integrated memory controllers, on-ship peripheral controllers, etc.) are operating. While the uncore frequency is scaled automatically by the hardware, it tends to be aggressive [10] and leads to unneeded overconsumption. Furthermore, uncore frequency scaling remains a frequent blind spot within the literature.

While prior research has explored the energy efficiency of individual architectures, like DPUs [44,73], CPUs [11,14,39,48,60], and GPUs [64], to the best of our knowledge, we present the first systematic and comprehensive comparison of these xPUs, evaluating their trade-offs across both performance and energy efficiency under a unified framework. Particularly, we expose the impact of the uncore even when the CPU is bypassed.

3 Implementation

In this section, we present the design and implementation of xPUBench and the processing models it supports. Since most of the state-of-the-art methods are unavailable or unmaintained, as shown in Table 1, we cannot easily rerun them.

Therefore, we implement these ideas from scratch to review them on a similar baseline.

We implement state-of-the-art communications patterns and our proposals for CPU-based methods (including CPU-GPU co-processing) in FastClick [5], an extended version of the Click Modular Router [35], when applicable. We considered other NFV-oriented processing frameworks such as BESS [21] or VPP [16], but FastClick provides most of the intrinsic features for high-speed, including kernel bypassing with DPDK [70], I/O batching and ARM support, comes with a richer set of features and has been the subject of recent academic works to improve its performance [15,18,49]. As the Click framework is not suitable for CPU-less platforms, we later detail the GPU-only approach, based on an NVIDIA sample, as well as the RISC-V implementation for the BlueField DPA, built on top of the samples provided by Chen *et al.* [9].

3.1 Automated Workload Generation and Measurements

xPUBench automates measurements using NPF [3]. NPF is responsible for orchestrating experiments, including defining the experimental design, deploying it, and collecting the data.

We integrate all the aforementioned processing models, as well as workload generation and energy measurements, into xPUBench. We contributed around 1600 lines of code (LoC) for the scripts used by NPF.

xPUBench and all implementations are available at https://github.com/ UCLouvain-ENSG/xPUBench.

3.2 CPU-GPU FastClick Pipelines

In our proposals, we stick to FastClick's best practices for multithreading [5] and follow a run-to-completion multithreaded processing path. In such a model, each packet is processed by the CPU core that received it, from reception to transmission. We added or modified 3662 LoC in FastClick. We built new FastClick template elements to implement a full-copy, ROI or zero-copy approach. These templates also hide the communication with the GPU to ease the development. Internally, we base the communication on the DPDK [70] GPU library. We also enable packet payloads to be received directly on GPU memory or on CPU memory mapped to the GPU. As in previous work, GPU elements themselves are rewritten from scratch in CUDA. Automatically compiling an existing CPU code to GPU, for instance, P4 to GPU [37], is orthogonal to our study.

The GPU workload is performed in parallel on all packets of a batch. One packet is processed with one GPU thread. When the processing of all packets from the batch is done, a shared flag is set. During GPU processing, the CPU alternates between processing packets from the NIC and polling the GPU completion flag, allowing packets to be enqueued while batches are being processed. When the GPU has processed the batch, the CPU retrieves it and continues processing in the pipeline. As in Batchy [36], we can configure both a minimal batch size and a maximum waiting delay for packets in the pipeline, but we prefer to show the tradeoff in this work and do not set any waiting time limit in our study.

3.3   Decoupling CPU and GPU Scalability

With the combination of processing models, memory models, and kernel models discussed in Sect. 2.1, we can effectively compare all previous work shown in Table 1. We further notice that if the application is computationally or memory intensive, new packets can arrive and be enqueued to the GPU in less time than it takes to process a single batch on the GPU.

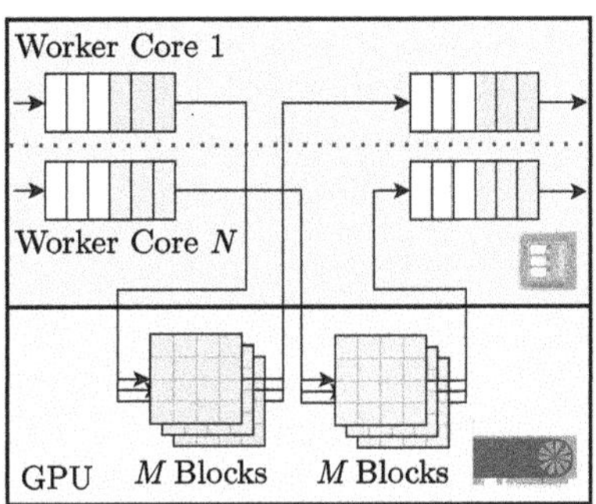

Fig. 5. Decoupled Parallel, our proposed processing model.

We propose a new, more scalable and resource-efficient CPU-GPU model that extends the parallel workers model. In this approach, GPU utilization can be tuned in two ways, as shown in Fig. 5: either by adjusting the number of CPU cores used to receive packets, or by increasing the number of queues a CPU core uses to communicate with the GPU. The latter increases GPU utilization while keeping the same CPU utilization, decoupling I/O scaling from computation scaling.

Batches from a queue are processed sequentially, but multiple queues are processed simultaneously, thanks to GPU *multi-stream* capabilities [50]. A stream defines an in-order sequence of operations. While all operations associated with a stream are executed in sequence, multiple streams can run on the same device simultaneously, allowing for parallel GPU kernel execution. The CPU fills the queues in a round-robin fashion. The GPU, however, processes the current batch of packets in all queues in parallel, using one stream per shared queue.

3.4   GPU-Only

The DOCA framework from NVIDIA provides GPUNetIO [54], a CPU-bypass implementation similar to GPU-Ether [28] working with NVIDIA NICs [52,53, 55]. As the GPU-only version is, of course, only running on GPU, it is a different code than FastClick based on an NVIDIA sample [54]. We contributed around 1364 LoC to implement the various applications.

The application is launched from the host CPU. Once it is started, all packet payloads and descriptors are received in GPU memory. Some GPU threads perform the packets' I/O and some others perform workloads. No CPU core is thus used when the traffic is being handled. This reduces latency, as there is no need to issue transactions to pass packets' info from the CPU to the GPU. Receive and send queues residing in GPU memory are used to transfer packets from the NIC to the GPU and the other way around. Each queue has a dedicated GPU block to process its packets. Packets are received per batch and packets of a batch are processed in parallel by up to 1024 packets [50]. Increasing the number of queues thus both spreads the load between multiple queues and increases GPU utilization. This work is the first to evaluate DOCA GPUNetIO performance at high speed.

As the NIC has to directly access GPU memory, the PCIe BAR of the GPU must be resizable, which limits the platforms that can run this implementation, as it is a BIOS-specific option.

3.5 DPU-Only

ARM Cores. We slightly modified FastClick to enable compilation on both BlueField-2 (BF2) [52] and BlueField-3 (BF3) [53] ARM cores. This allows to compare the performance of the CPU with that of the onboard ARM processor because they both run the same FastClick pipeline. The BlueField-2 is equipped with up to 8 ARMv8 A72 cores and 16 GB of DDR4 RAM. The BlueField-3 is equipped with up to 16 ARMv8.2+ A78 Hercules cores (64-bit) and 32 GB of DDR5 RAM.

DPA Cores. We build our applications on top of the datapath proposed by Chen *et al.* [9]. As recommended in their work, we use buffers allocated in ARM memory as opposed to DPA memory to receive packets, which enables us to sustain the line rate for an Ethernet mirroring application. The DPA can then access the packets using MMIO. Compared to DPDK which is used on the ARM cores, this datapath is particularly efficient. It leverages a shared RX-TX ring, eliminating the need for pointer copies between separate rings. In addition, its memory management is simpler: assuming run-to-completion execution, it can safely reuse the same buffers without relying on a memory pool. Following the approach of Chen *et al.* [9], we balance traffic across DPA threads using the destination MAC address. This approach is necessary due to the lack of documentation on using RSS with the DPA. Out of the 256 available threads, we were able to utilize 254. The DPA implementation adds around 300 LoC to the Chen *et al.* sample.

3.6 Limitations

In this work, we focus on simple stateless functions, an approach that facilitates similar implementations across different device architectures. Exploring stateful application performance would require complex, device-specific data structures and is left for future work. Particularly, DPU cores often exhibit architectural differences from traditional cores, such as smaller and slower caches in the case of the DPA [9]. We expect these differences to result in greater performance gaps in more complex, stateful workloads. Finally, we exclude all specialized accelerators present on the DPU, such as pattern-matching or compression engine [52], which are heavily task-specific.

4   Evaluation

In this section, we use xPUBench to evaluate the performance of all implementations. We first independently evaluate multiple VNFs processed on the CPU using standard FastClick, on the GPU using its various processing models, and on the DPUs. We also evaluate how important different factors are for each platform. We finally explore the energy efficiency of the various approaches.

4.1   Testbed

The server under test has an AMD EPYC 9124 16-core Processor at 3 GHz and 128 GB of RAM. An NVIDIA L4 GPU and an NVIDIA Mellanox ConnectX-6 100GbE NIC are connected on the same NUMA node, both on a PCIe 4.0 x16 slot. The second CPU on another NUMA node is only used for control. Simultaneous multithreading is disabled. The server runs the Linux kernel 5.15.0-113-generic. DPDK 23.11.0 is used in conjunction with CUDA 12.4, NVIDIA driver version 550.54.15 and DOCA 2.8.0082.

The BlueField-2 and BlueField-3 are running in standalone, externally powered. We stress the fact that for this study they can run in standalone, as packets do not ever reach the host CPU.

Packets are generated from another server, using Pktgen-DPDK [75] 23.06.1 with DPDK 23.03.0. The generator server is equipped with an Intel Xeon E-2378 octa-core Processor at 2.60 GHz, with 32 GB of RAM, and a single NUMA node. The NIC is an Intel Ethernet Controller E810-CAM1/2 100GbE, connected to the machine on a PCIe 4.0 x16 slot. The server runs the Linux kernel 5.15.0-113-generic.

Every run is repeated 3 times, and the standard deviation is always shown on the graph. When invisible, it should be assumed to be very low. When showing latency versus throughput, each point is only run once, as the variability is visible through the many measurements.

4.2   Workloads

We evaluate three workloads that stress different parts of the systems under review.

Ethernet Mirroring (labeled MAC) swaps the frame's source and destination Media Access Control (MAC) addresses. It is a baseline example application with a light workload, as only 12 B are read and modified for each received packet, regardless of its size. Furthermore, no memory lookup is required apart from accessing the packet.

Cyclic Redundancy Check computation (labeled CRC) computes a checksum on the full packet. It is an interesting proxy use case because it processes the whole packet. Therefore, the amount of data processed depends on the size of the frame.

IP Lookup (labeled IP1K or IP10K) looks up the destination IP address of the packet in a routing table. We used a linear search for its simplicity and ease of implementation. We perform IPv4 lookup exclusively. In this work, we do not look at faster implementation for CPU [65] or GPU [40] but simply consider it as a workload highly dependent on the routing table size. The table size therefore acts as a factor of complexity, similar in all implementations. Only 4 B of the IPv4 address is needed for each packet. The routing table used comes from the RIPE RIS database [62]. We obtained the data from collector 01 on 8 April 2024. We then take the top-N entries to form a routing table of size N, with $N = 1000$ in the IP1K cases and $N = 10000$ in the IP10K cases.

4.3   CPU Scalability

We first evaluate the scalability of the CPU implementation, where increasing the number of cores enables to run the VNF in parallel. We use RSS [27] to spread the load. Techniques such as RSS++ [4] could be used to ensure an even more balanced load between cores, but our synthetic workload ensures enough entropy for RSS to work efficiently.

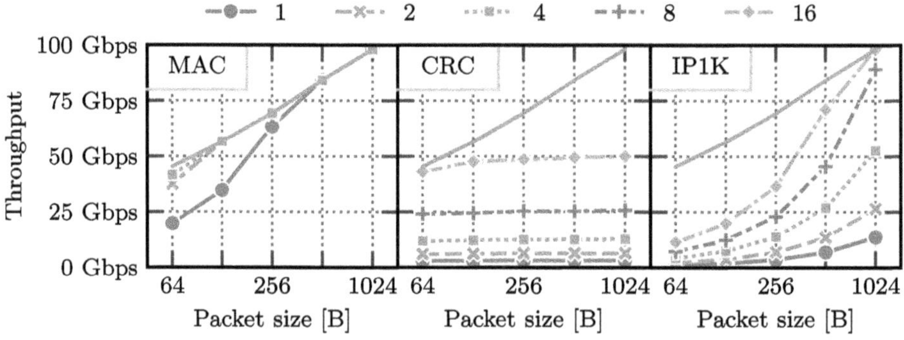

Fig. 6. Performance of the CPU implementation acc. to the number of CPU cores. Gray lines indicate the generator rate.

The throughput of the CPU implementation as the number of CPU cores increases is shown in Fig. 6. Four CPU cores are needed to handle Ethernet Mirroring on all packet sizes, but with large packets only one core is enough, as there are fewer packets received per second. For CRC computation, whose complexity is a function of the size of the packets, 16 CPU cores saturate the generator rate only for packets of 64 B. Recall that CPU cores handle both receiving and sending packets, as well as performing the workload: if it is heavy, there are fewer CPU cycles available to receive packets, leading to greater losses that are mitigated by spreading the load across more CPU cores. For IP lookup, independently of the packet size, increasing the number of cores by a factor of N leads to an increase of $\sim N$ times in the throughput, as our VNF under test does not share state between flows and can almost linearly scale.

⊙ **Takeaway 1.** CPUs struggle for even a relatively simple task such as CRC computation.

4.4   CPU-GPU Scalability

We then evaluate processing models in a CPU-GPU hybrid approach.

CPU Cores. We evaluate how performance scales in regard to the number of CPU cores used. The performance of the MW processing model, as well as the ROI, Z-C on CPU and Z-C on GPU memory models for the parallel processing model, are shown in Fig. 7. We do not evaluate separately full packet copy, as the ROI for the CRC actually showcases a complete packet copy.

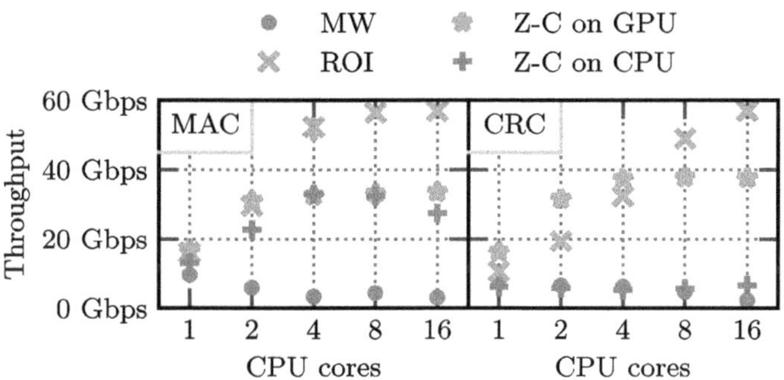

Fig. 7. Performance based on processing and memory model, with one CPU-GPU communication queue per core. Packet size is 128 B.

We notice the extremely poor performance of the MW processing model. Indeed, it saturates around 10 Gbps, and does not scale with the number of cores receiving packets. This threading strategy [19,22] is no longer viable at today's network speeds, as only one CPU core handles all communication with the GPU. Even with larger packets, the model fails to scale.

⊙ **Takeaway 2.** The Master-Workers processing model (PacketShader, APUNet) does not scale to modern speeds.

On the other hand, both the ROI and Zero-Copy using parallel workers scale with the number of cores, as they increase GPU utilization. We see that the Z-C on GPU plateaus after 2 cores for the Ethernet Mirroring and 4 cores for the CRC. We believe the bottleneck to be the number of PCIe transactions for the NIC-GPU interface. The ROI implementation continues to scale as it sends the bytes with a single DMA transaction per batch. Z-C on CPU matches Z-C on GPU for Ethernet mirroring, where only 16 bytes need to be written from and to CPU memory by the GPU. For the CRC workload where the whole packet needs to be fetched from the CPU memory by the GPU, Z-C on CPU offers poor performance. We measure the PCIe bandwidth with AMD uPerf and observe the Z-C on CPU leads to a 4× PCIe bandwidth increase. We believe it is because the GPU accesses the CPU transparently, always in cacheline-sized bursts. From now on, we only consider Z-C on GPU as it always provides better or equal performance.

⊙ **Takeaway 3.** ROI and full packet copy can still reach 100 Gbps, even with small packets.

⊙ **Takeaway 4.** While Z-C on GPU decreases the CPU PCIe utilization and slightly improves the per-core performance with regard to ROI when the full packet is needed, sending packet payloads from NIC to GPU leads to many PCIe transactions, leading to a plateau for small packets.

⊙ **Takeaway 5.** Accessing transparently the CPU memory from the GPU (as GASPP for large packets) is much less efficient than directly sending packets payloads to GPU memory.

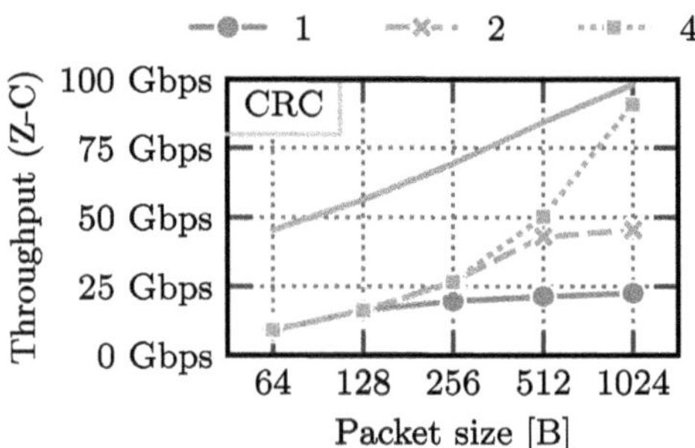

Fig. 8. Performance of the Z-C on GPU memory model on the CRC workload with a single CPU core, acc. to the number of CPU-GPU shared queues.

GPU Decoupled Parallelism. We then evaluate the performance of our new decoupled parallel model presented in Sect. 3.3. By balancing the load across CPU-GPU queues, we reduce the number of CPU cores needed. In the ROI model, increasing the number of queues does not lead to any improvement. As the implementation uses explicit copies, using multiple queues will lead to interleaved copies that cannot overlap, as the GPU only has a limited number of copy engines (2 in the L4 GPU we use) [50]. For cases that are more computationally intensive, more queues enable an increase of parallelism on the GPU, and thus a better throughput at constant CPU cores, as can be seen in Fig. 8 for the CRC use case.

⊙ **Takeaway 6.** Our new decoupled scaling strategy enables better use of GPU parallelism.

GPU Batching Size. We finally evaluate the performance based on the GPU batching size. We see in Fig. 9 that increasing the batching size always induces greater latency, as the Round-Trip Time (RTT) of the first packet in the batch includes the time taken to receive as many packets as there are in the batch, and leads to an equivalent or better throughput, as packets in a batch are processed in parallel.

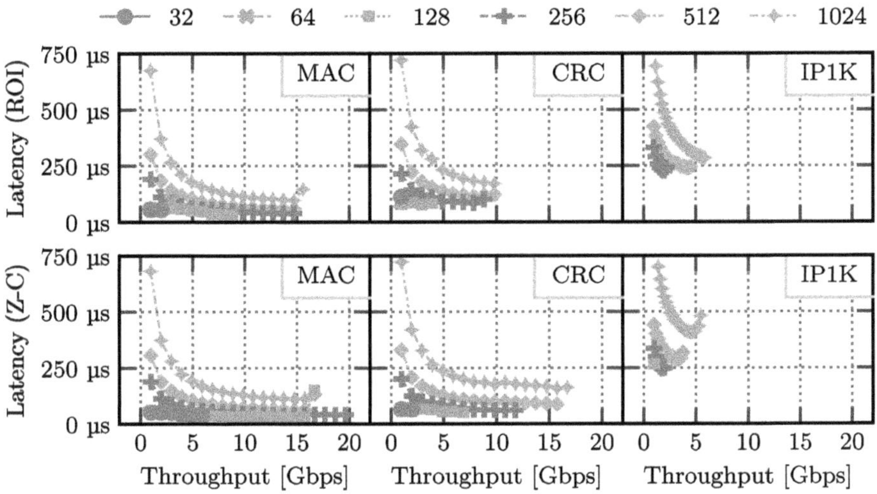

Fig. 9. Performance acc. to the GPU batching size. Packet size is 128 B, one CPU core retrieves packets and communicates with the GPU using a single queue.

⊙ **Takeaway 7.** In all implementations, using small batches results in poor throughput. Dynamic batch size adjustment is needed to avoid unnecessarily high latency.

⊙ **Takeaway 8.** While Takeaway 3 found parallel ROI (used by Snap) and full copies (both Snap and NBA) are efficient in terms of throughput, they induce a high latency due to the high need for batching to realize this throughput.

4.5 GPU-Only Scalability

We now evaluate the GPU-only implementation, analyzing both the impact of the number of queues used to spread the load and the batching size. We see in Fig. 10a that a high number of queues is needed to achieve a high throughput for all workloads. Using a low number of queues can make the implementation unable to handle a high volume of packets per queue, depending on the complexity of the use case. The problem arises when GPU processing is faster than the NIC and overwrites the NIC descriptors. This is a feature of the DOCA GPUNetIO library, stating that, for performance reasons, it is the developer's responsibility to ensure the NIC can flush the TX rings quickly enough before the CPU enqueues new packets. A heavier workload makes it more difficult to overwrite NIC descriptors because it processes more packets.

With small packets, the implementation is unable to saturate the generator rate, as already observed in Sect. 4.4 with the Z-C on GPU model. We also see that the throughput scales perfectly with the number of queues, as increasing it also extends the GPU utilization: one persistent kernel is running per queue. Furthermore, we see in Fig. 10b that the batching size does not influence much the latency, but has a steady impact on throughput for heavy workloads.

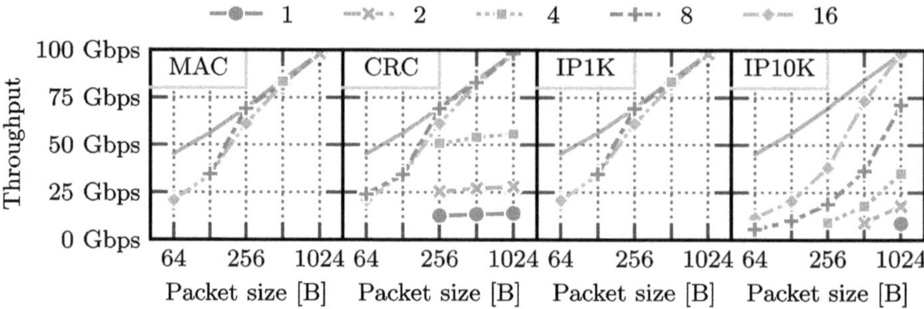

(a) Throughput acc. to the number of GPU queues, using a batching size of 1024.

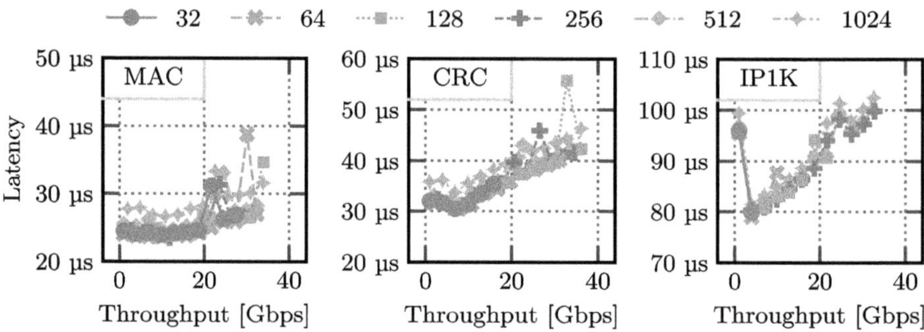

(b) Performance acc. to the GPU batching size. Packet size is 128 B. Y-axis is truncated to highlight the results.

Fig. 10. Performance of the GPU-only implementation.

We finally measured the same benchmark on another testbed in Appendix A. With newer generations of NICs and GPU, the limit in messages per second is alleviated.

⊙ **Takeaway 9.** Processing packets entirely on GPU is extremely efficient for large packets.

⊙ **Takeaway 10.** However, previous work at lower speeds failed to demonstrate the NIC has a modest packet rate when sending small packets directly to the GPU (both in Z-C or in GPU-Only).

⊙ **Takeaway 11.** To take advantage of GPU parallelism, a high number of queues is needed. GPU-Ether speed did not bring up such a need.

4.6 DPU Scalability

We evaluate the performance of CPU-based DPUs for executing NFV pipelines. We evaluate the ARM cores on both the BlueField-2 and BlueField-3, as well as the RISC-V cores (DPA) available on the BlueField-3.

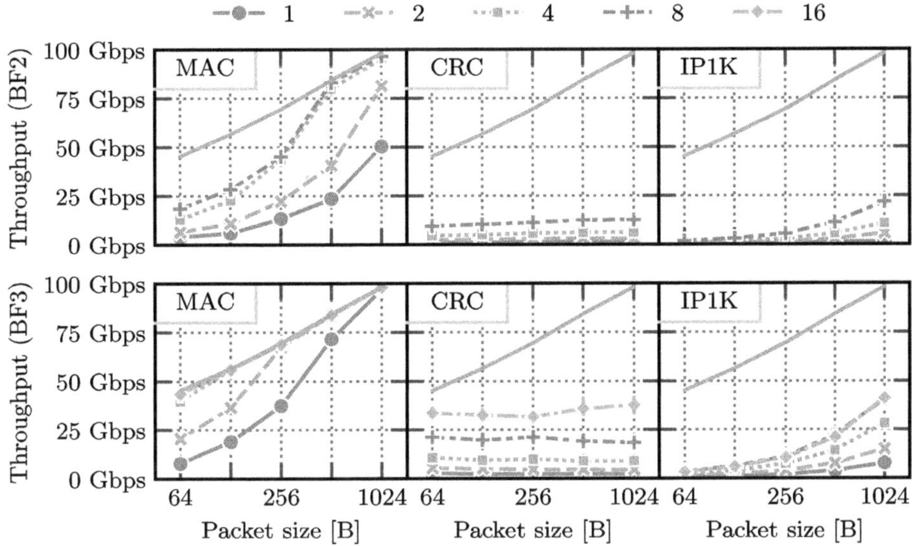

Fig. 11. Performance of the DPU implementations acc. to the number of ARM cores, running on the BlueField-2 (BF2) and BlueField-3 (BF3).

ARM Scalability. We see in Fig. 11 that performance differs drastically between the two DPUs. The BF2 is not able to saturate the NIC for small packets using its 8 ARM cores, even with a processing as lightweight as Ethernet Mirroring. With heavier workloads, the BF2's ARM cores performance is even more degraded.

The BF3, on the other hand, can reach the generator rate, doing Ethernet Mirroring for all packet sizes with only 8 of its embedded ARM cores. Using all 16 ARM cores provides a throughput close to the CPU implementation for the CRC computation and IP lookup. The performance of this DPU enables offloading even intensive tasks directly, thereby avoiding the host CPU entirely.

⊙ **Takeaway 12.** The BlueField-2 ARM cores are unable to reach the generator rate for small packets.

⊙ **Takeaway 13.** The BlueField-3 ARM cores provide similar throughput to a (x86) CPU-only implementation.

DPA Scalability. As shown in Fig. 12, DPA performance scales linearly with the number of threads. For both CRC and IP Lookup operations, increasing the number of threads continuously improves performance, even beyond the 190-thread limit used in previous work [9]. We observe that the DPA on the BF3 is on par with the ARM cores on the BF2, the previous generation of BlueField cards.

⊙ **Takeaway 14.** The BlueField-3 DPA performance is similar to that of the BlueField-2 weaker ARM cores.

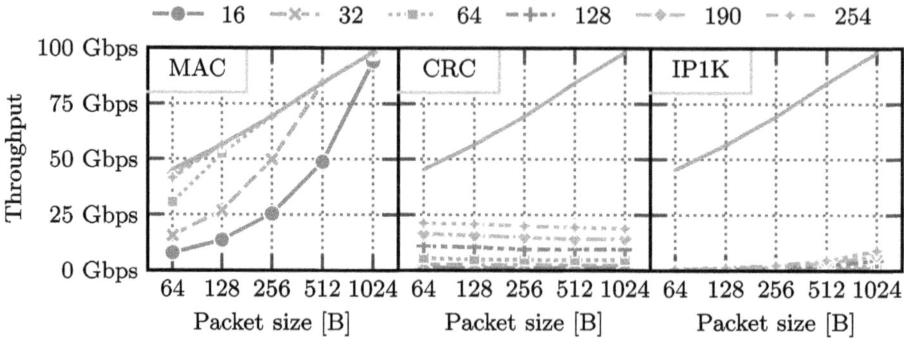

Fig. 12. Performance of the DPA implementations on the BlueField-3 with a variable number of threads.

4.7   Comparison of Processing Models and Devices

We compare in Fig. 13 the performance of the CPU-only, DPU-only (both BlueField-2 ARM cores and BlueField-3 ARM and DPA cores), two scalable CPU-GPU techniques (ROI and Z-C on GPU), and GPU-only (GPU Direct) approaches. Each implementation is tuned to its best-performing point, based on all previous evaluations of parameters. We see that, in the Ethernet Mirroring use case, the generator rate is easily reached by the CPU, ROI, BF3 and DPA implementations. As explained before, the Z-C and GPU-only implementations cannot sustain the rate offered with small packets.

Regarding CRC computation, only a GPU can sustain the computation load, except for small packets where the CPU and BF3 ARM cores can saturate the generator.

On a 1K IP lookup, as the amount of data needed on the GPU is small, the ROI is advantageous. GPU Direct can sustain the computation but is still limited with small packets. It is, however, the only one able to handle the 10K lookup. By removing the CPU bottleneck, performing the packet I/O on GPU turns out to be highly beneficial for such high-load use cases.

Regarding latency, the CPU and DPU implementations generally perform the best; however, they are unable to deliver high throughput. The CPU-GPU implementations are the most latency-prone, suffering from the additional communication between the two devices and the need to batch many packets to realize this throughput.

Regarding the BF3 DPA, we see that for intensive workloads its performance is comparable to the BF2 ARM cores. From this observation, we conclude that the DPA on the BF3 can be used to offload tasks from the BF3's ARM cores, similar to how DPUs can offload tasks from the host.

⊙ **Takeaway 15.** DPU and DPA implementations provide low latencies thanks to their on-NIC positions, but struggle to sustain high throughput.

⊙ **Takeaway 16.** The CPU-GPU hybrid models' latency is high because of the added communication between the two devices.

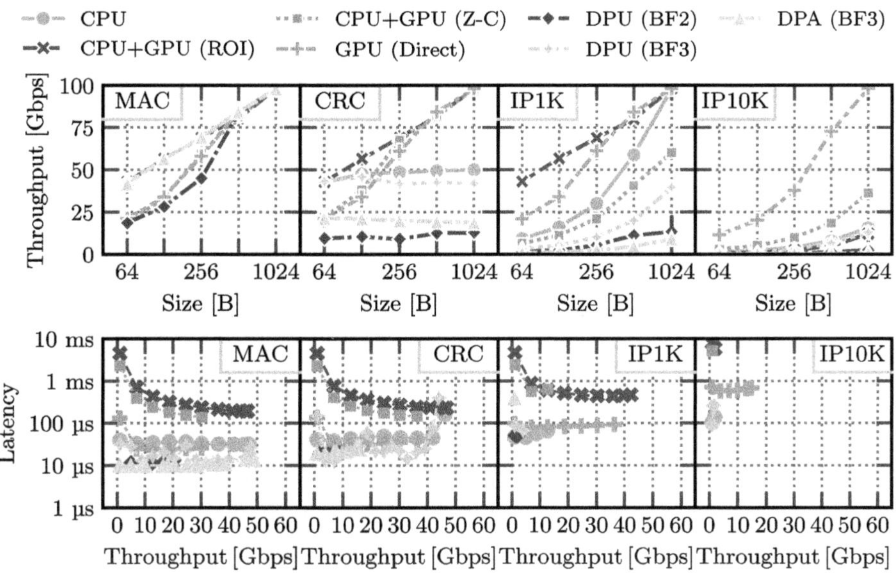

Fig. 13. Performance of each implementation on different applications. Latency is measured with packets of 128 B, and its scale is logarithmic.

⊙ **Takeaway 17.** GPU Direct performs best for large packets and intensive workloads while maintaining a small latency.

4.8 Energy Efficiency

This section addresses the energy efficiency of the different implementations. First, we focus solely on the impact of various factors of the CPU power consumption. Then, we consider the total (CPU + GPU) energy consumption with regard to the application workload. We report the CPU power consumption using RAPL [32] and the GPU power consumption using the NVIDIA System Management Interface [51] tool. We observed a delta of approximately 100 W between the sum of our counters and the actual power drawn by the server reported by IPMI. This difference can be explained by other components, such as the cooling system, the motherboard and disks. For the DPUs, we use a Benchlab and its PCIe adapter [6] that cuts down the PCIe power from the motherboard and replaces it with a monitored power supply connected through USB.

CPU Down-Scaling. When the host CPU is processing packets, as DPDK is polling, the CPU is always busy at 100 % and consumes a significant amount of power. In addition to the approach of Sloth [11] that uses core count and core frequency scaling as levers to reduce energy consumption, we introduce the study of uncore frequency scaling.

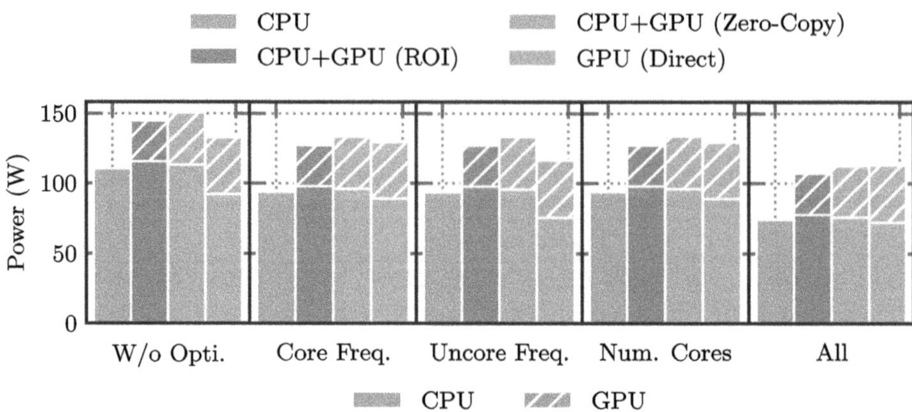

Fig. 14. Impact of core and uncore frequency scaling and core count on the power consumption of the CPU and GPU running Ethernet mirroring. The rate is fixed at 100 Gbps. DPA and DPU implementations are not included due to their insensitivity to the host CPU.

Section 2.4 explained how DVFS can be used to slow down the cores of a CPU, or the uncore (memory controller, PCIe root complex, and so on). While the core frequency can be adjusted through built-in tools within the Linux kernel, the uncore frequency relies on vendor-dependent tools to interact with hardware components. On AMD processors, such changes require communicating with the hardware through the HSMP mailbox system to adjust *fabric* and *memory* clocks [1].

Figure 14 presents the impact of core count and core/uncore frequency scaling on power consumption. Except from GPU Direct, each implementation benefits from all these optimizations and further power reduction can be achieved through a combination of these techniques. Following this approach, the power consumption of the CPU implementation is reduced by more than 30 W.

Although the GPU Direct implementation bypasses the CPU, therefore canceling any effort to reduce energy consumption by reducing core count or core frequency, adjusting the uncore frequency leads to a ~ 15 W reduction as packets still flow through the PCIe root complex. Even with the uncore at its minimal frequency, the CPU draws more than ~ 70 W, although it is not processing a single packet.

⊙ **Takeaway 18.** CPU core and uncore frequency scaling, and/or core count scaling, benefits to all implementations' power consumption.

⊙ **Takeaway 19.** The CPU power consumption is still high even when it is completely bypassed.

⊙ **Takeaway 20.** Adjusting the uncore frequency can further reduce the power consumption, although it remained essentially unexplored in previous work.

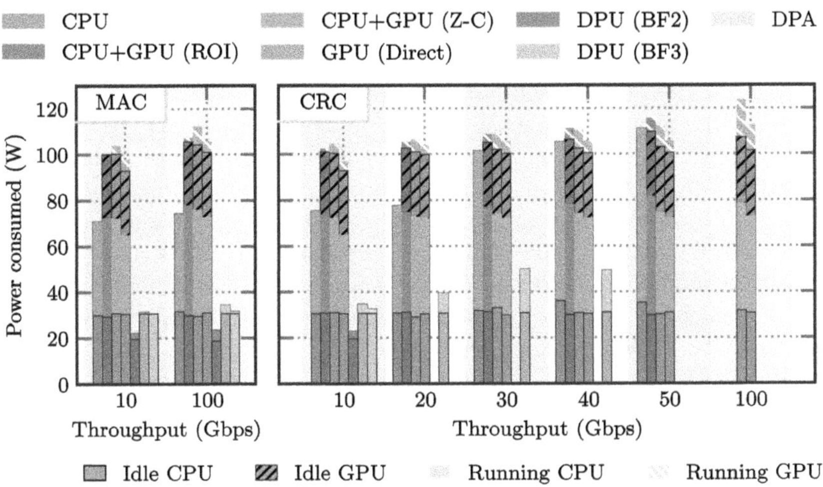

Fig. 15. Power consumed by the different processing models at various speeds, on 1024 B packets. The missing bars at different rates indicate that the system cannot sustain the generator rate, so there are no valid data points.

Energy Tradeoff. Figure 15 shows the consumption of the system under test at various input rates, with 1024 B packets. Bars are only displayed for systems that can keep up with the input rate. We run the Ethernet Mirroring use case, where all proposed implementations can forward traffic at 100 Gbps, and the CRC use case.

The CPU+GPU approaches are less energy-efficient, as they pay the price of being a hybrid system with two relatively high idle consumption. The CPU draws up to 35 W when idle while the GPU consumes around 25 W idling.

The DPU approaches are by far the most energy-efficient ones. However, they can only sustain a relatively low rate. For the CRC use case, the BF2 is limited to 11 Gbps, and the BF3 to 43 Gbps, at which point they respectively draw 24 W and 50 W. Moreover, the power consumption of the DPU includes the whole board capable of running in standalone mode, whereas for other methods, we only report the power of the CPU and/or the GPU. The CPU approach follows in terms of efficiency, but fails to reach 100 Gbps.

⊙ **Takeaway 21.** DPU ARM and DPA cores are the most power efficient, but are limited in terms of performance.

⊙ **Takeaway 22.** The DPU power consumption is dominated by idle consumption. Therefore, for the BF3, using the more efficient DPA instead of the ARM cores does not significantly reduce the consumption.

⊙ **Takeaway 23.** In terms of power consumption, GPU Direct is best when heavy computations are needed.

5   Conclusion

We propose xPUBench, a benchmarking environment that allows us to review the current body of research on packet processing using GPUs and DPUs. Our analysis shows that there is no one-size-fits-all solution. Each approach has its own strengths and drawbacks. Some existing models rely on a single master core to interface with the GPU. This approach struggles to scale with the speeds of modern NICs. Parallel models make each worker communicate directly with the GPU, removing the single core bottleneck. We evaluate the use of new capabilities of recent NICs such as Zero-Copy on GPU memory, and introduce a new model of scalability by allowing each worker to communicate with the GPU through multiple queues. Our approach achieves over a $2\times$ improvement in throughput compared to a 16-cores CPU implementation on heavy computations, reaching 100 Gbps with a single CPU core.

Our evaluation demonstrates that the use of a GPU to run the entire pipeline, without CPU involvement, provides higher throughput than hybrid solutions that rely on the CPU for I/O operations, while offering a highly reduced latency. However, current hardware fails to handle small packets at high rate. Even when avoiding CPU processing entirely, GPU solutions rely on CPU resources during PCIe transfers, which prevents the CPU from entering low-power states. While this limitation can be partially mitigated by slowing down the CPU uncore frequency, it remains a significant burden on the system's power consumption.

Finally, we showed that DPUs like the BlueField-2 and 3 can be used as coprocessors for NFV workloads. They offer the lowest latencies, as the ARM CPUs and DPA reside directly on the NIC. While the BF2 ARM cores and the DPA are very limited in terms of compute capacity, we observe that the more powerful BF3 ARM cores put the whole card on par with the host CPU in terms of performance, using less than half the power consumed by the host CPU alone.

Acknowledgments. The authors would like to acknowledge the anonymous reviewers for their valuable feedback. This work was supported by the Walloon region's CyberExcellence program under Grant № 2110186, and by the UCLouvain FSR. It was also supported by the Fonds de la Recherche Scientifique – FNRS MIS Grant № 40020886. Maxime Vanliefde is a Research Fellow of the FNRS. Clément Delzotti is a FRIA grantee of the FNRS. We also thank NVIDIA for granting a BlueField-2 used in prototyping.

Ethical Considerations. This work does not raise any ethical concerns.

Disclosure of Interests. The authors have no competing interests to declare that are relevant to the content of this article.

A   Hardware Impact on GPU-Only

We also evaluate the performance of the GPU-only implementation on another testbed. A HPE server is equipped with an NVIDIA L40S GPU and a BlueField-3 in NIC mode, connected via a PCIe 5.0 x16 system bus. The two are not

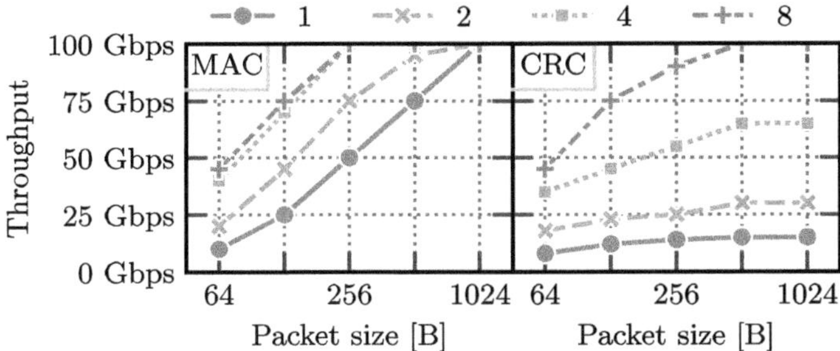

Fig. 16. Throughput of the GPU-only implementation using an NVIDIA L40S GPU and a BlueField-3 acc. to the number of queues.

connected through a dedicated PCIe switch. Results are shown in Fig. 16. In this situation, performance results are different with respect to the main testbed. There are no more points where the implementation is unable to answer, as the NIC is faster to flush the descriptors in its rings. Overall, benchmarks show better numbers in terms of throughput, as implied by the better GPU used.

References

1. Advanced Micro Devices Inc.: AMD HSMP. https://github.com/amd/amd_hsmp
2. Ahmed, M.R., Shatabda, S., Islam, A.M., et al.: Intrusion detection system in software-defined networks using machine learning and deep learning techniques–a comprehensive survey. Authorea Preprints (2023)
3. Barbette, T.: Network performance framework. https://github.com/tbarbette/npf
4. Barbette, T., Katsikas, G.P., Maguire, G.Q., et al.: RSS++: load and state-aware receive side scaling. In: CoNEXT 2019. ACM, New York, NY, USA (2019). https://doi.org/10.1145/3359989.3365412
5. Barbette, T., Soldani, C., Mathy, L.: Fast userspace packet processing. In: ANCS 2015, pp. 5–16. IEEE Computer Society, USA (2016)
6. BENCHLAB: Measuring PCIe slot power consumption (2024). https://benchlab.io/blogs/technical/measuring-pcie-slot-power-consumption
7. Bonfim, M.S., Dias, K.L., Fernandes, S.F.L.: Integrated NFV/SDN architectures: a systematic literature review. ACM Comput. Surv. **51**(6) (2019). https://doi.org/10.1145/3172866
8. Chaurasia, A.K., Garg, A., Raman, B., et al.: Simmer: rate proportional scheduling to reduce packet drops in vGPU based NF chains. In: ICPP 2022. ACM, New York, NY, USA (2023). https://doi.org/10.1145/3545008.3545068
9. Chen, X., Zhang, J., Fu, T., et al.: Demystifying datapath accelerator enhanced off-path SmartNIC. In: 2024 IEEE 32nd International Conference on Network Protocols (ICNP 2024), pp. 1–12. IEEE (2024)
10. Corbalan, J., Vidal, O., Alonso, L., et al.: Explicit uncore frequency scaling for energy optimisation policies with EAR in Intel architectures. In: 2021 IEEE International Conference on Cluster Computing (CLUSTER 2021), pp. 572–581 (2021). https://doi.org/10.1109/Cluster48925.2021.00089. iSSN: 2168-9253

11. Delzotti, C., Maistriaux, P., Barbette, T.: Sloth: a kernel-bypass scheduler maximizing energy efficiency under latency constraints. In: IFIP 2025 Slices Workshop-International Federation for Information Processing (IFIP 2025) Networking 2025 Conference (2025)

12. Di Girolamo, S., Kurth, A., Calotoiu, A., et al.: A RISC-V in-network accelerator for flexible high-performance low-power packet processing. In: In: ISCA 2021, pp. 958–971. IEEE (2021)

13. DPDK: Generic flow API (rte_flow) (2026). https://doc.dpdk.org/guides-24.07/prog_guide/rte_flow.html

14. Faltelli, M., Belocchi, G., Quaglia, F., et al.: Metronome: adaptive and precise intermittent packet retrieval in DPDK. In: CoNEXT 2020, pp. 406–420. ACM, New York, NY, USA (2020). https://doi.org/10.1145/3386367.3432730

15. Farshin, A., Barbette, T., Roozbeh, A., et al.: PacketMill: toward per-core 100-Gbps networking. In: ASPLOS 2021. ACM, New York, NY, USA (2021). https://doi.org/10.1145/3445814.3446724

16. FD.io: VPP. https://wiki.fd.io/view/VPP/

17. Feng, Y., Panda, S., Kulkarni, S.G., et al.: A SmartNIC-accelerated monitoring platform for in-band network telemetry. In: 2020 IEEE International Symposium on Local and Metropolitan Area Networks LANMAN, pp. 1–6. IEEE (2020)

18. Ghasemirahni, H., Farshin, A., Scazzariello, M., et al.: FAJITA: stateful packet processing at 100 million PPS. In: CoNEXT 2024 (2024)

19. Go, Y., Jamshed, M., Moon, Y., et al.: APUNet: revitalizing GPU as packet processing accelerator. In: Proceedings of the 14th USENIX Conference on Networked Systems Design and Implementation. In: NSDI 2017, pp. 83–96. USENIX Association, USA (2017)

20. Guo, Z., Lin, J., Bai, Y., et al.: LogNIC: a high-level performance model for smart-NICs. In: Proceedings of the 56th Annual IEEE/ACM International Symposium on Microarchitecture, pp. 916–929 (2023)

21. Han, S., Jang, K., Panda, A., et al.: SoftNIC: a software NIC to augment hardware. EECS Department, University of California, Berkeley, Technical report. UCB/EECS-2015-155 (2015)

22. Han, S., Jang, K., Park, K., et al.: PacketShader: a GPU-accelerated software router. ACM SIGCOMM Comput. Commun. Rev. **40**(4), 195–206 (2010)

23. Harris, S.L., Chaver, D., Piñuel, L., et al.: RVfpga: using a RISC-V core targeted to an FPGA in computer architecture education. In: 2021 31st International Conference on Field-Programmable Logic and Applications (FPL), pp. 145–150. IEEE (2021)

24. Hasanth, K.M., Basu, S., Nadig, D.: Data processing unit (DPU) based network process offloading for efficient service meshes. In: 2024 IEEE 10th International Conference on Network Softwarization (NetSoft), pp. 319–321, June 2024. https://doi.org/10.1109/NetSoft60951.2024.10588912

25. Huang, D., Costero, L., Atienza, D.: Is the powersave governor really saving power? In: 2024 IEEE 24th International Symposium on Cluster, Cloud and Internet Computing (CCGrid), pp. 273–283, May 2024. https://doi.org/10.1109/CCGrid59990.2024.00039. iSSN: 2993-2114

26. Humphries, J.T., Natu, N., Kaffes, K., et al.: Wave: Offloading resource management to SmartNIC cores. In: Proceedings of the 30th ACM International Conference on Architectural Support for Programming Languages and Operating Systems, vol. 3, pp. 264–281 (2025)

27. Intel Corporation: Improving network performance in multi-core systems (2007). https://www.intel.com/content/dam/support/us/en/documents/network/sb/318483001us2.pdf. White Paper
28. Jung, C., Kim, S., Yeom, I., et al.: GPU-Ether: GPU-native Packet I/O for GPU applications on commodity ethernet. In: IEEE INFOCOM 2021 - IEEE Conference on Computer Communications, pp. 1–10 (2021). https://doi.org/10.1109/INFOCOM42981.2021.9488699
29. Kalia, A., Zhou, D., Kaminsky, M., et al.: Raising the bar for using GPUs in software packet processing. In: NSDI 2015. USENIX Association USA (2015)
30. Katsikas, G.P., Barbette, T., Chiesa, M., et al.: What you need to know about (smart) network interface cards. In: International Conference on Passive and Active Network Measurement, pp. 319–336. Springer (2021)
31. Kfoury, E.F., Choueiri, S., Mazloum, A., et al.: A comprehensive survey on Smart-NICs: architectures, development models, applications, and research directions. IEEE Access (2024)
32. Khan, K.N., Hirki, M., Niemi, T., et al.: RAPL in action: experiences in using RAPL for power measurements. ACM Trans. Model. Perform. Eval. Comput. Syst. (TOMPECS) **3**(2), 1–26 (2018)
33. Khazraee, M., Forencich, A., Papen, G.C., et al.: Rosebud: making FPGA-accelerated middlebox development more pleasant. In: Proceedings of the 28th ACM International Conference on Architectural Support for Programming Languages and Operating Systems, vol. 3, pp. 586–605 (2023)
34. Kim, J., Jang, K., Lee, K., et al.: NBA (network balancing act): a high-performance packet processing framework for heterogeneous processors. In: Proceedings of the Tenth European Conference on Computer Systems, EuroSys 2015. ACM, New York, NY, USA (2015). https://doi.org/10.1145/2741948.2741969
35. Kohler, E., Morris, R., Benjie, C., et al.: The click modular router. ACM Trans. Comput. Syst. **18**(3), 263–297 (2000)
36. Lévai, T., Németh, F., Raghavan, B., et al.: Batchy: batch-scheduling data flow graphs with service-level objectives. In: NSDI 2020 (2020)
37. Li, P., Luo, Y.: P4GPU: accelerate packet processing of a p4 program with a CPU-GPU heterogeneous architecture. In: Proceedings of the 2016 Symposium on Architectures for Networking and Communications Systems, pp. 125–126 (2016)
38. Li, T.H., Chu, H.M., Wang, P.C.: IP address lookup using GPU. In: 2013 IEEE 14th International Conference on High Performance Switching and Routing (HPSR), pp. 177–184. IEEE (2013)
39. Li, X., Cheng, W., Zhang, T., et al.: Power efficient high performance packet I/O. In: ICPP 2018. ACM, New York, NY, USA (2019). https://doi.org/10.1145/3225058.3225129
40. Li, Y., Zhang, D., Liu, A.X., et al.: GAMT: a fast and scalable IP lookup engine for GPU-based software routers. In: Architectures for Networking and Communications Systems, pp. 1–12. IEEE (2013)
41. Lin, H., Wang, C.L.: Efficient low-latency packet processing using on-GPU thread-data remapping. J. Parallel Distrib. Comput. **133**, 51–62 (2019)
42. Lin, J., Guo, Z., Shah, M., et al.: Enabling portable and high-performance Smart-NIC programs with Alkali. In: NSDI 2025 (2025)
43. Liu, M., Cui, T., Schuh, H., et al.: Offloading distributed applications onto Smart-NICs using iPipe. In: Proceedings of the ACM Special Interest Group on Data Communication, pp. 318–333 (2019)

44. Mafioletti, D.R., Dominicini, C.K., Martinello, M., et al.: PIaFFE: a place-as-you-go in-network framework for flexible embedding of VNFs. In: ICC 2020 - 2020 IEEE International Conference on Communications (ICC), pp. 1–6 (2020). https://doi.org/10.1109/ICC40277.2020.9149240

45. Miano, S., Doriguzzi-Corin, R., Risso, F., et al.: Introducing SmartNICs in server-based data plane processing: the DDoS mitigation use case. IEEE Access **7**, 107161–107170 (2019)

46. Miano, S., Sanaee, A., Risso, F., et al.: Domain specific run time optimization for software data planes. In: Proceedings of the 27th ACM International Conference on Architectural Support for Programming Languages and Operating Systems (ASPLOS 2022), pp. 1148–1164 (2022)

47. Mijumbi, R., Serrat, J., Gorricho, J.L., et al.: Network function virtualization: state-of-the-art and research challenges. IEEE Commun. Surv. Tutorials **18**(1), 236–262 (2015)

48. Natori, K., Fujimoto, K., Shiraga, A.: Sleep control of packet receiving thread toward power saving. Ann. Telecommun. (2025). https://doi.org/10.1007/s12243-025-01084-2

49. Navarre, L., Michel, F., Barbette, T.: A high-speed robust tunnel using forward erasure correction in segment routing. In: ICNP 2024 (2024)

50. NVIDIA Corporation: CUDA C++ programming guide. https://docs.nvidia.com/cuda/cuda-c-programming-guide/

51. NVIDIA Corporation: System management interface smi, https://developer.nvidia.com/system-management-interface

52. NVIDIA Corporation: NVIDIA BlueField-2 DPU (2021). https://www.nvidia.com/content/dam/en-zz/Solutions/Data-Center/documents/datasheet-nvidia-bluefield-2-dpu.pdf

53. NVIDIA Corporation: NVIDIA BlueField-3 DPU (2021). https://www.nvidia.com/content/dam/en-zz/Solutions/Data-Center/documents/datasheet-nvidia-bluefield-3-dpu.pdf

54. NVIDIA Corporation: DOCA GPUNetIO (2024). https://docs.nvidia.com/doca/sdk/doca+gpunetio/index.html

55. NVIDIA Corporation: NVIDIA ConnectX-7 400G adapters (2024). https://www.nvidia.com/content/dam/en-zz/Solutions/networking/infiniband/connectx-7-datasheet.pdf

56. NVIDIA Corporation: DPA subsystem (2025). https://docs.nvidia.com/doca/sdk/dpa+subsystem/index.html

57. PCI-SIG: PCI Express Base Specification Revision 5.0 Version 1.0. PCI-SIG. https://picture.iczhiku.com/resource/eetop/SYkDTqhOLhpUTnMx.pdf

58. Poli, L., Saha, S., Zhai, X., et al.: Design and implementation of a RISC V processor on FPGA. In: 2021 17th International Conference on Mobility, Sensing and Networking (MSN), pp. 161–166. IEEE (2021)

59. Poutievski, L., Mashayekhi, O., Ong, J., et al.: Jupiter evolving: transforming Google's datacenter network via optical circuit switches and software-defined networking. In: Proceedings of the ACM SIGCOMM 2022 Conference, pp. 66–85 (2022)

60. Prekas, G., Primorac, M., Belay, A., et al.: Energy proportionality and workload consolidation for latency-critical applications. In: Proceedings of the Sixth ACM Symposium on Cloud Computing, SoCC 2015, pp. 342–355. ACM, New York, NY, USA, August 2015. https://doi.org/10.1145/2806777.2806848

61. Ring, W.: 100 Gbit interconnects and above: the need for speed (2007)

62. RIPE NCC: Routing information service (RIS) (2024). https://www.ripe.net/analyse/internet-measurements/routing-information-service-ris/
63. Rizzo, L.: Netmap: a novel framework for fast packet I/O. In: 21st USENIX Security Symposium (USENIX Security 12), pp. 101–112 (2012)
64. Romein, J.W.: Breaking the I/O barrier: 1.2 TB/S ethernet packet processing on a GPU. In: European Conference on Parallel Processing, pp. 225–238. Springer (2025)
65. Sahni, S., Kim, K.S.: Efficient construction of multibit tries for IP lookup. IEEE/ACM Trans. Network. **11**(4), 650–662 (2003)
66. Shoaib, N., Shamsi, J., Mustafa, T., et al.: GDPI: signature based deep packet inspection using GPUs. Int. J. Adv. Comput. Sci. Appl. **8**(11) (2017)
67. Silberstein, M., Kim, S., Huh, S., et al.: GPUNet: networking abstractions for GPU programs. ACM Trans. Comput. Syst. (TOCS 2016) **34**(3), 1–31 (2016)
68. Sonai, V., Bharathi, I., Noor Mahammad, S.: A perspective of IP lookup approach using graphical processing unit (GPU). In: International Conference on Distributed Computing and Intelligent Technology, pp. 98–103. Springer (2023)
69. Sun, W., Ricci, R.: Fast and flexible: parallel packet processing with GPUs and click. In: Architectures for Networking and Communications Systems, pp. 25–35. IEEE (2013)
70. The Linux Foundation Projects: DPDK. https://www.dpdk.org/
71. Vasiliadis, G., Koromilas, L., Polychronakis, M., et al.: GASPP: a GPU-accelerated stateful packet processing framework. In: 2014 USENIX Annual Technical Conference (ATC 2014), pp. 321–332 (2014)
72. Vasiliadis, G., Polychronakis, M., Ioannidis, S.: Parallelization and characterization of pattern matching using GPUs. In: 2011 IEEE International Symposium on Workload Characterization (IISWC), pp. 216–225. IEEE (2011)
73. Vogt, F.G., Rodriguez, F., Luizelli, M.C., et al.: Poster: Towards in-network resource scaling of VNFs. In: CoNEXT 2024, pp. 29–30 (2024)
74. Wang, Y., Zu, Y., Zhang, T., et al.: Wire speed name lookup: a GPU-based approach. In: NSDI 2013 (2013)
75. Wiles, K.: Pktgen-DPDK. https://github.com/pktgen/Pktgen-DPDK
76. Yi, X., Wang, J., Duan, J., et al.: FlowShader: a generalized framework for GPU-accelerated VNF flow processing. In: ICNP 2019 (2019)
77. Zhang, K., He, B., Hu, J., et al.: G-Net: effective GPU sharing in NFV systems. In: NSDI 2018 (2018)

Characterizing Bluefields' Memory Bandwidth Bottlenecks

Michał Piotr Podleś[1,2(✉)] (ID), Idelfonso Tafur Monroy[2] (ID),
Juan Jose Vegas Olmos[1] (ID), and Boris Pismenny[1] (ID)

[1] NVIDIA, Santa Clara, USA
mpodles@nvidia.com
[2] Eindhoven University of Technology, Eindhoven, Netherlands

Abstract. Emerging multi-hundred gigabit Ethernet speeds are out-pacing improvements in CPU performance and memory bandwidth, challenging host-based I/O processing capacity. SmartNICs, such as NVIDIA BlueField, promise to overcome this challenge by offloading network-intensive computation, freeing up host resources. We show, however, that SmartNICs fall short of this goal, offloading only a small portion of the host CPU and wire bandwidth for common tasks—BlueField-2 NVMe-over-TCP storage disaggregation offloads up to 4 host cores while BlueField-3 achieves up to 14 cores.

Prior work attributes this limitation to weaker SmartNIC cores; in contrast, in this work we identify SmartNIC memory bandwidth as the key bottleneck to line-rate performance. We then leverage SmartNIC support for direct cache access to overcome this bottleneck by constraining I/O buffers to the last-level cache (LLC). Our evaluation shows the benefits of this approach by improving BlueField-2 and BlueField-3 throughput on the previous benchmark by up to 56% and 20%, respectively.

1 Introduction

Server I/O speeds are rapidly increasing with PCIe bandwidth doubling every three years [39]. NIC speeds, in particular, are rising at an even higher pace with 100 GbE, 200 GbE, and 400 GbE already widely available and 800 GbE and 1.6 TbE NICs arriving in 2025 and 2026, respectively. The rapid growth in I/O speeds introduces bottlenecks for other host resources: CPU [8,50] and memory [24,34,35,43].

Figure 1 demonstrates that today's server I/O speeds already exceed CPU TCP and memory speeds. It shows I/O, memory, and CPU TCP bandwidth metrics for maximum core configurations of recent CPU architectures: Intel Emerald Rapids [15], AMD EPYC 9004 [2], and NVIDIA Grace (ARM) [29]. CPU bandwidth is calculated by multiplying the core number with typical TCP iperf throughput on Intel CPUs (i.e., 25 Gbps). I/O and memory bandwidth are based on the CPUs' PCIe and memory specifications. The data illustrates that in 2023 all CPU architectures' I/O bandwidth exceeds both memory bandwidth and

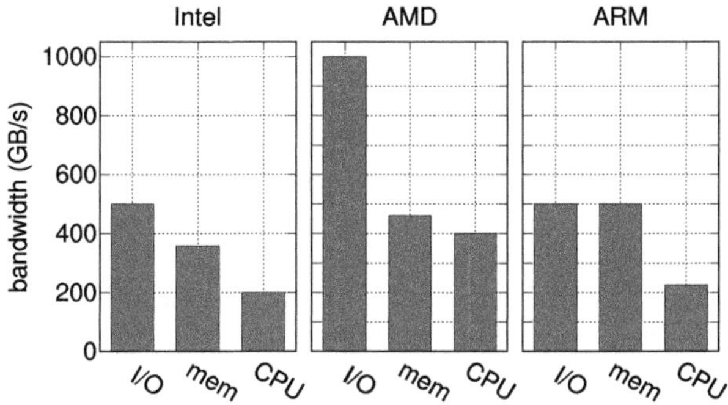

Fig. 1. I/O speeds exceed CPU TCP and memory speeds for all CPU architectures in 2023, motivating the offload of host compute and memory to SmartNICs.

CPU TCP bandwidth. This I/O imbalance has led to growing interest in Smart-NICs, such as the BlueFields, as a way to shift processing away from overwhelmed host CPUs and memory [12,19,21,25].

SmartNICs are a promising technology to overcome server I/O bottlenecks, as they combine NICs with additional generally programmable cores and dedicated memory, thus scaling compute and memory with each NIC attached to the server. SmartNICs also include dedicated accelerators for common I/O operations, such as data digest for deduplication, encryption, and compression, thus increasing SmartNIC compute performance for common tasks. However, SmartNIC cores are weaker than host cores and the cycle overhead of invoking SmartNIC accelerators to compute a function can exceed the cycles of computing the same function on the host CPU [1]. We illustrate the potential gains from offloading and the limitations of current SmartNICs by comparing the host and the BlueField-2 and BlueField-3 on NVMe-over-TCP storage disaggregation tasks (§2). Prior work has argued that SmartNICs process data at sub-line-rate speeds and offload fewer host CPU cores due to their limited compute capacity [7,22,40,49].

While true, in this work, we observe that limited SmartNIC memory bandwidth, and not compute, can be a key limiting or degrading factor to SmartNIC throughput (§3). SmartNIC memory bandwidth is insufficient to sustain even uni-directional line-rate writes—without reading the data. To demonstrate this, we investigate two successive generations of a widely deployed BlueField Smart-NIC: BlueField-2 and BlueField-3. We benchmark the SmartNIC's memory bandwidth from both the CPU and the RDMA engine. Our measurements reveal a significant generational difference in memory bandwidth limits: the BlueField-2 SmartNIC is limited to 10 Gbps, while the newer BlueField-3 achieves up to 60 Gbps. We use an NVMe-over-RDMA random 16 KiB read/write workload to show that I/O alone can saturate this bandwidth when data passes through the SmartNIC's memory. In contrast, when the I/O data fits within the last-level cache (LLC), RDMA can get much closer to the maximum duplex line rate of

400 Gbps on BlueField-2 and 800 Gbps on BlueField-3 because the SmartNIC can leverage the ARM's cache stashing mechanism.[1]

Fitting I/O data in the LLC has been shown to be effective for I/O intensive server workloads before [24,34,35,43], but our work is the first to employ this technique on SmartNICs. SmartNICs are well-suited for this optimization because they run dedicated infrastructure workloads and do not compete with user applications for cache resources [11].

We demonstrate that the gains from fitting I/O data in SmartNIC LLC can be used to unlock the performance scaling of TCP on BlueField-2 and that this optimization increases the throughput of NVMe-over-TCP storage disaggregation over the baseline NVIDIA SNAP [27] on both platforms by 56% and 20%, respectively (§4).

2   BlueFields SmartNIC Offload Potential

System-on-chip (SoC) of the BlueField-2 [30] and BlueField-3 [31] SmartNICs is well positioned to offload host applications. Depending on the configuration, it can be positioned in-line between the host and the network, enabling selective interception of I/O traffic. Application development is simplified by the Smart-NIC's support for a general-purpose Linux OS (e.g., Ubuntu), which provides a familiar and flexible software environment. We focus on the BlueFields for their developer-friendly Linux environment and integration with widely used software stacks.

The BlueField-2 SoC features 8 general-purpose ARMv8 CPU cores with 6 MiB last-level cache (LLC), a single 16 GiB DDR4 memory channel at 3200 MT/s and several hardware accelerators including RDMA and SHA-based data digest. The BlueField-3 has double the networking bandwidth of it's predecessor and features 16 ARMv8.2 cores, 16 MiB LLC and a dual 32 GiB DDR5 (see full characteristics in Table 2).

Prior work has demonstrated that the BlueFields effectively offload routing, switching, firewall, virtual private networking, monitoring [28,37], remote block storage [33,41], and distributed file systems [19]. These works emphasize using hardware accelerators efficiently, as the BlueFields' ARM cores are significantly less powerful than host CPU cores [22,23].

In this work, we use storage disaggregation as a running example because it is: (1) highly I/O intensive; (2) well suited for the BlueFields' accelerators, such as RDMA and deduplication; and (3) well studied [19,33,41,46].

As the storage disagregation stack we use NVMe-over-TCP due to it's generality, high-performance, and offloading potential.

Experimental Setup. We use two separate setups for BlueField-2 and BlueField-3 SmartNICs that differ in the CPU used but are otherwise identical in terms of connections.

---

[1] Cache stashing is ARM's equivalent of Intel's DDIO [6].

	BlueField-2	**BlueField-3**
CPU	8 ARMv8 A72 cores 2.5 GHz	16 ARMv8.2+ A78 cores
Cache	6 MiB LLC with cache stashing	16 MiB LLC with cache stashing [3]
	2 MiB L2 for every two cores	512 KiB L2 per core
	48 /32 KiB I/D-cache per core	64 /64 KiB I/D-cache per core
Memory	16 GiB single channel	32 GiB dual channel
	DDR4 at 3200 MT/s	DDR5 at 5600 MT/s
Network	two 100 Gbps ports	two 200 Gbps ports
	Ethernet or Infiniband	Ethernet or Infiniband

Fig. 2. BlueField-2 and BlueField-3 SmartNICs characteristics.

The first setup consists of two servers, each equipped with a 16-core 2.4 GHz Intel Xeon Silver 4314 CPU and 128 GB of memory (4×32 GB), running Linux 5.15. These servers are connected back-to-back using the BlueField-2 SmartNICs, with jumbo frames enabled.

The second setup also uses two back-to-back connected servers, but these feature a 64-core 2.2 GHz Intel Xeon Gold 6438M CPU and 630 GB of memory, running Linux 6.8. This setup employs the BlueField-3 SmartNICs and also has jumbo frames enabled.

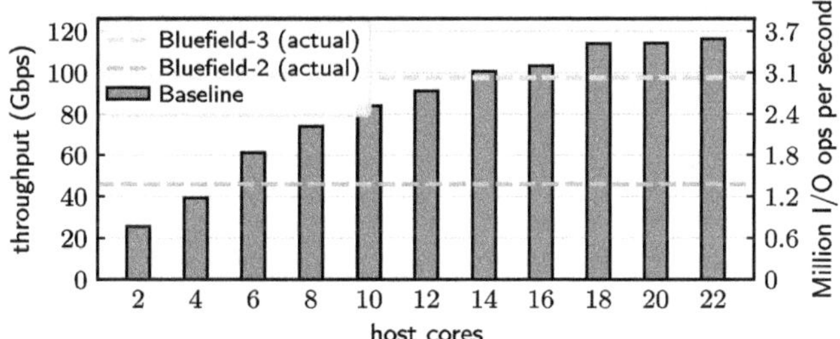

Fig. 3. NVMe-over-TCP random read host (bars) and BlueField-2/BlueField-3 (horizontal line) throughput using 4 KiB blocks. The BlueField-2 can offload up to 4 host cores while BlueField-3 can go as high as 16 cores. The performance on both platforms is 4x lower than their available RX bandwidth.

NVMe-Over-TCP Storage Disaggregation. In NVMe-over-TCP storage disaggregation, virtual machines (VMs) access remote storage through a virtualization backend that communicates over NVMe-over-TCP with a remote storage server. This backend can run either on the host hypervisor or on a SmartNIC.

To estimate the potential throughput and CPU utilization gains of virtualization backend SmartNIC offload, we measure SPDK nvme-perf [16] random 4 KiB read throughput on the VM, while varying the number of host cores assigned to the backend. To maximize performance, we run NVMe-over-TCP on SPDK

25.05 [16], and we make sure that the remote storage server is never the bottleneck.

We compare this with the performance of the virtualization backend running entirely on the BlueField SmartNIC using NVIDIA's storage-defined network accelerated processing (SNAP) [27].

Figure 3 presents the results. On the host, two cores achieve 25 Gbps, suggesting that—under ideal linear scaling—8 cores could reach 100 Gbps. However, performance scales sub-linearly due to LLC and memory bandwidth contention: 10 cores achieve only 77 Gbps and 100 Gbps can be reached only around 14 cores.

These results show that SmartNIC offload can save host CPU resources, but performance is limited: the BlueField-2 caps at 40 Gbps, equivalent to just 4 host cores. The BlueField-3 achieves close to 100 Gbps—more than double its predecessor—which, due to the sub-linear backend scaling equates to a more considerable 16 host cores.

We revisit those offloads in §4 and demonstrate that improved SmartNIC cache and memory bandwidth usage can boost throughput by up to 56% on BlueField-2 on a benchmark with the same block size and on BlueField-3 for larger 16 KiB blocks by 20%.

3   SmartNIC Memory Bandwidth Wall

The theoretical memory bandwidth for the BlueField-2 SoC is approximately 25 GB/s^2 and that of the BlueField-3 is $90GB/s^3$. Sustaining line-rate I/O performance (e.g., 100 Gbps per port) requires significant memory bandwidth; for two ports with bidirectional traffic, this can exceed 50 GB/s, which is 2× what the BlueField-2 can theoretically provide. This bottleneck stems from typical SmartNIC application behavior, which involves at least two memory accesses per I/O operation: one to store incoming data and another to read and send the processed data to the host or network. Some applications bypass SmartNIC memory entirely by transferring data directly between host memory and the network [41]. However, this approach is limited to inline NIC accelerators (i.e., IPsec and TLS encryption) and cannot support data-dependent computations or leverage SmartNIC-side accelerators. For instance, data deduplication requires the SmartNIC to hash data using the SoC before deciding whether to transmit it—necessitating full memory access and processing.

However, our measurements show that the bottleneck is even more acute: the actual memory bandwidth is capped at only 10 GB/s for BlueField-2. The successor, BlueField-3, improves this limit significantly, but is still capped at a measured 60 GB/s, as demonstrated in this section.

These limitations directly constrain the SmartNIC's ability to operate at line-rate speeds and must be understood to design effective offload strategies. To this end, we perform experiments accessing memory from SoC cores and from

---

[2] A single DDR4 channel at 3200 MT/s provides $3200 \times 10^6 \times 8B = 25.6\,GB/s$.

[3] Dual DDR5 channel at 5600 MT/s provides $5600 \times 10^6 \times 2 \times 8B = 89.6\,GB/s$.

RDMA-based I/O to empirically characterize SmartNIC memory bandwidth and assess it's implications for real-world workloads.

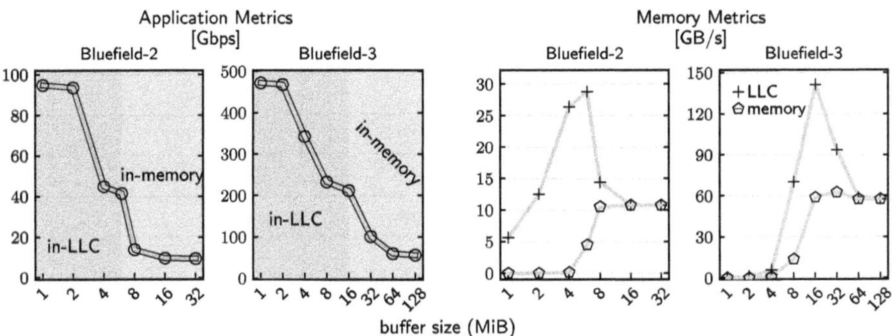

Fig. 4. Pmbw application and LLC bandwidth of running on BlueField-2 6 SoC and BlueField-3 16 SoC cores reading and writing data from a shared buffer split evenly between the cores.

Compute Induced Memory Bandwidth Bottlenecks. To evaluate the BlueFields' SoC memory bandwidth, we run a modified pmbw microbenchmark [4] with varying working set sizes. The total working set is split evenly between the cores to be accessed separately from others. Each core repeatedly reads and writes to its own private buffer as fast as possible. During these experiments, we measure system-level memory reads and writes which show both those incoming towards LLC and those that need to go towards DRAM due to LLC miss [32]. To minimize measurement interference, we isolate the cores that run the benchmarks from the rest of the system.

Figure 4 shows buffer read/write throughput as reported by PMBW and the LLC and memory bandwidth as reported by the performance counters on BlueField-2 and BlueField-3, respectively. As buffer size increases, throughput drops and eventually flattens, indicating the transition from cache to memory.

For BlueField-2, buffers smaller than 2 MiB are served from the L2 cache, producing some LLC traffic. Buffers between 2–6 MiB fit in the LLC, leading to rising LLC traffic. Buffers larger than 6 MiB spill into memory, reducing LLC traffic and exposing the system's effective memory bandwidth limit—10,GB/s. This is far below the theoretical 25,GB/s limit, suggesting that core-side memory access throughput is the bottleneck.

Similarly, for BlueField-3, buffers smaller than 8 MiB are served from the L2 cache and buffers between 8–16 MiB fit in the LLC, leading to rising LLC traffic. Buffers larger than that spill into memory, showing the memory bandwidth limit to be—60,GB/s, 6 times that of BlueField-2.

To determine whether other subsystems (e.g., I/O) can better utilize memory bandwidth, we next examine RDMA performance targeting the same SoC memory.

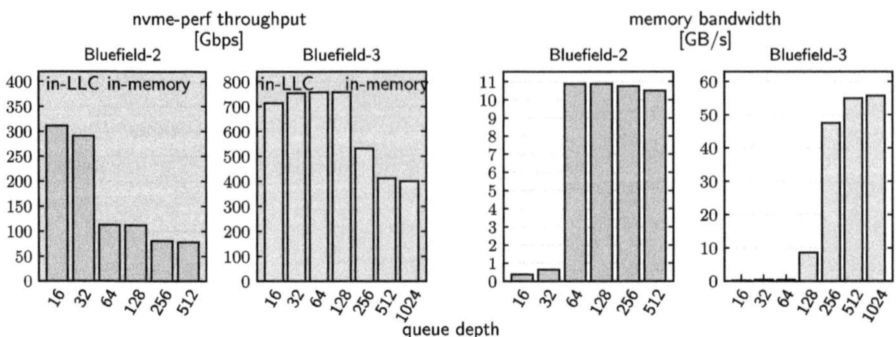

Fig. 5. SPDK nvme-perf 16 KiB random read/write throughput and memory bandwidth on the BlueField-2 and BlueField-3.

I/O Induced Memory Bandwidth Bottlenecks. To measure the BlueField SoC's memory bandwidth using I/O, we ran the SPDK nvme-perf benchmark on four SoC cores while varying the queue depth to control the I/O working-set size. To achieve maximum memory throughput, the BlueField-2 required the use of two 100 Gbps ports for full 200 Gbps TX/RX bandwidth, whereas the BlueField-3 could achieve its full TX/RX bandwidth using just one 400 Gbps port. We chose this benchmark because it effectively simulates real-world cloud applications, allows for careful control of the working-set size, and is computationally efficient, ensuring the measurement won't be bottlenecked by the CPU performance. We make sure that the x86 storage server runs enough storage devices that it is not the bottleneck. The resulting I/O working set consists of the ports × remote storage devices × queue depth × 16 KiB. Each core repeatedly issues RDMA reads as fast as possible according to the NVMe-over-RDMA protocol. As in the prior experiment, we use separate, isolated cores to measure LLC read/write bandwidth and minimize interference.

Figure 5 shows RDMA read/write throughput and memory bandwidth as reported by the performance counters for both platforms. When the I/O working set fits in the LLC, throughput achieved by BlueField-2 is slightly above 300 Gbps and that of BlueField-3 is close to 800 Gbps, while memory bandwidth is low in both cases. Once the working set across all cores and devices, exceeds the LLC—which for the 6 MiB LLC of BlueField-2 happens approximately at 48 entries[4] and for 16 MiB LLC of BlueField-3 at 128 entries[5]—throughput drops sharply to 80 Gbps and 400 Gbps, respectively, as a result of a sustained memory bandwidth limit of 10 GB/s and 60 GB/s of those two platforms.

This sharp transition is explained by ARM cache stashing [3], which allows DMA operations to access the LLC directly. Specifically, DMA writes update existing cache lines or allocate new ones by evicting others, while DMA reads

---

[4] 6 MiB ÷ (2 ports × 4 remote storage devices × 16 KiB) = 48.

[5] 16 MiB ÷ (1 port × 8 remote storage devices × 16 KiB) = 128.

are served from the LLC if the data is present. When the working set fits in the LLC, main memory bandwidth is bypassed, eliminating the bottleneck.

The failure of the BlueField-2 to achieve 400 Gbps even when the working set fits within the LLC aligns with the previous PMBW experiment, which demonstrates that even the available LLC bandwidth cannot sustain the full-duplex 200 Gbps line rate (400 Gbps = 50 GB/s).

Collectively, these findings confirm that the shared memory bandwidth of the BlueField SmartNICs is the critical bottleneck for line-rate workloads that necessitate memory access. Conversely, workloads with working sets contained entirely within the LLC may achieve full throughput, although on BlueField-2 for full-duplex operation even that won't be enough. This performance gap motivates our subsequent exploration of application designs engineered to retain their I/O working sets within the LLC's capacity.

4 Overcoming the Memory Wall via LLC-Aware Design

We explore LLC-aware applications that fit their I/O working sets entirely within the LLC, avoiding memory bandwidth bottlenecks via ARM cache stashing. We focus on TCP-based applications due to their complexity and ubiquity in data centers. A representative example is request-response protocols such as NVMe-over-TCP, used for remote storage virtualization.

While previous work has optimized the I/O working set of network functions (NFs) [10,35,36,43,44], this is, to our knowledge, the first to target TCP applications, SmartNICs, and remote storage workloads.

In typical network applications, the minimal I/O working set consists of the total memory allocated to NIC receive ring (Rx) buffers. These buffers are consumed in strict order and cannot be reused until all prior entries are processed.

As a result, network applications face a challenging trade-off. On one hand, Rx rings must be large enough to absorb packet bursts—often requiring at least 1 Ki entries per core [35]. On the other hand, such large per-core rings increase the I/O working set, making it harder to fit within the LLC. For example, on the BlueField-2, eight cores each with 1 Ki Rx ring entries and a 1.5 KiB MTU result in an I/O working set that exceeds the 6 MiB LLC capacity. The situation is slightly better on the BlueField-3 because, although its bandwidth and core count are doubled, its LLC size is more than doubled($16 \div 6 = 2\frac{1}{3}$).

The nature of request-response applications enables us to break this trade-off. In contrast to other network applications, the I/O working set size of request-response applications is determined by the size of all in-flight requests and responses. Furthermore, by admitting only requests (and responses) that fit in the LLC alongside previously admitted requests and responses, we can ensure that the I/O working set remains within the LLC. Additionally, the size of incoming bursts in request-response applications can be controlled per-core as the mapping between requests and responses to Rx rings is known. Moreover, since SmartNICs are typically used to offload network operations from the host, the network stack requesting the data runs entirely on the ARM SoC. This offloading enables the combined working-set size of the requesting applications running on the host to be arbitrarily large (i.e., larger than the SmartNIC's LLC capacity). This is possible because the SmartNIC only receives the comparatively small request from the host and the resulting response from the network. After the response is received into LLC-limited buffers on the SmartNIC, it can then be efficiently DMA'ed to host buffers of arbitrarily large size, effectively bypassing the SmartNIC's memory bandwidth bottleneck for the large data transfer.

This mechanism is especially effective in multi-tenant environments because tenant workloads are separated into distinct hardware domains (the host vs. the SmartNIC). The SmartNIC can be fully dedicated to running only the cloud provider's network stack (e.g., the virtualization layer) without interference from tenant applications on the host, ensuring predictable and high-performance I/O isolation.

We now apply this insight to limit the I/O working set in both the netperf request-response microbenchmark and the NVMe-over-TCP storage virtualization macrobenchmark.

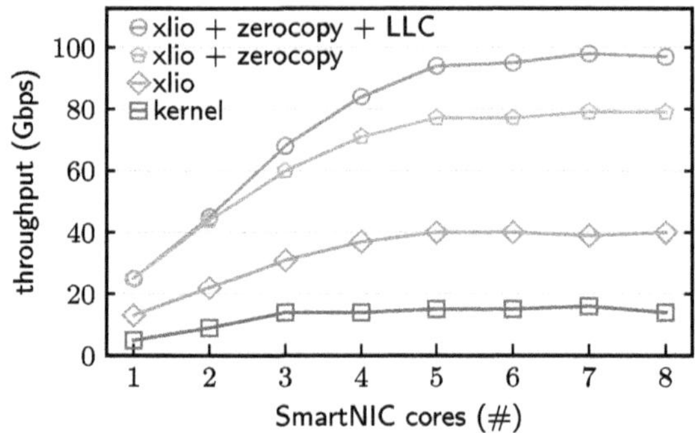

Fig. 6. BlueField-2 single-port netperf request-response throughput. Only xlio + zerocopy + LLC attains line-rate by overcoming memory bandwidth bottlenecks.

LLC-Aware Netperf. Previous work attributes poor TCP performance of BlueField-2 to weak SoC cores [22,49], but we find that for sufficiently optimized TCP stacks, the memory bandwidth—not compute—becomes the primary bottleneck.

We run the netperf [18] request-response benchmark using all BlueField-2 cores. To emulate the NVMe-over-TCP read protocol, we use 72 B requests and 4 KiB + 24 B responses. We use batches of 96 operations, which we empirically find to be sufficient to saturate the 100 GbE link.

We compare four levels of TCP optimizations: (1) Linux kernel TCP—the baseline; (2) NVIDIA xlio—a userspace TCP stack that avoids context switches, but still copies data; (3) NVIDIA xlio with zerocopy support (xlio

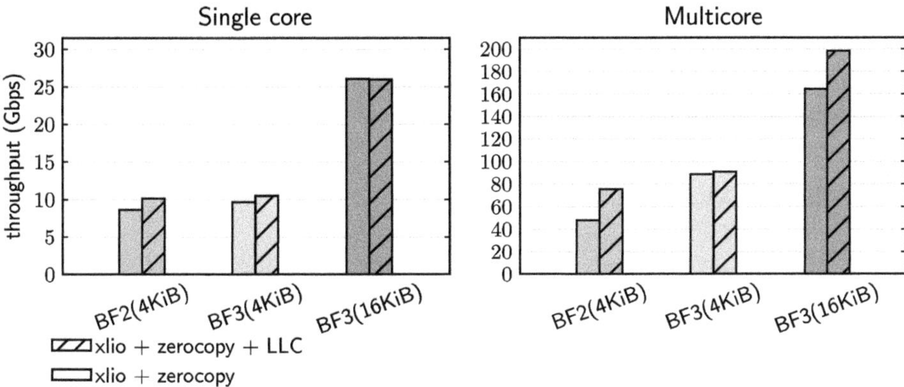

Fig. 7. NVMe-over-TCP 4 KiB random read throughput offloaded on BlueField-2 and BlueField-3 with default and LLC-optimized configurations.

+ zerocopy)—eliminates memory copies by passing application buffers directly to NIC rings; (4) NVIDIA xlio with zerocopy support that fits the I/O working set in the LLC (xlio + zerocopy + LLC)—further constrains the I/O working set to the LLC via admission control.

Figure 6 shows the results. Kernel TCP throughput is the lowest with a maximum of 16 Gbps due to the high cost of copying and context switches. Userspace xlio TCP improves throughput by up to 2.5x, reaching 40 Gbps. Adding zerocopy eliminates memory copies, increasing throughput by up to 1.97x to 79 Gbps— limited by memory bandwidth, consistent with our pmbw measurement of a 10 GB/s memory bandwidth limit. Finally, limiting the I/O working set to the LLC lifts the bottleneck entirely, achieving line-rate throughput of the port with a further 1.24x improvement.

With BlueField-3's much larger memory bandwidth, the performance of TCP is limited by compute before memory becomes a bottleneck so we skip it for this microbenchmark.

LLC-Aware NVMe-Over-TCP Offload. We apply our LLC-aware I/O working set optimization to the BlueFields' NVMe-over-TCP storage disaggregation workload described in §2. Specifically, we compare the baseline NVIDIA SNAP implementation—which already employs optimizations like xlio with zero-copy— against a variant that additionally constrains the I/O working set to fit within the LLC (i.e., LLC-aware). For the BlueField-3, we perform an additional experiment with a block size of 16 KiB to put higher stress on its significantly improved memory subsystem. Figure 7 shows the results for both single-core and multi-core configurations. For the BlueField-2, fitting the I/O working set to the LLC improves throughput by 17% for the single-core case and by 56% in the multi-core case. The BlueField-3 single and multi-core performance with 4 KiB blocks benefits by a small 5%. Its single-core performance with 16 KiB blocks does not improve, but after scaling the number of cores reading these larger blocks, the memory stress becomes large enough that the LLC-aware configuration improves the performance by 20%.

These gains highlight the effectiveness and, in some cases, the necessity of LLC-aware design even atop an already optimized baseline.

5   Related Work

SmartNIC Performance Analysis. Extensive prior work has characterized Smart-NIC performance across various dimensions, focusing primarily on compute and network throughput [14,21,22,40,45,47]. However, these studies largely overlooked memory bandwidth as a critical bottleneck for high-throughput workloads. While a few recent works have begun to examine memory subsystem performance [5,13,25], they have not systematically investigated the relationship between LLC bandwidth requirements and line-rate I/O performance, which is the focus of our work.

Application Offloading to SmartNICs. SmartNICs have emerged as attractive platforms for offloading data-intensive applications, including distributed file systems [12,19], network protocol processing [26,38], and storage systems [20,49]. While these systems demonstrate the potential of SmartNIC offloading, most operate at throughputs well below line-rate speeds and thus do not encounter memory bandwidth bottlenecks. The notable exception is IO-TCP, which achieves line-rate performance but saturates SmartNIC memory bandwidth; however, this work did not investigate LLC behavior or requirements.

Cache-Aware System Design. A substantial body of work has explored LLC analysis, monitoring, and management techniques [9,10,17,24,42–44,48]. These studies have primarily focused on CPU-centric systems and have not considered the unique characteristics of SmartNICs, where the substantial mismatch between available memory bandwidth and line-rate network speeds makes it so that the sizing I/O buffers to fit within the LLC working set transitions from being merely beneficial to absolutely essential for maintaining line-rate performance. Our work bridges these gaps by providing the first systematic analysis of LLC bandwidth requirements for line-rate SmartNIC applications, demonstrating how memory subsystem design becomes the critical bottleneck in high-throughput network processing.

6   Conclusion

SmartNIC offloads are often limited by memory bandwidth constraints. We show that fitting I/O buffers within the LLC alleviates this bottleneck by increasing the effectiveness of ARM cache stashing, improving CPU efficiency, and enabling higher-throughput offloading to the SmartNIC.

References

1. Altaf, M.S.B., Wood, D.A.: LOGCA: a high-level performance model for hardware accelerators. In: ACM International Symposium on Computer Architecture (ISCA), pp. 375–388 (2017). https://doi.org/10.1145/3079856.3080216
2. AMD: Epyc 9754 (2023). https://www.amd.com/en/products/processors/server/epyc/4th-generation-9004-and-8004-series/amd-epyc-9754.html
3. ARM: Cache stashing (2024). https://developer.arm.com/documentation/102407/0100/Cache-stashing. Accessed 15 Jan 2025
4. Bingmann, T.: PMBW (2013). https://panthema.net/2013/pmbw/. Accessed 15 Jan 2025
5. Chen, X., et al.: Demystifying datapath accelerator enhanced off-path smartnic. In: IEEE International Conference on Network Protocols (ICNP), pp. 1–12 (2024). https://doi.org/10.1109/ICNP61940.2024.10858560
6. Corporation, I.: Intel Data Direct I/O technology (intel DDIO): a primer. https://www.intel.com/content/dam/www/public/us/en/documents/technology-briefs/data-direct-i-o-technology-brief.pdf (2012). Accessed 18 July 2020
7. Cui, T., Zhao, C., Zhang, W., Zhang, K., Krishnamurthy, A.: Laconic: streamlined load balancers for smartnics (2024). https://arxiv.org/abs/2403.11411
8. Farshin, A., Barbette, T., Roozbeh, A., Maguire Jr., G.Q., Kostić, D.: PacketMill: toward per-core 100-Gbps networking. In: ACM International Conference on Architectural Support for Programming Languages and Operating Systems (ASPLOS), pp. 1–17 (2021). https://doi.org/10.1145/3445814.3446724
9. Farshin, A., Jr, G.Q.M., Roozbeh, A., Kostic, D.: Reexamining direct cache access to optimize I/O intensive applications for multi-hundred-gigabit networks (2020)
10. Farshin, A., Roozbeh, A., Maguire, G.Q., Kostić, D.: Make the most out of last level cache in intel processors. In: ACM Eurosystem (2019). https://dl.acm.org/doi/10.1145/3302424.3303977
11. Fried, J., Ruan, Z., Ousterhout, A., Belay, A.: CALADAN: mitigating interference at microsecond timescales. In: USENIX Symposium on Operating System Design and Implementation (OSDI), pp. 281–297 (2020). https://www.usenix.org/conference/osdi20/presentation/fried
12. Gootzen, P.J., Pfefferle, J., Stoica, R., Trivedi, A.: DPFS: DPU-powered file system virtualization. In: Proceedings of the 16th ACM International Conference on Systems and Storage, pp. 1–7. ACM, Haifa Israel (2023). https://doi.org/10.1145/3579370.3594769
13. Hu, J., et al.: dpBento: benchmarking DPUs for data processing (2025). Accessed 18 July 2025
14. Huang, J., Lou, J., Sun, Y., Wang, T., Lee, E.K., Sung Kim, N.: Making sense of using a SmartNIC to reduce datacenter tax from SLO and TCO perspectives. In: IEEE International Symposium on Workload Characterization (IISWC). IEEE, Ghent, Belgium (2023). https://ieeexplore.ieee.org/document/10289567/
15. Intel: Xeon platinum 8592+ processor (2023). https://www.intel.com/content/www/us/en/products/sku/237261/intel-xeon-platinum-8592-processor-320m-cache-1-90-ghz/specifications.html
16. Intel: SPDK (2024). https://spdk.io/. Accessed 15 Jan 2025
17. Jia, H., Wang, M., Li, B., Liu, Y., Guo, J., Zhang, P.: 5gc^{2}ache : improving 5G UPF performance via cache optimization. http://arxiv.org/abs/2404.13991 (2024). Accessed 17 July 2025

18. Jones, R.A.: NetPERF: a network performance benchmark (Revision 2.0). http://www.netperf.org/netperf/training/Netperf.html (1995). Accessed Aug 2016
19. Kim, J., et al.: Linefs: efficient SmartNic offload of a distributed file system with pipeline parallelism. In: ACM Symposium on Operating Systems Principles (SOSP), pp. 756–771. SOSP 2021, Association for Computing Machinery, New York, NY, USA (2021). https://doi.org/10.1145/3477132.3483565
20. Kim, T., Ng, D.M., Yu, M., Gong, J., Park, K., Kwon, Y.: Rearchitecting the TCP Stack for I/O-Offloaded Content Delivery. In: USENIX Symposium on Networked Systems Design and Implementation (NSDI) (2021). https://www.usenix.org/conference/nsdi23/presentation/kim-taehyun
21. Li, Y., Kashyap, A., Guo, Y., Lu, X.: Characterizing lossy and lossless compression on emerging BlueField DPU architectures. In: IEEE Symposium on High Performance Interconnects (HOTI) (2023). https://ieeexplore.ieee.org/document/10287290/
22. Liu, J., Maltzahn, C., Ulmer, C., Curry, M.L.: Performance characteristics of the BlueField-2 SmartNIC. http://arxiv.org/abs/2105.06619 (2021). Accessed 15 Jan 2025
23. Liu, M., Cui, T., Schuh, H., Krishnamurthy, A., Peter, S., Gupta, K.: Offloading distributed applications onto smartNICs using iPipe. In: ACM SIGCOMM Conference on Applications Technologies Architecture and Protocols for Computer Communications. pp. 318–333. ACM, Beijing China (2019). https://doi.org/10.1145/3341302.3342079
24. Marinos, I., Watson, R.N., Handley, M., Stewart, R.R.: Disk|Crypt|Net: rethinking the stack for high-performance video streaming. In: ACM SIGCOMM Conference on Applications Technologies Architecture and Protocols for Computer Communications (2017). https://dl.acm.org/doi/10.1145/3098822.3098844
25. Michalowicz, B., Suresh, K.K., Subramoni, H., Panda, D.K.D., Poole, S.: Battle of the BlueFields: an in-depth comparison of the BlueField-2 and BlueField-3 Smart-NICs. In: IEEE Symposium on High Performance Interconnects (HOTI), pp. 41–48. IEEE, CA, USA (2023). https://doi.org/10.1109/HOTI59126.2023.00020, https://ieeexplore.ieee.org/document/10287294/
26. Moon, Y., Lee, S., Jamshed, M.A., Park, K.: AccelTCP: accelerating network applications with stateful TCP offloading (2020)
27. NVIDIA: Mellanox introduces breakthrough NVME snap technology to simplify composable storage (2019). Accessed 15 Jan 2025
28. NVIDIA: DPU power efficiency. https://resources.nvidia.com/en-us-accelerated-networking-resource-library/nvidia-dpu-power-efficiency-white-paper (2022). Accessed 15 Apr 2025
29. NVIDIA: Grace CPU superchip datasheet (2023). https://resources.nvidia.com/en-us-grace-cpu/data-center-datasheet
30. NVIDIA: BlueField-2 DPU. https://resources.nvidia.com/en-us-accelerated-networking-resource-library/bluefield-2-dpu-datasheet (2024). Accessed 15 Jan 2025
31. NVIDIA: BlueField-3 DPU. https://www.nvidia.com/content/dam/en-zz/Solutions/Data-Center/documents/datasheet-nvidia-bluefield-3-dpu.pdf (2024). Accessed 15 Jan 2025
32. NVIDIA: Performance monitoring counters. https://docs.nvidia.com/networking/display/bluefielddpuosv385/performance+monitoring+counters (2024). Accessed 15 Jan 2025

33. NVIDIA: Supermicro launches NVIDIA BlueField-powered JBOF to optimize AI storage. https://developer.nvidia.com/blog/supermicro-launches-nvidia-bluefield-powered-jbof-to-optimize-ai-storage/ (2024). Accessed 15 Apr 2025
34. Pismenny, B., Liss, L., Morrison, A., Tsafrir, D.: The benefits of general-purpose on-NIC memory. In: Proceedings of the 27th ACM International Conference on Architectural Support for Programming Languages and Operating Systems, pp. 1130–1147. ACM, Lausanne Switzerland (2022). https://doi.org/10.1145/3503222.3507711
35. Pismenny, B., Morrison, A., Tsafrir, D.: ShRing: networking with shared receive rings. In: USENIX Symposium on Operating System Design and Implementation (OSDI) (2023). https://www.usenix.org/conference/osdi23/presentation/pismenny
36. Pismenny, B., Morrison, A., Tsafrir, D.: Disentangling the dual role of NIC receive rings. In: USENIX Symposium on Operating System Design and Implementation (OSDI) (2025). https://www.usenix.org/conference/osdi25/presentation/pismenny
37. Schulz, M., Schoent, M., Roesch, J., Ganesan, K., Kim, J.F., Castanos, J.: Optimizing networking and security performance using VMware vSphere and NVIDIA BlueField DPU with BWI (2023). https://vm-guru.com/ext/pdf/optimizing-networking-and-security-performance-using-vmware-vsphere-and-nvidia-bluefield-dpu-with-bwi.pdf. Accessed 15 Apr 2025
38. Shashidhara, R., Stamler, T., Kaufmann, A., Peter, S.: FlexTOE: flexible TCP Offload with Fine-Grained Parallelism. In: USENIX Symposium on Networked Systems Design and Implementation (NSDI) (2022). https://www.usenix.org/conference/nsdi22/presentation/shashidhara
39. Smith, R.: PCI express 6.0 specification finalized: x16 slots to reach 128 GBps (2024). https://www.anandtech.com/show/21335/full-draft-of-pcie-70-spec-available-512-gbs-over-pcie-x16-incoming. Accessed 14 May 2025
40. Sun, S., et al.: A comprehensive study on optimizing systems with data processing units. http://arxiv.org/abs/2301.06070 (2023)
41. Sun, X., Zhang, M., Shan, Y., Chen, K., Jiang, J.: Scalio: scaling up DPU-based JBOF Key-value store with NVMe-oF Target Offload. In: USENIX Symposium on Operating System Design and Implementation (OSDI) (2025)
42. Thomas, S., McGuinness, R., Voelker, G.M., Porter, G.: Dark packets and the end of network scaling. In: ACM/IEEE Symposium on Architectures for Networking and Communications Systems (ANCS), pp. 1–14. ACM, Ithaca, New York (2018). https://doi.org/10.1145/3230718.3230727
43. Tootoonchian, A., Panda, A., Lan, C., Walls, M., Argyraki, K., Ratnasamy, S., Shenker, S.: ResQ: enabling SLOs in network function virtualization. In: USENIX Symposium on Networked Systems Design and Implementation (NSDI) (2018). https://www.usenix.org/conference/nsdi18/presentation/tootoonchian
44. Wang, M., Xu, M., Wu, J.: Understanding I/O direct cache access performance for end host networking. In: ACM on Measurement and Analysis of Computing Systems (2022). https://dl.acm.org/doi/10.1145/3508042
45. Wang, Z., Wang, C., Wang, L.: DPUBench: an application-driven scalable benchmark suite for comprehensive DPU evaluation. In: BenchCouncil Transactions on Benchmarks, Standards and Evaluations. No. 2 (2023). https://linkinghub.elsevier.com/retrieve/pii/S2772485923000376

46. Wei, X., Cheng, R., Yang, Y., Chen, R., Chen, H.: Characterizing off-path Smart-NIC for accelerating distributed systems. In: USENIX Symposium on Operating System Design and Implementation (OSDI), pp. 987–1004. USENIX Association, Boston, MA (2023). https://www.usenix.org/conference/osdi23/presentation/wei-smartnic

47. Xing, T., Tajbakhsh, H., Haque, I., Honda, M., Barbalace, A.: Towards portable end-to-end network performance characterization of SmartNICs. In: ACM Asia-Pacific Workshop on Systems (APSYS), pp. 46–52. ACM, Virtual Event Singapore (2022). https://doi.org/10.1145/3546591.3547528

48. Yuan, Y., et al.: Don't forget the I/O when allocating your LLC. In: ACM International Symposium on Computer Architecture (ISCA) (2021). https://ieeexplore.ieee.org/document/9499850/

49. Zhang, Q., Bernstein, P.A., Chandramouli, B., Hu, J., Zheng, Y.: DDS: DPU-optimized Disaggregated Storage [Extended Report]. In: ACM on VLDB Endowment (2024). https://dl.acm.org/doi/abs/10.14778/3681954.3682002

50. Zhao, Z., Sadok, H., Atre, N., Hoe, J.C., Sekar, V., Sherry, J.: Achieving 100 Gbps intrusion prevention on a single server. In: USENIX Symposium on Operating System Design and Implementation (OSDI), pp. 1083–1100 (2020). https://www.usenix.org/conference/osdi20/presentation/zhao-zhipeng

Author Index

GPSR Compliance
The European Union's (EU) General Product Safety Regulation (GPSR) is a set
of rules that requires consumer products to be safe and our obligations to
ensure this.

If you have any concerns about our products, you can contact us on

ProductSafety@springernature.com

In case Publisher is established outside the EU, the EU authorized
representative is:

Springer Nature Customer Service Center GmbH
Europaplatz 3
69115 Heidelberg, Germany